Second Edition

Delinquency
and **Juvenile Justice**
in **American Society**

Second Edition

Delinquency
and Juvenile Justice
in American Society

Randall G. Shelden
University of Nevada–Las Vegas

WAVELAND
PRESS, INC.
Long Grove, Illinois

For information about this book, contact:
Waveland Press, Inc.
4180 IL Route 83, Suite 101
Long Grove, IL 60047-9580
(847) 634-0081
info@waveland.com
www.waveland.com

CONTENTS

2   The Extent of Delinquency

3   The Nature of Delinquency

PART II
EXPLAINING DELINQUENCY   199

6 Individualistic Theories of Delinquency   201

7 Sociological Theories of Delinquency   233

PREFACE TO THE SECOND EDITION

The writer of a textbook, no matter what the subject, never knows if there will be another edition. There is no way of predicting how many copies will be sold, nor how many of his or her fellow professors will assign the book for a class. The fact that there is a second edition to this text is one of the best rewards a textbook writer has. It means, simply, that someone out there likes what you have to say! It also means that the publisher also likes what you have to say—or at least likes the fact that others like what you have to say. After all, publishers like Waveland want to sell books.

Writing a second edition of a book may seem like a simple process, like updating some statistics for the tables and graphs, plus adding a few recent studies on the subjects covered. Believe me it is not that easy, for it is almost like writing a new book! Even I was surprised at all the new information collected since the first edition was written. I completed the bulk of the research for the first edition in 2005; there were now five years of new research to review. Thankfully the Internet is available and especially that magical invention called Google Scholar!

In addition to updating each chapter, I eliminated chapter 14 ("Recent Trends"). When teaching my classes on delinquency, I soon realized that trends were no longer "recent" within a year or two. By the time the year 2010 rolled around most of the "recent" was the past! Some of the sections now appear in other chapters (e.g., the discussion of boot camps is now in chapter 12, the discussion of *Roper v. Simmons* is now in chapter 11, and the subject of "zero tolerance" is in chapter 10). Speaking of "zero tolerance" there has been some relief from the perspective that resulted in more and more youths charged with petty offenses (or no offenses at all) and sent to juvenile court—with children as young as 6 or 7 taken away in handcuffs.

New topics explored include what has come to be called the "school to prison pipeline," which entails various processes inside public schools (some stemming directly from "zero tolerance" policies) that make it easier to suspend and expel students, which in turn often leads directly to the juvenile justice system and eventually to the adult prison system. Such procedures disproportionately target minorities.

I have added some new material in the solutions chapter (now chapter 14), including some promising programs for girl offenders and have added some recent events in California concerning what used to be called the California

Youth Authority (chapter 12). The scandals within this system resulted in a large lawsuit, which eventually led to the closing of several institutions and a name change. More abuse scandals have surfaced in recent years within youth prisons, and these are also discussed in chapter 12. I have found several websites devoted to this issue and discuss the problem frequently on my own website.

The important issue of social inequality is updated with new material in chapter 8. Since the publication of the first edition, the United States has suffered the greatest economic collapse since the Great Depression of the 1930s. So much has happened and the inequality has grown so much that I added a section discussing the economic collapse in some detail.

Once again, I want to thank my colleagues at UNLV for creating a nurturing environment, even though the university and the department have been negatively impacted by the recent economic collapse. I also want to thank the thousands of researchers and writers who make the writing of a textbook possible. I also want to thank Carol and Neil Rowe at Waveland Press. I have never found a more congenial pair of publishers and their assistants. It is so rare to find such support and continued confidence in my work.

Finally, to the people closest to me: Virginia and Marcie. Your love and unyielding faith in me cannot be measured. I love you both.

INTRODUCTION

In September 2010 fifteen-year-old Otilio Rubio and three other teens attempted to burglarize a central Florida home. They broke in through a window, and the homeowner shot Rubio and William Murphy. Rubio died two days later. Murphy (16), Zachary Mathew Garcia (17), and Austin Michael Clements (15) have been charged with burglary and felony murder. Under Florida law, individuals involved in a felony that results in death can be charged with murder, even if they are not directly responsible for the killing.[1]

In August 2010 seventeen-year-old India Spellman and 14-year-old Von Combs attempted to rob an 87-year-old man in Philadelphia. During a struggle, the victim was fatally shot. Spellman and Combs were charged with murder.[2] Under Pennsylvania law, juveniles charged with murder are automatically considered adults unless a judge decides to move the trial to juvenile court. Pennsylvania has more juveniles sentenced to life in prison without parole than any other state.[3]

In July 2010 Abelino Mazaniego was sitting on a bench in a park after finishing his shift at a restaurant. Three teenagers approached and beat him unconscious, while a fourth recorded the beating on a cell phone camera. The video circulated among teenagers in Summit, New Jersey, where the beating occurred. Mazaniego died several days later, and police arrested Nigel Dumas (19), Khayri Williams-Clark (18), and a 17-year-old (whose name was not released) for the murder.[4]

On January 14, 2010, Christian Romero was sentenced to psychiatric treatment for an indefinite period of time; he was ten years old and will remain on probation until age 18.[5] At the age of eight in November 2008, the third-grader shot his father (Vincent Romero, 29, who had full custody of his son) and a family friend (Timothy Romans, 39, who was renting a room from Romero) multiple times with his .22-caliber rifle, which his father had taught him to use. The boy confessed to the murders without an attorney or guardian being present during police questioning. The police released the video confession, and the rural Arizona town (population 4,000) was immediately besieged by television media.[6] The police alleged that Christian planned the killings while riding the bus home from school, that he ambushed his father inside the house, and that he killed Romans as he entered the front door. During questioning, Christian told police he shot the two men because someone else had wounded them and he needed to put them out of their misery. He later told a social worker that he had kept track of his spankings and had decided to take action after the 1,000th (the claim

1

was never validated).[7] Arizona law allows adult prosecution for anyone eight or older who commits murder. At the age of nine in February 2009, Christian (Arizona's youngest homicide defendant) signed a plea agreement that dropped the initial two counts of murder and charged him with one count of negligent homicide in the death of Romans. Judge Michael Roca had accepted the plea agreement with a proposed sentence of intensive probation and community treatment but later changed his mind and attempted to rescind the deal. The defense attorney alleged that local politics had motivated the change of mind and was successful in removing Roca from the case. Until the sentencing in 2010 Christian was in the custody of his birth mother while authorities addressed legal problems, including whether he was old enough to comprehend the proceedings.

On February 20, 2009, a four-year-old found her mother, 26-year old Kenzie Houk, murdered in her bed. She was eight months pregnant. She lived in rural Pennsylvania (Wampum) with her fiancée, his son, and her two daughters. Jordan Brown, the son of her fiancée, was charged with her murder and the murder of her unborn son; he was 11 years old. He allegedly hid his shotgun (a Christmas gift from his father) in his blanket when he went downstairs to shoot Houk, who was sleeping in her first-floor bedroom. After the shooting, he caught the bus for school. Judge Dominick Motto ruled that Brown should be tried as an adult, saying he doubted rehabilitation could be accomplished before Brown reached the age of 21 (when he would be released from the juvenile system). The Pennsylvania Superior Court agreed to hear an appeal to move the case to juvenile court; on March 11, 2011, it remanded the case to the trial court for a new transfer hearing. Cynthia Orr, of the National Association of Criminal Defense Attorneys stated: "It's simply inappropriate to put a 12-year-old child in the adult prison system. It won't work. It won't benefit society or this child." Laurence Steinberg, whose research about a child's brain not being fully developed in the areas that control decision making, risk taking, and impulse control influenced the Supreme Court to ban the death penalty for juveniles in *Roper v. Simmons*, said: "The idea of taking a child this age and locking him up for life is pretty repugnant. What he allegedly did is repugnant also. But the heinousness of the crime does not make him an adult."[8]

The media thrive on tragic events like those listed above ("if it bleeds, it leads"), horrifying the audience and priming public opinion to embrace policies with little contemplation of the consequences. The Internet offers constant access to stories about such tragedies—past and present. The news media, along with politicians from coast to coast, take advantage of public fear, suggesting an "epidemic" of youth violence. A more accurate analysis tells us something else: such incidents, horrific as they are, represent the exception rather than the rule. Contrary to the hype projected by the media and politicians, serious violent crimes are committed predominately by adults. In fact, the most serious forms of violence are committed by adult white males—such as Timothy McVeigh (convicted of blowing up the Alfred P. Murrah Federal Building in Oklahoma City, killing over 150 people).

For many years, youths have been the scapegoats for a variety of societal ills created by adults. How often have you heard the phrase "It was probably kids" when some deviant act was committed in your neighborhood? One writer astutely commented that "American adults have always believed that youth in their time are more violent than kids in the past."[9]

The Reality of Juvenile Delinquency

When we speak of the phenomenon of "juvenile delinquency," we are referring to a wide variety of mostly harmless behaviors, often done on the spur of the moment, involving a group of youngsters with no one receiving serious harm. The typical delinquent does not make the headlines, and he (most of the offenses are committed by males, although a substantial minority—about 25%—are committed by females) is rarely arrested and rarely makes an appearance in one of the thousands of juvenile courts in the country. Even among those referred to court, at least half never come back on another offense. The incidents listed above are hardly typical of the "crimes" committed by children. In fact, several myths need to be challenged before proceeding.

Myth 1: Today's youth are more criminal than ever

As chapter 2 makes clear, the overall crime rate for youths declined dramatically during the 1990s. If any one age group is more criminal, it is adults. During the 1990s the arrest rates for Index crimes (murder, rape, robbery, aggravated assault, burglary, larceny, motor vehicle theft, arson) went down by 15% for those under 18. It went up for those in their 30s by 36% and by 20% for those in their 40s. Despite this data, many noted criminologists, officials, and journalists predicted a huge rise in youth violence in the 1990s. James Q. Wilson stated in 1994 that crime had declined in the past decade with the exception of homicides by juveniles. In November 1995 criminologist John Diiulio published a report titled "The Coming of the Super-Predators."[10] President Bill Clinton said in 1996 that the crime rate had declined the previous three years, while "violence among young people under eighteen is up." Northeastern University's James Alan Fox predicted in 1996 that we would see an explosion of superpredators in the near future, dramatically stating, "We are facing a potential bloodbath of teenage violence in years ahead." That same year an attorney for New York City, Peter Reinharz, warned that "we must prepare for the onslaught of juvenile violence," while Pulitzer Prize winner Edward Humes stated, "We have an army forming on the horizon."[11]

A study by Mike Males, Daniel Macallair, and Megan Corcoran documented some amazing differences between adults and juveniles during the period 1980 and 2005. Examining data from Criminal Justice Statistics Center of the California Department of Justice, they found that in Los Angeles County the overall rate of felony arrests for juveniles declined by 66 percent; the arrest rate for violent felonies declined by 55 percent. What is most interesting is the fact that during this same period of time, the rate of felony arrests for those between 40 and 59 went up by 250%.[12]

Myth 2: As the number of teenagers rises so does the crime rate

As suggested above, the proportion of teenagers in so-called crime-prone years has little to do with overall crime. In fact, quite often just the opposite is true. For example, the study discussed above found that homicides in Los Angeles in the late 1980s rose rapidly as the young male population declined. The researchers found that between 1980 and 2005 the number of juveniles in the population of Los Angeles County rose by 34 percent, while their overall crime rate declined.

Despite the widespread demographic fallacy, the percentage of those under 20 peaked in 1969 and has declined since then. Yet James Q. Wilson warned in his often-quoted 1975 book *Thinking about Crime* that there is a "critical mass" of young people that "creates an explosive increase in the amount of crime, addiction, and welfare dependency." In fact, during the late 1980s the overall murder rate in the U.S. went up quite dramatically from around 8.5 to over 10 (per 100,000 population), while at the same time the percentage of males between 15 and 19 (supposedly the most violent age group) steadily declined.[13]

Myth 3: Youth of today are using more guns and committing more violent crime than ever

This myth is based on purely anecdotal evidence, especially the headline stories about the rare youth who uses a gun in a killing. During a ten-year period from 2000 to 2009, arrest rates for violent crime among juveniles declined 15%; arrests for possession of weapons dropped 7.5% (see chapter 2).[14] James Alan Fox wrote in 1996 that teenagers are "temporary sociopaths, impulsive and immature" and suggested that a 45-year-old with a gun is less likely to use it than a 14-year-old (calling 14-year-olds "trigger happy"). The homicide rate for the 13–14 age group at that time was 4.7—exactly the same as the rate for the age group between 40 and 49.[15] Juveniles are far more likely to be killed by their own parents at home than killed by one of their peers at school by a ratio of 15 to 1. A related myth is that the rise of "gangsta rap" has caused a rise in homicides by youth. Quite the opposite is true, as throughout the 1990s the number of rap music albums sold doubled (from 74 million to 125 million), while the number of teenage males arrested for murder decreased by half.[16]

Myth 4: Teenagers are the biggest part of the drug problem

Drug emergency cases contradict this commonly held belief. In 2007, people under the age of 18 accounted for 6.3% (the lowest percentage of those aged 12 or older) of all illicit drug emergency cases in the nation's hospitals. In contrast, the 34–44 age group constituted 26.5% (the highest percentage) of drug emergency cases.[17] Prescription drug abuse is more prevalent than illicit drug use for those under the age of 18. [18] Drug arrests for juveniles declined 14.8% between 2000 and 2009. In 2000 juveniles accounted for almost 13% of all drug arrests, while in 2009 the percentage was 10.4.[19]

Myth 5: Youths who commit murder and other serious crimes need to be treated as adults

Every major study has found that certifying children as adults does more harm than good. Certification has been applied to only 2% or 3% of all juveniles who are arrested, but the vast majority of those are minority youths.[20] National data show that 7,200 cases were waived in 1985; waivers peaked in 1994 at 13,100 and declined 35% to 8,500 cases in 2007. Of the waived cases, 47% were charged with a person offense in 2007, while 27% were charged with a property offense, and 13% were charged with a drug offense.[21]

A closely related myth says that tougher laws will reduce juvenile crime. This is not true. One example of getting tough is curfew laws, periodically touted as a cure-all for juvenile crime. Contrary to popular beliefs and pronouncements by law enforcement agencies, enforcement of curfew laws has no impact on juvenile crime. One study found that in several California cities, teenage crime was far more likely to decrease when curfew laws were *not* enforced. Similar results have been found for crackdowns on teenage driving. In California, before a new law went into effect (mandating that they not drive alone but with friends or adults) the rate of serious crashes involving those under 18 was going down. After the crackdown, the rates went up.[22] A careful review of the literature by Kenneth Adams found that most of the research done on the subject found that the enforcement of these laws has little or no impact on crime.[23]

Normal Adolescent Behavior or Deviance?

These and other myths about juvenile crime will be discussed throughout this book as we survey the various behaviors typically committed by individuals legally classified as "juveniles" (in most states those under the age of 18). As you will see in chapter 2, it is rather "normal" for individuals to violate some law or ordinance. In fact, surveys have consistently shown that virtually all youngsters commit some act that could theoretically result in an arrest by the police and a referral to the local juvenile court. In this sense, there is nothing "deviant" about "delinquency." It is very common adolescent behavior. When the offenses involve serious loss of property or serious harms to other human beings and when they are repeatedly committed over an extended period of time, then the behavior becomes something other than "normal." Youngsters whose behavior falls in this category are the ones whose files at the juvenile court are so thick that you need extra file folders, or extra space on a computer program.

What needs to be pointed out at the outset, however, is that with few exceptions these persistent delinquents—some call them chronic delinquents—do not appear out of nowhere for no apparent reason. With few exceptions, if one is confronted with a "hardened delinquent," one is also confronted with a youngster who has been victimized repeatedly, often starting as young as infancy. Those who work with these youngsters can corroborate a sad fact: the victimizer of today is the victim of yesterday.

Cultural Influences

What also needs to be pointed out is that the nature of the crime problem in the United States is directly related to our culture. The overall rate of crime—especially violent crime—is much higher in this country than in any other in the world. Any serious effort to reduce the problem must confront this fact and seriously consider some drastic changes in our way of life and our attitudes about children.

These youngsters—even the most hardened—can be salvaged. This is the lesson given to us by the authors of *Reclaiming Youth at Risk.*[24] The authors of this very unique book borrow heavily from Native American culture in exploring the ways youth who are at risk can be reclaimed.

It is time that we consider that we adults are just as much a part of the problem as are troubled youths, perhaps more so. After all, we seem to forget that *adults* created this world; it is *adults* who modeled the behavior, attitudes, and beliefs that young people follow. If we make even a cursory list of the incredible harms adults have committed over the centuries, the misdeeds of our modern adolescents—including the most hardened who sit in our jails, detention centers, and training schools—pale by comparison. It was not our adolescents who started the two World Wars, the Korean War, and the Vietnam War, which collectively took the lives of well over a million people; it was not our adolescents who engaged in the greatest theft and kidnapping and enslavement in human history, the theft of Native American lands, the kidnapping of Africans and their enslavement in the South; and none of our troubled youth were responsible for the bombing in Oklahoma City. Finally, none of America's youth carefully planned, backed up with one lie and distortion after another, what amounts to an invasion of a foreign country, Iraq, costing thousands of lives. And what are today's youth gangs in our inner cities doing if not mirroring the defense of "turf" done by adults in the Middle East and many other places around the globe?

In short, if we want to know where the answers lie and where to begin to look for solutions, we should start by looking in the mirror. We should ask: Is there anything that *I* can do differently? Is there something wrong with *my* attitudes, *my* beliefs, and *my* actions that contribute to the problem? If we want some answers, we should start the search *within ourselves*.

Fear Colors Reaction

Another crucial point is the recognition that the reaction to the offenses of young people is way out of proportion to the harm. Part of this overreaction stems from the extreme *fear* of young people—especially minorities. One particular case that illustrates such overreaction occurred in Las Vegas, home of the author. It was well publicized and involved a nine-year-old boy accused of vandalism. His "crime" consisted of writing his initials, the names of some of his friends, and some other markings in a cement sidewalk next to a construction site. According to testimony in the case, the child said that one or two workers at this site told him that he could write on the sidewalk, and so he did.

Apparently, the child overdid it a little and charges were filed. The police subsequently came to his school and arrested him in front of his classmates—handcuffs and all! One of the district attorneys charged him with a felony, calling this a very serious crime! The child was eventually placed on probation. The "zero tolerance" mentality can lead to extremes, and we will have more to say about this trend in later chapters.

Jennifer Taylor thoughtfully analyzed the overreaction of many states and legislation to punish juveniles as adults. She quoted a newspaper editorial at the beginning of her article about Proposition 21 in California, the Gang Violence and Juvenile Crime Prevention Initiative, which voters passed in March 2000 by a 62% majority.

> In our zeal to capture the hardened teen criminal, we spread the net too wide.
> In it we have caught the child who is too young to understand the difference
> between reality and fantasy, the first-time offender, the hormone-driven ado-
> lescent, the abused youth lashing out at the world. We have rewritten the
> rules: No more second chances, kid. It's one strike and you're out. [25]

Proposition 21 gave prosecutors—not judges—the power to decide whether juveniles as young as fourteen would be tried as adults for major felonies. Taylor notes that the reaction to crimes "that stick in your mind forever and break your heart: kids killing kids, lives wasted, and lives lost due to teen violence" has resulted in a dramatic shift away from attempts to rehabilitate young lives to punishment and incarceration.[26]

Critics of such measures as Proposition 21 have repeatedly noted that they target mostly the poor and especially racial minorities. The general issue of race will be one of the central themes of this book. Indeed, one cannot realistically examine the problem of delinquency—especially our reaction to it—without considering race. The "war on drugs" and the "war on gangs" launched during the 1980s became blatant examples of some of the most racist policies in U.S. history. As will be pointed out in several chapters, these "wars" (why is it that we so often use the "war" metaphor?) have consistently targeted racial minorities and, of course, the poor. Whether categorized as "collateral" damage, the result of unintended consequences, or the primary intention of those who established the policies, the effects on minorities and the poor have been devastating.

There are many examples of the trend toward punishment. The state of Oregon, traditionally known as a liberal state, passed one of the toughest pieces of legislation in the entire country in 1994. Known as "Measure 11," it amounts to a "one strike, you're out" form of punishment. It is about as draconian as we have ever witnessed, and it takes us back to the days of Puritanism in the seventeenth century. According to this legislation, if a child is 15 years of age and is charged with one of several specific crimes, he will automatically be tried as an adult and if convicted will spend years behind bars. Some of the offenses include: Sodomy I (8 years, 4 months), Sodomy II (6 years, 3 months), Unlawful Sexual Penetration I (8 years, 4 months), and Unlawful Sexual Penetration II (6 years, 3 months). As recently as May 2003, fully one-half of all of those locked up in juvenile institutions in Oregon had been committed for sex offenses.[27]

Understanding Juvenile Delinquency

Before we can seriously consider any solutions, we must begin by first trying to develop a general *understanding* of the phenomenon of juvenile delinquency. Part I reviews the nature and the extent of delinquency. Chapter 1 reviews the historical record of how the problem of delinquency began to be defined and the responses to it during the early years of the nineteenth century. The history of our response to the behaviors committed by children has not been a very glorious one. In fact, adult society has imposed on its youth some of the most egregious harms ever inflicted on one group of people. We find the roots of our somewhat contradictory responses to delinquency in the early days of the nineteenth century: benevolence mixed with loathing and cruelty; a "velvet glove" cloaked in an "iron fist." And the targets of the most repressive policies have consistently been those deemed the most "dangerous"—starting with Irish immigrants in the early nineteenth century and ending with African Americans and Hispanics in the twenty-first century.

In chapters 2 through 5, delinquency will be explored in some detail, starting with a general survey of how much delinquency there is, its nature, and the variety of behaviors labeled delinquent. Two specific forms of delinquency will be covered in chapters 4 and 5: "gang" delinquency and female delinquency.

Part II considers the very important question of why there is delinquency and crime. The most common theories of delinquency are summarized in chapters 6 and 7. Chapter 8 explores one of the most important variables related to crime and delinquency—social class and inequality—in its many forms. Over 100 years of research has revealed the importance of social class and the corresponding inequality. As will be noted, U.S. society is highly unequal; in fact, it is the most unequal among all the industrialized democracies. Inequality determines not only rates of juvenile offending but also, and especially, the official response. For several years beginning in 2008, the American economy suffered the greatest decline since the Great Depression of the 1930s; the impact on the urban poor has been particularly difficult. National unemployment in September 2010 hovered near 10%, while the hardest hit areas experienced much higher rates.

Chapters 9 and 10 will present a detailed look at two of our most important institutions that are strongly correlated with delinquency: the family and the schools.

In Part III of the book, we explore some of the most common responses to crimes committed by our youth. Chapter 11 describes the processing of cases from the police to the juvenile court. Chapter 12 explores the double standard of juvenile justice with a close look at how girls fare within this system. Chapter 13 takes a detailed, critical look at juvenile institutions, with an emphasis on their failure for more than 150 years to adequately deal with the problem.

The book ends with a detailed look at some alternative responses and some suggestions to reduce the number of children labeled delinquent (chapter 14). One particular program that the author evaluated, known as the Detention

Diversion Advocacy Project (DDAP), is covered along with many other model programs. It is hoped that the reader will come away with a better understanding of the phenomenon of juvenile delinquency. Ideally, if we can combine our understanding and energies to make the world a better place for children, everyone will benefit.

Conservative, Liberal, and Radical Views of Crime

In order to sort through the constructions and solutions discussed in this text, we need to be aware of ideologies that influence various perspectives. The media is one of many sources that present conflicting viewpoints. The reality perceived by the various parties is shaped by the lenses through which it is viewed. To conclude this chapter, I provide brief summaries of three very different perspectives on crime and criminal justice: conservative, liberal and radical. As the reader will see, these are also different perspectives on human beings and on the world itself.

Crime has always been and continues to be a hot political topic—the subject of countless commentaries by pundits and almost always an issue in state and local elections. Various perspectives and proposals are offered by both politicians and by scholars. These views fall into the three political and ideological perspectives mentioned above. Granted, the radical view is rarely expressed among politicians, although certain aspects of this perspective can be found among the various proposals for reducing crime. The two most common are, of course, the conservative and the liberal.

What follows is not to be seen as an exhaustive overview of the subject but rather a kind of "primer."[28]

The Conservative View

From a conservative perspective, democracy and the free enterprise system are working well, with most problems caused by individuals or groups of individuals who seem, mainly because of some character flaw(s), unable to succeed within the overall system. In essence, some individuals or groups make bad or irrational choices (it is assumed everyone has free will) that put them in problematic circumstances. Aside from some psychological and/or biological assistance (which can affect "choice"), the most effective way to address social problems such as crime is through the economic system. For example, cutting taxes on corporations is viewed as an incentive to create jobs, which will offer opportunities to earn money and thus avoid crime. The conservative view generally assumes that less government is better, except for enforcing the laws. The use of tax dollars for social programs to assist the general public is to be avoided whenever possible. Equality can be achieved mainly through hard work.[29] Part of the conservative philosophy is a strong belief in "rugged individualism," or the idea that you don't need help from others or the government.

The term conservatism has its roots in the Latin word *conservare*, which means to "save" or "preserve." Although the word has had a variety of meanings over the years (as has liberalism), in general it refers to a philosophy that supports "tradition" and the "status quo." One definition of conservatism is this: "Preference for the existing order of society—an opposition to all efforts to bring about rapid or fundamental change."[30]

A popular variation is "Libertarianism," which can be defined as a "belief that legitimate government should be small and should play only the most minimal possible role in economic, social and cultural life, with social relationships to be regulated as much as possible by voluntary contracts and generally accepted custom and as little as possible by statute law." Libertarians usually oppose government programs for the redistribution of income and other types of intervention to correct the ills of society.[31] Many libertarians find common ground with liberals when it comes to criminal justice, such as their opposition to the drug war and the overreach of the criminal law.[32]

Conservatism also refers to a belief that existing economic and political inequalities are justified and that the existing order is about as close as is practically attainable to an ideal order. One of the earliest conservatives was Edmund Burke, who supported the idea that the "proper formulation of government came from time-honored development of the state, piecemeal progress through experience, and the continuation of other important societal institutions such as the family and the Church." Another branch of conservatism originated from the Frenchman Joseph de Maistre who, writing in strong opposition to the French Revolution, "supported the restoration of hereditary monarchy, which he regarded as a divinely sanctioned institution, and for the indirect authority of the Pope over temporal matters."[33] From an economic standpoint, conservatives have generally supported a "modified free market" in contrast to a strictly "laissez-faire" system. Thus they support government intervention into the economy to "promote competition while maintaining the national interest."[34]

As the linguist George Lakoff explains, behind conservatism is a view of the family that can be described as the traditional nuclear family headed by the father as the major breadwinner. The society as a whole should operate based on this model of the family. There is, under this system, a "strict father morality" which is based in part on the belief that in order to become a "good" and "moral" person a child must learn to obey the rules and respect authority. Proper behavior is taught through the use or threat of punishment. Within such a system "the exercise of authority is itself moral; that is, it is moral to reward obedience and punish disobedience."[35]

For conservatives, the system of rewards and punishments has a higher purpose: in order to survive in a dangerous world, children must learn discipline and build character. Punishment, according to this philosophy, is the only way to become a self-disciplined and moral person. "Spare the rod, spoil the child" is a popular phrase. To be successful requires becoming self-disciplined. More importantly, rewarding someone who has not developed self-discipline is immoral. As a result, conservatives generally do not endorse welfare, affirmative action, or lenient punishments, all of which are considered rewards for laziness, failure to excel, and deviance.[36] There is often an erroneous assumption that those who are rich and famous became so through their own efforts, with little or no help from others.

According to the conservative view, there is a "morality of strength." Moral strength can be seen as a metaphor. The metaphor suggests that the world is divided into "good" and "evil," and in order to stand up to evil one must be morally strong; one becomes morally strong through a system of rewards and punishments that teach self-discipline. A person who is morally weak cannot fight evil. If one is too self-indulgent, he or she is immoral. It follows logically that crime and deviance are the result of moral weakness and indulgence. Teenage sex, drug use, and all sorts of other "deviant" behaviors stem from lack of self-control. A person with proper self-discipline should be able to "just say no." Those who do not must be and deserve to be punished.[37]

There has been a great deal of research supporting the connection between conservatism and the authoritarian personality.[38] Theodor Adorno[39] and his colleagues at what came to be called the Frankfurt School (a group of Germans who fled from Nazi Germany during World War II, first to Britain and then to Berkeley, California) first identified the authoritarian personality. The research explored the question of why some people easily succumb to fascism and eventually expanded to related issues such as anti-Semitism and ethnocentrism. The researchers developed the F Scale to measure fascism, authoritarianism, ethnocentrism, etc.[40] Among the key findings about the authoritarian personality were: a rigid adherence to rules (and to authority in general), an inability or unwillingness to accept ambiguity, superstition (which is in turn is often linked to religious beliefs),[41] the use of stereotypes, and punitiveness. The researchers also identified characteristics such as scapegoating and prejudice.[42]

The conservative view of crime and criminal justice can be summarized very simply. People commit crime because they think they can get away with it, largely because the pleasure they get from committing the crime is greater than the potential pain they would receive if caught and punished.[43] This is, of course, the popular "deterrence" perspective. From this perspective people refrain from committing crime mostly because of *fear* of getting caught and punished. In order to reduce crime, the pain must be increased so that it is greater than the pleasure received from committing the crime. In other words, to reduce crime, we should increase the odds of getting caught and the severity of punishment so that potential criminals will think twice before committing the crime. To use a popular phrase "if you can't do the time, don't do the crime."

Conservatives see criminals as having defective choice mechanisms. Specifically, they believe obeying rules and going to school are essential elements in eventually earning a living and becoming a productive member of society. Choosing not to participate in these behaviors leads to delinquency—substance abuse, crime, violence, or any number of deviant combinations.

Students of criminal justice may recognize this argument as being part of the "classical school" of criminology. This school of thought makes these assumptions: (1) All people are by their nature self-serving and therefore liable to commit crime. (2) In order to live in harmony and avoid a "war of all against all," people agree to give up certain freedoms in order to be protected by a strong central state. (3) Punishment is necessary to deter crime, and the state has the prerogative (which has been granted to it by the people through a social contract) to administer it. (4) Punishment should fit the crime and not be used to rehabilitate the offender. (5) Each individual is responsible for his or her actions; therefore, mitigating circumstances or excuses are inadmissible.[44]

Many on the extreme right have been complaining that their rights have been taken away from them and that the government has ignored them. They often feel a sense of powerlessness in the midst of rapid changes. It is no accident that almost all of them are white and one of their major complaints is that they are being discriminated against because of affirmative action, even though blacks as a group fare much worse on virtually every economic indicator.[45] Ron Walters, an emeritus professor of government and politics at the University of Maryland, believes that many citizens whose candidate lost the presidential election in 2008 are feeling disempowered and disenfranchised. "The movement of conservatism is dethroned. People are feeling, therefore, resentful about that and determined to demonstrate that resentment in ways that intimidate people, quite frankly." Drew Westen, a psychologist at Emory University, said these feelings of "victimhood" were reinforced by Republicans during Senate hearings for Obama's Supreme Court appointment of Sonia Sotomayor. He states that: "They attacked her as a racist, and where they scored points is with a lot of Americans—not only with conservatives, but a lot of Democratic white males—who have been on the losing end of affirmative action." He said that Republicans were able "to make the case that whites are getting a bad deal."[46]

It is interesting to note that back in 1964 historian Richard Hofstadter, writing about the "paranoid style of American politics," noted that in the mid-1950s conservative whites were complaining that:

> America has been largely taken away from them and their kind, though they are determined to try to repossess it and to prevent the final destructive act of subversion. The old American virtues have already been eaten away by cosmopolitans and intellectuals; the old competitive capitalism has been gradually undermined by socialistic and communistic schemers; the old national security and independence have been destroyed by treasonous plots, having as their most powerful agents not merely outsiders and foreigners as of old but major statesmen who are at the very centers of American power.[47]

Jonathan Simon has argued that starting in the late 1960s the elite in America have been engaged in "governing through crime" in that crime has become such a significant issue that many laws have extended governmental control into the lives of the majority of citizens (ironically quite contrary to conservative philosophy, and especially that of libertarians).[48]

The Liberal View

Modern liberalism has its roots in the period known as the Enlightenment in the eighteenth century and in particular in the works of John Locke (among others) whose writings had a profound impact on the leaders of the American Revolution. During this time period there was a rejection of many assumptions that dominated most theories of government, such as the "Divine Right of Kings," hereditary status, established religion, and free trade. The *Declaration of Independence* was a liberal document as it proclaimed that "all men are created equal; that they are endowed by their Creator with certain unalienable rights; that among these are life, liberty and the pursuit of happiness; that to insure these rights, governments are instituted among men, deriving their just powers from the consent of the governed."[49]

Liberals view the relationship between democracy and free-enterprise as problematic, with most benefits accruing to a small minority that has created a huge gap in both income and wealth. Some individuals are disadvantaged by problems with the system (not necessarily by their own choice), and should, therefore, be helped by those more fortunate, for whom the system does work. Liberals see plenty of flaws in the system and therefore support the use of tax dollars for various social programs for work, housing, health care, and so on. Liberals see the goal of government as providing for the general welfare of society or the "common good"—the philosophy of Roosevelt's "New Deal" during the 1930s, which instituted programs such as Social Security and the G.I. Bill.[50]

Liberals support the notion that many offenders come from disadvantaged situations related to the social structure rather than disadvantages resulting from individual choice. As a result, liberal responses to crime differ from conservative responses. For example, the liberal viewpoint believes prisons should focus on rehabilitation via education, work, and social skill enhancement. Prison rehabilitation should be followed by help after release for problems related to housing, schools, health clinics, etc. For liberals, this "systemic" approach, although costly at the outset, would be the only way to affect crime and, at the same time, improve society.[51]

Liberalism, in contrast to conservatism, views society as a "nurturant parent." According to George Lakoff, the liberal view of the family is one in which both parents are equally responsible for the moral development of children. The primary duty of such parents—and by extension the entire society—is to love and nurture their children. Nurturing includes two important aspects: empathy and responsibility—for both yourself and others. The element of "social responsibility" is a core value that stresses the importance of helping others and being concerned for the well-being of the community and the entire society. Rather than acting like an *authoritarian* parent, liberals stress the importance of acting like an *authoritative* parent.[52] Two very different approaches to responding to crime emanate from the liberal and conservative perspectives.

Throughout history, people have committed a variety of harms against their fellow human beings; societies have instituted a variety of procedures to identify those who harm others. Obviously no one wants serial rapists or murderers wandering the streets—even "leftists" like myself want something done about such crimes! Just as obvious, no one wants their homes burglarized, their cars stolen, their purses snatched, etc.

On the other hand, there is a lot left unsaid in the conservative argument. The most important omission is the question of "why do people commit crime in the first place?" Is it only the fear of getting caught and punished that keeps us from doing harm to others? Could it be possible that most of us are socialized to respect the rights of others, to believe that it is simply wrong to harm other people? And how do conservatives explain the consistently high rates of crime in America—especially violent crime—compared to all other countries (except a few in the Third World)? They cannot claim that we are not tough enough since our punishments are the most severe and we are among a few in the world that use the death penalty (again, except for a few Third World countries).[53] Quite often, conservatives describe crime as if it were simply a choice one makes, not unlike the choices we make of the food we eat.

The Radical View

A third viewpoint is often referred to as "radical," "critical," or "Marxist." From this point of view, the problem of crime stems from the very nature of capitalism. This view begins with the idea that capitalist societies are characterized by conflict—between classes (e.g., labor vs. management), races (black vs. white), and gender. Inequality is created and perpetuated by the capitalist system, largely because profits do not "trickle down" very far. In fact, in recent years there has been the greatest upward shift of wealth and income since the 1920s.[54]

From this perspective, the role of government is not neutral but rather tends to support the capitalist system and those who benefit from it. Currently (2010) most of the efforts of the Obama administration (and the previous administration) are directed toward saving the capitalist system. Radicals will also argue that even the New Deal during the Roosevelt years of the Great Depression aimed to save capitalism, although millions of working people received assistance.

Karl Marx is the best known proponent of the radical view. He saw capitalism as a system that exploits workers for the benefit of the owners. For Marx, true democracy cannot coexist with capitalism. Government represents the interests of those in power. In his words, the state is the instrument of the ruling class. According to Marx, the capitalist system must be replaced (and indeed will naturally be replaced) by socialism whereby the state "withers away" and those who perform the labor will control the government and all the major industries.[55]

Although Marx was not particularly focused on crime, it is not hard to see that from his analysis, the plight of the criminal becomes tied to the plight of the general, exploited society. Crime is the result of living in a system where access to success goals are limited and even restricted. A radical perspective focuses on "those social structures and forces that produce both the greed of the inside trader as well as the brutality of the rapist or the murderer. And it places those structures in their proper context: the material conditions of class struggle under a capitalist mode of production."[56] The material conditions include the class and racial inequalities produced by the contradictions of capitalism (which produce economic changes that negatively affect the lives of so many people, especially the working class and the poor).[57]

The importance of the capitalist system in producing inequality and hence crime is apparent when examining recent economic changes in American society and the effects of these changes. In recent years particularly, many scholars have begun to seek an explanation of crime and delinquency by examining changes in the economic structure of society and how such changes have contributed to the emergence of what some have called an "underclass," which in many ways represent what Marx called the "surplus population."[58] Moreover, the amount of injustices caused by a system that serves only those in power may well result in even more violent behavior, as this is what inconsistencies and contradictions often induce. Here again, to legitimately address the problem of crime, this view argues that the capitalist system must go.[59]

Social policy is essentially the management of varying interests. When viewpoints conflict, there is a tendency to dismiss those who do not agree with us as misinformed rather than reflecting on the foundations for the differences of opinion. Rarely is there a single answer to complex social problems. An engaged participant can look at the evidence presented as "facts" and evaluate the foundation on which it is based. Does the argument present potential for resolving a problem or does it contribute to myths about issues that create fear and misunderstanding? Misinformation is as readily accessible as reliable information, and the Internet disseminates both at dizzying speeds. Without the necessary background, we may make poor decisions that ignore the long-term implications of policies that address difficult issues. I hope this brief introduction to three perspectives help you navigate the complexities of the nature of juvenile delinquency and potential policies to address problems.

NOTES

[1] Associated Press (2010, September 23). "Florida Teen Dead, 3 Others Charged with Murder." *Miami Herald.* Retrieved from http://www.miamiherald.com/2010/09/24/1840252/fla-teen-dead-3-others-charged.html

[2] Steele, A. (2010, August 23). "Teens, 14 and 17, Charged in Murder of Navy Vet, 87." *Philadelphia Inquirer.* Retrieved from http://www.philly.com/philly/news/breaking/101323349.html?cmpid=15585797

[3] Canning, A. and M. Burbank (2010, April 28). "Jordan Brown Murder Case Takes Emotional Toll." Retrieved from http://abcnews.go.com/Nightline/jordan-brown-murder-case-12-year-adult/story?id=10288704

[4] Associated Press (2010, July 28). "Teens Charged with Murder of Immigrant." Retrieved from http://www.cbsnews.com/stories/2010/07/28/national/main6720148.shtml

[5] Dearing, S. (2010, January 15). "10 Year Old Arizona Boy Who Killed 2 to Receive Treatment." Retrieved from http://www.digitaljournal.com/article/285770; CNN (2010, January 15). "Arizona Boy Who Admitted Killing Father Sentenced to Treatment." Retrieved from http://www.cnn.com/2010/CRIME/01/15/arizona.boy.homicide/index.html?hpt=Sbin

[6] Powers, A. (2009, February 20). "Arizona Boy, 9, Pleads Guilty in Shooting." Retrieved from http://articles.latimes.com/2009/feb/20/nation/na-kidkiller20; Associated Press (2008, November 8). "8-Year-Old Arizona Boy Kills Father." Retrieved from http://www.cbsnews.com/stories/2008/11/08/national/main4586103.shtml

[7] Wagner, D. (2010, January 15). "St. John's Boy Is Sentenced to Treatment." *The Arizona Republic.* Retrieved from http://www.azcentral.com/arizonarepublic/local/articles/2010/01/15/20100115stjohns0115.html

[8] Mail Foreign Service (2010, March 31). "Fury in U.S. as Boy to Be Tried as Adult for Shooting Dead His Father's Fiancée." Retrieved from http://www.dailymail.co.uk/news/worldnews/article-1262271/US-boy-Jordan-Brown-tried-adult-killing-fathers-pregnant-fiance.html

[9] Gluckman, R. (2002). "The Scapegoating of America's Youth." Retrieved from www.zmag.org/Youth/gluckman_ scapegoating.cfm

[10] DiIulio, J. (1995, November 27). "The Coming of the Super-Predators." *Weekly Standard*, p. 23.

[11] Males, M. (1999). *Framing Youth: Ten Myths about the Next Generation.* Monroe, ME: Common Courage Press, p. 32; Elikann, P. (1999). *Superpredators: The Demonization of Our Children by the Law.* Reading, MA: Perseus, p. 25.

[12] Males, M., D. Macallair, and M. D. Corcoran (2006). "Testing Incapacitation Theory: Youth Crime and Incarceration in California." San Francisco: Center on Juvenile and Criminal Justice; see also an updated version of this paper in: Shelden, R. G. and D. Macallair (Eds.) (2008). *Juvenile Justice in America: Problems and Prospects.* Long Grove, IL: Waveland Press, pp. 63–81.

[13] Males, *Framing Youth*, pp. 29, 47–48; Males, M. and D. Macallair. (2000). "Dispelling the Myth: An Analysis of Youth and Adult Crime Patterns in California over the Past 20 Years." San Francisco: Justice Policy Institute (www.cjcj.org/themyth).

[14] *FBI Uniform Crime Reports, 2009.* Retrieved from http://www.fbi.gov/ucr/cius2009/data/table_32.html

[15] Males, *Framing Youth*, p. 49.

[16] Males, M. (2005). "Dubious Demography: The Myth that 'More Youth Means More Crime.'" Unpublished manuscript.

[17] Substance Abuse and Mental Health Services Administration (2010). Office of Applied Studies. *Drug Abuse Warning Network, 2007: National Estimates of Drug-Related Emergency Department Visits,* table 5. Rockville, MD. Retrieved from http://dawninfo.samhsa.gov/files/ED2007/DAWN2k7ED.pdf

[18] Drug Addiction Treatment (2010). "National Study Shows 1 in 5 Teens Abuses Prescription Drugs." Retrieved from http://www.drugaddictiontreatment.com/types-of-addiction/adolescent-drug-abuse/national-study-shows-1-in-5-teens-abuses-prescription-drugs/

[19] *FBI Uniform Crime Reports, 2009*, table 32.

[20] For a review see Fagan, J. and F. Zimring (Eds.) (2000). *The Changing Borders of Juvenile Justice: Transfer of Adolescents to the Criminal Court.* Chicago: University of Chicago Press; Bishop, D. and C. Frazier (1991). "Transfer of Juveniles to Criminal Court: A Case Study and Analysis of Prosecutorial Waiver." *Notre Dame Journal of Law, Ethics and Public Policy* 5: 281–302, and Bishop, D. and J. Henretta (1989). "Prosecutorial Waiver: Case Study of Questionable Reform." *Crime and Delinquency* 35: 179–201.

[21] Adams, B. and S. Addie (2010, June). "Delinquency Cases Waived to Criminal Court, 2007." Washington, DC: Office of Juvenile Justice and Delinquency Prevention, p. 2. Retrieved from http://www.ncjrs.gov/pdffiles1/ojjdp/230167.pdf

[22] Males, M. and D. Macallair (1998). "The Impact of Juvenile Curfew Laws in California." San Francisco: Center on Juvenile and Criminal Justice.

[23] Adams, K. (2003). "The Effectiveness of Juvenile Curfews at Crime Prevention." *The ANNALS of the American Academy of Political and Social Science* 587: 136–59.

[24] Brentro, L. K., M. Brokenleg, and S. Van Bockern (2002). *Reclaiming Youth at Risk: Our Hope for the Future* (2nd ed.). Bloomington, IN: National Education Service.

[25] Taylor, J. (2002). "California's Proposition 21: A Case of Juvenile Injustice." *Southern California Law Review*, 75: 983. Retrieved from http://www-bcf.usc.edu/~usclrev/pdf/075405.pdf

[26] Ibid.

[27] Data supplied by the Oregon Youth Authority (www.oya.state.or.us).

[28] Jim Palombo inspired me to write about this topic. He discusses the three perspectives in his book *Criminal to Critic: Reflections Amid the American Experiment.* Lanham, MD: Rowan and Littlefield, 2009. Jim's book is an excellent place to begin a more in-depth study, as are the other references in this section.

[29] The *Student News Daily* website provides a good chart comparing the conservative and liberal views on a number of current issues. Retrieved from http://www.studentnewsdaily.com/other/conservative-vs-liberal-beliefs/

30 Retrieved from http://www.information-entertainment.com/Politics/polterms.html

31 Ibid.

32 One example is a book called *The Tyranny of Good Intentions: How Prosecutors and Law Enforcement Are Trampling the Constitution in the Name of Justice* by Paul Craig Roberts and Lawrence M. Stratton. New York: Three Rivers Press, 2008. See also Gene Healy, *Go Directly to Jail: The Criminalization of Almost Everything.* Washington, DC: The Cato Institute, 2004. The Cato Institute is a libertarian think tank in Washington, DC.

33 For more detail on the connection between punitiveness and religion, see my book *Our Punitive Society: Race, Class, Gender and Punishment in America.* Long Grove, IL: Waveland Press, 2010 and an article on my website at http://www.sheldensays.com/Res-two.htm

34 Retrieved from http://en.wikipedia.org/wiki/Conservatism

35 Lakoff, G. (1996). *Moral Politics: What Conservatives Know that Liberals Don't.* Chicago: University of Chicago Press, p. 67. His latest book is: *The Political Mind: A Cognitive Scientist's Guide to Your Brain and Its Politics.* New York: Penguin, 2009.

36 Ibid., p. 68.

37 Ibid., pp. 74–75.

38 For a more complete discussion see Marshall, G. (1998). "The Authoritarian Personality." *Dictionary of Sociology.* Retrieved from http://www.encyclopedia.com/doc/1O88-authoritarianpersonality.html

39 Ibid; "Adorno, Theodor Wiesengrund." Retrieved from http://www.encyclopedia.com/topic/Theodor_Wiesengrund_Adorno.aspx#1O88-AdornoTheodorWiesengrund

40 Retrieved from http://en.wikipedia.org/wiki/F-scale; the definitive work on this subject is: Adorno, T. W., E. Frenkel-Brunswik, D. J. Levinson, and R. N. Sanford (1950). *The Authoritarian Personality.* New York: Harper and Row.

41 Randerson, J. (2008, May 13). "Childish Superstition: Einstein's Letter Makes View of Religion Relatively Clear." *The Guardian.* Retrieved from http://www.guardian.co.uk/science/2008/may/12/peopleinscience.religion

42 The key findings from their research can be found in Adorno et al., *The Authoritarian Personality.* A modern descendent of the F Scale is Robert Altemeyer's Right-Wing Authoritarianism Scale (http://en.wikipedia.org/wiki/Right-wing_authoritarianism). A more recent look at the connection between this type of personality and conservatism is found in John Dean's excellent book *Conservatives without Conscience.* New York: Viking, 2006. Dean refers to a study that explored personality characteristics of nursery school children and followed them for two decades. What the researchers found was that "little girls who are indecisive, inhibited, shy, neat, compliant, distressed by life's ambiguity, and fearful will likely become conservative women. Likewise, little boys who are unadventurous, uncomfortable with uncertainty, conformist, moralistic, and regularly telling others how to run their lives will then become conservatives as adults" (Dean, p. 31). The study he is referring to is: Block, J. and J. H. Block (2005). "Nursery School Personality and Political Orientation Two Decades Later." *Journal of Research in Personality.* Retrieved from http://berkeley.edu/news/media/releases/2006/03/block.pdf

43 The classic statement of this view is found in Beccaria, C. (1963). *On Crimes and Punishment.* New York: Bobbs-Merrill; reprinted by Transaction Publishers in 2009 (edited by Graeme Newman and Pietro Maronqui). Retrieved from http://www.crimetheory.com/Archive/Beccaria/index.html

44 For examples of the conservative approach to crime see the following: Wilson, J. Q. (1985). *Thinking About Crime.* New York: Vintage; one of the most simplistic, error-filled books was: Bennett, W., J. DiIulio, and J. P. Walters (1996). *Body Count: Moral Poverty . . . And How to Win America's War Against Crime and Drugs.* New York: Simon and Schuster.

45 A great deal of research documents these discrepancies. On the issue of affirmative action see the following: Wise, T. (2005). *Affirmative Action: Racial Preference in Black and White.* New York: Routledge; Katznelson, I. (2005). *When Affirmative Action Was White.* New York: W.W. Norton. On racial differences in wealth and income see: Oliver, M. and T. Shapiro (Eds.) (2006). *Black Wealth/White Wealth: A New Perspective on Racial Inequality* (2nd ed.). New York: Routledge; Massey, D. and N. Denton (1998). *American Apartheid: Segregation and the Making of the Underclass.* Cambridge, MA: Harvard University Press; Bonilla-Silva, E. (2006). *Racism Without Racists: Color-Blind Racism and the Persistence of Racial Inequality in the United States.* New York: Routledge. For

an excellent discussion of the "hidden dimension" of racism in America see Loewen, J. W. (2005). *Sundown Towns*. New York: Simon and Schuster. One of the best treatments of race and punishment is by Western, B. (2006). *Punishment and Inequality in America*. New York: Russell Sage Foundation. On race and the drug war see Provine, D. M. (2007). *Unequal Under Law: Race in the War on Drugs*. Chicago: University of Chicago Press. Updated information about the distribution of wealth and income can be found at http://www.demos.org/inequality/

[46] Abcarian, R., K. Linthicum, and R. Fausset. (2009, September 17). "White Conservatives Say It's Their Turn for Empowerment." *Los Angeles Times*. Retrieved from http://articles.latimes.com/2009/sep/17/nation/na-white-victimhood17

[47] Hofstadter, R. (1964, November). "The Paranoid Style in American Politics." *Harper's Magazine*, pp. 77–86. Retrieved from http://karws.gso.uri.edu/jfk/conspiracy_theory/the_paranoid_mentality/the_paranoid_style.html

[48] Simon, J. (2007). *Governing Through Crime*. New York: Oxford University Press.

[49] Retrieved from http://en.wikipedia.org/wiki/Liberalism

[50] Schlesinger, A. (2003). *The Coming of the New Deal, 1933–1935 (The Age of Roosevelt, Vol. 2)*. New York: Mariner Books; Badger, A. (2002). *The New Deal: The Depression Years, 1933–1940*. Chicago: Ivan Dee; Smith, J. E. (2008). *FDR*. New York: Random House. An excellent source on the G.I. Bill is: Humes, E. (2006). *Over Here: How the G.I. Bill Transformed the American Dream*. New York: Harcourt. There are many websites concerning the New Deal, including http://newdeal.feri.org/index.htm.

[51] A good summary of this approach to addressing the crime problem is provided by Currie, E. (1998). *Crime and Punishment in America*. New York: Metropolitan Books.

[52] For a more concise summary of Lakoff's two models, see the following: Lakoff, G. (2006). *Thinking Points: Communicating our American Values and Vision*. New York: Farrar, Straus and Giroux; and Lakoff, G. (2004). *Don't Think of an Elephant: Know Your Values and Frame the Debate*. White River Junction, VT: Chelsea Green.

[53] See my essay "Imprisonment and Crime Rates." Retrieved from http://www.sheldensays.com/Res-sixteen.htm

[54] See the following website for details: http://www.demos.org/inequality/numbers.cfm

[55] There are many sources that give an overview of Marxist perspectives. For an introduction visit http://www.marxists.org/subject/students/index.htm; more detail is available at http://www.marxists.org/. A brief definition is available at http://www.britannica.com/EBchecked/topic/367344/Marxism. Also see the following: Callari, A., S. Cullenberg, and C. Biewener (Eds.) (1994). *Marxism in the Postmodern Age: Confronting the New World Order*. New York: Guilford Press; D'Amato, P. (2006). *The Meaning of Marxism*. New York: Haymarket Books; Singer, P. (2001). *Marx: A Very Short Introduction*. New York: Oxford University Press; an excellent source for understanding the current economic crisis from a Marxist perspective is Foster, J. B. and F. Magdoff (2009). *The Great Financial Crisis: Causes and Consequences*. New York: Monthly Review Press.

[56] Quinney, R. and J. Wildeman (1991). *The Problem of Crime: A Peace and Social Justice Perspective* (3rd ed.). Mountain View, CA: Mayfield, p. 77.

[57] A good example of applying some of these ideas to the study of crime—and in particular one prominent theory of crime, that of "anomie" theory—is Messner, S. F. and R. Rosenfeld (2006). *Crime and the American Dream* (4th ed.). Belmont, CA: Wadsworth.

[58] It is important to emphasize that Marx did distinguish between these two terms. The "lumpenproletariat" was seen by Marx as the bottom layer of society, the "social junk," "rotting scum," and so on. In short, they were described as the "criminal class." The "surplus population" referred to working-class men and women who, because of various fluctuations in the market (caused chiefly by contradictions within the capitalist system), were excluded, either temporarily or permanently, from the labor market. It is important to note that during the current recession more and more people have become part of the "surplus population" or "reserve army of labor" given all of the lost jobs and layoffs.

[59] For an excellent presentation of the "radical" perspective in criminology see Lynch, M. J. and R. Michalowski (2006). *Primer in Radical Criminology* (4th ed.). Monsey, NY: Criminal Justice Press.

PART I

THE NATURE AND EXTENT OF DELINQUENCY

THE HOUSE OF REFUGE.

HOOP-SKIRT FACTORY.

SHOE SHOP, NAILING THE SOLES.

SHOE SHOP, REMOVING THE LAST.

WIRE WORKS—COILING WIRE.

THE PLAY-GROUND.

WIRE WORKS, WEAVING WIRE.

SANDPAPERING SOLES, &c.

SHOEMAKERS, FILING THE SOLES.

WIRE WORKS—MAKING SILVER, &c.

BLACKING SHOES.

SHOEMAKERS, PACKING.

Delinquency and Juvenile Justice in Historical Perspective

This chapter traces the development of the juvenile justice system from colonial times to the present. It begins with a brief discussion of how the misbehavior of children and youth was dealt with in colonial society and then turns to the buildup of institutions dealing with "juvenile delinquents" in the early nineteenth century. The chapter closes with a discussion of the reforms that took place in the last half of the nineteenth century, culminating in the modern juvenile court and juvenile training schools.

From our current historical vantage point, this is not a story with a happy ending. Indeed, we have continued to succumb to what many refer to as an *edifice complex*—we have continued to view the solution to many human problems as requiring some form of "edifice"—a courthouse, an institution, a detention center, etc. The mantra in the movie, *Field of Dreams*, is chillingly accurate in this context: "If you build them, they will come." In other words, as soon as you construct these "edifices," they will be filled almost immediately.

Another major theme of the chapter is that each new institution (e.g., reform schools, training schools, etc.) has been established on the heels of the failure of old institutions that had become overcrowded, inhumane, and costly. Each new institution was supposed to alleviate some of the problems created by existing institutions, but the replacement institutions soon became equally harsh and overcrowded.

The third theme of this chapter is that the juvenile justice system has been used mostly to control the behavior of the children of the urban poor, especially racial and ethnic minority groups. More informal—and less repressive—mechanisms have been reserved primarily for the children of the more privileged classes.[1]

The Invention of Childhood

Once upon a time there were no "children" and no concept of "adolescence." This is not to say that there were not persons under the age of 18 or under the age of 10 for that matter. In his excellent book, *The Disappearance of Childhood*, Neil Postman notes that:

> It is quite possible for a culture to exist without a social idea of children. Unlike infancy, childhood is a social artifact, not a biological category. Our genes contain no clear instructions about who is and who is not a child, and the laws of survival do not require that a distinction be made between the world of an adult and the world of a child.

He further notes that the word "children" is no more than about 150 years old, and the custom of celebrating a child's birthday did not exist until around 1800. Until the late nineteenth century the terms "adolescence" and "teenager" were not part of the language.[2]

Another way of putting this is to say that puberty is a biological fact, while "childhood" and "adolescence" are social facts. There is no biological reason why young people cannot assume most adult roles several years after the onset of puberty. In fact, before the industrial revolution when farming was the dominant way of life, a boy was considered a man as soon as he could fire a weapon or plow the fields or do countless other things men did. Similarly, a girl became a woman soon after puberty, when she was able to get pregnant. A close examination of anyone's family history will show women giving birth starting as young as 13 or 14.

In recent years we have seen what can be described as an extension of childhood and adolescence well beyond what was considered normal 150 years ago. College males aged 20, 21, or 22 may be seen on any college campus acting rather childish, doing all sorts of idiotic things that would have been unthinkable a century ago, when there was no leisure time for such behavior. Nineteenth-century counterparts would have been married with two or more children and either working on the farm or, in the twentieth century, working in mines and factories. Starting at the age of 10, most youths were working 14 hours a day 150 years ago.[3] As more and more immigrants arrived in this country to fill the jobs previously held by 10–15 year olds, "child labor" laws were passed. "Compulsory schooling" came about during the same period of time; something had to be done to occupy the youths displaced by the new immigrant labor force.

This brief introduction is intended to highlight the fact that "juvenile delinquency" is nothing more than various forms of deviance committed by persons under a certain biological age, one which has been rather arbitrarily set by adult legislators in the various states. Much of the behavior that is brought to the attention of juvenile courts around the country would not be "crimes" if it were not for the fact that we have set an arbitrary age for dividing "childhood" from "adulthood." Just to give you an idea of the arbitrary nature of this age, while most states set the legal age for adulthood at 18, many set it at 17 and a few use 16, prompting the logical question: "Why the difference?" Is there something the states that use 16 or 17 know that the other states do not know? Note also that "adults" of 18 often cannot purchase alcohol.

Shortly we will introduce the concept of "status offenses" as those "crimes" that are specific to those under the age of adulthood. These are behaviors like running away from home, truancy (back in the nineteenth century we made it a "crime" to miss too much school), being "unmanageable" or "incorrigible," curfew violations, liquor or cigarette law violations, etc. Again these offenses depend on arbitrary designations. In one state you can drink at 16; in another you will be arrested for exactly the same behavior. In one state you can run away from home at age 17, but in another state you will be arrested (even if you had a very good reason for running away, such as fleeing from an abusive parent).

Little Adults

The concept of childhood is of relatively recent vintage. In the Middle Ages (AD 500 to 1400) "infancy" ended at around seven, and "adulthood" began immediately; there was no "intervening stage." Art in the Middle Ages depicted children as little men and women.[4] In the medieval world childhood was "invisible."[5]

In fact, the "family" as we know it today did not exist in the Middle Ages. Until about the fourteenth century, one's "family" meant one's lineage, with an emphasis on "blood ancestry" rather than the "conjugal unit."

> The family was composed of large numbers of people in a constant state of flux and, on the estates of noblemen, whole crowds of servants, vassals, musicians, people of every class as well as a good many animals, in the ancient patriarchal household tradition.[6]

People in the Middle Ages were not conscious of "children" as a distinct social category. Unlike today, the typical child had very limited contact with a biological parent. In most families "children" were sent to another family for a period of apprenticeship, usually some sort of domestic service. This usually lasted from about age 7 to 14 or 18. (Keep in mind that during this time, there were no special words to describe these "little adults.") The child never developed a heavy dependence on his or her parents, since the typical household included all sorts of adults, not just the immediate family—there were visitors, friends, distant relatives, servants, etc.[7]

More crucially, children were never segregated into special quarters, schools, or even activities. There was no separate world of childhood. Children shared the same clothing, the same games, and the same stories with adults. They lived their lives together, never apart. There was no concept of privacy. In the Middle Ages, children witnessed all adult behavior. They were not "innocent" as we understand the term today, nor did parents worry about "protecting" children. Paintings by various artists of the time showed how the culture of the period did not hide anything from children.

Literacy

A key reason for the lack of distinction between adults and children was the lack of literacy. Throughout the Middle Ages, communications were primarily oral. Childhood ended at around the age of seven—the age at which children have command over speech and are able to understand others. It should also be noted that during the Middle Ages the Catholic Church determined that the age of seven was when a person knew right from wrong and could reason.

People did what was necessary to survive. Children were valuable sources of labor for communities and families. There was a very high rate of child mortality in the Middle Ages.

> In part because of children's inability to survive, adults did not, and could not, have the emotional commitment to them that we accept as normal. The prevailing view was to have many children in the hope that two or three might survive. On these grounds, people obviously could not allow themselves to become too attached to the young.[8]

Simply put, childhood ended at seven and adulthood began at once, with no intervening stages—no "adolescence" and no "teenager." One historian notes: "Of all the characteristics in which the medieval age differs from the modern, none is so striking as the comparative absence of interest in children."[9]

Johann Gutenberg is generally attributed with inventing the printing press in 1456 in Mainz, Germany (although the Chinese and Koreans had earlier versions). Gutenberg's invention changed the course of Western history. It created a symbolic world. Prior to printing, all communication occurred in a social context. Reading is isolated and private; the reader and his or her response are separated from social interaction. Books became a way of achieving fame and fortune and having one's words and work last forever, which in turn created a new sense of self, a unique identity. The linearity of the printed book affected how humans thought about the world. The emphasis was on logic and clarity.

While the early Renaissance began in about 1350, the most sweeping changes began after the invention of the printing press in 1440.[10] The rebirth of Western civilization swept away old feudal customs and institutions, made huge gains in intellectual development, and paralleled the emergence of capitalism. The Renaissance was a period of learning, commerce, and exploration. The need for binding contracts, deeds to property, and maps required an educated public. Within about 100 years after the invention of the printing press the foundations of modern science were laid, with the year 1543 standing out. This was the year that Copernicus and Vesalius published their famous books on astronomy and anatomy respectively.[11]

With the coming of books came a sharp distinction between those who could read and those who could not. Soon the idea of "childhood" became part of the human vocabulary. Adults learned to read first, and eventually it was accepted that the young would have to *become* adults by learning to read. Before literacy, the only line of separation was the ability to communicate orally. Before the technology of the printing press exploded, literacy was restricted to the clergy and those wealthy enough to afford tutors. Books were copied by hand and available only to the most privileged. European society invented schools and in so doing invented childhood.[12]

Schools

To give you an idea of the impact of these developments, consider the growth of schools in England. During the sixteenth century, villages all over England built schools to provide instruction for their children. One survey found that whereas in 1480 there were 34 schools in England, by 1660 there were 444, a growth of more than 1200% in less than 200 years. Because schools were designed "for the preparation of a literate adult, the young came to be perceived not as miniature adults but as something quite different altogether—unformed adults. School learning became identified with the special nature of childhood." The word "schoolboy" became popular and was synonymous with the word "child."[13] *Infancy* was eventually seen as ending when the command of speech was achieved, while *childhood* began "with the task of learning how to read." In fact, adults who could not read were described as "intellectually childish."[14]

Once people were categorized based on one characteristic—in this case, the inability to read—other characteristics were noticed and amplified. As childhood became a distinct social category based on literacy, other stages of childhood became visible. One student of the history of schooling and childhood observed that children were "segregated at schools, receiving special printed materials geared to distinct stages of learning."[15] These stages soon emerged as separate peer groups and created a distinctive youth culture. Not surprisingly, a special children's jargon emerged and eventually books were written about child rearing. In the Middle Ages it had been common for the same name to be given to different children, followed by a number to indicate birth order. By the seventeenth century, children received distinct names. "Children's literature" began to appear in the mid-eighteenth century with the publication in 1744 of a book called *Jack the Giant Killer*.[16]

What must also be remembered is that learning in a school setting required the development of incredible self-control, which runs counter to the natural inclinations of children. Children's natural exuberance had to be slowed down and controlled. Starting around the sixteenth century, "both schoolmasters and parents began to impose a rather stringent discipline on children. The natural inclinations of children began to be perceived not only as an impediment to book learning but as an expression of an evil character." [17] One of the primary purposes of education was to teach children to overcome possibly evil natures and to control their behavior. The school's emphasis on overcoming unacceptable behavior was an early example of a social control mechanism for a group based on age and a forerunner to the modern juvenile justice system. In previous ages children had been almost totally independent. As the culture changed to differentiate children from adults, there was a corresponding evolution to almost total dependence. Although there had been no need to control the same age group in the Middle Ages, once childhood was created by adult society, there followed a need for new forms of social control—the public schools.

The school was one of the key institutions for segregating children from adults and perpetuating the differences. All of this came about simultaneously with the emergence of capitalism and a "market society" where a new generation of workers needed to be socialized to take their place in the coming industrial order. Merchants, the emerging capitalist class, needed their children to be able to read and write in order to handle the paperwork of their business enterprises.[18] Childhood began as a middle-class idea, in part because the middle class could afford it. It would be another century or so before this idea filtered down to the lower classes.

Remember that the cultural change in society that created childhood was influenced by important economic and political changes. Other significant developments after the printing press were industrial capitalism and the factory system. Although literacy, schooling, and childhood had developed rapidly in England until 1700, the demand for factory and mine workers restricted those developments—especially for the children of the poor who were used to keeping the new factories operating.

Punishment of Children in the Colonies

Prior to the nineteenth century any sort of "deviance" (however defined) on the part of children was dealt with on a relatively informal basis. Until the mid-1700s, there was not much serious crime to speak of, neither among adults nor children. For the most part, the behavior and the control of children was largely a responsibility of parents and perhaps other adults in the community. Although there were often strict laws governing the behavior of youth (especially in New England), they were rarely enforced and the corresponding punishments were rarely administered. The Quakers, for example, followed one of two patterns. "When a child misbehaved, either his family took care of his discipline or the Quaker meeting dispensed a mild and paternalistic correction."[19] Almshouses (a word used synonymously for workhouses and jails up until the nineteenth century) and other forms of incarceration were rarely used to handle the misbehavior of members of one's own community, and incarceration for long periods of time was almost nonexistent. In cases where children's misbehavior was especially troublesome, apprenticeship (this usually involved sending a youth away from home to live with someone who could teach him or her a trade) was often used as a form of punishment.[20] For the most part, the control and discipline of children was left up to the family unit.[21] This does not imply that all was well with the treatment of youths at that time. Children were, for example, subjected to some extreme forms of physical and sexual abuse.[22]

The *stubborn child law* was the first example of involving the state in the lives of youth. Passed in Massachusetts in 1646, it established a clear legal relationship between children and parents and, among other things, made it a capital offense for a child to disobey his or her parents. This statute stated in part:

> If a man have a stubborn or rebellious son, of sufficient years and understanding (viz) sixteen years of age, which will not obey the voice of his Father, or the voice of his Mother, and that when they have chastened him will not harken unto them: then shall his Father and Mother being his natural parents, lay hold on him, and bring him to the Magistrates assembled in court and testify unto them, that their son is stubborn and rebellious and will not obey their voice and chastisement, but lives in sundry notorious crimes, such a son shall be put to death.[23]

This law was grounded in the distinctly Puritan belief in the innate wickedness of humankind—wickedness that required that children be subjected to strong discipline. This law was unique in several other respects: it specified a particular legal obligation of children; it defined parents as the focus of that obligation; and it established rules for governmental intervention should parental control over children break down.

Until the late eighteenth century, young people had relatively close ties to their families and communities until about the age of puberty. Joseph Kett has noted that in agricultural communities "physical size, and hence capacity for work, was more important than chronological age." Autobiographies and biographies during the colonial period and even well into the nineteenth century are replete with instances of young people beginning to work at ages as young as six or seven. Typically a boy between 7 and 14 would engage in minor jobs (such as running errands, chopping wood, etc.); older boys generally served an apprenticeship into some trade.[24]

> Children provided parents in preindustrial society with a form of social security, unemployment insurance, and yearly support. As soon as children were able to work in or out of the home, they were expected to contribute to the support of their parents; when parents were no longer able to work, children would look after them.[25]

There were, of course, class distinctions during this period.

> Poor farm children were forced out of the home early, children of prosperous, landowning farmers left home at a somewhat later age and returned home more frequently; children of wealthy manufacturers and merchants left early, but because of parental preference rather than necessity. The degree of freedom also depended on social class. To the extent that poor households were more frequently disrupted than wealthy ones, poor children often had more de facto freedom (unless bound as paupers), although, it must be added, there was little that they could do with their freedom.[26]

Many poor children were "sentenced" (because of their economic situation rather than their misbehavior per se) to several years of hard labor as "apprentices," either to wealthy landowners or to ship captains.[27]

Parens Patriae

The appearance of adolescence as a social category coincided with an increasing concern for the regulation of the "moral behavior" of young people.[28] Although entirely separate systems to monitor and control the behavior of young people began to appear during the early part of the nineteenth century, differential treatment based on age did not come about overnight. The roots of the juvenile justice system can be traced to much earlier legal and social perspectives on childhood and youth. One of the most important of these was a legal doctrine known as *parens patriae*.

Parens patriae has its origins in medieval England's chancery courts. At that time it was essentially a property law—a means for the crown to administer landed orphans' estates.[29] *Parens patriae* established that the king, in his presumed role as the "father" of his country, had the legal authority to take care of "his" people, especially those who were unable, for various reasons (including age), to take care of themselves. The king or his authorized agents could assume the role of guardian of the child and thus administer the child's property. By the nineteenth century, this legal doctrine had evolved into the practice of the state's assuming wardship over a minor child and, in effect, playing the role of parent if the child had no parents or if the existing parents were declared unfit.

In the American colonies, for example, officials could "bind out" as apprentices "children of parents who were poor, not providing good breeding, neglecting their formal education, not teaching a trade, or were idle, dissolute, unchristian or incapable."[30] Later, during the nineteenth century, *parens patriae* supplied (as it still does to some extent), the legal basis for court intervention into the relationship between children and their families.[31]

It is important to consider the full implications of the notion of the state as parent, and more especially, father—a concept that is implied in both the *parens patriae* doctrine and, to some extent, in the *stubborn child law* discussed earlier. The objects of a patriarch's authority have traditionally included women in addition to children. The idea of patriarchy has also reinforced the sanctity and privacy of the home, and the power (in early years, almost absolute power) of the patriarch to discipline wife and children.[32] Further, the notion of *parens patriae* assumes that the father (or, in this case, the state or king) can legally act as a parent with many of the implicit parental powers possessed by fathers. As we shall see, governmental leaders would eventually utilize *parens patriae*, once a rather narrowly construed legal doctrine, to justify extreme governmental intervention in the lives of young people. Arguing that such intervention was "for their own good," the state during the nineteenth century became increasingly involved in the regulation of adolescent behavior.

The legal responsibility of children in the United States was formulated according to Common Law principles. Blackstone's commentary on children's criminal incapacitation, written in 1796, was incorporated in American law. Blackstone noted:

> The capacity of doing ill, or contracting guilt, is not so much measured by years and days, as by the strength of the delinquent's understanding and judgement . . . at eight years old he may be guilty of a felony. Also under fourteen . . . and could discern between good and evil, he may be convicted and sentenced to death. Thus a girl of 13 has burnt for killing her mistress, one boy of 10, and another of 9 years old, who had killed their companions have been sentenced to death, and he of 10 years actually hanged . . . Thus also in very modern times, a boy of ten years old was convicted on his own confession of murdering his bedfellow; there appearing in his whole behavior plain tokens of mischievous discretion; and as the sparing this boy merely on account of his tender years might be of dangerous consequence to the public, by propagating a notion that children might commit such

> atrocious crimes with impunity, it was unanimously agreed by all the
> judges that he was a proper subject of capital punishment.[33]

Children between the ages of 7 and 14 were presumed innocent unless evidence of a criminal state of mind could be presented. Youth at the age of 14 who participated in criminal or delinquent behavior were considered adults and treated as such.

Anthony Platt documents 14 cases (between 1806 and 1882) on the criminal responsibility of children in the United States. Seven children were indicted for homicide and one for manslaughter. Five children were indicted for various degrees of larceny and one for malicious trespass. The jury returned a verdict of not guilty in 10 of the cases. One child was found guilty of trespass, but the sentence was not reported. Two children—aged 11 and 12—were executed. In *State v. Aaron*, a young male slave of 11 years was accused of murdering another young child.[34] Before and during the trial he denied the crime, but he was convicted and sentenced to death. George Stage, who was 8 years old at the time he was arrested, was caught while trying to escape from a private house with a stolen bearskin. He was convicted and sentenced to three years in the state prison. Although these cases were unusual, they nevertheless suggest that the criminal law recognized at that time that some children under 14, particularly children of color, were held as responsible for their actions as adults.[35]

In the United States, interest in the state regulation of youth was directly tied to explosive immigration and population growth. Between 1750 and 1850, the population of the United States went from 1.25 million to 23 million. The population of some states (including Massachusetts) doubled, and New York's population increased fivefold between 1790 and 1830.[36] Many of those coming into the United States during the middle of the nineteenth century were of Irish or German background; the fourfold increase in immigrants between 1830 and 1840 was in large part a product of the economic hardships faced by the Irish during the potato famine.[37]

The influx of poor immigrants created a growing concern among prominent citizens about the "perishing and dangerous classes," as they would be called throughout the nineteenth century. The shift from agriculture to industrialism introduced the age of adolescence. With this age came the problem of "juvenile delinquency" and attempts to control it.

Defining a Juvenile Delinquent

The term "juvenile delinquent" originated in the early 1800s. Its meaning derives from the different meanings of the two words in the term: (1) "delinquent" means "failure to do something that is required" (as in a person being delinquent in paying taxes) and (2) "juvenile" means someone who is "malleable," not yet "fixed in their ways," subject to change and being molded (i.e., "redeemable"). By the 1700s, with colleges and private boarding schools developing, various "informal" methods of social control of more privileged youth emerged (this paralleled the emergence of capitalism and the need to reproduce the next generation of capitalist rulers). Eventually, more formal systems of control emerged to control working and lower class "delinquents" around the early 1800s, including the juvenile justice system and uniformed police.[38]

Informal systems of control have always been reserved for the more privileged youths, while the less privileged have been subjected to formal systems of control. If we examine history closely, it has almost always been the case that minority youth were much more likely to be viewed as "hardened criminals" rather than "juvenile delinquents" (i.e., "malleable and thus "redeemable"). Little has changed today; a majority of those certified or waived to adult court in recent years (i.e., viewed as "unredeemable" adult criminals) have been minorities. Thus, the kinds of behaviors and the people labeled as "delinquent" have always been subjective. Like beauty, delinquency is in the eye of the beholder.

The House of Refuge Movement

During the early nineteenth century, prominent citizens in the cities of the East began to notice the poor, especially the children of the poor. The parents were declared unfit because their children wandered about the streets unsupervised and committing crimes in order to survive. Many believed that the lack of social control over this group could be the source of even greater problems in the future. Poor and immigrant children, their lifestyles, and their social position soon became synonymous with crime and juvenile delinquency.

David Rothman notes that there was an assumption that the causes of criminality were found both in the social conditions of the cities and in family upbringing. One belief was prominent: "parents who sent their children into the society without rigorous training in discipline and obedience would find them someday in prison."[39] Reformers, upon examining the life histories of adult convicts, found that early childhood transgressions were the prelude to worse things to come. The concept of "pre-delinquency" remains popular today.[40]

As attention began to focus on the children of the poor, another problem was noticed. Many observers found that young children, some as young as six or seven, were locked up with adult criminals in jails and prisons and were also appearing with increasing regularity in criminal courts. Many children were confined in the Bellevue Penitentiary in New York City in close association with adult offenders.[41] Child reformers believed that such practices were inhumane and would inevitably lead to the corruption of the young and perpetuation of youthful deviance, perhaps to a full-time career in more serious criminality.

A number of philanthropic associations emerged in eastern cities to deal with these problems. One of the most notable was the *Society for the Reformation of Juvenile Delinquents* (SRJD), founded in the 1820s.[42] A member of this group, lawyer James Gerard, expressed a view that was typical of other members of this society when he commented that most of the children appearing in the criminal courts of New York were "of poor and abandoned parents" whose "debased character and vicious habits" resulted in their being "brought up in perfect ignorance and idleness, and what is worse in street begging and pilfer-ing."[43] The solution that was offered became one of the most common solutions to the problem of delinquency in years to come: remove the children from the corrupting environments of prisons, jails, "unfit" homes, slums, and other unhealthy environments and place them in theoretically more humane and healthier environments.

The SRJD, composed primarily of wealthy businessmen and professional people, convinced the New York legislature to pass a bill in 1824 that estab-lished the *New York House of Refuge*, the first correctional institution for young offenders in the United States.[44] The Act provided a place for the custody of

> all such children as should be taken up and committed as vagrants or con-victed of criminal offenses, in the City of New York, as the Court of the General Sessions of the Peace, the Court of Oyer and Terminer, the Police Magistrates, or the Commissioners of the Aims-House and Bridewell of said city, might deem proper objects. It also empowered the managers [of the house of refuge] to have custody of the children so committed during their minority, and to cause them to be instructed in such branches of use-ful knowledge and to be placed at such employments, as should be suited to their years and capacities. It also gave power to the managers to bind out the children so committed, with their consent, as apprentices during their minority.[45]

The following is taken verbatim from one of the original documents of the Soci-ety for the Reformation of Juvenile Delinquents, dated July 3, 1823. This will give the reader some insight into the actual goals of this institution, as envi-sioned by its founders:

> The design of the proposed institution is, to furnish, in the first place, an asylum, in which boys under a certain age, who become subject to the notice of our Police, either as vagrants, or houseless, or charged with petty crimes, may be received, judiciously classed according to their degrees of depravity or innocence, put to work at such employments as will tend to encourage industry and ingenuity, taught reading, writing, and arithmetic, and most carefully instructed in the nature of their moral and religious obli-gations, while at the same time, they are subjected to a course of treatment, that will afford a prompt and energetic corrective of their vicious propensi-ties, and hold out every possible inducement to reformation and good con-duct. It will undoubtedly happen, that among boys collected from such sources, there will be some, whose habits and propensities are of the most unpromising description. Such boys, when left to run at large in the city, become the pests of society, and spread corruption wherever they go.[46]

How did the founders decide on the design of the house of refuge and where did they get the idea that "reform" could take place within an enclosed institutional edifice? They may have been influenced by the writings of John Howard, one of the leading prison reformers of that era. In his famous work on prisons published in 1784 he made reference to St. Michael's Hospice in Rome. He visited this institution in 1778 and wrote about it as follows:

> The Hospital of S. Michael is a large and noble edifice. The back front is near
> three hundred yards long. It consists of several courts with buildings round
> them. In the apartments on three sides of one of the most spacious of these
> courts, are rooms for various manufactures and arts, in which boys who are
> orphans or destitute are educated and instructed. . . . Another part of the hos-
> pital is a Prison for boys or young men. Over the door is this inscription: For
> the correction and instruction of profligate youth: That they who when idle,
> were injurious, when instructed might be useful to the State. 1704. In the room
> is inscribed the following admirable sentence, in which the grand purpose of
> all civil policy relative to criminals is expressed. It is of little advantage to
> restrain the Bad by Punishment unless you render them Good by Discipline.[47]

Howard described an activity as follows: "Here were sixty boys spinning, and
in the middle of the room an inscription hung up, SILENTIUM" and continued: "In this hospital is a room also for women. On the outside is an inscription, expressing that it was erected by Clement XII in 1735, for restraining the
licentiousness and punishing the crimes of women."[48]

Thorsten Sellin described the historical development of this institution as
follows:

> Its origin goes back to some of the earliest attempts made in Rome to com-
> bat the increasing pauperism and the mendacity accompanying it. To its
> history, no fewer than six separate institutions made important contribu-
> tions: the home for boys founded by Leonardo Ceruso, called II Letterato, in
> 1582; the hospice for the poor, erected by Pope Sixtus V, in 1586–1588; the
> home for boys founded by Tomasso Odescalchi in 1684; the orphanage for
> girls and the home for the aged poor, founded by Pope Innocent XII in 1693;
> the house of correction for boys, founded by Pope Clement XI in 1703; and,
> the house of correction for women, founded by Pope Clement XII in 1735.[49]

The general aims of the institution and the routines within it were strik-
ingly similar to adult prisons and to houses of refuge throughout the late eighteenth and early nineteenth centuries in the United States. The founders may
also have been influenced by Jeremy Bentham and his *panopticon* design for
prisons, factories, hospitals, schools and other structures.[50] Religion was
another significant influence.[51]

Sellin noted that movement founders endorsed several goals.

> Existing prisons lacked reformative power over young offenders who
> should receive special care, since from their ranks the recidivists would oth-
> erwise be recruited. Second, the emphasis upon religious and moral instruc-
> tion as necessary elements in the work of reformation. Third, the demand
> for manual training under the direction of skilled artisans, in order to give
> to the offender a trade at which he might later earn his livelihood. Fourth,
> the adoption of something similar to a "state-use" system of labor, the
> Apostolic state, its court, army, and navy, being made the consumer of the
> goods manufactured in the institution.

The statutes contained vague descriptions of behaviors and lifestyles that
were synonymous with the characteristics of the urban poor. Wandering the
streets rather than being at school or at work, begging, vagrancy, and coming

from an "unfit" home (as defined from a middle-class view point) were behaviors that could trigger custody in the house of refuge. The legislation that was passed also established specific procedures for identifying the proper subjects for intervention and the means for the legal handling of cases. According to law, the state, or a representative agency or individual, could intervene in the life of a child if it was determined that he or she needed "care and treatment," the definition of which was left entirely in the hands of the agency or individual who intervened. The legislators who passed the bill apparently gave little thought to the rights of children or their parents. This issue would eventually arise with the case of *Ex Parte Crouse* (discussed below).

Immigrants received the brunt of the enforcement of these laws. One house of refuge superintendent accounted for a boy's delinquency because "the lad's parents are Irish and intemperate and that tells the whole story."[52] The results of such beliefs are reflected in the fact that 63% of commitments to the refuge were Irish between 1825 and 1855.

Of the 73 children received at the New York Refuge during its first year of operation, only one had been convicted of a serious offense (grand larceny). Nine were committed for petty larceny, and 63 (88%) were committed for "stealing, vagrancy and absconding" from the almshouse.[53] These numbers indicate that delinquency statutes more often described a way of life or social status (e.g., poverty) than misconduct. The major "crime" was simply being poor. It was common for the police to arrest young children on petty charges, such as stealing a "two-penny copy of the *New York Herald.*"

The New York House of Refuge officially opened its doors on January 1, 1825. The new superintendent, Joseph Curtis, brought with him a young girl who had no home of her own and had been living with him at the time. The police brought "seven waifs" to the front door to begin their incarceration.[54]

> On that day the Board met and opened the Institution in the presence of a considerable concourse of citizens, among whom were members of the Common Council who assembled to witness the ceremony of the introduction of a number of juvenile delinquents into a place exclusively intended for their reformation and instruction. The ceremony was interesting in the highest degree. Nine of those poor outcasts from society, three boys and six girls, clothed in rags, with squalid countenances, were brought in from the police office and placed before the audience. An address appropriate to so novel an occasion was made by a member of the Board. All present expressed the warmest sympathy with and approbation of the philanthropic views which led to the foundation of this House of Refuge.[55]

The parents of children committed to the New York House of Refuge who held jobs (and most did not) were most frequently listed as "common laborer." "Washerwoman" ranked second, and "masons, plasterers and bricklayers" ranked third. The occupation of "washerwoman" is indicative of the common phenomenon of the period among many urban dwellers when men were forced to leave their families in order to find work elsewhere, leaving children and their mothers to fend for themselves. The women took in other people's laundry to earn money.[56]

The rich and the powerful in New York became increasingly fearful of class differences. One notable reformer, Stephen Allen, remarked that the "rising generation of the poor" was a threat to society.[57] Historian Robert Mennel observed:

> Early nineteenth century philanthropists also undertook charitable work for their own protection. They feared imminent social upheaval resulting from the explosive mixture of crime, disease, and intemperance which they believed characterized the lives of poorer urban residents. Without relieving the poor of responsibility for their conditions, these philanthropists saw in their benevolences, ways of avoiding class warfare and the disintegration of the social order. The French Revolution reminded them, however, that the costs of class struggle were highest to advantaged citizens like themselves.[58]

Changing Conceptions of Delinquency

Mennel notes that juvenile delinquency in the eighteenth century "slowly ceased to mean a form of misbehavior common to all children and instead became a euphemism for the crimes and conditions of poor children."[59] By the nineteenth century, that perception dominated popular thinking. Managers of the New York House of Refuge believed that the major causes of delinquency were, in order of importance: ignorance, parental depravity and neglect, intemperance, theatrical amusements,[60] bad associations, pawnbrokers, immigration, and "city life in general." A crude environmental view prevailed throughout this period as poverty, family rearing practices (of the poor), and other social and psychological factors were typically associated with delinquency.[61] A report by a Unitarian minister in 1830 stated that three-fourths of the young picked up by the police were from families that looked to their children to help support them. Instead of citing the inequalities that existed at the time and the exploitation on the part of factory owners (who employed large numbers of children), the report said that this condition was due to the "idleness and intemperance of the parents." The report further noted that these children "are every day at once surrounded by temptation to dishonesty."[62]

Rothman notes that the family was generally considered a major source of the problem. He writes that such phrases as "poor upbringing," "bad habits," "drinking," and "immorality" (indicative of the anti-Catholic bias common at that time) were commonly heard. Other factors commonly associated with crime and delinquency included the lack of respect for authority and failure to abide by the "work ethic" (even though the vast majority of the Irish immigrants worked hard, struggling to achieve the "American Dream"). All of these were characteristically associated with the behavior, lifestyles, and living conditions of the urban poor.[63]

It is generally true that reformers often blamed social conditions as the primary cause, and therefore beyond the control of individual youths. At the same time, however, they blamed the youngsters themselves (and their parents as well), at least indirectly. Time and again reformers stressed that it was up to the individual to avoid the "temptations" that such social conditions produced. A report by the SRJD noted that the youths in the refuge were "in a situation where there is no temptation to vice . . . and where, instead of being left to prey on the public, they will be *fitted* to become valuable members of society."[64] It was as if the evil conditions of the inner cities were like "bacteria" that were "in the air" and that some were "immune" while others were not. Therefore, the goal of reformation was to "immunize" individuals who had come down with the "disease" of delinquency or pre-delinquency. The physical analogy has been with us ever since.[65]

Social reformers, such as the SRJD and the "child savers" of the late nineteenth century (discussed below), have often been described as "humanitarians" with "love" in their hearts for the "unfortunate children of the poor." According to the SRJD: "The young should, if possible, be subdued with kindness. His heart should first be addressed, and the language of confidence, although undeserved, be used toward him." The SRJD also said that the young should be taught that "his keepers were his best friends and that the object of his confinement was his reform and ultimate good."[66]

The results of the actions by these reformers suggest that the "best interests of the child" were usually not served. Children confined in the houses of refuge were subjected to strict discipline and control. A former army colonel working in the New York House of Refuge said: "He (the delinquent) is taught that prompt unquestioning obedience is a fundamental military principle."[67] It was strongly believed that this latter practice would add to a youth's training in "self control" (evidently to avoid the "temptations" of evil surroundings) and "respect for authority" (which was a basic requirement of a disciplined labor force). Corporal punishments (including hanging children from their thumbs, the use of the "ducking stool" for girls, and severe beatings), solitary confinement, handcuffs, the "ball and chain," uniform dress, the "silent system," and other practices were commonly used in houses of refuge.[68]

A report on the existing penitentiary system in New York (specifically Newgate and Auburn) issued by the organization when they called themselves the Society for the Prevention of Pauperism helps explain attitudes at the time. The report advocated solitary confinement (practiced at the Eastern State Penitentiary in Philadelphia) and stated that prisons should be "places which are dreaded by convicts" and "generally productive of terror."[69] Such beliefs, prominent among even the most "benevolent" reformers of the period, influenced what went on inside the New York House of Refuge.

Religion played a key role in the development of this institution, as it had throughout the history of American prisons for both youths and adults.[70] Quakers were among the leaders of the refuge movement. The reformers of the late eighteenth and early nineteenth centuries spent a good deal of time and energy complaining about the "moral decline" of the country, especially in New York City. Two "vices" were identified as the leading causes of delinquency: theatres and saloons. "Immorality" would be a common charge leveled against juveniles throughout the nineteenth century and beyond.[71]

Superintendent Curtis of the New York House of Refuge was reportedly a kind person who believed in leniency toward the inmates. Even he, however, succumbed to the temptation to deal with any sign of disorder with severe punishment, including locking the inmates up in a small cage known as the "side table" where they ate in isolation. He also lashed boys' feet to one side of a barrel and their hands to the other; their pants were removed, and they were whipped with a "cat-o-nine tails."[72] Even so, the board of directors of the SRJD felt that Curtis was not tough enough. After his resignation (as a result of some pressure to get rid of him), he was replaced by a stern disciplinarian named Nathaniel C. Hart.

As would be the case for most other institutions for juveniles and adults alike throughout the nineteenth and into the twentieth century, houses of refuge contracted the labor of its inmates to "local entrepreneurs." The inmates "made brass nails, cane chairs, and cheap shoes," while girls "were occupied with domestic chores."[73] After they had been trained for "usefulness," they were released—boys to farmers and local artisans and girls bound out as maids. The more hardened boys were indentured to ship's captains.[74]

Following the lead of New York, other cities (including Rochester, NY) constructed houses of refuge in rapid succession. Within a few years there were refuges in Boston, Philadelphia, and Baltimore. It soon became evident, however, that the original plans of the founders were not being fulfilled, for crime and delinquency remained a problem. Also, many of the children apparently did not go along with the "benevolence" of the managers of the refuges. Protests, riots, escape attempts, and other disturbances became almost daily occurrences.[75] While at first limiting itself to housing first offenders, youthful offenders, and pre-delinquents, the refuges in time came to be the confines of more hardened offenders (most of whom were hardened by the experiences of confinement) and soon succumbed to the problem of overcrowding. The cycle continued to plague institutions built throughout the nineteenth and twentieth centuries and continues to the present day.

While the early nineteenth-century reforms did not have much of an impact on crime and delinquency, they did succeed in establishing methods of controlling children of the poor (and their parents as well). "The asylum and the refuge were two more bricks in the wall that Americans built to confine and reform the dangerous classes."[76] While the poor and the working classes were usually viewed as lazy, shiftless, and dangerous, the trait that tended to strike the most fear into the hearts and minds of the privileged was "idleness." Indeed, an idle mass of underprivileged and deprived people was an obvious threat to the security of the upper class. The major assumptions about the causes of crime and delinquency included idleness, lack of a "work ethic," and lack of "respect for authority." Authority generally means those in power: those who do the hiring and firing—the ruling class and its representatives. To achieve respect for authority is to "legitimize" a particular social order and set of rulers. When one lacks respect for authority one has, among other things, not granted legitimacy to the existing order and ruling class. Because of this, it becomes important to instill such values in the minds of citizens, especially those who violate the law or otherwise behave contrary to role expectations.

The SRJD asked citizens to visit the House of Refuge in New York "and see that idleness has become changed to industry, filth and rags to cleanliness and comfortable appearance, boisterous impudence to quiet submission."[77] Ideally, the result of orderly asylums such as these would be the production of passive, happy, contented workers who would, upon release, submit to authority and accept their assigned place at the bottom of the social order and cause no further trouble. In the following quotation Rothman describes the function of the prison, but his description could very easily apply to houses of refuge: "The functioning of the penitentiary . . . was designed to carry a message to the community. The prison would train the most notable victims of social disorder to discipline, teaching them to resist corruption."[78]

The rhetoric of the founders and managers of houses of refuge obviously fell far short of the reality experienced by the youth held in these facilities. A look at one of the most significant court challenges to the refuge movement provides additional insight into the origins of the juvenile justice system.

Ex Parte Crouse: Court Decisions and Effects

Argued in 1838, *Ex Parte Crouse* arose from a petition of habeas corpus filed by the father of Mary Ann Crouse. Without her father's knowledge, Crouse had been committed to the Philadelphia House of Refuge by her mother on the grounds that she was "incorrigible." Her father argued that the incarceration was illegal because she had not been given a jury trial. The court noted that Mary had been committed on a complaint stating "that the said infant by reason of vicious conduct, has rendered her control beyond the power of the said complainant [her mother], and made it manifestly requisite that from regard to the moral and future welfare of the said infant she should be placed under the guardianship of the managers of the House of Refuge."[79]

Ironically, there were several occasions where parents of children in the New York House of Refuge sought to get their children removed from the refuge. Many of these parents were apparently unaware of the fact that the Society for the Reformation of Juvenile Delinquents (SRJD) had, in effect, "usurped their parental rights and privileges." Many just pleaded for the SRJD to give them another chance at providing for their children. There were some cases, however, that were almost identical to what the father of Mary Crouse faced. Robert Pickett gives the example of a father, "on returning from the hinterland, found that his wife had committed his daughter during his absence. He went directly to the Refuge and requested her discharge." This they did, although they also warned him to "pay attention to her morals."[80]

In the case of Mary Crouse's father, the Pennsylvania Supreme Court rejected the appeal, saying that the Bill of Rights did not apply to juveniles. Based upon the *parens patriae* doctrine, the court asked, "May not the natural parents, when unequal to the task of education, or unworthy of it, be superseded by the *parens patriae* or common guardian of the community?" Further, the court observed that: "The infant has been snatched from a course which must have ended in confirmed depravity."[81] Note here that the logic was accepted, even though one of Crouse's parents (her father) felt able to care for her. Also note that they were making predictions of future behavior based on vague criteria, a practice that became increasingly common over the years.

The ruling assumed that the Philadelphia House of Refuge (and presumably all other houses of refuge) had a beneficial effect on its residents. It "is not a prison, but a school," the court said, and therefore not subject to procedural constraints. Further, the aims of such an institution were to reform the youngsters in their care "by training . . . [them] to industry; by imbuing their minds with the principles of morality and religion; by furnishing them with means to earn a living; and above all, by separating them from the corrupting influences of improper associates."[82]

What evidence did the justices use to support their conclusion that the House of Refuge was not a prison but a school? They solicited testimony only from those who managed the institution. This was probably because the justices of the Pennsylvania Supreme Court came from the same general class background as those who supported the houses of refuge; they believed the rhetoric of the supporters. In short, they believed the "promises" rather than the "reality" of the reformers.

A more objective review of the treatment of youths housed in these places, however, might have led the justices to a very different conclusion. For instance, subsequent investigations found that there was an enormous amount of abuse within these institutions.[83] Work training was practically nonexistent, and outside companies contracted for cheap inmate labor. Religious instruction was often little more than Protestant indoctrination (many of the youngsters were Catholic). Education, in the conventional meaning of the word, was almost nonexistent.[84]

Elijah DeVoe, who served for a short time as an assistant superintendent for the New York House of Refuge, got into a heated dispute with the SRJD and was fired. DeVoe eventually wrote a scathing critique of the refuge. Among other things, DeVoe charged:

> The New York House of Refuge has more features of a penitentiary than an asylum, and that its most characteristic name would be a *State Prison for Youthful Culprits;* or a HIGH SCHOOL WHERE MERE VAGRANTS ARE INDUCTED INTO ALL THE MYSTERIES OF CRIME [caps in the original]. Any boy over fourteen years of age, acquainted with the two institutions, would unhesitatingly prefer being sentenced to the penitentiary on Blackwell's Island to a commitment to the House of Refuge.[85]

People v. Turner

People v. Turner (1870) provided a most intriguing addendum to the history of the houses of refuge—and to the *Crouse* case. A young boy named Daniel O'Connell was incarcerated in the Chicago House of Refuge because he was "in danger of growing up to become a pauper." His parents, like Mary Crouse's father, filed a writ of habeas corpus, charging that his incarceration was illegal. Although the facts were almost identical to the *Crouse* case, the outcome was the exact opposite.

The case went to the Illinois Supreme Court. The court concluded that, first, Daniel was being *punished*—not treated or helped by being in this institution. (Recall that the Pennsylvania court had concluded that Mary Crouse was being *helped*.) Second, the Illinois court based its ruling on the *realities* or *actual practices* of the institution, rather than merely on "good intentions" as in the *Crouse* case. Third, the Illinois court rejected the *parens patriae* doctrine because they concluded that Daniel was being "imprisoned." They based their reasoning on traditional legal doctrines of the criminal law and emphasized the importance of *due process* safeguards. In short, while the court in the *Crouse* case viewed the House of Refuge in a very rosy light, praising it uncritically, the court in the O'Connell case viewed the refuge in a much more negative light, addressing its cruelty and harshness of treatment.[86] Because of the O'Connell case, only children who had committed felonies could be sent to reform schools. One reason for the different rulings in these two cases may stem from gender. Mary Ann Crouse was committed to a House of Refuge, and the court deemed this appropriate for her moral and future welfare.[87]

People v. Turner played a significant role in the push to establish a juvenile court in Chicago in 1899, which will be discussed in more detail shortly. The founders of the juvenile court established this institution in part as a method of getting around the argument in the O'Connell case. The Pennsylvania courts, meanwhile, continued to defend the decision in the *Crouse* case. In 1905, the Pennsylvania Supreme Court ruled in *Commonwealth v. Fisher*:

> To save a child from becoming a criminal, or continuing in a career of crime, to end in maturer [sic] years in public punishment and disgrace, the legislatures surely may provide for the salvation of such a child, if its parents or guardians be unwilling or unable to do so, by bringing it into one of the courts of the state without any process at all, for the purpose of subjecting it to the state's guardianship and protection.[88]

The reasoning would not be overturned until 1967 in the *Gault* case (see chapter 11).

Mid-Nineteenth Century Reforms

The United States in the mid-nineteenth century was a nation constantly moving west. The settlements in newly conquered territories needed labor, including farm laborers, helpers in retail stores, "washerwomen," and "kitchen girls." Simultaneously the eastern cities like New York, Boston, and Philadelphia were overpopulated with immigrants from all over Europe. Fleeing economic ruin, political repression, starvation, and religious persecution, they came to the United States by the millions.[89] The capitalist class promised jobs for everyone, along with freedom and the "good life." But for most, the reality was quite different. The immigrants in the overcrowded tenements and slums soon became the "dangerous classes," a term applied to them by those in power.[90]

Especially troublesome for those in power were the very young, those labeled as "street urchins," "abandoned waifs," and the children of the urban poor. They, along with their adult counterparts, needed to be controlled in some way. The newly emerging justice system—both the adult and juvenile—would provide this function, along with schools and other institutions and programs. One such program was the "placing out" system introduced by the New York Children's Aid Society (see below).

About the same time, many began to complain about the conditions of the houses of refuge. Not satisfied that these institutions were doing an adequate job of reformation, new methods were recommended. In Massachusetts, for instance, the first compulsory school law was passed in 1836, thereby creating a new category of delinquent, the "truant," and a new method of controlling youths. New York passed a similar law in 1853. As Robert Bremner noted about the New York law) "This legislation was an instrument for placing abandoned and neglected children [of the poor] in institutions." The goal was more about control than about educating the children of the poor.

In New York the Association for Improving the Conditions of the Poor established the New York Juvenile Asylum in 1853. The primary aim of this association was to create a "suitable House of Detention" for "beggars, truants, waifs," and other "morally exposed children and youth." It would remove them from "dangerous and corrupting associates and place them in such circumstances as will be favorable to reform, and tend to make them industrious, virtuous, and useful members of society."[91] Not much changed in the almost three decades since the opening of the first house of refuge.

Some reformers, such as Charles Loring Brace who founded the New York Children's Aid Society in 1853, believed that a family-type setting, preferably in the country, would offset the often brutalizing and impersonal setting of houses of refuge.[92] The beginnings of the placing-out movement took place in Boston in the1830s when prominent citizens felt the need to establish a reform school for boys who had not yet been convicted of a crime but were roaming the streets "in need of discipline." In 1849 the Massachusetts State Reform School for Boys, an institution positioned somewhere between the houses of refuge and the public school system, opened. A similar school was opened for girls in Lancaster in 1855, the first of many such institutions based on the "family system."[93] The Ohio State Reform Farm was a family system for boys and opened in 1857.[94]

The "cottage" or "family plan" was based on a belief in "rural purity," a dominant theme at that time.[95] Robert Mennel makes the following assessment of this system:

> The end result was hardly a smooth-running system. Institutionalists and advocates of placing out bickered constantly. Nativist Protestants expressed their preferences, thus hastening the development of Roman Catholic institutions. Delinquent girls did institutional housework and often were sexually abused when placed out. Negro children were initially more fortunate, since few institutions accepted them. Once admitted, they were usually segregated. By the Civil War, several institutions had experienced rioting and incendiarism, which usually began in the workshops where contract labor encouraged exploitation.[96]

A "placing out" system had emerged in the New York area, the most famous of which was the one operated by the New York Children's Aid Society, which placed children "out west" (their phrase referred to any location west of the Allegheny Mountains) in family-type institutions (such as the Ohio Reform School), in actual residences (similar to what today we know as foster homes) or on farms. Millions of children came west in what were commonly referred to as "orphan trains."[97] Economic factors played an important role, and many of these children provided landowners with a cheap source of labor:

The Children's Aid Society divided New York City into sections and assigned to each section a "visitor" (part of the Friendly Visitor program popular throughout the nation; visitors eventually evolved into "social workers").

> The visitors would go from house to house, trying to persuade the families to send their children to the public schools or to the industrial schools of the Children's Aid Society. When a visitor found a homeless or neglected child, he took him to the central office of the society, where, after securing the parent's consent—if they could be found—it prepared to send him to a farmer's home in the West.[98]

Usually the parents could not be found because they were away during the day (when the visitors called) either working or seeking work. What happened if the parents refused to cooperate with the "visitors"? The records of the reactions of those on the bottom of the social order are typically incomplete, if known at all. A few notable cases suggest that parents and their children did not always passively succumb to the "benevolences" of the reformers.[99]

For example, the Baltimore House of Refuge had a case in which a mother attempted to regain custody of her daughter who had been placed in a home by the refuge. The officials reported:

> After we had found a home for the little girl, the mother made an application for her, which we refused. She succeeded in finding where the child was, and demanded it. The man with whom we had placed her was quite firm, and refused to surrender her, but told the mother that if she conducted herself well, the mother might visit her. She threatened legal proceedings, but our power over the child was superior to hers and thus the injudicious interference of the parents was prevented.[100]

During the last half of the nineteenth century, the number of court cases challenging the state's power over children increased. Most commitments were for either poverty or "poverty plus" (begging, poverty, destitution, neglect, and dependency). In some cases, it was difficult to tell why children had been taken away from their parents. Court decisions give evidence that children were not committed to institutions because of any violation of the law or because of failings by parents, "but simply because the parents were poor and behaved as poor people always have." There was "an unspoken assumption that the state had an equal if not superior interest in the children and the burden was on the parents to show to the contrary."[101]

Late-Nineteenth Century Reforms

Toward the end of the nineteenth century it was clear to many that earlier reforms and the existing institutions were doing little toward the reformation of delinquents and the reduction of crime. The asylums constructed during the early and middle years of the nineteenth century had failed in their original intention to reform. They remained in place, however, with the new goal of custody. The "dangerous classes" could no longer be banished as they had been during the colonial period. They had to be controlled physically, for to banish them might result in their being a danger to another community.[102]

While it is certainly true that custody became the order of the day, some reformers never gave up and soon began to agitate for more effective reformation. Upset with the ruling in the O'Connell case, they sought ways of getting around it. They began to argue for an extension of the current system to include a special court for hearing children's cases. But in believing that reformation was not working, reformers were saying, in effect, that *control* was ineffective. Hence, additional "reforms" were merely new measures to control and regulate the "deviants," potential deviants, and the poor in general.[103]

Part of the new upswing in reform activities was a result of the changes occurring in the United States during the last half of the nineteenth century: greater industrialization and urbanization, a new wave of immigrants, general unrest and revolt by workers, periodic economic crises in the capitalist system, and other problems. Chicago, the main site of the "child-saving" movement, had grown from a small town of around 5,000 in 1840 to a huge city of a million and a half, mostly through immigration.[104]

There was also a noteworthy change in the labor market structure, especially as it affected youth. With the growth of factories in the 1880s came the movement of both journeymen and apprentices into the ranks of the industrial proletariat. Teenage helpers posed a constant threat to the wage-earning abilities of young adult journeymen. Skilled crafts began to exclude teenage youth, who were then forced to take factory jobs, most of which were dead-end jobs. Many of these youths became redundant workers[105] or what Marx referred to as the relative surplus population.

New theories of crime and delinquency had emerged by this time, heavily influenced by the positivist school of criminology. This school of thought popularized the so-called medical model of deviance. The Progressive Era ushered in a new series of reforms commonly known as the child-saving movement and resulted in the establishment of new institutions to "care for," "control," and "protect" errant and wayward youth. One such institution was the juvenile court.

The Child Saving Movement and the Juvenile Court

Like their earlier nineteenth century counterparts, the *child savers* were a group of upper-middle and upper-class whites with business and professional backgrounds threatened by the deleterious social conditions in the slums of Chicago and other cities. Surveys by noted reformers Z. R. Brockway and Enoch Wines found that children were still being kept in jails and prisons with adult offenders. The child savers dedicated themselves to "saving" these children and "diverting" them from the adult criminal justice system.

The result of their efforts was the establishment of the juvenile court. The new legislation of the period (first in Chicago and Denver in 1899, then elsewhere) created new categories of offenses and extended the state's power over the lives of children and youth. Because of the O'Connell case, only children who had committed felonies could be sent to reform schools. A method of "nipping the problem in the bud" was needed. The logic the reformers used was to define the new juvenile court as a sort of "chancery court," upon which the doctrine of *parens patriae* was based. Only in such a court, argued the child savers, could "the best interests of the child" be served. The 1899 Illinois Juvenile Court Act removed all cases involving juveniles (at first the upper age was 16; later it was raised to 17) from the jurisdiction of the criminal courts and formally established the juvenile court. Thus, the "problem" arising out of the O'Connell case was immediately solved.[106]

The new laws that defined delinquency and pre-delinquent behavior were broad in scope and quite vague: (1) the laws covered the usual violations of laws also applicable to adults; (2) the laws covered violations of local ordinances; and (3) the laws included such catchalls as "vicious or immoral behavior," "incorrigibility," "truancy," "profane or indecent behavior," "growing up in idleness," "living with any vicious or disreputable person," and many more. These would eventually be known as *status offenses*.[107]

To this list of status offenses should be added a specific charge of "immorality." This is important since it almost always applied to girls. A detailed examination of the case files of the first three decades of the Cook County Juvenile Court revealed that immorality constituted between 20 and 55 percent of all charges made against girls. Most of the remainder of the charges were "incorrigibility"—a charge that typically masks various kinds of sexual behavior by girls and/or child abuse.[108]

Prior to the passage of the Juvenile Court Act in Chicago in 1899 several states already had laws defining status offenses. For instance, Tennessee passed an act in 1895 to establish county reformatories that could commit "infants under the age of 16" if:

> by reason of incorrigible or vicious conduct, such infant has rendered his control beyond the power of such parent guardian or next friend, and made it manifestly requisite that from regard to the future welfare of such infant, and for the protection of society he should be placed under the guardianship of the trustees of such reformatory institution.

Children could also be committed as "vagrants" or if they were "without a suitable home and adequate means of obtaining an honest living, and who are in danger of being brought up to lead an idle or immoral life."[109] The Tennessee code reproduced, almost word-for-word, the original act that had created the New York and Philadelphia Houses of Refuge.

Reformers believed that delinquency was the result of a wide variety of social, psychological, and biological factors. They believed that one must look into the life of the child offender in intimate detail in order to know the "whole truth" about the child. The judge of the juvenile court was to be like a benevolent, yet stern, father. The proceedings were to be informal without the traditional judicial trappings. There was neither a need for lawyers nor constitutional safeguards because (1) the cases were not "criminal" in nature and (2) the court would always act "in the best interests of the child." The court was to be operated like a "clinic," and the child was to be "diagnosed" in order to determine the extent of his "condition" and to prescribe the correct "treatment" plan, preferably as early in life as possible.[110]

Even the terminology of the juvenile justice system was, and to some extent still is, different. Children in many parts of the United States are "referred" to the court rather than being arrested; instead of being held in jail pending court action, they are "detained" in a "detention center" or "adjustment center"; rather than being indicted, children are "petitioned" to court; in place of a determination of guilt, there is an "adjudication"; and those found guilty (i.e., adjudicated) are often "committed" to a "training school" or "reform school" rather than being sentenced to a prison.

Envisioned as a "benevolent" institution that would emphasize treatment rather than punishment, the juvenile court turned out to be a mixture of the two orientations: that of a social welfare agency (with an emphasis on treatment) and a legal institution (with an emphasis on punishment). The confusion can be traced to the mixed legacy of the court that combined a puritanical approach to stubborn children and parental authority with the Progressive Era's belief that children's essential goodness can be corrupted by undesirable elements in their environments. James Finckenauer termed the mixture "ambivalent" or "even schizophrenic."[111]

The attention of the juvenile court and its supporters was fixed primarily on the children of the poor, especially immigrants. Steven Schlossman has suggested that the juvenile court served "as a literal dumping ground." The court provided an arena "where the dependent status of children was verified and reinforced, and where the incapacities of lower-class immigrant parents were, in a sense, certified."[112]

The juvenile court system extended the role of probation officer, a role originally introduced in the mid-nineteenth century in Boston.[113] This new role was one of the primary innovations in the twentieth-century juvenile justice system, and the role became one of the most crucial in the entire system. Schlossman writes that "nothing in a child's home, school, occupation, or peer-group relations was, at least in theory, beyond" the purview of the probation officer. The probation officer "was expected to instruct children and parents in reciprocal obligations, preach moral and religious verities, teach techniques of child care and household management."[114] Part of the probation officer's role was likened to that of an "exorcist," for he was required to, in a sense, "ward off" or "exorcize" the "evil temptations" of the city. One reformer, Frederic Almy, wrote in 1902: "Loving, patient, personal service" would provide the "*antiseptic* which will make the *contagion* of daily life harmless."[115]

Many of the child savers suggested a number of social factors as causal forces of delinquency, but few carried their arguments to the logical conclusion—changing the harmful environmental factors. The solution continued to focus on the control, "rehabilitation," or "treatment" of individual offenders or groups of offenders from a particular segment of the population (including those identified as pre-delinquents). The existing social structure was accepted as good and necessary, but there was a need to lead those who went astray back so that they could "fit" into the existing social order and class system. Unfortunately, the only place they were permitted to fit was at or near the bottom of that order.

Most of the programs advocated during this period placed primary emphasis on the individual and his or her moral and other personal shortcomings and received justification from psychological, psychiatric, and psychoanalytic theories of delinquency just beginning to emerge during the late nineteenth century. The works of G. Stanley Hall and William Healy, both of whom worked closely with the juvenile courts in various cities, were based on such theories. These writers advocated a "clinical" approach (using the medical model), one that stressed the need for a "scientific laboratory" to study delinquents. One such laboratory was the juvenile court.

The child savers claimed that they had ushered in new innovations in penology, especially with the establishment of industrial and training schools. Actually, the methods used were variations of earlier methods used in houses of refuge and other institutions. Most of the "new" institutions of the twentieth century were placed in rural areas—a product of the popular antiurban bias among so many child savers. It was assumed that the "temptations" of city life would be offset by placement in such a setting. The juvenile court was to be the primary placing agency, thus serving a function similar to that of the Children's Aid Society when it placed children "out west."

The emphasis within these institutions remained relatively unchanged from previous methods. Restraint, control, the teaching of "good work habits" (e.g., cleaning floors, waiting on tables, milking cows, cooking, etc.), respect for authority, and a quasi-military model continued to be the hallmark of these institutions.

An example of the kinds of institutions opened during this period was the Shelby County Industrial and Training School, located near Memphis, Tennessee. Opened in 1904 in a farming community, it emphasized farm labor and the development of "habits of industry" through various forms of work and education. A report in 1912 to the board of directors stated in glowing terms how "successful" this institution had become.

> The boys in the several departments of work and in the school room have shown commendable interest in work and study. All are in school half of every weekday, under the instruction of a thoroughly competent lady school teacher. In the several departments of work, habits of industry have been cultivated which must prove a helpful training for future usefulness. The half-day work and half-day school, which has been in practice in these

institutions for years, is now appealing to our public school authorities as a necessary advance in youthful development.

There has been no attempt in the past to indulge in expensive and often impracticable methods. Our work in all departments is necessary, practical and productive. On the farm and in the garden the actual use of the implement in the hand of the boy, under intelligent supervision, must produce results—and does—which means an abundance of fresh vegetables in their season for our tables and feed for our dairy cows and other stock.

In the bakery and kitchen . . . the boys, under the supervision of a lady teacher of domestic science, are kept exceedingly busy. . . . The laundry force and the boys who do the endless scrubbing, sweeping and dusting are all being taught the necessity of work.[116]

Thus, even the most menial work was made "respectable," so that these youths would fit into their appropriate labor force position after release. This institution was closed in 1935 amid a great deal of controversy, with two grand jury reports criticizing its methods and lack of results (in terms of a high recidivism rate and overcrowding).[117]

The "new penology" (as it was called at the time), perhaps best represented by state and county "reformatories," "industrial and training schools," and the like, emphasized menial labor that helped produce profits for both the state and private industry. For instance, the Illinois State Reform School (opened in 1871 at Pontiac) signed contracts with a Chicago shoe company, a company that manufactured brushes, and a company manufacturing cane-seating chairs— yet the production of commercial products was referred to as the "educational" program at this institution.[118] The "training" in such institutions was supposed to, in the words of the famous penal reformer Frederick Wines, "correspond to the mode of life of working people," and should "be characterized by the greatest simplicity in diet, dress and surroundings, and *above all by labor*."[119]

In many of these institutions (such as the one in Memphis) a lot of emphasis was placed on agricultural training, despite the fact that the United States was fast moving toward an industrial society. The reformatory regime aimed to teach middle-class values but lower-class skills. "Bookishness" was expressed as something undesirable, while menial labor was described as an "educational" experience. Waiting on tables, cleaning, cooking, and the like were to be taught to the "colored boys" in these institutions, according to the National Conference of Charities and Correction. Reformers aimed to "get the idea out of the heads of city boys that farm life is menial and low."[120]

Delinquency, Public Schools, and Industry

Social reformers in the United States accepted a form of "soft determinism"—the idea that behavior is sometimes determined by forces outside the individual's control. "If criminal behavior was determined by knowable biological or psychological or social conditions, those conditions could be identified and changed, *at least at the individual level*."[121] Although causal factors were external to the individual (such as poverty, bad housing, inequality), the emphasis was and would continue to be on the individual offender.

Most of the reformers tended to accept the version of *Social Darwinism* known as *Reform Darwinism*—the view that man was not completely helpless and that man's progress enabled him, through "positive science," to step in and improve his lot. With the help of such writers as Charles Cooley and Charles Henderson, reformers tended to accept the "nature vs. nurture" view, with heavy emphasis on the "nurture" side of this dichotomy.[122] However, taken as a whole, the environmental view that combined "bad homes and evil surroundings" dominated the thinking throughout the nineteenth and early twentieth centuries. There is little evidence that the prevailing views have changed very much.

The beliefs that intervention should be stressed and that "potential criminals and delinquents" could and should be identified and treated at the earliest age possible continued to be dominant themes. The juvenile court was supposed to be one of the chief means through which intervention would be made. The court also enlisted the help of other programs and institutions to carry out such a program. Public schools, recreation programs, public playgrounds, boys' clubs, YMCAs, and other organizations all helped in dealing with the problem of delinquency, especially in their role of identifying and "containing" so-called "pre-delinquents."[123]

The desire to use public schools for social control had been stated early in their development. Brace declared in 1880:

> We need, in the interests of public order, of liberty, of property, for the sake of our own safety and the endurance of free institutions here, a strict and careful law, which shall compel every minor to learn to read and write, under severe penalties in case of disobedience.[124]

It can certainly be argued that the school system ultimately meant upward mobility for some (usually those already from privileged classes). For the majority, however, it meant remaining in their original class position.

The general images or stereotypes of delinquents and criminals had not changed much since the early nineteenth century. In his first report in 1854 about the efforts of The Children's Aid Society, Brace warned:

> This "dangerous class" has not begun to show itself, as it will in eight or ten years, when these boys and girls are matured. Those who were too negligent or too selfish to notice them as children, will be fully aware of them as men. They will vote—they will have the same rights as we ourselves, though they have grown up ignorant of moral principle, as any savage or Indian. They will poison society. They will perhaps be embittered at the wealth, and the luxuries, they never share. Then let society beware, when the outcast, vicious, reckless multitudes of New York boys, swarming now in every foul alley and low street, come to know their power and *use it*.[125]

As this quotation suggests, the images of "delinquents" were often contradictory. On the one hand they were viewed sympathetically as needing help; on the other hand, they were feared and described viciously and in racist terms.

The connection between compulsory schooling, the new factory system, and various forms of punishment in penal institutions is apparent. Although writing about England, historian Lawrence Stone's comments are relevant for the United States. He notes that one of the effects of industrial capitalism was "to add support for the penal and disciplinary aspects of school, which were seen by some largely as a system to break the will and to condition the child to routinized labor in the factory."[101]

Public school reforms would continue to have a close connection to juvenile justice reforms. In his book, *Education and the Rise of the Corporate State*, Joel Spring writes:

> The more general concern of industrialists was that schools produce an individual who was cooperative, knew how to work well with others, and was physically and mentally equipped to do his job efficiently. A cooperative and unselfish individual not only worked well with his fellows in the organization *but was more easily managed.*[102]

William H. Tolman, co-founder of the American Institute of Social Service, commented in 1900 on the importance of the kindergarten program, saying:

> The lessons of order and neatness, the discipline of regulated play . . . are acquisitions, making the child of greater value to himself, and, if he can follow up the good start which has been made for him, tending to make him of greater wage earning capacity.

Tolman further stated that children would be coming into the shops of the employers "in a few years; how much better for you [the employers] that their bodies have been somewhat strengthened by exercise, and their minds disciplined by regulated play."[103]

Such innovations in public schooling as kindergarten, extracurricular activities, home room, and organized playgrounds combined to teach children the benefits of cooperative work, discipline, and respect for authority, not to mention submission to the needs of the group. (Individual initiative was apparently not encouraged.) It was not by accident that many of these programs were also established to prevent and control delinquency.

Representatives of the business world began a concerted campaign to support new forms of education that would train the future workers of the United States.[104] At first they began with their own educational programs along the lines of improving employee morale and relations between management and the worker. For instance, corporations brought about such programs as the "social secretary" (to "maintain constant personal contact with the workers"), employee associations and clubs, periodic employee benefit gatherings, Sunday School programs, company magazines, and even their own public schools (including day-nurseries and kindergartens). The establishment of nurseries and kindergartens functioned to free "both parents for work either in the factory or home." The Plymouth Cordage Company used such a system because: "The company believed that by removing the children from the house for part of the day the mother could give her undivided attention to housework." The rationale given by this company was that the husband would function better at work coming from a clean home with hot meals. Another function of kinder-gartens was to promote the role of women as the "natural caretakers" of children, as they enabled teachers to get into the homes of workers and thus interest mothers in children's work.[105]

Eventually corporations began to put pressure on local communities to have the public school system perform some of these functions. Obviously to do so would save business a great deal of money. As Spring concludes:

> These industrial programs for the management of workers became models for the type of activities adopted by the public school. . . . In some cases actual programs, like home economics, were transferred from factory education activities to the public schools to produce workers with the correct social attitudes and skills.[106]

In short, the school system evolved "to meet the needs of capitalist employers for a disciplined labor force, and to provide a mechanism for social control."[107]

Rather than eliminating inequality and increasing upward social mobility, the school system effectively maintained class differences. A report by the National Education Association in 1910 stated: "The differences among children as to aptitudes, interests, economic resources, and prospective careers furnish the basis for a rational as opposed to merely a formal distinction between elementary, secondary, and high education."[108] Ellwood Cubberly, an educational reformer, wrote in 1909:

> Our city schools will soon be forced to give up the exceedingly democratic idea that all are equal, and our society devoid of classes . . . and to begin specialization of educational effort along many lines in an attempt to adapt the school to the needs of these many classes.[109]

As noted earlier, reforms in public schooling were closely related to the problem of juvenile delinquency.[110] Henry Goddard, one of the leaders in the development of the Alfred Binet Intelligence Test implemented in 1916, believed that intelligence testing was the key to reducing delinquency and claimed that the public schools could be used as "clearing houses" to pick out "potential delinquents," especially the category he called the low intelligent, "defective delinquent."[111] Teachers, guidance counselors, truant officers, school social workers, and school psychologists became part of this vast network of social control within the school system.

Twentieth-Century Developments in Juvenile Justice

During the period roughly between 1920 and the 1960s there were relatively few structural changes within the juvenile justice system. In Illinois, beginning around 1909, the juvenile court began experimenting with the intensive psychological study and treatment of youthful deviance. The Juvenile Protective League, under the leadership of such notables as Julia Lathrop (head of the U.S. Children's Bureau), Jane Addams (reformer and founder of Hull House[112]), Julian Mack (judge of the Boston juvenile court), and William Healy (psychologist), established a child guidance clinic. The clinic embodied the medical model of delinquency. Under the direction of Healy, child guidance clinics focused their attention and energies on the individual delinquent, one who was generally viewed as "maladjusted" to his or her social environment. By 1931 there were over 200 such clinics around the country.[113]

During the 1920s and 1930s the profession of social work grew to prominence.[114] This field began to dominate the treatment of individual delinquents and interpreted delinquency as stemming from conflicts within the family. Even today, social work methodology has a strong influence within the juvenile justice system.

The Chicago Area Project, theoretically based on the works of the Chicago School of Sociology and those of Clifford Shaw, focused on community organization to prevent delinquency. From this perspective, delinquency stemmed from the social disorganization of slum communities rather than from the exploitation inherent in the capitalist system. Hence, the solution would be found in "fostering local community organizations to attack problems related to delinquency," such as poverty, inadequate housing, and unemployment.[115] Much of the effort focused on reducing gang delinquency, which was prevalent in Chicago and other large cities.[116] But such programs did little to alter the social reality of economic deprivation and other structural sources of delinquency. Barry Krisberg and James Austin comment:

> Chicago at that time was caught in the most serious economic depression in the nation's history. Tens of thousands of people were unemployed, especially immigrants and blacks. During this period, a growing radicalization among impoverished groups resulted in urban riots. The primary response by those in positions of power was an expansion and centralization of charity and welfare systems. In addition, there was considerable experimentation with new methods of delivering relief services to the needy [e.g., Hull House]. No doubt, Chicago's wealthy looked favorably upon programs like the Area Project, which promised to alleviate some of the problems of the poor without requiring a redistribution of wealth and power.[117]

The decade of the 1960s brought about some hope for significant changes, but such hope lasted barely into the 1970s. At least two developments stand out during this period of time. One was intervention by the United States Supreme Court through rulings in cases including *In re Gault* (1967),[118] *Kent v. United States* (1966)[119], and *In re Winship* (1970)[120]. Sadly, most of the promise of reform inherent in these rulings was never realized, especially with regard to institutionalizing youth (more will be said on these and other cases in chapter 11).

The second development came on the heels of the efforts of Jerome Miller, who managed to close most of the reform schools opened in the nineteenth century in the state of Massachusetts.[121] Despite the success of the closure of these types of institutions and the development of workable alternatives throughout the country, recent "get tough" policies threaten the progress made. Krisberg and Austin have observed that: "Most jurisdictions still rely on placement in institutions, with conditions reminiscent of reform schools 100 years ago. Children continue to be warehoused in large correctional facilities, receiving little care or attention."[122] "Get tough" policies target minorities; more and more institutions are populated with urban African Americans.[123] Moreover, young women continue to be subject to a "double standard." Minor offenses too often result in some form of incarceration.[124] Also, many institutional systems have become huge bureaucracies with a vested interest in keeping a certain percentage of youth incarcerated.

Into the Twenty-First Century

As we shall see in chapters 11 and 12, the late 1990s witnessed a continuing trend toward getting tougher and tougher with young offenders, highlighted by "zero tolerance" policies and the war on drugs. As the new century dawned, however, it became obvious to most observers that getting tough was not working. Scandals surrounding juvenile "training schools" and local detention centers drew attention to the abusive practices of these institutions and how counterproductive they had become. The situation became so bad within the California Youth Authority that they were forced to close many institutions and even changed their name to one that represented the many improvements that were coming (see chapter 12).

New models for dealing with juvenile crime began to emerge, highlighted by alternative programs in the community and a nationwide attempt to reduce minority overrepresentation inside juvenile institutions. Among the most popular models was one that emerged in the state of Missouri as they began to close down their large institutions and institute community-based programming and one in San Francisco called the Detention Diversion Advocacy Project (DDAP). Several large foundations, such as the Annie E. Casey Foundation, began to fund alternative programs. The results so far have been promising, as recidivism rates have declined significantly and youth crime continued its decrease from the highs reached in the early 1990s. These and other model programs will be discussed in more detail in the last chapter of this book.

Summary

The history of the juvenile justice system in the United States demonstrates that a class, race, and gender bias has pervaded the institution since its inception. The standard definitions of "delinquency" reflect such biases. The roots of this pattern can be traced to colonial embellishments of the *parens patriae* doctrine. The first and most significant legal challenge to this doctrine, *Ex Parte Crouse*, involved the incarceration of a girl on the grounds that she was "incorrigible."

With changes in the labor market structure and several other structural changes in society during the nineteenth century came changes in conceptions of and responses to youthful deviance. The House of Refuge movement during the first half of the nineteenth century was one result of those changes. The primary function of these institutions (and those that followed) was to control and reform children of the poor. The general aim of "reform" was to inculcate "habits of industry" and respect for authority, which would help maintain the existing class structure.

With more changes in the social structure came more reforms of the juvenile justice system during the last half of the nineteenth century. Youth became more and more dependent, and many were relegated to the surplus labor population. With thousands flocking to large cities in the Northeast and Midwest, unemployment and vagrancy became widespread. Juvenile delinquency became a problem for reformers as the juvenile system as we know it today began to take shape. One of the most notable changes was the establishment of the juvenile court system and industrial and training schools. Thus, by 1900 to 1910 the basic structure of modern juvenile justice was created, with the *parens patriae* doctrine and the medical model of deviance providing the philosophical justification for state intervention into the lives of youth. Child guidance clinics and the Chicago Area Project were two significant forms of youth control that followed the establishment of the juvenile court.

NOTES

[1] For more detail on the history of juvenile justice see the following: Platt, A. M. (2010). *The Child Savers: The Invention of Delinquency* (40th anniversary edition). Chicago: University of Chicago Press; Mennel, R. (1973). *Thorns and Thistles: Juvenile Delinquents in the U.S., 1820–1940.* Hanover, NH: University Press of New England; Bernard, T. J. (1992). *The Cycle of Juvenile Justice.* Oxford: Oxford University Press.

[2] Postman, N. (1994). *The Disappearance of Childhood.* New York: Vintage, p. xi.

[3] Ibid., p. 53.

[4] Ariès, P. (1962). *Centuries of Childhood.* New York: Knopf.

[5] Postman, *The Disappearance of Childhood*, p. 18.

[6] Firestone, S. (1970). *The Dialectic of Sex.* New York: Bantam Books, p. 75.

[7] Postman, *The Disappearance of Childhood*, pp. 15–16.

[8] Firestone, *The Dialectic of Sex*, p. 78.

[9] Tuchman, B. (1978). *A Distant Mirror.* New York: Alfred A. Knopf, p. 53.

[10] For background on the invention of the printing press see the following website: http://inventors.about.com/od/gstartinventors/a/Gutenberg.htm

[11] Firestone, *The Dialectic of Sex*, p. 35; see also: http://en.wikipedia.org/wiki/Nicolaus_Copernicus and http://www.faqs.org/health/bios/60/Andreas-Vesalius.html

[12] Postman, *The Disappearance of Childhood*, p. 36.

[13] Ibid., p. 41.

[14] Ibid., p. 42.

[15] Eisenstein, E. (1979). *The Printing Press as an Agent of Change.* Cambridge, England: Cambridge University Press, pp. 133–34.

[16] Postman, *The Disappearance of Childhood*, p. 43.

[17] Ibid., p. 46.

[18] Spring, J. (1972). *Education and the Rise of the Corporate State.* Boston: Little, Brown, pp. 37–38.

[19] Hawes, J. (1971). *Children in Urban Society.* New York: Oxford University Press, p. 18. See also Rothman, D. J. (1971). *The Discovery of the Asylum: Social Order and the Disorder in the New Republic.* Boston: Little, Brown; Sutton, J. R. (1988). *Stubborn Children: Controlling Delinquency in the United States.* Berkeley: University of California Press.

[20] Bremner, R. H. (Ed.) (1970). *Children and Youth in America.* Cambridge: Harvard University Press; Bernard, *The Cycle of Juvenile Justice*, pp. 44–45; Rendleman, D. (1979). "*Parens Patriae:* From Chancery to Juvenile Court." In F. Faust and P. Brantingham (Eds.), *Juvenile Justice Philosophy* (2nd ed.). St. Paul, MN: West.

[21] Krisberg, B., and J. Austin (1993). *Reinventing Juvenile Justice*. Thousand Oaks CA: Sage, p. 9.

[22] de Mause, L. (Ed.) (1974). *The History of Childhood*. New York: Psychohistory Press; Empey, L. T. (Ed.) (1979). *The Future of Childhood and Juvenile Justice*. Charlottesville: University Press of Virginia.

[23] Sutton, *Stubborn Children*, p. 11.

[24] Kett, J. F. (1977). *Rites of Passage: Adolescence in America, 1790 to the Present*. New York: Basic Books, pp. 13–18.

[25] Ibid., p. 23.

[26] Ibid., p. 29.

[27] Bremner, *Children and Youth in America*.

[28] Platt, *The Child Savers*; Empey, *The Future of Childhood and Juvenile Justice*; Postman, *The Disappearance of Childhood*.

[29] Sutton, *Stubborn Children*.

[30] Rendleman, "Parens Patriae," p. 63.

[31] Teitelbaum, L. E. and L. J. Harris (1977). "Some Historical Perspectives on Governmental Regulation of Children and Parents." In L. E. Teitelbaum and A. R. Gough (Eds.), *Beyond Control: Status Offenders in the Juvenile Court*. Cambridge, MA: Ballinger.

[32] Dobash, R. E. and R. Dobash (1979). *Violence against Wives*. New York: Free Press, ch. 1.

[33] Blackstone, W. (1796). *Commentaries on the Laws of England*. Oxford: Clarendon Press, pp. 23–24.

[34] *State v. Aaron* 4. N.J.L. 263, 1818

[35] Platt, *The Child Savers*.

[36] Empey, *The Future of Childhood and Juvenile Justice*, p. 59.

[37] Brenzel, B. (1983). *Daughters of the State*. Cambridge: MIT Press, p. 11.

[38] Bernard, *The Cycle of Juvenile Justice*, pp. 49–55.

[39] Rothman, *The Discovery of the Asylum*, p. 70.

[40] One of the persistent problems in our response to crime and delinquency is that when trying to make predictions based on certain "risk factors" (as done with various health problems such as cancer), there are too many "false positives" where you predict that someone will become a delinquent and the prediction turns out to be false. Most kids, even those at "high risk," will never become adult criminals.

[41] Pickett, R. (1969). *House of Refuge*. Syracuse: Syracuse University Press, p. 48; Lewis, W. D. (2009). *From Newgate to Dannemora. The Rise of the Penitentiary in New York, 1796–1848*. Ithaca, NY: Cornell University Press (originally published in 1965), p. 47.

[42] This group was formerly called the Society for the Prevention of *Pauperism* (another word for poverty). For a discussion of this group and a detailed description of its upper-class backgrounds see Pickett, *House of Refuge*, pp. 21–49. A complete list of all of those associated with the Society can be found in the publication of a reception for the outgoing president of the association on December 15, 1851. Called "Society for the Reformation of Juvenile Delinquents, Reception," the document can be viewed and downloaded at: http://books.google.com/books?id=-NUXAAAAYAAJ&pg=PA3&output=text. The list of members reads like a "who's who" of New York Society.

[43] Hawes, *Children in Urban Society*, p. 28.

[44] "An Act to Incorporate the Society for the Reformation of Juvenile Delinquents in the City of New York," Chap. 126, Laws of 1824, passed on March 29, 1824.

[45] "Society for the Reformation of Juvenile Delinquents, Reception."

[46] "Documents relative to the House of Refuge: Instituted by the Society for the Reformation of Juvenile Delinquents." Retrieved from http://books.google.com/books?id=YrkqAAAAMAAJ&printsec=frontcover&output=text

[47] The title of Howard's book was: *State of the Prisons in England and Wales with Preliminary Observations and an Account of Some Foreign Prisons and Hospitals*. This quotation (the inscriptions have been translated into English) is taken from a piece written by criminologist Thorsten Sellin: "The House of Correction for Boys in the Hospice of Saint Michael in Rome." (1930, February). *Journal of the American Institute of Criminal Law and Criminology* 20(4): 533–53. Retrieved from http://www.jstor.org/pss/1134675

[48] Ibid.

[49] Ibid.

[50] For more on Bentham and the panopticon design see Shelden, R. G. (2008). *Controlling the Dangerous Classes: A History of Criminal Justice in America* (2nd ed). Boston: Allyn & Bacon, ch. 4.

[51] Thomas Eddy, a wealthy businessman and Quaker, was influential in designing the New York House of Refuge. He had helped design and build the first penitentiary in New York—Newgate—and had been influenced by Howard and Bentham. For further background on Eddy see Pickett, *House of Refuge* and Lewis, *From Newgate to Dannemora*.

[52] Pickett, *House of Refuge*, p. 15 for quote.

[53] Abbott, G. (1938). *The Child and the State*. Chicago: University of Chicago Press, p. 362.

[54] Pickett, *House of Refuge*, p. 68.

[55] "Society for the Reformation of Juvenile Delinquents, Reception."

[56] Pickett, *House of Refuge*, p. 14.

[57] Ibid., p. 15.

[58] Mennel, *Thorns and Thistles*, p. 6.

[59] Ibid., p. xxvi.

[60] The upper class apparently did not approve of the lower classes attending theatres, which were growing in popularity. In their 1938 annual report, the managers of the House of Refuge claimed that theatres played a major role in the "depravity" of 59 out of 130 children committed to the refuge. It was noted that one boy sold his father's Bible in order to get money for tickets (Pickett, *House of Refuge*, p. 18). The city eventually levied a tax on theatres to help finance the refuge. Religious fanaticism was prevalent. Frances Trollope, a European traveler who observed the fulmination over theatres, came to the conclusion that "religious enthusiasm and narrow provincialism combined to freeze out cultural activities" (pp. 19–20). Religious instruction took on a primary role in the daily routine of the refuge.

[61] Pickett, *House of Refuge*, p. 191.

[62] Bremner, *Children and Youth in America*, p. 613.

[63] Rothman, *The Discovery of the Asylum*, p. 58.

[64] Hawes, *Children in Urban Society*, p. 44, emphasis added.

[65] Platt, *The Child Savers*, p. 107. Platt was writing about the later nineteenth century but his comments applied to the next century as well. "If, as the child savers believed, criminals are conditioned by biological heritage and brutish living conditions, then *prophylactic* measures must be taken early in life." Famous prison reformer Enoch Wines commented that "They are born to it, brought up for it. They must be saved" (p. 45, emphasis added).

[66] Hawes, *Children in Urban Society*, pp. 45–46.

[67] Mennel, *Thorns and Thistles*, p. 103.

[68] Pisciotta, A. (1982). "Saving the Children: The Promise and Practice of *Parens Patriae*, 1838–98." *Crime and Delinquency* 28: 410–25.

[69] Society for the Prevention of Pauperism (1822). *Report on the Penitentiary System in the United States*. New York. Retrieved from http://books.google.com/books?id=yNHf851WemcC&pg=PP8&ots=EK7H0ewdjn&dq=Report+on+the+Penitentiary+System+in+the+United+States&output=text. This quote was first seen in Lewis, *From Newgate to Dannemora*, p. 64.

[70] For a discussion of the connection between religion and punitiveness see Shelden, R. G. (2010). *Our Punitive Society: Race, Class, Gender and Punishment in America*. Long Grove, IL: Waveland Press, pp. 9–12.

[71] Pickett, *House of Refuge*, pp. 21–49. The charges that brought juveniles into the early juvenile courts included "immorality." This was especially true for girls, as discussed later in the chapter.

[72] Ibid., pp. 72–73.

[73] According to an annual report found on the Internet, multiple shops created many different items in 1828. For example, the shoe shop completed 1,214 pair of pumps, closed 4,341 pump uppers, completed 39 boots, crimped and closed 4,262 boot legs, and closed 1,555 brogans and shoes. The chair shop completed 9,834 cane seats for plain frames, 864 for maple frames, 330 backs for large arm chairs, and caned 132 settee bottoms. The brass nail shop completed 14,976 brass nails, 228 dozen bits, 2,196 pair of stirrups, and 396 holster tips. "Documents Relative to the House of Refuge." Retrieved from http://books.google.com/books?id=YrkqAAAAMAAJ&pg=PA145&dq=Nathaniel+C.+Hart&output=text#c_top

[74] Bremner, *Children and Youth in America*, p. 672.

[75] Ibid., pp. 689–91; Hawes, *Children in Urban Society*, pp. 47–48.

[76] Rothman, *The Discovery of the Asylum*, p. 210.

[77] Hawes, *Children in Urban Society,* p 44.

[78] Rothman, *The Discovery of the Asylum*, pp. 107–8.

[79] The wording used here is taken *verbatim* from the law, passed in Pennsylvania in 1826, which authorized the House of Refuge "at their discretion, to receive into their care and guardianship, infants, *males under the age of twenty-one years, and females under the age of eighteen years*, committed to their custody . . ." (emphasis added). Note the obvious distinction based upon gender. This exact same statute was reproduced in numerous state laws throughout the nineteenth century. I found an example in my own study of Memphis, Tennessee: Shelden, R. G. (1976). "Rescued from Evil: Origins of the Juvenile Justice System in Memphis, Tennessee, 1900–1917." Ph.D. dissertation, Southern Illinois University, Carbondale; Shelden, R. G. and L. T. Osborne (1989). "'For Their Own Good': Class Interests and the Child Saving Movement in Memphis, Tennessee, 1900–1917." *Criminology* 27: 801–21.

[80] Pickett, *House of Refuge*, pp. 76–77. Pickett also notes that on some occasions where the parents challenged the Refuge officials legally, officials backed off to "save face" and avoid further legal problems. In hindsight, we might wonder what would have happened if several dozen or more parents filed a class action lawsuit. In all likelihood, most parents were too poor and or too unaware of their rights to challenge the officials.

[81] *Ex Parte Crouse*, 4 Wharton (Pa.) 9 (1938); for the significance for girls see Shelden, R. G. (1998). "Confronting the Ghost of Mary Ann Crouse: Gender Bias in the Juvenile Justice System." *Juvenile and Family Court Journal* 49: 11–26.

[82] *Ex Parte Crouse.*

[83] See Mennel, *Thorns and Thistles*; Hawes, *Children in Urban Society*; Bremner, *Children and Youth in America*; Pisciotta, "Saving the Children." Abuses within the juvenile justice system have continued to the present, with one scandal after another in multiple jurisdictions. See, for example, Confessore, N. (2010, July 14). "Federal Oversight for Troubled N.Y. Youth Prisons." Retrieved from http://www.nytimes.com/2010/07/15/nyregion/15juvenile.html; and Davis, A. (2010, August 12). "O'Malley Touts Possible End to Federal Oversight of Md. Juvenile Facilities." Retrieved from http://voices.washingtonpost.com/annapolis/2010/08/omalley_touts_possible_end_to.html

[84] Pisciotta, "Saving the Children."

[85] DeVoe, E. P. (1848). *The Refuge System; or Prison Discipline Applied to Juvenile Delinquents.* New York: John R. McGown, p. 9, quoted in Pickett, *House of Refuge, 159.*

[86] Bernard, *The Cycle of Juvenile Justice*, pp. 70–72.

[87] For further discussion of this issue see Chesney-Lind, M. and R. G. Shelden (2004). *Girls, Delinquency and Juvenile Justice* (3rd ed.). Belmont, CA: Wadsworth.

[88] *Commonwealth v. Fisher*, 213 Pa. 48 (1905).

[89] While during the decade of the 1830s just under 600,000 arrived, during the following decade about 1.7 million arrived, followed by another 2.6 million in the 1850s. Most came from northern and western Europe (especially Ireland and Germany). In Ireland the potato famine in 1845 created misery and death by the thousands and resulted in an estimated 1.5 million coming to America between 1845 and 1860. Blum, J. M., B. Catton, E. S. Morgan, A. M. Schlesinger, Jr., K. M. Stampp, and C. V. Woodward (1963). *The National Experience: A History of the United States.* New York: Harcourt, Brace and World, p. 203. New York City alone accounted for between 62 and 70 percent of all immigrants between1846 and 1855 (http://www.latinamericanstudies.org/immigration-statistics.htm). For a general discussion of the movement to the Midwest, see http://www.wisconsinhistory.org/turningpoints/tp-018/. The Midwest experienced massive population growth between 1820 and 1840: Ohio grew by 140%; Indiana went up by 308%; Illinois grew by 765% (http://www.connerprairie.org/Learn-And-Do/Indiana-History/America-1800-1860/Western-Immigration.aspx). See also Litcht, W. (1995). *Industrializing America: The Nineteenth Century.* Baltimore, MD: Johns Hopkins University Press.

[90] Brace, C. L. 1872. *The Dangerous Classes of New York.* New York: Wynkoop and Hallenbeck.

[91] Bremner, *Children and Youth in America*, pp. 456, 739, 820.

[92] The Children's Aid Society Website. Retrieved from http://www.childrensaidsociety.org/about/history

[93] Brenzel, B. (1975). "Lancaster Industrial School for Girls: A Social Portrait of a Nineteenth Century Reform School for Girls." *Feminist Studies* 3: 40–53.

[94] Bremner, *Children and Youth in America*, p. 705.

[95] Platt, *The Child Savers*, pp. 61–66. One supporter of this plan stated that such cottages would be "furnished with all the necessities and comforts of a well ordered home, presided over by a Christian gentleman and lady . . ." Platt, p. 63.

[96] Mennel, R. (1983). "Attitudes and Policies toward Juvenile Delinquency in the United States: A Historiographical Review." In M. Tonry and N. Morris (Eds.), *Crime and Justice: An Annual Review of Research (Vol. 4)*. Chicago: University of Chicago Press, pp. 191–224.

[97] Holt, M. I. (1992). *The Orphan Trains*. Lincoln: University of Nebraska Press.

[98] Hawes, *Children in Urban Society*, p. 101.

[99] In a study of the origins of the juvenile justice system in Memphis, Shelden found several instances where commitments to the county training school were challenged in court, some successfully. See Shelden, "Rescued from Evil," and Shelden, R. G. (1992). "A History of the Shelby County Industrial and Training School." *Tennessee Historical Quarterly* 51: 96–106.

[100] Bremner, *Children and Youth in America*, pp. 693–94.

[101] Rendleman, "*Parens Patriae*," pp. 104–6.

[102] Rothman, *The Discovery of the Asylum*, p. 240.

[103] Piven, F. F. and R. Cloward (1972). *Regulating the Poor: The Functions of Social Welfare*. New York: Vintage Books.

[104] Bernard, *The Cycle of Juvenile Justice*, p. 84.

[105] Schwendinger, H. and J. Schwendinger (1976). "Delinquency and the Collective Varieties of Youth." *Crime and Social Justice* 5 (Spring–Summer): 13.

[106] Bernard, *The Cycle of Juvenile Justice*, pp. 88–89.

[107] Platt, *The Child Savers*, p. 138.

[108] Knupfer, A. M. (2001). *Reform and Resistance: Gender, Delinquency, and America's First Juvenile Court*. New York: Routledge, p. 199.

[109] Shannon, R. T. (Ed.) (1896). *Code of Tennessee*. Nashville: Marshall and Bruce, pp. 1087–88.

[110] Platt, *The Child Savers*, ch. 6.

[111] Finckenauer, J. O. (1984). *Juvenile Delinquency and Corrections*. New York: Academic Press, p. 116; Feld, B. (1999). "A Funny Thing Happened on the Way to the Centenary." *Punishment and Society* 1: 187–214.

[112] Schlossman, S. (1977). *Love and the American Delinquent: The Theory and Practice of "Progressive" Juvenile Justice, 1825–1920*. Chicago: University of Chicago Press, p. 92.

[113] The origins of probation can be traced to the efforts of a man named John Augustus, a Boston shoemaker who, during the 1840s, volunteered to take on the responsibility of supervising offenders in the community as a substitute to sending them to prison or jail. Since then this rather unique idea has become highly bureaucratized with the average probation officer supervising between 50 and 100 offenders. The spirit of volunteerism and the offering of a helping hand in the name of true benevolence toward another human being has turned into a job as a career bureaucrat. Many who engage in this line of work are overwhelmed by the responsibilities and often care little about the persons they supervise. In fact, the "supervision" is often little more than surveillance, which usually consists of a few phone calls. In many instances probation officers follow the motto found on the wall of a California probation office, which reads: "Trail 'em, Surveil 'em, Nail 'em, and Jail 'em." Miller, J. G. (1996). *Search and Destroy: African-Americans Males in the Criminal Justice System*. Cambridge University Press, p. 131.

[114] Schlossman, *Love and the American Delinquent*, p. 99.

[115] Ibid., emphasis added.

[116] *Memphis Commercial Appeal*, July 16, 1912.

[117] Shelden, "A History of the Shelby County Industrial and Training School."

[118] Platt, *The Child Savers*, p. 105.

[119] Ibid., p. 50, emphasis added.

[120] Ibid., pp. 59–60.

[121] Faust and Brantingham, *Juvenile Justice Philosophy*, p. 3, emphasis added.

[122] Cooley, C. H. (1974). "Nature vs. Nurture in the Making of Social Careers." In Faust and Brantingham, *Juvenile Justice Philosophy*; Henderson, C. R. (1974). "Relation of Philanthropy to Social Order and Progress." In Faust and Brantingham, *Juvenile Justice Philosophy*.

[123] Shelden, "Rescued from Evil"; and Shelden and Osborne, "For Their Own Good."

124 Brace, C. L. (1872). *The Dangerous Classes of New York and Twenty Years' Work among Them*. New York: Wynkoop & Hallenbeck, p. 352. Available on Google Books.

125 Ibid., pp. 321–22.

126 Stone, L. (1969). "Literacy and Education in England, 1640–1900." *Past and Present* 42 (February): 92, quoted in Postman, *The Disappearance of Childhood*, p. 53.

127 Spring, *Education and the Rise of the Corporate State*, p. 43, emphasis added.

128 Ibid., pp. 36–37.

129 Bowles, S. (1975). "Unequal Education and the Reproduction of the Social Division of Labor." In M. Carnoy (ed.), *Schooling in a Corporate Society*. New York: David McKay.

130 Spring, *Education and the Rise of the Corporate State*, p. 36.

131 Ibid., p. 22.

132 Bowles, "Unequal Education," p. 219.

133 Cohen, D. K. and M. Lazeron (1972). "Education and the Corporate Order." In R. C. Edwards, M. Reich, and T. E. Weisskopf (Eds.), *The Capitalist System*. Englewood Cliffs, NJ: Prentice-Hall, p. 186.

134 Ibid., p. 187.

135 For a fuller discussion of this topic from the perspective of an active reformer of the period see J. Addams, *The Spirit of Youth and the City Streets* originally published in 1909. The University of Illinois Press reissued the book in 2001.

136 Mennel, *Thorns and Thistles*, pp. 96–99.

137 See Addams, J. (1910). *Twenty Years at Hull-House*. New York: Macmillan. Also available from the University of Illinois Press.

138 Krisberg and Austin, *Reinventing Juvenile Justice*, pp. 32–35.

139 Lubove, R. (1965). *The Professional Altruist: The Emergence of Social Work as a Career, 1880–1930*. Cambridge, MA: Harvard University Press.

140 Krisberg and Austin, *Reinventing Juvenile Justice*, pp. 35–42.

141 Liazos, A. (1974). "Class Oppression: The Functions of Juvenile Justice." *Insurgent Sociologist* (Fall): 12; Thrasher, F. (1927). *The Gang*. Chicago: University of Chicago Press.

142 Krisberg and Austin, *Reinventing Juvenile Justice*, p. 33.

143 The case of *In Re Gault* involved a 15-year-old Arizona boy named Gerald Gault who was adjudicated as a "delinquent" in juvenile court and committed to the Arizona Industrial School for the "period of his majority" (21 years old) because he and some friends made an "obscene" phone call to a neighbor. The U.S. Supreme Court ruled that Gault had been denied certain fundamental rights (similar to the ruling by the Illinois court in the O'Connell case), such as the right to counsel. Writing for the majority, Justice Abe Fortus stated that "Under our Constitution, the condition of being a boy does not justify a kangaroo court." For the full text of this case (and many others, including the O'Connell case) see Faust and Brantingham, *Juvenile Justice Philosophy*; see also Platt, *The Child Savers*, pp. 161–63.

144 *Kent v. United States* (383 U.S. 541, 1966).

145 *In re Winship* (397 U.S. 358, 1970).

146 Miller, J. G. (1998). *Last One Over the Wall* (2nd ed.). Columbus: Ohio State University Press.

147 Krisberg and Austin, *Reinventing Juvenile Justice*, p. 49.

148 Pope, C. and W. Feyerherm (1990). "Minority Status and Juvenile Justice Processing: An Assessment of the Research Literature" (Parts I and II). *Criminal Justice Abstracts* 22 (2, 3); Miller, *Search and Destroy*.

149 Chesney-Lind and Shelden, *Girls, Delinquency and Juvenile Justice*.

THE EXTENT OF DELINQUENCY

The actual amount of crime committed in the United States today is not known and is probably unknowable. There are several reasons for this. First, there are literally hundreds of acts that are prohibited by law. Many of these acts lack precise definition, such as "disorderly conduct" and "disturbing the peace."[1] Second, many illegal acts are committed out of public view, such as possession and/or sale of illegal drugs. These and other "victimless crimes" usually do not involve a complaining victim. Third, determining the true extent of crime would mean that each individual would have to be monitored 24 hours a day, which would be an admittedly horrible—and impossible—state of affairs. Therefore, the only realistic sources of knowledge about crimes are those that come to the attention of local police or other authorities (from actual observation or reported by citizens) and those admitted by perpetrators and/or victims to sources other than criminal justice practitioners (that is, responses to people administering victimization surveys).

Measuring Delinquency

It is not easy to find out how much delinquent behavior there is in the United States. As an example, consider the measurement of youth "gang" activities. Youth gang activity has long been viewed as criminal behavior. In April 2001 the Office of Juvenile Justice and Delinquency Prevention (OJJDP) released a report claiming that gang problems for communities had increased by more than 1,000% between 1970 and1998.[2] Such figures can be alarming if people accept the figures uncritically, but the data generate some obvious questions. First, how can these data be collectivized when the definition of gang varies across jurisdictional lines? Where did these researchers find the "list" of gangs to consider? (Gangs do not keep paper or electronic records that can be searched.) The numbers were generated largely from law enforcement agencies—the same agencies that improve their chances of receiving additional funding by making a case that their communities have gang problems. The fact is that many of the youth labeled as gang members in this study were probably not gang members at all. Some of the activities were not even related to youth gang activities; indeed, some of the acts were committed by people legally classified as adults. As revealed in the Rampart scandal in Los Angeles[3] some of the activities may never have occurred in the first place. We are not suggesting that people should disregard government reports, but it is essential to employ critical analysis before reaching any conclusions.[4]

Before discussing the extent of delinquency in the United States, we will take a close look at where we obtain the information on this subject and how crime and delinquency are measured. The four most frequently consulted sources of data are: (1) *Crime in the United States* (also known as the *Uniform Crime Reports*) published annually by the Federal Bureau of Investigation; (2) Juvenile Court Statistics, which provides data from the various juvenile courts in the country[5] (3) various kinds of "self-reports" where young people are asked to tell, through anonymous questionnaires and interviews, what kinds of delinquent activities they have engaged in recently; and (4) victimization surveys.

FBI Uniform Crime Reports

Since 1930 the Federal Bureau of Investigation (FBI) has published statistics on crime in the United States. The reports began as monthly publications, changed to quarterly in 1932, and became annual in 1959. The report is based on data sent to the FBI by local police departments and covers about 93% of the population. Much of the data is channeled through state- level Uniform Crime Report (UCR) Programs (there are currently 41 such programs). However, the accuracy of the data depends primarily on local police departments and how well they adhere to the annual reporting procedures suggested by the FBI.

Crime in the United States consists of two major sections: (1) "Offenses Known to Law Enforcement" (crimes that are reported or otherwise come to the attention of local police departments) and (2) "Persons Arrested." The first category consists of eight different crimes (formerly referred to "index crimes") and is divided into two parts: violent crimes and property crimes. The arrest category includes the eight crimes in the first category plus 21 other crimes (formerly referred to as "Part II offenses).

Two kinds of data are presented: the actual *number* of incidents known to law enforcement and the *crime rate* per 100,000 people in the general population (based on the most recent census). The crime rate is established by dividing the number of crimes by the population and multiplying by 100,000. For instance, if a particular area has a population of 350,000, and 30,000 crimes were known to law enforcement during the year, the crime rate would be 8,571.4. The data for arrests are categorized according to age, sex, race, and location (urban, rural, and suburban).

The FBI provides breakdowns of arrests according to race, sex, and age, but it does not cross-tabulate by race and sex. In other words, we do not know how many black males or white females, for example, are arrested. There are cross-tabulations of sex and age, but not race and age (so, for instance, we don't know the arrest rate of black males between the ages of 15 and 17). One of the most egregious shortcomings of the FBI report is that Hispanics *are grouped with whites rather than appearing in a separate category.*[6] Because of the categorization, the numbers reported underplay the disparity in arrests of minorities (which would usually include Hispanics) compared to non-Hispanic whites.[7]

Serious Crimes (formerly Part I)

Crimes known to law enforcement include the following classifications: (1) murder, (2) forcible rape, (3) robbery, (4) aggravated assault, (5) burglary, (6) larceny-theft, (7) motor vehicle theft, and (8) arson. Both the media and law enforcement refer to these eight offenses as "serious crime." The media generally cover the FBI's annual release (usually mid-September) of the numbers for the previous year, reporting whether the numbers or rate of serious crime decreased or increased.

Crime in the United States also includes a section called "crimes cleared by an arrest." It details the percentage of those crimes "known to the police" that result in (or are "cleared" by) an arrest. The noteworthy fact is that relatively few crimes known to the police are ever cleared by an arrest. Despite steady improvement in technology and the growth in police professionalism, the percentage of crimes cleared by an arrest has been steadily declining over the years. The percentage varies according to the type of crime committed. For instance, in 2009, 47.1% of the 1,142,108 violent crimes known to the police were cleared by an arrest (66.6% of murders; 41.2% of rapes; 28.2% of robberies; and 56.8% of assaults). Of the 8,229,516 property crimes know to the police, 18.6% were cleared by arrest (12.5% of burglaries; 21.5% of larcenies; 12.4% of motor vehicle thefts; and 18.5% of arsons).[8] For crimes known to the police involving persons less than 18 years of age, more property crimes than violent crimes were cleared. Of the 458,914 violent crimes involving juveniles, 11% were cleared (4.8% of murders; 11.4% of rapes; 14.9% of robberies, and 17.2% of aggravated assaults). Of the 1,337,882 property crimes involving juveniles, 17.2% were cleared (15.1% of burglaries; 17.7% of larceny thefts; 14.7% of motor vehicle thefts; and 34.7% of arsons).[9]

Other Crimes (formerly Part II)

Arrests for what used to be called Part II crimes include such offenses as drug law violations, fraud, embezzlement, and driving under the influence. In terms of monetary losses and deaths/injuries, many of these offenses are a great deal more serious than some of the eight offenses included in the "serious" crimes category. Many of the offenses are not specific *crimes* per se; rather, they are *categories* of different kinds of crimes. For example, there is no such crime as "aggravated assault." This is usually referred to in state legal codes as "felonious assault" or "assault with a deadly weapon" or something similar. This particular offense should be distinguished from the category known as "other assaults," which is a catchall term referring to a variety of altercations and/or threats (ranging from a barroom brawl to a couple of teenagers fighting after school).[10] The category "all other offenses" includes such crimes as public nuisance, failure to appear on a warrant, bigamy, and—strangely enough—kidnapping, which can carry a penalty harsher than murder or rape if there is a ransom demand.

Other kinds of data in this report include changes over time (for both crimes known to police and persons arrested), geographic location (crime by state, region, etc.), the number of full-time law enforcement personnel, police officers killed, and other kinds of information. (An electronic copy is available on the Internet and most public and university libraries have paper versions.)

Critique of the FBI Report

FBI data should be interpreted with extreme caution since there are a number of shortcomings. The first and most important problem is that the accuracies of the data depend on the work done by local police departments. This fact alone raises concerns about official reports of crime. Law enforcement agencies (like other bureaucracies) need to protect themselves—to prove that they are doing their job. They are not above manipulating crime statistics in order to obtain more local, state, or federal funding or to improve their "public" image. Crime statistics are just about the easiest statistics to manipulate. For instance, some crimes are never counted officially. An audit of arrests for 196 police departments found an error rate of around 10%; moreover, virtually all police departments make numerous errors in their UCR reporting procedures.[11] Another study found serious problems in the reporting of arson, since many fire departments do not report suspicious fires to the UCR and those that do omit many fires that may have been set by arsonists.[12] Some police administrators may knowingly falsify crime reports by undervaluing the cost of stolen goods. Conversely they may report an ordinary pickpocketing incident as a "robbery" (especially if they want to show that "violent crime" is rising to justify an increase in the police budget). The number of "gangs," "gang members" and "gang-related" crime can be inflated to receive federal funding to create or increase the size of a "gang unit" or to divert the public's attention away from internal problems within the police department.[13]

Henry Brownstein found that in the mid-1990s the media, politicians, and criminal justice officials in New York exaggerated a relatively modest fluctuation of reported crime to further private and political ambitions. His analysis demonstrates how easily local data can be miscounted. Consider that data are sent on a monthly basis from more than 600 local law enforcement agencies to a central data collection agency, the Division of Criminal Justice Services (DCJS). At the time of the study, DCJS had a staff of only four data entry clerks, one supervisor, and one administrator to handle about 800 forms every month. Perhaps more important, Brownstein (who was the head of DCJS for several years) reports that there had been major staff cutbacks earlier in the decade, including decreases in the staff who trained UCR clerks in local police departments. As a result, many local clerks never had any training; constant turnover among several positions was another problem. All of this resulted in problems with the data, not the least of which was the constant backlog of forms submitted to the DCJS. Looming deadlines for submitting the forms increased stress levels. "Even diligent and hardworking people have difficulty maintaining their usual standard of quality control under these circumstances."[14]

Space does not permit a complete reporting of Brownstein's fascinating study, but his discoveries about perhaps the most easily manipulated category of crime—drug offenses—create serious doubts about official statistics. Brownstein notes that in New York City in 1980 there were a reported 14,339 drug sales, while in 1981 there were only 4,317, a decrease of 70%! Brownstein dismissed the possibility of a misprint since in 1979 there were a reported 14,007 arrests for drug sales (almost identical to the 1980 number), and in 1982 the number was 3,950 (very close to the 1981 number). It turned out that there were "two informal, unwritten policy-shifts around that time" that essentially "refined how drug sales were counted." The first change was that phone calls from citizens reporting drug sales were no longer counted. The second change was that instead of counting an arrest of one drug dealer as one crime, the police began counting each drug sales *scene* as one crime, *no matter how many people were arrested*. Crime reporting and data collection are *human enterprises and hence subject to ordinary human error*; critical analysis is essential when using data to make decisions about policies.

A 1998 report revealed scandals in several police departments in Philadelphia, Boca Raton (Florida), Atlanta, and Buffalo (New York). Police departments in those cities were accused of falsely reporting crime statistics, resulting in resignations and demotions of high-ranking police officials. In Boca Raton a police official downgraded a total of 385 felonies (11% of the total serious crime). In one example, he reclassified as "vandalism" a case where a burglar stole $5,000 in jewelry and did more than $25,000 in damage.[15] Philadelphia's problem was so bad that they had to withdraw their crime figures from the FBI reports for 1996, 1997, and the first half of 1998. The report notes that this city accounts for 2% of all homicides in the country and thus can have a significant impact on the national homicide rate. Also in Philadelphia, a police captain reported an 80% decrease in serious crime in his district, caused in part by his downgrading many robberies, burglaries, and thefts to "missing property" cases.

The FBI also investigated inflated crime numbers in Detroit. In 1999, the city reported 415 killings and 1,152 murder arrests. The number of murders and arrests should be about equal. Officials blamed outdated computers for their problems—an excuse that ignores the trauma experienced by innocent people booked for murder. The most recent report comes from a series of articles in the *New York Times* published in February of 2010.[16] According to one report, a survey of 100 senior and retired officers found that many had raised questions on the accuracy of crime data collection within the NYPD. Many complained of pressure to "cook the books" by, for instance, classifying certain felonies as misdemeanors, thereby showing a drop in serious crime in the city. Are the cities of Detroit, Philadelphia, New York and Boca Raton isolated cases? Critical analysis would suggest an alternative explanation: they are the jurisdictions whose failings have been exposed.

The second problem with UCR data is that many crimes are never reported to the police at all. In fact, it has been estimated that there may be more than twice as many index crimes committed than are actually reported to the police. It should be noted that most unreported crimes are relatively minor crimes. Citizens may be reluctant to report crimes because they believe that nothing can be done, that the police do not want to be bothered, that the incident was essentially a private matter, or that reporting the crime will bring retaliation. In the case of rape, the victims fear (justifiably so) that the criminal justice system will not take their victimization seriously and will further victimize them, primarily by blaming them for their own victimization.[17] This problem is even more significant when we consider all of the part II offenses. Our only measurement for the extent of these crimes is through arrest data (which, as shown below, leave much to be desired). How many frauds and embezzlements really occur each year? How many DUIs occur? How many drug offenses are committed? How many minor assaults ("other assaults") actually occur? How much domestic violence happens? No one knows.

The third problem revolves around the arrest figures. If someone is arrested and charged with more than one crime, only the most serious of these crimes is counted in the final tabulation of arrest data. Further, in some cases each *act* is counted as a separate offense, while in others multiple acts are counted as a single offense. If several people are robbed in an incident at a restaurant, it would be counted as one robbery. However, if the same offender physically attacked four people, the attacks would be listed as four assaults. Also, in the case of an arrest for the crime of murder, the reader should remember that these data pertain to *persons arrested—not the number of murders*. In other words, we have no idea how many murders the person arrested has actually committed. Someone like the "Unabomber" or serial killers David Berkowitz, Edward Cunnan, or John Wayne Gacy, and those charged with multiple killings on college campuses will be listed as one person arrested for homicide, not several homicides.

The fourth significant problem is that we have no idea, from reading the FBI's report, what eventually happened to each arrest. Were any charges dropped by the police department or the district attorney? In many cases, *all* the charges are dropped. What does that tell us about the arrest figures? Moreover, was the person convicted, and if so of what crime? As we will note in our chapter on prosecution, the vast majority of all arrests are dismissed by the district attorney's office, or the original charge is reduced to some other charge. Further, many arrestees are *overcharged* by the police because they anticipate that the district attorney will "bargain down" the charges. Thus, we have no idea how many of the millions of arrests the police make each year are a true reflection of what really happened.

The fifth problem is the interpretation of crime *rates*. First, these rates are based on the *total* population (in the most recent UCR this meant about 230 million people), which is far different from the population *at risk* of a particular crime (that is, the population of potential victims). For instance, rates of forcible rape are not based on the number of women in the population (since they are the major at-risk group). Since the female population is about 50% of the total population, the actual rate of reported rapes should be about double that reported by the FBI. Similarly, motor vehicle theft should be based on the number of motor vehicles, since not every person owns a motor vehicle (at a minimum, the rate should be based only on the population 16 and over). Second, changes in crime rates may be more a reflection of changes in the population, or various demographic characteristics (e.g., increases or decreases in the proportion of youth), rather than the number of crimes committed. Quite often the actual number of specific crimes may increase, while the rate will decrease during a given period (and vice versa).

Finally, there are several types of crimes that are excluded from the report. For example, federal crimes are excluded. More importantly, the report focuses almost exclusively on "street crimes" involving a direct, "one-on-one" harm. Why are corporate crimes and crimes of the state largely ignored? The common definitions of "crime" and the popular images of "crime" are shaped and determined by the dominant classes in society and the state itself. [18] It would not make sense for the powerful to define some of their own harmful behaviors as "crimes" nor would it seem logical for the state to define itself as "criminal." There are built-in class and racial biases in the very definition of "crime."[19]

In response to many of these criticisms, the FBI developed the National Incident-Based Reporting Program (NIBRS). This is an additional form to be filled out by local police departments that allows for a much wider variety of data. All crimes would be reported, not just the index crimes, while attempted crimes would be distinguished from completed crimes. Although some states already have such a system, it is still far from uniform. But such a huge database has many potential problems as well, and most of this new system does not insure against misuse by police departments. Too much information on citizens is a problem waiting to happen. We have seen how databases on "gangs" can be misused, especially against minorities.[20]

How Much Delinquency Is There?

FBI figures provide data on the number of arrests of people under the age of 18. Juveniles commit a wide variety of offenses, ranging from the most serious (such as murder and assault) to the most trivial (such as curfew violation and loitering). As will be noted shortly, self-report studies indicate that practically every youth at some point in their teenage years does something that could theoretically result in an arrest. Most are never arrested, and only a very small percentage end up in the juvenile justice system. What about those arrested? What are they arrested for? What are the distribution of arrests in terms of race and gender?

Arrest Figures

Table 2-1 shows the total numbers and percent distribution of juvenile arrests in 2009, based on the FBI crime categories. Tables 2-2 and 2-3 show some recent trends for juvenile arrests.

As shown in table 2-1, the majority of juvenile arrests are for part II offenses, with "all other offenses" constituting the largest chunk of these arrests, followed by "other assaults," drug offenses, disorderly conduct, and curfew and loitering. Among the part I offenses, the majority of juveniles are

Table 2-1   Total Arrests, Under 18, 2009

	Number	Percent
Total Arrests	**1,161,830**	**100.0**
Index Crimes*		
Murder	652	**
Rape	1,820	**
Robbery	19,336	1.7
Aggravated assault	29,932	2.6
Burglary	46,637	4.0
Larceny-theft	196,863	17.0
Motor vehicle theft	11,354	**
Arson	3,615	0.3
Violent crime totals	51,740	4.5
Property crime totals	258,469	22.2
Total index crime	310,209	26.7
Part II Offenses*	—	—
Other assaults	135,125	11.6
Forgery & counterfeiting	1,277	**
Fraud	4,091	0.4
Embezzlement	393	**
Stolen property	11,990	1.0
Vandalism	55,757	4.8
Weapons	20,696	1.8
Prostitution	791	**
Sex offenses	7,799	0.7
Drugs	103,657	9.0
Gambling	312	**
Offenses against the family and children	2,689	0.3
Driving under the influence	8,085	0.7
Liquor laws	67,859	5.9
Drunkenness	9,837	0.8
Disorderly conduct	92,754	8.0
Vagrancy	1,047	**
Curfew & loitering	72,203	6.2
Runaways	59,223	5.1
All other offenses***	196,036	16.8

* In 2003 the FBI stopped using the terms Index and Part II Offenses. They are being used here to retain some continuity.

** Less than .1%

***All Other refers to such offenses as trespassing, public nuisance, failure to appear on warrants, contempt and, for juveniles especially, violation of probation and certain status offenses.

Source: FBI (2010). *Crime in the United States, 2009*. Washington, DC: U.S. Department of Justice. Retrieved from http://www2.fbi.gov/ucr/cius2009/data/table_32.html

arrested for property offenses (some serious, but mostly minor). Larceny-theft constitutes the largest category, which includes shoplifting.

Table 2-2 shows the trends in arrest rates during the 10-year period from 1999 to 2008 (rates for 2009 not available as of this writing). There were significant decreases in juvenile arrests in almost every category. The only notable category that did not decline was robbery, which increased 15% (the change in disorderly conduct was extremely small). For the first time in several years there was a decrease in the arrest rate for drug offenses. This is somewhat puzzling in that the number of drug offenders referred to juvenile courts increased slightly. Other assaults are mostly minor personal crimes, resulting in few injuries. The bulk of these offenses occurs near or around schools and in the home and mostly involves fighting with other youth. There was a very slight decline in the overall arrest rate for these offenses. However, as we will see shortly, there was a slight increase in referrals to juvenile court for this offense.

The number of arrests for "other assaults" depends on the willingness to resort to a formal arrest for minor forms of fighting on and off school grounds and for domestic disturbances. The "zero tolerance" mentality of recent years contributes to arrests. This is especially true for fighting on school grounds. In Las Vegas, where the author lives, school police make thousands of arrests each year, and most of the "crimes" are ordinary fighting among students. A generation ago, such fighting was broken up by teachers and other school employees, and an arrest was a rare occurrence.

It is important to note that there is a danger in misinterpreting reports of "violent crime" from annual reports about juvenile crime, especially when such reports cite juvenile court statistics. National statistics, like those reported in *Juvenile Court Statistics*, often lump together homicide, aggravated assault, rape, robbery, and "simple assaults" under the category "person crimes." Most referrals to juvenile court (see below) are for "simple assault." Very often, however, news reports will show data on the broad category of "person crimes" or even use the more value-loaded term "violent crime" without pointing out that the bulk of the offenses are simple assaults. The author has seen such reports in newspapers on numerous occasions, with such headlines as "Violent Crime Up among Juvenile Court Referrals."

Table 2-3 shows the rank order of juvenile arrests for the years 2003 and 2009. Note that in both years "all other offenses" and "larceny-theft" ranked first and second, constituting around one-third of all arrests. Other assaults ranked third in both years, while drugs and disorderly rounded out the top five. In both years, the top five offense categories constituted about 60% of all arrests.

Overall trends are depicted in figure 2-1. After reaching a peak around 1994, juvenile arrests for violent crime declined until 2001 and have remained about the same since that time. Total arrests for juveniles declined 20% in the decade beginning 2000; every offense category declined except for robbery, which increased 18% and prostitution, which increased 8.5%. The percentage decline from 2008 to 2009 was 9%, and every category declined (including robbery, which decreased 11%) except for gambling, which increased 13.4%.[21]

Table 2-2   Juvenile Arrest Rates (per 100,000 ages 10–17), 1999–2008

	1999	2008	% Change
Total	7888	6317.7	-20
Index Crimes*			
Murder	4.6	3.8	−17
Rape	15.8	9.8	−38
Robbery	93.8	107.6	+15
Aggravated assault	223.1	166.9	−25
Burglary	317.7	250.3	−21
Larceny–theft	1231.5	979.9	−20
Motor vehicle theft	167.1	74.7	−55
Arson	25.5	18.5	−27
Selected Part II Offenses*			
Other assaults	747.4	688.2	−8
Vandalism	368.6	317.1	−14
Weapons	136.7	119.2	−13
Drugs	645.2	540	−16
Driving under the influence	69.1	46.9	−32
Liquor laws	522.1	394.8	−24
Drunkenness	70.6	46.5	−34
Disorderly conduct	564.5	564.6	0
Curfew & loitering	571.8	406.7	−29
Runaways	479.4	327	−32

*In 2003 the FBI stopped using the terms Index and Part II Offenses.

Source: National Center for Juvenile Justice (2009, October 31). *Juvenile Arrest Rates by Offense, Sex, and Race* http://ojjdp.ncjrs.org/ojstatbb/crime/excel/JAR_2008.xls

Table 2-3   Rank Order of Juvenile Arrests, 2004 and 2009 (percent distribution)

2004	2009
1. All Other Offenses (17.3%)	1. All other offenses (17.4%)
2. Larceny-theft (15.1)	2. Larceny-theft (17.0)
3. Other assaults (11.3)	3. Other assaults (11.6)
4. Disorderly conduct (8.8)	4. Drugs (9.0)
5. Drugs (8.5)	5. Disorderly conduct (8.0)
Sub-total 60% of all juvenile arrests	63% of all juvenile arrests

Source: FBI, *Uniform Crime Reports* (2009). Retrieved from: http://www.fbi.gov/ucr/cius2009/data/table_32.html

Figure 2-1   Juvenile Violent Crime Index Arrest Rate Trends, 1980–2008

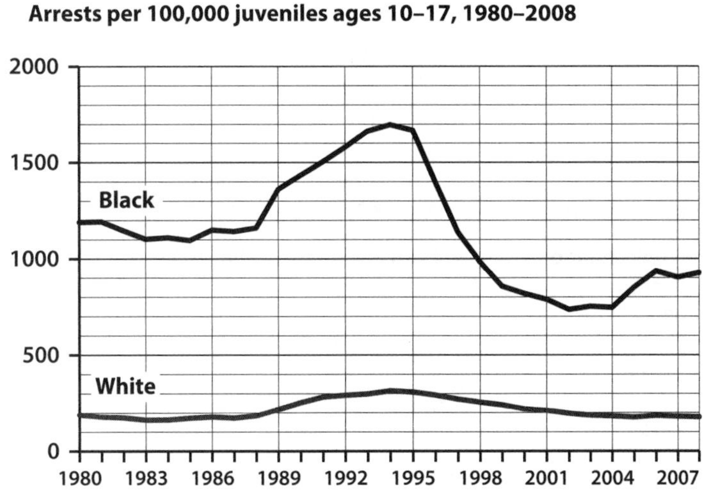

Arrests per 100,000 juveniles ages 10–17, 1980–2008

Source: Office of Juvenile Justice and Delinquency Prevention: www.ojjdp.gov/ojstatbb/crime/JAR_Display.asp?ID=qa05261

Racial Differences

Both race and gender have consistently figured prominently in delinquency rates. Table 2-4 shows some trends in the arrest rates for white and black youths for selected offense categories. This table shows trends dating back to 1988 during the peak years of the "war on drugs." The overall arrest rate for blacks exceeded that for whites by slightly more than a 1.9:1 ratio in 1988; 1.8:1 in 1998; and almost 2.2:1 in 2008. The ratio has fluctuated for violent crimes; black-white ratios went from 6.3:1 in 1988; then to 3.9:1 in 1998; then 5.2:1 in 2008. For property crimes, the ratios increased very slightly during this period of time from 2:1 in 1988 to almost 2.4:1 in 2008. Note the significant increases in drug arrest rates for whites between 1988 and 1998 and from 1988 to 2008, compared to blacks. (Gender differences will be covered in chapter 5.)

Juvenile Court Statistics

The most common source for national figures has been OJJDP, which publishes surveys of juvenile court case processing based on the voluntary submission of data from both state and local agencies. The most recent figures are from 2007 (even though the report was issued in June 2010). The data are grouped into the following major categories: person, property, drugs, and public order (see table 2-5).

In 2007 there were an estimated 1,666,100 delinquency cases processed in juvenile courts across the nation. The majority were either property offenses (36%) or public order offenses (28%). Relatively few were serious violent

Table 2-4   Juvenile Arrest Rates (per 100,000 ages 5–17), for Selected Offenses, by Race, 1988–2008

	1988		1998		2008	
	White	**Black**	**White**	**Black**	**White**	**Black**
Index Crimes						
Violent	185	1161	255	984	178	926
Property	2203	4466	1721	3283	1131	2689
Drugs	256	1026	556	1381	503	921
Total (all arrests)	6947	13,575	7621	13,996	5550	12,161

Percent Change:	**1988–1998**	**1998–2008**	**1988–2008**
Violent			
White	+38	−30	−4
Black	−15	−6	−20
Property			
White	−22	−35	−49
Black	−26	−18	−40
Drugs			
White	+117	-10	+ 96
Black	+35	−33	−10
All Offenses			
White	+10	−27	−20
Black	+3	−13	−10

Note: Between 1980 and 1989 the drug arrest rate for blacks increased by 249%; for whites there was a decrease of 33%.

Source: National Center for Juvenile Justice (2009). *Juvenile Arrest Rates by Offense, Sex, and Race*. http://ojjdp.ncjrs.org/ojstatbb/crime/excel/JAR_2008.xls

offenses (homicide, rape, robbery and aggravated assault, constituting only 5% of all cases). The most common offense against the person was that of "simple assault" (totaling 17% of all delinquency cases and 67% of all "person offenses"). Drugs accounted for about 11% of the total. Public order offenses increased 13% between 1998 and 2007, while person offenses increased only 1%, drug violations decreased 2%, and property offenses decreased 24%. Within the public order category, the most noteworthy increases were disorderly conduct and liquor law violations.

What is clear from this picture is the relatively minor nature of most juvenile crime. Thus, within the property offense category, larceny-theft (chiefly shoplifting) leads the way, accounting for almost half of the total (43%). Between 1998 and 2007 all of the property offenses declined. As noted above, violent crimes accounted for 5% of the total delinquency offenses. This is quite different from the media image of juvenile predators running wild.

The only data available about offenses are the cases that are actually petitioned to court, rather than all status offense referrals. In 2007 a total of 150,700 cases were petitioned, an increase of 31% over the number of cases in 1995. The most common status offense was truancy (38% of the total, an increase of 67%

Table 2-5   Referrals to Juvenile Court, 1998–2007

Most serious offense	Number of cases (2007)	Percent change	
		1998–2007	2003–2007
Total delinquency	**1,666,100**	**–7%**	**–2%**
Person offenses	**409,200**	**1**	**0**
Criminal homicide	1,400	–31	5
Forcible rape	4,300	–10	–3
Robbery	31,000	4	45
Aggravated assault	49,600	–16	1
Simple assault	274,900	4	–4
Other violent sex offenses	15,700	20	–3
Other person offenses	32,300	3	5
Property offenses	**594,500**	**–24**	**–6**
Burglary	105,300	–22	0
Larceny–theft	255,500	–28	–11
Motor vehicle theft	26,600	–39	–29
Arson	8,100	–5	–1
Vandalism	108,800	–2	+11
Trespassing	54,300	–14	6
Stolen property offenses	17,900	–43	–14
Other property offenses	18,000	–38	–16
Drug law violations	**190,100**	**–2**	**1**
Public order offenses	**472,300**	**13**	**2**
Obstruction of justice	214,700	2	–2
Disorderly conduct	124,600	39	7
Weapons offenses	40,900	–3	11
Liquor–law violations	36,600	76	4
Nonviolent sex offenses	11,400	–1	–15
Other public order offenses	44,000	–3	0

Note: Detail may not add to totals because of rounding. Percent change calculations are based on unrounded numbers.

Source: Knoll, C. and M. Sickmund (2010, June). "Delinquency Cases in Juvenile Court, 2007," p. 2. Bureau of Justice Statistics. Retrieved from http://www.ncjrs.gov/pdffiles1/ojjdp/230168.pdf

over 1995) with liquor-law violations ranking second (22%, up 23% over 1995), followed by ungovernability and runaway (13% and 12%, respectively).[22]

Self-Report Studies

One of the most popular methods of determining the extent of crime is the self-report survey. These are surveys that ask people to talk to a researcher about the crimes they have committed. Since the 1940s there have been a number of such studies, which have come in several different forms. Some rely on anonymous questionnaires. Some ask people to sign their names, and then the answers are compared to police records. Other studies check the accuracy of the answers to the questionnaires with follow-up interviews and the threat of the use of lie-detector tests (a rather dubious method). Some studies use interviews plus validation by looking at police records.[23]

As long ago as the mid-1930s researchers have noted that there is a large amount of delinquent behavior that never comes to the attention of the police and juvenile court officials. For instance, in a book published in 1936, Sophia Robison observed that about one-third of delinquent behaviors known to social service agencies in New York City never became juvenile court cases.[24] A study of boys in a counseling program found that many had committed delinquent acts but were never arrested, while many others were handled informally by the police. A mid-1940s study of college students discovered that they committed a variety of delinquent offenses while in high school. Self-report studies continued to be published in the 1950s and 1960s. One study compared the delinquent behaviors of a group of high school students with those of institutionalized delinquents and found that the behaviors were quite similar.[25]

A study conducted by Martin Gold and his associates at the Bureau of Social Research in Ann Arbor, Michigan, was, at the time, one of the most sophisticated surveys ever completed. They selected a national sample of 847 youths and conducted in-depth interviews that lasted an average of about 105 minutes. Each interview covered a wide variety of both delinquent and nondelinquent activities. It was discovered that 88% had committed at least one delinquent act during the previous three years. While most were rather trivial acts, some were quite serious felonies. What was most interesting was that only 9% ever came into contact with the police. Moreover, higher status white male youth committed more serious delinquencies than lower status youth.[26]

Several different agencies and organizations have investigated various forms of youth behavior over the past couple of decades. The Office of Applied Studies in The Substance Abuse and Mental Health Services Administration (SAMHSA) conducts an annual survey of the population age 12 and older to collect information on health issues, primarily the prevalence, patterns, and consequences of substance abuse. The survey is called the National Survey on Drug Use and Health; it also asks youths if they have engaged in delinquent behaviors in the past year. Some of the key findings are found in table 2-6. Note the low prevalence of most of these behaviors and that the most common was engaging in a fight. Notice too that there were few differences among the races for drug sales.

One of the most comprehensive surveys is conducted by the Centers for Disease Control and Prevention. Some of the results from the Youth Risk Behavior Surveillance 2009 survey are summarized in table 2-7. Note the similarities for most behaviors across races. As other surveys have shown, there are few racial differences in drug usage. As we have already seen, however, the arrest rates for drugs show significant differences, with blacks and Hispanics far more likely to be arrested.

In general, these studies have demonstrated that just about everyone has committed some act that could be designated as "criminal" or "delinquent,"

Table 2-6 Participated in a Physical Delinquent Behavior in the Past Year among Persons Aged 12 to 17, 2008 and 2009

	Got into a serious fight at school or work		Took part in a group-against-group fight		Attacked someone with intent to seriously harm	
2009	21.1%		14.4%		7.2%	
2008	21.4%		14.5%		7.3%	
	2008	**2009**	**2008**	**2009**	**2008**	**2009**
Male	24.5	24.6	15.6	15.9	8.7	8.7
Female	18.1	17.5	13.3	12.7	5.8	5.6
White	18.9	18.3	12.4	12.6	6.1	5.8
Black	28.5	29.1	19.2	19.3	12.3	11.8
Hispanic	24.7	24.8	17.4	16.9	7.3	8.4

	Carried a Handgun		Sold Illegal Drugs		Stole or Tried to Steal Anything Worth More Than $50	
2009	3.2%		3.2%		4.4%	
2008	3.2%		3.0%		4.6%	
	2008	**2009**	**2008**	**2009**	**2008**	**2009**
Male	5.2	5.3	4.2	4.4	5.9	5.6
Female	1.1	1.0	1.8	2.0	3.3	3.1
White	3.2	3.3	3.0	3.2	4.1	3.9
Black	3.6	3.3	3.6	3.0	6.3	5.0
Hispanic	2.9	3.2	2.9	3.7	5.0	5.6

Substance Abuse and Mental Health Services Administration (2010). 2009 SAMHSA National Survey on Drug Use and Health: Detailed Tables 3.11B and 3.12B. Retrieved from http://oas.samhsa.gov/NSDUH/2k9NSDUH/tabs/Sect3peTabs1to25.htm#Tab3.11B; http://oas.samhsa.gov/NSDUH/2k9NSDUH/tabs/Sect3peTabs1to25.htm#Tab3.12B

but few people have been caught. Most juveniles have not committed serious forms of criminal or delinquent behavior, and they have not committed these acts on a regular basis. Crime and delinquency are distributed throughout the social class structure, and blacks and whites have about the same average of deviance. Class and racial differences are most apparent when considering serious (a term, as we have noted, which may itself be class or racially biased) and persistent forms of lawbreaking.

Self-report studies can be criticized on several grounds. First, there are problems with the research methods used. The social settings where the research is conducted differ (e.g., some in high school classrooms, some at institutions, some in the home, etc.). Also, there are problems inherent in asking people questions about their past behavior. This is especially the case when asking about behaviors that violate the law. There is the problem of the loss of memory (e.g., we often tend to forget an experience that was unpleasant), some people just like to lie or exaggerate (e.g., youths may want to seem "tough"), the wording of questions and even the meaning of different acts may be interpreted differently by different people, and there is always the problem of bias on the part of the interviewer. Another problem is how to measure social class.

Table 2-7   Proportion of High School Students Engaging in Delinquent Behavior, by Race and Gender, 2009

Behavior	Male			Female		
	White	**Black**	**Hispanic**	**White**	**Black**	**Hispanic**
Carried weapon	29%	21%	27%	7%	8%	8%
Carried gun	10	13	8	2	2	2
Carried weapon to school	8	7	8	2	4	4
Got in a physical fight	36	48	44	18	34	29
Ever used alcohol	72	65	75	76	70	79
Current alcohol use	44	31	42	46	36	44
Ever used pot	37	44	44	34	38	36
Current use pot	23	26	25	18	19	18
Tried pot before age 13	7	16	13	4	4	8
Ever used cocaine	7	4	10	5	2	9
Current use cocaine	3	3	5	2	1	4
Ever used heroin	3	4	4	2	1	3
Ever used meth	4	5	6	3	1	5
Offered, sold or given illegal drug at school	23	26	35	17	19	27
Ever had sexual intercourse	40	72	53	45	58	45
Before age 13	4	25	10	2	6	4

Source: Centers for Disease Control and Prevention (2010, June 4). "Youth Risk Behavior Surveillance—United States, 2009" Vol. 59, SS-5, tables 8, 10, 14, 36, 40, 42, 46, 53, 59, 61. Retrieved from http://www.cdc.gov/mmwr/pdf/ss/ss5905.pdf

Some surveys use income levels of individuals (or their parents), some use median income of census tracts, and some use occupation.

Many of these surveys have been validated through one or more methods. The most common methods include: comparing incarcerated youth with "normal" youth groups; asking friends about a subject's delinquent acts; longitudinal testing where the same questions are asked at different points in time; and comparing self-reports with official arrest or juvenile court records. These methods have shown that most of the youths responding to self-report questionnaires have been telling the truth.[27]

Juveniles as Victims

The victimization of juveniles takes two forms. First, there is the traditional victimization from a standard "crime"—an assault, a theft, etc. Second, there is the victimization by a member of one's own family, commonly referred to as *abuse and neglect*. While both of these areas will be discussed in this section, the latter will receive the most attention because it is the most devastating to the victims.

Child Abuse and Neglect

A few figures are cited here to give the reader an idea of how widespread this problem is. While data are readily available and have been for some time, this issue is largely ignored by the two major sources of information about crime and delinquency: the UCR and *Juvenile Court Statistics*. The reasons are not clear, but one might reasonably guess that it may have something to do with the fact that the perpetrators are mostly adults, and adults have more power and status than children. It may also be because of the fact that other organizations are involved in the collection of such data, as noted below.

Government publications often use the umbrella term "maltreatment" to refer to six major types of child abuse and neglect. The categories are outlined below.

Types of Child Abuse and Neglect

One of the major sources of data about child abuse and neglect is the National Child Abuse and Neglect Data System (NCANDS) and the Child Welfare Information Gateway.[28]

According to The Child Abuse Prevention and Treatment Act of 1998 (CAPTA) child abuse and neglect refer to: "Any recent act or failure to act on the part of a parent or caretaker, which results in death, serious physical or emotional harm, sexual abuse, or exploitation, or an act or failure to act which presents an imminent risk of serious harm." CAPTA defines sexual abuse as follows: "The employment, use, persuasion, inducement, enticement, or coercion of any child to engage in, or assist any other person to engage in, any sexually explicit conduct or simulation of such conduct for the purpose of producing a visual depiction of such conduct; or the rape, and in cases of caretaker or interfamilial relationships, statutory rape, molestation, prostitution, or other form of sexual exploitation of children, or incest with children." [29]

The following typologies are derived from the Child Welfare Information Gateway:[30]

Physical Abuse.   Physical abuse is generally defined as "any nonaccidental physical injury to the child" and can include striking, kicking, burning, or biting the child, or any action that results in a physical impairment of the child. In approximately 36 States and American Samoa, Guam, the Northern Mariana Islands, Puerto Rico, and the Virgin Islands, the definition of abuse also includes acts or circumstances that threaten the child with harm or create a substantial risk of harm to the child's health or welfare.

Neglect.   Neglect is frequently defined in terms of deprivation of adequate food, clothing, shelter, medical care, or supervision. Approximately 21 States and American Samoa, Puerto Rico, and the Virgin Islands include failure to educate the child as required by law in their definition of neglect. Seven States further define medical neglect as failing to provide any special medical treatment or mental health care needed by the child. In addition, four States define as medical neglect the withholding of medical treatment or nutrition from disabled infants with life-threatening conditions.

Sexual Abuse/Exploitation.   All States include sexual abuse in their definitions of child abuse. Some States refer in general terms to sexual abuse, while others specify various acts as sexual abuse. Sexual exploitation is an element of the definition of sexual abuse in most jurisdictions. Sexual exploitation includes allowing the child to engage in prostitution or in the production of child pornography.

Emotional Abuse.   All States and territories except Georgia and Washington include emotional maltreatment as part of their definitions of abuse or neglect. Approximately 22 States, the District of Columbia, the Northern Mariana Islands, and Puerto Rico provide specific definitions of emotional abuse or mental injury to a child. Typical language used in these definitions is "injury to the psychological capacity or emotional stability of the child as evidenced by an observable or substantial change in behavior, emotional response, or cognition," or as evidenced by "anxiety, depression, withdrawal, or aggressive behavior."

Parental Substance Abuse.   Parental substance abuse is an element of the definition of child abuse or neglect in some States. Circumstances that are considered abuse or neglect in some States include:

- Prenatal exposure of a child to harm due to the mother's use of an illegal drug or other substance
- Manufacture of a controlled substance in the presence of a child or on the premises occupied by a child
- Allowing a child to be present where the chemicals or equipment for the manufacture of controlled substances are used or stored
- Selling, distributing, or giving drugs or alcohol to a child
- Use of a controlled substance by a caregiver that impairs the caregiver's ability to adequately care for the child

Abandonment.   Many States and territories now provide definitions for child abandonment in their reporting laws. Approximately 18 States and the District of Columbia include abandonment in their definition of abuse or neglect. Approximately 13 States, Guam, Puerto Rico, and the Virgin Islands provide separate definitions for establishing abandonment. In general, it is considered abandonment of the child when the parent's identity or whereabouts are unknown, the child has been left by the parent in circumstances in which the child suffers serious harm, or the parent has failed to maintain contact with the child or to provide reasonable support for a specified period of time.

In fiscal year 2008 there were an estimated 3.3 million referrals to Child Protective Services agencies alleging child abuse and neglect, involving about 6 million children (more than double the 2 million in 1986). About 22% of these cases were substantiated. During that year an estimated 1,740 children died due to child abuse or neglect. Almost 80% were under 4 years of age; 39% were white; almost 30% were African American; almost 16% were Hispanic.[31]

Of the children subjected to abuse or neglect, 38.3% were maltreated by their mother acting alone; 18% were victimized by their father acting alone; and

17.9% were victimized by both parents. The most common type of maltreatment was neglect (71.1%), while about 16% were physically abused, 9% were sexually abused, 7.3% were psychologically maltreated, and the rest were victims of multiple maltreatments.[32] There is a correlation between maltreatment and lower socioeconomic status; maltreatment is also more likely within single-parent families—making poverty a contributing factor to maltreatment.[33]

The connection between child abuse and neglect and future behavioral problems has been clearly established. There are at least six long-term effects: *Emotional trauma* results in low self-esteem, guilt, anxiety, depression, and such physical problems as sleep disturbances, significant weight gain or loss, numerous illnesses, poor social relationships, and overall difficulties functioning in society.[34] *Running away* is a two-word outcome, and the important word is "away"—not running *to* something but running *away* from what is often an unbearable situation (many who are placed in foster homes or some other alternative living arrangements continue to run, since they often experience further abuse and neglect). *Disruptive and truant behavior in school* is a perfectly understandable outcome—children spend a huge amount of their lives in school, and problems at home spill over into the schools. The problems these children experience at school run the gamut from language deficiencies to learning problems to conflict with peers and teachers and the school itself (e.g., fights, vandalism, arson), not to mention poor academic performance and dropping out. *Drug and alcohol abuse* are often efforts to block the pain; this is especially common among sexual abuse victims. *Sexual behavior* involves promiscuity, prostitution, and early pregnancy; the connection between girls' sexual abuse and later prostitution has been extensively documented. *Violence and abuse* is a frequent pattern for those who have been abused themselves; they often abuse others, sometimes with severe violence, as in the case where children kill their parents. One important gender difference is that whereas boy victims generally take out their anger on others in the form of violence, girl victims tend to engage in self-destructive behavior. The adage that "sparing the rod spoils the child" is one of the greatest myths ever, as study after study show the clear connection between corporal punishment and children's deviance.[35] Finally, studies have shown that those who have experienced abuse are far more likely to end up somewhere in the juvenile justice system.[36]

Juvenile Victims of Crime

Perhaps the most dramatic statistic about juvenile victims of crime is that homicide is the second leading cause of death for those between the ages of 15 and 19; it is the third leading cause of death for those aged 10–14 and 1–4.[37] In 2006, the murder rate for black male teens (66.4 per 100,000) was 20 times greater than for whites (3.4); in fact, homicide was the leading cause of death for black teenagers. The rate for Hispanics (28.4) was 8 times greater than for whites. Firearms were involved in 85% of the cases. In 2009 1,348 juveniles under the age of 18 were murdered; of those, almost 40% were under age 4.[38] Most (80%) of the perpetrators were adults.[39] Previous reports have found that

62% of the murders of children aged 5 or younger and 40% of the murders of children aged to 6 to 11 were committed by family members.[40]

The *Los Angeles Times* tracks homicides in Los Angeles County and issues a detailed report.[41] Their analysis looks at variables in the homicides such as race, age, location of the event, circumstances, day of the week, etc. From January 1, 2007 through September 29, 2010, there were 3,047 homicides. Of that number, 387 (13%) were under the age of 18; in fact, 84 (3%) were 5 years or age of under—and 32 of the victims were killed before reaching their first birthday. A total of 613 (20%) were between 18 and 21; 450 (15%) were between the ages of 22 and 25. In other words almost half (48%) were 25 years or younger. Not surprisingly, the bulk of the homicide victims were minorities, with Latinos leading the way at 52%, while blacks constituted another 32%. Most were males (85%) and most of the homicides were concentrated in the poorest neighborhoods in the county, especially those areas with high concentrations of gangs (e.g., Long Beach, Compton, Inglewood, Boyle Heights, and Pomona). The city of Long Beach had the most with 162, followed by Compton with 132. Also not surprisingly, most (75%) were killed by guns.

Juveniles also have a high rate of victimization from assault. However, it must be stressed that the majority of all assaults can be classified as "simple assaults" where no weapon is used and no serious injuries result. This fact is demonstrated not only in victimization and self-report surveys but also in arrest statistics.[42]

Research has also documented the close connection between being a victim and offending. A large study of delinquent careers in Denver (see below) found that the victimization of males predicted greater levels of violence and the victimization of girls predicted a greater level of delinquency in general (but not violence in particular).[43]

Victimization Surveys

The National Crime Victimization Survey (NCVS) provides data on crime incidents, victims, and trends. Twice a year, U.S. Census Bureau personnel interview members of a nationally representative sample of about 42,000 households—approximately 75,000 people age 12 or older. Households remain in the sample for three years. The interviewers ask a series of questions regarding household members' experiences as victims of crime, whether or not they reported a crime if they were victimized, and if they did not report it, why not. They are also asked to describe their offenders (in cases of personal crimes) and how they reacted (did they resist, etc.).

The NCVS program began in 1972 and was redesigned in 1992. The redesign was based on the need to improve the questions asked, to update survey methods, and to broaden the scope of crimes measured. The survey focuses on the crimes of rape, sexual assault, personal robbery, assault (aggravated and simple), household burglary, theft, and motor vehicle theft. The results of the survey have consistently shown some rather significant differences from the annual FBI report.

What is particularly striking about the survey is that the most common crime reported by victims is "simple assault." This is true for all age groups, but particularly for those between 12 and 15 and 16 and 19, where the rates per 1,000 exceed 35 (see table 2-8). Note also that the rates for simple assault are quite similar for whites and blacks and for males and females. The rates for simple assault dwarf all of the other offenses included in this survey. Juveniles between the ages of 12 and 15 (for example) are more than three as likely to be the victim of a "simple assault" than any of the other three crimes combined. It appears that "fighting" is the true "all-American crime."

NCVS data point to potential future problems. *The victim of today is the offender of tomorrow.*[44] Many youths who joined gangs had been victimized and believed that gang affiliation would protect them from future victimization.[45] An analysis of birth cohort data in Philadelphia found that offenders were far more likely to have been victims. This was especially the case for nonwhite offenders, with almost half (46%) having been victims, compared to only 19% of the white offenders.[46]

A major problem with NCVS is that many crimes are *underreported*, as is the case with UCR. Crime is obviously a sensitive topic for many people, and they may understandably keep some information away from both the police and researchers. If they live in an area where there is a lot of crime, they might not remember the particulars of each and every theft, for example. When it comes to crimes committed by family members, there is a tendency to withhold information. If the victim is young enough, he or she might not even recognize that the behavior is "criminal." Similarly, women who are victims of abuse by their husbands often rationalize or minimize abusive behavior; in some cases the abuse may be so frequent it is regarded as "normal." Women who are raped are often reluctant to report such incidents, even to researchers.

People who move frequently may never have the opportunity to be part of the national sample. If you are homeless or a runaway, you are at increased risk for victimization but very unlikely to be included in the annual survey. The number of homeless children has increased in recent years. According to the National Center on Family Homelessness one in every 50 children in the United States is homeless—an estimated 1.5 million children.[47]

Finally, a common criticism is that many questions on the NCVS are about relatively minor offenses. The same can be said about UCR data, since the majority of crimes reported to the police are relatively minor offenses. However, NCVS specifically excludes homicide, arson, commercial crimes, and crimes against children under the age of 12. Survey respondents are never asked "if toxic chemicals were dumped in the creek behind their house, if they were cheated out of a month's rent by the local bank or rental agent, if their children were made sick by companies selling lead-based crayons, or if they lost their union retirement benefits when the local savings and loan closed down after the president left for the Cayman Islands with $100 million." Nor are they asked about racial or sexual harassment in their schools, at work, or even on the street.[48] Moreover, children are never asked if their parents or some other adult sexually or physically abused them. This is especially important to know, since abuse and neglect have been found by many researchers to be an important link to delinquency.[49]

Although the subject will be discussed in more detail in chapter 10, some mention should be made of school violence. Despite media attention to the rare instances of school shootings, the school grounds continue to be the safest places for kids to be. A study published in the *Journal of the American Medical Association* found that during the school years 1992–1993 and 1993–1994, 63 students were murdered in school. During the *calendar* years 1992 and 1993, a total of 7,294 youngsters between 5 and 19 were murdered *away from school*.[50] The most recent data show that the rate of crime (per 1000 students) on school grounds went from 144 in 1992 to 47 in 2008; the rate of crime away from school also dropped, from 138 to 38. Moreover, the number of kids murdered on school grounds went from 34 to 15 during the same period.[51]

Delinquent Careers

The past several decades have witnessed considerable interest in delinquent "careers" and an increasing concern over the "chronic" delinquent. One of the most famous studies was authored by Marvin Wolfgang and his colleagues at the University of Pennsylvania.[52] Their study and a subsequent update traced the delinquent behavior of a group of adolescents over time.[53] Other researchers have completed similar longitudinal studies to explore the extensiveness of involvement in delinquent behavior. Most studies have measured delinquency by using contact with police or courts.[54]

The method of using a *cohort* (which can be all those born in a particular year, all who graduated in the same year, all those first arrested in the same year, etc.) has been one, among several, varieties of longitudinal studies. This type of analysis is especially helpful in examining the extent, prevalence, and incidence of delinquency, since these rates may vary among specific individuals. This is important from both a practical and theoretical perspective. For instance, it is important to be able to distinguish between youths who come into contact with the juvenile court only once and those who have repeated contacts with the court. We also need to distinguish between those who cease their delinquent activities prior to their 18th birthday and those who persist into their adult years. A longitudinal approach also tells us at what age a "career" actually begins. In other words, we learn about the "onset, duration and termination" of delinquent careers.[55]

The data for these studies have come from a variety of sources. The study by Wolfgang and his associates used arrest records of youths in two different birth cohorts of Philadelphia; Lyle Shannon used police arrest records for three different birth cohorts in Racine, Wisconsin.[56] The Cambridge Study in Delinquency used self-report data, arrest and convictions, plus interview data.[57] Others have used self-report data, juvenile court data, and records of commitments to institutions.[58]

One of the most often quoted of these kinds of studies included in-depth surveys in three cities: Pittsburgh, Rochester, and Denver.[59] These longitudinal studies have examined a number of questions, including: (1) What factors are most strongly related to the onset, duration, and termination of delinquent careers? (2) What factors best predict who persists in their delinquent careers into their adult years? (3) Are there "early warning signs" for the onset of a delinquent career? (4) Do delinquents "specialize" in certain offense types? (5) Do delinquents "progress" from minor to more serious offenses during their careers?

Longitudinal research has revealed several factors that predict the length of one's "career." The age at which an individual first has contact with the juvenile justice system has been shown to be one of the most powerful predictors of the extent of his or her delinquent career. In general, research has found that the earlier one's contact, the greater the extent of one's career. Strongly related to this factor is exhibiting antisocial behavior at an early age (what researchers call "early onset"). Several studies have documented that such behavior in school, at home, and in the youth's own neighborhood are strong predictors of extensive delinquent behavior. More specifically, aggressiveness and theft at a very early age are particularly strong predictors. The importance of "early onset" should be underscored (see figure 2-2). The research is clear that the later one begins getting into trouble, the less likely he or she will continue such behavior into their adult years.[60]

Gender, race, and social class are also related to delinquent careers. Both of the Philadelphia cohort studies, in addition to several others, suggest that African-American youths not only have more extensive careers but also begin their careers at a younger age.[61] While social class (or socioeconomic status) is not apparently correlated with self-reported delinquency, it is related to *official* delinquency (partly because class is related to the seriousness of offenses committed and because class is related to police response). This fact has been noted by several researchers.[62]

Gender differences appear to be the most pronounced among all the variables examined.[63] Males are more actively involved in delinquent behavior (in terms of number and seriousness of offenses that bring them to official attention); their "careers" also go on longer than those of females. In the 1958 Philadelphia cohort study, about 33% of the males had at least one police contact compared to 14% of the females. Male delinquency, as measured by arrest, was also more serious. The male offense rate overall was four times greater than that for females, but the ratio was almost 9:1 for index offenses and 14:1 for violent index offenses. Girls were also one-and-a-half times more likely to be "one-time delinquents."[64] Research done in the 1960s and 1970s arrived at similar results.[65] Interestingly, the overwhelmingly most common aggressive offense for girls was hitting other students.

The most recent data on arrests show the same trends in gender. Of the total number of juveniles arrested in 2009, 70% were males. The ratio for violent offenses was 4.5 male (42,418) for each female (9,322) arrest. The ratio for property crime was 1.6:1 (160,299 male arrests versus 98,170 female). The most frequent offense for both males and females was larceny theft (13% of male and 25% of all female arrests) followed by other assaults (11% of male and 13% of all female arrests). For males, both categories declined from 2000 to 2009. Lar-

Figure 2-2   Early-Onset Offenders Will Place a Burden on Justice Resources

Snyder (2001) studied the juvenile court records of more than 150,000 urban juveniles who aged out of the juvenile justice system (i.e., turned age 18) between 1980 and 1995. The study found that the earlier a youth enters the juvenile justice system, the more likely he or she is to acquire an extensive juvenile court record. The younger the juvenile is at first referral to court, the more likely he or she is to have at least four separate referrals to juvenile court intake, at least one referral for a serious offense, and at least one referral for a violent offense by the time he or she reaches age 18. Juvenile court career patterns depend on whether offenders begin their careers before or after age 13.

Number of youth out of a typical 1,000:

	First referral	
Career Type	**Before Age 13**	**Age 13 or Older**
Single referral	411	629
Serious	473	312
Chronic	317	116
Violent	130	72
Chronic and violent	104	31

The likelihood of becoming a violent offender declines with the age of first referral to juvenile court.

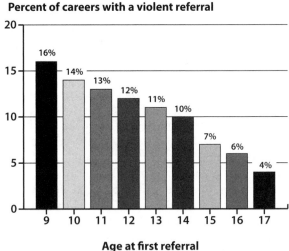

Percent of careers with a violent referral

Age at first referral

• Of those referred to juvenile court for the first time at age 9, 16% had at least one referral for a violent offense before they turned 18. Child offenders under the age of 13 had a greater proportion of serious, violent, and chronic careers than older-onset youth

Source: Snyder, H. (2001). "Epidemiology of Official Offending." In R. Loeber and D. Farrington (eds.), *Child Delinquents: Development, Intervention, and Service Needs.* Thousand Oaks, CA: Sage. See also Puzzanchera, C., B. Adams, and M. Sickmund (2010, March). *Juvenile Court Statistics 2006–2007,* pp. 9–11. Retrieved from http://www.ojjdp.gov/ojstatbb/njcda/pdf/jcs2007.pdf

ceny theft declined 27% from 146,160 arrests in 2000 to 106,852 in 2009; other assaults declined by 10% from 98,731 to 88,631. For females, larceny theft increased 5% from 85,599 arrests in 2000 to 90,011 in 2009; other assaults increased 6% from 43,968 to 46,494.[66]

Researchers have noted that status offenders rarely returned to court; and when they do return, it is almost always for another status offense. This is particularly true for female offenders.[67]

The important point is that the vast majority of "problem behaviors" are intermittent or transitory. The OJJDP report on the surveys in Denver, Rochester, and Pittsburgh notes that most juveniles "who exhibit problem behaviors do so only during a single year," and this pattern holds true for all problem behaviors. The next most common pattern lasts for only two years. The report did find, however, a large proportion (20–30%) could be classified as "serious delinquents." However, these surveys also found that "more than half of the male serious delinquents in Denver and Pittsburgh and more than half of the female serious delinquents in Denver display no other problems; in Rochester, the figure is roughly 40% for both genders." The authors of this study conclude that

> a large proportion of persistent serious delinquents are not involved in persistent drug use, nor do they have persistent school or mental health problems. Although a significant number of offenders have other problems and are in need of help, persistent offenders as a group cannot be characterized as having other problems.

In short, as already noted, even those involved in "serious delinquency" generally engage in the behavior for a limited amount of time.[68]

Summary

This chapter focused on the extent of delinquency in the United States. While it is impossible to determine the true extent of delinquency, many sources provide estimates, including the FBI's annual UCR data, self-report studies, victimization surveys, and statistics from juvenile courts. Each source of data can be criticized on several grounds. The FBI report in particular has great potential for abuse, especially at the local level.

The two major categories in the UCR that include data on delinquency are "crimes known to the police" and "persons arrested." Victimization surveys were designed to estimate crimes that are not reported to local police departments. Although these self-report studies focus primarily on minor behavior, they do reveal that a great deal of criminal behavior never gets reported, much less results in an arrest.

Total arrests of juveniles declined 20% in the past decade. The bulk of offenses juveniles are charged with have consistently been mostly minor offenses. Contrary to popular opinion and media accounts, there has been no "wave of violence" among girls, and the highest arrest rates continue to be for males. Black juveniles are far more likely than whites to be subjected to arrests for drugs.

The several forms of juvenile victimization categorized as maltreatment become important predictors of future delinquency. Juveniles are often victimized within their own families. Rates of abuse have been increasing in recent years.

Studies that focus on delinquent careers have found several predictors. Aggressive behavior in school, at home, or in the neighborhood is one indicator, as is theft at an early age. Gender, race, and social class also affect delinquent careers.

NOTES

[1] Similarly, the concept of "high crimes and misdemeanors" went through a very heated debate among politicians while considering impeachment against Bill Clinton. The fact that the interpretations often vary according to political party alignment demonstrates not only the inherent vagueness of the concept of "crime" but the political nature as well. Incidentally, "high crimes and misdemeanors" are not covered in state criminal codes and hence are not part of the purview of the criminal justice system.

[2] Miller, W. B. (2001, April 24). *The Growth of Youth Gang Problems in the United States: 1970–98.* Washington, DC: U.S. Department of Justice, Office of Justice Programs, Office of Juvenile Justice and Delinquency Prevention.

[3] The scandal involved police officers from a special gang unit (CRASH) in the Rampart Division, which covered an area that includes, among other towns, Hollywood. The corruption was first identified in 1999, and the probe soon expanded to other divisions. In March 2005 the city of Los Angeles agreed to pay $70 million to settle lawsuits that alleged misconduct or brutality by corrupt police officers. The corruption scandal involved the investigation of 82 incidents involving 50 officers and the reversal of more than 100 criminal convictions because of police misconduct. The Rampart Scandal was the principal cause for a decade-long federal consent decree that ended in July 2009. The Blue Ribbon Rampart Review Panel issued its findings on the extent of the corruption in July 2006, seven years after the scandal was discovered (http://www.lacp.org/2006-Articles-Main/RampartReconsidered.html).

[4] For a more complete critique of the measurement of "gang" activities see Shelden, R. G., S. Tracy, and W. B. Brown (2004). *Youth Gangs in American Society* (3rd ed.). Belmont, CA: Wadsworth.

[5] National Center for Juvenile Justice (2010). Easy Access to Juvenile Court Statistics (EZAJCS). Retrieved from http://www.ojjdp.gov/ojstatbb/ezajcs/; see also Puzzanchera, C., B. Adams, and M. Sickmund (2010, March). *Juvenile Court Statistics 2006–2007.* Pittsburgh, PA: National Center for Juvenile Justice. Retrieved from http://www.ncjjservehttp.org/ncjjwebsite/pdf/jcsreports/jcs2007.pdf

[6] There are four categories for race: white; black; American Indian or Alaskan Native; Asian or Pacific Islander.

[7] Sources that publish prison statistics have recently begun to include a separate category for the Hispanic population.

[8] FBI (2010). *Crime in the United States, 2009,* table 25. Retrieved from http://www.fbi.gov/ucr/cius2009/data/table_25.html

[9] FBI, *Crime in the United States, 2009,* table 28. Retrieved from http://www.fbi.gov/ucr/cius2009/data/table_28.html

[10] Legal codes distinguish between "assault" and "battery" as specific crimes. A simple example will help. If someone should come up and threaten you with bodily harm, that act is technically an "assault"; all that is necessary is the threat. For example, the statement, "The next time you cross me, I'll bash your face in!" is an assault. If a person carries through on the threat, it is "assault and battery." If there were no threat but simply a case of someone attacking you without a weapon, the charge would be "battery" (but for statistical purposes it would be counted as an assault). Also, if someone threatens you and points a gun or other weapon at you, a charge of "assault with a deadly weapon" can be made. If the threat is carried out it can result in a charge of "felonious assault."

[11] Sherman, L. and B. Glick (1984). "The Quality of Arrest Statistics." *Police Foundation Reports* 2: 1–8.

[12] Jackson, P. (1988). "Assessing the Validity of Official Data on Arson." *Criminology* 6: 181–95.

[13] This assertion is based on personal observations of the author, confidential conversations with members of police departments in two different cities and internal memos obtained. Documentation about using "gangs" to divert attention away from internal problems is found in McCorkle, R. C. and T. D. Miethe (2001). *Panic: The Social Construction of the Street Gang Problem.* Upper Saddle River, NJ: Prentice-Hall.

[14] Brownstein, H. H. (1996). *The Rise and Fall of a Violent Crime Wave: Crack Cocaine and the Social Construction of a Crime Problem.* Guilderland, NY: Harrow and Heston, p. 22.

[15] Butterfield, F. (1998, August 3). "Possible Manipulation of Crime Data Worries Top Police." *New York Times.*

[16] See, for example, Rashbaum, W. K. (2010, February 7). "Retired Officers Raise Questions on Crime Data." (http://www.nytimes.com/2010/02/07/nyregion/07crime.html?ref=nyregion); Baker, A. (2010, February 8). "Former Commander Recalls Pressure to Alter Reports." (http://www.nytimes.com/2010/02/08/nyregion/08captain.html).

[17] Allison, J. and L. Wrightsman (1993). *Rape: The Misunderstood Crime.* Newbury Park, CA: Sage; Madigan, L. and N. Gamble (1989). *The Second Rape: Society's Continual Betrayal of the Victim.* New York: Lexington Books.

[18] Reiman, J., and P. Leighton (2010). *The Rich Get Richer and the Poor Get Prison* (9th ed.). Boston: Allyn & Bacon.

[19] For a further discussion of this issue see Shelden, R. G. (2008). *Controlling the Dangerous Classes: A History of Criminal Justice in America* (2nd ed.). Boston: Allyn & Bacon.

[20] Shelden et al., *Youth Gangs in American Society.*

[21] FBI, *Crime in the United States, 2009,* tables 32 and 36.

[22] Puzzanchera, et al. *Juvenile Court Statistics 2006–2007,* p. 72.

[23] DeKeseredy, W. S. and M. D. Schwartz (1996). *Contemporary Criminology.* Belmont, CA: Wadsworth, p. 135.

[24] Robison, S. (1936). *Can Delinquency Be Measured?* New York: Columbia University Press.

[25] The studies referred to here are: Short, J. F., Jr. and F. I. Nye (1958). "Extent of Unrecorded Juvenile Delinquency: Tentative Conclusions." *Journal of Criminal Law, Criminology and Police Science* 49: 296–302; Murphy, F. J., M. M. Shirley, and H. L. Witmer (1946). "The Incidence of Hidden Delinquency." *American Journal of Orthopsychiatry* 16: 686–96; Porterfield, A. (1946). *Youth in Trouble.* Fort Worth, TX: Leo Potishman Foundation.

[26] Gold, M. (1970). *Delinquent Behavior in an American City.* Pacific Grove, CA: Brooks/Cole.

[27] Farrington, D., R. Loeber, M. Stouthamer-Loeber, W. Van Kammen, and L. Schmidt (1996). "Self-Reported Delinquency and a Combined Delinquency Seriousness Scale Based on Boys, Mothers, and Teachers: Concurrent and Predictive Validity for African-Americans and Caucasians." *Criminology* 34: 501–25.

[28] Federal legislation addressing child abuse and neglect was passed in 1974. *The Child Abuse Prevention and Treatment Act* (CAPTA) authorized the National Center on Child Abuse and Neglect (NCCAN) to collect data annually on cases reported to child protective services. The act has been amended several times, most recently in June 2003 by the *Keeping Children and Families Safe Act.* NCCAN was also authorized by CAPTA to conduct a periodic national incidence study, which is designed to estimate the actual number of abused and neglected children. It includes data from community professionals who encounter maltreated children as well as official reports from child protective service agencies. NIS-1 was conducted in 1979/1980 (published in 1981). NIS-2 and NIS-3 (authorized by amendments) were conducted in 1986/1987 (published in 1988) and 1993/1994 (published in 1995). NCCAN was replaced by the National Child Abuse and Neglect Data System (NCANDS). Its first report on child maltreatment was based on data for 1990. The data are collected annually and published two years later. NIS04 (mandated by the *Keeping Children and Families Safe Act of 2003*) collected data from 2004/2005. Another source is the Child Welfare Information Gateway (http://www.childwelfare.gov/index.cfm). The data in this section are from these sources.

[29] Child Welfare Information Gateway (2008). "What Is Child Abuse and Neglect?" Retrieved from http://www.childwelfare.gov/pubs/factsheets/whatiscan.cfm

[30] Ibid.

[31] U.S. Department of Health and Human Services, Children's Bureau (2010). "Child Maltreatment 2008." Retrieved from http://www.acf.hhs.gov/programs/cb/pubs/cm08/cm08.pdf

[32] Ibid.

[33] See Zielinski, D. S. (2005). "Long-term Socioeconomic Impact of Child Abuse and Neglect: Implications for Policy." Retrieved from http://familyimpactseminars.org/s_nmfis02c03.pdf; Berger, L. M. and J. Brooks-Gunn (2005). Socioeconomic Status, Parenting Knowledge and Behaviors, and Perceived Maltreatment of Young Low-Birth-Weight Children. Retrieved from http://www.jeffreylonghofer.com/page121/page108/assets/quantiative_ssr_child%20maltreatment.pdf

[34] I have personally seen firsthand hundreds of incarcerated youth (in detention centers and training schools) who are very small for their age, often shorter than normal, and who have numerous serious physical ailments, including dental problems (many never saw a dentist until they were detained) and eating disorders (for many, incarceration is their first experience with three meals a day). No wonder they are angry, confused, depressed, anxious, and so often express these problems outwardly either against themselves (e.g., suicide attempts) or others (e.g., fighting, theft). A visit to a local detention center or training school quickly brings the problem into focus.

[35] Straus, M. (1994). *Beating the Devil Out of Them: Corporal Punishment in American Families.* New York: Lexington Books.

[36] Ryan, J. P., D. Herzb, P. M. Hernandeza, and J. M. Marshall (2007). "Maltreatment and Delinquency: Investigating Child Welfare Bias in Juvenile Justice Processing." *Children and Youth Services Review 29*: 1035–50.

[37] "Child Trends Databank. Teen Homicide, Suicide and Firearms Deaths, 2006." Retrieved from http://www.childtrendsdatabank.org/?q=node/174

[38] FBI, *Crime in the United States, 2009.* Expanded Homicide Data table 2. Retrieved from http://www.fbi.gov/about-us/cjis/ucr/crime-in-the-u.s/2009

[39] Ibid.

[40] Snyder, H. N. and M. Sickmund (2006). *Juvenile Offenders and Victims: 2006 National Report.* Washington, DC: Office of Juvenile Justice and Delinquency Prevention, p. 22. Retrieved from http://ojjdp.ncjrs.gov/ojstatbb/nr2006/downloads/NR2006.pdf; http://www.childstats.gov/pdf/ac2009/ac_09.pdf

[41] "The Homicide Report." *Los Angeles Times* (site is updated frequently). Retrieved from http://projects.latimes.com/homicide-report/map/

[42] Snyder and Sickmund, *Juvenile Offenders and Victims.*

[43] Huizinga, D., R. Loeber, T. P. Thornberry, and L. Cothern (2000). "Co-occurrence of Delinquency and Other Problem Behaviors." Washington, DC: Office of Juvenile Justice and Delinquency Prevention. http://www.ncjrs.org/html/ojjdp/jjbul2000_11_3/contents.html

[44] Nofziger, S. (2003). *Correlates and Consequences of Juvenile Exposure to Violence: A Replication and Extension of Major Findings from the National Survey of Adolescents.* Washington, DC: U.S. Department of Justice; Anderson, N. and O. Rodriguez (1984). "Conceptual Issues in the Study of Hispanic Delinquency." *Research Bulletin 7* (Hispanic Center, Fordham University); Fagan, J., E. S. Piper, and Y. Cheng (1987). "Contributions of Victimization to Delinquency in Inner Cities." *Journal of Criminal Law and Criminology 78.*

[45] Shelden et al., *Youth Gangs in American Society.*

[46] Singer, S. (1987). "Victims in a Birth Cohort." In M. E. Wolfgang, T. P. Thornberry, and R. M. Figlio (Eds.), *From Boy to Man, from Delinquency to Crime.* Chicago: University of Chicago Press, pp. 163–79.

[47] Associated Press (2009, March 10). "1 in 50 U.S. Children Experiences Homelessness." Retrieved from http://www.msnbc.msn.com/id/29602056/. See also Prather, S. (2010). "A Comparative Analysis of Incarcerated Homeless." MA Thesis, Department of Criminal Justice, UNLV, 2010.

[48] DeKeseredy and Schwartz, *Contemporary Criminology*, pp. 132–33.

[49] The literature on this subject is vast. Examples include the following: Widom, C. S. (1989). "Child Abuse, Neglect, and Violent Criminal Behavior." *Criminology 27*: 251–71; Smith, C. and T. Thornberry (1995). "The Relationship between Childhood Maltreatment and Adolescent Involvement in Delinquency." *Criminology 33*: 451–77; Zingraff, M. (1993). "Child Maltreatment and Youthful Problem Behavior." *Criminology 31*: 173–202.

50 Brener, N. D., T. R. Simon, E. G. Krug, and R. Lowry (1999). "Recent Trends in Violence-Related Behaviors among High School Students in the United States." *Journal of the American Medical Association* 282: 440–46.

51 Robers, S., J. Zhang, and J. Truman (2010, November). *Indicators of School Crime and Safety: 2010.* National Center for Education Statistics, p. 72. Retrieved from http://nces.ed.gov/pubs2011/2011002.pdf

52 M. E. Wolfgang, R. M. Figlio, and T. Sellin (1972). *Delinquency in the Birth Cohort.* Chicago: University of Chicago Press.

53 Tracy, P. E., M. E. Wolfgang, and R. M. Figlio (1985). *Delinquency in Two Birth Cohorts.* Washington, DC: U. S. Department of Justice.

54 Farrington, D. (1983). "Offending from 10 to 25 Years of Age." In K. Van Dusen and S. A. Mednick (Eds.), *Prospective Studies of Crime and Delinquency.* Boston: Kluwer-Nijhoff, pp. 17–37; Farrington, D. (1987). "Early Precursors of Frequent Offending." In James Q. Wilson and Glenn C. Loury (Eds.), *From Children to Citizens, Vol. 3: Families, Schools, and Delinquency Prevention.* New York: Springer-Verlag, pp. 27–50; Carrington, P. J. (2009). "Co-offending and Offending and the Development of the Delinquent Career." *Criminology* 47: 1295–1329.

55 Farrington, D., D. L. Ohlin, and J. Q. Wilson (1986). *Understanding and Controlling Crime: Toward a New Research Strategy.* New York: Springer-Verlag, pp. 40–44.

56 Shannon, L. W. (1982). *Assessing the Relationship of Adult Criminal Careers to Juvenile Careers.* Washington, DC: U.S. Department of Justice.

57 West, D. (1982). *Delinquency: Its Roots, Careers and Prospects.* Cambridge: Harvard University Press; West, D. and D. P. Farrington (1977). *The Delinquent Way of Life.* London: Heinemann; West, D. and D. P. Farrington (1973). *Who Becomes Delinquent.* London: Heinemann.

58 This research is too vast to cite here, but a good representation would be: Loeber, R. (1987). "The Stability of Antisocial and Delinquent Child Behavior: A Review." *Child Development* 53: 1431–46; Loeber, R. and T. Dishion (1983). "Early Predictors of Male Delinquency: A Review." *Psychological Bulletin* 94: 68–99.

59 Huizinga et al. "Co-occurrence of Delinquency and Other Problem Behaviors."

60 Although somewhat dated, a very good literature review is provided by Dryfoos, J. G. (1990). *Adolescents at Risk: Prevalence and Prevention.* New York: Oxford University Press.

61 Huizinga et al. "Co-occurrence of Delinquency and Other Problem Behaviors."

62 For a discussion of class as a key variable, see Reiman and Leighton, *The Rich Get Richer and the Poor Get Prison.*

63 For a comprehensive review of girls and delinquency see Chesney-Lind, M. and R. G. Shelden (2004). *Girls, Delinquency and Juvenile Justice.* Belmont, CA: Wadsworth; one of the latest surveys is: Girls Study Group (2009). *Resilient Girls—Factors That Protect Against Delinquency.* Washington, DC: Office of Juvenile Justice and Delinquent Prevention. Retrieved from http://www.ncjrs.gov/pdffiles1/ojjdp/220124.pdf

64 Tracy et al., *Delinquency in Two Birth Cohorts*, p. 6.

65 Mulligan, D. G., J. W. Douglas, W. A. Hammond, and J. Tizard (1963). "Delinquency and Symptoms of Maladjustment." *Proceedings of the Royal Society of Medicine* 56: 1083–86; Douglas, J. W., J. M. Ross, W. A. Hammond, and D. G. Mulligan (1966). "Delinquency and Social Class." *British Journal of Criminology* 6: 294–302; Ouston, J. (1984). "Delinquency, Family Background, and Educational Attainment." *British Journal of Criminology* 24: 2–26.

66 FBI, *Crime in the United States, 2009*, table 33.

67 Datesman, S. and M. Aickin (1984). "Offense Specialization and Escalation among Status Offenders." *Journal of Criminal Law and Criminology* 75: 1246–75. Almost identical findings were reported in a longitudinal study of juvenile court referrals in Las Vegas. See Shelden, R. G., J. Horvath, and S. Tracy (1989). "Do Status Offenders Get Worse? Some Clarifications on the Question of Escalation." *Crime and Delinquency* 35: 202–16; see also Kempf-Leonard, K., P. E. Tracy, and J. C. Howell (2001). "Serious, Violent, and Chronic Juvenile Offenders: The Relationship of Delinquency Career Types to Adult Criminality." *Justice Quarterly* 18: 449–78; Tracy, P. E., K. Kempf-Leonard, and S. Abramoske-James (2009). "Gender Differences in Delinquency and Juvenile Justice Processing." *Crime & Delinquency* 55: 171–215.

68 Huizinga et al., "Co-occurrence of Delinquency and Other Problem Behaviors."

THE NATURE OF DELINQUENCY

As we saw in chapter 1, the term "delinquency" evolved from early nineteenth-century state codes based, at least in part, on the *parens patriae* doctrine. To review, the term "juvenile delinquent" referred to both the failure to do something that is required and someone who is not yet fixed in his or her ways and is thus subject to change and redemption.

The Illinois Juvenile Court Act of 1899 created the first juvenile court and delineated three major areas for its jurisdiction: (1) juvenile acts that violated laws applicable to adults (e.g., burglary, larceny, assault, etc.); (2) juvenile violations of local ordinances; and (3) behaviors that would eventually be called "status offenses" (e.g., running away from home, truancy, underage drinking, curfew violations, etc.). In time, juvenile and family courts would oversee three broad areas: (1) *delinquency*, which refers to violations of laws applicable to any age group; (2) *status offenses*, which are offenses because of the age of the offender; and (3) *abuse and neglect* (or "dependency and neglect"), which are cases in which the juvenile is the victim. Violations of various court orders (e.g., contempt of court, conditions of probation or parole) also fall under the umbrella of "delinquency." This is important because it can override certain restrictions. For example, status offenders cannot be placed in detention, subjected to incarceration in correctional institutions, or placed in adult facilities. However, if a youth violates a court order, even if the original behavior was a status offense, he or she could be subject to detention. We will revisit this issue later in this chapter.

While juvenile codes have changed a great deal since the founding of the modern juvenile court, there are still numerous vaguely worded statutes governing the behavior of juveniles. Words such as "idle," "immoral," or "dissolute" appear in statutes that prohibit loitering or sleeping in alleys and begging—in other words, being poor.

An important component of modern juvenile codes is the term "juvenile" itself. State law determines the oldest age at which a juvenile court has original jurisdiction over an individual for violating the law. In 37 states and the District of Columbia, 18 is the upper age limit. Ten states use 17, while New York and North Carolina use 16.[1] Connecticut previously used 16 but changed its definition to 18 in 2009.[2] This means that a person who reaches the age of 19, 18, or 17 (depending on the state) is legally an adult. A complete summary of the multitude of behaviors that can bring juveniles to the attention of the juvenile court is beyond the scope of this book. The remainder of this chapter will be devoted to a broad overview of some of the major types of delinquency behavior and the patterns that such behavior takes. Some of the most distinctive features of delinquency are the incredible range of behaviors covered, the degree to which such behaviors reflect various social and personal problems, the actual extent of such behavior, and the significance of such behaviors.[3]

Varieties of Delinquent Behavior

We can segment "delinquency" and "delinquents" into eight categories. Within the categories, there is a continuum of behavior.

1. From Mentally Disturbed to Well Adjusted

At one extreme are acts committed by young people that are behavioral responses to a perceived threatening environment by persons ill equipped to cope with that environment (ranging from children who demonstrate minor forms of mental disturbances to fully developed psychopathology).[4] At the other extreme are youths who appear to be well adjusted to their environment and who may be acting in accordance with the prevailing system of norms (whether a middle-class youth who gets "high" at a party or a gang member who commits a crime as part of an initiation ritual). In fact, in the latter instances, failure to act in any other manner would be considered "deviant" by his or her peers and would no doubt result in rejection by the group. The vast majority of those juveniles who violate some law or status offense are rather well-adjusted young people who will invariably "grow out of it" and become fully functioning adults. As we saw in chapter 2, self-report studies show that over 90% of all juveniles commit some crime before they reach adulthood.

2. From Striving for Acceptance to "Just Business"

Some juveniles "act out" to gain personal recognition and/or acceptance. Growing numbers of young people are finding that the only way they can get any attention from the significant adults in their lives is to do something outrageous—which may, by the way, include wearing "outlandish" clothes, doing something "wild" with one's hair color or style, or getting multiple body piercings or tattoos. Quite often young people are just testing the boundaries of what they can do. Or, more likely, they got carried away at a party or group gathering and committed a crime (perhaps on a dare). Or they merely made a mistake, like we all do from time to time. These examples constitute the "typical" or "normal" form of "delinquency" engaged in by millions of adolescents the world over.

At the other extreme, there is a small minority who engage in very "business-like" criminal behavior, such as repeatedly breaking into cars, homes, businesses, or schools in order to steal things; dealing in drugs; systematically shoplifting at malls. As discussed in chapter 2, a very small minority of juveniles (known as "chronic offenders") is responsible for a disproportionate amount of the crime committed by this age group.

3. From Means of Survival to Hedonistic Behavior

Some youths engage in a variety of delinquent activities—especially theft and drug dealing—as a means of surviving in a very deprived environment. The proceeds help support their families, who are often living on the edge and barely surviving.[5] The typical delinquent, however, engages in behavior that more often than not reflects consumerist behavior in a capitalist society, where wants are artificially created and obtaining material things (e.g., clothes, cosmetics, cars, etc.) is linked to status. Young people often engage in minor forms of theft where the objects stolen are not necessary for survival but are "needed" to "be somebody," to "fit in," or to attract the opposite sex. As we will see later in the chapter, most theft by juveniles is of this kind. Part of this kind of criminal activity is merely a natural by-product of the relentless pursuit of the American Dream, a cultural ethos that places intense pressures on most people to "formulate wants and desires that are difficult, if not impossible, to satisfy within the confines of legally permissible behavior."[6]

4. From Individual to Highly Organized Behavior

One truism in the field of criminology is that the vast majority of delinquent activities take place among groups of two or more youths. The lone delinquent offender is the exception, rather than the rule.[7] He or she lies at one extreme of the continuum and acts alone for a variety of reasons. Most delinquent behavior is highly disorganized and occurs on the spur of the moment, with little or no planning involved. More often than not, a group of youths are "out and about" with little sense of direction, perhaps merely "hanging out" where teenagers normally gather—on a street corner, in a park or playground, at the movies, at a mall, at video arcades, or just "cruising" around, with "no particular place to go."[8] Numerous studies have confirmed that little planning takes place during most delinquent activities.[9] At the other end of the continuum are the few who engage in highly organized behavior, sometimes for profit and sometimes just for "kicks"—because of the "thrill" or the "charge" they might get from the behavior.[10]

5. From Restricted Acts to Generic Deviation

Some juveniles tend to "specialize" in one form of delinquency or another. Some may engage in status offenses only or shoplift, while others steal cars, deal drugs, commit burglaries, or participate in other forms of crime. More often than not, those who engage in persistent delinquent activities engage in more than one type. Some will commit a variety of property crimes involving little or no violence; others may engage in violent types of crimes only, such as assaults (including rapes) or robberies. An examination of the "rap sheets" of juvenile offenders usually finds a variety of mostly property crimes, some status offenses, and some referrals to court for abuse and neglect.

6. From Prankish Behavior to Intended Harm

The vast majority of delinquent activities do not involve a victim who suffers a direct harm or, if harm does occur, it is not serious and/or intentional. Most acts are of the "public order" variety (disturbing the peace, loitering, curfew violations, truancy, running away from home, drug and/or alcohol use, etc.). *Joyriding* (where youths "borrow" someone's car, usually a neighbor's, and take it for a short ride) is an example of an offense where usually no one is physically harmed or no property damage occurs (unless of course there is an accident). "Pranks" have been a normal part of adolescence for hundreds of years and are usually viewed as an acceptable method of "letting off steam." The "zero tolerance" (see chapter 14) mentality so much in evidence today seems to have closed off many outlets for youthful expression.

At the other extreme are activities where harm, often very serious harm, is the express purpose. Examples include gang retaliations, such as "drive-by shootings." People may be killed or injured—sometimes bystanders rather than the intended victim.[11]

7. From the Isolated Act to Chronic Behavior

Delinquents range from those youth who are involved in one single act of deviance (or at least one act where they are caught) to those who engage in repeated, often called "habitual" or "chronic" criminal behavior. The typical "delinquent" engages in just a few acts in his or her lifetime. Most longitudinal studies have found that the majority of youths who are arrested and referred to the juvenile court usually have no subsequent official contact or have perhaps one or two additional arrests or referrals to court. The author's study of a cohort of youth referred to the juvenile court of Las Vegas found that out of more than 800 youths, about half had no subsequent referrals; the vast majority of the remainder had fewer than two or three more contacts. The "chronic" offender is in the minority, constituting no more than 3–5% of all offenders.[12] Numerous studies have confirmed another fact about the "careers" of juvenile offenders: most never become adult offenders (see chapter 2).

8. From Status Offenses to Criminal Law Violations

The two main categories of behavior that may result in a referral to juvenile court are committing an offense that is unlawful for all age groups ("delinquent offenses") and committing an offense that applies to juveniles only ("status offenses"). While most chronic youths have engaged in both types of behaviors at one time or another, most of those referred to juvenile court specialize in one form or the other. In the Las Vegas study, there were two major categories of chronic offenders. The "chronic serious" offender committed mostly felonies (robbery, burglary, grand larceny, assault, etc.); this type of offender was in the minority. Most chronic offenders were in the "chronic nuisance" category. Most of their "crimes" were so minor that they were more of a nuisance than a serious threat to lives and property. Typically, these youths will be involved in either status offenses or minor misdemeanors (shoplifting, disturbing the peace, vandalism, minor assaults, etc.). Most of these minor offenders, by the way, never "escalated" or "graduated" into more serious forms of behavior.[13] Several other longitudinal studies have confirmed these findings (see chapter 2).

These eight dimensions are but a few of the factors that must be considered when explaining juvenile delinquency. The interrelationships and overlapping of the categories make this subject even more complex. These variations have been presented merely to illustrate that "delinquents," like humans in general, are not one-dimensional. There is no "typical delinquent." In fact, as we review some of the more common varieties of delinquent behavior in the remainder of this chapter, we will discover that no one single act is the same as another (e.g., no two cases of shoplifting are identical, no two assaults are identical). We need to keep this in mind throughout this book, because the surrounding context of an act must be known in order to more fully understand it. We cannot say, in other words, "an assault is an assault is an assault." Even the most emotionally charged crime—such as a drive-by shooting or a kidnapping—is the result of a complex set of factors. The author has heard numerous stories over the years about assaults—lumped together as "violent crime" and tabulated and categorized as if every one of them were alike. A young girl who has been habitually running away from home (often for a very good reason, such as sexual abuse) attempts to run one more time, but her mother gets in her way and the girl "bumps" into her on the way out the door. According to the law, the mother can file an "assault" charge against the daughter, which immediately transforms what is really a "status offense" into a "delinquent" offense, which carries a more serious punishment.

As noted above, juveniles engage in a wide variety of delinquent offenses. The remainder of this chapter consists of a general review of the main categories of these offenses: property crimes, violent crimes, public order offenses, and status offenses.

Property Crimes

Shoplifting

As we saw in chapter 2, the most common offense for which juveniles are arrested is larceny-theft. This category constitutes about 17% of all juveniles arrested (and more than 63% of all arrests for index crimes); it accounted for 13% of all male juvenile arrests (and about 21% of all index crimes committed by males)[14] and 25% of all female arrests (and 84% of all female index crimes).[15]

Since there are important gender differences in shoplifting, this subject will be explored in much more detail in chapter 5 when discussing female delinquency. Shoplifting falls in this category. In a capitalist society like the United States, being a consumer is most important. If there are not enough funds to match the desire to acquire the latest fashion or gadget, shoplifting might be viewed as a solution.

For teenagers, going shopping (including hanging out at the shopping mall) is a very common activity. It is normal and healthy for adolescents to want to be with their peers. By the time a child has reached puberty, the peer group has already begun to take over in terms of influencing behavior. In fact, teenagers in the United States spend more time each day talking with friends than any other activity, and high school students spend more time with their friends than with their parents.[16] Teens spend a considerable amount of time in shopping malls. One study found that this behavior stems in part from loneliness and the need to associate with friends.[17] A simple Google search finds numerous web sites devoted to the encouragement of teenage shopping, especially for girls.[18] Same-sex cliques are extremely popular among youth, and the bulk of delinquency occurs within these groups. Indeed, peer influences have long been recognized as a factor in delinquency causation.[19]

Ronald Huff noted:

> Because adolescents go to dances together, party together, shop together (and, in many cases, shop*lift* together), it should not be surprising that some of them join together in one type of social group known as a gang. Group experience, then, is a familiar and normative phenomenon in adolescent subculture, and gangs represent an extreme manifestation of that age-typical emphasis on being together and belonging to something.[20]

Most teenagers engage in some form of theft, as revealed by numerous self-report surveys. Contrast this type of behavior known as *occasional property criminal behavior* with the more fully developed "career criminal" who has a strong identification with crime, a self-conception as a criminal, and strong group support for criminal activities "in the form of extensive association with other criminals and with criminal norms and activities."[21] Few occasional property offenders make a career out of crime; in fact, the majority engages in property crimes on an irregular basis.

The most common forms of property crimes other than shoplifting include check forgery, use of fake identification (e.g., to use to purchase alcohol or cigarettes), vandalism (including graffiti), burglary, theft from automobiles and vending machines, and motor vehicle theft. Youths are consistently involved in all of these, with the exception of forgery, which is mostly an adult crime.

Vandalism

As noted in chapter 2 (table 2-1), there were about 56,000 arrests for vandalism, constituting about 5% of all arrests for juveniles in 2009. This has consistently been mostly a male offense. Vandalism is defined as follows:

> To willfully or maliciously destroy, injure, disfigure, or deface any public or private property, real or personal, without the consent of the owner or person having custody or control by cutting, tearing, breaking, marking, painting, drawing, covering with filth, or any other such means as may be specified by local law.[22]

Vandalism covers a wide range of malicious behavior directed at property, such as: slashing automobile tires, drawing obscene pictures on public restroom walls, smashing windows, destroying school records, tipping over gravestones, defacing library books, etc.[23]

Vandalism is associated with more affluent societies, as it rarely occurs in poor countries (mainly because there is not much property to be destroyed). The term itself was first used to describe the behaviors of a group called the Vandals, an East German tribe that attacked Rome in the fifth century. They engaged in what was described as the senseless destruction of objects that had aesthetic appeal or were completed with great effort.[24] The concept was also used to describe the destruction of Paris during the French Revolution (the word used was *Vandalisme*).

Vandalism of school property is perhaps the most common offense. Parks, public transportation facilities, libraries, churches, houses, automobiles, and traffic lights are also common targets. Benches, markers, flags, and putting greens at golf courses are often vandalized, as are vacant houses and movie theaters.[25]

Vandalism is often characterized as a "teenage problem." Most research has studied young populations.[26] A website called "Family First Aid" provides statistics about teen vandalism and suggestions for preventing the behavior.[27] Contrary to the frequent assumption that vandalism is a youthful activity, most of those arrested are adults. In fact, vandalism has become less of a problem in recent years among juveniles as the number arrested dropped by 21.8% between 2000 and 2009, while arrests for those 18 and older increased 8.2%.[28]

There are three categories of vandalism: wanton, predatory, and vindictive. *Wanton vandalism* is defined as "nonutilitarian" or just plain "ornery." It is usually sporadic and done on the spur of the moment, often on a dare. *Predatory vandalism* is economically oriented; it includes breaking into parking meters, public telephones, and vending machines to collect change. *Vindictive vandalism* is, as the name implies, a kind of "hate" crime directed at a specific individual or group, often of a different race, religious orientation, or social class.[29]

The majority of those who commit vandalism are not serious offenders and do not view themselves as criminals. More often than not they view their actions as mere pranks. Most of the time, such acts are a form of entertainment or rebellion and are viewed as exciting.[30]

Graffiti[31]

As every parent knows, adolescents strive to create their own unique world—separate and distinct from the adult world. Modes of dress and communication styles draw the boundaries between themselves and adults. Youth gangs often employ graffiti as a unique form of communication.

Graffiti is the primary form of communication used by gangs today, although historically a wide variety of groups have used graffiti. Not all graffiti is the product of gangs. As several studies have shown, many respectable artists began with graffiti. The goal of such artwork (for example, the murals in many New York City subways) is to establish an individual artist's reputation and to display one's own style of art. In contrast, the purpose of gang graffiti is usually (but not always) to expand the reputation of the gang, rather than that of an individual. Gangs use graffiti to identify their existence (to tell others who they are), to mark a specific area as their turf (for example, by writing on a wall, a building, or other structure), to challenge rival gangs, and to commemorate members who have died in battles. Graffiti can be used as a "newspaper of the street" or a community memo.

Gang graffiti may be viewed as a form of artistic expression because it follows established styles and makes use of sophisticated principles of graphic design. One of the most common styles is the use of large block lettering. This is especially common when writing the name or initials of the gang. The style of gang graffiti in Los Angeles, for instance, especially the form of lettering used, is quite similar to the styles used in the 1960s. Much of it, in fact, has been appropriated by commercial artists and the adolescent subculture in general.

Modern gang graffiti serves several different purposes. Seven distinctive qualities are discussed below.

1. Identifying the Neighborhood of the Gang.   Usually graffiti will identify a neighborhood or varrio (barrio is Spanish for neighborhood; varrio is slang for barrio), often by merely the letter V or B. One example was found in a suburb of Los Angeles, the city of La Puente. VP-13 was used to identify a local gang. The 13 refers to the 13th letter of the alphabet, or M, and within the gang subculture has normally referred to Sur, or Southern California. This method of gang reference is believed to have originated with prison gangs in California as a way to distinguish gangs in the southern part of the state from those in the northern part. (The number 14 stands for the 14th letter of the alphabet, or N, and refers to Norte, or Northern California.) A variation of this usage is to place the word barrio or varrio before, after, or in the middle of the gang name. For instance, a gang in south central Los Angeles located in the area of Grape Street is known as Watts Varrio Grape.

2. Making Pronouncements.   Gangs use graffiti to communicate with one another. One of the most common messages is to use the letter R or to simply write out the words Rifa, Rifan, or Rifamos, followed or preceded by the name of the gang. One of the most common pronouncements is to challenge or to show disrespect for a rival gang. Often gang members will travel into a rival's territory and cross out graffiti of the rival. (The police study this process to measure the extent of conflict between gangs or to predict a pending battle.) A variation of this is the targeting of a rival gang for retaliation. An example would be using the number 187, which stands for the California Penal Code number for murder and is often used by gangs in their graffiti to target a rival.

Sometimes a gang will put down one of their own members, as when they write the word Leva next to a member's name. This means that the member is being given the silent treatment because of associating with another gang, disrespecting the gang, or some other infraction.

3. Commemorating the Dead.   Death is an ever-present reality for gang members, and much of their graffiti is used to commemorate their fallen brothers. Examples include printing the letters RIP (rest in peace) on walls and buildings in a neighborhood along with the name of the deceased.

4. Using Numbers.   Much gang graffiti involves the use of various kinds of abbreviations, typically letters or numbers that stand for something related to the gang. The numbers may be written in English, Spanish, Roman numerals, or a combination. Numbers usually refer to a specific street where most of the gang members live. This becomes part of the actual gang name, such as 18th Street or XVIII Street. A variation is to replace numbers with words, especially common among African-American gangs. Thus, the numbers 1, 2, and 3 are replaced by Ace, Deuce (often written as Duce), and Trey (or Tray). In Los Angeles, for example, 73rd Street is written as 7 Trey St., and 101st Street is written as 10 Ace St. Specific examples are Eight Tray Gangster Crips (found on 83rd Street), Eleven Deuce Crips (located on 112th Street), and Ace Deuce Crips (found on 12th Street).

5. Subgroups, Cliques, and Sets.   Gangs are often subdivided into age-graded cliques or sets, and graffiti often reflects this. For instance, TDS would stand for the Tiny Dukes (a younger version of the Dukes gang), MLS would refer to the Midget Locos, and LL or LxL would stand for Little Locos. Also, Spanish names differentiate male from female gangs: Chicos = male and Chicas = female.

6. Location.   Gangs often identify with either a small area (for example, a housing project or a park) or a very large area within a city. Typically, they use names like West, Westside, South, Southside, North, and so on to refer to a wide area of a city, followed by the name of the gang itself. A common method is to use letters to stand for the location, or the side, of the area within which they are located. Thus the symbol n/s or n will stand for the northside, and s/s or s will stand for the southside. This notation will be followed by an abbreviation of the gang name. Some examples are as follows: w/s V13 = Venice 13, a gang on the westside of Los Angeles within the city of Venice near 13th Street; e/s BP (Eastside Baldwin Park) and n/s BP (Northside Baldwin Park) are two rival gangs within the same city. Often, as in the Baldwin Park example, landmarks are used to differentiate east and west and north and south. These can be streets, canals, rivers, freeways, railroad tracks, and, in Los Angeles, washes (dry river beds). For instance, the Harbor Freeway in Los Angeles separates east from west for African-American gangs. In Las Vegas, I-15 separates the West Coast Bloods from the East Coast Bloods.

7. Taggers.   The phenomenon of tagging has been growing rapidly in most urban areas in recent years. This form of graffiti is not usually associated with specific gangs, although some people refer to groups of youths who do this as gangs. Tagging is usually an announcement of the presence of a gang (typically by using a nickname). Some common examples (found in Las Vegas, Nevada) include the following names: ACME, BNEE, ASTRO, DAZE, POUR, TRASH, LEEN, REAM, and SMIRK. Diego Vigil notes that tagger graffiti has muddled the general idea of boundary markers between gang neighborhoods. Rival gangs now often carry a "roving notion of gang turf with them into any place where they might run into an enemy."[32]

Graffiti is a way of gaining attention and recognition from the public. A Chicano gang member in Los Angeles remarked: "I always wonder what people think of when they ride by and see the name 'Puppet' (his nickname) there. Do they think of me?" Another stated: "I know the guys from that barrio know who I am. They've seen my placas in their neighborhood."[33]

Joyriding

There are generally four motivations for motor-vehicle theft: (1) joyriding, (2) transportation, (3) commission of other crimes, and (4) commercial theft.[34] The *New World Law Dictionary* defines joyriding as: "The temporary appropriation of another's vehicle for use, typically without the intention of selling or destroying it."[35] The law distinguishes between two types of auto theft based on intent. In joyriding, the car is "borrowed." Often the formal charge is "operating a motor vehicle without the owner's permission."[36] The other type of auto theft involves an intent to permanently deprive the owner of his or her automobile. The car can be stolen as a means of transportation, used during the commission of a crime, or stripped and the parts sold on the black market. While most auto thieves have extensive records, those who engage in joyriding do not. This is typically a teenage crime, and the perpetrators are not "career criminals." It is a very spur-of-the-moment offense, usually done in groups where either the keys are in the car or the car belongs to a neighbor (often a parent or relative of one of the youths involved).[37]

Quite often joyriding offers validation of the perpetrator's "toughness," "skill," or "personal autonomy." It brings momentary excitement to the daily routine. The behavior is mostly expressive and spontaneous, often rationalized as a flippant "why walk when you can drive?"[38] In many cases, the thefts are committed by youths who are strangers to their victims. As mentioned above, there are some occasions where the victims are known. Examples include cases where children drive their parents' cars without their permission (perhaps stemming from family conflicts), vehicles are "liberated" by ex-spouses or ex-lovers (usually adults rather than juveniles), or youth groups or gangs steal from their rivals. Often, joyriders will "steal and trash the cars of people who have mistreated them," such as neighbors.[39]

Overall, arrests for motor vehicle theft constitute a small proportion of arrests among juveniles (less than 1% in 2009); it is primarily an adult activity (more than 3 times the number of arrests as for juveniles).[40] The automobile is extremely important in U.S. culture. Having one means freedom and independence, especially for juveniles not yet able to leave home, vote, and engage in a number of other activities. Obtaining a driver's license represents a very important rite of passage. Having a license and having access to a vehicle are important indicators of maturity. It is no accident that the peak age for many juvenile crimes is 16.

Violent Crimes

Violence, it has been said, is "as American as apple pie." We fear it yet are fascinated by it. We pay billions of dollars to view it on television and on the movie screen. It brings in billions of dollars in advertising revenue for the nightly news—hence the popular phrase, "If it bleeds, it leads." It seems that nothing stirs up so much debate, fear, and distortion than the alleged violence committed by youths. This has never been more evident than with the exaggerated concept of juvenile "superpredators."[41] Indeed, starting in the mid-1980s and running throughout the decade of the 1990s, pundits, politicians, and even some criminologists (who should have known better) continued to exaggerate the amount of violence committed by teenagers. In the introduction, we touched on the frenzy of predictions in 1996 about a rising tide of juvenile violence. In a book filled with hyperbole and gross misuse of statistics, William Bennett, John DiIulio, and John Walters presented dire warnings.[42]

> A new generation of street criminals is upon us—the youngest, biggest, and baddest generation any society has even known. . . . They live by the meanest code of the meanest streets, a code that reinforces rather than restrains their violent, hair-trigger mentality. In prison or out, the things that superpredators get by their criminal behavior—sex, drugs, money—are their own immediate rewards. *Nothing else matters to them.*

Bret Easton Ellis, in an article in *George* magazine, stated, "There's something far more insidious infesting America: kids are ruining our lives."[43] Ellis, however, appeared to have an extended definition of "kids"; he referred to the growing violent crime rate among those under the age of 25. Then Congressman William McCollum of Florida stated in 1997 that today's youth are "the most dangerous criminals on the face of the earth."[44]

In his book, *The Culture of Fear*, Barry Glassner gives more examples of the incendiary rhetoric, noting such headlines as "Alarming Rise in Kids Who Kill" (*Los Angeles Times*, August 1992), "Life Means Nothing" (*Newsweek*, July 1993), "Wild in the Streets" (*Newsweek*, August 1993), "A New Wave of Mayhem" (*Los Angeles Times*, September 1995), and "Superpredators Arrive" (*Newsweek*, January 1996). The headlines report rare incidents, but the media treat them as if they were everyday occurrences. Almost invariably, journalists (both television and print) note, erroneously, "it could happen anywhere to anyone." Glassner discusses a study of the media's treatment of children's issues; during one month in the early 1990s, only 4% of newspaper and television stories covered health and economic issues, while 40% of the news was about crime and violence. For the evening news on ABC, CBS, and NBC, the figure was 48%.[45]

The actual figures on homicide (the crime most often linked to youthful "superpredators") tell another story. While arrests for juveniles on homicide charges grew between 1987 and 1993, they declined substantially thereafter.[46] The number of juveniles arrested for murder declined by about 11% from 1999 to 2009.[47] Remember also that *numbers* of juveniles arrested can be very misleading. We need to consider the *rate* of juvenile homicide arrests. In 1993 the juvenile arrest rate for homicide was 14.4 per 100,000 juveniles ages 10 through 17; in 2008, the rate was 3.8—a 74% decrease.[48]

In 2009, 1,348 people under the age of 18 were murder victims; 51% of the murders involved firearms.[49] In 2008, 38% of juvenile murder victims were younger than 5; 50% of juveniles were killed with a firearm—17% of those younger than 13 and 80% of those older than 13.[50] Homicide was the third leading cause of death for juveniles ages 12–17 in 2007, and suicide was the fourth leading cause. Persons in this age group were about equally likely to be the victims of suicide as homicide. Sixty percent of all juvenile suicides were committed with a firearm.[51]

The Demographic Fallacy: More Kids Does Not Equal More Crime

Mike Males and Dan Macallair noted that arrest rates for violent crimes for youths between 13 and 17 went up by 56% in California between 1983 and 1992 but then dropped by about 14% between 1992 and 1998. Interestingly, the violent crime arrest rates between 1978 and 1998 *increased the most for those between the ages of 30 and 49*, rather than the 10–17 age group. The older group's arrest rate went up by 97%, compared to a decrease of 32% for the 10–17 age group.[52] Between 1993 and 2002 the overall arrest rate for juveniles *declined* by 30% (7,479 to 5,249), while the population (age 10–17) *increased* by almost the same amount (28%). The arrest rate for violent felonies declined by 43%.[53] Thus, despite an increase in the number of juveniles ages 10–17, the rate of juvenile crime declined.

Males and Macallair also dispelled the myth of the "growing menace" from future children by noting that the average age of those arrested for felonies in California in 1978 was 21.5, while the average age in 1998 was 27.7. Moreover, arrest rates had nothing to do with the proportion of young people in the population, a favorite theory among many criminologists who steadfastly support this demographic fallacy. In the words of John DiIulio: "More teenaged boys, more crime. Period."[54] During the 1980s the violent crime rate for juveniles went up, yet California's teenage population declined. Then in the 1990s the violent crime rate went down, while the teen population was going up.[55]

As shown in table 3-1, arrests for violent crimes declined by 8.6% among those under 18; the decline among those 18 and over was 4.2%. For property crimes, arrests for those under 18 went down by almost 20%, compared to a 12% increase by those 18 and over. Note too that their respective populations both declined during this period of time.

Table 3-1   Arrest Trends by Age (percent change, 2000–2009) and Change in Population

	Arrests	
	Under 18	**18 and Over**
Violent Crime*	–15.0	–5.1%
Property crime**	–20.3	+21.1
Total	–20.2	+2.7
Population change	–7.7	–9.2

*Murder, forcible rape, robbery, aggravated assault
**Burglary, larceny–theft, motor-vehicle theft, arson

Source: FBI, Crime in the United States, 2009, table 32. Retrieved from http://www2.fbi.gov/ucr/cius2009/data/table_32.html
Population changes retrieved from the U.S. Census: http://www.census.gov/

Gang Violence: A Special Case

A great deal of the violence committed by juveniles occurs within the context of youth gangs. The National Gang Center reported that 36.5% of gang members were younger than 18 in 2006. Other demographic statistics about gangs are that 93.4% of gang members are males; 49.5% are Hispanic; 35.2% are black, and 8.5% are white.[56] The number of cities and counties reporting gang problems declined from 1996 to 2001; there was a 25% increase in reported problems from 2002–2007.[57]

Membership in youth gangs can increase the probability of violence in two ways. First, being in a gang increases the probability of offending in general. The greater the number of offenses one commits over one's lifetime, the greater the possibility that more of the offenses will be violent.[58] Second, certain features of gangs may facilitate violence.

> Street socialization generally produces a street subculture of violence, and . . . areas with a high concentration of crime undergird a pattern of violence. The potential for street mayhem and violence in such places is a product of opportunity. A youth who spends more time with criminal offenders is more likely to participate in offending activities. In short, motivated offenders, suitable targets, and an absence of capable guardians converge in certain times and places to increase the possibility of a crime.[59]

A study by Joan Moore compared the rate of violence between two generations of gang members in East Los Angeles gangs: those growing up in the post-World War II era (1950s and 1960s) and those growing up mostly in the 1970s and 1980s. She reported that between 1970 and 1979 gang homicides accounted for 16% of all Hispanic-related homicides; gang homicides accounted for only 7% of the homicides among other ethnic groups.[60]

Moore cited the following reasons for gang fights: invasion of gang territory by a rival gang, rivalry over dating, fights related to sporting events, and personal matters in which the gang supports a member. She listed two factors contributing to the increase in the number of deaths among gang members during the 1970s: (1) more guns were available in the 1970s than in the 1950s; (2) the goal of intimidation was replaced with intention to harm. There was also a more impersonal aspect to inflicting harm with the emergence of the drive-by shooting. This is related to the demise of the fair fight, in which combatants fought but shook hands after the fight and then went their separate ways.

It may be tempting to explain the increase in gang violence by pointing to exaggerated masculine behavior, or machismo. This term, says Moore, refers just as much to control as it does to aggressiveness. "Locura is the 'craziness' or wildness that is stereotypically associated with Chicano gangs and their vatos locos (crazy guys)."[61] It is especially related to unrestrained conduct on the part of a member. But even the definitions of locura have changed over time, often becoming linked to violence among the younger members. As Vigil notes,

> In the most marginalized and impoverished communities, for some individuals, a series of personal traumatic experiences and influences have generated a sense of rage and aggression such that lashing out violently becomes a generally predictable and expected type of behavior. In this context of social determinants and psychological propensities, street gangs have become a street-created medium and vehicle to encourage and vent this aggression.[62]

Moore comments that "younger members often want to match or outdo the reputation of their predecessors. Respondents from the more violent cliques were significantly more likely to believe that their clique was more violent than its immediate predecessor."[63]

> In general the elevated level of violence over time had some relationship to each clique's sense that it must outdo its predecessor and also with some elements of the changing definitions of locura. Violence also puts the gang under considerable strain. This is a consequence of the "code of the barrio." In part, this translates into a norm that homeboys back one another up in all situations, especially fights. This "code of the barrio" is one of the prime sources of lethal violence, especially i more recent times when guns replaced one-on-one fighting to establish a pecking order.[64]

In the next section, Elijah Anderson explains the code of the barrio in more detail and calls it the "code of the streets."

Gang researcher Ruth Horowitz summarizes the important relationship between insults, honor, and violence. This is especially important for young men without many personal accomplishments or valued social roles to create self-worth. In a culture that emphasizes machismo and "defines violations of interpersonal etiquette in an adversarial manner, any action that challenges a person's right to deferential treatment in public can be interpreted as an insult and a potential threat to manhood."[65] This situation demands that the offended male be able to respond. Horowitz states that this situation is particularly acute for youths because of their lack of educational and occupational success. Further, dishonor is something that is perceived as a loss of manhood, and the response to this, according to this subculture, must be physical. In short, "violence is triggered by the norms of the code of personal honor."[66]

The National Youth Gang Survey Analysis found that conflict between gangs and drug-related factors directly affected levels of gang violence in half of the jurisdictions reporting in 2006. Less frequently reported factors were gang-member migration, jurisdictions, emergence of new gangs, and the return of gang members from secure confinement.[67] The Los Angeles Police Department reported in 2010 that gang-related index crime declined 20.3% from 2008.[68] Gang homicides declined 16.9%. From 2002 to 2007, gang-related homicides were most likely to occur in larger cities; 13% of those jurisdictions reported a total of 10 or more homicides for those six years; 31.5% of the larger cities reported no homicides. More than three-quarters of the smaller cities and rural counties predominantly reported no homicides during those years, as did more than half of the suburban jurisdictions. The most frequently reported number for all jurisdictions was one to two homicides in those six years.[69]

Gang-related homicides in Los Angeles are an interesting case because of the fluctuations during the past 20 years. Data collected by Malcolm Klein and Cheryl Maxson cover the years 1980 through 1997, and they reveal that gang-related homicides increased dramatically in the mid-1980s, exactly the time when crack cocaine became a staple on the streets of Los Angeles.[70] There was also a noteworthy increase in the availability and lethality of weapons during this time. The number of gang-related homicides went from 212 in 1983 to more than 800 by 1992; the percentage of all homicides that were gang-related went from 10 to around 45 during that time. Part of this increase was directly related to the increase in drive-by shootings. Between 1989 and 1991 the number of these incidents went from 1,112 to 1,543, with the number of victims increasing from 1,675 to 2,222 and the number of deaths going from 78 to 141.[71] The numbers declined from 1992 to 1993, followed by a slight increase through 1995, and a significant decrease after that. In Los Angeles County, gang-related homicides went from a high of 807 in 1995 to 587 in 2001 (a drop of 27%). In the city of Los Angeles, gang-related homicides went from a high of 430 in 1992 to 157 in 2009 (a decline of almost two-thirds).[72]

The Code of the Streets

In a fascinating study, Elijah Anderson explored a culture that differed substantially from common expectations.[73] He noted that in poor environments the negative influences are everywhere and have become part of an oppositional culture he calls "the streets." The street subculture operates on norms in direct opposition to those of mainstream society, which is "committed to middle-class values." The existence of such an oppositional culture means that even youths from "decent" homes must be able to handle themselves in a street-oriented environment. The parents of such youths actually encourage them to at least become familiar with the *code of the streets*, which Anderson defines as a

> set of informal rules governing interpersonal public behavior, including violence. The rules prescribe both a proper comportment and a proper way

to respond if challenged. They regulate the use of violence and so allow those who are inclined to aggression to precipitate violent encounters in an approved way.[74]

The heart of the code is respect, which is defined as being treated with proper deference. Unfortunately, the definition is not precise. Moreover, respect is something that is "hard-won but easily lost," and thus one must constantly guard against someone taking it away. If one has respect, then one can go about one's business without being bothered by others. If one *is* "bothered" in public, it is a disgrace, in addition to any physical danger. In current slang, one has been "dissed" or disrespected. While many of the examples of what constitutes dissin' (e.g., maintaining eye contact for too long) may seem trivial to middle-class people, these incidents are of major importance to those involved in the subculture of the gang. Anderson suggests that the reason can be found in the fact that so many inner-city African Americans (especially the young) feel totally alienated from mainstream society and its institutions. The code is nothing more than a subcultural adaptation to the lack of faith in the justice system (especially the police), which they believe does not respect or protect them. Many residents have taken on the responsibility of protecting themselves. The code of the streets, therefore, takes over where the police and judicial system end.

Anderson distinguished between two polar extremes among families in the inner city—the decent and the street family, titles used by residents themselves. (They may even exist simultaneously within the same family.) The decent families accept mainstream values and try to instill them in their children. Most are among the working poor, and they place a high value on hard work and self-reliance. They want their children to stay in school and to better themselves. They tend to be strict parents and warn their children to be on the lookout for bad people and bad situations.

In contrast, street parents tend to show a lack of consideration for others and are often unable to cope with the demands of parenthood. They strongly believe in the code and try to instill it in their children. Their lives are often disorganized, and they often engage in self-destructive behavior, largely as a result of their lowly status and their frustration over unpaid bills, lack of jobs and food, and so on. Many of the women get involved in drugs and abusive relationships with men. They often become bitter and angry, and they have short fuses, causing them to lash out at anybody who irritates them.

The women (too often at home with children and no man in the house) can be very aggressive with their children, yelling and striking at them with little or no explanation. Such verbal and physical punishment teaches children to solve any interpersonal problems by resorting to hitting or other violent behavior. These mothers may love their children, but this is the only way they know how to control them. Many of these women believe, for example, that there is a "devil in the boy" and that this must be "beaten out of him" or that "fast girls need to be whupped."[75]

The children are often ignored by their mothers, and so they often learn to fend for themselves at a very early age. They become children of the street, and, as a popular saying goes, they "come up hard."[76] Many become employed by drug dealers and learn to fight at an early age. In such environments, says Anderson, children learn that might makes right and that in order to protect oneself "it is necessary to marshal inner resources and be ready to deal with adversity in a hands-on way. In these circumstances physical prowess takes on great significance."[77] In the most extreme cases, a street-oriented mother may leave her children alone for several days. This is most common among women with drug and/or alcohol problems. For these children, a very harsh lesson is learned: "Survival itself, let alone respect, cannot be taken for granted; you have to fight for your place in the world."[78]

Beginning at a very early age, these children begin to hang out on the streets. After school they will come home, then walk right out the door and spend the afternoons and evenings (often as late as 9 or 10 PM—much later for teenagers) on the streets with their peers. Children from decent homes are more closely supervised, with curfews imposed on them and lessons given by their parents on how to avoid trouble. When children from decent families meet children from street families, there is always tension and a social shuffle in which the decent children are tempted. Their choice depends on how well they have already been socialized by their parents. Street children rarely develop the values of decent families; when they do it is almost always from sources in another setting, such as church or school, and often as a result of involvement with a caring adult.

While on the street, children continually witness disputes, and the resolution usually reinforces the might-makes-right belief. They see that "one child succumbs to the greater physical and mental abilities of the other. . . . In almost every case the victor is the person who physically won the altercation, and this person often enjoys the esteem and respect of onlookers."[79] The children learn to admire toughness rather than humility.

The messages are reinforced verbally by other family members, neighbors, and friends:

> "Watch your back" "Protect yourself." "Don't punk out." "If somebody messes with you, you got to pay them back." "If someone disses you, you got to straighten them out." Many parents actually impose sanctions if a child is not sufficiently aggressive. For example, if a child loses a fight and comes home upset, the parent might respond, "Don't you come in here crying that somebody beat you up; you better get back out there and whup his ass. I didn't raise no punks. If you don't whup his ass, I'll whup your ass when you come home."[80]

Even some decent parents give similar warnings about the need for self-defense. Although youths are ambivalent about fighting, they feel pressured to fight by the code. Both street-oriented and decent parents believe that a primary component of self-defense is looking as though you are capable of taking care of yourself.

The essence of the code centers on the presentation of self. The major requirement is to prove to others that one is willing and able to use violence to defend oneself. One communicates this message through facial expressions and a certain way of walking and talking (including the words one selects). Physical appearance is also important—jewelry, certain kinds of clothing (jackets, sneakers, and so on), and the way one is groomed. In order to be respected, one must have the right look. There are always going to be challenges to one's respect, or "juice" (as it is often called). If one is assaulted or otherwise challenged, one must avenge oneself. According to the code, maintaining one's honor or respect is crucial.

There is a widespread feeling that within this environment there is a limited amount of respect and that everyone must compete for affirmation. If one violates another and there is no response, it merely encourages further violations against that person. Thus one must be constantly on guard against not only direct violations but even the appearance of potential violation. This is especially true among teenagers, whose self-esteem is by definition already vulnerable. There are many young males who so desperately want respect that they are willing to die in order to maintain it.[81]

One major assumption is that everyone should know the code of the streets. Thus, even the victim of a mugging who does not act according to the code may cause the mugger to feel no remorse for his violence—the victim "should have known better."[82] Because even youths from decent families are familiar with the code, they too may have to resort to violence to defend their honor or respect.

One of the core beliefs associated with this concept of manhood is that one of the best ways of gaining respect (therefore proving one is a real man) is to exhibit nerve. The concept of nerve refers to the ability to take someone else's possessions, mess with someone's woman, get in someone's face, or fire a weapon. The show of nerve, however, is a very forceful method of showing disrespect—it can very easily offend others and result in retaliation.[83]

The issue of self-respect is very important to understand in terms of the extent to which a young person has the potential for violence. Most individuals in mainstream society are able to retreat and not seek revenge against an attack; they have gained enough self-esteem from other sources (e.g., education, jobs, and family) to withstand the insult. Other sources of self-esteem are absent for inner-city youths; thus, they have to seek revenge (even going so far as to enlist the aid of relatives or fellow gang members). In short, being a man means being in control, being in charge. This is not to say that within middle- and upper-class society being a man does not mean the same basic thing. The main difference is that within the inner city it comes down to the physical aspect of this equation because there are few nonviolent means to maintain respect and to prove that one is a real man.

Sex Offenses

Media reports about juvenile sex offenders have been replete with misinformation and have contributed to national hysteria—and public policy—about the issue. During the past two decades far-reaching legislation has widened the net of social control over a vast array of "sexual" behaviors that heretofore had been virtually ignored. While the impetus for the legislation was extremely serious crimes (e.g., the rape and murder seven-year-old Megan Kanka, discussed below), the reality is that "sex offenses" and "sex offenders" has been defined so broadly that even the most innocuous acts have been criminalized—in particular, the rather innocent behavior of children. Consider the following cases:

- A 14-year-old boy was arrested and placed in a juvenile facility because a "13-year-old girl had told her mother the boy touched her bottom during a game of tag." The boy pled guilty to "sexual assault."

- A fourth-grade boy was charged with "sexual assault" for putting his hand in the pants of a female fourth-grader.

- An 11 year-old boy was arrested after a girl of the same age "told her parents they were on the playground swing together and she could feel his genitals." He was convicted of "sexual harassment" and had to register as a "sex offender."[84]

- Ten-year-old Leah DuBuc was adjudicated for "sexual experimentation." She and her two stepbrothers—ages eight and five—"were caught flashing each other and pretending to have sex with their clothes on." After pleading guilty to "first and second degree sexual conduct," she was sentenced to eighteen months in a residential treatment program and was required to register as sex offender for twenty-five years.[85]

- Three girls and three boys at a Pennsylvania high school were charged with "child pornography"—they took pictures of themselves, nude or seminude. "One father complained that his daughter was pictured simply wearing a bathing suit," but the local DA called the photo "provocative," while in another case two girls age 13 "were photographed lying side by side in their thick white training bras."[86]

- In Oregon, a girl who spent the majority of her time in the Oregon Youth Authority (OYA) for petty theft, running away, and other minor crimes, declared herself to be a lesbian while at a juvenile institution. "A member of the staff saw her putting her arm around another girl and based on this action, she was sent to the sex offender unit." She must register as a "sex offender."[87]

These examples represent merely a small sampling of the overreach of sex offender laws. According to the Justice Policy Institute: "In most states, intercourse with a child under the age of 14, 15, or 16 is considered sexual assault regardless of consent. However, according to the National Longitudinal Survey of Youth, slightly more than three-quarters of youth in the survey reported having had sexual intercourse. Of those youth, more than 80 percent reported having had sex by age 15."[88] The Justice Policy Institute also notes that: "Many of the behaviors reported are status offenses, including things such as 'parking' and 'necking,' which would not be a crime if committed by an adult."[89]

In *Moral Panic: Changing Concepts of the Child Molester in Modern America*, Philip Jenkins talks about the role of the media. Although the overwhelming majority of offenses against children are committed by someone the victim knows, the news media focuses on the rare and chilling rapes and murders of the young by strangers. Sensational stories heightened public concern, and children as sex offenders became the next focus in our national anxiety about sex crimes. As Jenkins states, "First it's adult predators, and then it's what about children? To draw attention, you have to up the ante. The issue moves up a notch, and you can't move it back easily.[90]

The first significant piece of legislation was the Wetterling Act in 1994, which was a provision in the Federal Violent Crime Control and Law Enforcement Act that required states to "implement a sex offender and crimes against children registry." In 1996, Megan's Law was an amendment to the Wetterling Act and required states to establish a "community notification system." The next amendment was the Pam Lychner Sexual Offender Tracking and Identification Act of 1996 which required "lifetime registration for recidivists and offenders who commit certain aggravated offenses."[91]

All fifty states had sex offender registration lists, but only 28 required juveniles adjudicated for a sex offense to register as sex offenders; five required juveniles tried as adults to register, and seventeen required all juvenile sex offenders to register. The Adam Walsh Child Protection and Safety Act, title I of the Sex Offender Registration and Notification Act (SORNA), was enacted in July 2006.

The Act was designed to create a publicly posted national sex offender registry and to make failure to register a crime. The contentious issues involved juveniles. The Act eviscerates a central tenet of the juvenile justice system. For more than a century, the records of youthful offenses have generally been sealed and unavailable to the public. The rationale for this protection has been that children are less responsible for their actions and more amenable to rehabilitation.[92] The Act requires juveniles 14 and older convicted of serious sex crimes to register with authorities and to remain on the national registry *for the rest of their lives*.[93] States had until July 2010 to comply, but only Ohio met the deadline. The Federal Register posted revised rules in May 2010 (open to public comment) that would let states decide whether to include teen offenders in their public registries.

States vary in the requirements for young sex offenders. Twenty-one states require juvenile sex offenders to register. Nineteen other states require only juveniles convicted as adults (or juveniles who move from a state that requires registration) to register. Community notification law frequently means that websites post juveniles' names, addresses, photos, and sometimes birth dates and maps to their homes in addition to the detailed profiles of pedophiles and adult rapists.[94] Four states do not publish such details for juveniles online. In Nevada, a juvenile sex offender can petition a judge to set aside registration requirements.[95]

Proponents of registration argue that children must be protected from predators, even if they are minors. Juvenile justice advocates want rehabilitation instead of registration. Valerie Arnold, a child and adolescent psychiatrist, states: "These kids can get better and here you are punishing them for life without offering any treatment. That to me is unethical. Even convicted murderers aren't put on a list like this."[96] Timothy Kahn, a Seattle therapist who has worked with thousands of juveniles with sex offenses, states:

> It is morally wrong to do nothing to educate kids about the laws and then have them have to register as sex offenders and they haven't even hit puberty. I've been arguing for a classification called "puberty in the first degree," which gives them a break for what they do when they are 12, 13, 14.[97]

Another concern is that juveniles are subject to the same registration requirements as adults without the benefit of a jury trial or similar protections.[98]

Laws such as those mentioned above are what may be described as "exception-based" or "legislation by anecdote."[99] They are typically passed after a particularly heinous crime that, although extremely rare, provokes public fear and reactions from politicians who seize the opportunity to appear "tough on crime." In California, Proposition 83 (Jessica's Law) was passed by the voters in 2006 amid a great deal of controversy and criticism. The law banned "all released sex offenders from living within 2,000 feet of a school or park." What this did, in effect, is prohibit sex offenders from living anywhere in San Francisco, Los Angeles, or any other urban area. One report noted that it "would banish the former convicts from urban settings that offer the services, jobs and family connections that help them remain law-abiding—and dump them on rural communities ill-equipped to supervise them."[100]

Debra Lee Cochrane notes that, among other problems, "public notification of juvenile sex offenders hinders rehabilitation efforts in many ways. By requiring notification to an offender's school this public outing could lead to peer harassment causing social isolation, emotional and physical harm."[101] She related the following incident.

> A nine-year-old boy convicted of raping a younger boy was adjudicated and spent three years in a detention center. Seven years later the family moved to Missouri to get away from the constant public attention and persecution. The boy was now sixteen and had never committed another sex offense. The residents of Missouri found out about the boy's past criminal history. Following the notification to the school he lost his privacy, all his friends, and his right to attend school. The school claimed they feared for the safety of other students and suggested the family tutor him at home.[102]

In 2009 a total of 7,799 juveniles were arrested for "sex offenses" (except forcible rape and prostitution). These offenses represented less than .7% of all juvenile arrests, and the number of arrests declined 28.1% from the number in 2000.[103] It is obvious from these numbers that the national hysteria over "sex offenders" is highly exaggerated when it comes to juveniles.[104]

Public Order Offenses

Behaviors that fall under this category are "victimless crimes" (crimes without a "complaining victim") or crimes that offend some vague sense of "public order." Among the most common charges in this category are drug abuse violations, prostitution, pornography, illegal gambling, liquor-law violations (these are sometimes classified as "status offenses," discussed in the next section), public drunkenness, disorderly conduct, and vagrancy. Some public order offenses are subsumed within the category known as "all other offenses," discussed below. *Juvenile Court Statistics* includes the following offenses under the heading of "public order": obstruction of justice, disorderly conduct, weapons offenses, liquor-law violations, nonviolent sex offenses, and "other" public order offenses. Drugs are treated as a separate category.

Rarely discussed in the literature on delinquency cases is the catch-all offense generally called "obstruction of justice." In the UCR, these charges are usually included in the "all other offenses" category. They represent a sizeable proportion of cases processed through the juvenile court. As noted in table 2-1, there were 196,036 arrests in this category. Simple assaults was the only category with more arrests (an additional 827). What exactly is "obstruction of justice"?

> intentionally obstructing court or law enforcement efforts in the administration of justice, acting in a way calculated to lessen the authority or dignity of the court, failing to obey the lawful order of a court, escaping from confinement, and violating probation or parole. This term includes contempt, perjury, bribery of witnesses, failure to report a crime, and nonviolent resistance of arrest.[105]

The description clearly covers a wide variety of behaviors. Personal observations and conversations with court personnel and juveniles over many decades suggest that this charge often stems from occasions when a youth angers a judge or court officer (e.g., his or her parole officer), fails to display an acceptable attitude (which also can add the charge of "resisting arrest"), or gets caught violating one or more of the myriad rules of probation and parole. As will be noted in chapter 11, it appears that more and more juveniles are either becoming more defiant or the court is increasingly more likely to respond with formal charges. There were 153,100 obstruction of justice cases petitioned in 2007 (71% of all the obstruction of justice cases processed by the courts—a percentage that ranks it with violent crimes, burglary, and motor vehicle theft); 60% of these cases were adjudicated. For both petitioned and adjudicated cases, more than 40% were juveniles younger than 16, about 25% were female, and 60% were white.[106]

While obstruction of justice covers diverse behaviors, there are several commonalities.[107] First, many are "victimless crimes" where both participants are technically violating the law. Second, many involve the generic "public" as victim, as in disturbing the "peace" of the surrounding community. Third, many involve a simple exchange of goods or services that are in demand. Fourth, there is no consensus on the seriousness of these offenses. Fifth, some of the offenses resemble legitimate behaviors engaged in by adult citizens. This is especially the case with drunkenness and illegal drug use.[108] While the public may condemn such behavior for others and for juveniles, they may also secretly indulge in similar behavior.

Tens of thousands of juveniles are picked up by the police and at least momentarily detained, if not brought directly to juvenile court, for offenses that could be considered "hanging out" or "partying." In 2009, almost 355,000 juveniles were arrested for such offenses as drunkenness, disorderly conduct, curfew violation/loitering, liquor-law and drug violations, prostitution, and other sex offenses (except rape). An additional 196,000 were arrested for "all other offenses" (which includes "obstruction of justice").[109] These high numbers should come as no surprise given that the police historically have been charged with maintaining order within a community. A ride in the back of a squad car during any given evening (especially a weekend) will demonstrate this very clearly, with a large amount of time consumed responding to various kinds of "disturbances," including "rowdy kids." In 2007, there were 472,300 public order case referrals to juvenile court plus another 190,100 drug case referrals for a total of 662,400. Public order offenses accounted for 54% of the growth in delinquency caseloads between 1985 and 2007.[110]

Status Offenses

As we noted in the first chapter, the earliest juvenile codes strongly emphasized offenses applicable to those under a certain age, commonly known as *status offenses* because the violation is linked to the "status" of *age*. Hundreds of thousands of young people—70% of whom are between the ages of 14 and 16—are arrested each year, and many end up in court, although they have not committed a criminal offense.[111] "These adolescents often come from families in crisis, feel unsafe in or alienated from their homes or schools, run away, skip school, or act out in other ways that involve them with the court system. They may be called "unruly teens," "chronic runaways," "truants," "children in need of services" or any one of a dozen other terms."[112]

Every state's juvenile code contains several of these kinds of offenses. Many status offenses are related to academic difficulties, abuse and neglect in the home, substance abuse, or physical and mental health problems. Girls and youth of color are disproportionately confined for status offense behavior. [113] Some states include vague descriptions such as "beyond the control of parents" or "child in need of supervision."

In many states guardians can file a status offense petition when a youth is "unruly," "ungovernable," or "incorrigible." Such behaviors range from refusing to obey parental curfews to repeated arguments with family members to a child physically abusing a parent—cases in which the parent or guardian perceives the situation to be unmanageable and is looking for help.[114] Virginia distinguishes between a "Child In Need Of Services" and a "Child In Need Of Supervision." The former "refers to a child whose behavior, conduct or condition presents or results in a serious threat to the well-being and physical safety of the child." The latter "refers to a child who either while subject to compulsory school attendance, is habitually and without justification absent from school, or without reasonable cause and without the consent of his parent or lawful custodian, remains away from home."[115]

There are four major types of status offenses: (1) running away, (2) truancy, (3) curfew violations, (4) liquor-law violations. The catch-all categories of "incorrigible" and "unmanageable" cover other status offense behaviors. Title II of the Juvenile Justice and Delinquency Prevention Act (passed in 1974) prohibited the placement of status offenders in locked detention in states receiving federal funds. The Act was modified in 1980 to allow judges discretion if status offenders violated a valid court order (VCO). [116] Between 1974 and the 1980, status referrals decreased by 21% and the detention of juveniles for status offenses was cut in half.[117]

> The VCO exception allows courts to hold juvenile status offenders in a secure juvenile facility without violating the DSO [deinstitutionalizing status offenders] requirement, either under the traditional contempt authority of the court or if the state delinquency code allows judges to adjudicate a status offender as delinquent after he violates a VCO. This approach is commonly known as "bootstrapping," as it takes what had been nondelinquent behavior, protected under the DSO requirement of the JJDPA, and converts it into a category of behavior that loses that protection. For example, a runaway ordered by the court to stay in her home could be placed in secure detention if she runs again. Because many states did not increase services to address the underlying problems facing status offenders, repeat offending was common.[118]

Status offender detentions increased dramatically after the VCO modification, and the number of incarcerated status offenders quickly doubled.

In large part, the separation of status offenders from other delinquent youths has emerged in response to concerns about the rights of youths charged with status offenses. Status offense laws have been objected to on constitutional grounds. One of the most common grounds is that the statutes are too vague. For example, what is the precise meaning of "habitual disobedience" or "lawful parental demands"? Another concern is that status offense laws violate the Eighth Amendment in that punishment ensues from status rather than behavior. A major source of the bias in contemporary juvenile courts is undoubtedly parental use (some might say abuse) of the status offense category. Recent national data show that law enforcement agencies referred only 40% of runaway cases and only 10% of all truancy and unmanageable or incorrigible cases. Thus status offenses are clearly the products of conflicts with the family and school system.

As we will note in chapter 5, one of the distinguishing characteristics of female delinquency is the role played by status offenses. Running away and curfew violation constitute a higher percentage of female delinquency arrests (15% in 2009) than male delinquency arrests (9.5%).[119] The majority of curfew (67%), liquor law violation (63%), ungovernability (56%), and truancy (54%) cases petitioned to the court in 2007 were male juveniles.[120] The only status offense category in which there were more female (59%) than male cases was runaway. Truancy cases outnumbered all other status offense cases for both males and females from 1997–2007. Case rates for ungovernability increased 7% for both males and females from 1995 to 2007.

Adolescents are less likely than adults to think about the future consequences of their actions; they are generally more focused on the present and immediate gratification. They have an imbalanced perception of risk and lack impulse control. In addition, most adolescents respond to peer influence and may gain higher social status for engaging in antisocial behavior. A truant, disruptive, or runaway youth focuses on the immediate benefits rather than long-term effects.[121]

Runaways

Youths who leave home without permission are runaways; youths who are forced out of their homes or refused permission to return are thrownaways. Runaway youth often leave their homes because of intense family conflict or abuse (physical, sexual or psychological). Most of these children are between the ages of 15 and 17.[122]

The recession that began in 2008 has fueled an increase in runaways.

> Over the past two years, government officials and experts have seen an increasing number of children leave home for life on the streets, including many under 13. Foreclosures, layoffs, rising food and fuel prices and inadequate supplies of low-cost housing have stretched families to the extreme, and those pressures have trickled down to teenagers and preteens.

Experts estimate that approximately 1.6 million juveniles run away from or are thrown out of their homes each year; most return home within a week. The government does not conduct a comprehensive survey, but the number of contacts with runaways that federally-financed outreach programs make provides one means of measuring the number of runaways. Those contacts rose to 761,000 in 2008, up from 550,000 in 2002.[123]

Most youths who run away remain within 10–50 miles from home (usually staying with friends nearby). Runaways often feel unwanted, abused, neglected, and rejected by their parents.[124] Many believe their parents have unrealistic expectations of them, are overly strict, and use excessive punishment. Many runaways have experienced poor relationships outside of the home, often ostracized by both teachers and peers. They have also experienced failure at school, and many have had to repeat grades. In-school problems and habitual truancy are also common. Not surprisingly, most have very negative feelings toward school in general.

Runaway statutes often include phrases such as "voluntary absence" and "without consent," which are vague, subjective, and open to interpretation.

> There is often a very active parental role in a child's running away. In many cases where a child is alleged to have stayed away from home overnight or longer—i.e., to have run away—the youth has a very different take on the events that caused her to leave, insisting that she was actually "put out of the house" by the parent. Many cases involve an argument between the parent and youth that eventually escalates to the point that the parent

insists the youth leave the house. Rather than back down or lose face by apologizing, the youth leaves angrily. Most kids don't wander the streets. Usually the parent knows exactly where the youth went—to a relative, neighbor, or friend's home. . . .

Occasionally, kids run away from stable, healthy homes to wander the streets in search of drugs or to pursue a romantic relationship that their parents forbid. In many instances, however, children's actions are justified. The desire for a safe, loving home is innate. Under normal circumstances, obstinacy alone will not motivate a child to leave her home and fend for herself. If she does, she may be running away *from* something with good cause.[125]

The runaway statutes in some states are more defined. For example, Florida's statute requires proof that the youth has "*persistently* run away." Other states insert a "good cause" requirement.[126] In Arkansas, running away consists of leaving home *without sufficient cause, permission, or justification.* Connecticut uses the phrase *without just cause,* and Virginia uses *without reasonable cause.* Terms such as *sufficient, just,* and *reasonable* are also very general, but they do direct the juvenile court to determine the reason for running away. Certainly, abuse or neglect by another household member would qualify as "good cause." Some judges also might find good cause where a parent has kicked the child out of the home, or even in cases of persistent, but nonviolent, parent-child conflict.

Physically leaving a difficult situation is a common coping mechanism for many youths. Repeated runaway behavior frustrates judges, service providers, and parents—who often hope that a one-time intervention will end the behavior. Research shows that the most successful responses tackle the underlying issues that prompted the runaway behavior.[127] Some guardians are misdirected to the status offender system. They want their children located and returned but are unaware of the other components of the status offender process. When probation or child welfare brings the petition, they may believe that court involvement is required, although voluntary services or reuniting the family might also be an option.

If the case is petitioned, several issues should be explored. For example, did the parent breach a legal obligation to the child? Was the child's behavior threatening or was it only a poor response after being placed in a difficult situation by the person who is supposed to provide care and guidance? [128]

A Final Word on Status Offenses

Status offenses can be viewed as ways of regulating and controlling children. The state, in effect, sides with schools and the family. But what if the children are victimized by either the family or the school? Which side does the state take? The state (Juvenile Court, etc.) is supposed to be acting "in the best interest of the child." However, do the constraints of the legal system work against doing so (think of the differences between social work and the law)? Are we engaging in the overregulation of children? Here's what a writer in England had to say on this subject:

There's a widespread belief that children grow up faster today. In fact, though they may adopt adult cultures and attitudes, their daily lives are far more controlled and overseen than a couple of decades ago. . . . Why have the horizons of childhood shrunk so much? While parents set the limits, their actions are just the beginning of the story. Many social and cultural trends—traffic growth, longer working hours, more fragmented communities, greater fear of crime and a pervasive climate of anxiety—all reinforce the logic of containment. . . .

Whatever the reasons, we now have a norm of parenting that equates being a good parent with being a controlling parent. We do not just ferry children everywhere, we also supervise nearly every move they make.

The overregulation of children's lives has a big downside. Many experiences children used to enjoy—boisterous physical play, street play, verbal jousting, even climbing trees—are now seen as deeply troubling. The parents who allow those activities are labelled irresponsible. But children need everyday challenges and adventures if they are to learn how to manage their own safety and sort out their problems for themselves. Today, many preadolescent children don't get those opportunities. How will they develop the skills they need to deal with the wider world?

I don't think parents are solely to blame. Most are well aware they should be preparing their offspring for life as autonomous adults. I speak as a parent myself. We do not need more experts telling us what to do. One thing I have found helpful is simply to share views with other parents, looking back on our own childhoods to remind ourselves of the value of tasting freedom. While we cannot recreate our childhoods, we can reject the culture of overprotection and come up with practical steps to give our children more responsibility. This could be walking to school once a week with an older child on the street, or trying to sort out minor spats for themselves or simply climbing trees in the park.

This is not a job parents can do by themselves. Parents, teachers, child-carers and providers of organized activities all need to accept that children do not need adults watching their every move. As a society, we need to move from a philosophy of protection to a philosophy of resilience. The role of adults in childhood is not just to protect, but to help children build their coping mechanisms and take on more responsibility for their everyday lives.

This will not be easy. I believe government leadership is needed to reverse this trend. Alongside new policies in schools and services, politicians should be making the creation of more child-friendly communities a high priority. By these I mean neighbourhoods that are safe, supportive, welcoming and tolerant as children gradually extend their lives beyond home and school.

Ultimately, this is a question of balance. Of course we need to protect children from serious threats, but we also need to give them the freedom to learn how to get to grips with the world for themselves.[129]

The enforcement of status offense laws plus the emergence of "zero tolerance" polices has added to the overregulation of children.

Summary

Delinquent behavior encompasses a wide variety of prohibited behaviors, ranging from the petty to the most serious, from offenses applicable to youths under a certain age (status offenses) to behaviors that apply to adults as well. Many of the behaviors are motivated by the desire to obtain various kinds of property, with shoplifting from retail stores being the most common—not a surprising motivation given how much emphasis our culture places on material goods. There are also a variety of personal crimes involving some physical contact with the victim, ranging in seriousness from minor altercations to serious assaults with weapons, which can result in serious injury and in a few cases death.

Youngsters spend a lot of time together in public. Therefore, public order offenses are common, often known by such names as disturbing the peace, loitering, and curfew violation. Another category of offenses have no complaining victim, such as drug use and possession of liquor. Finally, there are millions of youngsters who suffer some form of abuse, sometimes running away to escape or exhibiting similar abusive behavior and being labeled as "incorrigible." Runaway behavior often leads to the commission of various criminal behaviors as a means of survival.

NOTES

[1] Puzzanchera, C., B. Adams, and M. Sickmund (2010, March). *Juvenile Court Statistics 2006–2007*. Pittsburgh, PA: National Center for Juvenile Justice, p. 103. Retrieved from http://www.ncjjservehttp.org/ncjjwebsite/pdf/jcsreports/jcs2007.pdf

[2] Birckhead, T. R. (2008, September). "New Research Analyzes North Carolina's Century-Long Refusal to Include 16- and 17-Year-Olds in Juvenile Court," endnote ii. Retrieved from http://www.ncchild.org/action/images/stories/JoshDocuments/Juvenile_Court_Jurisdiction_Reform_Fact_Sheet_11_17_08.pdf

[3] I'm indebted to my former professor, Charles H. Newton (now deceased). These are part of his lecture notes from his course on juvenile delinquency taught at Memphis State University during the late 1960s and early 1970s. They contain much information that remains relevant today; not much has changed in terms of the various dimensions of "delinquent behavior" over the past 40 years.

[4] As we will see in chapter 12, growing numbers of youth with serious mental issues are being detained all across the country waiting for placement in a mental health agency.

[5] Brown, W. B. (1998). "The Fight for Survival: African-American Gang Members and Their Families in a Segregated Society." *Juvenile and Family Court Journal* 49: 1–14.

[6] Messner, S. F. and R. Rosenfeld (2001). *Crime and the American Dream* (3rd ed.). Belmont, CA: Wadsworth, p. 76.

[7] Reiss, A. (1988). "Co-offending and Criminal Careers." In M. Tonry and N. Morris (Eds.), *Crime and Justice*, Vol. 10. Chicago: University of Chicago Press, pp. 117–70.

[8] Many songs over the years have been based on the theme of kids just "hangin' out," including "I Get Around," "Fun, Fun, Fun," and "No Particular Place to Go."

[9] Gove, W. R. (1994). "Why We Do What We Do: A Biopsychosocial Theory of Human Motivation." *Social Forces* 73: 374–88; Paternoster, R. (1989). "Absolute and Restrictive Deterrence in a Panel of Youth: Explaining the Onset, Persistence/Desistence, and Frequency of Delinquent Offending." *Social Problems* 36: 289–309; Thomas, C. W. and D. Bishop (1984). "The Effect of For-

mal and Informal Sanctions on Delinquency: A Longitudinal Comparison of Labeling and Deterrence Theories." *Journal of Criminal Law and Criminology* 75: 1222–45. Recent research has found that kids with Attention-Deficit/Hyperactivity Disorder (ADHD) are very likely to commit petty crimes on the spur of the moment, compared to kids without ADHD. Fletcher, J. and B. Wolfe (2009). "Long-term Consequences of Childhood ADHD on Criminal Activities." *Journal of Mental Health Policy and Economics* 12: 119–38.

[10] Katz, J. (1988). *Seductions of Crime: Moral and Sensual Attractions in Doing Evil.* New York: Basic Books; McCarthy, B. (1995). "Not 'Just for the Thrill of It': An Instrumentalist Elaboration of Katz's Explanation of Sneaky Thrill Property Crime." *Criminology* 33: 519–38; Matsueda, R. L., D. Kreager, and D. Huizinga (2003). "Deterring Delinquents: A Rational Choice Model of Theft and Violence." Paper presented at the annual meeting of the American Sociological Association, Atlanta. This study found some evidence that the perceived likelihood of psychic rewards from crime (i.e., excitement and being seen as "cool") related to the commission of delinquent acts.

[11] Shelden, R. G., S. Tracy, and W. B. Brown (2004). *Youth Gangs in American Society* (3rd ed.). Belmont, CA: Wadsworth; Sanders, W. (1994). *Gangbangs and Drivebys.* New York: Aldine DeGruyter.

[12] Shelden, R. G. and M. Chesney-Lind (1991). "Gender and Race Differences in Delinquent Careers." *Juvenile and Family Court Journal* 44: 73–90.

[13] Ibid.

[14] Federal Bureau of Investigation (2010). *Crime in the United States, 2009*, table 39. Retrieved from http://www2.fbi.gov/ucr/cius2009/data/table_39.html

[15] Ibid., table 40. Retrieved from http://www2.fbi.gov/ucr/cius2009/data/table_40.html

[16] Steinberg, L. (1999). *Adolescence* (5th ed.). New York: McGraw-Hill, p. 152.

[17] Kim, Y., E. Y. Kim, and J. Kang (2003). "Teens' Mall Shopping Motivations: Functions of Loneliness and Media Usage." *Family and Consumer Sciences Research Journal* 32: 140–67; see also: Mangleburg, T. F., P. M. Doneya, and T. Bristol (2004). "Shopping with Friends and Teens' Susceptibility to Peer Influence." *Journal of Retailing* 80: 101–16.

[18] Here's a website for Los Angeles shopping: http://discoverlosangeles.com/play/shopping/apparel/los-angeles-shopping-for-teenagers-top-shops-for-teens.html. This is just one of many examples.

[19] Agnew, R. and T. Brezina (1997). "Relational Problems with Peers, Gender and Delinquency." *Youth and Society* 29: 84–111; Merriman, J. (2008). "Linking Risk-Taking Behavior and Peer Influence in Adolescents." *Neuropsychiatry Review* 9(1).

[20] Huff, C. R. (1993). "Gangs in the United States." In A. P. Goldstein and C. R. Huff (Eds.), *The Gang Intervention Handbook.* Champaign, IL: Research Press, pp. 5–6, emphasis in the original.

[21] Clinard, M., R. Quinney, and J. Wildeman (1994). *Criminal Behavior Systems* (3rd ed.). Cincinnati: Anderson, p. 59.

[22] FBI, *Crime in the United States, 2009,* Offense Definitions. Retrieved from http://www2.fbi.gov/ucr/cius2009/about/offense_definitions.html

[23] Miethe, T. D. and R. McCorkle (1998). *Crime Profiles* (2nd ed.). Los Angeles: Roxbury Press, p. 207.

[24] Ward-Perkins, B. (2005). *The Fall of Rome and the End of Civilizations.* New York: Oxford University Press, referenced in Wikipedia: http://en.wikipedia.org/wiki/Vandalism#cite_note-klossowski-1.

[25] Clinard et al., *Criminal Behavior Systems,* pp. 62–63.

[26] See, for example, Horowitz, T. and D. Tobaly (2003). "School Vandalism: Individual and Social Context." *Adolescence* 38 (Spring): 131–39.

[27] http://www.familyfirstaid.org/teen-vandalism.html.

[28] FBI, *Crime in the United States, 2009,* table 32. Retrieved from http://www2.fbi.gov/ucr/cius2009/data/table_32.html

[29] Clinard et al., *Criminal Behavior Systems,* p. 65.

[30] Goldstein, A. P. (1996). *The Psychology of Vandalism.* New York: Plenum Press; Moser, G. (1992). "What Is Vandalism?" In H. Christenson, D. R. Johnson, and M. Brookes (Eds.), *Vandalism: Research, Prevention and Social Policy.* Washington, DC: U.S. Department of Agriculture Forest Service, pp. 49–70; Casserly, M. D., A. S. Bass, and J. R. Garrett (1982). *School Vandalism.* Lexington, MA: Lexington Books.

[31] The following section is adapted from Shelden et al., *Youth Gangs in American Society,* ch. 4.

[32] Vigil, J. D. (2010). *Gang Redux: A Balanced Anti-Gang Strategy.* Long Grove, IL: Waveland Press, p. 62.

[33] Vigil, J. D. (1988). *Barrio Gangs: Street Life and Identity in Southern California.* Austin: University of Texas Press, p. 115.

[34] Miethe and McCorkle, *Crime Profiles*, p. 156.

[35] http://www.yourdictionary.com/law/joyriding.

[36] Clinard et al., *Criminal Behavior Systems*, p. 63.

[37] Miethe and McCorkle, *Crime Profiles*, p. 151.

[38] Ibid., pp. 156–57.

[39] Ibid., p. 157.

[40] FBI, *Crime in the United States, 2009*, table 32.

[41] Elikann, P. (1999). *Superpredators: The Demonization of Our Children by the Law.* Reading, MA: Perseus.

[42] It is highly recommend that you read the book by Bennett, DiIulio, and Walters. It is an eye-opening example of not only the alarmist rhetoric noted here but also the misuse of crime statistics, especially the tendency to look only at *numbers* (e.g., going from 1 homicide to 3 homicides represents a 300% increase) rather than *rates*, plus the tendency to use "maximum starting and stopping points" to back up an exaggerated claim. It is also interesting to note that both Bennett and Walters held the office of Director of the Office of National Drug Control Policy. Criminologist John DiIulio was briefly Director of the White House Office of Faith-based and Community Initiatives. Bennett, W., J. DiIulio, and J. P. Walters (1996). *Body Count: Moral Poverty and How to Win America's War against Crime and Drugs.* New York: Simon and Schuster.

[43] Quoted in Elikann, *Superpredators*, p. 25.

[44] Males, M. and D. Macallair (2000). "Dispelling the Myth: An Analysis of Youth and Adult Crime Patterns in California over the Past 20 Years." San Francisco: Justice Policy Institute. Retrieved from http://www.cjcj.org/files/Dispelling/pdf

[45] Glassner, B. (1999). *The Culture of Fear.* New York: Basic Books, pp. 68–70.

[46] Puzzanchera, C. (2009, December). *Juvenile Arrests 2008*, p. 1. Retrieved from http://www.ncjrs.gov/pdffiles1/ojjdp/228479.pdf

[47] FBI, *Crime in the United States 2009*, table 32.

[48] Puzzanchera, *Juvenile Arrests 2008*, p. 1.

[49] FBI, *Crime in the United States, 2009*, table 9. Retrieved from http://www2.fbi.gov/ucr/cius2009/offenses/expanded_information/data/shrtable_09.html

[50] Puzzanchera, *Juvenile Arrests 2008*, p. 3.

[51] Puzzanchera et al., *Juvenile Court Statistics 2006–2007*, pp. 20, 25.

[52] Males and Macallair, "Dispelling the Myth."

[53] Judicial Council of California, Administrative Office of the Courts (2004, April 20). *California Juvenile Statistical Abstract.* Retrieved from http://courtinfo.ca.gov/programs/cfcc/programs/description/abstract.htm

[54] Cited in Males, M. (n.d.). "The Demographic Fallacy." Unpublished manuscript.

[55] Males and Macallair, "Dispelling the Myth."

[56] National Gang Center (2009). *National Youth Gang Survey Analysis.* Retrieved from http://www.nationalgangcenter.gov/Survey-Analysis/Demographics

[57] Ibid.; http://www.nationalgangcenter.gov/Survey-Analysis/Prevalence-of-Gang-Problems#prevalenceyouthgang

[58] Wolfgang, M., R. Figlio, and T. Sellin (1972). *Delinquency in a Birth Cohort.* Chicago: University of Chicago Press.

[59] Vigil, *Gang Redux*, p. 61.

[60] Moore, J. (1991). *Going Down to the Barrio: Homeboys and Homegirls in Change.* Philadelphia: Temple University Press, pp. 57–58.

[61] Ibid., p. 62.

[62] Vigil, *Gang Redux*, p. 24.

[63] Moore, *Going Down to the Barrio*, p. 60.

[64] Ibid., p. 65.

[65] Horowitz, R. (1983). *Honor and the American Dream.* New Brunswick, NJ: Rutgers University, pp. 81, 247.

66 Ibid., p. 82.

67 National Gang Center (2009). *National Youth Gang Survey Analysis*. Retrieved from http://www.nationalgangcenter.gov/Survey-Analysis/Gang-Related-Offenses#crime

68 LAPD (2010). Los Angeles Department Crime Statistics Snapshot. Retrieved from http://www.lapdonline.org/crime_snapshot

69 National Gang Center (2009). *National Youth Gang Survey Analysis*. Retrieved from http://www.nationalgangcenter.gov/Survey-Analysis/Measuring-the-Extent-of-Gang-Problems#homicidesnumber

70 Figures through 1992 found in Klein, M. (1995). *The American Street Gang*. New York: Oxford University Press, p. 120; figures from 1993–1997 from Cheryl Maxson, personal communication with author.

71 Klein, *The American Street Gang*, pp. 116–18.

72 Data supplied by both the county sheriff's office and the LAPD. Retrieved from http://www.laalmanac.com/crime/cr03x.htm#LA

73 Anderson, E. (1994, May). "The Code of the Streets." *The Atlantic Monthly*. Retrieved from http://www.theatlantic.com/past/politics/race/streets.htm

74 Ibid., p. 82.

75 Ibid.

76 This has also been noted by Vigil, *Barrio Gangs*.

77 Anderson, "The Code of the Streets," p. 86.

78 Ibid.

79 Ibid.

80 Ibid., p. 87.

81 The author connected a local example with similar behavior at the national level. A gang member at a local alternative school attacked someone else merely because he heard a rumor that the other person was out to get him for some reason. The code he lived by dictated that he attack this person before he was attacked in order not to be embarrassed or "dissed." Perhaps you also think this behavior sounds familiar. It reminded me of the U.S. government's "preemptive" attack against Iraq based on the assumption that they might, in the future, attack us with their "weapons of mass destruction." In this case, one "gang" (the U.S. government and its military) attacked another "gang," although the latter gang was clearly no match.

82 Anderson, "The Code of the Streets," p. 89.

83 Ibid., p. 92.

84 The above three incidents were reported in Johnson, B. (2007, October 27). "It's a Crime What Courts Do to Kids Just Being Kids." *Rocky Mountain News*.

85 Moore, M. T. (2006, July 10). "Sex Crimes Break the Lock on Juvenile Records." *USA Today*. Retrieved from http://www.usatoday.com/news/nation/2006-07-10-juvenile-offenders_x.htm. See also Cochrane, D. (2010). "Attitudes Toward Megan's Law and Juvenile Sex Offenders." *UNLV Theses/Dissertations/Professional Papers/Capstones*. Paper 2, p. 11. Retrieved from http://digitalcommons.library.unlv.edu/thesesdissertations/2

86 Wypijewski, J. (2009, May 1). "Super Prude Prosecutors Charge Teenagers with Pornography and Worse for Sexy Text Messages." *The Nation*. Retrieved from http://www.alternet.org/story/139272/

87 Cochrane, "Attitudes Toward Megan's Law." This particular girl was once interviewed by this author and Professor William Brown of Western Oregon University. At this institution there was a special building housing "female sex offenders."

88 Justice Policy Institute (2008, November 21). "Registering Harm: How Sex Offense Registries Fail Youth and Communities," p. 21. Retrieved from http://www.justicepolicy.org/images/upload/08-11_RPT_WalshActRegisteringHarm_JJ-PS.pdf

89 Ibid., p. 5.

90 Jones, M. (2007, July 22). "How Can You Distinguish a Budding Pedophile from a Kid with Real Boundary Problems?" *New York Times Magazine*. Retrieved from http://www.nytimes.com/2007/07/22/magazine/22juvenile-t.html?pagewanted=all

91 Bureau of Justice Statistics (n.d.). "Overview and History of the Jacob Wetterling Act." Retrieved from http://www.ojp.usdoj.gov/BJA/what/2a1jwacthistory.html

92 Jones, "How Can You Distinguish a Budding Pedophile?"

93 Koch, W. (2010, May 17). "Changes Would Give Sex-Offender Law Flexibility." *USA Today.* Retrieved from http://www.usatoday.com/news/washington/judicial/2010-05-17-walsh-act_N.htm?csp=obinsite

94 Jones, "How Can You Distinguish a Budding Pedophile?"

95 Associated Press (2010, May 6). "New Divide Over How to Treat Young Sex Offenders." Retrieved from http://www.cbsnews.com/stories/2010/05/06/national/main6464820.shtml

96 Ibid.

97 Jones, "How Can You Distinguish a Budding Pedophile?"

98 Ibid.

99 For another critique of SORNA see: Walsh, N. and T. Velazquez (2009, December). "Registering Harm: The Adam Walsh Act and Juvenile Sex Offender Registration." National Association of Criminal Defense Lawyers. Retrieved from http://www.nacdl.org/public.nsf/0/49866029f7f8475c852576d6005aad6a?OpenDocument

100 Warren, J. (2006, September 18). "Sex Offender Crackdown Measure Ties Into a National Trend." *Los Angeles Times.* Retrieved from http://articles.latimes.com/2006/sep/18/local/me-offender18

101 Cochrane, "Attitudes Toward Megan's Law," p. 11.

102 Ibid.

103 FBI, *Crime in the United States, 2009,* table 32.

104 More information can be obtained from the National Center for Sexual Behavior of Youth at: http://www.ncsby.org/pages/publications/What%20Research%20Shows%20About%20Adolescent%20Sex%20Offenders%20060404.pdf

105 Puzzanchera et al., *Juvenile Court Statistics 2006–2007,* p. 104.

106 Ibid., pp. 7, 9, 37, and 45.

107 See Miethe and McCorkle, *Crime Profiles,* ch. 8.

108 Clinard et al., *Criminal Behavior Systems,* p. 101.

109 FBI, *Crime in the United States, 2009,* table 32.

110 Puzzanchera, et al. *Juvenile Court Statistics 2006–2007,* pp. 6–7.

111 Shubik, C. (2010). "What Social Science Tells Us about Youth Who Commit Status Offenses: Practical Advice for Attorneys," p. 18. In S. Inada and C. Chiamulera (Eds.), *Representing Juvenile Status Offenders.* Chicago: American Bar Association, pp. 15–36. Retrieved from http://www.americanbar.org/content/dam/aba/migrated/child/PublicDocuments/RJSO_FINAL.authcheckdam.pdf

112 Inada and Chiamulera, *Representing Juvenile Status Offenders,* p. v.

113 Bilchik, S. and E. Pinheiro (2010). "What the JJDPA Means for Lawyers Representing Juvenile Status Offenders," p. 4. In Inada and Chiamulera, *Representing Juvenile Status Offenders,* pp. 1–14.

114 Shubik, "What Social Science Tells Us," pp. 23–24.

115 Department of Social Services, City of Newport News (n.d.). Retrieved from http://www.nngov.com/human-services/social-services/adult-and-family-services/children-in-need-of-services-supervision

116 Hornberger, N. (2010, Summer). "Improving Outcomes for Status Offenders in the JJDPA Reauthorization." *Juvenile and Family Justice Today,* p. 15. Retrieved from http://www.juvjustice.org/media/announcements/announcement_link_156.pdf

117 Bilchik and Pinheiro, "What the JJDPA Means for Lawyers," pp. 5–6.

118 Ibid., pp. 6–7.

119 FBI, *Crime in the United States, 2009,* table 33.

120 Puzzanchera et al., *Juvenile Court Statistics 2006–2007,* p. 77.

121 Shubik, "What Social Science Tells Us," pp. 19–20, 22.

122 Ibid., p. 29.

123 Urbina, I. (2010, October 26). "Recession Drives Surge in Youth Runaways." *New York Times.* Retrieved from http://www.nytimes.com/2009/10/26/us/26runaway.html?_r=1&hp

124 Swaim, F. F. and B. A. Bracken (1997). "Global and Domain-Specific Self-Concepts of a Matched Sample of Adolescent Runaways and Nonrunaways." *Journal of Clinical and Child Psychology* 26: 397–403.

[125] Smith, T. J. (2010) "Preadjudication Strategies for Defending Juveniles in Status Offense Proceedings," pp. 69, 70. In Inada and Chiamulera, *Representing Juvenile Status Offenders*, pp. 59–76.

[126] Ibid.

[127] Shubik, "What Social Science Tells Us," p. 31.

[128] Smith, "Preadjudication Strategies," p. 69.

[129] Gill, T. (2008). "We Don't Need No Supervision." *Ode Magazine* (UK), Jan.–Feb. Retrieved from http://www.odemagazine.com/doc/50/we-dont-need-no-supervision/

YOUTH GANGS

Youths have formed groups (usually with their own age cohorts) from the beginning of time. Some of these groups have committed various kinds of harmful activities, including crimes. Some of these groups have been called "gangs"; many have been labeled with other negative terms such as "rowdies," "bad kids," "troublemakers," "punks," or "hoodlums."

A Brief History

Youth groups known as "gangs" are not recent inventions of U.S. society. Such groups have existed since at least the fourteenth and fifteenth centuries in Europe, possibly much earlier. For instance, Mike Davis notes that gangs were a prominent feature of early Roman society.[1] Descriptions of life in England in the 1700s included references to gangs committing various forms of theft and robbery, along with extortion and rape.[2] One report noted that citizens in London were

> terrorized by a series of organized gangs calling themselves the Mims, Hectors, Bugles, Dead Boys . . . who found amusement in breaking windows, demolishing taverns, assaulting the watch . . . The gangs also fought pitched battles among themselves dressed with colored ribbons to distinguish the different factions.[3]

In France during the Middle Ages, there were groups of youths who fought with rival groups from other areas and schools, and who committed a variety of crimes. Youth gangs or groups reportedly existed in Germany during the seventeenth and eighteenth centuries.[4]

Deviant youth groups (and no one knows for certain the extent to which these groups were referred to as gangs) did not exist in any large number in the United States until the nineteenth century. An early study by the Illinois State Police noted that a gang called the Forty Thieves was founded in New York around 1820; this is believed to be the first youth gang in the United States.[5] A study of articles in a Philadelphia newspaper from 1836 to 1878 found information on 52 different gangs and reports that Philadelphia was "plagued" by gangs during the pre-Civil War era. The *New York Tribune* reported that the northern suburbs of Philadelphia during the years 1849 and 1850 were crawling with loafers who "herd together in squads" defacing property. Irving Spergel estimates that in New York City in 1855 there were "30,000 men who owed allegiance to gang leaders and through them to the political leaders of Tammany Hall and the Know Nothings or Native American Party."[6] With the rapid expansion of the capitalist system following the Civil War, some citizens in cities such as Philadelphia and New York expressed a concern about the problem of delinquency in general and gangs in particular. Herbert Asbury wrote about various youth gangs in and around the Five Points area of New York City in the late 1800s. Among the most famous gangs were the Plug-Uglies, Dusters, Bowery Boys, Roach Guards, Shirt Tails, and Kerryonians.[7]

Public concern about gangs was reinvented during the 1980s and continues today. The escalation of media presentations about youth gangs—particularly those gangs located in inner cities—has raised the public's level of fear about youth gangs. Gangs were a hot topic in the media with the amount of coverage increasing tremendously until 1996. Richard McCorkle and Terance Miethe note that during the 1980s:

> Newspapers, television, and films were suddenly awash with images of gun-toting, drug-dealing, hat-to-the-back gangstas. With the hue-and-cry came a massive mobilization of resources. Federal, state, and local funds were allocated to create anti-gang units in law enforcement and prosecution agencies.[8]

The rapid deployment of technology and databases augmented the proliferation of gang "experts" (typically police officers or former gang members). The alarm was sounded that gangs were everywhere. "In public schools across the country, gang awareness and resistance techniques were incorporated into the curriculum, gang-related clothing was banned from campuses, and teachers instructed on how to identify gang members and spot concealed weapons."[9]

A search of a database that accesses the files of major newspapers and magazines substantiated the growth in media coverage. The number of articles on the subject of gangs between 1983 and 2002 increased from 33 references in 1983 to more than 1,300 in 1996; media coverage then decreased. In 1996 there were an average of 3.6 stories per day compared to 1.5 items per day in 2002. A detailed study of the role of the media in Nevada (specifically in the two largest cities, Las Vegas and Reno) showed a similar pattern.[10] Researchers who studied news reports on gangs in the *Dallas Morning News* from January 1991 to December 1996 noted that one theme stood: "no longer could anyone be considered safe from the violence of street gangs."[11] This is similar to the more general theme of violence in the media that reproduces the idea that "it can happen anywhere" (as noted in chapter 1).

Media coverage continues; the National Gang Center website offered access to 14,242 articles from each state and all the provinces in Canada written between March 12, 2003, and May 16, 2011.[12] Media coverage of most major topics rarely conforms to the importance of an issue to the community; instead, it conforms to the need for profits. There is abundant research showing that the media portray a reality according to the perceptions of groups in power who control the media.[13] One of the major roles of the corporate-dominated media is to divert the public's attention away from real problems and to keep them entertained.[14]

More often than not, the media totally ignore the surrounding social context of issues like gangs. Debra Seagal's research about a prime-time television "real crime" show (videotapes of real police arrests) illustrates this problem. Seagal discusses how focusing on individual criminals diverts our attention away from the social context of crime and communicates the idea that these offenders exist in a social vacuum.

> By the time our 9 million viewers flip on their tubes, we've reduced fifty or sixty hours of mundane and compromising video into short, action-packed segments of tantalizing, crack-filled, dope-dealing, junkie-busting, cop culture. How easily we downplay the pathos of the suspect; how cleverly we breeze past the complexities that cast doubt on the very system that has produced the criminal activity in the first place.[15]

Gangs have become somewhat permanent institutions of large urban areas with a heavy concentration of the poor and racial minorities. Youth gangs exist, in some form, in all 50 states.[16] As Émile Durkheim once proposed, there is a certain inevitability of crime.[17] So too there will probably always be some groups in society that will be labeled "gangs." Gang members come from an array of economic and ethnic backgrounds (for example, African American, Asian, Latino, and a multiplicity of European ethnic groups). Each of these ethnic groups, at various junctures in history, has been viewed as representing a threat to the existing order. Gang behavior has habitually been portrayed as destructive and/or violent.

Violence and crime are not the innovations of contemporary youth gangs. Substantive attributes of youth gangs have not changed significantly since the early part of the twentieth century.[18] However, gangs have taken advantage of modern technological advancements (the abundance of automatic weapons), become more willing to expand their business-venture options (drug dealing), and increased their level of violence to protect their interests (drive-by shootings). These changes in gang activities parallel economic, social, and technological transformations that shape social change in the greater society (for example, declining employment opportunities, widespread acceptance of violence promoted by the mass media, social fascination with draconian modes of punishment, and the development and sanitized/impersonal use of high-tech war machinery). Gangs are also an adaptation to "racial and ethnic oppression, as well as poverty and slums, and are reactions of despair to persisting inequality."[19]

Fifty years ago, membership in gangs was a transitory experience of recent immigrant groups. Most members eventually matured out of the gangs and settled down to jobs and families. Recent studies indicate that this is no longer the case. More and more gang members remain within the gang well into their adult years because there are few opportunities for well-paying jobs. Virtually all the research within the past 20 years documents the fact that gangs have become a more permanent part of the underclass of marginalized minority youth.[20] During a follow-up study of the original 47 gang founders in Milwaukee, John Hagedorn found that over 80% of them were still involved in the gang despite having reached their mid-20s, an age when previously most members would have matured out of the gang.[21] A report from the Royal Canadian Mounted Police notes that ages of gang members ranges from 8 to 50 and older.[22] Although adult gang members are now more common, youths typically do not stay with gangs for very long. A detailed study in Rochester, New York found that membership in a gang was a rather brief experience for most of these youth. Half of the males were in a gang 1 year or less, while two-thirds of the females were in a gang for 1 year or less.[23]

What Is a Gang?

What exactly constitutes a gang or gang membership? If four youths are standing on a street corner or are simply walking down the street, are they a gang? If these same youths hang out together frequently and occasionally engage in some form of deviant activity, are they gang members? Suppose this same group invents a name for itself and even purchases special shirts or jackets and invents slogans or hand-signs—does this mean it is a gang? If a young person is seen giving special hand signals or heard uttering gang phrases because he thinks it is cool or hip to do so (whether he fully understands the implications or not), should he be considered a gang member? Or, if a youth lives in a neighborhood that has an established gang (but no one in the gang considers him a member) and is passing the time on a street corner with a gang member he has known for several years, will the police officer who decides to question the group fill out a field investigation card on him? Should he be counted as a gang member? How does race enter into the picture of defining gangs? We suspect that the average white citizen (and many police officers) would respond to a group of three or four white youths differently than they would to a group of three or four African-American teenagers hanging out together (for example, at a shopping mall). Perhaps this is one reason why most official estimates of gangs and gang members tell us that less than 10% are white, and the majority of gang members are African American or some other minority group (usually Hispanic). These few examples illustrate the difficulty in defining gangs and gang members.

The term *gang* can have many different definitions. Gil Geis has provided one of the most interesting comments about the etymology of the term, noting that the early English usage of *gang* was "a going, a walking, or a journey."[24] The definition given by the Random House College Dictionary provides similar meanings of a positive or neutral nature, such as "a group or band," "a group of persons who gather together for social reasons," "a group of persons working together; squad; shift; *a gang of laborers*," along with the more negative meanings. The thesaurus of the WordPerfect program used to type these words gives such synonyms as "pack," "group," "company," and "team."

Not surprisingly, there has existed little consensus among social scientists and law-enforcement personnel as to what these terms mean. One writer defined gangs as "groups whose members meet together with some regularity, over time, on the basis of group-defined criteria of membership and group-defined organization."[25] Researchers have often used a police definition of the term. Many researchers have apparently confused the term *group* with the term *gang* and have proceeded to expand the definition in such a way as to include every group of youths who commit offenses together. One of the most accepted definitions comes from Malcolm Klein, who has studied gangs for more than thirty years:

> [A gang is] any denotable . . . group [of adolescents or young adults] who (a) are generally perceived as a distinct aggregation by others in their neighborhood, (b) recognize themselves as a denotable group (almost invariably with a group name), and (c) have been involved in a sufficient number of [illegal] incidents to call forth a consistent negative response from neighborhood residents and/or enforcement agencies.[26]

The most recent survey by the National Gang Center finds a general consensus on the following elements in defining a gang:[27]

- The group has three or more members, generally aged 12–24.
- Members share an identity, typically linked to a name, and often other symbols.
- Members view themselves as a gang, and they are recognized by others as a gang.
- The group has some permanence and a degree of organization.
- The group is involved in an elevated level of criminal activity.

The National Gang Center adds: "In general, law enforcement agencies report that group criminality is of greatest importance and the presence of leadership is of least importance in defining a gang."[28] Omitted from this definition were such groups as motorcycle gangs, hate/ideology groups, prison gangs, and "exclusively adult gangs."

The dominant law-enforcement perspective is that gangs are essentially criminal conspiracies with a few hard-core members (often described as sociopaths) and that arrest and imprisonment of these individuals are required as a viable social policy. One example is the California Penal Code (the Street Terrorism Enforcement and Prevention Act passed in 1988), which defines a criminal street gang as

> any ongoing organization, association, or group of three or more persons, whether formal or informal, having as one of its primary activities the commission of [specific criminal acts] . . . having a common name or common identifying sign or symbol, and whose members individually or collectively engage in or have engaged in a pattern of criminal gang activity. . . . In order to secure a conviction, or sustain a juvenile petition, pursuant to subdivision (a), it is not necessary for the prosecution to prove that the person devotes all, or a substantial part of his or her time or efforts to the criminal street gang,

nor is it necessary to prove that the person is a member of the criminal street gang. Active participation in the criminal street gang is all that is required.[29]

Many states use almost identical wording in their definitions of "criminal gangs." Other researchers distinguish between the terms *gang, street gang, traditional youth gang*, and *posse/crew*. A *gang* is

> a group or collectivity of persons with a common identity who interact in cliques or sometimes as a whole group on a fairly regular basis and whose activities the community may view in varying degrees as legitimate, illegitimate, criminal, or some combination thereof. What distinguishes the gang from other groups is its communal or fraternal, different, or special interstitial character.[30]

In contrast, *street gang* is "a group or collectivity of persons engaged in significant illegitimate or criminal activities, mainly threatening and violent." The emphasis is placed on the location of the gang and their gang-related activities. The *traditional youth gang*

> refers to a youth or adolescent gang and often to the youth sector of a street gang. Such a group is concerned primarily with issues of status, prestige, and turf protection. The youth gang may have a name and a location, be relatively well organized, and persist over time. [They] often have leadership structure (implicit or explicit), codes of conduct, colors, special dress, signs, symbols, and the like. [They] may vary across time in characteristics of age, gender, community, race/ethnicity, or generation, as well as in scope and nature of delinquent or criminal activities.[31]

Still another variation is the *posse* or *crew*, which, while often used in conjunction with the terms *street* or *youth gang*, is more commonly "characterized by a commitment to criminal activity for economic gain, particularly drug trafficking."[32]

Researchers have also distinguished between *delinquent groups* and *criminal organizations*. The former are far less organized and criminal than the gangs defined previously and do not have distinctive dress, colors, signs, and so on. The latter refers more to a relatively well-organized and sophisticated group of either youths or adults (often a combination of both) organized mainly around the illegal pursuit of economic gain. Finally, there are gang *cliques* or *sets* that are often smaller versions (or subgroups) of larger gangs, usually based on age.[33]

Ronald Huff distinguishes between gangs and organized crime. *Youth gangs* historically were largely groups of adolescents (mostly male) who engaged in a variety of deviant activities, especially turf battles and gang fights. Now they are increasingly involved in major crimes, especially those that are violent or drug related. *Organized crime* meant *adult* criminal enterprises operating businesses. Today such organized activities characterize many youth gangs. Huff defines a *youth gang* as a

> collectivity consisting primarily of adolescents and young adults who (a) interact frequently with one another; (b) are frequently and deliberately involved in illegal activities; (c) share a common collective identity that is usually, but not always, expressed through a gang name; and (d) typically

express that identity by adopting certain symbols and/or claiming control over certain "turf" (persons, places, things, and/or economic markets).[34]

He defines an organized crime group as a

> collectivity consisting primarily of adults who (a) interact frequently with one another; (b) are frequently and deliberately involved in illegal activities directed toward economic gain, primarily through the provision of illegal goods and services; and (c) generally have better defined leadership and organizational structure than does the youth gang.[35]

There are several key differences between these two groups. First, they differ significantly in terms of age, with youth gangs being much younger than organized crime groups. Second, whereas the organized crime group exists almost exclusively for the purpose of economic criminal activity, youth gangs engage in a variety of both legal and illegal activities, with their illegal activities usually committed by individuals or small groups of individuals, rather than by the entire group.

It is obvious that the majority of the definitions of gangs focus almost exclusively on delinquent or criminal behavior as the distinguishing feature that differentiates gangs from other groups. This is consistent with a strictly law enforcement perspective. Several researchers disagree and argue that gangs should not be defined as purely criminal or delinquent organizations. Huff regards group experience as a normative component in youth subculture. "In analyzing youth gangs, it is important to acknowledge that it is normal and healthy for adolescents to want to be with their peers. In fact, adolescents who are loners often tend to be maladjusted."[36] Hagedorn believes that gangs are not merely criminal enterprises or bureaucratic entities with formal organizational structures. Rather, as other researchers have noted, gangs are age-graded groups or cliques "with considerable variation within each age group of friends."[37] More recently Hagedorn has argued that gangs "are not stable, clearly defined entities. Today's youth gang might become a drug posse tomorrow or, in some places, even transform into an ethnic militia or a vigilante group the next day.[38]

It is difficult to conceive of gangs as purely criminal organizations. Most gang members spend the bulk of their time simply hanging out or engaging in other nondelinquent activities. Many researchers have spent a considerable amount of time (perhaps months) "waiting for something to happen."[39]

An equally difficult task is trying to determine what constitutes a *gang-related offense*. If a gang member kills another gang member in retaliation for the killing of a fellow gang member, few would argue over whether this would be gang related. However, what if a gang member is killed as a result of some sort of love triangle, or if a gang member is killed by someone not in a gang, or if a gang member kills someone while committing a robbery on his own? Decisions about these kinds of incidents must be made, and police officials have procedures for such reporting. However, as Malcolm Klein and Cheryl Maxson observe, such procedures are conducted "not always according to reliable criteria, not always with adequate information regarding the motive or circumstances of the crime, not always with extensive gang-membership information on file, and *most clearly*—not by the same criteria from city to city."[40]

Klein and Maxson reviewed reporting procedures in five cities and found that each city had somewhat different methods for defining gang-related incidents. For example, in two cities, only violent incidents were counted. In one city the policy was to include only gang-on-gang crimes, but the authors found that robberies where the offenders (but not the victims) were gang members constituted gang-related crimes. In another city any offense committed by a gang member was counted as gang related.[41]

A police official in Chicago expressed the following common view: "'Gang-related' simply means that the offender or victim has gang ties, either self-admitted or distinguishing tattoos."[42] The Los Angeles Police Department maintains a website providing a citywide gang crime summary that lists gang statistics by month without providing a definition or a way to distinguish these crimes from crimes that are not gang related.[43] The National Gang Center states: "Larger cities were most likely to indicate regularly recording *any* [emphasis added] criminal offenses as "gang-related," although more than one-third reported not doing so in 2006. Of the other three categories of agencies, approximately half reported regularly recording any criminal offenses as "gang-related."[44]

How Many Gangs and Gang Members Are There?

Gangs exist in all cities with populations of 100,000 or more, as well as in federal and state prison systems and most juvenile correctional systems. Gangs are found within almost every major urban high school in the United States.[45] Gang activity inside schools, however, fluctuates quite a bit. For example, one study noted that between 1995 and 1999 gang activity within schools declined and that the claim of high rates of gang activity within schools is highly exaggerated.[46] In January 2010 state lawmakers in Washington were debating how to deal with gangs in schools. A department of health survey conducted by the state reported that 25,000 students responded that they were "gang members or affiliated with a gang." Lost in the concern to do something about the gang problem was that there were about 1 million students in the school system at that time—2.5% of all students admitting being a gang member or "affiliated" with a gang. A Washington legislator introduced two bills aimed at suppressing gangs. One defined the circumstances under which schools could suspend or expel students who engage in gang activity or hate crimes on school grounds. It would also allow schools to reject a student who had a record of gang involvement to transfer from another district. As noted above, the sticking point is that there is no clearly defined way to define gang involvement. A task force that researched the rise in gang activity at Washington schools in 2009 had noted: "Despite research and years of experience that demonstrates the relative ineffectiveness of suppression as a long-term solution to gangs, programs designed to reduce gang activity in this country and our state lean heavily toward police suppression."[47] The proposed legislation was a reaction to a problem that has been exaggerated by the media. Rather than helping to prevent a problem, it would be far more likely to introduce other problems, including profiling of students for expulsion.

Exactly how many gangs and how many gang members there are in the country is not known with any degree of certainty. In fact, there are as many estimates as there are estimators![48] In the 1920s Frederic Thrasher estimated that there were 1,313 gangs in Chicago alone.[49] Walter Miller's nationwide survey in the 1970s estimated anywhere from 700 to almost 3,000 gangs in the largest cities in the country.[50] Estimates come almost exclusively from law enforcement sources. Until 1997, the estimated numbers showed yearly increases. During those years the amount of money going to police departments increased as well, in addition to the number of "gang units" and police officers assigned to these units. As noted earlier, in virtually every survey in recent years the definition of "gang" and "gang member" has been left entirely up to the reporting law enforcement agencies. This enables local criminal justice agencies to vary their estimates depending on their goals. Some provide conservative estimates to preserve a safe image of their city or to promote tourism, while others exaggerate the numbers to obtain more funding.

In 2008 there were an estimated 27,900 gangs and approximately 774,000 gang members. The number of gangs increased 28% since 2002, and the number of gang members increased 6%. The estimated number of gang members had decreased 14% between 1996 and 2002.[51] Gangs have also become common in schools, which sometimes serve as a gathering place for gangs. More than one-third (37%) of a nationally representative sample of students reported gang presence in their schools in 1995, a 100% increase over 1989.[52] Small cities had the largest proportion of gangs with mixed race/ethnicity and included more females, Caucasians, and younger members than gangs in larger cities.[53]

In the late 1970s, the Los Angeles Police Department created specialized anti-gang units called CRASH—Community Resources Against Street Hoodlums. These units were eventually assigned to each police division, including the Rampart division, which covers almost 8 square miles just west of downtown Los Angeles. It is the city's most densely populated community and has a heavily immigrant and transient population of about 300,000. The community had a history of high crime rates; by the mid-1980s, it was the city's most violent community. In addition to CRASH units, the city instituted a controversial tool to fight street gangs—gang injunctions. The injunctions prohibited named gang members from congregating or carrying pagers within certain geographic boundaries. Sworn statements from police officers—usually officers in CRASH units—identified the gang members targeted for injunction. CRASH officers enjoyed a great deal of discretion, and many abused their powers. The Rampart corruption scandal involved officers making false arrests, extorting money from drug dealers, giving perjured testimony, and falsely accusing many individuals of being "gang members." In March 2000 the CRASH units were disbanded (replaced by Special Enforcement Units). The Rampart scandal casts doubt on the authenticity of the gang data for Los Angeles. For example, of the alleged 112,000 gang members in Los Angeles County, 62,000 of them had been identified by a disbanded CRASH unit. Police officials and police gang "experts" claimed that the data were accurate, but this is a dubious claim. At least 100 convictions of "gang" members have been overturned, and 20 officers have been fired or have quit.[54]

The percentage of youths who self-report being in a gang or engaging in gang-related behavior has not changed significantly during the past two decades. Typically, no more than 10 to 15% of all youths report being in a gang (and this estimate includes areas with a high rate of crime and gang membership). According to the 1997 National Longitudinal Survey of Youth (unfortunately, the latest survey available) only 8% of a representative sample of 9,000 youths between the ages of 12 and 16 had belonged to a gang by age 17.[55] In cities with a higher number of gangs, the percentage increased to 11 for current gang members and to 17% for those reporting having been gang members at one point in their lives.[56]

A word of caution is in order. In must be stressed that the numbers coming from law enforcement sources should be treated with some skepticism since there is no way to verify them independently. Field researchers emphasize that local politics shape gang intelligence and record-keeping on gangs in law enforcement agencies. The National Youth Gang Center cautions that gang problems can be exaggerated or denied in law enforcement reporting depending on local political considerations. Other researchers have noted that official data on gangs more often reflect "the organization of social control agencies than empirical realities about gang membership or gangs," and police data "provide rather subjective assessments of gang behavior."[57] The Justice Policy Institute observes:

> It is difficult to find a law enforcement account of gang activity that does not give the impression that the problem is getting worse by the day. . . . The most comprehensive survey of law enforcement data on gang activity shows no significant changes in estimated gang membership or the prevalence of gang activity—both of which are down significantly since the late 1990s. Further, law enforcement depictions of the gang population are sharply at odds with youth survey data when it comes to the geography of gang activity as well as the race and gender of gang members."[58]

Gangs and Crime

There is some evidence that gang members commit a disproportionate amount of crime, especially violent crime. It is quite probable that this aspect of the problem is exaggerated, since violence captures the public imagination and makes the headlines. Also, the violence is heavily concentrated within certain neighborhoods in large cities. If we consider an entire city or county, we find that gang members do not contribute significantly to the overall crime problem. In Chicago, for instance, it was estimated that gang crime constituted less than 1% of all index crimes between 1986 and 1988.[59] More recent estimates suggest the same, although in certain neighborhoods gangs contribute to the overall crime problem.[60] A large-scale study (the Rochester Youth Development Study) of 1000 youths (both gang and non-gang members) found that gang members committed a great deal more crime than their non-gang counterparts. Moreover, the longer they remained in the gang, the greater the prevalence of criminal activity.[61] Most of the offenses committed by gang members continue to be property crimes (often committed by gang members independently, rather than as part of an organized gang activity).

Between 1993 and 2003, victims in rural areas perceived that about 5.9% of those who committed a violent crime against them were gang members; in urban settings the percentage was 8.6%; in suburban areas, the percentage was 7.3%.[62] The victims believed that gang members were involved in 12% of aggravated assaults, 4% of the rapes, 10% of the robberies and 6% of the simple assaults. The FBI's supplementary homicide reports indicated from 5% to 7% of all homicides and from 8% to 10% of homicides committed with a firearm were gang related. In Rochester, New York, self-reports revealed that gang members committed 68% of all adolescent violent offenses, while in Denver, gang members committed 79% of all serious violent adolescent offenses; in Seattle, gang members committed about 85% of teenage robberies.[63]

The stereotype of the gang member and the gang revolves around criminal activity—a characterization perpetuated by both the media and the police (recall the discussion above about recording any crime as "gang related").[64] In the case of the media, this is no doubt because the daily activities of the typical gang member are rather boring and hence not newsworthy. As for the police, their historic role in society is to catch people who have committed crime. Because of this role, information from the police about gangs (printed up and handed out at literally hundreds of "gang workshops" throughout any given year) focuses almost exclusively on the criminal activities of gangs and methods of identifying gang members (e.g., graffiti, dress styles, hand signals, gang slang) in order to help officers make arrests or engage in "proactive policing" (i.e., keeping tabs on gang members). It is important to keep this in mind as we discuss the various crimes committed by gang members. Most gang members spend their time doing the things—sleeping, eating, going to school, "hanging out," etc.—that occupy the time of adolescents everywhere.

The criminal activities of gangs vary according to the type of gang, with some committing little crime and others heavily involved in criminal activity. Overall, the typical crimes committed by gangs have consistently been a "garden variety" or "cafeteria style" of offenses (for example, burglaries, petty theft, vandalism, fighting, and truancy). The major victims of gang violence are other gang members. Innocent bystanders are rarely the victims, despite claims from law enforcement and other officials to the contrary.[65] However, it is true that certain periods of time are marked by a sharp rise in gang violence and innocents are killed. Such was the case in Los Angeles during the late 1980s and early 1990s. One study focused on the time period from 1989 to 1993 and found that almost half (47%) of those "shot at" and 23% of actual victims of homicide were innocent bystanders.[66] If an innocent bystander is killed by a gang member, the media report the tragedy in a highly sensational manner.[67] Sometimes a report does not mention that violence against a victim was gang related but the audience, conditioned by previous shocking reports, assumes it was.[68]

The study by McCorkle and Miethe mentioned earlier sheds further light on the subject. Examining court records in Las Vegas, Nevada, for the years 1989 through 1995, they discovered that the proportion of defendants charged with index crimes who were identified as gang members was quite low. For violent index crimes, for instance, the proportion who were gang members ranged from 2% to 6%. Gang members were most often involved in murder cases; yet in a typical year gang members were involved in about 15% of all homicides. As for property offenses, gang members constituted 2%–7% of the total; they were most likely to be involved in motor vehicle theft (ranging from 4% to 12%). The myth that gangs dominate the drug scene was shattered by this study, as the researchers found that gang members constituted 2%–8% of all felony drug defendants. These figures were in stark contrast to local media and law enforcement reports that gangs had "taken over" the drug market.[69]

In the most recent National Youth Gang Survey (NYGS) covering the period 2002-2007, more than half of the jurisdictions did not report a single gang-related homicide—this includes 77% of the rural counties and 80% of the smaller cities reporting gang problems.[70] Most gang-related homicides occur in larger cities.

> Excluding Chicago and Los Angeles (which, on average, have accounted for roughly one-quarter of all gang homicides recorded in the NYGS over the past seven years), gang homicides increased 8.5 percent in very large cities (with populations of 100,000 or more) from 2002 to 2008. To illustrate the difficulties associated with making generalizations about gang homicide trends, the annual number in Chicago increased 22.5 percent, while the annual number in Los Angeles decreased by 52.3 percent in the 7-year time frame.[71]

It should be emphasized that for most gangs the bulk of their time is *not* spent committing crimes. The gangs Hagedorn studied spent most of their time partying and hanging out.[72] Klein has observed that "For the most part, gang members do very little—sleep, get up late, hang around, brag a lot, eat again, drink, hang around some more."[73] Klein notes that it is a rather boring life and in fact "the only thing that is equally boring is being a researcher watching gang members." When gang members hang out, it is usually by a park, by a taco stand, and they are "smoking, drinking, roughhousing, playing a pickup ball game, messing with a few girls, or sauntering up a street in a possessive, get-outta-our-way fashion."[74] When they do get involved in crime, it is either fighting (mostly with other gangs) or hustling, which includes petty theft and drug sales. Drugs will be discussed in a later section, but it should be noted here that, as Hagedorn found for Milwaukee gangs, selling drugs "for most gang members is just another low-paying job—one that might guarantee 'survival,' but not much else."[75] The minimal amount of violence actually engaged in by gangs has been corroborated by other studies. Property crimes remain the major type of offense committed by gangs.[76] A more recent study found that aside from just "hanging out," the consumption of alcohol was the most common activity of gang members.[77]

The commission of crime is rarely an activity in which the entire gang participates; rather, it is usually committed by a small group of gang members. The gang does not condone such activity. In fact, most gangs discourage it. Moreover, "the crimes themselves are not committed on behalf of the gang, nor are proceeds shared. The individuals (or groups, which may include non-gang members as well as homeboys) who commit such crimes do so for their own reasons and by their own rules—and that includes drug dealing."[78] This fact is extremely important. It contradicts the theory underlying most gang-enhancement statutes, which increase the punishment if the crime is gang related. The implication of such statutes is crimes classified as gang related are committed on behalf of the gang.

Gang and Gang Member Typologies

Gangs and gang members can be differentiated by multiple criteria including: age, race or ethnicity, gender, setting, type of activity, purpose of the gang activity, degree of criminality, level of organization, and group function.[79] Remember that much of the terminology used to discuss gangs is the invention of outside observers, and the terms applied can be influenced by the backgrounds of those observing.

Klein found that a number of police gang experts he surveyed knew little about the structural nature of the gangs in their cities. "Because they were concentrating on crime patterns and investigative issues, they found little relevance in the forms that their gangs took."[80] In his call for more careful research on gang structures, Klein commented, "What struck me in these conversations with the officers was that the terminology was far more varied than the substance to which it was being applied. . . . Officials are applying self-satisfying terms to arbitrary distinctions." Klein also cautioned about the terminology applied to gang members. "The dismaying array of terms makes it clear that consensus is not a feature of the current American police knowledge of gangs."[81]

Most gangs are rather loosely structured groups who "come together for periods of weeks, months, or as long as a year, but then disintegrate."[82] One of the more stable types is the traditional area gang, often described as a vertical organization because of its age-graded structure of cliques within the group. Characterized by a common territory, these gangs are typically all-male (often with female auxiliary groups) ethnic minorities (usually African American and Hispanic, but often Asian).

Another variation is the horizontally organized groups in which divisions cut across different neighborhoods and include youths in different age brackets. Many have spread across cities, states, and even countries. Often they are referred to as supergangs and nations. Examples of these horizontal alliances include the Crips and Bloods (who started in Los Angeles) and the People and

Folks (starting in Illinois). It should be emphasized that these large groupings often consist of gangs with very little in common with one another, other than their name. To a gang member, the particular *set* or neighborhood of origin is of prime importance. "See, 'Crip' doesn't mean nothin' to a membership. Like 'I'm a Crip, you're a Crip—so what? What set are you from? What neighborhood are you from? What street do you live on? I may live on Sixty-ninth, he may live on Seventieth.'"[83]

Small groups clustered by age or friendship are the basic building blocks of gangs. Gangs are loosely organized into small age/friendship cohorts or cliques. Age groupings vary by location and time frame. In the early 1960s in New York City, age divisions included Tots (11 to 13 years of age), Juniors (13 to 15 years of age), Tims (15 to 17 years of age), and Seniors (17 and older). By the 1970s the most common groupings in New York included the Baby Spades (9 to 12 years), the Young Spades (12 to 15 years old), and the Black Spades (16 to 30 years of age). In Philadelphia the age groupings were identified as: Bottom-Level Midgets (12 to 14 years), Middle-Level Young Boys (14 to 17), and Upper-Level Old Heads (18 to 23 years old). Members of gangs are often further categorized by levels of participation. Hard-core, confirmed members spend more time with the gang than fringe, associates, marginals, and wannabes. The latter group is normally composed of the very young (usually 12 or younger).[84] In Los Angeles, barrios sometimes have at least two or three cohorts defined by age and status: 12–16-year-olds who are just getting into the gang; 14–18-year-olds who are somewhat proven gang members; and 18–20-year olds who are seasoned. Diego Vigil notes: "This age grading, with its informal and formal processes of socialization and enculturation, ensures that the barrio gang always has a new clique to take over the duties of defending the turf."[85]

Leadership in gangs can best be described as a shifting, elusive target, permeable and elastic, and thus inherently resistant to outside intervention. It presents not a cohesive force but, rather, a sponge-like resilience."[86] Gang leadership is usually divided among a number of members depending on the type of activity. "Gang leadership is functional, not positional. It exists more, and less, because of its context."[87] If the gang is involved in protecting its turf, the leader will be someone who is cool under pressure and has the skills required for protection. If the gang needs a spokesperson, the leader will be someone with good verbal skills. If the gang is involved in an athletic contest, the leader will be someone who can manage the team and is respected by other members. Leadership is also a function of time and the availability of members. Members could be incarcerated; as time passes members could get married or be unavailable because of work. The stereotype of the gang leader is someone who is tough, with a long criminal history, and a strong influence over the members. In actuality, the typical leader does not maintain influence over a long period of time for the reasons described above. The belief that to eliminate the gang all you need to do is "cut off the head" and the rest will die off is based on incorrect stereotypes. Gangs with centralized authority are probably a small minority, but they fit a convenient stereotype. As Klein noted:

One possible reason that gangs with centralized authority are seen as more prevalent is that they appear to be more amenable to methods of gang control frequently advocated by the police and the courts. If one attributes crime by gang members primarily to the presence and influence of a single strong leader (key-personality model), all one has to do is to locate and remove that leader to curb or eliminate crime.[88]

The reality is that if one gang leader is removed, there will be someone else to fill the needed function.

One of the most important distinguishing features of gangs has been territory or *turf*. However, there have been changes. Klein's most recent research notes that most cities surveyed reported the existence of "single or autonomous gangs." These are gangs that occupy smaller territories than was once the pattern. Examples include single blocks, a school, the "projects," etc. These gangs tend to have shorter histories, fewer ties to neighborhoods or "barrios," and to be less cohesive than the more traditional gangs. Klein also describes "geographically connected gangs." These are "branches" of another gang located in a neighboring territory or sharing an affiliation but residing in totally separate geographical areas.[89] The declining importance of turf for some gangs could be a function of growing sophistication and the increasing use of the automobile.

Turf or neighborhood remains of critical importance to the more traditional gangs. In many areas, especially in Los Angeles, the term *gang* is often synonymous with *barrio* or *neighborhood*.[90] The notion of turf centers around two important ideas—identification and control—with control being the most important. There are three primary types of turf rights. The first is basic ownership rights; the gang "owns" a particular area and attempts to control practically everything that occurs there. The second is occupancy rights; different gangs share an area or tolerate one another's use. The third is enterprise monopoly; one gang controls certain criminal activities within a specified area.[91] Contested areas between gangs can consist of actual territory involving homes and family or "symbolic space or 'turf' that must be defended from pecuniary intruders."[92] Disputes over market space are somewhat recent developments.

When categorizing gangs, there are two prevalent methods: types of *gangs* and types of gang *members*. More than a dozen types of gangs have been identified, and about an equal number of categories of gang *members*. This coincides with a point made previously; namely, there are a variety of adolescent groups existing at any one time. In fact, the adolescent subculture is famous for the infinite variety of groupings.[93]

It should be noted at the outset that the following typologies should be considered as *ideal types*, to use Max Weber's famous concept.[94] Ideal types are used frequently by researchers in all fields of study to organize a vast array of research findings. Ideal types do not necessarily reflect reality in that there are no "pure" types of anything (e.g., no person is a pure "authoritarian personality" type; there are no pure democracies). What normally happens is that the researcher suggests that a phenomenon *tends to fit into one or another type*. For instance, using "democracy" as an ideal type, a researcher can compare different political systems in terms of the extent to which they are "democratic," realizing that there will be no perfect "democracy." Or, to use gangs as an example, there may not be a pure "hard-core" gang member nor a pure "predatory" gang, but a particular individual may come close to the pure type of "hard core" but also have certain characteristics that could place him in the category of "peripheral" member. Similarly, a specific gang could be characterized as "predatory" despite having some characteristics of a "territorial" gang. However, it would show more "predatory" tendencies than other gangs, and the territorial characteristics would be less defining.

The most commonly used criteria to classify types of gangs are behavioral characteristics, especially deviant and/or criminal behavior, although certain nondeviant or traditional group behaviors are also factors. Research in six different cities by three different researchers identified the following major types of gangs.[95]

Types of Gangs

1. *Hedonistic/social* gangs. With only moderate drug use and offending, these gangs like having a good time, use drugs to get high, and have little involvement in crime, especially violent crime.

2. *Party* gangs. These groups have relatively high use and sales of drugs but only one major form of delinquency (vandalism).

3. *Instrumental* gangs. The main criminal activity of these gangs is committing property crimes. Most members use drugs and alcohol but seldom engage in the selling of drugs.

4. *Predatory* gangs. These gangs are heavily involved in serious crimes (for example, robberies and muggings) and in the abuse of addictive drugs such as crack cocaine. Some may engage in the selling of drugs, although not in any organized fashion, and some have lower involvement in drug use and drug sales than the party gang.

5. *Scavenger* gangs. These loosely organized groups of youths are "urban survivors," preying on the weak in the inner cities, engaging in petty crimes (but sometimes violent) often just for fun. The members have no greater bond than their impulsiveness and the need to belong. They have no goals and are low achievers, often illiterate, with poor school performance.

6. *Serious delinquent* gangs. Although heavily involved in both serious and minor crimes, these gangs have much lower involvement in drug use and drug sales than the party gang.

7. *Territorial* gangs. Gangs associated with a specific area or turf and are often involved in conflicts with other gangs over their territories (see "barrio territorial" gangs below).

8. *Organized/corporate* gangs. Resembling major corporations, with separate divisions handling sales, marketing, discipline, and so on, these gangs

are heavily involved in all kinds of crime including sales of drugs. Discipline is strict, and promotion is based on merit; drug use is also heavy.

9. *Drug* gangs. These gangs are smaller than other gangs and focused on the drug business. They are much more cohesive with strong, centralized leadership.

Many prefer to use the all-inclusive term, *street gang*, to describe most of the above gangs (except for drug gangs).[96]

Types of Gang Members

The most common method of distinguishing types of gang *members* is based on the *degree of attachment to and involvement in the gang*. Think of a continuum running from very little attachment to complete involvement. The following gang *member* types have been identified by researchers.[97]

1. *Regulars/hard core*. These members are strongly attached to the gang, participate regularly, and have few interests outside of the gang (in other words, the gang is practically their whole life). Vigil describes these individuals as having "had a more problematic early life. They became street oriented earlier. They became gang members sooner, and they participated in the destructive patterns over a longer period of time."[98] These individuals also lacked a consistent male adult in their lives, which made the streets even more attractive as they began to emulate other gang members. For these persons, getting into the gang was seen as a rite of passage. They also began experimenting with drugs and engaging in street fighting at a much earlier age than other kinds of members. The small number of hard-core (or simply core) members of the gang are the most influential and active; they interact frequently and relate easily to one another, thriving on the gang's activity. Individuals in the inner clique are the key recruiters, make key decisions, and set standards.[99] Hard-core members are "the most gang-bound in terms of lifestyle. For these young men, life outside pretty much ceases to exist. They have few friends outside the gang and recognize no authority beyond its existence."[100]

2. *Peripheral* members. Also known as *associates*, these individuals have a strong attachment to the gang but participate less often than the regulars because they have other interests outside the gang. Although the peripheral member can be just as intense as a regular once he is in the gang, "his level of commitment is mediated less by a problematic early life and more by a life-turning event (for example, incarceration), which causes him to contemplate pursuing another lifestyle."[101] The *associates* are sometimes called *fringe* members. They may belong to the gang but are not considered part of the hard-core group. Using a fraternity analogy, these members are like those students who recently completed "hell week" and have just been initiated into the fraternity.

3. *Temporary* members. Marginally committed, these members join the gang at a later age than the regulars and peripherals; they remain in the

gang only a short period of time. This individual "is neither as intense nor as committed as the others and primarily associates with the gang during a certain phase of his development."[102]

4. *Situational* members. These members are very marginally attached and join the gang only for certain activities (avoiding the more violent activities whenever possible).

5. *At Risk*. These *pre-gang* youths are not really gang members. They do not yet belong to a gang but have shown some interest. They live in neighborhoods where gangs exist. They often fantasize about being members and also might have friends or relatives whom they admire who belong to the gang. Often they begin experimenting with certain gang attire and/or language. This may begin as early as the second grade.[103]

6. *Wannabe*. Gangs themselves use this term to describe "recruits," who are usually in their preteen years and know and admire gang members. They are perhaps one notch above the "at risk" youths in terms of commitment and involvement. They have already begun to emulate gang members in terms of dress, gang values, and so on. Such young people are mentally ready to join a gang and perhaps just need an invitation or opportunity to prove themselves in some way. They may be called *Pee Wees* or *Baby Homies*. An analogy may be made to freshmen college students aspiring to join fraternities. One researcher called this type an *emulator*.[104]

7. *Veteranos/O.G.s*. This group usually consists of men in their 20s or 30s (or even much older) who still participate in gang activities (sometimes referred to as *gang banging*). There are two major subtypes within this category. *Veteranos* have traditionally been regarded as elder statesmen who are somewhat retired but still command respect. The title is more honorable within Chicano gangs than African-American gangs. O.G.s are *original gangsters*. In African-American gangs, they are men who have earned respect through a combination of longevity and achievement. Often they are expected to teach younger members the ways of the gang and/or to straighten out younger members causing trouble within the gang. Sometimes they are literally the founding member or members of the gang.

8. *Auxiliary*. These members hold limited responsibility within a gang; this is a very common role for female members. These individuals do not participate in all gang activities. A related type is the *adjunct* member, who is a permanent part-time member by choice, often because of holding down a regular job.[105]

Gang Classifications

Gangs are most commonly characterized by ethnicity or race. After discussing an example of a supergang, we will look at the most frequent ethnic groupings (Chicano/Hispanic, Asian, African American, and White). Some gangs have united into "supergangs" to achieve certain uniform objectives (especially self-protection). Still others have simply been described as "gang nations" or "gang sets." Examples of the latter often include the famous (or infamous) Bloods and Crips that began in the Los Angeles area. The most popular terms for "gang nations" or "supergangs" are People and Folks, originating in Chicago in the 1970s.

The Supergangs of Chicago: People and Folks

This grouping actually began in the 1960s in Chicago when a "youth group" known as the Black P-Stone Rangers evolved into a criminal organization, largely through the efforts of Jeff Fort.[106] He eventually organized a group of about 50 gangs into one "nation" called the Black P-Stone Nation. The leaders (21 in all) described themselves in a more positive light, saying they were a "socially conscious, self-help organization that would help uplift themselves and their community." They were able to obtain $1.4 million in federal anti-poverty money, but the funds were used to finance their criminal enterprises. Eventually Fort was indicted by a federal grand jury, convicted, and sent to prison.

Shortly thereafter, two other Chicago gangs (Black Disciples and Gangster Disciples) combined to form the Black Gangster Disciple Nation. Throughout the decade of the 1970s these two groups—Black P-Stone Nation and Black Gangster Disciple Nation—fought over control of the illegal drug market in Chicago. Many from each nation ended up in prison. At the end of that decade, the informal alliances and rivalries merged to form two major supergangs (or nations) known as People and Folks.[107] Gangs that were originally part of the Black P-Stone Nation became aligned with the People Nation; those that were part of the Black Gangster Disciple Nation aligned with the Folk Nation.

Among the gangs aligned with People were: Black P-Stone, Latin Kings, Vicelords, Spanish Lords, El Rukns, Bishops, and the Gaylords. Gangs aligned with Folk included: Black Gangster Disciples, Black Disciples, Gangster Disciples, La Raza, Latin Disciples, and the Simon City Royals. The People Nation is often distinguished by the use of the 5-point crown.[108]

The Folk Nation is often associated with the 6-point star and pitchfork.

Even when aligned with a nation, individual gangs retained their own distinguishing characteristics, tattoos, and symbols (e.g., Vicelords use the top hat and cane).

According to the National Gang Intelligence Center, there were about 10,000 gangs in the city of Chicago in 2008. The most prominent gangs (and the estimated number of members) were: Gangster Disciples (6,000 to 8,000), Latin Kings (numbers in Chicago not given, but it was estimated that they and their sister gang Queen Nation had about 20,000 to 35,000 members in and "make up more than 160 structured chapters operating in 158 cities in 31 states"), Vice Lords (based in Chicago, they had an estimated 30,000 to 35,000 members in 74 cities in 28 states), and Black P. Stones (6,000 to 8,000 members mostly in the Chicago area).[109]

Chicano Gangs

Chicano gangs in Southern California have perhaps the longest history of any gangs in the United States; some have existed for over 70 years. The economic boom of the 1920s attracted thousands of primarily rural and poor Mexican immigrants to the area. They brought with them a tradition known as *palomilla* (Spanish for a covey of doves). Young men in a village would join together to form a coming-of-age cohort. In the Los Angeles area, the young men would identify with a particular neighborhood (barrio) or parish.

During the Depression, thousands of Mexican immigrants were repatriated, a process that had a very negative effect on the Mexican-American population. Many positive role models were deported, and those who remained felt unwanted. Thousands more left the neighborhoods when they were drafted for World War II. After the war, many returning veterans took advantage of GI benefits and purchased homes in the growing suburbs. The old neighborhoods suffered from racist policies and widespread discrimination.

On August 1, 1942, a murder at a party in East Los Angeles near a reservoir known as Sleepy Lagoon (frequented mostly by Mexican-American youths denied access to public recreation facilities) resulted in a violent clampdown by the police against Mexican-American young people. The police arrested 22 youths for conspiracy to commit murder; 17 were tried in *People v. Zammora*, which resulted in 5 being found guilty of assault and 12 guilty of murder.[110] Sensational press coverage included stereotypical descriptions of Chicano gangs. Police began periodic sweeps of gang areas, and white servicemen on leave began harassing youths dressed in zoot suits.[111] The violent clashes were known as the Zoot Suit riots of 1943. Mexican Americans who fought in the riots "were seen by their younger brothers as heroes of a race war."[112]

Two of the oldest gangs in East Los Angeles are White Fence and El Hoyo Maravilla. White Fence traces its beginnings to the 1930s as a sports group associated with a local church. The younger brothers and cousins of the original group started the gang in 1944 after most of the founders were drafted into World War II. By that time, there were already several established gangs in the area. White Fence was considered more violent than other gangs, probably because they challenged older boys from other gangs (such as the "Veteranos" from El Hoyo formed in 1933).[113]

In the Maravilla neighborhood there were several gangs, mostly named after streets (Arizona Maravilla, Kern Maravilla, Ford Maravilla, etc.). The first clique of El Hoyo was actively involved in sports and often competed with White Fence neighborhood kids. The early Hoyo gang was more like a modern gang than the original White Fence group. These were the "pachucos" or "zoot-suiters." Like the original White Fence group, World War II separated them and left many younger kids to carry on the tradition.[114]

By the late 1940s the gangs became permanent fixtures, essentially agents of socialization in the form of peer groups. An age-graded structure developed as the older members matured and broke with the gang, and younger kids formed their own cliques. For instance, the White Fence Monsters, formed in 1946, were followed by a gang called the Cherries in 1947, and then the Tinies in 1949. Later cliques went by such names as the Santos (1960–1963), Locos (and the girl branch of Las Locas, 1964–1968), Jokers (1970–present) and Cyclones (1973–present) The Veteranos in El Hoyo Maravilla were followed by the Cherries in 1939, the Jive Hounds in 1943, the Lil Cherries in 1945, the Cutdowns in 1946, the Midgets in 1950, and both the Lil Spiders and Winitos in 1974.[115]

Unlike the gangs Thrasher studied in the 1920s, Chicano gangs (particularly in Los Angeles) are not a transitory phenomena. They are based in neighborhoods where Chicanos have lived for several generations. These gangs are *Mexican American*, meaning that they have not assimilated into mainstream U.S. society as did the Europeans. Also, some Chicano gang members remain affiliated with their gang well into middle age.[116]

Vigil has written extensively on Chicano gangs in the barrio and notes a process of *choloization*.[117] Street gangs are the result of marginalization—the relegation of certain persons to the fringes of society, where social and economic conditions result in powerlessness.

> It is a process that begins with where people live and raise their families; what type of work and status they've attained; how place and status, in

turn, shape the patterns of parenting, schooling, and policing; and finally, the personal and group identities that emerge in this marginalized context. A broad linking and sequencing of these features show the additive and cumulative nature of the emergence of gangs and the generation of gang members.[118]

Various cultural changes and conflicts have made some Chicano youth especially vulnerable to becoming gang members. Vigil mentions several "stressors" in the barrios, including economic, social, cultural, psychological, and ecological. Those who suffer from more than one stressor constitute victims of what he terms *multiple marginality*; these youths are the most likely to become gang members.[119]

> The most multiply marginal youths are often the most unsupervised and reside in crowded housing conditions where private space is limited. These youngsters are driven into the public space of the streets where peers and teenaged males, with whom they must contend, dominate. . . . Thus, because of the situations (e.g. exposure only to run-down and spatially separate enclaves; lack of or limited access to and identity with dominant institutions; social and cultural conflicts between first- and second-generation family members; and so on) and *conditions* (e.g. inferior, crowded housing; low or inadequate income; and so on) many urban youths are compelled to seek the dynamics of the street.[120]

Joan Moore studied three major Chicano gangs in the Los Angeles area, finding evidence of some traditional sociological theories, especially those of Thrasher. She observes that: "The age-graded gang is one among many barrio structures in which boys play a role; it may be the only structure in which they play a reasonably autonomous role." She also notes that the Chicano subculture is more than just "machismo," as there is a sense of belongingness, a feeling of family. No wonder they refer to themselves as "homies" or "homeboys."[121] Family and community ties are most apparent among Chicano gangs. The individual gang member is expected to assist other gang members in times of need and to uphold the neighborhood gang name.

Moore, Vigil, and Robert Garcia divide Chicano gangs into two distinctive categories: institutionalized and noninstitutionalized. *Institutionalized* extensions of gang membership are intertwined with the Chicano traditions of kinship and alliance. Kinship is self-explanatory; alliance occurs when others "come to the rescue" or exhibit loyalty and an interest in friendship with gang members. Other categories include an expansion of boundaries (absorbing small nearby barrios) and the formation of branches (occurring when gang members move into new neighborhoods). *Noninstitutionalized* categories include family motives for moving out of the barrio, ecological displacement (making way for public improvements), and factional struggles within a particular group or *klika/clique*.[122]

It has been estimated that there are more than 500 Chicano gangs in Los Angeles County, constituting about half of all gangs in this area. They appear to be more geographically distributed throughout the region than other gangs.

They are found predominantly in the San Fernando Valley, San Gabriel Valley, Long Beach (and other beach communities), and in South Central Los Angeles.[123]

Most of these gangs do not identify with specific colors the way Bloods and Crips do. Black, white, brown, and tan are favored colors; Dickie pants and Pendleton shirts are popular attire. Some use red bandannas, which stand for North California Hispanic gang allegiance (signified by the notation *Norte 14* from the California prison subculture); others wear a blue bandanna, which stands for Southern California Hispanic gang allegiance (signified by the notation *Sur 13* from the California prison subculture).

William Sanders has observed that African-American and Chicano gangs differ in the use and sale of drugs, the size of the gangs, and their various alliances, business dealings, and relation to turf.[124] African-American gangs are more likely to sell but less likely to use drugs than are Chicano gangs. Most African-American gangs frown on heavy use of drugs, since it is "bad for business," whereas Chicano gangs use drugs mostly for recreational purposes. Moreover, the African-American gangs tend to cover more territory and are divided into two supergangs (Bloods and Crips), whereas Chicano gangs are more oriented around the barrio and do not usually have allegiance outside this area. While this is the case in Los Angeles, most Chicano gangs in Chicago are grouped into either the People or Folks nations.[125] There are at least two web sites that have been established to keep track of Chicago gangs, one of which includes maps showing exactly where the gangs are located.[126]

Asian Gangs

In the United States there are several varieties of gangs of Asian descent. Asians immigrating into the United States enter gang life and often pursue the same kind of activities that they pursued in their native countries, resulting in differing activities for Chinese, Korean, Japanese, Vietnamese, or Filipino gangs. Police find that Asian gangs are difficult to penetrate, as they are extremely secretive. Asian gangs generally victimize people from their own culture, and the victims usually do not report the crimes to the police. The gangs are highly entrepreneurial in nature.[127]

The socioeconomic environment of the Southeast Asians, such as Vietnamese gangs, more closely resembles that of non-Asian gangs. Due partially to the desire to provide a safe haven to South Vietnamese who wished to emigrate as the Vietnam War escalated, U.S. immigration policy eased to allow a large number of Asians to enter the United States. Many were young, unskilled, and unable to speak English. Gang members were usually relatively recent immigrants, from very poor backgrounds, and subjected to much racism and discrimination. They developed gangs partly as a response to these conditions.

Currently the ages of Vietnamese gang members range from mid-to-late teens to the early 20s. They have been described as youths who are frustrated by their lack of success in both school and the community and by their inability to acquire material goods. Despite socioeconomic similarities, these gangs differ from their African-American or Hispanic counterparts. They do not claim turf, nor do they adopt particular modes of dress; they often do not have a gang name. Fighting is infrequent, and drug dealing, wearing tattoos, and using hand signs are avoided because of the attention that would draw to their activities. They are organized very loosely, and membership changes constantly.[128]

Money is the focal point within these gangs. Their crimes include mostly auto theft, burglary, robbery, and extortion. They travel rather extensively. They are very pragmatic in that they victimize other Vietnamese citizens because of this group's inability to understand and/or utilize the legal system. (About half of the robberies go unreported.)[129] Many Vietnamese Americans:

> keep large amounts of cash and gold within their homes. Knowing this, the youth gangs survey a residence and enter the home armed with handguns, usually in small groups of four or five persons. Victims are beaten and coerced into revealing the location of their valuables.[130]

Armed robbery of small stores employing Asian clerks or Vietnamese-owned jewelry and grocery stores is also common. These types of store owners are often victims of extortion by the gang members. Female members are the go-betweens for various gangs, and they often engage in prostitution. Small body markings and earrings are used by both male and female members more for purposes of intimidation than as signs of a particular group affiliation.[131]

Chinese gangs are now common in San Francisco, Los Angeles, Boston, Toronto, Vancouver, and New York City. In the 1960s and 1970s most Chinese gang members were from Hong Kong. Many started to come after the passage of the Immigration and Naturalization Act in 1965, after which thousands of Chinese Americans sent for family members. Thus, a new generation (second generation) of Chinese youth was either born in this country or was brought here at an early age. As with other second generation adolescents, many formed gangs. Unlike other groups, Chinese gangs already had an existing organized crime network in which to operate or to emulate. Some new Chinese gangs allow Korean, Taiwanese, or other non-Chinese youth to participate.[132]

Chinese gangs are composed predominantly of males whose ages range from 13 to 37, with an average age of 22. Most of the youths who are recruited are vulnerable, not doing well in school, or are dropouts. Their English is usually very poor, and they have few job skills. Each gang has between 20 and 50 hard-core members. They tend to have a hierarchical structure nearly parallel to the Mafia or other organized crime groups. Many of the gang members are used by older gang members as "muscle." Most gangs have two or more cliques constantly at battle with each other, so the intergang conflicts are more threatening (gang members are most often killed by other members of the same group) than attacks from external sources, such as rival gangs or the police.[133] Between 80 and 90% of Chinese businessmen pay gangs on a regular or occasional basis for protection. There are four distinct types of extortion common to Chinese gangs: monetary gain, symbolic (used as a display of power to indicate control of a territory), revenge, and instrumental (to intimidate the victim into backing down in certain business or personal conflicts).[134]

Filipino neighborhood gangs are similar in structure and operation to Hispanic gangs and often affiliate with them in the western United States. They are
located mostly in Los Angeles and San Francisco, but also in cities in Alaska,
Washington, and Nevada (Las Vegas). The largest gangs include the Santanas,
Taboos, and the Temple Street Gang. Their crimes include burglaries, muggings, drug sales, and assaults.[135]

These gangs began in the 1940s in the prison system of California. Many
left the Philippines during the 1970s and early 1980s at the height of political
unrest in that country. As the children of these immigrants began to attend
school, there were cultural confrontations and confrontations with street
gangs. To defend themselves, they began to form their own gangs with other
members of their families. These family groupings became cliques or sets
within each gang.[136]

African-American Gangs

The origins of African-American gangs in Southern California are similar
to those of the Chicano gangs, even though they emerged a little later. Group
members came from rural areas (mostly the rural South) to Southern California, a sprawling urban and industrial society. Their traditions included close-
knit families, often centered around the church. However, the second-generation children (like the cholo youths) faced many pressures in the new culture in
Los Angeles. By the late 1960s African-American youths (concentrated in a few
areas near downtown Los Angeles and in the San Fernando Valley)

> found themselves alienated from the old rural values that had sustained
> their parents. They were racially locked out of the dominant Anglo culture
> and, in most cases, economically locked out of the African-American mid-
> dle class. Their futures were as bleak as any cholo's, maybe bleaker.[137]

Families came in search of the "American Dream" of good-paying jobs in
the booming aerospace, automobile, and construction industry, only to find
most of the jobs filled by whites. From the late 1950s to1965, unemployment
among African Americans in south-central Los Angeles went from around 12%
to 30%, while median incomes dropped by about 10%.[138] Racial intimidation
by whites, residential and school segregation, and exclusion and isolation from
mainstream Los Angeles increased steadily after World War II. This process
was the result of restricted covenants legalized back in the 1920s that kept
blacks from moving into white neighborhoods. Blacks challenged such laws
and also school segregation, which resulted in a white backlash.[139]

Several Los Angeles area high schools during the late 1940s and early
1950s experienced racial conflicts. African-American gangs emerged as a *defensive* response to discrimination, much like the response by Hispanic youths to
the Zoot Suit riots. One example was a white gang called the "Spook Hunters"
who intimidated and attacked blacks who ventured into white communities.[140] Some of the earliest African-American gangs were often car clubs (common throughout the LA area) that went by names such as the Slausons,

Gladiators, Watts, Flips, Rebel Rousers, Businessmen, and the like.[141] These groups consisted of "guys who banded together for camaraderie and, to a certain extent, for protection."[142] These gangs differed from current gangs. They usually did not consider neighborhoods where they lived as their territory or turf. They did not commonly fight other gangs; they had no colors; they did not paint graffiti.

Some of these groups divided themselves into two factions, one group on the "West Side" (usually with more money and more sophistication) and the other on the "East Side" (less money and less sophistication). Some were merely the extension of intramural athletic rivalries, common in those days.[143] As white clubs began to disappear (most whites began migrating to all-white areas like Orange County (to the southeast of Los Angeles), Santa Clarita, Simi Valley and Antelope Valley (all to the west and northwest), black clubs began to fight each other, leading to six murders in 1960.

The Watts riots of 1965 created similar circumstances for African-American gangs as did the Zoot Suit riots for Chicano gangs. Young African Americans were seen in a more negative light by the media and by the rest of society. At the same time, African-American youths began to see themselves differently. Many banded together to fight police brutality and other injustices.[144] It is important to note that although African-American youths did not have the *palomilla* tradition of their Mexican counterparts, they were aware of the benefits Chicano gangs derived from the bonding of cohorts in the barrio.

> Given the emasculating circumstances of ghetto life a quarter-century ago, it is small wonder that the cocky, dangerous style of the Latino gangs had a strong appeal for African-American youths. It responded perfectly to the need for repackaging defeat as defiance, redefining exclusion as exclusivity.[145]

During the mid- to late-1960s the emergence of groups that eventually called themselves Crips transformed the gang landscape. There is some debate as to the exact origin of the name. Some link it to the movie, *Tales from the Crypt*. Others say it comes from the word cripple because the original gangs crippled their enemies or suffered a similar fate. Another version is that the Crips were founded by a group of youths from Fremont High School. One of them was referred to as a "crip" (short for cripple) because he walked with the aid of a stick. Still another version alleges that because walking sticks were a symbol for the original gang, the police and the media began to apply the name, and the gang eventually adopted it.[146] Several imitators emerged from the city of Compton. Raymond Washington and Stanley "Tookie" Williams founded the Westside Crips there in 1971.[147] They borrowed one of the cholo traditions of wearing bandannas and emphasized the color blue. Other Crip sets soon began to imitate them by wearing blue bandannas and other blue clothing to set themselves apart. One version of the origin of the Crips gang was that the first set formed in reaction to the destruction of housing and neighborhood ties when the Century Freeway was built. One member claimed Crip originally stood for "Continuous Revolution in Progress."[148] Another version of the origin of the Crips is that they emerged in the wake of the demise of the Black Panther Party.[149] Many believe that the decline of the Panthers led directly to a resurgence of gangs, including the Bloods and Crips, in the early 1970s.[150]

The next important development was a reaction to the emergence of Crip gang sets on both the east and west sides of Figueroa Street. One group of African-American youths who lived on a street called Piru in Compton began to get together for protection from attacks by Crip sets. They called themselves the Compton Pirus and are believed to be the first gang to apply the term *blood brothers* to their gang name. Independent gangs such as the Brims, Bounty Hunters, and Denver Lanes, among others, joined together and wore red handkerchiefs, calling themselves "Blood."[151] The term suggested, of course, the color red, which they selected as their gang's color. Soon Blood sets wore red bandannas, shoes, and jackets to set themselves apart from the Crips.

The continuous deteriorating economic situation in black communities throughout Los Angeles, plus the added forces of segregation, fueled a continued growth of black gangs. Whereas in 1972 there were about 18 black gangs, by 1996 there were an estimated 270.[152] Alonso concludes that the emergence of black gangs in LA were the result of "efforts to maintain White privilege and racial exclusion throughout a period of turbulent social and geographic change in Los Angeles."[153]

Within just a few years Blood and Crip sets spread throughout the Los Angeles area. These gangs began to borrow other traditions of Hispanic gangs—flying colors, defending their turf, using graffiti, hanging with homeboys, and jumping in new members. Crips currently outnumber Bloods by about three to one in Los Angeles. The Crips and Bloods have so influenced African-American street gangs in Los Angeles that the only distinction between the thousands of gang members is the blue and the red colors. Crips do not use words starting with the letter "B," and Bloods do not use words starting with the letter "C." Crips often refer to themselves as "cuzz," while bloods often call each other "Piru." They often include rival gang abbreviations along with the slant sign and the letter "K," which means killers. Thus the letters C/K may mean Crip killers and the letters B/K will stand for Blood killers. Typically African-American gang members will ask the question, "What set you from?" This is asking for the individual's gang affiliation.[154]

Useni Perkins studied Chicago's African-American street gangs and raised the issue of institutional racism playing a major role in the development and perpetuation of these gangs. He also suggested that African-American youth are drawn into gangs in order to develop a sense of belonging, identity, power, security, and discipline.[155]

White Gangs

According to the National Gang Center, white gangs make up 8.4% of the gangs in larger cities, 14% in the suburbs and smaller cities, and about 17% in rural areas.[156] Nationally, whites make up 9% of all gang members.[157] Since the late 1970s, white teenagers have been forming groups based on an interest in punk rock music and the social attitudes it represents. These attitudes include helplessness, anger, and rebellion. Many of these youth view the world as offering scant opportunity for individual self-expression. Both the listeners and the performers in the punk rock scene exhibit behavior that is both angry and violent, mostly for shock value. There are, however, groups of punkers who are very involved in drugs and alcohol, which leads to more involvement in crimes.

Usually white youth gangs (some of which include mixed ethnicities) express their delinquent behavior in ways different from other street gangs. Some are involved in the "skinhead" movement, identified as a militant racist organization. Skinheads have been described by some as "the kiddie corps of the neo-Nazi movement."[158] Youths have belonged to these kinds of organizations since the early 1980s. However, skinhead groups are not all avowed racists. The racist skinheads advocate white supremacy, and the nonracist skinheads have a multiracial membership. They are rivals and often engage in violent confrontations. These groups are scattered and have erratic membership, although in some areas they claim territory and are classified as a street gang. One example of a nonracist skinhead gang is the SHARPs (Skinheads Against Racial Prejudice) or SARs (Skinheads Against Racism).[159] A variation is the kind of group known as a "separatist" group. These are youths who consider themselves "survivalists, concerned only with their own personal welfare and survival in the likelihood of a nuclear holocaust or natural disaster." These groups do not care much about what is going on around them and try to avoid overt racial violence.[160]

A group similar to the racist skinheads is known as "political skinheads." These are youth who take orders from such groups as WAR (White Aryan Resistance) or the Aryan Brotherhood. Members are perhaps the most avowedly racist and are very critical of the U.S. government, claiming that minorities are given preferential treatment over whites. Skinheads are common in most prisons and frequently join forces with the White Aryan Brotherhood or the KKK.[161]

The skinhead movement in Southern California began in the late 1970s. Music was an important component, with music bands like Sham 69, Skrewdriver, and The Four Skins. They were not very organized at first, and many groups dissolved quickly. Eventually they became very aggressive groups with shared interests, which was pivotal to their development. These groups resembled other gangs in that they identified with specific turfs. So, for instance, there were the Huntington Beach Skins, Chino Hills Skins, South Bay Skins, Norwalk Skins and the like. Sometimes they marked parks as their turf and used graffiti "tags" to identify themselves.

Other groups in Southern California played a part in the formation of the skinheads. The most important were the "punks." So-called "punk rock" provided a subcultural foundation for the development of skinheads. In fact, most of the original skinhead groups came directly from the punk scene. Other groups included surfers, skaters, bikers, stoners, and peckerwoods. All of these groups were white youth subcultures. But the punks were the most important connection. Punks can be viewed as a rejection of left-wing political movements—a result of the anxiety of a rapidly changing world that ignored the white working class. Although they held a variety of views on social issues, one of the most important was the perception that white youth were victimized by several outside social forces (e.g., minority street gangs, affirmative action programs, etc.).[162] The shaved heads of many of these individuals was a strong statement, an "in your face" protest. Much of the punk subculture evolved into a more aggressive attitude, often expressed through random violence. Punk rock music reflected this aggressiveness, with very loud and hard tones. Skinhead music is as important to these youths as rap is to African-American youths. This music is radical and often reflects the racial and political attitudes of the skinheads.

Eventually, skinheads began to construct a racist ideology that included, in part, neo-Nazism. Some of the early skinhead gang members became involved with Nazism when they were punks and long before they shaved their heads and became skinheads. Furthermore, some of the surfers, such as those living in La Jolla (a very up-scale town just north of San Diego) were a version of "Nazi punks." The skinheads in Los Angeles were reacting to some very specific trends that they perceived as threatening to them and their class and especially their race. Increased immigration was one of the most important of these changes occurring in Southern California.

Modern skinheads usually dress in a polo or T-shirt, suspenders (that match the color of the bootlaces), pants (usually Dickies or Levis) that are rolled up or tailored (so the entire boot is exposed), flight jackets (often with personalized graffiti), and boots. If the boots are scuffed on the steel tips, the gang member is considered tough; the more scuffs on his boots, the tougher he is considered to be. If one is seen with his suspenders down, this means he is ready to fight. If he wears white laces in his boots, this means that he upholds "white pride," while red laces stand for a more aggressive type of white power, and yellow laces signify hatred for the police or a claim that he has killed a police officer.[163]

Their graffiti is similar to that of other street gangs, with the addition of a racial and political orientation. Hand signs are given as well. Tattoos are common, appearing on the face, neck, and inside of the lips. American skinhead gangs have "jumping in" initiations for new members, during which the recruit is attacked with fists by between 4 and 12 other members for a certain period of time.[164]

Skinheads are highly likely to engage in violent acts and to direct such acts against those they perceive as the most different or a threat to the white majority—homosexuals, racial and ethnic groups, and religious minorities. There are two other types of white gangs, which are very different from skinheads.

Youths known as *stoners* are distinguishable from traditional street gangs by their secretiveness and the difficulty in identifying them. Often referred to as "cults," they engage in many ritualistic activities. They are white suburban youths from a higher socioeconomic background than most other gangs. Stoner gangs constitute only about 5% of all gangs in California and an even smaller percentage of all white youths in the correctional system.[165]

Stoner gangs are heavily involved in the use of various drugs (e.g., speed, LSD, rock cocaine, PCP) and have an especially high rate of toxic vapor use. They are almost always into heavy metal music. Stoners use graffiti to mark territory, not necessarily geographic, but to claim music groups or types of music. They generally do not have any organized leadership, are anti-establishment, and often dabble in Satanism, participating in animal sacrifice and ritual crimes (e.g., grave or church desecrations). Stoners typically dress in red or black clothing, with athletic jersey tops depicting heavy metal music stars, metal-spiked wrist cuffs, collars and belts, earrings, long hair, and tattoos. They often wear Satanic relics or sacrilegious effigies.[166]

The final variation of white gangs is *taggers*. It seems that everywhere one travels in urban and suburban areas one sees a form of graffiti known as "tagging." Such graffiti is not done to mark "turf, but rather it is a way these mostly white and middle-class youths call attention to themselves." Wayne Wooden, who has studied these groups extensively, quotes one 17-year-old tagger who says: "It's addictive, once you get started. It's like a real bad habit."

> The addiction has drawn thousands of teenagers—who call themselves and their rivals "toys," "taggers" or "pieces"—to devote their time to "getting up" to attain "fame" by tagging poles, benches, utility boxes, signs, bridges and freeway signs in the San Fernando Valley with graffiti.[167]

Police estimate that in Los Angeles County there are at least 600 tagger "crews" with about 30,000 youths. One crew, who call themselves NBT or "Nothing But Trouble," claims a membership of 400 or more. These groups are also referred to by such names as "graffiti bands," "posses," "pieces" (so-called because they believe that they draw "masterpieces" of art), and "housers" (because they like to tag houses). What specifically is tagged varies by age. Younger taggers (10–15) usually tag around school grounds. Older youths will go after bigger targets, such as freeway overpasses or bridges, public transportation (especially buses), streetlight poles, etc. "Less geographically bound to protecting a particular neighborhood turf than are ethnic and inner-city gangs, the taggers spread their marks far and wide on their nightly runs."[168]

Taggers, like regular street gangs, have their own slang. For instance, a "toy" is someone who is a novice or amateur tagger; to "kill a wall" is to cover a wall completely with graffiti. Taggers will go on a "bombing run" where members of a crew will go out and try to mark as many places as possible with their "tag names" and the names of their crew. Sometimes crews will "slash" or cross out rival crews or taggers' names, which is considered an insult or challenge.[169]

Wooden's interviews with tagger crews found that they typically do not have much of a formal organizational structure, that most members are not "jumped in" or otherwise go through a formal initiation process, that members often drift in and out of the groups, and they often change their names when they get tired of the old one. Often these groups will do "battle" with each other; the battles are contests to see whose name will appear most often.[170]

Although more and more tagger members are carrying weapons for protection from rival crews, tagging is primarily a form of fun and play. Most members do not choose to call what they do a crime; they see it as an art form and a way to express themselves. They are insulted when others (e.g., the police) call their work "graffiti." On the other hand, many become increasingly destructive in order to achieve some form of notoriety with other taggers.

Police in Southern California have recently noticed two other types of tagger crews. One is known as the *dance and party crews*. Many of these crews are associated with street gangs with whom they get together at parties and coexist peacefully. They may use this association as intimidation against rival crews. There has been an increase in violence associated with "dance battles" where crews dance against each other for recognition. Rivalries may lead to confrontation and violence. Many times parties are held at a private residence, usually ransacking and stealing property.[171]

Skating crews are a recent phenomenon linked to the popularity of skateboarding and rollerblading. These crews form when a group feels the need to adopt a name and/or nickname. Some crews claim certain parking areas and alleys as their own. They may begin tagging their group's name to claim an area or for recognition. Fights among rival skating crews are increasing, according to police reports.

While there is little doubt that dance and skating groups exist, what are the criteria used by the police to label some of these groups "gangs"? There should be some very specific criteria to distinguish among the literally thousands (perhaps millions) of teenagers who engage in skateboarding and rollerblading in virtually every city and small town in the country. Similarly, one should have some very good criteria to distinguish street gangs bent on criminal activity and kids who go to parties. Certainly kids will attend parties and engage in activities that incur the wrath of many adults. But are these "gangs"? Given the elusive definitions of "gangs" and "gang members" plus the millions of dollars in funding to fight gangs, is there a tendency on the part of some law enforcement agencies to add every sort of teenage grouping and activities to the term "gang," whether or not it is warranted?

Summary

Gangs are not something new to the social arena. They existed in fourteenth- and fifteenth-century Europe and colonial America. In this chapter we have pointed out that public perception (and fear), crucial to policy development, is shaped largely by the mass media. It is clear that the media have done little to differentiate fact from fiction in the portrayal of youth gangs; they have contributed to the stereotypical images of how we think about gangs and gang members.

The only agreement about what constitutes a gang, its members, and its activities is disagreement. Often, this discord is linked to location (e.g., type of neighborhood), age (e.g., adolescent versus young adult), and purpose (e.g., play group, organized crime, drugs). We have found that one of the major problems associated with the study of gangs is the identification of gang-related crime. Each jurisdiction seems to create its own criteria to determine whether or not a crime is gang related.

This chapter also addressed the issue of *how many*. How many gangs are currently active in the United States? How many individuals are in these groups? There are a significant number of projections and estimates related to these questions. Frequently, the argument is raised that because gangs come and go, it is difficult to determine accurately the number of gangs and gang members. It is our contention, however, that the most critical factor in determining how many gangs or gang members are active is to first determine what exactly a gang or gang member is.

We reviewed attempts to categorize "gangs" and "gang members." It is impossible to provide a profile of a gang member that covers all socioeconomic factors and motivations for affiliation. It is equally difficult to precisely identify a pure type of gang. Any attempt to identify a "typical" gang falls short. While many gangs are identified by ethnic composition, others cross gender, racial, and ethnic boundaries. Organizational structures are difficult to categorize. The fairly traditional idea of a vertically organized street gang contrasts dramatically with loosely organized taggers. Social scientists have created several typologies to describe the many varied groupings, but there are no universally applicable labels.

NOTES

[1] Davis, M. (2008). "Foreword" to J. M. Hagedorn, *A World of Gangs: Armed Young Men and Gangsta Culture.* Minneapolis: University of Minnesota Press, pp. xi–xii.

[2] Hay, D., P. Linebaugh, J. Rule, E. P. Thompson, and C. Winslow (Eds.) (1975). *Albion's Fatal Tree: Crime and Society in Eighteenth-Century England.* New York: Pantheon; Pearson, G. (1983). *Hooligan: A History of Reportable Fears.* New York: Schoeken Books.

[3] Pearson, *Hooligan*, p. 188.

[4] Covey, C., S. Menard, and R. Franzese (1992). *Juvenile Gangs.* Springfield, IL: Charles S. Thomas, pp. 90–91.

[5] Goldstein, A. P. (1991). *Delinquent Gangs: A Psychological Perspective.* Champaign, IL: Research Press, p. 8.

[6] Spergel, I. A. (1995). *The Youth Gang Problem: A Community Approach.* New York: Oxford University Press, p. 7.

[7] Asbury, H. (1927). *The Gangs of New York.* New York: Alfred Knopf. A movie of the same title and based partly on the book was released in 2002 and was nominated for several academy awards.

[8] McCorkle, R. and T. Miethe (2001). *Panic: The Social Construction of the Street Gang Problem.* Upper Saddle River, NJ: Prentice-Hall, p. 3.

[9] Ibid.

[10] Ibid.

11 Thompson, C. Y., R. L. Young, and R. Burns (2000). "Representing Gangs in the News: Media Constructions of Criminal Gangs." *Sociological Spectrum* 20: 409–32.

12 National Gang Center (2011, May 16). "Gang-Related News Articles." Retrieved from http://www.nationalgangcenter.gov/Gang-Related-News

13 See the following studies of the media that support this contention: Bagidikian, B. (2002). *The Media Monopoly* (6th ed.). Boston: Beacon Press; Chomsky, N. (1989). *Necessary Illusions: Thought Control in Democratic Societies.* Boston: South End Press; Herman, E. and N. Chomsky (1988). *Manufacturing Consent: The Political Economy of the Mass Media.* New York: Pantheon.

14 Fox, R. L., R. W. Van Sickel, and T. L. Steiger (2007). *Tabloid Justice: Criminal Justice in an Age of Media Frenzy.* Boulder, CO: Lynne Reinner.

15 Quoted in Reiman, J. (2007). *The Rich Get Richer and the Poor Get Prison: Ideology, Crime, and Criminal Justice* (8th ed.). Boston: Allyn & Bacon, p. 175.

16 Shelden, R. G., S. Tracy, and W. B. Brown (2004). *Youth Gangs in American Society* (3rd ed.). Belmont, CA: Wadsworth.

17 Durkheim, É. (1950). *Rule of the Sociological Method.* Glencoe, IL: Free Press (originally published in 1895).

18 Shaw, C. and H. D. McKay (1942). *Juvenile Delinquency in Urban Areas.* Chicago: University of Chicago Press; Thrasher, F. (1927). *The Gang.* Chicago: University of Chicago Press.

19 Hagedorn, *A World of Gangs*, p. xxiv.

20 For an extensive review see Shelden et al., *Youth Gangs.*

21 Hagedorn, J. M. (1998). *People and Folks: Gangs, Crime and the Underclass in a Rustbelt City* (2nd ed.). Chicago: Lakeview Press.

22 Royal Canadian Mounted Police (2004). "A Research Report on Youth Gangs: Problems, Perspective and Priorities." Retrieved from http://www.rcmp-grc.gc.ca/pubs/ccaps-spcca/gangs-bandes-eng.htm

23 Thornberry, T. P., D. Huizinga, and R. Loeber (2004). "The Causes and Correlates Studies: Findings and Policy Implications." *Juvenile Justice*, 10: 3–19. Retrieved from http://www.ncjrs.gov/pdffiles1/ojjdp/203555.pdf

24 Quoted in Klein, M. (1995). *The American Street Gang.* New York: Oxford University Press, p. 22.

25 Short, J. F. (1990). "Gangs, Neighborhoods, and Youth Crime." *Criminal Justice Research Bulletin* 5: 3.

26 Klein, M. (1971). *Street Gangs and Street Workers.* Englewood Cliffs, NJ: Prentice-Hall, p. 111.

27 National Gang Center (n.d.). Retrieved from http://www.nationalgangcenter.gov/About/FAQ#q1

28 Retrieved from http://www.nationalgangcenter.gov/Survey-Analysis/Defining-Gangs

29 California Penal Code sec. 186.22[f], [i]. Retrieved from http://www.iir.com/nygc/gang-legis/gang-related%20definitions.htm. The "East Coast Gang Investigators Association" defines a gang this way: "A group or association of three or more persons who may have a common identifying sign, symbol, or name and who individually or collectively engage in, or have engaged in, criminal activity which creates an atmosphere of fear and intimidation." Retrieved from http://www.ecgia.org/faq.asp

30 Spergel, I. A. and G. D. Curry (1990). "Strategies and Perceived Agency Effectiveness in Dealing with the Youth Gang Problem." In C. R. Huff (Ed.), *Gangs in America.* Newbury Park, CA: Sage, p. 388.

31 Ibid., p. 389.

32 Ibid.

33 Ibid.

34 Huff, C. R. (1993). "Gangs in the United States." In A. P. Goldstein and C. R. Huff (Eds.), *The Gang Intervention Handbook.* Champaign, IL: Research Press, p. 4.

35 Ibid.

36 Ibid., p. 5.

37 Hagedorn, *People and Folks*, p. 86.

38 Hagedorn, *A World of Gangs*, p. xxv.

39 Jackson, P. G. (1989). "Theories and Findings about Youth Gangs." *Criminal Justice Abstracts* (June): 314; Klein has made the same point, noting that the only thing more boring than watch-

ing gangs is watching researchers watching gangs (Klein, *American Street Gangs*); a close friend and colleague, Bud Brown, who spent a considerable amount of time hanging out with a Detroit gang, noted the same thing.

[40] Klein, M. and C. Maxson (1989). "Street Gang Violence." In M. E. Wolfgang and N. A. Weiner (Eds.), *Violent Crime, Violent Criminals*. Newbury Park, CA: Sage, p. 206.

[41] Ibid., p. 208.

[42] Chaney, K. (2009, August 26). "Gang-Related Crime More Visible, Not More Prevalent." *Chicago Defender*. Retrieved from http://www.chicagodefender.com/article-6185-gang-related-crime-more-visible-not-more-prevalent.html

[43] Retrieved from http://www.lapdonline.org/get_informed/content_basic_view/24435

[44] National Gang Center (2009). *National Youth Gang Survey Analysis*. Retrieved from http://www.nationalgangcenter.gov/Survey-Analysis/Gang-Related-Offenses#gangrelated

[45] Shelden et al., *Youth Gangs*, ch. 1.

[46] Beres, L. S. and T. D. Griffith (2005). "Gangs, Schools and Stereotypes." *Loyola of Los Angeles Law Review* 37: 935–78. Retrieved from http://llr.lls.edu/volumes/v37-issue4/documents/beres.pdf

[47] Slovan, M. (2010, January 28). "State Lawmakers Want to Rid Schools of Gangs, but Will Their Proposals Hurt Kids More Than They Help?" Olympia Newswire. Retrieved from http://www.olympianews.org/2010/01/28/state-lawmakers-want-to-rid-schools-of-gangs-but-will-their-proposals-hurt-more-schools-than-they-help/

[48] This apparent obsession over how many gangs and gang members there are is typical of the positivistic orientation in the social sciences—and in the larger society in general. Numbers assume enormous importance. Part of the obsession is the need to "control" or "manage" gangs. For this to be done, it is apparently important to know the exact size of the "problem." What is lost in this procedure are people (both the victims and the victimizers) and their circumstances—often masked by social disadvantage and oppression. Also lost are the various social conditions that create gangs. Imagine doctors having the attitude that we just need to "control" or "manage" cancer or AIDS, and spending their time counting the number of cases rather than trying to locate and eliminate the causes.

[49] Thrasher, *The Gang*.

[50] Miller, W. B. (1975). *Violence by Youth Gangs and Youth Groups as a Crime Problem in Major American Cities*. Washington, DC: U.S. Department of Justice; see also Miller, W. B. (1982). *Crime by Youth Gangs and Groups in the United States*. Washington, DC: U.S. Department of Justice.

[51] Egley, A. E., J. C. Howell, and J. P. Moore (2010, March). "Highlights of the 2008 National Youth Gang Survey." Retrieved from http://www.ncjrs.gov/pdffiles1/ojjdp/229249.pdf

[52] Howell, J. C. and J. P. Lynch (2000). *Youth Gangs in Schools*. Washington, DC: Office of Juvenile Justice and Delinquency Prevention.

[53] Starbuck, D., J. Howell, and D. Lindquist (2001, December). *Hybrid and Other Modern Gangs*. Washington, DC: OJJDP, Juvenile Justice Bulletin, p. 2.

[54] O'Connor, A. (2000, March 25). "Police Scandal Clouds List of Gang Members." *Los Angeles Times*; Jablon, R. (2000, February 19). "L.A. Prepares for Worst as Police Scandal Grows." Associated Press.

[55] Snyder, H. N. and M. Sickmund (2006). *Juvenile Offenders and Victims: 2006 National Report*. Washington, DC: U.S. Department of Justice, Office of Juvenile Justice and Delinquency Prevention. Retrieved from http://ojjdp.ncjrs.gov/ojstatbb/nr2006/

[56] Esbensen, F. A. and E. P. Deschenes (1998). "A Multisite Examination of Gang Membership: Does Gender Matter?" *Criminology* 36(4): 799–827.

[57] Curry, D. (2000). "Self-Reported Gang Involvement and Officially Recorded Delinquency." *Criminology* 3: 1254–55.

[58] Greene, J. and K. Pranis (2007). "Gang Wars: The Failure of Enforcement Tactics and the Need for Effective Public Safety Strategies." *Justice Policy Institute*, p. 33. Retrieved from http://www.justicepolicy.org/content-hmID=1811&smID=1581&ssmID=22.htm

[59] Spergel, *The Youth Gang Problem*. Recall from chapter 2 that index crimes include homicide, rape, robbery, aggravated assault, burglary, larceny, motor vehicle theft, and arson.

[60] Egley et al., "Highlights"; Howell, J. C., A. Egley, Jr., and D. K. Gleason (2002). *Modern Day Youth Gangs*. Washington, DC: OJJDP; Howell, J. C., J. P. Moore, and A. Egley, Jr. (2002). "The

Changing Boundaries of Youth Gangs." In C. R. Huff (Ed.), *Gangs in America III*. Thousand Oaks, CA: Sage, pp. 3–18.

[61] Thornberry, T. P., M. D. Krohn, A. J. Lizotte, C. A. Smith, and K. Tobin (2003). *Gangs and Delinquency in Developmental Perspective*. Cambridge: Cambridge University Press.

[62] Harrell, E. (2005, June). "Violence by Gang Members, 1993–2003." Bureau of Justice Statistics. Retrieved from http://www.helpinggangyouth.com/violent_crimes_by_gangs-2003.pdf

[63] Thornberry et al., "The Causes and Correlates Studies."

[64] The website of a defense attorney in Orange County, California, gives specific instructions to other attorneys on how to provide a defense against an offender when the prosecutor alleges gang involvement. "It should be noted that many agencies receive funding for investigation and arrest for suspect gang members. This creates a conflict of interest that should be exposed to the public. There are many instances where a person commits a criminal offense and should be punished but the prosecutor decides to allege gang charges in addition to the substantive offense (e.g., drug sales, assault with a firearm) because he or she knows that when a jury hears about a gang, jurors will fold their hands in laps and wait to convict." Retrieved from http://www.williamweinberg.com/lawyer-attorney-1472296.html

[65] Klein, *The American Street Gang*, p. 22. Data collected by Klein and Maxson found that only 2% to 5% of gang homicides involved innocent, non-gang victims (Klein and Maxson, "Street Gang Violence," p. 231).

[66] Hutson, H. R., D. Anglin, and M. Eckstein (1996). "Drive-by Shootings by Violent Street Gangs in Los Angeles: A Five-year Review from 1989 to 1993." *Academic Emergency Medicine* 3: 300–3.

[67] Troshynski, E. I. and L. Finley (2006). "Gang Violence, Against Bystanders." In L. Finley (Ed.), *Encyclopedia of Youth Violence*. Santa Barbara, CA: Greenwood Press, p. 90.

[68] See for instance this story: DiIonno, M. (2009, July 21). "Newark Violence Claims Life of Innocent Bystander Nakisha Allen." Retrieved from http://blog.nj.com/njv_mark_diionno/2009/07/newark_violence_claims_life_of.html

[69] McCorkle and Miethe, *Panic*.

[70] National Gang Center (2009). *National Youth Gang Survey Analysis*. Retrieved from http://www.nationalgangcenter.gov/Survey-Analysis/Measuring-the-Extent-of-Gang-Problems#homicidesnumber

[71] National Gang Center (2009). *National Youth Gang Survey Analysis*. Retrieved from http://www.nationalgangcenter.gov/About/FAQ#q5

[72] Hagedorn, *People and Folks*, p. 94; a similar finding was reported by Huff, C. R. (1989). "Youth Gangs and Public Policy." *Crime and Delinquency* 35: 524–37.

[73] Klein, *The American Street Gang*, p. 11.

[74] Ibid., p. 22.

[75] Hagedorn, *People and Folks*, p. 103; see also Klein, *The American Street Gang*, and Padilla, F. (1992). *The Gang as an American Enterprise*. New Brunswick, NJ: Rutgers University Press.

[76] Horowitz, R. (1983). "The End of the Youth Gang." *Criminology* 21: 585–600; Horowitz, R. (1987). "Community Tolerance of Gang Violence." *Social Problems* 34: 437–50; Miller, W. B. (2001, April 24). *The Growth of Youth Gang Problems in the United States: 1970–98*. Washington, DC: U.S. Department of Justice, Office of Justice Programs, Office of Juvenile Justice and Delinquency Prevention.

[77] Fagan, J. (2004). "Gangs, Drugs and Neighborhood Change." In R. D. Peterson (Ed.), *Understanding Contemporary Gangs in America*. Upper Saddle River, NJ: Prentice-Hall.

[78] Reiner, I. (1992). *Gangs, Crime and Violence in Los Angeles: Findings and Proposals from the District Attorney's Office*. Arlington, VA: National Youth Gang Information Center, pp. 58–59.

[79] Spergel, *The Youth Gang Problem*, p. 60.

[80] Klein, *The American Street Gang*, p. 101.

[81] Ibid., p. 102.

[82] Klein and Maxson, "Street Gang Violence," pp. 209–10.

[83] Bing, L. (1992). *Do or Die*. New York: Harper/Perennial, p. 244.

[84] Spergel, *The Youth Gang Problem*, pp. 55–56.

[85] Vigil, J. D. (2010). *Gang Redux: A Balanced Anti-Gang Strategy*. Long Grove, IL: Waveland Press, p. 62.

[86] Klein and Maxson, "Street Gang Violence," p. 211.

[87] Klein, *The American Street Gang*, p. 64.

[88] Ibid., p. 64.

[89] Ibid., p. 102.

[90] Moore, J. W. (1978). *Homeboys: Gangs, Drugs, and Prisons in the Barrio of Los Angeles*. Philadelphia: Temple University Press; and Moore, J. W. (1991). *Going Down to the Barrio: Homeboys and Home-girls in Change*. Philadelphia: Temple University Press.

[91] Spergel, *The Youth Gang Problem*, pp. 71–72.

[92] Vigil, *Gang Redux*, p. 61.

[93] There is plenty of literature on adolescent groups and subcultures. For a good review see Schwendinger, H. and J. Schwendinger (1985). *Adolescent Subcultures and Delinquency*. New York: Praeger. For an overview of the gang subculture in particular, see Shelden et al., *Youth Gangs*.

[94] Perhaps most famous for his work *The Protestant Ethic and the Spirit of Capitalism* (1958), German-born Max Weber (1864–1920) was a prolific writer on subjects ranging from law to economy to religion. Within the academic world he is also popular for developing the notion of the *ideal type*.

[95] Huff, "Youth Gangs and Public Policy"; Fagan, J. A. (1989). "The Social Organization of Drug Use and Drug Dealing among Urban Gangs." *Criminology* 27: 633–67; Taylor, C. S. (1990). *Dangerous Society*. East Lansing: Michigan State University Press.

[96] Klein, *American Street Gang*, p. 132.

[97] Vigil, J. D. (1988). *Barrio Gangs*. Austin: University of Texas Press; Vigil, J. D. (1990). "Cholos and Gangs: Culture Change and Street Youths in Los Angeles." In Huff, *Gangs in America*, pp. 116–28; Vigil, J. D. and J. M. Long (1990). "Emic and Etic Perspectives on Gang Culture: The Chicano Case." In Huff, *Gangs in America*, pp. 55–70; and Reiner, *Gangs, Crime and Violence in Los Angeles*.

[98] Vigil, *Barrio Gangs*, pp. 66, 81–85.

[99] Spergel, *The Youth Gang Problem*, p. 84.

[100] Reiner, *Gangs, Crime and Violence in Los Angeles*, p. 42.

[101] Vigil, *Barrio Gangs*, p. 66.

[102] Ibid.

[103] Reiner, *Gangs, Crime and Violence in Los Angeles*, pp. 40–44.

[104] Taylor, *Dangerous Society*.

[105] Ibid.

[106] Florida Department of Corrections (n.d.). "Gang and Security Threat Group Awareness." Retrieved from http://www.dc.state.fl.us/pub/gangs/chicago.html; National Youth Gang Center; Hagedorn, *People and Folk*; Knox, G. (2004). "The Problem of Gangs and Security Threat Groups." Retrieved from http://www.ngcrc.com/ngcrc/corr2006.html.

[107] Bobrowski, L. J. (1988). *Collecting, Organizing and Reporting Street Gang Crime*. Chicago: Chicago Police Department, Special Functions Group; see also Hagedorn, *People and Folks*.

[108] Florida Department of Corrections, "Gang and Security Threat Group Awareness."

[109] National Gang Intelligence Center (2009, January). *National Gang Threat Assessment 2009*. Retrieved from http://www.justice.gov/ndic/pubs32/32146/appb.htm#start

[110] One year later, the convictions were overturned because of a biased judge and lack of evidence. The parents of the five other indicted youths had sufficient resources to pay for defense attorneys who won separate trials for their clients; all were acquitted.

[111] Initially an African-American fashion connected to jazz culture, the zoot suit attracted Mexican-American youths, who adapted it as their trademark. The amount of material and tailoring required made the suits luxury items, especially at a time when fabric was being rationed for the war effort. In the face of widespread discrimination, the suit was both an outrageous style and a statement of defiance. The following website presents a timeline concerning the Zoot Suit riots: http://noemigarcia.tripod.com/lapaint/zootline.htm

[112] Moore, *Homeboys*, p. 62.

[113] Moore, J. W. (1993). "Gangs, Drugs, and Violence." In S. Cummings and D. J. Monti (Eds.), *Gangs: The Origins and Impact of Contemporary Youth Gangs in the United States*. Albany: SUNY Press, pp. 25–44.

[114] Moore, *Going Down to the Barrio*, p. 27.

[115] Ibid., p. 31.

[116] Ibid.

[117] The term *cholo* is used to describe a Chicano gang member or the Chicano subculture itself. It is derived from a term used to describe a marginal position between two cultures—the older Mexican culture and the newer Mexican-American culture. To better understand marginalization, think of the margins on typical notebook pages, which are on the side of the page and not part of the main body of the page. Marginalization of dissent refers to the fact that alternative perspectives are rarely discussed in the mainstream media or political discourse.

[118] Vigil, *Gang Redux*, p. 3.

[119] Vigil, *Barrio Gangs*.

[120] Vigil, *Gang Redux*, p. 6.

[121] Moore, *Homeboys*, pp. 52–53.

[122] Moore, J. W., J. D. Vigil, and R. Garcia (1983). "Residence and Territoriality in Chicano Gangs." *Social Problems* 31: 182–94.

[123] http://www.streetgangs.com/hispanic/htm

[124] Sanders, W. (1994). *Gangbangs and Drivebys*. New York: Aldine DeGruyter, p. 148.

[125] Hagedorn, *People and Folks*.

[126] http://www.chicagogangs.org/ and http://www.gangresearch.net/ChicagoGangs/latinkings/latindex.html; see also the website for Alex Alonso: http://www.streetgangs.com/resume.html

[127] Reiner, *Gangs, Crime and Violence in Los Angeles*, p. 46.

[128] Vigil, J. D. and S. C. Yun (1996). "Southern California Gangs: Comparative Ethnicity and Social Control." In Huff, *Gangs in America III*, pp. 139–56; Chin, L. (1990). "Chinese Gangs and Extortion." In Huff, *Gangs in America*, pp. 129–45; Goldstein and Huff, *The Gang Intervention Handbook*, pp. 15–16.

[129] Reiner, *Gangs, Crime and Violence in Los Angeles*, p. 48.

[130] Vigil and Yun, "Southern California Gangs," p. 157.

[131] Ibid.

[132] Reiner, *Gangs, Crime and Violence in Los Angeles*, p. 49.

[133] Chin, "Chinese Gangs and Extortion."

[134] Ibid., pp. 134–42.

[135] Jackson, R. and W. D. McBride (1992). *Understanding Street Gangs*. Placerville, CA: Copperhouse, p. 50.

[136] Los Angeles County Sheriff's Department (1992). *L.A. Style: A Street Gang Manual of the Los Angeles County Sheriff's Department*. Los Angeles: Los Angeles County Sheriff's Department, p. 1.

[137] Reiner, *Gangs, Crime and Violence in Los Angeles*, p. 5.

[138] Davis, M. (1992). *City of Quartz*. New York: Vintage Books, p. 296.

[139] Alonso, A. A. (2004). "Racialized Identities and the Formation of Black Gangs in Los Angeles." *Urban Geography* 25: 658–74. For more information, download this fascinating, historical study from http://www.streetgangs.com/academic/2004ug_gangsla.pdf

[140] Ibid. Alonso also notes that the same thing happened in Chicago in the 1920s, as a white gang called the "Dirty Dozen" attacked black people. White intimidation of and attacks on blacks ignited the race riots in 1919 in Chicago. Similarly a white gang called the "Dukes" attacked blacks in New York City.

[141] Alonso quotes the founder of the "Businessmen" saying that "You couldn't pass Alameda Blvd. because those white boys in South Gate would set you on fire." This group was based in the Central Vernon area (near downtown Los Angeles). South Gate is just a few miles southeast. This section, along with Huntington Park and Inglewood, were mostly white and they literally surrounded the black community in South Central Los Angeles. Today these areas are predominantly black and Hispanic. This group, like similar groups of blacks in Chicago, began to function as a defense against whites. See also Suttles, G. (1968). *The Social Order of the Slum*. Chicago: University of Chicago Press.

[142] Bing, *Do or Die*, pp. 148–49.

[143] Davis, *City of Quartz*, pp. 294–96. Davis provides an insightful analysis of the role of the Los Angeles Police Department in helping to perpetuate gangs, particularly with their efforts to eliminate them. Chief William Parker in the 1950s engaged in a war on narcotics in both the south-central and East Los Angeles areas, which translated into a war on gangs. This included an attack on the Group Guidance Unit of the Los Angeles Probation Department, which had been set up after the Zoot Suit riots to help young offenders. To Parker, these youths were unreformable criminals who needed stiff prison sentences. Chief Daryl Gates in the 1980s and early 1990s took a similar hard line.

[144] Alonso, "Racialized Identities." See also Davis, *City of Quartz*, p. 297 and Baker, B. (1988, June 26). "Homeboys: Players in a Deadly Drama." *Los Angeles Times*.

[145] Reiner, *Gangs, Crime and Violence in Los Angeles*, p. 5.

[146] Davis, *City of Quartz*, p. 299; Reiner, *Gangs, Crime and Violence in Los Angeles*, p. 6.

[147] Washington was killed in 1979. Williams was convicted of murdering four people in 1979; he was sentenced to death in 1981. From San Quentin's death row, he wrote nine children's books warning about the dangers of gang life, for which he was twice nominated for the Nobel Peace Prize. Williams acknowledged the glamorous lifestyle that gangs allowed him but also regretted the pain and destruction caused. Well aware of the seductive nature of the gang, he wrote his books to warn young people about potential consequences and to alert them to alternatives to gang life. He received more than 50,000 e-mails from youths, parents, teachers, and law enforcement officers stating that his writings changed and saved lives. In 2004, Jamie Fox played the title role in a movie, *Redemption: The Stan Tookie Williams Story*. Williams was executed by lethal injection on December 13, 2005.

[148] Davis, *City of Quartz*, p. 299.

[149] The FBI and other police organizations engaged in a systematic elimination of the Black Panther Party in the 1960s largely through COINTELPRO, a counterintelligence program established by the FBI to "disrupt, harass, and discredit groups that the FBI decided were in some way 'un-American.'" This included the American Civil Liberties Union and just about every African-American political organization in the country whose views were in any way militant. Chambliss, W. (1993). "State Organized Crime." In W. Chambliss and M. Zatz (Eds.), *Making Law: The State, the Law and Structural Contradictions*. Bloomington: Indiana University Press, p. 308; Chomsky, N. (1999). "Domestic Terrorism: Notes on the State System of Oppression." *New Political Science* 21: 303–24.

[150] Davis, *City of Quartz*, p. 298; Alonso ("Racialized Identities") also makes this argument.

[151] Ibid.

[152] Alonso, "Racialized Identities."

[153] Ibid.

[154] Shelden et al., *Youth Gangs*, ch. 2.

[155] Perkins, U. E. (1987). *Explosion of Chicago's Black Street Gangs: 1900 to the Present*. Chicago: Third World Press, pp. 54–55.

[156] National Gang Center (2009). *National Youth Gang Center Survey Analysis*. Retrieved from http://www.nationalgangcenter.gov/Survey-Analysis/Demographics#anchorregm. Such a low estimate may be a reflection of both the standard definitions of "gangs" and a racial bias or stereotype of what gangs are. There would probably be more white gangs and white gang members if the criteria that are used to define "gang" were expanded. This would especially be the case if groups known as "taggers" were included in the definition of "gang," not to mention biker groups, which are not included in the standard definitions.

[157] Ibid. Retrieved from http://www.nationalgangcenter.gov/About/FAQ

[158] Wooden, W. S. (1995). *Renegade Kids, Suburban Outlaws*. Belmont, CA: Wadsworth, p.129.

[159] Ibid., p. 131.

[160] Ibid., p. 136.

[161] Ibid.

[162] Simi, P. (2003). "Rage in the City of Angels: The Historical Development of the Skinhead Subculture in Los Angeles." Unpublished doctoral dissertation, Department of Sociology, University of Nevada-Las Vegas. Unless otherwise noted, the remainder of the discussion on skinheads is taken from this source.

163 Wooden, *Renegade Kids*, pp. 133–34.

164 Los Angeles County Sheriff's Department, *L.A. Style*, p. 39.

165 Ibid., pp. 160–64.

166 Jackson and McBride, *Understanding Street Gangs*, pp. 42–45.

167 Wooden, *Renegade Kids*, p. 115.

168 Ibid., p. 118.

169 Ibid., p. 119.

170 Ibid., p. 124.

171 Los Angeles County. (1999, August). *Gangs*. Santa Clarita Valley, Cobra Unit, Los Angeles County Sheriff's Department.

FEMALE DELINQUENCY

More than 350,000 girls were arrested in 2009, about 30% of all arrests of people under the age of 18.[1] Who is the typical female delinquent? What behavior brings her in contact with the juvenile justice system? How do her violations differ from those committed by boys? How are they similar? What causes her to get into trouble? What happens to her if she is arrested? These are questions that few members of the general public could answer quickly. When the public talks about delinquency or youth crime, they generally mean male behavior.

Although there are many similarities between male and female delinquency, there are also significant differences. First, and most important, girls tend to be arrested for offenses that are less serious than those committed by boys. Half of all girls are arrested for one of two offenses: larceny theft (usually shoplifting) and running away from home. Crimes committed by boys are more varied.

Running away from home points to another significant aspect of female delinquency. Girls are often arrested for offenses that are not actual crimes—running away from home, being incorrigible, or being beyond parental control. This is not a recent development. In the early years of the juvenile justice system, most of the girls in juvenile court were charged with status offenses—a trend that continues. In 2009, for example, girls made up 55% of arrests for running away from home (see table 5-3). The most recent census of juvenile correctional facilities (2007) shows that 11% of the confined girls were in for status offenses, compared to only 3% of the boys (compared to 21% of girls in 1997 and 4% of boys).[2]

Why are girls more likely to be arrested than boys for running away from home? There are no easy answers to this question. Studies of actual delinquency (not simply arrests) show that girls and boys run away from home in about equal numbers. There is some evidence to suggest that parents and police may be responding differently to the same behavior. Parents may be calling the police when their daughters do not come home, and police may be more likely to arrest a female than a male runaway.

The reasons that boys and girls have for leaving home can also contribute to the differing responses to running away. Girls are much more likely than boys to be the victims of child sexual abuse; some experts estimate that roughly 70% of the victims of such abuse are girls. Not surprisingly, the evidence also suggests a link between sexual abuse and girls' delinquency—particularly running away from home. Several studies indicate that a large number (often two-thirds to three-quarters) of the girls in runaway shelters or juvenile detention facilities have been sexually abused. The numbers of girls who experience serious problems with physical abuse are also high. The relationship between girls' problems, their attempts to escape victimization by running away, and the traditional reaction of the juvenile justice system are all unique aspects of girls' interaction with the system.[3]

The Extent of Female Delinquency

Like all criminal and delinquent behavior, female delinquency encompasses a very wide range of activities. Girls can be labeled as delinquent for the commission of crimes (e.g., burglary, larceny, assault) or for status offenses. As mentioned in previous chapters, these are offenses for which only juveniles can be taken into custody and include an array of behaviors (running away from home, being a truant, violating a curfew, being incorrigible or "beyond control"). Status offenses play a major and controversial role in female delinquency.

This section looks at data from a variety of sources to determine not only how much female delinquency exists but also its manifestations. We compare the portraits of girls' offending drawn by official agencies like the police and the juvenile courts with those based on anonymous, self-report studies. We also look at gender differences in delinquency and trends in girls' delinquency over time.

Recent Trends: National Arrest Data

Crime in the United States includes information on persons under the age of 18 arrested for a variety of offenses. The 2009 arrest figures (table 5-1) reveal that there are considerable gender differences in official delinquency (that is, the picture of delinquency derived from statistics maintained by law enforcement officers). Most obvious is that far fewer girls than boys are arrested for delinquent behavior. Although 354,012 girls were arrested in 2009, more than twice as many males were arrested (807,818). Boys are far more likely than girls to be arrested for violent crimes and for the most serious property crimes (burglary, motor vehicle theft, and arson). Because of these arrest patterns, serious violent and property offenses have traditionally been considered "masculine" offenses.

Girls are more likely to be arrested for running away from home (55% of arrests; see table 5-3) and prostitution (79% of all arrests, not included in table 5-3 because the number of arrests was so small). These are the only two categories in which female arrests outnumber male arrests (see table 5-1). The male-to-female ratios are fairly close for larceny-theft (54% male; 46% female; females have narrowed the gap in recent years); this category had the largest number of arrests (196,863) in 2009. Girls approach the percentages for boys in the commission of some status offenses, such as liquor-law violations—this category is the seventh highest in number of arrests (see table 2-1). Boys outnumber girls by a considerable margin for drug law violations (boys constituted about 84% of arrests for this offense).

Arrest statistics provide a portrait of the character of official delinquency for both females and males. The distribution of arrests within each sex cohort (table 5-1) shows that the bulk of offenses for which both males and females are arrested are relatively minor; many do not have a clearly defined victim. For example, larceny-theft represented the highest percentage of arrests for girls

Table 5-1 Arrests of Persons under 18, by Sex, 2009

	Male		Female	
	Number	**Percent**	**Number**	**Percent**
Total	**807,818**	**100.0**	**354,012**	**100.0**
Index Crimes				
Homicide	599	*	53	*
Forcible rape	1,792	*	28	*
Robbery	17,342	2.1	1,994	*
Aggravated assault	22,685	2.8	7,247	2.0
Burglary	40,897	5.1	5,740	1.6
Larceny-theft	106,852	13.2	90,011	25.4
Motor vehicle theft	9,412	1.2	1,942	*
Arson	3,138	*	477	*
Total violent	42,418	5.3	9,322	2.6
Total property	160,299	19.8	98,170	27.7
Total index	202,717	25.1	107,492	30.4
Part II Offenses				
Other assaults	88,631	11.0	46,494	13.1
Forgery/counterfeiting	889	*	388	*
Fraud	2,637	*	1,454	*
Embezzlement	224	*	169	*
Stolen property	9,670	1.2	2,320	*
Vandalism	48,203	6.0	7,554	2.1
Weapons	18,553	2.3	2,143	*
Prostitution	167	*	624	*
Other sex offenses	7,061	*	738	*
Drugs	86,857	10.8	16,800	4.7
Gambling	304	*	8	*
Offenses against the family	1,701	*	988	*
DUI	6,033	*	2,052	*
Liquor laws	41,879	5.2	25,980	7.3
Drunkenness	7,381	*	2,456	*
Disorderly conduct	61,616	7.6	31,138	8.8
Vagrancy	824	*	223	*
Curfew and loitering	50,288	6.2	21,915	6.2
Runaway	26,800	3.3	32,423	9.2
All other offenses	145,385	18.0	50,653	14.3

*Less than .1%

Source: Federal Bureau of Investigation (2010). *Crime in the United States, 2009*. Retrieved from http://www2.fbi.gov/ucr/cius2009/data/table_33.html

(25%) and the second highest for boys (13.2%). In contrast, only 5.3% of boys' arrests and 2.6% of girls' arrests in 2009 were for serious violent crime.

Status offenses play a more significant role in girls' arrests than in boys' arrests. The status offenses of running away and curfew/loitering accounted for about 15% of all girls' arrests in 2009, but only 9.5% of boys' arrests. The gap in status offense arrests narrowed somewhat in the last decade. The status offense of running away accounted for 9.2% of all girls' arrests, compared with 3.3% of boys' arrests. The UCR arrest figures understate the extent of status offense arrests. They compile separate statistics for only running away and curfew violations. Other status offenses (such as "incorrigibility," "unmanageability," and truancy), which are important components of both male and female delinquency, are lumped in the "all other offenses" category. As shown in table 5-1, 14.3% of girls' arrests and 18% of boys' arrests fall into this category—the highest percentage of arrests for males, and the second highest for females.

Both girls and boys are arrested in large numbers for alcohol-related offenses, but burglary and vandalism (which account for about 11% of boys' offenses) are relatively unimportant in the delinquency of girls (accounting for less than 4% of their arrests). Generally, official delinquency is dominated by less serious offenses, and this is particularly true of female delinquency. A 10-year compari-

Table 5-2   Rank Order of Arrests for Juveniles, 1999 and 2008
(Figures based on percent distribution within each sex cohort)

Male		Female	
2000	**2009**	**2000**	**2009**
1. All other (17.8)	All other (18.0)	Larceny-theft (21.0)	Larceny-theft (25.0)
2. Larceny-theft (14.0)[1]	Larceny-theft (13.2)	All other (16.1)	All other (14.3)
3. Drug violations (9.8)	Other assaults (11.0)	Runaway (13.1)	Other assaults (13.1)
4. Other assaults (9.4)	Drugs (10.8)	Other assaults (10.8)	Runaway (9.2)
5. Disorderly con.(6.7)	Disorderly con. (7.6)	Liquor laws (7.5)	Disorderly con. (8.8)

	Male		Female	
	2000	**2009**	**2000**	**2009**
Arrests for serious violent offenses[2]	4.7	5.3	2.8	2.6
Arrests for all violent offenses[3]	14.2	16.2	13.5	15.8
Arrests for status offenses[4]	10.0	9.5	20.5	15.3

Notes

[1] "All other" refers to a variety of offenses, usually state and local ordinances. Among the most common include public nuisance, trespassing, failure to appear on warrants, contempt of court, and, for juveniles especially, violation of various court orders (e.g., probation, parole) and certain status offenses. This category does not include traffic offenses.

[2] Arrests for murder, robbery, rape, and aggravated assault.

[3] Also includes arrests for other assaults, a part II crime.

[4] Arrests for curfew and runaway.

Source: Federal Bureau of Investigation (2010). *Crime in the United States, 2009*. Retrieved from http://www2.fbi.gov/ucr/cius2009/data/table_33.html

Table 5-3   Girls' Share of all Juvenile Arrests, 2000 and 2009 (Index Crimes and Selected Part II Offenses)

	2000	2009
Part I Crimes		
Homicide	12.2	8.1
Rape	.8	1.5
Robbery	9.3	10.3
Aggravated assault	23.3	24.2
Burglary	11.9	12.3
Larceny-theft	36.9	45.7
Motor vehicle theft	17.1	17.1
Arson	11.9	13.2
Total violent	18.4	18.0
Total property	30.2	38.0
Selected Part II Offenses		
Other assaults	30.8	34.4
Stolen property	15.6	19.3
Vandalism	12.4	13.5
Weapons	10.2	10.4
Drugs	15.4	16.2
Liquor laws	31.6	38.3
Disorderly conduct	29.4	33.6
Curfew	30.8	30.4
Runaway	58.7	54.7
All other	26.1	25.8

Federal Bureau of Investigation, *Crime in the United States, 2009*. Retrieved from http://www2.fbi.gov/ucr/cius2009/data/table_33.html

son of offenses that accounted for the greatest number of girls' and boys' arrests in 2000 and 2009 (table 5-2) shows this clearly. Boys were most likely to have been arrested for "all other" and larceny-theft offenses. Larceny-theft ranks first among girls' arrests for both 2000 and 2009, accounting for about a quarter of all girls' arrests in both years. The largest percentage decreases in categories with significant numbers of arrests during this decade were motor vehicle theft (–59.6%), runaways (–35.1%), liquor law violations (–30.3%), curfew violations (–25.8%), and vandalism (–21.8%).[4] In the last decade, drug offenses have appeared in the top five for boys' arrests, but not for girls.

What are the trends in female delinquency? Are there more female delinquents today? Are they more likely than their counterparts of a previous time period to commit "masculine offenses"? FBI data for the past few decades reveal some interesting patterns. First, the number of girls arrested rose dramatically during the 1960s and early 1970s. Between 1960 and 1975, for example, the number increased 250%. Statistics like these, particularly when coupled with increases in the arrests of girls for nontraditional offenses, such as a 503.5% hike in the arrests of teenage girls for serious, violent crimes, encouraged many to believe that the women's movement had triggered a crime wave among young women.[5] The contention has since been discredited.[6]

The share of total arrests of girls went from 28% in 2000 to 30% in 2009. Arrests for most offenses decreased, but disorderly conduct increased 7.3%, other assaults 5.7%, and larceny-theft 5.2% (while the percentages for males decreased 11.7%, 10.2%, and 26.9% respectively). Girls still lag behind boys in number of arrests by a considerable margin for all offenses, with the exceptions of running away and prostitution as mentioned above.

As for overall trends in arrests of girls, the rates per 100,000 (see table 5-4) for most serious crimes have been decreasing for both males and females. Arrests for violent crime went steadily down for boys during the past 20 years and fluctuated slightly for girls.

The largest increases in girls' arrests since 1990 have been in the categories drugs, disorderly conduct, "other assaults," and curfew. The latter category increased 46% since 1990, but increased 212% in the first decade before declining in the second. Similarly, drugs increased 178% then declined to an overall increase of 148%. Both disorderly conduct and other assaults increased signifi-

Table 5-4   Juvenile Arrest Rate Trends (per 100,000 population aged 10–17)

	Female			Male		
	1990	1999	2008	1990	1999	2008
Part I Crimes						
Homicide	*	*	*	22	8	7
Rape	*	*	*	42	30	19
Robbery	27	17	21	277	167	191
Aggravated assault	75	104	81	395	336	250
Burglary	84	74	62	920	549	430
Larceny-theft	987	910	888	2333	1537	1068
Motor vehicle theft	76	56	24	604	272	123
Arson	5	6	5	45	44	32
Total violent	105	122	102	736	542	465
Total property	1152	1046	979	3903	2401	1652
Selected Part II Crimes						
Other assaults	258	473	485	803	1008	882
Vandalism	78	92	87	803	631	536
Weapons	19	27	24	268	241	210
Drugs	69	192	171	527	1075	892
Liquor laws	334	333	305	808	701	480
Disorderly conduct	187	326	381	687	790	740
Curfew	179	559	261	453	774	546
Runaway	723	586	377	522	379	279
Total	3754	4429	3878	12,090	12,136	8642

*Less than 1 per 100,000.

Source: U.S. Department of Justice, OJJDP, Statistical Briefing Book. http://www.ojjdp.ncjrs.gov/ojstatbb/crime/JAR_Display.asp?ID=qa05230

cantly in the first decade and then grew more slowly, reaching increases of 88% and 104% respectively.

There are several possible explanations for the increases in arrests for other assaults. First, many of these increases could be attributed to the increase in girls' involvement in gang-related offenses. (It is also possible that the increase in arrests is the result of increased police attention to the gang problem, rather than a real increase in violent behavior.) Second, some of the increase could be attributed to greater attention given to the problem of domestic violence, which has resulted in more arrests for both males and females. Third, and perhaps more important, it is possible that many of the recent arrests on assault charges are due to greater attention to normal adolescent fighting and/or girls fighting with parents.[7] Previously this type of aggression was ignored or dealt with informally.

Taking the decade of the 1990s as a whole, we see a huge contradiction between media representations, the "law and order" rhetoric of most politicians, and reality. Despite media images of "wild, uncontrollable youths" preying on citizens everywhere, in actuality there was a significant *decrease* in youth crime for both sexes in that decade. And this drop continued throughout the following decade, as clearly shown in tables 5-2, 5-3, 5-4, and figure 5-1. With significant declines in almost all categories of offenses, there is little data to support the belief that girls are becoming more violent. What the arrest figures may demonstrate more than anything else is a change in official crime control policies that, among other consequences, have resulted in targeting certain kinds of youthful behaviors (e.g., drug use, schoolyard fights, and domestic disturbances.)

Arrest statistics tell only part of the story. An obvious problem is that the FBI's figures are based on police contacts that result in an arrest; however, the police do not arrest everyone who has committed an offense. Further, police officers "contact" many more youths than they arrest.[8] These two facts make it possible that arrest statistics are as much a measure of police behavior as they are of criminal behavior. For a more complete picture of the extent of female delinquency, it is also necessary to examine a very popular alternative source of information on the volume of delinquency: self-report surveys. In such surveys people respond anonymously to questionnaires or participate anonymously in interviews about their delinquent activities, especially about acts that never come to the attention of the police.

Self-Report Surveys

Researchers have long used self-report surveys to attempt to gain information about the extent of juvenile delinquency. Typically, the surveys reveal that female delinquency is more common than arrest statistics indicate and that there are more similarities than official statistics suggest between male and female juvenile delinquency. They also show males are more involved in delinquency, especially the most serious types of offenses. These findings point to some possible gender biases operating within the juvenile justice system, because self-report data show about as many boys as girls committing status offenses.

Figure 5-1

Arrests per 100,000 males ages 10–17, 1980–2008

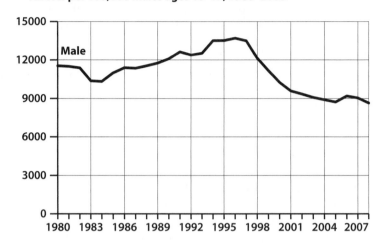

Arrests per 100,000 females ages 10–17, 1980–2008

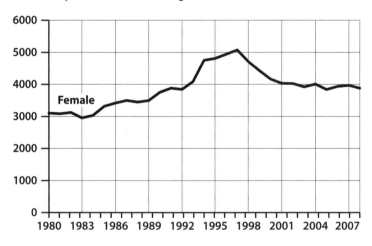

Source: U.S. Department of Justice, OJJDP, Statistical Briefing Book. http://www.ojjdp.gov/ojstatbb/crime/
JAR_Display.asp?ID=qa05230&text=yes

Concerning the volume of unreported female delinquency, surveys have found that although the ratio of male to female arrestees was approximately 4:1 in the late seventies, that ratio was twice as large as the mean ratio of just over 2:1 found in self-report data.[9] Similar findings have also been reported in other self-report studies.

In a comprehensive review of self-report studies published between 1955 and 1977, Darrell Steffensmeier and Renée Steffensmeier noted that male–female differences tend to be greater for crimes of violence and serious property crimes.

Males and females report similar rates (especially in more recent surveys) for such offenses as truancy, driving without a license, running away from home, and minor forms of theft. The fact that males and females are about equally as likely to admit running away is interesting because females are much more likely to be arrested (as already indicated) and to be referred to the juvenile court for this offense.[10] A study that compared girls' arrests for running away and incorrigibility with girls' self-reports of these two activities underscored these results. It found a 10% overrepresentation of girls arrested for running away and an astounding 31% overrepresentation in arrests for incorrigibility.[11]

It might be useful to consider in some detail a picture of female delinquency drawn from various self-report surveys. Rachelle Canter analyzed data from the National Youth Survey over time and found much similarity between female and male delinquency. There was no behavior in which girls were significantly more involved than boys—even in offenses traditionally ascribed to girls (such as prostitution and running away from home).[12]

In the 1970s Stephen Cernkovich and Peggy Giordano analyzed a self-report survey of Midwestern youths. Their study divided self-reported delinquency into three categories: one in which the proportion of males admitting commission of the offense exceeds the female proportion by a considerable margin, one in which the proportion of males only moderately exceeds females, and one in which almost equal numbers of girls and boys admit having committed the offense.[13]

The unexpected similarity in girls' and boys' violence against parents highlights another problem with some of the offense categories used in arrest statistics: categories can obscure significant differences in specific behaviors and in responses to those behaviors. Consider, for example, property damage. The National Youth Survey found that girls damage family property and males tend to damage other kinds of property (e.g., school property). A similar pattern appears in the area of assault, with girls closing the gender gap when simple assault against parents is considered. This pattern suggests that the setting in which delinquent behavior occurs and the relationship between victim and assailant differ for males and females in many offenses. These differences may have important implications for reporting and for the reactions of juvenile justice officials.[14]

The 2009 National Survey on Drug Use and Health also reported similar findings for male and female involvement in a number of activities. The male percentage of youths who self-reported trying to steal anything worth more than $50 in the past year was 5.6%, versus 3.1% of females.[15] Serious fights at school or work had fairly similar percentages, with 24.6% of males reporting such activity and 17.5% of females. The numbers for participation in a group-against-group fight in the past year were even more similar: 15.9% of males and 12.7% of females. Attacks with intent to seriously harm others were reported by 8.7% of male respondents and 5.6% of females.[16] A higher percentage of females (27% versus 19% of males) reported arguing or fighting with at least one parent 10 times or more in the past year.[17]

The Nature of Female Delinquency

The remainder of this chapter will look at some of the major forms of delinquent behavior committed by girls: shoplifting, status offenses, running away and the corresponding problem of prostitution, and violent offenses. A detailed look at the many dimensions of these offenses reveals a great deal about the lives of the girls who become enmeshed in the juvenile justice system.

Shoplifting: The Prototypical Girls' Crime?

As discussed in the previous section, one-fourth of girls arrested are charged with "larceny-theft," which consists primarily of shoplifting. In such a consumer culture, this is not a surprising statistic; in fact the category of larceny-theft dominates the FBI's index crime list every year.[18] Studies, including one in New Mexico of those appearing in a "teen court" program, consistently document the frequency of this crime.[19] In England, a survey found that there were more than 4 million shoplifting incidents reported to the police each year and about 1.3 million arrests.[20] Women in Great Britain tend to shoplift fewer and less costly items than do men; they also tend to be less sophisticated or professional.

As we saw in chapter 3, there have been significant increases in shoplifting during the past several years. We also noted the contribution our consumer culture makes to the problem, especially focusing on the encouragement of girls to go shopping. Is it any wonder, then, that girls are far more likely to engage in shoplifting? Or are they?[21]

The few studies of shoplifters have focused more on adults and on the decision of store personnel to prosecute than on shoplifters' motives. According to self-report studies, however, males are more likely to shoplift. An English self-report study found they outnumbered females by a 2:1 ratio. Another study also found males to be more likely than females to shoplift, but the male to female ratio for youths "cautioned by the police" or actually sentenced was only 1.7:1. Allison Morris suggests that females are more often detected by store personnel because the latter expect women to shoplift more than men and therefore watch women more closely. She cites research that found that British police believe more girls shoplift than boys and that the items stolen differ. Yet, official statistics revealed that females constituted only 36% of those cautioned or found guilty of shoplifting.[22]

Ruth Horowitz and Ann Pottieger found a similar pattern when they compared girls' self-reports of delinquency in Florida with official arrests. The police tended to arrest fewer girls than boys for major felonies, but they arrested more girls than boys for petty property crimes. The researchers suggested that this might have been a product of police bias because shoplifting is seen as a "stereotypical female crime."[23]

Several recent self-report studies have shown little or no difference in shoplifting between girls and boys and a few show boys with slightly higher rates. A survey of adolescents in Montana found that males were more likely than females to engage in shoplifting.[24] A study in the Netherlands found similar rates of shoplifting among girls and boys.[25] Another European study found that males were more likely to shoplift than girls.[26] A study of college students also found that males were more likely than females to shoplift.[27]

Explanations of male and female shoplifting have generally been simplistic and gender biased. A common explanation for female shoplifting is that it is a result of subconscious motivations, depression, or poverty.[28] Another explanation is that shoplifting among girls is explained as "outlets for sexual frustration." Also girls' shoplifting has been explained as the result of being "led astray," or being "sick" or "evil," while shoplifting by males is usually seen as "rational" and based upon economic considerations. Pamela Davies makes the point that: "Traditional explanations never recognized the economic motivation or the fact that money might be equally a motivating factor for women as for men. The possibility of rationality being a female criminal attribute has never been systematically explored."[29] A common explanation of male shoplifting is that it results from "peer-group pressure and the search for excitement."[30] An English study concluded that shoplifters are under both personal and physical stress, tend to be depressed, suffer from low self-esteem, and have various personality problems.[31] A study in Buffalo, New York, cited lack of "self-control" as the principle cause.[32]

Note that the above studies focused on the alleged "defects" of those who shoplift, as if stealing something from a store is "abnormal" or indicative of some "underlying problem." One consideration that rarely appears in work on shoplifting is that young people, especially girls, may be inordinately sensitive to the consumer culture: they steal things they feel they need or may actually need but cannot afford. For example, Anne Campbell notes that women—young and old—are the targets of enormously expensive advertising campaigns for a vast array of personal products. They also constitute a large proportion of those who shop, spend more time doing it as a pastime, and consequently are exposed to greater temptation.[33] Temptation is probably most pronounced for girls, who feel that popularity is linked to physical appearance and participation in fashions and fads. Perhaps this may partly explain the fact that about one in every 10 to 15 shoppers has shoplifted at least once in their lives.[34] JoAnne Sweeney offered a more nuanced perspective in her study of college students. She found that those who engaged in shoplifting had personality characteristics and belief systems that placed greater emphasis on "individualist values" (e.g., hedonism) and less emphasis on such "collectivist values" as benevolence and conformity that were shared by those who did not shoplift.[35]

Shoplifters do not exhibit mental illness, and they are typically not "kleptomaniacs" as defined by the DSMIV.[36] Shoplifting behavior is most likely to be influenced by peers who also shoplift, especially those who have not yet been caught. The most influential factor in the decision to shoplift for those in Sweeney's study was money (mentioned by 41% of the shoplifting subjects), while 21% reported that they shoplifted for the "thrill," and another 18% did so because of "peer pressure."[37]

Participation in the teen consumer subculture is costly. If a young woman cannot afford to participate, she may very well steal what she wants. Studies spanning two decades have documented that girls in both Europe and America are more likely than boys to shoplift cosmetics and clothes. Boys, in contrast, are much more likely to steal electronic items.[38] Moreover, because girls spend more time shopping, they undergo more scrutiny by store detectives, who report they are suspicious of young people in groups, particularly if they are not dressed well.[39] In short, the teenage subculture may be particularly hard on girls from poor families. They are bombarded daily with the message that they are acceptable only if they look a particular way, and yet they may not have the money to purchase the "look." These pressures can be seen in the comments of one delinquent girl:

> I took everything. I mean from pins to makeup, and fingernail polish and fake fingernails. Even toothbrushes [laughs]. We went over there to go shopping, but I told them, "Nah, I shop for you guys," and what I went away with . . . was almost $300. I had two packages full.[40]

It is also important to note how shoplifting often occurs within the context of serious life problems among some girls. For instance, a study of 38 drug-addicted women found a direct link between early life trauma and later criminal activities, including shoplifting and prostitution. Most of the women in this study were African American and grew up in some of the worst kinds of circumstances imaginable in the inner cities of Philadelphia and Camden, New Jersey. Their early lives were marked by constant abuse, both physical and sexual (many victimized by alcoholic parents), and they began to engage in drug use at an early age and eventually were drawn into the world of crime, as shoplifters and "sex workers." Most started drinking and using drugs at around the age of 12 or 13 and some even younger.[41]

In general, shoplifting by girls must be placed within the context of girls' lives in a youth- and consumer-oriented culture. The drawbacks of not having money are evident, and for girls there are few avenues to teenage success. Shoplifting, then, is a social cost attributable to the bombarding of young people with images of looks and goods most cannot afford.

Status Offenses

As emphasized earlier, one of the distinguishing characteristics of female delinquency is the role played by status offenses. Arrest statistics consistently show that running away and curfew violation constitute a major portion of official female delinquency. These two offenses accounted for 15% of all arrests of girls in 2009 and 9.5% of all arrests for boys (in 2000, the percentages were 21% and 10%).

As discussed in chapter 3, the early juvenile justice system developed the concept of status offenses specifically to distinguish between delinquent and criminal behavior.[42] Despite the intent, status offenses have subjected many youths to court action. Legislation to curb the courts' authority was enacted in 1974. As mentioned in chapter 3, The Juvenile Justice and Delinquency Prevention Act (JJDPA) required that states receiving federal delinquency-prevention money divert and deinstitutionalize youth arrested and/or referred to court for status offenses. Proponents of the act argued that community agencies rather than police departments and juvenile courts were more appropriate entities to deal with youths who are not guilty of criminal behavior.[43]

After more than a century, girls are still much more likely to be referred to court after an arrest for a status offense. Running away is the fourth most common offense for which girls are arrested, and girls are more than three times more likely as boys to be detained for a status offense. Girls are four times more likely than boys to be placed in a correctional facility for a status offense (14% versus 4%)[44]

For many years statistics showing large numbers of girls arrested and referred to court for status offenses were taken as evidence of the different types of male and female delinquency. However, as we have seen, self-report studies of male and female delinquency do not reflect the differences in misbehavior found in official statistics. A persuasive explanation for the differences between official and unofficial rates of female delinquency is that the juvenile justice system's historic commitment to the idea of the state as parent has encouraged abuse of the status offense category. Because parents are likely to set different standards of obedience for their male and female children, and because there are few legal guidelines concerning what constitutes a reasonable parental request, parents are able to refer their children to court for a variety of activities. Research dating back many decades has affirmed this.[45]

Gender-specific socialization patterns have not changed very much over the years, and this is especially true for parents' relationships with daughters. A study conducted in the 1970s found that even parents who opposed sexism in general, felt "uncomfortable tampering with existing traditions."[46] More recent research confirms that not much has changed. Barrie Thorne found parents have new reasons to enforce a sexual double standard. Concerned about sexual harassment, rape, and HIV/AIDS, parents and other adults mix protection with punishment and "often tighten control of girls when they become adolescents, and sexuality becomes a terrain of struggle between the generations."[47] Thorne also noted that as girls use sexuality as a proxy for independence, they reinforce their status as sexual objects seeking male approval—ultimately ratifying their status as the subordinate sex. Girls were still using "cosmetics, discussions of boyfriends, dressing sexually, and other forms of exaggerated 'teen' femininity to challenge adult, and class and race-based authority in schools." She also found that "the double standard persists, and girls who are overtly sexual run the risk of being labeled 'sluts.'"[48] Peggy Orenstein's observations also point to the durability of the sexual double standard; at the schools she observed sex "ruins girls" but "enhanced boys."[49] The most recent research exploring a variety of socialization issues still finds evidence of gender differences and traditional sex role expectations.[50]

Childhood sexual abuse often leads girls into behaviors such as running away from home or other status offenses.[51] Girls experience sexual abuse at an earlier age than boys do. Their abuse is more likely to be perpetrated by family members (usually the father or the stepfather); consequently, it has a longer duration than abuse of boys. All of these factors are associated with more severe trauma, causing dramatic short- and long-term effects in victims, which include "fear, anxiety, depression, anger and hostility, and inappropriate sexual behavior." Other effects include running away from home, difficulties in school, truancy, and early marriage.[52] The vast majority of girls who run away have been sexually abused, with many suffering post-traumatic stress disorder.[53] The most recent research has reinforced these findings. For instance, one recent study found that girls who have experienced sexual abuse have a much higher incidence of suicide attempts, PTSD, abnormal brain development, aggression and drug and alcohol problems.[54]

National research on the characteristics of girls in the juvenile justice system clearly shows the role played by physical and sexual abuse in girls' delinquency. Although somewhat dated, a study of girls in juvenile correctional settings conducted by the American Correctional Association in the late 1980s showed that a very large proportion of these girls—about half of whom were of minority backgrounds—had experienced physical abuse (61%), with nearly half saying that they had been abused 11 or more times. Most were 9 years of age or younger when the abuse began. Although many had reported the abuse, either nothing changed (30%) or the reporting made things worse (25%).[55] The vast majority of girls surveyed had run away from home (81%), and 39% had run away 10 or more times. Over half (54%) said that they had attempted suicide; when asked why, they replied they "felt no one cared." Girls who had used running away as a survival or coping strategy found that their self-protective behavior was criminalized. Their first arrests were typically for running away from home (21%), and they eventually were confined in a juvenile correctional facility.[56]

Detailed studies of youth entering the juvenile justice system in Florida have compared the problems of girls and boys entering detention. Female youth were more likely than male youth to have abuse histories and contact with the juvenile justice system for status offenses, while male youth had higher rates of involvement with a variety of delinquent offenses. Further research on youths admitted to an assessment center in Tampa concluded that "girls' problem behavior commonly relates to an abusive and traumatizing home, life, whereas boys' law violating behavior reflects their involvement in a delinquent life style."[57]

Study after study documents the devastating effects of abuse on subsequent behavior. Prostitution is one outcome; in one study 60% of the street prostitutes interviewed had been sexually abused as juveniles.[58] Girls who had been adjudged guilty of either status or delinquent offenses in Arkansas reported high levels of sexual and physical abuse: 53% had been sexually abused; 25% had scars; 38% recalled bleeding from abuse.[59] A survey of girls in the juvenile justice system in Wisconsin found that 79% had been subjected to physical abuse that resulted in some injury, 50% had been sexually assaulted, and 32% had been sexually abused by parents or persons closely connected to their families.[60] A study of youths in a runaway shelter in Toronto reported that 73% of the females and 38% of the males had been sexually abused.[61]

More recent research arrives at the same results—running away is linked with negative home environments consisting of both physical and sexual abuse.[62] One recent study found that girls in correctional institutions were more often diagnosed with major types of depression than were boys.[63] A study of youth in a Hawaii Youth Correctional Facility found that girls are more likely than boys to have histories of neglect, sexual abuse, and also foster care placement; they also had more parents involved in the criminal justice system and relationships with older men, in addition to more drug use and self-injurious behaviors."[64]

A profile of girls in the Illinois youth correctional system found that: "Over half of these females had experienced either physical and/or sexual abuse at least once in their lifetime. Over 95 percent of the females who reported physical, emotional, or verbal abuse and nearly three-quarters of the females reporting past sexual abuse reportedly knew their victimizers (e.g., family members, boyfriends, other relatives, etc.)." Not surprisingly these girls had many of the problems normally linked with abuse, such as school troubles (the report noted that 45% had been suspended at least once and 23% had dropped out) and mental health issues (about 75% had been diagnosed with a mental health disorder) and suicide (38% had reported suicidal thoughts and more than 25% had attempted suicide).[65] A report by Human Rights Watch on girls in the New York youth prison system also found the exact same background characteristics, noting in particular that their "history of abuse may be the most significant underlying cause of behaviors leading to girls' delinquency."[66]

A study of the backgrounds of adult women in prison underscores the important link between childhood victimization and later criminal careers. Meda Chesney-Lind and Noelie Rodriguez interviewed female offenders and found that most were victims of physical and/or sexual abuse as youngsters: over 60% had been sexually abused, and about 50% had been raped. Their situations prompted them to run away from home (75% were arrested for this and other status offense charges) and to engage in prostitution and petty property crimes for survival. Many also started what would become lifetime problems with drugs. With little education and almost no marketable occupational skills, the women were trapped in this type of criminal behavior and eventually were imprisoned.[67]

Cathy Widom found that abused or neglected females were twice as likely as a matched group of control subjects to have an adult criminal record: 16% compared with 7.5%. The difference among men was not as dramatic: 42% compared with 33%. Men from abusive backgrounds were also more likely than members of the control group to contribute to the "cycle of violence," with more arrests for violent offenses as adults. In contrast, when women with abusive backgrounds entered the criminal justice system, their arrests tended to involve property and public order offenses, such as disorderly conduct, curfew violation, and loitering.[68] Another study found that child sexual abuse victims were more likely to be arrested for prostitution as adults than were non-sexually abused juveniles.[69] Similar conclusions were found in a study of adolescent runaways and homeless women.[70]

In summary, girls may well have several legitimate reasons to differ with their parents—reasons that may bring them into court as status offenders. The juvenile justice system, because of its history and structure, has tended to ignore children's rights in favor of judicial support for family authority and power over offspring. Girls who may in fact be victims find themselves arrested and referred to court for noncriminal offenses.

Runaways

As discussed in chapter 3, about 1.6 million youths run away from home each year; more than 12,000 run away from juvenile facilities; over half are girls.[71] The previous section pointed to the problems young women face on the streets after fleeing to escape sexual victimization at home. Some resort to crime in order to survive, but they do not have much attachment to their delinquent activities. The Wisconsin study noted that 54% of the girls who ran away found it necessary to steal money for food and clothing. A few exchanged sexual contact for money, food, and/or shelter.[72] The Toronto study found that sexually abused female runaways were significantly more likely than their nonabused counterparts to engage in delinquent or criminal activities such as substance abuse, petty theft, and prostitution. No similar pattern was found among male runaways. Not surprisingly, girls tend to exhibit more negative physical self-concepts than males.[73] A study of prostituted children in Malaysia found multiple problems among these girls that prompted them to run away from home, including: emotional neglect, violence within the family, physical neglect and parental substance abuse and/or gambling.[74]

Regarding prostitution, the recent literature merely reinforces what has been said for decades, namely that girls who run away and get involved in prostitution have histories of abuse, particularly sexual abuse. Anywhere from 35 to 73% of runaway children have been sexually abused. One recent study found that 59% ran away from home because they were neglected, while 81% were pushed or grabbed in anger by their parents, 64% were threatened with a gun or knife, and almost one-fifth were pressured to have sex by a caregiver.[75]

As already noted most runaways have fled homes where abuse was an everyday event; yet their lives on the streets are almost always even more abusive. Trafficking of children for sexual gratification is an enormous worldwide problem. A recent study estimated that "600,000 to 800,000 men, women, and children trafficked across international borders each year, approximately 80 percent are women and girls, and up to 50 percent are minors." There are also an estimated 12.3 million people "in forced labor, bonded labor, forced child labor, and sexual servitude at any given time."[76] In the U.S. alone, the FBI estimates that "over 100,000 children and young women are sex trafficked every day. Many victims are not runaways or kids who have been abandoned but rather have been lured or coerced by clever predators."[77] One report noted that sexual trafficking of children is a "$67 billion annual worldwide business larger than Nike, Starbucks and Google combined."[78]

Prostitution

As already suggested above, running away and abandonment are two primary risk factors for prostitution. Accurate data on the number of active prostitutes are difficult to obtain. As noted earlier, only 791 juveniles were arrested for prostitution in 2009, 79% of whom were girls. The most recent estimate is that there are around 300,000 children who are active prostitutes, according to the Department of Justice.[79] Most experts believe this is a low estimate. One estimate put the total at 650,000 who "exchange sex for favors," most of them boys.[80]

How is it that thousands of teenage girls end up as prostitutes? There are several interrelated reasons. The first was discussed in the previous section: it is a form of survival. Consistent with the research cited earlier, numerous studies have noted that between 40% and 75% of teenage prostitutes have been the victims of physical and/or sexual abuse. The most common form of teenage prostitution today may be what some have called "survival sex"—sex in return for that which one needs immediately: warm shelter for a night, drugs, or perhaps a few Big Macs."[81] The director of Children of the Night (an agency in Hollywood, California, that tries to help teenage prostitutes) deplores that rhetoric, finding that it softens or renders acceptable what is in reality "sexual exploitation" and a criminal offense. Whatever term one applies, teenage prostitution is widespread. According to the director of Children's Hospital High Risk Project in Los Angeles, its practitioners are getting younger; many are under the age of 15. Most are from dysfunctional families characterized by alcoholism or drug abuse, physical abuse, and neglect. Many can be classified as chronic homeless (three or more months on their own). They often live in abandoned buildings with no bathrooms or utilities. One estimate is that in Hollywood alone there are as many as 4,000 runaways on any given day, and about 10,000 in Los Angeles County; most ply the prostitution trade.

Several additional factors may lead to prostitution. Girls may be coerced, tricked, seduced, or even blackmailed by a pimp. Further, a lack of shelters may leave few alternatives to prostitution.[82] Family conditioning could have caused very low self-esteem, resulting in the belief that prostitution is deserved. Some girls may move from a few isolated sexual encounters for money to a situation in which they feel they have no access to more acceptable roles such as housewife or student. In other words, being a prostitute becomes a girl's major role. "Typically, the adolescent does not at first recognize her acts as constituting prostitution. At some point, however, she begins to realize that the behavior she has adopted signifies that she is a prostitute."[83]

Detailed information on the lives of these girls is often available only in journalistic accounts. For instance, *New York Times* columnist Nicolas Kristol describes teenage prostitution this way:

> The business model of pimping is remarkably similar whether in Atlanta or Calcutta: take vulnerable, disposable girls whom nobody cares about, use a mix of "friendship," humiliation, beatings, narcotics and threats to break the girls and induce 100 percent compliance, and then rent out their body parts. It's not solely violence that keeps the girls working for their pimps.

Jasmine fled an abusive home at age 13, and she said she—like most girls—stayed with the pimp mostly because of his emotional manipulation. "I thought he loved me, so I wanted to be around him," she said. That's common. Girls who are starved of self-esteem finally meet a man who showers them with gifts, drugs and dollops of affection. That, and a lack of alternatives, keeps them working for him—and if that isn't enough, he shoves a gun in the girl's mouth and threatens to kill her.[84]

Another recent report tells a story about a 14-year-old girl who was brought to the Los Angeles program Children of the Night. "Raised in the city of Oakland, she lived with a friend of her mother's, whose boyfriend started molesting her when she was four. Authorities intervened and placed the girl with a foster family, who later adopted her. But Monica ran away repeatedly, starting at age 10, and turned to prostitution at the urging of her older boyfriend." The report also details the story of a girl from Seattle. Her mother, a drug addict, died earlier in the year of an overdose. Amanda had lived with her father and was sexually abused by his roommate. When she was 14, she met a man in his mid-30s, who persuaded her to run away from home.

She was soon in another city, selling herself on the street—on the track, as she calls it—the stretch of street where she routinely worked. She gave her earnings to the pimp, who would often beat her. "He made me make a schedule for myself. I think it was 11 [a.m.] to 7 [p.m.], I would work one track," said Amanda. "And I would take a break from 7 to 9, and then at 9 to 2, I would work a different track, 9 to 2 at night. And every time I made $300, I would have to call him and give it to him. I would make an average of 600 or 700 [dollars] a day."[85]

Here's a story from Las Vegas:

Miranda is 14 years old and angry as she stands in court. She's spent a month in juvenile detention, even though she wasn't charged with a crime. No, this time Miranda's locked up because she agreed to testify against her pimp, and juvie is where she must wait for the trial to start—it's the only place in Clark County for a young victim witness with a history of running away.

So she waited. Then the trial was postponed. More waiting. Then, two days before Miranda was due in court, her pimp took a deal. He pleaded guilty to pandering in late February and avoided trial. Miranda spent 38 days in juvenile detention, and never testified.

Here's what the jury didn't hear: Miranda was 13 when Metro vice cops caught her milling outside a truck stop on Tropicana Avenue last August. She was wearing a short brown dress. She climbed into a passing car. Police pulled the car over. Miranda said the driver was paying her $30 for a blow job. Then she started to sob.

Miranda came to Vegas from LA with her pimp and another prostitute on a Greyhound bus—she turned tricks to pay for their tickets. Now she was working Tropicana to pay for their motel room. She had to make $500 a night or her pimp, Tony, denied her food and sleep. Miranda said Tony bought her from another pimp two months earlier. He gave her clothes, a fake ID, and a warning: Charge at least $80 for sex, make clients buy condoms, and work for me or die.

> Miranda is a ward of the state in California. She has no family to go home to. When she didn't want to turn tricks, Tony beat her, then sent her to the hospital under a fake name. So when Miranda agreed to help vice detectives build a case against Tony, it was a tremendous thing—not just the brave choice, but also the hard choice.[86]

Prostitution among girls, then, is not so much a choice as a survival mechanism for those who have few other options once forced onto the streets. Despite the obvious need, programs like Children of the Night are the exception rather than the rule. For many young people who cannot stay at home, there is little help from the social service and criminal justice systems.

Girls and Violence

According to media reports and statements by many politicians (and even a few criminologists), girls are getting progressively more violent each year. Hardly a week passes without a feature story about some girls committing "violent" acts, or statements to the effect that girls are getting just as violent as boys. In the past decade we have been flooded with news stories with essentially the same theme: girls are in gangs, they are "meaner" than girls in earlier generations, and their behavior does not fit the traditional stereotype of female delinquency.

Throughout the 1990s a multitude of new stories regurgitated the same line: girls are getting out of hand and more violent. Stories with headlines like "Delinquent Girls Achieving a Violent Equality in D.C." or "Ruthless Girlz," or "Troubled Girls, Troubling Violence" are common. The *Philadelphia Inquirer* published the following story that centered on a single incident in which an African-American girl attacked another girl (who was described as middle-class and appeared white in the photo that accompanied the story) in a subway:

> Girls are committing more violent crimes than ever before. Girls used to get in trouble like this mostly as accomplices of boys, but that's no longer true. They don't need the boys. And their attitudes toward their crimes are often as hard as the weapons they wield—as shown in this account based on documents and interviews with participants, parents, police, and school officials. While boys still account for the vast majority of juvenile crime, girls are starting to catch up.[87]

In large bold red letters, the headline of a lead article in the *Boston Globe Magazine* proclaimed "BAD GIRLS":

> Until about 10 years ago, teenage girls seldom fought each other, even with fists. They did not carry knives and razors and box cutters. They did not form roaming packs and attack other girls. They did not fight with sticks, bats, and bricks. Though most of them still aren't likely to carry guns, girls are moving into the world of violence that once belonged to boys.[88]

The writer presents caricatures of girl offenders. Although the isolated cases are true, the story does not emphasize the infrequency of such violence. Instead, it suggests that we are being confronted with a new breed of violent female offenders who are just as wicked and evil as their male counterparts. This is nothing new; sensationalistic accounts have appeared in newspapers throughout their existence. Newspaper archives would provide similar accounts of female lawlessness (including violence) dating back to the early years of the twentieth century.

Labeling girls as "violent" or "more violent" than at some point in the past is a process of social construction. Feminist criminologists have criticized traditional schools of criminology for assuming that male delinquency, even in its most violent forms, was somehow an understandable if not "normal" response. Girls who shared the same social and cultural milieu as delinquent boys but who were not violent were somehow abnormal or "over-controlled."[89] Essentially, law-abiding behavior on the part of at least some boys and men is taken as a sign of character, but when women avoid crime and violence, it is an expression of weakness.[90] The other side of this equation is that *if* girls engage in even minor forms of violence, they are somehow more vicious than their male counterparts. The construction of an artificial, passive femininity lays the foundation for the demonization of young girls of color, as the media have done in reporting on the activities of girl gang members. The media also often react to increases in male violence with the attitude of "so what else is new?" However, when reporting an increase in girls' violence, the conclusion is that something fundamental is wrong or there is a "new breed" of "violent women" roaming the streets and threatening the social order.

Such is clearly not the case, as shown in a detailed study by Meda Chesney-Lind and Katherine Irwin. Their analysis clearly shows that the media attention to girls' violence was based on exaggerated reports and anecdotal evidence. They note that "the institutions that have historically socialized and controlled girls *informally* (families, schools, peer groups) are changing the way they monitor and control girls—with bad consequences for girls."[91] The authors present a wide arrange of news stories claiming that girls are getting meaner and more violent, with headlines such as "Girls Just Want to Be Mean" (*New York Times Magazine*); "For Gold Earrings and Protection, More Girls Take the Road to Violence" (*New York Times*); "Troubled Girls, Troubling Violence" (*Philadelphia Inquirer*); "BAD Girls" *(Boston Globe Magazine)*; "In a New Twist on Equality, Girls Crimes Resemble Boys" (*San Jose Mercury*).[92] Lead stories on such popular talk shows as *Larry King Live, Oprah* and *Geraldo* also trumpeted the theme. *Newsweek* featured a story with the title: "Bad Girls Go Wild."[93] Popular books like *Odd Girl Out* and *Queen Bees and Wannabees* were big sellers; both reinforced the hype of the violent female offender.[94]

James Garbarino authored a book entitled *See Jane Hit: Why Girls Are Growing More Violent and What We Can Do About It*.[95] Mike Males critiqued the exaggerated claims in the book, noting that the author:

> rests his case on the claim that girls' violence has increased steadily and sharply in recent years, especially the last decade. Yet, virtually all of his sources for this alarming claim consist of secondhand citations; Garbarino shows no evidence of having looked at original data.

In response to Garbarino's claim that girls are "assaulting themselves, cutting and stabbing, poisoning and shooting themselves, in record numbers," Males states:

> Records of self-inflicted (suicidal) injuries are not available for past decades. Girls' deaths from drug overdoses, other poisonings, gunshots, cutting instruments, and suicides and possible suicides are much lower today than in the 1970s, `80s, or `90s. California posts hospital ER cases on self-inflicted injuries, whose rates among girls have dropped 10% to 15% since 1991, while Center for Health Statistics figures show girls' suicide rates have fallen by more than 50% (yes, you read that right) and are now at historical low levels.[96]

Virtually all news stories on girls and violence follow the same pattern. Typically, an egregious example of female violence is described, followed by a quick review of the FBI's latest arrest statistics showing what appear to be large increases in the number of girls arrested for violent offenses, accompanied by quotations from "experts"—usually police officers, teachers, or various social service workers, and occasionally criminologists. Much of the "evidence" cited is anecdotal, and the focus is almost always on a few, isolated and exceptional cases (otherwise it would not be "news") followed by gross generalizations.

Jerry Kurelic offers a unique acronym to explain the framing of sensational events by the media and political pundits: W.I.S.E. *Withhold* information that is contrary to their opinion; *identify* that which is consistent with their opinion; *sensationalize* that which illustrates your perspective; *expand* it as if it represents the whole. So in the case of girls and violence, journalists will seek out (identify) a few cases that fit their preconceived notions that girls are getting more violent; withhold any information that contradicts this position; sensationalize it with inflammatory headlines in bold, large type; and finally, make it seem as if this is typical all over the country.[97]

Before looking at whether girls are becoming as violent as boys, note that words like "violence" and "assault" are value laden and cover a wide variety of behaviors, most of which is relatively harmless. As suggested in chapter 3, juvenile court reports should be scrutinized to find more specific details about offenses beyond the broad categories commonly reported. A typical example is the broad category of "person crimes" (sometimes called "crimes against the person" or "personal crimes") or the largest single category "other assaults" or "simple assaults" (which do not involve the use of a weapon nor result in serious injury). As shown below, the term "violent crime" lumps together assaults with deadly weapons leading to serious injuries (aggravated assaults) with minor fistfights on high school campuses or fights between children and their parents (simple assaults).[98]

Contrary to arrest data, self-report data of youthful involvement in violent offenses suggests that girls' violence and aggression is decreasing at a substantially greater rate than that of boys. The Centers for Disease Control (CDC) publishes The Youth Risk Behavior Survey every two years. In the spring, it surveys students in grades nine through twelve in public and private schools, asking questions about a number of topics, including violence. In 1991, 34.4% of girls and 50.2% of boys surveyed said that they had been in a physical fight one or more times in the 12 months before the survey; in 2001, that figure dropped to 23.9% for girls and 43.1% for boys. In 2009, the percentages were 22.9% for girls and 39.3% for boys.[99] The number of girls who reported carrying weapons and guns declined from 10.9% in 1991 to 6.2% in 2001 before increasing to 7.1% in 2009 (the percentages for boys were 40.6%, 29.3%, and 27.1%.) Earlier research also revealed significant decreases in girls' involvement in felony assaults, minor assaults, and hard drugs, and no change in a wide range of other delinquent behaviors—including felony theft, minor theft, and index delinquency.[100] Self-report data showing increased involvement of girls in assaultive behavior needs to be viewed with a very clear idea of what behavior is included in each category. For example, the percentage of students who were injured in a physical fight and had to be treated by a doctor or nurse averaged 4% in the years from 1991 to 2009, which means many of the self-reported fights were minor.[101]

Arrest statistics for 2009 show approximately a 3:1 ratio (male/female) for "aggravated assault" and about a 2:1 ratio for "other assaults." As noted in table 5-2, the proportion of all arrests of girls for serious violent crimes declined from 2.8% to 2.6%; the percentages for "other assaults" increased 3% (as noted above, the increase may be due to changes in public policies concerning domestic violence and school fighting).

One enlightening bit of data comes from hospitals and public health reports. For instance, research on girls' violence in San Francisco, which utilized vital statistics maintained by health officials (rather than arrest data), found that there had been a 63% drop in teen girl fatalities between the 1960s and the 1990s and that girls' hospital injuries were dramatically underrepresented among those reporting injuries, including assaults.[102] This trend has been reported elsewhere. Chesney-Lind and Irwin note that the increasing number of arrests for girls on relatively minor offenses like simple assaults stems from what they term "hyper policing," rather than a change in actual behavior.[103] They summarize this increased hyper-vigilance as follows:

> The media-driven "gangsta girl" hype of the eighties and nineties, the millennium mean girl, and "bad girls go wild" of the new century have all served to justify increased control of girlhood. Girls' increased arrests came, we argue, not because they were becoming more like boys, but instead because girls would bear the brunt of an intensified system of social control . . . girls who were "acting out" in the home, in their peer groups, or in the school are now being punished formally, and often labeled as violent criminals in the process.[104]

In sum, the idea that girls have "gone wild" in recent years is a complete fraud. Males and Chesney-Lind put it this way:

> We have examined every major index of crime on which the authorities rely. None show a recent increase in girls' violence; in fact, every reliable measure shows that violence by girls has been plummeting for years. Major

offenses like murder and robbery by girls are at their lowest levels in four decades. Fights, weapons possession, assaults and violent injuries by and toward girls have been plunging for at least a decade.[105]

Relabeling Status Offenses

Why is it that arrest data show an increase in female juvenile delinquency, while self-reports indicate a decrease? Research suggests that this stems from official policy changes at the federal, state, and local levels, which in turn cause changes in enforcement practices. Policy change and corresponding law enforcement procedures have narrowed the gap in delinquency between girls and boys. Behaviors that were once categorized as status offenses—non-criminal offenses like running away, person in need of supervision, and domestic violence cases—have been increasingly relabeled as "violent" offenses, resulting in increases in the arrests of girls.

Changes in police practices with reference to domestic violence have resulted in an increased number of arrests of girls and women for assault. For example, a study of domestic violence arrests in California that included both juvenile and adult arrests revealed that girls' and women's shares of these arrests nearly tripled in the decade of the 1990s.[106] One study found that policy changes for domestic violence ended up lowering the risk of arrest for men and increasing the risks for women and girls.[107]

Girls' case files in various states highlight a similar trend of relabeling domestic violence incidents as more serious offenses. In a review of over 2,000 cases of girls referred to Maryland's juvenile justice system for "person-to-person" offenses, virtually all of these offenses involved "assault"; about half of them were "family centered" and involved such activities as "a girl hitting her mother and her mother subsequently pressing charges."[108] Similarly, a review of nearly 1,000 girls' files from four California counties found that a majority of their offenses involved assault. However, a close reading of these girls' case files revealed that most of their assault charges were the result of "nonserious, mutual combat situations with parents."[109] Case descriptions ranged from self-defense (e.g., "father lunged at [daughter] while she was calling the police about a domestic dispute, and [daughter] hit him") to trivial arguments (e.g., girl arrested "for throwing cookies at her mother").[110] Some critics have called the trend toward criminalizing behaviors previously ignored or treated informally as "upcriming."[111]

What previously would have been classified as disagreements are now taken as evidence of increased violence in schools. In Canada, for instance, 21% of 703 adolescent girls surveyed in schools and 52% of 763 adolescent boys reported having "beaten up another kid" at least once or twice in the year in which the survey was conducted.[112] A summary of two studies on self-reported aggression also reflects that while about a third of girls reported having been in a physical fight in the last year, this was true of over half of the boys in both samples.[113]

Barry Feld analyzed data on changes in arrests and confinement for boys and girls who were charged with simple and aggravated assault and arrived at the conclusion that the charges were mostly a relabeling of status offenses. He found that in many cases this relabeling stemmed from the fact that the passage of the 1974 Juvenile Justice and Delinquency Prevention Act failed to give states enough money to develop the necessary programs that would meet the needs of girls. As lawmakers tried to find options without any additional funding, they found it easier to relabel status offenders from incorrigibility to "simple assault" (such cases often involve pushing and shoving matches between parents and their daughters).[114] Changes in New York's domestic violence policies resulted in an increase in arrests of girls, mostly charged with simple assault.[115] Time-series analyses of victimization data (1980 through 2003) supported this trend.[116] Much of the increase in girls' arrests for violent crimes is an artifact of policy changes, rather than actual behavior. There is not, nor has there ever been, a "new wave" of violent girls.

Aggression and Gender

Is there any truth to the claim that girls are getting just as aggressive as boys? Research literature largely refutes this claim; it also reveals the unique aspects of girls' aggression.

The psychological literature, which considers forms of aggression other than physical aggression (or violence), is also relevant here. For example, results from a large national longitudinal survey of children and youth (aged 4 to 11 years) in Canada indicate that while boys exhibit higher levels of physical aggression at all ages, girls demonstrate higher levels of *indirect aggression* (defined as "behavior aimed at hurting someone without the use of physical aggression").[117] While boys and men are more likely to be physically aggressive, differences begin to even out when considering verbal aggression (yelling, insulting, and teasing). Further, girls in adolescence may be more likely than boys to use "indirect aggression," such as gossip, false stories, or telling secrets. The use of indirect aggression increases with age for girls and boys. When this broad definition of "aggression" is utilized, only about 5% of the variance in aggression is explained by gender.[118]

Research has identified gender-specific forms of aggression in childhood and adolescence. Boys' aggression tends to be more "overt," such as hitting, pushing, or threatening to beat others up; girls' aggression tends to be more "relational," focused on damaging another child's friendships or feelings of inclusion by the peer group. Relationally aggressive youth experience more difficulties with social adjustment, because they are significantly more disliked and lonelier than non-relationally aggressive peers.[119] These findings suggest that girls' aggression is rooted in significant relationships within childhood and adolescence. It also highlights the historically patriarchal context of how terms like "aggression" and "violence" are defined; in this case, it is defined from a male standpoint, without an acknowledgement of gender-specific manifestations.

Research suggests that trauma, particularly in the form of physical and sexual abuse has a profound impact on the development of female juvenile delinquency. Sibylle Artz found that "violent" girls in Canada reported signifi-

cantly greater rates of victimization and physical abuse (20%) than their nonviolent counterparts (6.3%), and reported great fear of sexual assault, especially
from their boyfriends. Roughly one out of four violent girls had been sexually
abused compared to one in ten of nonviolent girls.[120]

The research is also quite clear that aggression among girls usually occurs
within the context of the home or "intrafemale" (girl-on-girl). Traditionally this
kind of violence was rarely reported to authorities. Recently, however, such
aggression has been "discovered" by the news media and some scholars, as
discussed above.

Finally, girls' behavior, including violence, needs to be put in the context of
a patriarchal society. The analysis of self-reported violence among girls in Canada discussed above did precisely that, and the results were striking. Follow-
up interviews with a small group of violent girls found that they had learned at
home that "might makes right" and engaged in "horizontal violence" directed
at other powerless girls (often with boys as the audience). Certainly, these findings provide little ammunition for those who would contend that the "new"
violent girl is a product of any form of "emancipation."[121]

Criminologist Walter DeKeseredy supports these contentions in noting
that the "ideology of familial patriarchy . . . supports the abuse of women who
violate the ideals of male power and control over women." This ideology is
acted out by those males and females who insist on women being obedient,
respectful, loyal, dependent, sexually accessible and sexually faithful to
males.[122] Girls who behave aggressively tend to "buy into" these beliefs and
"police" other girls' behaviors, serving and preserving the status quo, including, ironically, their own continued oppression.[123]

In case studies of the life experiences of girls in custody in British Columbia, the girls were largely male focused, wanting very much to have boyfriends
and always making sure they had at least one—both in and out of jail. One girl
strongly identified with the boys and saw herself as "one of the guys," also
admitting that she had "always wanted to be a boy." Only one girl spoke little
about boys—at 18 years of age she was the oldest girl in the center. All the girls
used derogatory terms to describe other girls, and when they spoke about girls,
their words reflected views of females as "other." Many girls saw other girls as
threats, particularly if they were pretty or "didn't know their place" (i.e.,
thought they were better than other girls). A girl to whom boys pay attention
was a primary target for girl-to-girl victimization because she had the potential
to unseat those who occupied the top rung on the "pretty power hierarchy." An
"ugly" or "dirty" girl (a girl designated as a "slut") was also a primary target
for girl-to-girl victimization because she "deserved" to be beaten for her unap-
pealing looks and for her "unacceptable" behavior.[124] These beliefs correspond
to the "code of the streets" discussed in chapter 3. Those in oppressed situations or who suffer various forms of prejudice and discrimination typically take
it out on those similarly situated rather than on the true objects of their oppression, as noted in the classic work by Gordon Allport, *The Nature of Prejudice.*[125]

In their study of relational-aggression among girls, Chesney-Lind and
Irwin conducted focus group interviews with 27 young adult women from sev-

eral states about their adolescent experiences. All of them agreed that they had encountered girls who were often very mean to each other, often in very physically aggressive ways. The common context for such aggression revolved around competition with other girls to fit in and be accepted. The authors described dramatic retellings of encounters characterized as "living hell, catastrophic, or the end of the world." Several described cases of bullying, but only one said that it broke into actual violence. Despite these experiences, the meanness "did not drive girls into horrible risk-taking behaviors, nor did it propel them into the depths of depression." Chesney-Lind and Irwin further point out that meanness, pettiness and nastiness is not unique among girls—it is also common among boys. Why, therefore, so much attention toward this behavior on the part of girls at the exclusion of boys?

> It is because the rules of the game seriously disadvantage girls. If they conform to feminine ideals such as being kind to everyone and attractive, they are negatively labeled as shallow creatures who are overly concerned with popularity and appearances. And if they reject or challenge these impossible feminine goals, they are "fat cows," "bitches," or "mean girls." Even covert social skills, like the ability to recognize and deploy indirect aggression, is demonized in girls while in the adult male world, it is seen as an extremely clever political strategy (think Karl Rove). In a world where people are regularly nasty to one another, it is girls who become the focus of our attention and the subject of books, television shows, and newspaper articles. For girls, it shows clearly and poignantly that the game is rigged against them.[126]

Indeed, aggression and meanness is a huge part of the business world, a world dominated by men. Whenever women "act like men" (which they have to do to survive in a world dominated by men), they are subjected to negative labels ("bitch," etc.).

Girls and Robbery

The crime of robbery has traditionally been included in the broad category of violent crime. While typically a masculine crime, in recent years increasing numbers of women and girls have been charged with this offense, contributing to sensational reports of "violent girls and women." Yet girls' share of arrests for robbery remain low, constituting just over 10% (see table 5-3). While the arrest rate increased slightly since 1999 (from 17 to 21), this followed a significant decrease (from 27). The arrest rate for boys is significantly higher (191) but followed a similar trajectory of decreasing in the first decade before increasing in the second decade.

In order to investigate whether girls now participate more frequently in the traditionally male offense, we must first examine the concept of robbery. There are many more nuances than the stereotypes of this crime suggest. Offenses such as robbery often fit the "low-yield," criminal "mischief" category of offenses. Because of the increased risk of a felony charge and the relatively low yield involved in robbery, its appeal decreases as youths mature.

Popular youth culture, which stresses the importance of name brand clothing, gold jewelry, and expensive electronic gear, often visibly separates the "haves" from the "have-nots." It also appears to play a major role in robbery, particularly juvenile robbery. Youth status, then, coupled with economic marginality of many urban youth, creates a fertile environment for robbery. In short, at least some youths resort to victimizing their peers in order to obtain the material goods they could not otherwise afford.

Other research has amplified these findings, noting that youths also commit robbery offenses for reasons less related to economics. The thrill and excitement associated with street robbery, coupled with a desire to target individuals who are perceived as "show-offs" motivates some to participate in robberies. Research also indicates that juvenile robberies are not sophisticated and planned offenses; rather they are impulsive and spontaneous events. Juvenile robbers are less likely to victimize the elderly and most likely to victimize their peers; most juvenile robberies are committed by two or more people.[127]

It is also clear that robbery is closely related to gender. Boys tend to commit the vast majority of offenses, perhaps because the robbery setting provides the ideal opportunity to construct a tough and masculine posture.[128] Typically, male-on-male robberies occur on the streets and entail more physical violence. Female robberies are less frequent. While also occurring on the streets, they do not usually involve serious physical violence; they can, however, involve physical contact such as hitting, shoving, and fighting with the victim. Although females commit fewer robbery offenses than do males, both males and females express similar reasons for engaging in robbery. In a qualitative review of the role of gender in robbery, Jody Miller analyzed interviews with youthful robbers in St. Louis. She concluded that the acquisition of money and "status-conferring goods," such as jewelry, are the primary motivations for committing the offense for both males and females.[129]

Males are most likely to use weapons when committing a robbery. In Miller's study, for example, all of the males in the sample reported using a gun. Males use physical violence and weapons as a way of accomplishing gender and displaying masculinity. Female robberies tend not to include weapons because females typically prey on other females, and female victims tend to be more submissive and less likely to fight back.[130]

A recent study on another subject (needs and services provided to African-American girls in the juvenile justice system) noted an observation made by a service provider who stated that among many African-American girls "they pick up robbery charges, not because they're the person that's actually, you know, robbing, but because they're there. They're a participant. They're following along with what the boys do. Or they're doing what the boys tell them to do."[131]

Chesney-Lind and Irwin researched this issue by analyzing robbery arrests in Honolulu between 1991 and 1997. In 1991 almost all arrests (95%) were male; in 1997, the percentage dropped to 83%—the percentage of girls arrested for robbery had tripled. Probing a little deeper, they found that there was no major change in the overall pattern of robberies committed. Rather, they found that less serious kinds of robberies were swept up into the system, including many by girls. They noted that the age of offenders declined as did the value of the items taken (from a median of $10 in 1991 to $1.25 in 1997). What they also discovered was that while there was an increasing use of a weapon, this did not involve guns. More often than not these robberies were committed by "slightly older youth bullying and 'hijacking' younger youth for small amounts of cash and occasional jewelry" and that these kinds of robberies constituted almost all of the increases. Finally, they found that the key to such increases were changes in school policies, which involved calling the police versus handling the problem within the school as they had done before. This was confirmed by conversations Chesney-Lind and Irwin had with police officers. The police began to label these kinds of offenses ("hijacking," etc.) as robberies, whereas before they would have been labeled as thefts. Also, most of the increases in these arrests took place within schools serving inner-city youth.[132]

In short, as with virtually all offenses, close attention must be paid to the many dimensions and the surrounding social context. Even "violent" crimes must be analyzed within a social context.

Summary

This chapter has reviewed the extent of girls' involvement in delinquency. Measures of female delinquency reveal that it is more varied than official statistics indicate. Girls commit a variety of offenses but are less likely than boys to engage in serious, violent delinquency. Some research (especially self-report studies) suggests that there are more similarities than previously imagined in male and female delinquency. In essence, most delinquency is quite minor, and the differences between boys' and girls' misbehavior are not pronounced. Discussions that focus on very serious violent offenses exaggerate the gender differences in delinquency because males are more likely to commit these offenses.

Evidence indicates that female delinquency has changed little in the past three decades. Both official arrest statistics and self-report data suggest that the changes we have seen in girls' misbehavior have been in minor and traditionally female offenses. Girls are still arrested and referred to court for minor property offenses and status offenses. There is some evidence from cohort studies that more girls are being arrested, but there is little or no evidence that there has been any major change in girls' delinquent behavior.

Like studies of other forms of gender difference, studies of female and male delinquency tend to make more of dissimilarities than they do of similarities. Both are interesting from a theoretical standpoint, but to date only the gender difference in violent crime has attracted attention. Also of interest is the fact that although girls commit many offenses, only some of the offenses result in arrest. Later chapters will help us further address crimes that typically bring girls into the juvenile justice system and examine what happens to them there.

Status offenses have always been closely identified with female delinquency. Running away from home and being unmanageable or incorrigible have long been seen as typical female offenses. The prevalence of status offenses in girls' delinquency stems in part from the parental desire to control the behavior of girls. Self-report studies show that boys and girls are about equally as likely to commit status offenses, yet referrals to juvenile court show an obvious gender bias, with more girls facing detention for such charges.

The bias is even more troubling when one considers that persistent status offense behavior in girls, notably running away, appears to be linked to abuse, especially sexual abuse, within the home. Running away very often leads girls to commit a variety of crimes in order to survive. Girls who join the ranks of street youth often end up in the world of prostitution, where their abuse continues at the hands of pimps and customers alike.

Shoplifting has consistently been the most common property offense committed by girls. From the few available studies, it appears that girls and boys are about equally as likely to shoplift, but girls are more likely to be detected by store personnel, arrested by the police, and referred to juvenile court. Items stolen by girls are of lesser value than those stolen by boys, and girls are more apt to be amateurs. Most of the items girls steal are for personal use and may be linked to their desire to conform to a standard of female beauty and appearance that is otherwise inaccessible to poor girls.

Our understanding of girls' delinquency is sketchy at best. Very little is known about the few girls who commit serious, violent crimes. Also, little is known about girls and property crime, aside from shoplifting (and even here the evidence is scanty). Even in areas extensively researched, as in the case of status offenses, a review of the literature reveals the need for objective inquiry. In essence, investigation of girls' lives and their troubles, uncluttered by stereotypical thinking, has begun only within the past few decades.

NOTES

[1] Federal Bureau of Investigation (2010). *Crime in the United States, 2009.* Retrieved from http://www2.fbi.gov/ucr/cius2009/data/table_33.html

[2] Sickmund, M., T. J. Sladky, and W. Kang (2011). "Detailed Offense Profile by Sex (column percent)." Retrieved from http://www.ojjdp.gov/ojstatbb/ezacjrp/asp/Offense_Sex.asp?state=0&topic=Offense_Sex&year=2007&percent=column

[3] For a more complete analysis, see Chesney-Lind, M. and R. G. Shelden (2004). *Girls, Delinquency and Juvenile Justice* (3rd ed.). Belmont, CA: Wadsworth, chs. 2 and 3. In order to understand why girls become involved in activities that are likely to land them in the juvenile justice system, it is essential to consider gender in all its dimensions. Girls undergo a childhood and adolescence that is heavily colored by their gender (a case can be made that the lives of boys are also affected by gender roles). Girls and boys do not have the same choices. This is not to say that girls do not share some problems with boys (notably the burdens of class and race), but even the way in which these similarities affect the daily lives of young people is heavily mediated by gender.

[4] FBI, *Crime in the United States, 2009.* Retrieved from http://www2.fbi.gov/ucr/cius2009/data/table_32.html

[5] Adler, F. (1975). *Sisters in Crime.* New York: McGraw-Hill.

[6] See Chesney-Lind and Shelden, *Girls, Delinquency and Juvenile Justice,* ch. 2.

[7] Although there are no hard data on this, several sources inside the juvenile justice system have told me about the following trend. Because juvenile courts have been restrained in recent years from responding vigorously to cases of runaways, some police and probation officers are sug-

gesting that parents do the following: when a girl threatens to run away, the parent should stand in her way; if she runs into the parent or pushes the parent out of the way, then the parent can call the court and have the girl arrested on "simple assault" or "battery" or some other "personal" crime that would fit into the FBI category "other assaults." Although it is uncertain how often this happens or how this could shape arrest figures that are reported to the FBI, I mention it to illustrate that FBI categories are just that: "categories" representing a wide variety of behaviors and different social contexts. As discussed in chapter 2, official arrest statistics like those discussed in this chapter should be interpreted cautiously.

[8] Chesney-Lind and Shelden, *Girls, Delinquency and Juvenile Justice*, ch. 7.

[9] Canter, R. J. (1982). "Sex Differences in Self-Report Delinquency." *Criminology* 20: 373–93; Cernkovich, S. and P. Giordano (1979). "A Comparative Analysis of Male and Female Delinquency." *Sociological Quarterly* 20: 131–45.

[10] Steffensmeier, D. J. and R. H. Steffensmeier (1980). "Trends in Female Delinquency: An Examination of Arrest, Juvenile Court, Self Report, and Field Data." *Criminology* 18: 62–85.

[11] Teilmann, K. and P. Landry (1981). "Gender Bias in Juvenile Justice." *Journal of Research in Crime and Delinquency* 18: 47–80.

[12] Canter, "Sex Differences in Self-Report Delinquency."

[13] Cernkovich and Giordano, "A Comparative Analysis of Male and Female Delinquency."

[14] Canter, "Sex Differences in Self-Report Delinquency."

[15] Substance Abuse and Mental Health Services Administration (2010). 2009 SAMHSA National Survey on Drug Use and Health: Detailed Tables. Retrieved from http://oas.samhsa.gov/NSDUH/2k9NSDUH/tabs/Sect3peTabs1to25.htm#Tab3.12B

[16] Ibid. Retrieved from http://oas.samhsa.gov/NSDUH/2k9NSDUH/tabs/Sect3peTabs1to25.htm#Tab3.11B

[17] Ibid. Retrieved from http://oas.samhsa.gov/NSDUH/2k9NSDUH/tabs/Sect3peTabs1to25.htm#Tab3.13B

[18] The classic study of shoplifting is still Mary Cameron's (1964) *The Booster and the Snitch*. New York: Free Press. This is probably the most often cited work on the subject.

[19] Harrison, P., J. Maupin, and G. L. Mays (2001). "Teen Court: An Examination of Processes and Outcomes." *Crime and Delinquency* 47: 243–64.

[20] Farrington, D. (1999). "Measuring, Explaining, and Preventing Shoplifting: A Review of British Research." *Security Journal* 12: 9–27.

[21] An interesting history of shoplifting is presented by Segrave, K. (2001). *Shoplifting: A Social History*. New York: McFarland & Company. Here it is noted that up until the 1920s shoplifting was mostly a male activity. Then it shifted to a mostly female activity, in part because of the significant increase in women shoppers.

[22] Morris, A. (1987). *Women, Crime and Criminal Justice*. New York: Basil Blackwell, pp. 29–31, 196.

[23] Horowitz, R. and A. E. Pottieger (1991). "Gender Bias in Juvenile Justice Handling of Seriously Crime-Involved Youths." *Journal of Research in Crime and Delinquency* 28: 75–100.

[24] Astroth, K. A. and G. W. Haynes (2002). "More Than Cows & Cooking: Newest Research Shows the Impact of 4-H." *Journal of Extension* 40.

[25] Weerman, F. M. and C. Bijleveld (2007). "Birds of Different Feathers." *European Journal of Criminology* 4: 357–83.

[26] Zauberman, R. (2010). *Self-Reported Crime and Deviance Studies in Europe: Current State of Knowledge and Review of Use*. Brussels: Brussels University Press.

[27] Sweeney, J. (2007). "The Impact of Individualism and Collectivism on Shoplifting Attitudes and Behaviors." *The UCI Undergraduate Research Journal*. Retrieved from http://www.urop.uci.edu/journal/journal99/08_joanne/Joanne%20Sweeney.pdf

[28] Morris, *Women, Crime and Criminal Justice*, p. 65.

[29] Davies, P. (1997). "Women, Crime and an Informal Economy: Female Offending and Crime for Gain." *The British Criminology Conferences: Selected Proceedings* (Vol. 2). Queens University, Belfast, July 15–19.

[30] Salmelainen, P. (1995). "The Correlates of Offending Frequency: A Study of Juvenile Theft Offenders in Detention." *Criminal Justice Abstracts*. Sydney: New South Wales. Bureau of Crime Statistics and Research, pp. 9–17

[31] Day, L., J. Maltby, and D. Giles (2000). "Psychological Predictors of Self-Reported Shoplifting." *Psychology, Crime and Law* 6: 77–79.

[32] Deng, X. and L. Zhang (1998). "Correlates of Self-Control: An Empirical Test of Self-Control Theory." *Journal of Crime and Justice* 21: 89–110.

[33] Campbell, A. (1981). *Girl Delinquents*. New York: St. Martin's Press, pp. 122–23.

[34] Lo, L. (1994). "Exploring Teenage Shoplifting Behavior: A Choice and Constraint Approach." *Environment and Behavior* 26: 613–39.

[35] Sweeney, "The Impact of Individualism and Collectivism." Sweeney explains: "Individualism is a multifaceted outlook on life that emphasizes, among other things, independence and self-reliance. In contrast, collectivism focuses on duty and obedience."

[36] Sarasalo, E., B. Bergman, and J. Toth (1997). "Kleptomania-like Behavior and Psychosocial Characteristics among Shoplifters." *Legal and Criminological Psychology* 2: 1–10.

[37] Ibid.

[38] Campbell, *Girl Delinquents*; Sarasalo, E., B. Bergman, and J. Toth (1998). "Repetitive Shoplifting in Stockholm, Sweden: A Register Study of 1802 Cases." *Criminal Behavior and Mental Health* 8: 256–65.

[39] May, D. (1977). "Delinquent Girls Before the Courts." *Medical Science Law Review* 17: 203–10, and May, D. (1978). "Juvenile Shoplifters and the Organization of Store Security: A Case Study in the Social Construction of Delinquency." *International Journal of Criminology and Penology* 6: 137–60.

[40] Chesney-Lind and Shelden, *Girls, Delinquency and Juvenile Justice*, p. 29.

[41] Caputo, G. (2009). "Early Life Trauma among Women Shoplifters and Sex Workers." *Journal of Child and Adolescent Trauma* 2: 15–27.

[42] Feld, B. C. (1988). "The Juvenile Court Meets the Principle of Offense: Punishment, Treatment and the Difference It Makes." *Boston University Law Review* 68: 821–915; Platt, A. M. (1977). *The Child Savers* (revised edition). Chicago: University of Chicago Press, p. 38; Sutton, J. R. (1988). *Stubborn Children: Controlling Delinquency in the United States, 1640–1981*. Berkeley: University of California Press, pp.162–63.

[43] Chesney-Lind and Shelden, *Girls, Delinquency and Juvenile Justice*, ch. 3.

[44] Sickmund, Sladky, and Kang, "Census of Juveniles in Residential Placement Databook." Data on detention and placement in institutions will be presented in chapters 11 and 12.

[45] Andrews and Cohn found that in New York parental concerns varied from serious problems (like running away from home) to "sleeping all day" and "refusing to do household chores." Despite the petty nature of some complaints, court personnel routinely failed to make independent determinations about youthful behaviors and typically responded to parental wishes. Andrews, R. H. and A. H. Cohn (1974). "Ungovernability: The Unjustifiable Jurisdiction." *Yale Law Journal* 83: 1404.

[46] Katz, P. (1979). "The Development of Female Identity." In C. Kopp (Ed.), *Becoming Female: Perspectives on Development*. New York: Plenum, p. 24.

[47] Thorne, B. (1994). *Gender Play: Girls and Boys in School*. New Brunswick, NJ: Rutgers University Press, p. 156. Observations of students in my classes, plus conversations with colleagues, reinforce these research findings, showing that such behaviors extend into the university setting.

[48] Ibid.

[49] Orenstein, P. (1994). *Schoolgirls*. New York: Doubleday, p. 57.

[50] A small sample of the research includes: Cassano, M., C. Perry-Parrish, and J. Zeman (2007). "Influence of Gender on Parental Socialization of Children's Sadness Regulation." *Social Development* 16: 210–31; Leaper, C. and C. K. Friedman (2007). "The Socialization of Gender." In J. E. Grusec and P. D. Hastings (Eds.), *Handbook of Socialization: Theory and Research*. New York: Guilford Publications; Chaplin, T. M., P. M. Cole, and C. Zahn-Waxler (2005). "Parental Socialization of Emotion Expression: Gender Differences and Relations to Child Adjustment." *Emotion* 5: 80–88; Baillargeon, R. H., M. Zoccolillo, K. Keenan, S. Côté, D. Pérusse, H. Wu, M. Boivin, and R. E. Tremblay (2007). "Gender Differences in Physical Aggression: A Prospective Population-Based Survey of Children before and after 2 Years of Age." *Developmental Psychology* 43: 13–26; Eschenbeck, H., C. Kohlmann, and A. Lohaus (2007). "Gender Differences in Coping Strategies in Children and Adolescents." *Journal of Individual Differences* 28: 18–26; Hastings, P. D., K. H. Rubin,

and L. DeRose (2005). "Links among Gender, Inhibition, and Parental Socialization in the Development of Prosocial Behavior." *Merrill-Palmer Quarterly* 51: 467–93.

[51] The literature is nicely summarized in Dorne, C. K. (2002). *An Introduction to Child Maltreatment in the United States* (3rd ed.). Monsey, NY: Criminal Justice Press.

[52] Browne, A. and D. Finkelhor (1986). "Impact of Child Sexual Abuse: A Review of Research." *Psychological Bulletin* 99: 69.

[53] Ackerman, P. T., J. E. O. Newton, W. B. McPherson, J. G. Jones, and R. A. Dykman (1998). "Prevalence of Post Traumatic Stress Disorder and Other Psychiatric Diagnoses in Three Groups of Abused Children (Sexual, Physical, and Both)." *Child Abuse & Neglect* 22: 759–74; Boney-McCoy, S. and D. Finkelhor (1996). "Is Youth Victimization Related to Trauma Symptoms and Depression after Controlling for Prior Symptoms and Family Relationships? A Longitudinal, Prospective Study." *Journal of Consulting and Clinical Psychology* 64: 1406–16; Kendall-Tackett, K. A., L. M. Williams, and D. Finkelhor (1993). "Impact of Sexual Abuse on Children: A Review and Synthesis of Recent Empirical Studies." *Psychological Bulletin* 113: 164–80; Neumann, D. A., B. M. Houskamp, V. E. Pollock, and J. Briere (1996). "The Long-Term Sequelae of Childhood Sexual Abuse in Women: A Meta-Analytic Review." *Child Maltreatment* 1: 6–16; Herman, J. L. (1981). *Father–Daughter Incest.* Cambridge: Harvard University Press; Meiselman, K. (1978). *Incest.* San Francisco: Jossey-Bass.

[54] Roy, A. and M. Janal (2006). "Gender in Suicide Attempt Rates and Childhood Sexual Abuse Rates: Is There an Interaction?" *Suicide and Life-Threatening Behavior* 36: 329–35; Feiringa, C. and C. Cleland (2007). "Childhood Sexual Abuse and Abuse-Specific Attributions of Blame over 6 Years Following Discovery." *Child Abuse and Neglect* 31: 1169–86; Andersen, S. L., A. Tomada, E. S. Vincow, E. Valente, A. Polcari, and M. H. Teicher (2008). "Preliminary Evidence for Sensitive Periods in the Effect of Childhood Sexual Abuse on Regional Brain Development." *Journal of Neuropsychiatry and Clinical Neuroscience* 20: 292–301; Cullerton-Sen, C., A. R. Cassidy, D. Murray-Close, D. Cicchetti, N. R. Crick, and F. A. Rogosch (2008). "Childhood Maltreatment and the Development of Relational and Physical Aggression: The Importance of a Gender-Informed Approach." *Child Development* 79: 1736–51; Nelson, E. C., A. C. Heath, M. T. Lynskey, K. K. Bucholz, P. A. F. Madden, D. J. Statham, and N. G. Martin (2006). "Childhood Sexual Abuse and Risks for Licit and Illicit Drug-Related Outcomes: A Twin Study." *Psychological Medicine* 36: 1473–83.

[55] American Correctional Association. (1990). *The Female Offender: What Does the Future Hold?* Washington, DC: St. Mary's Press.

[56] Ibid., pp. 46–71.

[57] Dembo, R., L. Williams, and J. Schmeidler (1993). "Gender Differences in Mental Health Service Needs among Youths Entering a Juvenile Detention Center." *Journal of Prison and Jail Health* 12: 73–101; Dembo, R., S. C. Sue, P. Borden, and D. Manning (1995). "Gender Differences in Service Needs among Youths Entering a Juvenile Assessment Center: A Replication Study." Paper presented at the Annual Meeting of the Society of Social Problems, Washington, DC, p. 21.

[58] Silbert, M. and A. Pines (1981). "Sexual Child Abuse as an Antecedent to Prostitution." *Child Abuse and Neglect* 5: 409.

[59] Mouzakitas, C. M. (1981). "An Inquiry into the Problem of Child Abuse and Juvenile Delinquency." In R. J. Hunner and Y. E. Walkers (Eds.), *Exploring the Relationship between Child Abuse and Delinquency.* Montclair, NJ: Allanheld, Osmun.

[60] Phelps, R. J., M. McIntosh, V. Jesudason, P. Warner, and J. Pohlkamp (1982). *Wisconsin Juvenile Female Offender Project.* Madison: Youth Policy and Law Center, Wisconsin Council on Juvenile Justice, p. 86.

[61] McCormack, A., M. Janus, and A. Burgess (1986). "Runaway Youths and Sexual Victimization: Gender Differences in an Adolescent Runaway Population." *Child Abuse and Neglect* 10: 387–95.

[62] Kurtz, P. D., G. L. Kurtz, and S. V. Jarvis (1991). "Problems of Maltreated Runaway Youth." *Adolescence* 26: 543–55; Sullivan, P. M. and J. F. Knutson (2000). "The Prevalence of Disabilities and Maltreatment among Runaway Children." *Child Abuse and Neglect* 24: 1275–88; Warren, J. K., F. A. Gary, and J. Moorhead (1994). "Self-Reported Experiences of Physical and Sexual Abuse among Runaway Youths." *Perspectives in Psychiatric Care* 30: 23–28; Kaufman, J. G. and C. S.

Widom (1999). "Childhood Victimization, Running Away and Delinquency." *Journal of Research in Crime and Delinquency* 36: 347–70.

[63] Fazel, S. M., H. Doll, and N. Langstrom (2008). "Mental Disorders among Adolescents in Juvenile Detention and Correctional Facilities: A Systematic Review and Metaregression Analysis of 25 Surveys." *Journal of the American Academy of Child & Adolescent Psychiatry* 47:1010–19.

[64] Pasko, L. (2006). "Female Juvenile Offender in Hawaii: Understanding Gender Differences in Arrests, Adjudications, and Social Characteristics of Juvenile Offenders." Washington, DC: Office of Juvenile Justice and Delinquency Prevention.

[65] Alderden, M. B. and A. Perez (2003). "Female Delinquents Committed to the Illinois Department of Corrections: A Profile." Chicago: Illinois Criminal Justice Information Authority. Retrieved from http://www.icjia.state.il.us/public/pdf/ResearchReports/FemaleDel_IDOC.pdf

[66] Human Rights Watch (2006). "Custody and Control: Conditions of Confinement in New York's Juvenile Prisons for Girls." New York: Human Rights Watch. Retrieved from http://www.hrw.org/en/reports/2006/09/24/custody-and-control-0

[67] Chesney-Lind, M. and N. Rodriguez (1983). "Women Under Lock and Key." *Prison Journal* 63: 47–65.

[68] Widom, C. S. (1988). "Child Abuse, Neglect and Violent Criminal Behavior." Unpublished manuscript, p. 17.

[69] Widom, C. S. and M. A. Ames (1994). "Criminal Consequences of Childhood Sexual Victimization." *Child Abuse and Neglect* 18: 303–18.

[70] Simons, R. L. and L. B. Whitbeck (1991). "Sexual Abuse as a Precursor to Prostitution and Victimization among Adolescent and Adult Homeless Women." *Journal of Family Issues* 12: 361–79.

[71] Hammer, H., D. Finkelhor, and A. Sedlak (2002). *Runaway/Thrownaway Children: National Estimates and Characteristics*. Washington, DC: Office of Juvenile Justice and Delinquency Prevention. Kaufman and Widom, "Childhood Victimization, Running Away and Delinquency"; Swaim, F. F. and B. A. Bracken (1997). "Global and Domain-Specific Self-Concepts of a Matched Sample of Adolescent Runaways and Nonrunaways." *Journal of Clinical and Child Psychology* 26: 397–403.

[72] Phelps et al., *Wisconsin Juvenile Female Offender Project*, p. 67.

[73] McCormack et al., "Runaway Youths and Sexual Victimization," pp. 392–93; Swaim and Bracken, "Global and Domain-Specific Self-Concepts"; Crain, R. M. (1996). "The Influence of Age, Race, and Gender on Child and Adolescent Multidimensional Self-Concept." In B. A. Bracken (Ed.), *Handbook of Self-Concept: Developmental, Social and Clinical Considerations*. New York: Wiley.

[74] Lukman, Z. M. (2009). "The Prevalence of Running Away from Home among Prostituted Children in Malaysia." *Journal of Social Sciences* 5: 157–62.

[75] Whitbeck, L. B. and D. R. Hoyt (1999). *Nowhere to Grow: Homeless and Runaway Adolescents and their Families*. Hawthorne, NY: Walter de Gruyter; Walker, N. E. (2002). "Prostituted Teens: More than a Runaway Problem." Michigan Family Impact Seminars Briefing Report No. 2002-2. East Lansing: Institute for Children, Youth and Families, Michigan State University. Retrieved from http://www.familyimpactseminars.org/s_mifis06report.pdf. Among earlier studies showing the same results include: Janus, M., F. X. Archambault, S. Brown, and L. Welsh (1995). "Physical Abuse in Canadian Runaway Adolescents." *Child Abuse and Neglect* 19: 433–47; Rotheram-Borus, M. J. (1993). "Suicidal Behavior and Risk Factors among Runaway Youths." *American Journal of Psychiatry* 150: 103–7; Koopman, C., M. Rosario, and M. J. Rotheram-Borus (1994). "Alcohol and Drug Use and Sexual Behavior Placing Runaways at Risk for HIV Infection." *Addictive Behaviors* 19: 95–103; Campagna, D. S. and D. L. Poffenberger (1988). *The Sexual Trafficking in Children*. Dover, MA: Auburn House.

[76] U. S. Department of State (2009). *Trafficking in Persons Report 2009*. Retrieved from http://www.state.gov/g/tip/rls/tiprpt/2009/

[77] Gore, M. R. (2008, November 10). "Sex Trafficking of Children in America." Retrieved from http://crime.suite101.com/article.cfm/sex_traffficking_of_children_in_america

[78] Sarnoff, C. (2009, December 21). "Selling Children in America." *Huffington Post*. Retrieved from http://www.huffingtonpost.com/conchita-s-sarnoff/selling-children-in-ameri_b_399974.html

[79] Couric, K. (2009, July 22). "Criminal Networks Prey on Teen Prostitutes." CBS News with Katie Couric. Retrieved from http://www.cbsnews.com/stories/2009/07/22/eveningnews/main5181151.shtml; the same number is noted in an article by Marian Wright Edelman in the *Huffington Post*, "The Girls Next Door May be on the Corner Now." Retrieved from http://www.huffingtonpost.com/marian-wright-edelman/the-girl-next-door-may-no_b_175239.html

[80] Rosen, D. (2008, August 2). "Teen Prostitution in America." *Counterpunch*. Retrieved from http://www.counterpunch.org/rosen08022008.html

[81] Beyette, B. (1988, August 21). "Hollywood's Teen-age Prostitutes Turn Tricks for Shelter, Food." *Las Vegas Review-Journal*.

[82] Campagna, D. S. and D. L. Poffenberger (1988). *The Sexual Trafficking in Children*. Dover, MA: Auburn House, pp. 65–66.

[83] Boyer, D. and J. James (1982). "Easy Money: Adolescent Involvement in Prostitution." In S. Davidson (Ed.), *Justice for Young Women*. Tucson, AZ: New Directions for Young Women, p. 93.

[84] Kristol, N. (2009, May 6). "Girls on Our Streets." *New York Times*. Retrieved from http://www.nytimes.com/2009/05/07/opinion/07kristof.html?_r=2

[85] O'Sullivan, M. (2010, June 9). "Former US Teenage Prostitutes Escape Brutal Street Life." http://www1.voanews.com/english/news/a-13-2009-06-18-voa70-68740097.html

[86] Goldman, A. (2010, March 18). "Throwaway Kids: What to Do with Teenage Prostitutes?" *Las Vegas Weekly*. http://www.lasvegasweekly.com/news/2010/mar/18/throwaway-kids-teenage-prostitutes/

[87] Lewis, N. (1992, December 23). "Delinquent Girls Achieving a Violent Equality in D.C." *Washington Post*, pp. A1, A14; Marinucci, C., S. Winokur, and G. Lewis (1994, December 12). "Ruthless Girlz." *San Francisco Examiner*, p. A1; Santiago, D. (1992, February 23). "Random Victims of Vengeance Show Teen Crime." *The Philadelphia Inquirer*, p. A1.

[88] Ford, R. (1998, May 24). "Bad Girls." *The Boston Globe Magazine*.

[89] Cain, M. (Ed.) (1989). *Growing Up Good: Policing the Behavior of Girls in Europe*. London: Sage.

[90] Naffine, N. (1987). *Female Crime: The Construction of Women in Criminology*. Sydney, Australia: Allen and Unwin.

[91] Chesney-Lind, M. and K. Irwin (2008). *Beyond Bad Girls: Gender, Violence and Hype*. New York: Routledge, p. 4.

[92] Ibid., pp. 11–17.

[93] Scelfo, J. (2005, June 13). "Bad Girls Go Wild: A Rise in Girl-on-Girl Violence Is Making Headlines Nationwide and Prompting Scientists to Ask Why." *Newsweek*.

[94] Ibid., pp. 18–20. Simmons, R. (2002). *Odd Girl Out: The Hidden Culture of Aggression in Girls*. New York: Harcourt; and Wiseman, R. (2002). *Queen Bees and Wannabees: Helping Your Daughter Survive Cliques, Gossips, Boyfriends and Other Realities of Adolescence*. New York: Crown.

[95] Garbarino, J. (2006). *See Jane Hit: Why Girls Are Growing More Violent and What We Can Do about It*. New York: Penguin Group.

[96] The review by Mike Males is found on my website: http://www.sheldensays.com/review_of_see_jane_hit.htm

[97] Kurelic, J. (2005). *Our Indispensable Delusions: Why Humans Can't Handle the Truth*. Unpublished manuscript, on file with author.

[98] Brener, N. D., T. R. Simon, E. G. Krug, and R. Lowry (1999). "Recent Trends in Violence-Related Behaviors among High School Students in the United States." *Journal of the American Medical Association* 282: 440–46.

[99] Centers for Disease Control and Prevention (2010). *Youth Risk Behavior Surveillance—United States, 2009*. Surveillance Summaries, June 4, MMWR; 59 (No. SS-5). Centers for Disease Control and Prevention (2002). *Youth Risk Behavior Surveillance—United States, 2001*. Surveillance Summaries, MMWR; 51 (No. SS-4). Retrieved from http://www.cdc.gov/mmwr/preview/mmwrhtml/ss5104a1.htm; Kann, L., W. Warren, J. L. Collins, J. Ross, B. Collins, and L. J. Kolbe (1993). Results from the National School-Based 1991 *Youth Risk Behavior Survey* and Progress toward Achieving Related Health Objectives for the Nation. *Public Health Rep.* 108 (Suppl 1): 47–67. Retrieved from http://www.ncbi.nlm.nih.gov/pmc/articles/PMC1403309/pdf/pubhealthrep00063-0049.pdf

[100] Huizinga, D. (1997). *Over-Time Changes in Delinquency and Drug Use: The 1970s to the 1990s.* Boulder: University of Colorado, Research Brief.

[101] Centers for Disease Control (2010). Trends in the Prevalence of Behaviors that Contribute to Violence. National YRBS: 1991–2009. Retrieved from http://www.cdc.gov/healthyyouth/yrbs/pdf/us_violence_trend_yrbs.pdf

[102] Males, M. and A. Shorter (2001). "To Cage and Serve." San Francisco: Center on Juvenile and Criminal Justice.

[103] Chesney-Lind and Irwin, *Beyond Bad Girls*, pp. 27–28.

[104] Ibid., p. 31.

[105] Males, M. and M. Chesney-Lind (2010, April 1). "The Myth of Mean Girls." *New York Times.* Retrieved from http://www.nytimes.com/2010/04/02/opinion/02males.html?ref=opinion

[106] Bureau of Criminal Information and Analysis (1999). *Report on Arrests for Domestic Violence in California, 1998.* Sacramento: State of California, Criminal Justice Statistics Center.

[107] Hovmand, P. S., D. N. Ford, I. Flom, and S. Kyriakakis (2007). "Women Arrested for Domestic Violence: Unintended Consequences of Pro and Mandatory Arrest Policies." Paper presented at the International System Dynamics Conference July 29–August 2, 2007, Boston, MA. Retrieved from http://www.systemdynamics.org/conferences/2007/proceed/papers/HOVMA376.pdf. They also report that women constitute about 20% of arrests for domestic violence. On this same issue see also: Finn, M. A. and P. Bettis (2006). "Punitive Action or Gentle Persuasion: Exploring Police Officers' Justifications for Using Dual Arrest in Domestic Violence Cases." *Violence Against Women* 12: 268–87.

[108] Mayer J. (1994). *Girls in the Maryland Juvenile Justice System: Findings of the Female Population Taskforce.* Presentation to the Gender Specifics Services Training. Minneapolis, Minnesota. The author became familiar with a case in Las Vegas where a 16-year-old girl was in juvenile court on a charge of "assault" that resulted from a confrontation with her mother inside the home one night. No weapon was used, and there were no injuries. In the courtroom the girl stood in front of the judge (who was particularly stern) crying and not understanding what was going on. She was being asked to make a plea and after the judge finally explained the difference between "no contest" and "guilt and innocence" she pleaded not guilty since she strongly felt that she did not do anything wrong. As I watched the proceedings, I thought of David Matza's description of juvenile court proceedings in a book written about 40 years ago that described in great detail the difficulties children usually have in understanding juvenile court procedures (Matza, *Delinquency and Drift*, John Wiley, 1964). It also made me think about the often absurd and meaningless terms like "assault" and "violent crime." I also wonder how many more cases like these end up being labeled "assault" and, even worse, become lumped together as "violent crimes." The girl in this case was placed on probation, and the charges were eventually dropped.

[109] Acoca, L. (1999). "Investing in Girls: A 21st Century Challenge." *Juvenile Justice* 6: 8.

[110] Recent statistics have identified the rising use of detention for girls and the disproportionate representation of girls of color in detention. These issues are discussed at length in Chesney-Lind and Shelden, *Girls, Delinquency and Juvenile Justice*, ch. 7.

[111] Chesney-Lind, M. and K. Irwin (2008). "Still the 'Best Place to Conquer Girls': Girls and the Juvenile Justice System." In R. G. Shelden and D. Macallair (Eds.), *Juvenile Justice in America: Problems and Prospects.* Long Grove, IL: Waveland Press.

[112] Artz, S. and T. Riecken (1997). "What, So What, Then What?: The Gender Gap in School-Based Violence and Its Implications for Child and Youth Care Practice." *Child and Youth Care Forum* 26 (4): 291–303.

[113] Girls, Incorporated (1996). *Prevention and Parity: Girls in Juvenile Justice.* Indianapolis: Girls, Incorporated National Resource Center.

[114] Feld, B. (2009). "Violent Girls or Relabeled Status Offenders? An Alternative Interpretation of the Data." *Crime and Delinquency* 55: 241–65. This quote is from p. 5. Feld points out that at least one early analysis predicted that this would happen and it did. See Handler, J. F. and J. Zatz (Eds.) (1982). *Neither Angels nor Thieves: Studies in Deinstitutionalization of Status Offenders.* Washington, DC: National Academy Press.

[115] Frye, V., M. Haviland, and V. Rajah (2007). "Dual Arrest and Other Unintended Consequences of Mandatory Arrest in New York City: A Brief Report." *Journal of Family Violence* 22: 397–405.

[116] Schwartz, J., D. J. Steffensmeier, and B. Feldmeyer (2009). "Assessing Trends in Women's Violence via Data Triangulation: Arrests, Convictions, Incarcerations, and Victim Reports." *Social Problems* 56: 494–525.

[117] Tremblay, R. E. (2000). "The Development of Aggressive Behavior during Childhood: What Have We Learned in the Past Century." *International Journal of Behavioral Development* 24: 129–41.

[118] Bjorkqvist, K. and P. Niemela (1992). "New Trends in the Study of Female Aggression." In K. Bjorkqvist and P. Niemela (Eds.), *Of Mice and Women: Aspects of Female Aggression.* San Diego: Academic Press, pp. 3–16; Bjorkqvist K., K. Osterman, and A. Kaukiainen (1992). "The Development of Direct and Indirect Aggressive Strategies in Males and Females." In Bjorkqvist and Niemela, *Of Mice and Women,* pp. 51–64.

[119] Crick, N. R. and J. K. Grotpeter (1995). "Relational Aggression, Gender, and Social-Psychological Adjustment." *Child Development,* 66: 710–22.

[120] Artz, S. (1998). *Sex, Power and the Violent School Girl.* Toronto: Trifolium Books.

[121] Ibid.

[122] DeKeseredy, W. (2000). *Women, Crime and the Canadian Criminal Justice System.* Cincinnati: Anderson, p. 46.

[123] Suggested by Artz, *Sex, Power and the Violent School Girl.*

[124] Artz, S., M. Blais, and D. Nicholson (2000). *Developing Girls' Custody Units.* Unpublished report. British Columbia Crime Trends, p. 31.

[125] Allport, G. (1954). *The Nature of Prejudice.* New York: Bantam Books.

[126] Chesney-Lind and Irwin, *Beyond Bad Girls,* pp. 55–56.

[127] Sommers, I. and D. R. Baskin (1993). "The Situational Context of Violent Female Offending." *Journal of Research on Crime and Delinquency* 30(2): 136–62.

[128] Messerschmidt, J. (1996). *Masculinities and Crime.* Lanham, MD: Rowman and Littlefield.

[129] Miller, J. (1998). "Up It Up: Gender and the Accomplishment of Street Robbery." *Criminology* 36: 37–65.

[130] Ibid.

[131] Brubaker, S. J. and K. C. Fox (2010). "Urban African American Girls at Risk: An Exploratory Study of Service Needs and Provision." *Youth Violence and Juvenile Justice* 8(3): 250–65.

[132] Chesney-Lind and Irwin, *Beyond Bad Girls,* pp. 148–50. See also Brubaker and Fox, "Urban African American Girls at Risk."

PART II

EXPLAINING DELINQUENCY

6

INDIVIDUALISTIC THEORIES
OF DELINQUENCY

Theory is an important part of any academic discipline. Two broad schools of thought have dominated the thinking about crime and criminal justice during the past 200 years: the *classical* and the *positivist*. Whereas the classical perspective has been the dominant theoretical backbone of the criminal justice system, the positivist paradigm has dominated most of the theories attempting to explain criminal behavior and has provided some of the major assumptions behind the juvenile justice system. Within the positivist tradition, there have been two major categories of theories that, for simplistic purposes, can be described as either *individualistic* (discussed in this chapter) or *sociological approaches* (chapter 7). When explaining crime and criminal behavior, one can emphasize two individualistic approaches—the offender's body (biological) or mind (psychological) and a sociological approach focusing on the environment.

The Classical School

This school of thought emerged during the late eighteenth century with the work of an Italian publicist named Cesare Beccaria and an Englishman named Jeremy Bentham. Their theories emerged at a time of great social changes, the most notable being the emerging capitalist order and the demise of the old feudal order throughout both Europe and America. Enlightenment thinkers such as Montesquieu, Rousseau, Hobbes, Helvetius, Diderot, and Locke provided the foundation for the core ideas of the classical school.[1] It is safe to say that just about everyone associated with this school of thought "affirmed their belief in the principles of reason, in the precision of the scientific method, and in the authority of nature."[2] From the perspective of the classical school, an unwritten "social contract" emerged during the Renaissance (1300–1600) a period during which a vast social movement swept away old customs and institutions and promoted intellectual development, while capitalism emerged throughout the Western world. The social contract, as described by philosophers such as Thomas Hobbes and Jean Rousseau, involves a *responsible* and *rational* person applying *reason*. Humans originally lived in a state of nature, grace, or innocence; escape from this state is the result of the ability to reason. Rational peo-

201

ple have reasoning powers that place them above animals. This perspective also stressed that humans have *free will*. Theoretically, there is no limit to what they can accomplish. Furthermore, humans are essentially *hedonistic*. By their very *nature*, humans will choose actions that *maximize pleasure and minimize pain*. More importantly, social contract thinkers claim that the main instrument of the control of human behavior is *fear*, especially fear of *pain*. Fear of punishment and the pains it causes influence humans to make the right choice. Punishment is viewed as the logical means to control behavior. In addition, society has a right to punish the individual and to transfer this right to the state to insure it will be carried out. Finally, some code of criminal law, or better, some system of punishment is deemed necessary to respond to crime.[3]

Social contract theorists based their theories on some unproven assumptions about human nature, yet their views were taken as given by the new democratic governments in the seventeenth and eighteenth centuries. "Social contract" became a convenient ideology for justifying a strong central government concerned with protecting the interests of private property and profits. The social contract theory justified the buildup of police forces and other formal methods of handling conflicts and disputes. The formal criminal justice system included a definition of crime as harm to the state and to the people—terms often used interchangeably.

Ironically, Rousseau wrote that the ultimate source of inequality was man taking a plot of ground and claiming it as his own. This is exactly what happened during the *Enclosure Movements* in England during the sixteenth century when powerful landlords built fences around common ground (land formally used by all and not legally "owned") and claimed it as their own or charged rent in the name of "private property." This resulted in thousands of vagrants (homeless people) flocking to European cities in search of work and eventually being labeled the "dangerous classes." The Elizabethan Poor Laws passed during the sixteenth century and declared two kinds of poor: (1) the *worthy*: those who could be reformed and be useful to society; and (2) the *unworthy*: those who were unreformable, useless, and requiring a sentence to the poorhouse/workhouse (early forms of jails and prisons). The prevailing view that crime was a *voluntary* violation of the social contract became an essential idea in much of the subsequent thinking about crime, especially classical views. Such a view largely ignored the gross inequalities existing at the time. The inequality included illiteracy, leading to the question of whether "the people" in the new social orders unanimously agreed on the social contract, since so few could read or write.

The classical school of criminology derives mainly from the work of Cesare Beccaria (1738–1794), who published *On Crimes and Punishment* in 1764.[4] For Beccaria and other liberal thinkers, the major governing principle of any legislation should be "the greatest happiness for the greatest numbers" (this supports the view that government should be "of the people, by the people, for the people"). This philosophical doctrine is known as *utilitarianism*—the idea that punishment is based on its *usefulness* or *utility* or *practicality*. On the last page of his book, Beccaria noted:

In order for punishment not to be, in every instance, an act of violence of one or of many against a private citizen, it must be essentially public, prompt, necessary, the least possible in the given circumstances, proportionate to the crimes, dictated by the laws.[5]

In other words, punishment should not be excessive; *it should fit the crime* (this is a key phrase, most commonly expressed as "let the punishment fit the crime"). Beccaria also argued that the punishment should closely follow the commission of a crime, making it more just and useful. The major thrust of the classical school, however, is that the purpose of the criminal justice system should be to *prevent* crime through *deterrence* (see below). A potential criminal, according to this line of thinking, will decide not to commit a crime because the punishment will be too costly.

Jeremy Bentham was one of Beccaria's contemporaries (1748–1832). He suggested that criminal behavior (like all human behavior) is a rational choice, born of man's free will. In order to prevent crime we must make the punishment (i.e., pain) greater than the criminal act. In summary, the classical school assumes that (1) all people by nature are hedonistic and self-serving; they are likely to commit crime to get what they want; (2) in order to live in harmony and avoid a "war of all against all" (as Thomas Hobbes stressed), the people agree to give up certain freedoms in order to be protected by a strong central state; (3) punishment is necessary to deter crime and the state has the prerogative (which has been granted to it by the people through a "social contract") to administer it; (4) punishment should "fit the crime" and not be used to rehabilitate the offender; (5) use of the law should be limited and due process rights should be observed; (6) each individual is responsible for his or her actions; mitigating circumstances or "excuses" are inadmissible.[6] The ideas of Beccaria and Bentham influenced one of the most popular perspectives on crime and crime control: deterrence.

Deterrence Theory

Deterrence comes from the word *deter*, which the *Random House Dictionary* defines as "to discourage or restrain from acting or proceeding, as through fear or doubt." It also means "to prevent; check; arrest." It is synonymous with such words as "hinder" and "stop." In large part the theory of deterrence is based on *fear*—fear of consequences. A young person might be warned by his or her parents "if you stay out past midnight, you'll be grounded" or "if you do that again, we'll take the car away!"

Applying the deterrence idea to the prevention of crime, we have two variations. The first is known as *general deterrence*; it is used to "send a message" to would-be law violators about what will happen if they break a law. The assumption is that the general public will be discouraged from law-breaking behavior.[7]

The second variation is known as *special (or specific) deterrence*; the punishment will prevent a specific offender from reoffending. The offender will think twice the next time he or she thinks about committing a crime.

The classical school and all of its modern variations are rooted in a conservative belief system that dominates in the United States. We need to look deep into the culture to understand the high degree of punitiveness that character-izes U.S. society.[8] At the heart of this philosophy is a simplistic view of the world—a world divided into rigid categories of "good" and "evil." This view includes the traditional nuclear family with the father in control as the major breadwinner. The "strict father morality" is based in part on the belief that in order to become a "good" and "moral" person, a child must learn to obey the rules and to respect authority. Proper behavior is taught through the use or threat of punishment. Within such a system, "the exercise of authority is itself moral; that is, it is moral to reward obedience and punish disobedience."[9]

This system of rewards and punishments is based on the belief that in order to survive in a dangerous world, children must learn discipline and build char-acter. Punishment, according to this philosophy, is the only way to become a self-disciplined and moral person. To be successful requires becoming self-disci-plined. More importantly, rewarding someone who has not earned it by devel-oping self-discipline is immoral. This is why conservatives reject welfare, affirmative action, lenient punishments, and the like; they view such actions as rewarding deviance, laziness, etc.[10] According to the conservative view, there is a "morality of strength." Moral strength can be seen as a metaphor. One must be morally strong to stand up to evil, and one becomes morally strong through a system of rewards and punishments that teach self-discipline. A person who is morally weak cannot fight evil. If one is too self-indulgent, he or she is immoral. Welfare is immoral. Crime and deviance are immoral and should be punished. Following this reasoning, crime and deviance are the result of moral weakness. Teenage sex, drug use, and all sorts of other "deviant" behaviors stem from lack of self-control. A person with proper self-discipline should be able to "just say no," and those who do not must be and deserve to be punished.[11]

Does deterrence work? Does putting fear into potential offenders keep them from committing crime? With some exceptions, the answer to this ques-tion is no.[12] Numerous studies have found that adding police officers or increasing patrols in certain areas of the city has little impact in overall crime rates.[13] The same is true for most other police practices, although there have been a few exceptions to this general rule.[14] Research on the deterrent effects of the death penalty have been conducted for at least 60 years, and the results show little if any effect on murder, although one recent study showed that in the month after a well-publicized execution the murder rate dropped.[15] The death penalty as a potential deterrent does not relate to juveniles since the Supreme Court in March 2005 ruled the penalty unconstitutional for anyone who committed a capital crime when under the age of 18.[16]

As for the deterrent effect of punishment in general on juveniles, most research has shown that there is little, if any, impact. One study found that instilling a sense of citizenship has a greater impact than simply increasing either the certainty or severity of punishment.[17] The strongest factors in pre-venting youths from committing crimes include: increasing employment, reducing poverty, increasing family income, and increasing family supervi-sion.[18] One study casts doubt on the impact of incarceration on youth crime. Mike Males, Dan Macallair and Megan Corcoran examined incarceration rates of juveniles in California during a 30-year period (1970-2000) and found that as these rates went down, the crime rate for juveniles also went down.[19] As will be shown in chapter 12, the number of youths incarcerated has declined during the past decade—as has the overall youth crime rate. The major problem with applying deterrence to juveniles is the fact that most of their crimes are done without much planning. The behavior is the result of spur-of-the-moment decisions; therefore, the threat of punishment has little impact.[20]

During the last half of the twentieth century, several variations to the classical approach appeared. One theory that became popular in the 1970s and 1980s took the position that crime was merely a product of "rational" choices and decisions that people made in their daily lives. Various terminologies have been used almost interchangeably, such as *criminal opportunity theory, routine activity theory,*[21] and *situational choice model.*

Rational Choice Theory

Modern versions of the classical approach to crime learned from the mistakes of the original classical school. Beccaria and Bentham erroneously assumed that all humans behave "rationally" all the time—that they consistently, carefully calculate the pros and cons of their behaviors. More recent examples of this view—including the *rational choice theory*—recognize that choices are often not based on pure reason and rationality; rather, they are determined by a host of factors. There are constraints on our choices because of lack of information, differing moral values, the social context of the situation, and other situational factors. In short, not everyone acts logically and rationally all the time, which may be especially true for young offenders. Indeed, it has been estimated that as much as two-thirds of delinquent acts are spur-of-the-moment with no advanced planning. Some planning does, of course occur, especially when the crimes are serious property crimes or systematic drug sales.[22]

Modern rational choice theory still makes the assumption that people freely choose to commit crime because they are goal oriented and want to maximize their pleasure and minimize their pain. In short, they are acting mostly out of self-interest. One modern variation, known as *routine activities theory,* suggests that criminals plan very carefully by selecting specific targets based on such things as vulnerability (e.g., elderly citizens, unguarded premises, lack of police presence) and commit their crimes accordingly. Thus people who engage in certain routine activities during the course of their daily lives place themselves at risk of being victimized, such as being out in high crime areas at night, not locking doors, leaving keys in the car, working at certain jobs during certain hours of the day (e.g., late-night clerk at a 7–11 store), and so on. Active criminals weigh the odds of getting caught when they select their targets. One of the flaws in this thinking is the assumption that people should stay home to avoid becoming a victim when, in fact, certain groups (especially women and children) are more vulnerable at home.[23]

Studies of gangs have noted that there are many "logical" reasons why a youth may want to join a gang.[24] Rational choice theory could be used to explain the motivation to join. On the other hand, the threat of punishment (e.g., so-called enhancement statutes that increase the penalty for the commission of a crime if a person is a gang member) could predict against joining a gang. Malcolm Klein used a crackdown on gangs by the Los Angeles Police Department (Operation Hammer) to illustrate the problem of deterrence. This operation resulted in mass arrests of almost 1,500 individuals who were subsequently booked at a "mobile booking" unit next to the Los Angeles Memorial Coliseum. About 90% were released with no charges filed. There were about 60 felony arrests, and charges were eventually filed on about half of those. Klein presents two possible scenarios when the gang member returns to his neighborhood following his release.

> Does he say to them [his homies], "Oh, gracious, I've been arrested and subjected to deterrence; I'm going to give up my gang affiliation." Or does he say, "Shit man, they're just jivin' us—can't hold us on any charges, and gotta let us go." Without hesitation, the gangbanger will turn the experience to his and the gang's advantage. Far from being deterred from membership or crime, his ties to the groups will be strengthened when the members group together to make light of the whole affair and heap ridicule on the police.[25]

In other words, human behavior is far more complex than the rather simplistic notion that we all use our free will to make choices. Decisions hinge on the availability of alternative choices. A good analogy is that of a menu at a restaurant. Some restaurants have several items to choose from, while others have a limited selection. Likewise, some youths may have a variety of choices (stemming mostly from their environment), while others may have extremely limited selections. A youth growing up in a community with gangs may have the choice of joining or getting attacked. Other youths in other communities may have other options, such as moving with their parents to a new community.[26] Two researchers have proposed a *situational choice model* that asserts criminal behavior is a function of choices and decisions that are made within a surrounding context of various opportunities and constraints.[27]

Each of the variations of the classical school eventually is reduced to the key notion of *free will*, an idea that has been debated for several centuries among philosophers and scientists. It is beyond the scope of this chapter to deal with this issue in any detail, but we will briefly raise several issues.

Every event in life has a *cause*.[28] Our world would be chaos, and science would not exist if there were effects without causes and effects. If a plane crashes, we immediately try to find what caused the crash. No one would think of suggesting that it may be "causeless." If there is a new disease, an effective cure is possible only after we have identified the cause. If the police find a dead body, they will try to discover who and what caused it. All the laws of nature and all our scientific advances are possible *only* because *all* effects have causes. Modern life itself would be impossible if there were effects without causes. If there were effects without causes the word "experience" would be nonsensical. Experience is all about the long slow process of learning which effects go with which causes.

When it comes to explaining certain human behaviors—especially crime—much of this kind of thinking is often tossed aside. For example, Dr. Laura Schlessinger discussed on her radio show the case of Susan Smith, the South Carolina woman who let her car slide into a pond with her two children in the back seat. Smith first blamed a black man, a complete stranger; eventually she confessed. Dr. Laura explained Susan Smith's actions by saying she was "evil." No further discussion was needed. To start to ask why she is "evil" opens you up to charges that you are some bleeding heart, soft-on-crime liberal, followed by the "abuse-excuse" mentality. It's almost as though trying to find a cause of this and similar tragedies is tantamount to approving Susan Smith's actions. To suggest that there is not a cause for what we describe as evil, however, is contrary to all the laws of science and logic. Quite often people confuse "explanation" with "excuse."

Is Dr. Laura saying there is no cause for "evil"? If so, then there is no way to protect ourselves against it. There is nothing to be on the lookout for if it just happens without cause. It's like contracting some rare disease for which there are no preventive measures. Let's suppose that that is exactly what happens. How then can we hold people accountable? Are there people who are just born evil? What could that person have done to avoid being born evil?

Are there people who are not born evil but who then somehow become evil? That seems more likely. The question of how they became evil demands finding a cause. It is unlikely that they were not evil on January eighteenth, but they were evil on January nineteenth without something happening, some cause.

Do youngsters just suddenly choose to commit a delinquent act with no antecedent events leading up to it? If we take two youths growing up in the same neighborhood, and one joined a local gang and the other one didn't, do we simply say one "freely chose" to be in a gang and the other one "freely chose" not to? If so, then we must ask *why* they chose different paths. There have to be *causes* for each of the two courses of action. I often ask students why they are attending my university, rather than Harvard or Stanford. They often say they "freely chose" to attend my university, but when asked why they didn't "freely choose" Harvard or Stanford, they typically begin talking about their family backgrounds, the income level of their parents, the communities where they grew up, their grades in high school, etc. Each of these variables in turn has their own *causes*, such as why one's parents are not rich or why the high school grades were not higher. If a peer received an athletic scholarship to a very prestigious school, we could ask why one person had athletic ability and the others did not.

The bottom line is that everything has a cause, and usually multiple causes. These causes can be simplified as being either genetic or environmental—the famous nature vs. nurture debate. To reduce the complexities of human behavior, delinquent or otherwise, to some simple formula of "rational choice" is patently absurd. The classical school perspective boxes us into a corner—it comes down to the idea that delinquent acts (and, in fact, all other acts) are merely "choices" we make with our "free will." Our entire legal system is based on deterrence. We have laws, police, and courts that mete out punishments for wrongdoing. All of these systems operate on the assumption that people make free choices to commit crime, and it is up to the legal system to prevent that from occurring by making the "pain" greater than the "pleasure" gained by committing a crime. Actions by the legal system—including the threat that legal agents may take action—are the foundation of the legal order. This system cannot handle the possibility that people may not have free will and that there are all sorts of causes beyond an individual's control.

The Crime Control and Due Process Models

The classical school of thought has generally led to two contrasting models of the criminal justice system, which are roughly the equivalent of two differing political ideologies, namely, conservatism and liberalism. These models have been termed the "crime control" and "due process" models.[29] From the conservative ideology comes the *crime control model*. Essentially, the crime control model is based on the assumption that the fundamental goal of the criminal justice system is the "repression of crime" through aggressive law enforcement, strict enforcement of the law and harsh punishments, including the use of the death penalty. From this point of view, it is better to emphasize protecting citizens from crime than protecting the civil liberties of citizens. In other words, supporters of this model would prefer that no criminals be set free on "technicalities," even at the expense of depriving innocent persons of their constitutional rights. The primary concern is public safety rather than individual rights. The appropriate response to crime is repression through arrest and conviction. Discussion of causes are ignored, dismissed, or reduced to clichés: "if you can't do the time, don't do the crime."[30]

From the liberal ideology comes the *due process model*. While the crime control model may resemble an "assembly line," the due process model resembles an "obstacle course." The due process model stresses the importance of individual rights and would support the general belief that it is better to let a few criminals go unpunished than to falsely imprison an innocent person. This model is based on the assumption that the criminal justice process is plagued by human error. Discretion by criminal justice personnel—especially the police—should be limited; the accused should receive equitable treatment at each stage of the proceedings and should have adequate legal counsel to safeguard individual rights.

The classical school and its modern derivatives are subject to several major criticisms. As we have noted already, the assumptions that people always act rationally and that all people are hedonists and self-serving can be challenged. Over 100 years of social science research has demonstrated that this is clearly not the case; humans are much more complex than such a simplistic view.[31]

The classical school of thought assumes that people are equal in the ability to reason and that they are equally likely to commit a crime. In point of fact, people in society (especially when the classical school emerged) are hardly equal by any method of measurement. You can't have "equal justice" in an unequal society. French philosopher Anatole France once praised the "majestic equality of the law" in that it "forbids rich and poor alike to sleep under bridges, to beg in the streets and to steal bread."[32]

This point leads us directly into the third objection, namely that the classical school does little to address the causes of crime. Classical writers particularly avoided any discussion of the relationship between inequality and crime and instead focused on problems associated with the control of crime.[33] Probing the multiple *causes* of crime would lead to an emphasis on *prevention*. The prevention of crime is reduced to finding ways to deter people through the threats of the legal system, usually in the form of more cops on the street and harsher punishments. What is really the topic is the *control* of crime, rather than true prevention. Over time, the classical approach became "administrative and legal criminology," during which justice became "an exact scale of punishments for equal acts without reference to the nature of the individual involved and with no attention to the question of special circumstances under which the act came about."[34]

The problems associated with the classical approach were evident as soon as legislatures attempted to put them in place. The French Code of 1791, for instance, tried to fix an exact amount of penalty for every crime.[35] Social determinants of human behavior were ignored, with courts proceeding as though "punishment and incarceration could be easily measured on some kind of universal calculus."[36] Eventually, lawyers and jurists primarily in Europe revised the classical approach to account for practical problems in the administration of justice (sometimes called the "neoclassical school"). Reformers attacked the French Code as unjust because of its rigidity and recognized the necessity of looking at factors other than the crime itself. The offender's past record, the degree of incompetence, insanity, and the impact of age on criminal responsibility were taken under consideration.[37] There was some recognition that all offenders did not possess the same degree of "free will" and because of this not every offender was suitable to imprisonment.

It is important to note, however, that the basic thrust of the classical school's vision of human beings and the proper response to crime was, for all practical purposes, left unchanged. Beccaria and Bentham's premises that criminals make willful decisions to commit crimes and thus must be held responsible continued to influence thinking about the criminal justice process. What began as a general theory of human behavior became a perspective on government crime control policy.[38] The administration of justice continued to be guided, as it is today, with one overriding principle: that human behavior, in this case criminal behavior, can be shaped, molded, changed, etc., through the *fear of punishment* and that all that is needed is to make the punishment (or rather the *pain* that is associated with it) exceed the *pleasure* (or profit from the crime), to prevent people from committing crime. Almost as soon as Beccaria's proposals were being debated, a rival school of criminology challenged the assumptions.

The Positivist School

In the nineteenth century, a new trend emerged that used observation and measurement to study social phenomena. The *scientific method* represented a sharp break from the past. Rather than relying on religious beliefs or "arm-chair" philosophy, answers to fundamental questions about human beings and the universe around them were investigated through "objective" *science*.[39] Charles Darwin, in his book *On the Origin of Species* (published in 1859), presented evidence that "humans were the same general kind of creatures as the rest of the animals, except that they were more highly evolved or developed." Most importantly, humans were beginning to be "understood as creatures whose conduct was influenced, if not determined, by biological and cultural antecedents rather than as self-determining beings that were free to do what they wanted."[40] The first "scientific" studies of crime and criminal behavior began at about the same time.

Positivism is a *method of inquiry* that attempts to answers questions through the scientific method. The researcher examines the "real world" of empirical facts by testing hypotheses, with the goal of arriving at the "truth" and deriving "laws" (e.g., the law of falling bodies, the law of relativity).[41] The positivist mode of inquiry gained respectability in the social sciences largely through the work of August Comte (1798–1857). "While Comte recognized that positive methods to study society cannot be completely identical to mathematical and physical science methods, he maintained that positive knowledge can be gained by using observation, experiment, comparison, and historical method."[42] Using the scientific approach, human beings are able to discover regularities among social phenomena resulting in the establishment of predictability and control.[43]

The positivist school of criminology argues that humans do not have free will—their behavior is determined by various biological, psychological, and sociological factors. Thus, responsibility for one's actions is diminished. The solution to the problem of crime, from this perspective, is to eliminate the various factors that are thought to be the most likely causes of why crime occurs. Such a task might include (but is not limited to) the reduction of poverty; greater emphasis on education, psychiatric, and or psychological testing and treatment; monitoring nutrition and adjusting or supplementing one's diet. The goal of the criminal justice system is to reduce crime by *making the punishment fit the offender* rather than fit the crime, as the classical school proposed. *Rehabilitation* of the offender is accomplished through the wide use of discretion among criminal justice officials and some form of *indeterminate* sentence.

The scientific study of crime began with Adolphe Quetelet (a Belgian astronomer and mathematician) and Andre-Michel Guerry (a French lawyer and statistician) in Europe during the 1830s and 1840s. The first annual national crime statistics were published in France in 1827; Guerry was appointed director of criminal statistics for the French Ministry of Justice. He used maps to indicate crime rates and to display social factors. He found higher rates of property crimes in wealthier regions and concluded that the primary contributing factor was opportunity—there was more to steal.[44] He also found that the areas with the highest levels of education had the highest rates of violent crime.

Quetelet used probability theory to search for the causes of crime and to predict future trends in criminal activity. His quest was to identify law-like regularities in society by applying traditional scientific methods to official crime data for France. He concluded that "criminal behavior was as much a product of society as of volition."[45] Looking at the years 1828 and 1829, he was able to identify over 2,000 crimes against the person committed by people who could not read or write. During the same period, he noted that only 80 similar offenses had been committed by people who had received "superior" academic instruction. He found that the educated were much less likely to commit property crimes than their uneducated counterparts. He identified 206 property offenses committed by the well educated compared to 6,617 like offenses committed by illiterate offenders during the same time period.

> The knowledgeable class implies more affluence and, consequently, less need to resort to the different varieties of theft which make up a great part of crimes against property; while affluence and knowledge do not succeed as easily in restraining the fire of the passions and sentiments of hate and vengeance.[46]

He also looked at the criminal justice process in France for crimes committed between 1826 and 1829. He found consistencies in the number of defendants who failed to appear in the courts and certain courts that were more likely to impose particular sanctions for particular offenses.

> So, as I have had occasion to repeat several times before, one passes from one year to the other with the sad perspective of seeing the same crimes reproduced in the same order and bring with them the same penalties in the same proportions.[47]

Later, he turned his attention to the propensities for crime, and found striking correlations between crime and independent variables such as age, sex, climate, and socioeconomic status of offenders. Young males between the ages of 21 and 25 were found to have the highest propensity for crime, while women had the lowest. When Quetelet compared female and male offenders he discovered that males committed nearly four times as many property offenses as women, and they were involved in over six times the number of violent offenses. He also noted that violent offenses were more likely to occur in the summer months, and property offenses were more commonly committed during the winter. The poor and the unemployed were found to have a higher propensity for crime than members of the working and upper classes.

He also discovered that economic changes were related to crime rates, surmising that society itself, through its economic and social attributes, was responsible for crime. While people may have free will there were, nevertheless, scientific laws to which criminal behavior responded. Recognizing that all people had the "capacity" to commit crime (an idea that would later be adopted by neo-Freudians), Quetelet argued that the average person rarely transferred that option into action. He eventually turned away from the social influences of criminal behavior (as most contemporary criminologists have done), and focused on the correlation between crime and morality, suggesting that certain people were more prone to criminal behavior than others (e.g., vagabonds, gypsies, and others with "inferior moral stock").

In 1876 an Italian doctor named Cesare Lombroso published *Criminal Man*.[48] He emphasized the *biological* basis of criminal behavior and argued that criminals had distinctive physical *stigmata* (characteristics common to more primitive people) that distinguished them from noncriminals.

His work was a breakthrough for positivist criminology, which has since branched out in several directions. There are now three major versions of positivist criminology: biological (which began with Lombroso), psychological, and sociological. Biological positivism locates the causes of crime within the individual's physical makeup; psychological positivism suggests the causes are in faulty personality development; sociological positivism stresses social factors within one's environment or surrounding culture and social structure.[49]

The positivist approach suffers from several problems. First, it assumes that pure objectivity is possible—that research is "value free" without any biases. Max Weber, perhaps fully understanding the potential for intellectual and/or academic arrogance, strongly cautioned researchers about the assumption of objective and/or value-free research.[50] Second, there is an assumption that the scientific method is the only way of arriving at the truth. Third, positivism takes for granted the existing social and economic order; that is, it generally accepts the status quo and the official definition of reality. Part of the reality that is accepted includes the standard definitions of crime—the state's definitions. Because of this, positivists have focused their research almost exclusively on those who violate the criminal law rather than on the law itself. Their efforts focus on controlling and/or changing the lawbreaker rather than the law or the social order. The positivist method does not assist us in seeking alternatives to the present social and economic order and the current method of responding to crime.[51] Finally, as David Shichor notes, there is the concern that "biological theorizing and research can lead to profiling, racial discrimination, selective law enforcement, discriminatory preventive policies, and sentencing based on 'dangerousness.'"[52] If "experts" use "science" to identify what types of people commit crimes or to prescribe punishment or treatment, the power granted to make such decisions could endanger the rights of others.

What is most interesting about both the classical and the positivist's perspectives is that they are primarily concerned with the *control* of crime, rather than the amelioration of the social conditions that create crime, although the positivist approach gives at least some lip service to the causes of crime. Even the positivists, however, have been concerned primarily with the offender and how he or she can be controlled and/or changed, rather than changing the existing social and economic order itself.

Biological Theories

The central thesis of this perspective is that criminals are biologically different from noncriminals—and that criminals are *inferior* to noncriminals because of those biological characteristics. As mentioned in the previous section, Cesare Lombroso is the most famous representative of this perspective.

Lombroso (1836–1909) and his followers, such as Enrico Ferri (1856–1928) and Rafaele Garofalo (1852–1934), have been referred to as the "Italian School." Criminal anthropologists following this school of thought believed that criminals had certain *atavistic* physical features—that they were biological throwbacks to a more primitive time.

Lombroso's theory included five propositions. (1) Criminals are, at birth, a distinct type of human being. (2) This type can be recognized by certain stigmata, anomalies such as high cheekbones, large jaws, deformed or oddly shaped ears, excessive body hair, etc. Lombroso arrived at these and other conclusions as a result of his work performing autopsies on the bodies of hundreds of Italian prisoners who had died in confinement. He never explored whether the physical conditions of these prisoners could have been the *result of their confinement* rather than the *cause* of their criminal behavior—an entirely plausible explanation given the horrible conditions in Italian prisons and jails of the time. (3) The "criminal type" can be easily identified if he or she exhibits five or more of these stigmata. Lombroso also believed that women offenders had "fallen from grace" so far that they were even more inferior than male criminals.[53] (4) These stigmata do not so much cause criminal behavior as they are indicators of someone who is *predisposed* to becoming a criminal. (5) Because of their personal natures, such offenders cannot help but become criminals unless they grow up under extremely favorable conditions.[54]

Although the popularity of being able to "spot" a criminal because of certain physical features has been thoroughly rejected within academic circles, certain variations exist today.[55] It is interesting to note that people in U.S. society (with the media playing a major contributing role) continue to subscribe to stereotypes of what criminals "look like."[56] Unfortunately many of these stereotypes center on race (mostly African American and Hispanic) and class (mostly lower or "underclass").

A variation of Lombroso's views is the general theory of *body types* (sometimes referred to as *physiognomy*), which gained popularity during the first half of the twentieth century.[57] According to this view, humans can be divided into three basic *somatotypes*. These body types correspond to certain *temperaments*. The first type is the *endomorph*, characterized by excessive body weight and having an extroverted personality (the stereotype of the "jolly fat man"). The second type is the *mesomorph*, who is athletically built and muscular. These individuals are described as being active and behaving aggressively. They are believed to be the most likely to be involved in serious criminal activity and to join gangs. The third type is the *ectomorph*, who is thin and delicate with an introverted personality (characterized as loners unlikely to engage in crime). Still another variation of these views focuses on women offenders and the *pre-menstrual syndrome* (PMS). Although popular in explaining women's crime, there is virtually no research proving that this is a factor, even though it is used as a form of insanity defense in France and has also been used as a defense in both England and the United States. Part of the problem is the lack of precise definition of the term itself.[58]

A closely related view is known as *phrenology*, which was popular for a time in the nineteenth century. According to this view, a person's character and behavior is determined in part by the shape of the head. There is an assumption (a false one at that) that a person's mental faculties are located in brain "organs" on the surface of the skull and "can be detected by visible inspection of the skull." The man most responsible for its popularity was Joseph Gall, who wrote the first book on the subject.[59] He argued that the organs of the brain "which were used got bigger and those which were not used shrunk, causing the skull to rise and fall with organ development. These bumps and indentations on the skull, according to Gall, reflect specific areas of the brain that determine a person's emotional and intellectual functions."[60] Although it has been discredited as a viable explanation of crime, it remains popular, as witnessed by the existence of a website devoted to the theory.[61]

The belief in the connection between physiological features of the body and human behavior persists, as indicated by an article that appeared in the *New York Times* on May 10, 2010.

> A small band of economists has been studying how height, weight and beauty affect the likelihood of committing—or being convicted of—a crime. Looking at records from the 19th, 20th and 21st centuries, they have found evidence that shorter men are 20 to 30 percent more likely to end up in prison than their taller counterparts, and that obesity and physical attractiveness are linked to crime.[62]

Gregory Price, an economist at Morehouse College, has written about height and crime. Rather than endorsing biological determinism or a genetic predisposition to crime, he argues that crime can be viewed, at least partially, as an alternative labor market. "If individuals with certain physical attributes are disadvantaged in the labor force, they may find crime more attractive."[63] In addition, height and weight can indicate a lack of nutrition or health care; smaller stature could be the result of impoverished conditions.

This area of study is sometimes called anthropometric economics. H. Naci Mocan, an economist at Louisiana State University, wrote a paper on crime and attractiveness.[64] He notes that employer discrimination or preference may account for someone who is overweight, unattractive, or short being disadvantaged in the labor market or more likely to commit a crime—but there is certainly no clear cause and effect. He also studied high school students and found that students ranked as unattractive (on a 5-point scale) had lower grade point averages and more problems with teachers. They were also more likely to commit crimes (such as burglary or selling drugs) than average or attractive students. Shorter students were less likely to participate in clubs, often resulting in lower self-esteem and underdeveloped social skills that could be useful later in life.

Some biological positivists focus on the functioning of the central nervous system. The central nervous system is involved in conscious thought and voluntary motor activities. Abnormal brain wave patterns, measured through electroencephalographs (EEGs), have been associated with various abnormal behavioral patterns in individuals. Additionally, researchers have studied neurological impairments, "minimal brain dysfunction" (MBD), hormonal influences, diet (especially sugar intake) and attention deficit hyperactivity disorder (ADHD), among biological variables. Trying to predict criminal behavior has never been easy. A large number of studies concerning predicting behavior have been conducted during the past 20 years and the conclusions have not been uniform.[65]

There has been some research suggesting a link between prenatal exposure to certain drugs and/or intoxicants from the mother and subsequent acting out behavior.[66] Also, the taking of an excessive amount of drugs over time has been shown to affect the biological system of individuals.[67]

Criminality as an Inherited Trait

Another popular variation of the biological approach claims that criminal behavior is genetically transmitted from one generation to another. Throughout the twentieth century, various researchers have ostensibly found evidence in support of this view, primarily in the studies of twins. While correlations have been found when studying identical twins raised in different geographical locations, the samples have been much too small to be able to generalize.[68] Criminality in the family is correlated with becoming an offender. For example, having a father with a criminal record is highly correlated with delinquency. This, however, could easily be the result of the behavior modeled by the father and/or lack of parenting skills rather than a genetic predisposition.

An additional view holds that certain individuals have an extra "Y" chromosome, and this genetic abnormality makes them "supermales" who exhibit more aggressive behavior than normal. However, this extra Y chromosome is only found in about one male out of every 1,000. Despite the hoopla surrounding this research (including the fact that these individuals are overrepresented in the criminal justice system), the vast majority of male offenders (including most violent offenders) do not have the extra Y chromosome.[69]

"Modern biological theories in criminology do not argue for biological determinism. . . . Only an increased probability is asserted, not an absolute prediction."[70] Biological factors should be viewed as one of multiple factors influencing behavior. They certainly do not influence whether or not certain behaviors will be *defined by society as criminal*. Perhaps more importantly, we should stress the idea that these kinds of theories, based as they are on notions of biological inferiority, have consistently been used to describe people of certain races and ethnic groups (e.g., European immigrants, African Americans). This can be seen more clearly in recent efforts to link genetics with certain kinds of "abnormal" behavior, especially with regard to poor and/or minority children. Critics of research to find a biological predisposition to crime warn that "society has a long, tragic history of using poorly understood genetic science to justify social policies designed to get rid of classes of people deemed unwanted, dangerous or inferior."[71]

A relatively recent variation of biological theories is that of *sociobiology*.[72] This line of thinking attempts to link genetic and environmental factors with criminality. Two specific lines of research have occurred in recent years. One tries to link neuropsychological factors with delinquency and another focuses on the relationship between temperament and delinquency.

Terrie Moffitt and her colleagues examined several hundred males in New Zealand (13-18 years of age) and found that poor neuropsychological scores were related to the early onset of delinquency; however, the scores were not related to delinquency that began in the adolescent years.[73] Moffitt offered a *developmental theory* based on her longitudinal research that suggested that there are two trajectories in the life pattern of delinquency. Some children develop a life-long pattern of delinquency starting as early as 3 years of age, and the anti-social behavior continues well into their 30s. Children on this trajectory have several neuropsychological problems, such as attention deficit hyperactivity disorders (ADHD), which lead to learning problems at school. For those on the second trajectory, delinquent behavior starts in adolescence and desists around the age of 18.[74] In another study Moffitt and her colleagues found that the delinquency of males was much more likely than females to stem from various neuropsychological problems. For females, the causes of delinquency were more social, especially relating to social relationships.[75] Moffitt also researched the MAOA gene that regulates such chemicals as dopamine and serotonin. Males with one form of the gene who had been severely mistreated in childhood were more likely to engage in antisocial behavior than males with the other common form of the gene who had also been mistreated. Moffitt urges a nuanced understanding of the interplay between genes and the environment. "In the absence of a person's lifestyle and social relationships, the gene was not a powerful force."[76]

A longitudinal study that focused on a sample of African Americans living in the inner-city found no evidence of a connection between neuropsychological deficits and criminality.[77] Guang Guo, a sociologist at the University of North Carolina, studied 1,000 men and found that several genetic variations were linked to delinquency and to social factors.[78] A laboratory at Vanderbilt University offers genetic testing to lawyers in criminal cases. One of the tests looks at the MAOA gene, and another tests anxiety and depression. In 1994, lawyers for Stephen Mobley in his murder trial asked to have him tested for MAOA deficiency. Since that time, lawyers have increasingly introduced genetic evidence in courtrooms. Nita Farahany, an associate professor at Vanderbilt Law School, tracks cases of behavioral genetics in the courtroom. Since 2004, there have been 200 cases in which lawyers used genetic evidence to claim a predisposition to violent behavior, depression, or drug and alcohol abuse. The efforts have generally not been successful, although some sentences may have been lighter.[79]

As with most biological explanations, the percentage of delinquents who exhibit various neuropsychological problems is extremely small. Most of those who engage in delinquent behavior are relatively normal and well-adjusted youth. Moreover, such explanations do not fit well with various social factors to be discussed in the next chapter.[80] More importantly, attempts to link various biological "defects" with criminality have some very serious negative side effects with important social and political ramifications, often linked to both class and race. Troy Duster, a New York University sociologist cautions: "Once we begin to screen for gene disorders, we open a door to making an assessment of what is normal. When that door is opened, when do you close it?"[81] He cautions that screening at the genetic level risks misses the complex interaction between genes and environment; the screening presumes a precision that does not exist.

Gene Warfare[82]

A social movement known as the *eugenics movement* developed during the late nineteenth and early twentieth centuries in the context of widespread fear and nativism.[83] The goal of the movement was to eliminate, or at least physically remove, so-called "bad seeds" from an otherwise healthy U.S. soil. The theory of eugenics holds that certain problem behaviors are inherited and can be reduced and perhaps eliminated by preventing the carriers from reproducing. This theory was based in part on the idea that there are certain *groups*—especially *racial* groups—who are inherently "defective" (it was during this same period of time that the term "defective delinquent" became popular).

Eugenics was based on the philosophy of social Darwinism, which looked at human society in terms of natural selection and believed science could engineer progress by attacking problems believed to be hereditary, including moral decadence, crime, venereal disease, tuberculosis, and alcoholism. Eugenicists believed science could solve social problems, and they looked at individuals in terms of their economic worth. If an individual possessed traits that through propagation would weaken society, the scientific remedy was sterilization.[84]

> Eugenics was, quite literally, an effort to breed better human beings—by encouraging the reproduction of people with "good" genes and discouraging those with "bad" genes. Eugenicists effectively lobbied for social legislation to keep racial and ethnic groups separate, to restrict immigration from southern and eastern Europe, and to sterilize people considered "genetically unfit." Elements of the American eugenics movement were models for the Nazis, whose radical adaptation of eugenics culminated in the Holocaust.[85]

The movement's research was funded in part by some of the wealthiest men in the United States at the time—including Andrew Carnegie, John Rockefeller, and Henry Ford. These and other "captains of industry" were feeling threatened by a growing labor movement. Eugenics fit in well with the prevailing ideology that white Protestant Europeans were naturally superior, and just about every other racial stock was inferior. The rich and powerful deserved to rule over the less fit. The unfit—generally, the poor and nonwhite races—could not compete. Just as nature weeds out the unfit, society should do the same. This view justified the vast discrepancies in the distribution of wealth in society; the rich deserve to be rich because they are "naturally" superior.

A study by André Sofair and Lauris Kaldjian of Yale University found that physicians participated in state-authorized sterilization programs to prevent people believed to possess undesirable characteristics from having children.[86] The alliance between the medical profession and the eugenics movement in the United States was not short-lived. The first state eugenics law was passed in

Indiana in 1907. Forced sterilization was legal in 18 states, and most left the decision to a third party. While it was once believed that eugenics had declined in popularity after the 1920s, the study found that more than 40,000 people classified as insane or feebleminded in 30 states had been sterilized by 1944; by 1963, another 22,000 had been sterilized.

> The U.S. practice of neutering "mentally defective" individuals was backed by most leading geneticists and often justified on grounds that it would relieve the public of the cost of caring for future generations of the mentally ill. Sterilizations also took place mainly in public mental institutions, where the poor and ethnic or racial minorities were housed in disproportionately high numbers. "It is better for all the world, if instead of waiting to execute degenerate offspring for crime, or to let them starve for their imbecility, society can prevent those who are manifestly unfit from continuing their kind," Supreme Court Justice Oliver Wendell Holmes wrote in the majority opinion of a landmark eugenics case in 1926.[87]

While eugenics was eventually discredited, the search for scientific solutions to social problems continues to target minorities and the poor. For example, *The Bell Curve* argued that social stratification and economic inequality depend on one criterion: cognitive ability as measured by IQ tests. By these measures, blacks and other minority races are "inherently inferior."[88]

In 1989, the Department of Health and Human Services and the Public Health Service issued a report calling for strategies of intervention in "minority homicide and violence." Ironically the report cited factors like poverty, unemployment, homelessness, the availability of guns, and the glorification of violence within U.S. culture as causes of violence. Yet its recommendation for prevention focused on identifying *individuals* and *modifying their behavior*—mostly, as it turned out, with medication. The report flatly stated that: "Targeting individuals with a predisposition to, but no history of, violence would be considered primary as in programs to screen for violent behavior." This would require "tools to facilitate screening out high-risk individuals for early intervention." Such screening would target hospital emergency rooms, health centers, jails, and schools "at the lowest levels" where "acting out" behavior can be identified and dealt with. Perhaps more importantly, the program would conduct research "on the biomedical, molecular, and genetic underpinnings of interpersonal violence, suicidal behavior, and related mental and behavioral disorders."[89]

Following the logic of this view, biological factors are believed present at birth that predict later violent behavior. Infants would be the central focus of interventions designed to prevent future violence. In fact, subsequent developments of these various violence initiatives often specifically stated that the children of the poor and racial minorities would be the target. Rather than seek out some of the most common social sources of violence—racism, poverty, poor schools, unemployment, etc.—and attempt to reduce or eliminate them, government—and drug-company-sponsored research—targeted individuals and designated precursors of violent behavior.

Soon thereafter, the Department of Justice sponsored the Program on Human Development and Criminal Behavior. The co-directors of this project were Felton Earls (Professor of Child Psychiatry at Harvard Medical School) and Albert Reiss (Professor of Sociology at Yale's Institute for Social and Police Studies).[90] As was the case with eugenics, academics led the search for the "genetic" source of criminal behavior. The program was designed to identify children who could be potential offenders and who were "in need of preventive treatment or control." Specifically, the research would target nine age groups: infancy, 3, 6, 9, 12, 15, 18, 21, and 24. The key question to be answered would be: "What biological, biomedical, and psychological characteristics, some of them present from the beginning of life, put children at risk for delinquency and criminal behavior?"[91]

A program called the Violence Initiative Project received funding from the National Institute of Mental Health. Led by psychiatrists and funded by some of the largest pharmaceutical companies (such as Lilly, Pfizer, Upjohn, Hoffman-La Roche, Abbott Laboratories and many more), the program continues to seek genetic explanations for violent crime. In her application for funding, Gail Wasserman claimed that "Genetic and neurobiological research holds out the prospect of identifying individuals who may be predisposed to certain kinds of criminal conduct . . . and of treating some predispositions with drugs and unintrusive therapies. . . . Such research will enhance our ability to treat genetic predispositions pharmacologically."[92]

Wasserman also stated "It is proper to focus on blacks and other minorities as they are overrepresented in the courts and not well studied." She and Daniel Pine selected male minority youth, ages 6 to 10, each of whom had an older sibling who had been ruled delinquent by family court. These children, who had no criminal record, were considered to be at "high risk" (often a code word for poor urban minorities) for future violence. They were given a dose of a dangerous drug called fenfluramine[93] to examine the effects of environmental stressors on serotonin levels. Some scientists correlated low serotonin levels with aggressive behavior. Administering fenfluramine was an attempt to counter genetic predispositions to violence by increasing serotonin levels to prevent future violent acts. Of course, the only "predisposition" was a family member who had been declared delinquent, and none of the children had committed any violent acts. In addition, their serotonin levels were normal.

> Children's disorders and disruptive or violent behavior in particular remain growth markets. Powerful vested interests, including giant pharmaceutical firms, stand to profit mightily from proposed applications of biological research. Biomedical researchers and their labs and institutes will not readily fold or refrain and retool for wholly different kinds of research.[94]

The research cited by such biological theories is very selective and ignores the vast research that disproves any linkage between biology (including genetics) and crime, especially violent crime. The causes are social, not biological. Indeed, numerous studies have shown that those who commit the most heinous acts of violence have suffered, from an early age, incredible humiliation and brutality from their caretakers (often witnessing one violent act after another). Inevitably they begin to engage in similar acts against others; the victim becomes the victimizer. It has nothing to do with genetics. It has everything to do with one's immediate environment, including the violence within our own culture.

To put it bluntly, the United States is a very violent society. Most of the violence has been committed by those in power (mostly white, by the way) against those without power. Americans have been responsible for a great deal of what has recently been called "ethnic cleansing," although politicians and the media have been applying the term very selectively. Examples abound: the genocide of the Native American population, the subjugation of African slaves, the eugenics movement of the late nineteenth and early twentieth centuries, the deportation of Chinese-Americans and Italian-Americans, the incarceration of Japanese-Americans in "relocation centers" during World War II, the murderous rampages of the Ku Klux Klan, the McCarthy era "witch-hunt," and the support (money, training, and ammunition) of totalitarian dictatorships around the world (especially in Latin America), primarily to protect corporate interests.[95]

Biological and genetic approaches to human behavior, including criminality, have a long history. Allan Burch noted that widely popular magazines (including *Life, Atlantic Monthly, New Republic, U.S. News and World Report, Time,* and *Newsweek)* ran cover stories in the late 1980s and throughout the 1990s

> emphasizing the contribution of genes to our social behavior. Coat-tailing on major advances in genetic biotechnology, these articles portray genetics as the new "magic bullet" of biomedical science that will solve many of our recurrent social problems. The implication is that these problems are largely a result of the defective biology of individuals or even racial or ethnic groups.[96]

Some see a connection between the modern use of the genome to solve certain problems and the old eugenics programs. Alex Capron warned of the dangers inherit in the use of genetics.[97] A series entitled "Against Their Will: North Carolina's Sterilization Project" explores the eugenics program in North Carolina under which 7,600 people between 1929 and 1974 were sterilized.[98] The website contains links to documents and current stories related to eugenics. For example, one story describes how the Southern Poverty Law Center, a civil rights organization that watches hate groups such as the Ku Klux Klan, began tracking university professors who suggested that a modern version of eugenics should be used to eliminate weak parts of the population.[99] Another article is entitled "Blaming the 'Defective' People." The website is one example of people concerned that eugenics may rear its ugly head again, albeit in somewhat different forms. Such views are natural offshoots of the attempt to explain criminality and other human problems as individual "defects" rather than the result of social conditions.

Recent Developments: The Adolescent Brain

On March 1, 2005, the Supreme Court ruled that the Eighth and Fourteenth Amendments forbid the execution of offenders who commit their crimes when younger than 18. The Court's ruling in *Roper v. Simmons* affected 72 juvenile offenders in 12 states. Justice Anthony Kennedy wrote the opinion and stated:

"When a juvenile offender commits a heinous crime, the State can exact forfeiture of some of the most basic liberties, but the State cannot extinguish his life and his potential to attain a mature understanding of his own humanity."[100] We will discuss this case in detail in chapter 11. Here we present some background information about the differences between adolescent and adult reasoning that was used by lawyers who opposed the imposition of the death penalty on juveniles. On May 17, 2010, in *Graham v. Florida*, the Supreme Court followed similar reasoning (that juveniles are less culpable than adults because they are not as capable of controlling their behavior) in ruling that a sentence of life without parole is cruel and unusual punishment for juveniles who commit a crime other than homicide.[101]

Adolescent years are filled with all sorts of trials and tribulations—storm and stress as it is often called. A friend once gave this definition of adolescence: "adults with less sense." Even the term "juvenile delinquent" and the mere existence of a "juvenile" court reflect the popular recognition that kids are still growing up. The term "juvenile" means "young, immature, redeemable, subject to change." We as a society have long recognized this, which is why we impose special restrictions on some behaviors, such as voting, serving on a jury, entering into contracts, getting married, consuming alcohol and tobacco, and many more. We even limit what kinds of movies young people can see without an adult present.

However, when it came to the death penalty, we were one of a small number of nations (Congo, Nigeria, Saudi Arabia, and Iran) that treated juveniles as adults. The United States ranked first in the world in the execution of juveniles in the decade beginning in 1995.[102]

Using technology such as magnetic resonance imaging, several studies have found that the *pre-frontal cortex* (called the "CEO" of the body, it enables mature humans to make good decisions) is not fully developed until around the ages of 18 to 21—and in many cases the mid-20s.[103] The prefrontal cortex is responsible for prioritizing thoughts, thinking in the abstract, anticipating consequences, planning, and controlling impulses. Researchers at the National Institute of Mental Health first identified that a significant growth of synaptic connections between brain cells was not complete until individuals reach their mid-20s.[104] Although teens are capable of thinking logically, the process is more easily derailed by emotions and other distractions than is the case for most adults.

Temple University psychologist Laurence Steinberg notes that the brain's facility for reasoning is as good at age 16 as it is in adult years. He explains why adolescents are more prone to errors in judgment: "We think the reason doesn't have to do with their basic intelligence. It has to do with ways in which emotional and social factors impair their judgment. This means that it takes longer than we probably thought for people to develop mature impulse control." He studied 950 people between the ages of 10 and 30 in five countries and found that reasoning powers mature early, but impulse control, thinking of future consequences, and resisting peer pressure take much longer—slowly maturing through the twenties.[105]

By tracing brain development throughout the teenage years, researchers at Harvard Medical School, the National Institute of Mental Health, and UCLA have found physiological changes that may help explain such typical adolescent behaviors as emotional outbursts and reckless behavior (taking enormous risks and violating rules). During most of the teenage years, there is a release of hormones (starting around puberty) that causes areas of the brain such as the amygdala (which governs our emotional, "gut" responses) to expand, prompting some very irrational and impulsive behavior.[106] Teenagers are especially bad "at the kind of thinking that requires looking into the future to see the results of actions, a characteristic that feeds increased risk-taking." More importantly, they tend to "have trouble generating hypotheses of what might happen," in part because "they don't have access to the many experiences that adults do."[107] Ronald Dahl at the University of Pittsburgh School of Medicine notes that passions in adolescence can derail the brain's ability to make decisions and control behavior. "The system is precarious, tipping on one side toward strong emotions and drives and on the other side not yet supported well enough by self-control." He urges parents, coaches, teachers and other responsible adults and social systems to support adolescents so that they can take some risks, experiment, and develop some self-control without spiraling into terrible outcomes.[108]

Despite the lack of brain development, every youth does not go out and kill someone. What factors are present in the cases that do result in murder? The background characteristics of people on death row who committed their crimes when under the age of 18 are revealing. Chris Mallett found that about 75% experienced various kinds of family dysfunction, 60% were victims of abuse and/or neglect, 43% had a diagnosed psychiatric disorder, 38% were addicted to drugs, and 38% lived in poverty.[109] Mallett also noted that 30% had experienced six or more "distinct areas of childhood trauma with an overall average of four such experiences per offender." Few children and adolescents experience even one of these kinds of trauma, yet these significant facts were presented to less than half of the juries who convicted the juveniles. Other studies had found equally distressing facts. One found that well over half of the 14 death row inmates studied had either a major neuropsychological disorder or a psychotic disorder, and all but two had IQ scores of under 90. Just three had average reading abilities, while three learned to read while on death row.[110]

Although we have developed a much greater understanding of brain development in general, there are still many unanswered questions. There is no universally accepted "normal" model of brain functioning. "Each individual is not an exact map," says an attorney who deals with these cases. "The difficulties in determining what the range of variations are is really dangerous and subject to a number of interpretations."[111]

Perhaps because of the inexact nature of science on this subject, groups that support the death penalty have dismissed most of the research. Dianne Clements, president of Justice for All, a Houston nonprofit victim-advocacy group, said: "There is science, and then there is junk science. This is an effort by those in the scientific community who oppose the death penalty to use science to argue their position." She argues that many teenagers who kill realize their actions are wrong "because they often try to cover up and destroy evidence to avoid getting caught. What's more, most relatives of murder victims don't think a killer's age at the time of the crime should result in a lesser sentence."[112] This is often a response from those who take a "hard line" approach to crime, advocating letting the punishment fit the crime—"old enough to do the crime, old enough to do the time" and similar clichés.

While it is probably true that many try to cover up their crimes, it should also be noted that this is the way immature minds often work: they do not plan their crimes very well and cannot seem to hypothesize likely results. When confronted with the often horrible results of their actions, they try to pretend it didn't happen. Also, labeling research coming from highly respectable sources such as Harvard Medical School as "junk" shows ignorance of the scientific method. Moreover, a lot of research dispels common myths and "common sense," which makes many people uncomfortable. Scientists who engage in research on human behavior, especially criminal behavior, are often accused of "excusing" the behavior, when in fact they are merely trying to *explain* the behavior. An attorney in Miami who has represented juveniles facing capital punishment noted that science is quite often ahead of the law. For instance, the courts did not immediately support the use of DNA evidence. "If you just focus on how horrible the crime was, a lot of people do not care how old the offender was. But the brain research begins to demonstrate that adolescents are less culpable than adults."[113]

Psychological Theories

Psychological theories of criminal behavior focus on the link between such factors as intelligence, personality, various abnormalities of the brain, and crime. As biological views stressed that criminals were biologically inferior, psychological views stress that criminals are psychologically or mentally inferior.

Feeblemindedness and Crime

Early in the twentieth century, psychologist Henry Goddard began to study intelligence and argued that there was a correlation between low intelligence and crime. He administered an IQ test to inmates at the New Jersey Training School for the Feebleminded and found that none of the inmates scored higher than a mental age of 13. Over the years, the link between feeblemindedness and crime has been discredited, primarily because of poor measurement tools and the recognition that the motivation for such tests could be the desire to control (or even eliminate) certain "undesirables." It is easier to justify controlling people if they are "proven" to be inferior. The Nazi genocides, the practice of slavery, the eugenics movement (and other more modern forms of sterilization) were all supported by "scientific" theories and research.[114]

Psychoanalytic Theories

While Sigmund Freud did not specifically study criminal behavior, a good deal of what he had to say about the human personality and the *id*, *ego*, and *superego* has been used to explain criminality. This view maintains that crime is a symptom of deep-seated mental problems, which in turn stem from defects in one's personality. Causes of criminal behavior include: (1) difficulties or problems during one of the psychosexual stages of development (e.g., anal, phallic, Oedipal); (2) an inability to sublimate (or redirect) sexual and aggressive "drives" or "instincts"; (3) an inability to successfully resolve the *Oedipal* (in men) or *Electra* (in women) complex and; (4) an unconscious desire for punishment.[115]

Often researchers claim that specific crimes are associated with certain stages of development. For example, problems during the so-called *phallic* stage (in which a child begins to understand the pleasure associated with his or her sexual organs) can be related to such crimes as sexual assault, rape, or prostitution. Problems during the *oral* stage may result in crimes associated with alcoholism or drug addiction. Other works related to criminal behavior that can be traced back to Freud's theories include studies of antisocial personalities, sociopaths, and psychopaths. These people are characterized as having no sense of guilt and no sense of right and wrong.[116]

Personality Trait Theories

Some researchers have resurrected versions of IQ and feeblemindedness tests and applied them to the study of "personality traits." Various standardized tests have been devised for this purpose, the most famous of which is the Minnesota Multiphasic Personality Inventory (MMPI), which consists of over 500 true and false questions. Several different "scales" have been used, corresponding to the responses to certain questions. One such scale is the so-called "psychopathic scale" or "Scale 4." One of the problems is that the scale for this test was determined by the responses of inmates and former inmates who scored lower, "proving" that they are "different" from the rest of us. A variation is the California Psychological Inventory (CPI).[117] There is an assumption that we can easily distinguish between "criminals" and "noncriminals." As self-report studies have shown, most high school and college students have done something that could have landed them in jail. Yet they are viewed in these kinds of research projects as the "nonoffender" control group. Ronald Akers concluded that research using personality inventories has not produced "strong findings that personality variables are major causes of criminal and delinquent behavior."[118]

It is interesting to note that psychiatrist Robert Hare not only extended the research into the psychopathic personality but linked these characteristics to the behavior of large corporations. This is highly unusual, for these kinds of traits are normally alleged to be associated with those occupying the lower socioeconomic sectors of society.[119]

Mental Illness and Crime

Occasionally someone or some group will "go berserk" and commit an outrageous crime that attracts widespread media attention. Examples include shootings at a middle school in Jonesboro, Arkansas, in 1998 by a 13-year-old boy (who had promised to kill all the girls who had broken up with him) and his 11-year-old cousin. Four girls and one teacher were killed, and 11 others were wounded.[120] On April 20, 1999, Eric Harris (18) and Dylan Klebold (17) killed 12 students and 1 teacher at Columbine High School in Littleton, Colorado. Seung-Hui Cho (23) killed 32 people and wounded many others at Virginia Polytechnic Institute and State University in Blacksburg, Virginia, on April 16, 2007. On January 8, 2011, Jared Lee Loughner (22) opened fire at a supermarket where constituents had gathered to meet U.S. Representative Gabrielle Giffords. He killed six, including a federal judge and a 9-year-old girl, and wounded 12. The images from these and other high-profile incidents sear into the national conscience and leave the impression of frequency, but compared to the thousands of serious crimes committed each year, they are aberrations. Yet, many in the media and some experts immediately attribute the criminal behavior to "mental illness," as if the term had a precise and agreed upon meaning.

Juvenile murderers—a very small minority—have often been described as "anxious," "depressed" and "overly hostile." Many have been labeled as schizophrenic and with other personality disorders.[121] Actually, there is serious question as to whether or not there is a direct link between mental disorders and criminality. The fact is that most people labeled as "mentally ill" (whatever the specific category) are far more likely to withdraw from other people or harm themselves rather than engage in aggressive behaviors with others. The recidivism rate of prisoners who had been hospitalized with mental disorders is actually lower than "normal" people. If they do commit more crime, they do so for the same reasons as normal offenders—long histories of crime, unemployment, lack of education, drug and alcohol abuse, etc.[122] This is not to say that juveniles do not suffer from some serious mental health problems, for indeed they do. As we will see in chapter 12, many are held in detention centers awaiting placement in mental health centers, even though few have committed serious crimes. Most delinquents are relatively normal youngsters.

Summary

The theories reviewed in this chapter focus on individual characteristics of offenders, specifically the human body and the mind. Many questions about biological and psychological theories remain unanswered. One problem is that cross-cultural research has failed to arrive at similar findings. Why is the risk of being a crime victim higher in the United States than in most other countries? Is there an "American crime gene" or "American personality trait"? One problem with these types of theories is what Elliott Currie has called the "fallacy of

autonomy"—the idea that people act totally on their own, without the influence of others, and totally unaffected by their surrounding culture and social
institutions.[123] If crime were caused by some inferior gene or a certain personality trait, then how do we explain the high rate of corporate and white-collar
crime by supposedly "normal" upper-class, white males? Why is it that the
crime rates have remained the highest in certain parts of large urban areas,
regardless of the kinds of people who live there, over about a 100-year period?
Why are crime rates higher in urban than in rural areas, and why do males have
a crime rate about four times the rate of females? For these and other questions,
we turn to sociological theories of crime discussed in the next chapter.

NOTES

[1] For a simple and easy-to-read overview of the Enlightenment, see Spencer, L. and A. Krauze
(2000). *Introducing the Enlightenment*. New York: Totem Books. The "Introducing" series provides overviews of topics ranging from Freud to Postmodernism and includes books on Marx,
Jung, Kant, Sartre, and many others.

[2] Bierne, P. (1993). *Inventing Criminology*. Albany: SUNY Press, p. 20. This book is an excellent
source for the early development of criminology. See also: Taylor, I., P. Walton, and J. Young
(1973). *The New Criminology*. London: Routledge & Kegan Paul.

[3] Taylor et al., *The New Criminology*, ch. 1.

[4] This classic book is available in many bookstores and libraries. One edition was published by
Bobbs-Merrill: Beccaria, C. (1963). *On Crimes and Punishment*. New York: Bobbs-Merrill.

[5] Ibid., p. 99.

[6] Taylor et al., *The New Criminology*, p. 2.

[7] Stafford, M. R. and M. Warr (1993). "A Reconceptualization of General and Specific Deterrence." *Journal of Research in Crime and Delinquency* 30: 123–35.

[8] Shelden, R. G. (2010). *Our Punitive Society: Race, Class, Gender and Punishment in America*. Long
Grove, IL: Waveland Press. The "get tough" approach will be discussed in more detail in chapter 14.

[9] Lakoff, G. (1996). *Moral Politics: What Conservatives Know that Liberals Don't*. Chicago: University
of Chicago Press, p. 67.

[10] Ibid., p. 68.

[11] Ibid., pp. 74–75.

[12] Bursik, R., H. Grasmick, and M. Chamlin (1990). "The Effect of Longitudinal Arrest Patterns on
the Development of Robbery Trends at the Neighborhood Level." *Criminology* 28: 431–50;
Nagin, D. and G. Pogarsky (2001). "Integrating Celerity, Impulsivity and Extralegal Sanctions
Theories into a Model of General Deterrence: Theory and Evidence." *Criminology* 39: 865–92; a
somewhat dated study, but still a good one, is: Chiricos, T. and G. Waldo (1970). "Punishment
and Crime: An Examination of Some Empirical Evidence." *Social Problems* 18: 200–17.

[13] One of the first studies to look at this issue was Tittle, C. and A. Rowe (1974). "Certainty of
Arrest and Crime Rates: A Further Test of the Deterrence Hypothesis." *Social Forces* 52: 455–62; a
study by Bayley found little evidence that adding more police officers had any impact on crime
rates. Bayley, D. (1994). *Policing for the Future*. New York: Oxford University Press; a more general review is provided by Marvell, T. and C. Moody (1996). "Specification Problems, Police
Levels, and Crime Rates." *Criminology* 34: 609–46. One famous experiment in Kansas City found
that increasing levels of policing had little impact on crime rates. Kelling, G., T. Pate, D. Dieck-
man, and C. Brown (1974). *The Kansas City Preventive Patrol Experiment: A Summary Report*.
Washington, DC: Police Foundation.

[14] Kovandzic, T. and J. J. Sloan (2002). "Police Levels and Crime Rates Revisited: A County-Level
Analysis from Florida (1980–1998). *Journal of Criminal Justice* 30: 65–76. For the most part, so-
called "police crackdowns" have not had much effect, with a few exceptions. Novak, K., J. Hart-

man, A. Holsinger, and M. Turner (1999). "The Effects of Aggressive Policing of Disorder on Serious Crime." *Policing* 22: 171–90; Smith, M. (2001). "Police-Led Crackdowns and Cleanups: An Evaluation of a Crime Control Initiative in Richmond, Virginia." *Crime and Delinquency* 47: 60–68.

[15] One of the oldest studies was Dann, R. (1935). "The Deterrent Effect of Capital Punishment." *Friends Social Service Series* 29; Sellin, T. (Ed.) (1967). *Capital Punishment.* New York: Harper & Row; a study in Texas, the state that leads the nation in executions, found that the death penalty had no impact on murder rates: Sorenson, J., R. Wrinkle, V. Brewer, and J. Marquart (1999). "Capital Punishment and Deterrence: Examining the Effect of Executions on Murder in Texas." *Crime and Delinquency* 45: 481–93. For more studies see the Death Penalty Information website: http://www.deathpenaltyinfo.org/

[16] *Roper, Superintendent, Potosi Correctional Center v. Simmons* No. 03–633. Retrieved from http://caselaw.lp.findlaw.com/cgi-bin/getcase.pl?court=US&navby=case&vol=000&invol=03–633

[17] Schneider, A. L. (1990). *Deterrence and Juvenile Crime: Results from A National Policy Experiment.* New York: Springer.

[18] Mocan, N. (1999). "Economic Conditions, Deterrence and Juvenile Crime: Evidence from Micro Data." *American Law and Economics Review* 7: 319–49.

[19] Males, M. A., D. Macallair, and M. D. Corcoran (2008). "Testing Incapacitation Theory; Youth Crime and Incarceration in California." In R. G. Shelden and D. Macallair (Eds.), *Juvenile Justice in America: Problems and Prospects*. Long Grove, IL: Waveland Press.

[20] Steinberg, L., E. Cauffman, J. Woolard, S. Graham, and M. Banich (2009). "Are Adolescents Less Mature Than Adults?" *American Psychologist* 64: 583–94.

[21] Cook, P. J. (1986). "The Demand and Supply of Criminal Opportunities." In M. Tonry and N. Morris (Eds.), *Crime and Justice*, Vol. 7. Chicago: University of Chicago Press; Cohen, L. and M. Felson (1979). "Social Change and Crime Rate Trends: A 'Routine Activities' Approach." *American Sociological Review* 44: 588–608; Einstadter, W. and S. Henry (1995). *Criminological Theory: An Analysis of Its Underlying Assumptions*. Fort Worth, TX: Harcourt Brace; Cornish, D. B. and R. V. Clarke (Eds.) (1987). *The Reasoning Criminal.* New York: Springer-Verlag.

[22] Gove, W. R. (1994). "Why We Do What We Do: A Biopsychosocial Theory of Human Motivation." *Social Forces* 73: 374–75; Wolfgang, M. E., T. P. Thornberry, and R. M. Figlio (1987). *From Boy to Man: From Delinquency to Crime*. Chicago: University of Chicago Press.

[23] Maxfield, M. (1987). "Household Composition, Routine Activities, and Victimization: A Comparative Analysis." *Journal of Quantitative Criminology* 3: 301–20. Messner, S. and K. Tardiff (1985). "The Social Ecology of Urban Homicide: An Application of the Routine Activities Approach." *Criminology* 23: 241–67.

[24] Shelden, R. G., S. T. Tracy, and W. B. Brown (2004). *Youth Gangs in American Society* (3rd ed.). Belmont, CA: Wadsworth.

[25] Klein, M. (1995). *The American Street Gang*. New York: Oxford University Press, p. 163.

[26] Agnew, R. (1995). "Determinism, Indeterminism, and Crime: An Empirical Exploration." *Criminology* 33: 87–88.

[27] Clarke, R. V. and D. B. Cornish (Eds.) (1983). *Crime Control in Britain: A Review of Policy and Research.* Albany: SUNY Press.

[28] The following discussion is taken from an unpublished manuscript by Jerry Kurelic called *Our Indispensable Delusions: Why Humans Can't Handle the Truth.*

[29] Packer, H. L. (1968). *The Limits of the Criminal Sanction*. Palo Alto, CA: Stanford University Press.

[30] I recall reading somewhere of a unique theory of crime articulated by a police officer in a criminology class. He called his "theory of crime" the "asshole theory of crime" to wit: "Assholes cause crime." Period. End of discussion. No need to seek why some people are "assholes" and others are not!

[31] For a good discussion of "human nature" and the fact that humans are not inherently "hedonistic" see Michalowski, R. (1985). *Order, Law and Crime*. New York: Macmillan, ch. 3. See also Taylor et al., *The New Criminology,* for a critique of the classical school of thought. For an excellent discussion of deterrence (which is a central feature of the classical school) see Zimring, F. and G. J. Hawkins (1973). *Deterrence: The Legal Threat in Crime Control.* Chicago: University of Chicago Press.

[32] Burtch, B. (1992). *The Sociology of Law*. Toronto: Harcourt Brace Jovanovich, p. 6.

[33] Taylor et al., *The New Criminology*, p. 5.

[34] Vold, G. and T. J. Bernard (1986). *Theoretical Criminology* (3rd ed.). New York: Oxford University Press, p. 25.

[35] Akers, R. and C. Sellers (2009). *Criminological Theories: Introduction, Evaluation, and Application* (5th ed.). New York: Oxford University Press, p. 17.

[36] Taylor et al., *The New Criminology*, p. 7.

[37] Ibid., p. 8.

[38] Shichor, D. (2010). "The French-Italian Controversy: A Neglected Historical Topic in Criminological Literacy." *Journal of Criminal Justice Education* 21(3): 1–18.

[39] The "scientific method" consists, generally, of four main stages: (1) identify a problem by observing something occurring in the universe (e.g., certain groups of people seem to commit more crime than others); (2) derive from this a hypothesis that suggests a possible answer (e.g., those from single-family homes commit more crime than those from two-family homes); (3) test this hypothesis through an experiment or some other kind of observations (e.g., collect data on court cases); and (4) draw conclusions from your research. A possible fifth step is to modify your original hypothesis and derive a competing hypothesis. From this procedure you eventually derive a "theory" to explain what you discovered. One of the great advantages of this method is that it is *unprejudiced* in that the conclusions are independent of religious persuasion, ideology, or the state of consciousness of the investigator and/or the subject of the investigation. In direct contrast, faith refers to a belief in something that does not rest on any logical proof or material evidence. Faith does not determine whether a scientific theory is adopted or discarded. Knowledge based on faith was the dominant paradigm until the discovery of the scientific method. For an excellent book on the subject see, Kuhn, T. (1970). *The Logic of Scientific Revolutions* (2nd ed.). Chicago: University of Chicago Press.

[40] Ibid., p. 36.

[41] The word *empirical* is defined in the Random House Dictionary as "derived from or guided by experience or experiment"; a related term is empiricism, which means "the doctrine that all knowledge is derived from sense experience." A *hypothesis* is a key ingredient of the *scientific method*, and it can be defined as a proposition about the expected or anticipated relationship between two or more variables, usually expressed as the dependent and independent variable. When using the scientific method you use a hypothesis in order to find out what causes something. It is sort of like testing a "hunch" you have about the cause of something, such as trying to determine why your car is not starting. In this case, the "car not starting" is the dependent variable in that it is dependent on some other variable—the independent variable. You might "hypothesize" that your car not starting is caused by being out of gas.

[42] Shichor, "The French-Italian Controversy," p. 214.

[43] Bottomore, T., L. Harris, V. G. Kiernan, and R. Miliband (Eds.) (1983). *A Dictionary of Marxist Thought*. Cambridge, MA: Harvard University Press, p. 382.

[44] Bernard, T., J. Snipes, and A. Gerould (2010). *Vold's Theoretical Criminology* (6th ed.). New York: Oxford University Press.

[45] Shichor, "The French-Italian Controversy," p. 215.

[46] Quetelet, A. (1984). *Research on the Propensity for Crime at Different Ages*. Cincinnati: Anderson, p. 69. (Originally published in 1831.)

[47] Ibid.

[48] Lombroso, C. (1911). *Criminal Man*. Montclair, NJ: Patterson-Smith. (Originally published in 1876.)

[49] Cullen, F. and K. Gilbert (1982). *Reaffirming Rehabilitation*. Cincinnati: Anderson, p. 33.

[50] Max Weber (1864–1920) was one of the pioneers in the early years of sociology, most famous for his book *The Protestant Ethic and the Spirit of Capitalism*, originally published in 1904 and translated by Talcott Parsons and published by Scribner's in 1958. A good summary of his works is found in Weber, M. (1946). *From Max Weber: Essays in Sociology* (trans. H. H. Gerth and C. W. Mills). New York: Oxford University Press.

[51] Quinney, R. and J. Wildeman (1991). *The Problem of Crime: A Peace and Social Justice Perspective* (3rd ed.). Mountain View, CA: Mayfield, pp. 32–33.

[52] Shichor, "The French-Italian Controversy," p. 224.

[53] Lombroso, C. and W. Ferrero (1895). *The Female Offender.* New York: Philosophical Library.

[54] Bohm, R. M. (1997). *A Primer on Crime and Delinquency.* Belmont, CA: Wadsworth, p. 35.

[55] Bernard et al., *Vold's Theoretical Criminology.*

[56] The television program *Cops* on Fox is a good representation of many stereotypes. For instance, nearly everyone they arrest is a black man who is shirtless; he is invariably shown spread-eagle on the ground or against the hood of a police car.

[57] Glueck, S. and E. Glueck (1956). *Physique and Delinquency.* New York: Harper and Row; Hooton, E. A. (1939). *The American Criminal: An Anthropological Study.* Cambridge: Harvard University Press; Sheldon, W. (1949). *Varieties of Delinquent Youth.* New York: Harper. Each of these authors was on the faculty of Harvard University at one time, lending credibility to the views expressed.

[58] Ibid., p. 180.

[59] Gall lived between 1758 and 1828. His most important book was called *On the Functions of the Brain and of Each of Its Parts* (2nd ed.), which was published after his death in 1835 (Boston: Marsh, Capen & Lyon). For more about Gall and Phrenology see the following website: http://www.whonamedit.com/doctor.cfm/1018.html

[60] The Skeptic's Dictionary. Retrieved from http://www.skepdic.com/phren.html

[61] Phrenology. Retrieved from http://www.phrenology.org/

[62] Cohen, P. (2010, May 10). "For Crime, Is Anatomy Destiny?" *New York Times.* Retrieved from http://www.nytimes.com/2010/05/11/books/11crime.html

[63] Ibid.

[64] Ibid.

[65] These studies are too numerous to mention here. A good overall review is found in Moffitt, T. (1990). "The Neuropsychology of Juvenile Delinquency: A Critical Review." In N. Morris and M. Tonry (Eds.). *Crime and Justice: An Annual Review* (vol. 12). Chicago: University of Chicago Press, pp. 99–169; Rowe, D. (2001). *Biology and Crime.* Los Angeles: Roxbury Press.

[66] Apel, R., et al. (2007). "Unpacking the Relationship between Adolescent Employment and Antisocial Behavior: A Matched Sample Comparison." *Criminology* 45: 67–97.

[67] Tubman, C. R. and D. Haerle (2008, March). "The Final Chance for Change: Recidivism among a Cohort of the Most Serious State Delinquents." Paper presented at the annual meeting of the Academy of Criminal Justice Sciences, Cincinnati, OH.

[68] English scientist Cyril Burt was discredited for using fabricated data in his studies of twins to prove that certain races are born with low intelligence, leading to the propensity to commit crime. Despite research debunking such theories, supporters continue to search for a crime gene, arguing that the environment is only indirectly responsible by triggering behaviors to which one is genetically predisposed.

[69] DeKeseredy, W. S. and M. D. Schwartz (1996). *Contemporary Criminology.* Belmont, CA: Wadsworth, p. 180.

[70] Bernard et al., *Vold's Theoretical Criminology*, p. 37.

[71] Tsouderos, T. (2010, February 26). "Genes, Crime and Ties that Bind." *Chicago Tribune*, p. 4.

[72] The most popular statement of this view is Wilson, E. O. (1975). *Sociobiology.* Cambridge: Harvard University Press.

[73] Moffitt, T. F., D. R. Lynam, and P. A. Silva (1994). "Neuropsychological Tests Predicted Persistent Male Delinquency." *Criminology* 32: 277–300.

[74] Moffitt, T. E. (1993). "Adolescent-Limited and Life-Course-Persistent Antisocial Behavior: A Developmental Taxonomy." *Psychological Review* 100: 674–701.

[75] Moffitt, T. E, A. Caspi, M. Rutter, and P. A. Silva (2001). *Sex Differences in Antisocial Behaviour.* Cambridge, England: Cambridge University Press.

[76] Tsouderos, "Genes, Crime and Ties that Bind."

[77] McGloin, J. M., T. Pratt, and A. R. Piquero (2006). "A Life-Course Analysis of the Criminogenic Effects of Maternal Cigarette Smoking During Pregnancy." *Journal of Research in Crime and Delinquency* 43: 412–26.

[78] The study was published in the *American Sociological Review* in 2008, as reported in Tsouderos, "Genes, Crime and Ties that Bind."

[79] Feresin, E. (2009, October 30). "Lighter Sentence for Murderer with 'Bad Genes.'" Retrieved from http://www.nature.com/news/2009/091030/full/news.2009.1050.html

[80] These approaches have received their share of criticisms over the years. See especially Messer-schmidt, J. W. (1993). *Masculinities and Crime: Critique and Reconceptualization of Theory.* New York: Rowan and Littlefield.

[81] Ibid.

[82] This section is taken from Shelden, R. G. (2000). "Gene Warfare." *Social Justice* 27: 162–67.

[83] Rafter, N. H. (Ed.) (1988). *White Trash: The Eugenic Family Studies, 1899–1919.* Boston: Northeast-ern University Press.

[84] Morgan, D. (2000, February 15). "Yale Study: U.S. Eugenics Paralleled Nazi Germany." *Chicago Tribune.*

[85] "The Eugenics Archive" developed by Elof Carlson of the State University of New York at Stony Brook. Retrieved from http://www.eugenicsarchive.org/eugenics/

[86] Sofair, A. and L. Kaldjian (2000). "Eugenic Sterilization and a Qualified Nazi Analogy: The United States and Germany, 1930–1945." *Annals of Internal Medicine* 132(4): 212–319.

[87] Morgan, "Yale Study."

[88] Space does not permit a complete examination of this controversy. It began in 1969 with the pub-lication of Arthur Jensen's "How Much Can We Boost IQ and Scholastic Achievement?" (*Harvard Educational Review* 39: 1–123). Richard Hernstein then wrote an article simply called "I.Q." (*The Atlantic,* September 1971, pp. 43–64). James Q. Wilson and Hernstein wrote *Crime and Human Nature: The Definitive Study of the Causes of Crime* in 1985 (New York: Simon and Schuster). This book resurrected some of the oldest biological theories from the nineteenth century and dressed them up in twentieth-century jargon. Note the subtitle, revealing a bit of elitism. The most controversial publication was by Hernstein and Charles Murray (1994). *The Bell Curve: Intelligence and Class Structure in American Life.* New York: The Free Press. The most damning cri-tiques of this work were: Gould, S. J. (1994, November 28). "Curveball." *The New Yorker,* pp. 139–49; and Herman, E. (1994, December). "The New Onslaught," *Z Magazine,* pp. 24–26; also there was a special in *Contemporary Sociology* (1995, March), "Symposium: The Bell Curve," 24: 149–61. An excellent source for the "eugenics" movement is Rafter, N. H. (Ed.) (1988). *White Trash: The Eugenic Family Studies, 1899–1919.* Boston: Northeastern University Press.

[89] Bregin, G. and P. Bregin (1998). *The War Against Children of Color: Psychiatry Targets Inner City Youth.* Monroe, ME: Common Courage Press, p. 15; Cohen, M. (2000, April). "Beware the Vio-lence Initiative Project." *Z Magazine.*

[90] This information comes from Bregin and Bregin, *The War Against Children of Color.*

[91] Ibid., p. 38.

[92] Cohen, "Beware the Violence Initiative Project."

[93] Fenfluramine was the main ingredient in the diet drug "fen phen." Shortly after this experiment was completed in late 1997, the drug was withdrawn from the market because it could cause potentially fatal heart valve impairments in many patients and brain cell death in others.

[94] Bregin and Bregin, *The War Against Children of Color,* p. 40. The violence targeted is that commit-ted by the poor and racial minorities. No one suggested testing the children of members of Con-gress or the children of Fortune 500 CEOs, despite the fact that some of those individuals have been responsible for a great deal of death and destruction around the world (as any cursory review of white collar and corporate crime research will reveal). But no one has put that type of violence under the microscope to determine genetic influences. Rather, the poor and racial minorities pose the same threat to those in power that European immigrants posed in the late nineteenth and early twentieth centuries.

[95] Ample documentation exists for this contention. One of the best is Blum, W. (2000). *Rogue State.* Monroe, ME: Common Courage Press.

[96] "Is a New Eugenics Afoot?" *Science* 294: 59–61. Retrieved from http://www.sciencemag.org/cgi/content/full/294/5540/59

[97] Capron, A. (2007). "Dark History, Bright Future: The Ethical Conundrum of Eugenics and Genomics." The public lecture was delivered in Edinburgh on April 26. Retrieved from http://www.docstoc.com/docs/28407272/Dark-History-Bright-Future-The-Ethical-Conundrum-of-Eugenics-and

[98] "Against Their Will: North Carolina's Sterilization Program." Retrieved from http://extras.journalnow.com/againsttheirwill/background/links.html

99 Deaver, D. (2002). "Stirring Up Academia." Retrieved from http://extras.journalnow.com/againsttheirwill/parts/five/story2.html

100 *Roper, Superintendent, Potosi Correctional Center v. Simmons* No. 03–633. Retrieved from http://caselaw.lp.findlaw.com/scripts/getcase.pl?court=us&vol=000&invol=03–633

101 Koppel, N. (2010, October 29). "Judges Forced to Revisit Juveniles' Life Sentences. *The Wall Street Journal*, p. A3.

102 Juvenile Justice Center (2004). "Adolescence, Brain Development, and Legal Culpability." Washington, DC: American Bar Association, March 16. Retrieved from http://www.abanet.org/crimjust/juvjus/Adolescence.pdf

103 Ibid.

104 Kotulak, R. (2006, April 24). "Teens Driven to Distraction." *Chicago Tribune*, pp. 1, 21.

105 Ibid.

106 Bowman, L. (2004, May 11). "New Research Shows Stark Differences in Teen Brains." *Scripps Howard News Service*. Retrieved from http://www.deathpenaltyinfo.org/new-research-shows-stark-differences-teen-brains

107 Ibid.

108 Kotulak, "Teens Driven to Distraction."

109 Mallett, C. (2003). "Socio-Historical Analysis of Juvenile Offenders on Death Row." *Juvenile Corrections Mental Health Report* 65, cited in Juvenile Justice Center, "Adolescence, Brain Development, and Legal Culpability," p. 3.

110 Lewis, et al. (1988). "Neuropsychiatric, Psychoeducational, and Family Characteristics of 14 Juveniles Condemned to Death in the United States." *American Journal of Psychiatry* 145, cited in Juvenile Justice Center, "Adolescence, Brain Development, and Legal Culpability," p. 3.

111 Bowman, "New Research."

112 Davies, P. (2004, May 26). "Psychiatrists Question Death for Teen Killers." *The Wall Street Journal*, p. B1.

113 Quoted in Ibid.

114 Kraska, P. (1989). "The Sophistication of Hans Jurgen Eysenck: An Analysis and Critique of Contemporary Biological Criminology." *Criminal Justice Research Bulletin* (4)5: 1–7.

115 Bohm, *A Primer on Crime and Delinquency*, p. 51; DeKeseredy and Schwartz, *Contemporary Criminology*, pp. 182–83.

116 Ibid.

117 Ibid., pp. 183–84.

118 Akers and Sellers, *Criminological Theories*, p. 76.

119 His original work is: Hare, R. D. (1996). "Psychopathy: A Clinical Construct Whose Time Has Come." *Criminal Justice and Behavior* 23: 25–54; his adaptation to the behavior of corporations is found in Bakan, J. (2004). *The Corporation: The Pathological Pursuit of Profit and Power*. New York: Free Press.

120 Bragg, R. (1998, March 25). "4 Girls and a Teacher Are Shot to Death in an Ambush at a Middle School in Arkansas." *New York Times*, p. 1.

121 Sorrells, J. (1977). "Kids Who Kill." *Crime and Delinquency* 23: 312–20; Steury, E. H. (1992). "Criminal Defendants with Psychiatric Impairment: Prevalence, Probabilities and Rates." *Journal of Criminal Law and Criminology* 84: 354–74.

122 Engel, R. S. and E. Silver (2001). "Policing Mentally Disordered Suspects: A Reexamination of the Criminalization Hypothesis." *Criminology* 39: 225–52; Bonta, J., M. Law, and K. Hanson (1998). "The Prediction of Criminal and Violent Recidivism among Mentally Disordered Offenders: A Meta-Analysis." *Psychological Bulletin* 123: 123–42.

123 Currie, E. (1998). *Crime and Punishment in America*. New York: Metropolitan Books.

SOCIOLOGICAL THEORIES OF DELINQUENCY

In order to evaluate theories about delinquency, we need to look at the various paths people take to find answers and the expectations they have about possible explanations. Chapter 6 looked at the search to find measurable characteristics of offenders that set them apart from those who do not commit delinquent behavior. The focus was on biological and psychological processes that affect behavior. The biological theories looked at genetics to determine if people are born with delinquent tendencies. The psychological theories looked at mental problems that affect behavior and learning. Learning is affected by more than personality traits and mental ability. Sociologists focus on the influence of society, culture, and groups on how we behave. The probable influences of social conditions are the point of focus rather than potential causal factors of individual traits.

This chapter presents a general overview of seven sociological perspectives: (1) social disorganization/social ecology, (2) strain/anomie, (3) cultural deviance, (4) social bond (also known as control theory), (5) social learning, (6) labeling, and (7) critical/Marxist perspectives. Figure 7-1 provides a summary of each of these perspectives.

Social Disorganization/Social Ecology Theory

Social disorganization theory has been one of the most popular and enduring sociological theories of crime and delinquency. Variations of this theory have been called the *social ecology* perspective, since it has a lot to do with the *spatial or geographical distribution* of crime and delinquency.[1] Modern versions of this perspective began with the work of sociologists at the University of Chicago during the first three decades of the twentieth century. The original idea behind the spatial distribution of crime can be traced to two scientists introduced in chapter 6: Adolphe Quetelet and Andre-Michel Guerry. Their work collecting and analyzing crime data and matching them with various socioeconomic variables (such as poverty, infant mortality, unemployment, etc.) became known as the Cartographic School of Criminology. It involved plotting the location of criminals and various social indicators on a city map with colored dots. Police departments do

---

Figure 7-1   Sociological Theories of Delinquency

Theory	Major Points/Key Factors
1. Social disorganization	Crime stems from certain community or neighborhood characteristics, such as poverty, dilapidated housing, high density, high mobility, and high rates of unemployment. *Concentric zone theory* is a variation that argues that crime increases toward the inner city area.
2. Strain/anomie	Cultural norms of "success" emphasize such goals as money, status, and power, while the means to obtain such success are not equally distributed. As a result of blocked opportunities, many among the disadvantaged resort to illegal means, which are more readily available.
3. Cultural deviance	Certain subcultures, including a gang subculture, exist within poor communities, which contain values, attitudes, beliefs, and norms that are often counter to the prevailing middle-class culture. An important feature of this subculture is the absence of fathers, thus resulting in female-headed households, which tend to be poorer. Youths are exposed to this subculture early in life and become *embedded* in it.
4. Control/social bond	Delinquency persists when a youth's bonds or ties to society are weak or broken, especially bonds with family, school, and other institutions. When this occurs a youth is likely to seek bonds with other groups, including gangs, to meet his/her needs.
5. Learning	Delinquency is *learned* through association with others, especially gang members, over a period of time. This involves a *process* that includes the acquisition of attitudes and values, the instigation of a criminal act based on certain stimuli, and the maintenance or perpetuation of such behavior over time.
6. Labeling	Definitions of "delinquency" and "crime" stem from differences in power and status in the larger society. Those without power are the most likely to have their behaviors labeled as "delinquent." Delinquency may be generated, and especially perpetuated, through negative labeling by significant others and by the judicial system. One may associate with others similarly labeled, such as gangs.
7. Critical/Marxist	Gangs are inevitable products of social (and racial) inequality brought about by capitalism; power is unequally distributed, and those without power often resort to criminal means to survive.

the same today when, for example, they plot the locations of certain crimes, such as the locations of a series of muggings, auto thefts, etc.[2]

This idea of mapmaking and the more general notion that crime is *spatially* distributed within a geographical area became the hallmarks of the *Chicago School* of sociology. Researchers noticed that crime and delinquency rates varied by areas of the city (just as Guerry and Quetelet had done almost a century earlier).

They found the highest rates of crime and delinquency in areas that exhibited high rates of many other social problems, such as single-parent families, unemployment, multiple-family dwellings, welfare cases, and low levels of education.

One of the key ideas of the social ecology of crime is that high rates of crime and other problems persist within the same neighborhoods over long periods of time *regardless of who lives there.* As several gang researchers have noted, some gangs have existed for as long as 50 or more years in certain neighborhoods, often spanning three generations. East Los Angeles is a prime example of this phenomenon.[3] Thus there must be something about the *places* themselves, perhaps something about the *neighborhoods,* rather than the people living there that produces and perpetuates high crime rates.[4]

The social ecology perspective borrows concepts from the field of plant biology, studying human life using ideas derived from studies of the interdependence of plant and animal life. From this perspective, people are seen as being in a relationship to one another and to their physical environment. Further, just as plant and animal species tend to *colonize* their environment, humans colonize their "geographical space."[5] The Chicago sociologists "argued that the urban topography of industry, railroads, crowded tenements, and vice districts influenced a person's alienation, detachment, and amorality."[6] In contrast, the suburbs away from the city's core had boulevards, spacious parks, and manicured lawns that reflected community stability and organization.

Robert Park and Ernest Burgess of the Chicago School developed the *concentric zone* model of city life to explain such patterns.[7] They identified five specific zones emanating outward from the central part of the city: (1) central business district, or the "Loop"; (2) zone in transition; (3) zone of working-men's homes; (4) residential zone; and (5) commuter zone.

According to this theory, growth is generated (from mostly political and economic forces) outward from the central business district. Expansion occurs in concentric waves, or circles. The expansion and movement affects neighborhood development and patterns of social problems. Studies of the rates of crime and delinquency, especially by sociologists Clifford Shaw and Henry McKay, demonstrated that over an extended period of time, the highest rates were found within the first three zones *no matter who lived there.* These high rates were strongly correlated with such social problems as mental illness, unemployment, poverty, infant mortality, and many others.[8]

The breakdown of institutional, community-based controls causes the higher rates, and the breakdown is the result of three general factors: industrialization, urbanization, and immigration. People living within these areas often lack a sense of community because the local institutions (e.g., schools, families, and churches) are not strong enough to provide nurturing and guidance for the area's children. It is important to note that there are important political and economic forces at work here. The concentration of human and social problems within these zones is not the inevitable "natural" result of some abstract laws of nature. Rather, they are the result of the actions of some of the most powerful groups in a city (urban planners, politicians, wealthy business leaders, etc.).

A subculture of criminal values and traditions develops in such environments and replaces conventional values and traditions. These criminal values and traditions persist over time regardless of who lives in the area. (This is part of the "cultural deviance" theory, discussed later.) One of the classic works about gangs from a social disorganization perspective was written by Frederic Thrasher. *The Gang,* published in 1927, is equally relevant today. For Thrasher, gangs originate from

> the spontaneous effort of boys to create a society for themselves where none adequate to their needs exists. What boys get out of such associations that they do not get otherwise under the conditions that adult society imposes is the thrill and zest of participation in common interests, more especially in corporate action, in hunting, capture, conflict, flight, and escape. Conflict with other gangs and the world about them furnishes the occasion for many of their exciting group activities.[9]

Thrasher's view of the origin of gangs was consistent with the social disorganization perspective. Thrasher noted that gangs are *interstitial*—situated within but not necessarily characteristic of the space occupied. In nature, there are cracks and crevices, where matter of a different nature collects. Similarly, there are fissures in social organization. Gangs are an interstitial element in the social framework of society; they are created in the cracks and boundaries of society and fill gaps when families and schools are weak in socialization. Gangland occupies an interstitial region in the geography of the city. Gangs collect in regions "characterized by the deteriorating neighborhoods, shifting populations, and the mobility and disorganization of the slum."[10] Gangs are most frequently found in areas bordering the central business district.

Thrasher found evidence of at least 1,313 gangs in Chicago, with an estimated 25,000 members. No two of these gangs were alike; they reflected the great diversity characteristic of the city of Chicago in the 1920s (even today Chicago and its gangs reflect this diversification). Much like today, gang delinquency in Thrasher's day ranged from the petty (such as truancy and disturbing the peace) to the serious (serious property crime and violent crime).

Thrasher summarized his theory of why gangs exist:

> The failure of the normally directing and controlling customs and institutions to function efficiently in the boy's experience is indicated by the disintegration of family life, inefficiency of schools, formalism and externality of religion, corruption and indifference in local politics, low wages and monotony in occupational activities; unemployment; and lack of opportunity for wholesome recreation. All these factors enter into the picture of the moral and economic frontier, and, coupled with deterioration in the housing, sanitation, and other conditions of life in the slum, give the impression of general disorganization and decay.[11]

The gang offers a substitute for what society fails to give, and it provides relief from suppression and distasteful behavior. It fills a gap and affords an escape.

Thrasher viewed gang membership as offering a young man the opportunity to acquire a personality and name—it conferred status and prescribed a role to play. The gang "not only defines for him his position in society . . . but it becomes the basis for his conception of himself."[12] The gang becomes the youth's reference group, that is, the group from which he obtains his main values, beliefs, and goals. In a sense the gang becomes his family. Moreover, groups of youths progressed from what Thrasher called "spontaneous play groups" to gang status when adults began to disapprove of them. When this occurs, particularly if coupled with legal intervention, the youths become closer and develop a "we" feeling.[13] Thrasher clearly believed that gangs provided certain basic needs for growing boys, such as a sense of belonging and self-esteem.

Several subsequent studies have focused on the community or neighborhood as the primary unit of analysis. Such a focus begins with the assumption that crime and the extent of gang activities vary according to certain neighborhood or community characteristics. In *Racketville, Slumtown and Haulberg*, Irving Spergel writes that the three neighborhoods he studied varied according to a number of criteria and had different kinds of traditions, including delinquent and criminal norms. For example, Racketville, a mostly Italian neighborhood, had a long tradition of organized racketeering. Gangs were mostly involved in the rackets because criminal opportunities for such activities existed in the neighborhood.[14] In contrast, the area Spergel called Slumtown was primarily a Puerto Rican neighborhood with a history of conflict and aggression. The gangs in this area were mostly involved in various conflict situations with rival gangs (usually over turf). Haulberg was a mixed ethnic neighborhood (Irish, German, Italian, and others) with a tradition of mostly property crimes; thus, a theft subculture flourished.

The ethnographic fieldwork of Mercer Sullivan provides a variation on this theme. He studied three neighborhoods in Brooklyn (which he called "Projectville," "La Barriada," and "Hamilton Park").[15] Socioeconomic indicators varied in the three communities, and the neighborhoods also had significantly different patterns of crime. La Barriada was a mixed Latino and white area; Projectville was a largely African-American neighborhood; Hamilton Park was predominantly white. The two neighborhoods with the highest crime rates (Projectville and La Barriada) also had (1) the highest poverty level, with more than half the families receiving public assistance; (2) the highest percentage of single-parent families; (3) the highest rate of renter-occupied housing; (4) the highest rate of school dropouts; and (5) the lowest labor-force participation rates (and correspondingly highest levels of unemployment).

Sullivan explained the concentration of high-risk, low return theft in the two impoverished, minority neighborhoods:

> The primary causes for their greater willingness to engage in desperate, highly exposed crimes for uncertain and meager monetary returns were the greater poverty of their households, the specific and severe lack of employment opportunities during these same mid-teen years, and the weakened local social control environment, itself a product of general poverty and joblessness among neighborhood residents.[16]

A key to understanding these differences, argues Sullivan, is that of personal networks rather than human capital.

> Personal networks derived from existing patterns of articulation between the local neighborhoods and particular sectors of the labor market. These effects of labor market segmentation were important for youth jobs both in the middle teens and during the ensuing period of work establishment. The Hamilton Park youths found a relatively plentiful supply of temporary, part-time, almost always off-the-books work through relatives, friends, and local employers during the middle teens, most of it in the local vicinity.[17]

When these youths reached their late teens, they were able to make use of these same contacts to get more secure and better-paying jobs. The minority youths from Projectville and La Barriada never developed such networks (see discussion below on social embeddedness).

Sullivan found that among the precursors to a criminal career among most of the youths studied was involvement in some gang or clique of youths. It typically began with fighting with and against other youths. Street fighting was motivated mostly by status and territory. Beginning in their early teens, these youths would spend a great amount of time within what they considered to be their own territory or turf. The cliques and gangs these youths belonged to "were quasi-familial groupings that served to protect their members from outsiders."[18]

Rodney Stark also suggested that criminal behavior persists within specific neighborhoods over time *because of certain characteristics of the neighborhoods*, rather than the people who inhabit them.[19] He argued that there are five key characteristics of perpetually high-crime neighborhoods: (1) high density, (2) high rates of poverty, (3) mixed-use (poor dense neighborhoods mixed together with light industry and retail shops), (4) a high rate of transience among residents, (5) dilapidation. His theory also incorporates the impact of these five characteristics on people's responses to the conditions. He identified (1) moral cynicism, (2) increased opportunities for crime, (3) an increase in the *motivation* to commit crime and, (4) diminished social control, especially among residents via informal methods of control. The neighborhood characteristics and people's responses to them drive away the least deviant people, further reducing social control and attracting "crime-prone" people into the area.

This theory impacts delinquency rates. In high-density neighborhoods, homes are crowded. As a result, more people congregate outside, and there is less supervision of children. Less supervision of children almost inevitably leads to poor school achievement, resulting in an increase in deviant behavior by such children. Moreover, with crowding in homes comes greater family conflict, further weakening attachments (see control theory, discussed below).[20]

More recent studies have continued to confirm the connection between neighborhoods, especially lower socioeconomic areas, and delinquency, and in general supporting the work that began with Quetelet and Guerry and later the Chicago School.[21]

The *Los Angeles Times* incorporates this perspective in its continuing series on homicides in Los Angeles. The newspaper compares two neighborhoods in close proximity to one another in South Central Los Angeles (where gangs are highly concentrated). During the past three years, one neighborhood (Vermont Knolls) has experienced no homicides. Another neighborhood about a mile away (Westmont) has had 28 homicides—a person "cannot walk a block outside its borders without coming across the site of a killing from the last three years."[22]

The explanation for this difference is that there has been a huge infusion of money for rebuilding in the Vermont Knolls area and the addition of several organizations, such as the Crenshaw Christian Center, a mega-church that now sits on the old Pepperdine University campus. "Most streets are lined with modest but appealing single-family houses. Front yards often have no fences, the lawns are green and well-maintained."[23] This area is also primarily inhabited by older residents.

> The predominance of single-family homes instead of apartments means a less densely packed population and less turnover. And many in the neighborhood own their homes and have had roots in the area for generations. The result is a place where people know each other, have an emotional and financial investment and don't take kindly to anything that might disturb the peace.[24]

In recent years, a substantial amount of research maps communities to show the geographic distribution of crime and criminals. James F. Austin and Associates is one organization that engages in this kind of research.[25] Also, a new academic journal began in 2009 called *Crime Mapping: A Journal of Research and Practice* published within the Department of Criminal Justice at UNLV.[26]

Strain Theory

Strain theory originated with Robert Merton, who borrowed the term *anomie* from the French sociologist Émile Durkheim[27] and applied it to the problem of crime in the United States.[28] The concept of *anomie* refers to inconsistencies between societal conditions and opportunities for growth, fulfillment, and productivity within a society (the term *anomia* has been used to refer to those who experience personal frustration and alienation as a result of anomie within a society). It also involves the *weakening of the normative order* of society—that is, norms (rules, laws, and so on) lose their impact on people. The existence of anomie within a culture can also produce a high level of flexibility in the pursuit of goals, even suggesting that it may at times be appropriate to deviate from the norms concerning the methods of achieving success.

Durkheim, writing during the late nineteenth century, suggested that under capitalism there is a more or less chronic state of "deregulation" and that industrialization had removed traditional social controls on aspirations. The capitalist culture produces in humans a constant dissatisfaction, a never-ending longing for more and more. There is never enough—whether this be money, material things, or power. There is a morality under capitalism that dictates "anything goes," especially when it comes to making money.

What Durkheim was hinting at (but never stated as forcefully as Karl Marx) was that a very strong social structure is needed to offset or place limits on the "anything goes" perspective. In other words, strong institutions, such as the family, religion, and education, are needed to place some limits on us. The failure of these institutions are reflected in our high crime rates and the fact that the economic institution dominates all others. (More will be said about this shortly.)

The basic thesis of strain theory is: Crime stems from the lack of articulation or "fit" between two of the most basic components of society: *culture* and *social structure*.[29] Culture in this sense consists of (1) the main value and goal orientations or "ends" and (2) the institutionalized or *legitimate means for attaining these goals.* Social structure consists of the basic *social institutions* of society, especially the economy, but also such institutions as the family, education, and politics, all of which are responsible for distributing *access* to the legitimate means for obtaining goals.

According to Merton, a "lack of fit" creates *strain* within individuals, who respond with various forms of deviance. People who find themselves at a disadvantage relative to legitimate economic activities are motivated to engage in illegitimate activities (perhaps because of unavailability of jobs, lack of job skills, education, and other factors). Within a capitalist society like the United States, the main emphasis is on success; there is less emphasis on the legitimate *means* to achieve that success. Moreover, success goals have become *institutionalized*—they are deeply embedded in the psyches of everyone via a very powerful system of corporate propaganda.[30] At the same time, the legitimate means are not as well defined or as strongly ingrained. In other words, there is a lot of discretion and a lot of tolerance for deviance from the means but not the goals. One result of such a system is high levels of crime.

Another important point made by strain theory is that our culture contributes to crime because the opportunities to achieve success goals are not equally distributed. The strong class structure creates incredible inequality within our society, which means that some are extremely disadvantaged compared to others.[31] Another way of saying the same thing is that the *culture promises what the social structure cannot deliver.* The strains of this contradiction cause people to seek alternatives.

Merton refers to the possible alternatives as "modes of adaptation." His typology of adaptations includes the following:

1. *conformity*—accepting both the legitimate means and the success goals;
2. *ritualism*—accepting the means but rejecting the goals (one goes to work every day but has given up on the goal of "success");
3. *innovation*—accepting the goals of success but rejecting the legitimate means to obtain them;
4. *retreatism*—rejecting both the goals *and* the means and more or less dropping out of society to become part of a subculture (such as the drug subculture);
5. *rebellion*—rejecting both the goals and the means, substituting *new* definitions of success and the means to obtain them.

Obviously, the adaptation known as *innovation* directly relates to criminal activity. Thus anomie/strain theory would suggest that participating in gang-related activities would be an example of being *innovative* in the pursuit of success.

According to Steven Messner and Richard Rosenfeld, in a recent revision of anomie theory, such strain explains high rates of crime not only among the disadvantaged but also among the more privileged. All are under strains to make more money, often by any means necessary. This theory helps explain corporate crime in this country.[32] Messner and Rosenfeld's revision of strain theory contains an important component that has usually been missing from writings on this particular theory—the emphasis on the importance of *social institutions* and the relationship with the *American Dream*.

Crime and the American Dream

The American Dream is an ethos deeply embedded into our culture. Generally, it refers to a commitment to the goal of material success. Within a capitalist society everyone is supposed to act in their own self-interest in this pursuit (this has been part of the mythology of "free enterprise" and the "free market"); this, in turn, will automatically promote the "common good." Somehow, the fruits of individual pursuits (part of the creed of "rugged individualism") in the free market system will eventually trickle down to benefit others.

The American Dream contains four deeply embedded core values summarized in figure 7-2. There is, however, a "dark side" to the American Dream that stems from a contradiction in U.S. capitalism: The same forces that promote progress and ambition also produce a lot of crime, since there is such an incredible pressure to succeed at any cost. The emphasis on competition and achievement produces selfishness that drives people apart, weakening a collective sense of community. The fact that monetary rewards are such a high priority results in the fact that tasks that are noneconomic receive little cultural support (e.g. homemakers and child-care workers). The existence of such a high degree of inequality produces feelings of unworthiness. Those who fail are looked down on, and their failure is too often seen as an *individual failure* rather than a failure attributed to institutional and cultural factors. Even education is seen as a means to an end—the end being a high-paying job or any secure job. The author saw an advertisement for a local university on a Boston subway. It encouraged people to "go back so you can get ahead," rather than encouraging people to obtain a degree for the sake of expanding their knowledge base and other noneconomic benefits.

One of the keys to understanding the link between the American Dream and crime is knowing the meaning and importance of the term *social institution*. Social institutions can be defined as a persistent set of organized *methods* of meeting basic human needs. There are relatively stable groups and organizations (complete with various norms and values, statuses, and roles) that help humans (1) adapt to the environment, (2) mobilize resources to achieve collective goals, and (3) be socialized to accept society's fundamental normative patterns.[33] The most important of these institutions include (1) the economy, (2)

Figure 7-2   Core Values of American Culture

1. *Achievement*—One's *personal worth*, which is typically evaluated in terms of monetary success and/or fame. This stems from a culture that emphasizes "doing" and "having" rather than "being." Failure to achieve is equated with the failure to make a contribution to society. This value is highly conducive to the attitude "it's not how you play the game; it's whether you win or lose." A similar attitude is "winning isn't everything; it's the *only* thing."

2. *Individualism*—People are encouraged to "make it" on their own. This value discourages a value that could (and has proven to) successfully reduce crime, namely cooperation and collective action. A corollary to this value is "I don't need any help." (Note how this is reinforced in many movies and television series, where one man conquers evil or solves a crime, etc.). Messner and Rosenfeld comment that "the intense individual competition to succeed pressures people to disregard normative restraints on behavior when these restraints threaten to interfere with the realization of personal goals."

3. *Universalism*—The value claims everyone has the same opportunity to succeed, as long as you "work hard." Part of the value derives from the Protestant work ethic.

4. *Fetishism of Money*—Money is so important in our culture that it often overrides almost everything else. It is often worshiped like a God. Money is the *currency* for measuring just about everything. Moreover, there is no end point; the striving is incessant. In the *consumerist culture* everyone is socialized from the day they are born to be a *consumer*. (Witness the emergence of corporate-sponsored programs within elementary schools, including the ever-present McDonald's.)

Messner, S. and R. Rosenfeld (2007). *Crime and the American Dream* (4th ed.). Belmont, CA: Thomson/Wadsworth, pp. 66–71.

---

the family, (3) schools, and (4) politics. Other important institutions include health care, media, religion, and the law (many would place law within the much larger political institution).

It is important to understand that when these institutions fail to meet the needs of members of the society (or a sizable proportion of the population), then alternative institutions will begin to develop—different forms or *methods* of meeting needs. For example, if the prevailing economic system is failing, more and more people will engage in alternative means of earning a living; if organized religion is not meeting such needs as answers to fundamental life questions, then people will seek out unorthodox religious forms (e.g., cults like the Branch Davidians or Heaven's Gate); if the legal institution is not perceived as providing justice, then people may "take the law into their own hands"; and if the mainstream media provide too much disinformation and do not allow dissenting views, then alternative media emerge.

Gangs are one example of alternative institutions. Note in figure 7-3 that all of the major institutions are connected by straight lines. Because every institution is connected in some way with all the others, problems in one cause problems in another. As suggested in chapter 4, gangs function as sort of *quasi-institutions* in many ways. For example, many gang members feel that their "homies" are like a "family." Gangs provide methods and incentives to seek alternative methods of earning money. They also provide an alternative media

Figure 7-3 Social Institutions and Gangs

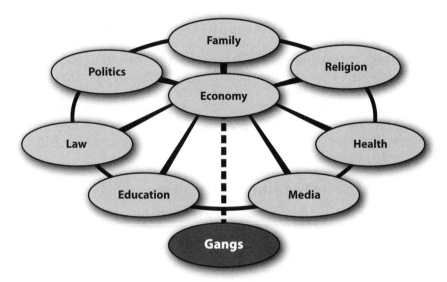

Shelden, R. G., S. Tracy, and W. B. Brown (2004). *Youth Gangs in American Society* (3rd ed.). Belmont, CA: Wadsworth.

(graffiti) and an alternative religion (putting "RIP" style of graffiti on walls). They even have their own informal legal system. In short, gangs provide many of the needs that are supposed to be provided by mainstream institutions.

As Messner and Rosenfeld suggest, what is unique about U.S. society is that the economic institution almost completely dominates all other institutions. John Dewey expressed a similar view when he stated that "politics [or government] is the shadow that big business casts over society."[34] American capitalism, unlike capitalism in other countries, emerged with virtually no interference from previously existing institutions. Unlike other societies, there were no other existing institutions that could tame or offset the economic imperatives.[35] European and Japanese cultures, in contrast, place almost equal importance on the family, religion, education, and other institutional concerns. Under U.S. capitalism, other institutions are subordinate to the economy (which it appears in the middle in figure 7-3). The goal is to make a *profit*, and everything else becomes secondary. Over time this has become a "market society," in contrast to a "market economy." In the former, the pursuit of "private gain" dominates all other pursuits (e.g., the arts or family support).[36]

The emphasis on economics can have devastating consequences. The *New York Times* reported on an unpublished study called the Milwaukee Area Renters Study (MARS), which addresses the growing problem of evictions—a major issue since the 2008 recession.[37] "Eviction is a particular burden on low-income black women, often single mothers, who have an easier time renting apartments than their male counterparts, but are vulnerable to losing them because their wages or public benefits have not kept up with the cost of housing." Matthew Desmond, a sociologist at the University of Wisconsin–Milwaukee, authored the study and states the problem succinctly: "Just as incarceration has become typical in the lives of poor black men, eviction has become typical in the lives of poor black women."[38] One out of every 25 renter-occupied households in Milwaukee as a whole is evicted, while in black neighborhoods the rate is one in 14. Women in black neighborhoods constitute 13% of Milwaukee's population but 40% of those evicted. Losing one's home can have a contagious effect. It can force a change in schools and perhaps threaten employment if the new residence is located too far from public transportation. This is one recent illustration of the links between institutions and the strain experienced by some members in society.

Differential Opportunity Structures

A variation of strain theory comes from the work of Richard Cloward and Lloyd Ohlin in *Delinquency and Opportunity*.[39] These authors argued (1) that blocked opportunity aspirations cause poor self-concepts and feelings of frustration and (2) that these frustrations lead to delinquency. A key concept here is *differential opportunity structure*, which is an uneven distribution of legal and illegal means of achieving economic success, especially as they are unequally divided according to class and race. Cloward and Ohlin argued that while legitimate opportunities are blocked for significant numbers of lower-class youths, the same cannot be said for illegitimate opportunities (e.g., selling drugs and other crimes).

> The disparity between what lower class youth are led to want and what is actually available to them is the source of a major problem of adjustment. Adolescents who form delinquent subcultures, we suggest, have internalized an emphasis upon conventional goals. Faced with limitations on legitimate avenues of access to these goals, and unable to revise their aspirations downward, they experience intense frustrations; the exploration of nonconformist alternatives may be the result.[40]

Among the specific assumptions of this theory is that blocked opportunities (or aspirations) create feelings of frustration and low self-esteem, which in turn often lead to delinquency. Cloward and Ohlin postulate that three different types of gangs emerge and that these types correspond to characteristics of the neighborhoods rather to the individuals who live there. *Criminal gangs* are organized mainly around the commission of property crimes and exist in areas where there are already relatively organized forms of adult criminal activity, which serve as models for the youths who live there. *Conflict gangs* engage mostly in violent behavior, such as gang fights over turf; they exist in neighborhoods where living conditions are unstable and transient, resulting in the lack of any adult role models, whether conventional or criminal. (3) *Retreatist gangs* engage mostly in illegal drug use and exist in neighborhoods dominated by a great deal of illegal drug activity; these youths are described as double failures by Cloward and Ohlin.

Social Embeddedness

John Hagan[41] borrows the term *social embeddedness* from economist Mark Granovetter[42] to describe a developmental view of involvement in delinquency, a very interesting variation of strain theory. Hagan notes that instead of unemployment *preceding* involvement in criminal behavior (a common view in criminology), *the reverse is actually the case* for young offenders. For these youths, involvement in crime begins well before they can legally be involved in the labor market. Granovetter asserts that becoming a regularly employed person involves much more than an individual's skills and education; it involves being connected to a social network of contacts that accrue over time. One needs to be socialized into the labor market at a very early age. This means, among other things, that a youth begins to earn money doing odd jobs such as mowing lawns, babysitting, washing windows, shoveling snow, delivering papers, and so on long before turning 16. These activities start the process of social embeddedness. Youths who live in declining neighborhoods, who do poorly in school, and who do not have a large support network rarely have the contacts to be socialized into the labor market.[43]

Hagan argues that just as one can become socially embedded in the world of work, so too can one become embedded in a network of crime and deviance. In most of the high-crime, inner-city neighborhoods, the odd jobs of middle-class youths noted above do not exist in large numbers (e.g., there are no lawns to be mowed in high-rise buildings). He notes that parental involvement in crime will integrate youths into networks of criminal opportunities. Likewise, association with delinquent peers or contacts with drug dealers can also integrate youths into criminal networks. Moreover, delinquent acts tend to cause youths to become further isolated from networks of employment. A snowballing effect takes place whereby each delinquent act and/or contact with the world of crime further distances a youth from the legitimate world of work. Thus the perspective of social embeddedness identifies "a process of separation and isolation from conventional employment networks" that has a time sequence with a "lagged accumulation of effect that should build over time."[44]

Hagan cites several examples of recent ethnographic research on delinquency that support this view. Elijah Anderson notes: "For many young men the drug economy is an employment agency. . . . Young men who 'grew up' in the gang, but now are without clear opportunities, easily become involved; they fit themselves into its structure, manning its drug houses and selling drugs on street corners."[45] Felix Padilla noted that gang youths he studied "began turning to the gang in search of employment opportunities, believing that available conventional work would not sufficiently provide the kinds of material goods they wished to secure." He also noted that youths were between the ages of 13 and 15 when they first became gang members. Increasing involvement in the gang further embedded them, making entry into the legitimate world of work a serious problem for them later in life.[46] The process of estrangement from the legitimate world of work and embeddedness in the world of criminal opportunities are amply documented by research in Chicago,

Los Angeles, Milwaukee, New York, Boston, and many other urban areas.[47] All of these studies found evidence of the socialization of inner-city youths (especially minority youths) into the world of criminal opportunities and their subsequent isolation from the social networks of legitimate work.

Cultural Deviance Theories

Cultural deviance theory proposes that delinquency is a result of a desire to conform to cultural values that are to some extent in conflict with those of conventional society. In part, this perspective is a direct offshoot of social disorganization theory. Remember that part of that theory suggests that criminal values and traditions emerge within communities most affected by social disorganization.

Cohen's Culture of the Gang

One of the most popular versions of cultural deviance theory was Albert Cohen's work, *Delinquent Boys: The Culture of the Gang*. Although somewhat dated (he conducted his research in the 1950s), his perspective is still relevant today. Cohen's view incorporates the following assumptions: (1) a high proportion of lower-class youths (especially males) do poorly in school; (2) poor school performance relates to delinquency; (3) poor school performance stems from a conflict between dominant middle-class values of the school system and values of lower-class youths; and (4) most lower-class male delinquency is committed in a gang context, partly as a means of meeting some basic human needs, such as self-esteem and belonging.

There are two key concepts in Cohen's theory: (1) *reaction formation*, openly rejecting what one wants or aspires to but cannot achieve or obtain, and (2) *middle-class measuring rod*, evaluations of behavior based on norms and values associated with the middle class, such as punctuality, neatness, cleanliness, nonviolent behavior, drive and ambition, achievement and success (especially at school), deferred gratification, and so on. Cohen argues that delinquents often develop a culture that is at odds with the norms and values of the middle class; they rebel against those norms by turning them upside down.[48]

This subculture remains real today, although with some variations, and it is important for those who deal with delinquents to understand it.[49] One famous application of this theory to the treatment of delinquents was a program established in Provo, Utah (called Pine Hills) in the late 1950s. A form of group therapy was used whereby the offenders themselves actively participated in their own changes. The program proved to be somewhat successful.[50]

Lower-Class Focal Concerns

As with Cohen's work, the perspective proposed by anthropologist Walter B. Miller remains relevant today even though his study was also done in the 1950s. Within certain communities in the Boston area, Miller discovered what he called the *focal concerns* of a distinctive "lower-class culture" (see figure 7-4). Miller argues specifically that (1) there are clear-cut focal concerns (norms and values) within the lower-class culture and (2) that *female-dominated households* are an important feature within the lower class and are a major reason for the emergence of street-corner male adolescent groups in these neighborhoods.[51]

Two key concepts here are (1) *focal concerns,* which include trouble, toughness, smartness, excitement, fate, and autonomy; and (2) *one-sex peer units,* which serve as alternative sources of companionship and male role model development outside the home. Such concerns are often at odds with main-

---

Figure 7-4   Miller's "Focal Concerns" of Lower-Class Culture

1. *Trouble* is a defining feature of lower-class life. Unlike the middle class, where judgment is usually based on one's achievements (e.g., education, career advancement), the lower-class concern is whether one will pursue the law-abiding route or its reverse. Further, membership in a gang is often contingent on demonstrating a commitment to law-violating behavior, acts that carry much prestige.

2. *Toughness* is associated with stereotypical masculine traits and behaviors, featuring an emphasis on physical prowess, strength, fearless daring, and a general macho attitude and behavior (or machismo). It also includes a lack of sentimentality, a disdain for art and literature, and a view of women as sex objects. Concern about toughness may derive from being reared in a female-headed household and a lack of male role models. The need to demonstrate toughness precludes behaviors that could be interpreted as feminine, such as caring for one's children or acting responsibly to avoid fathering children out of wedlock.

3. *Smartness* revolves around the ability to *con* or outwit others, to engage in hustling activities. Skills in this area are continually being tested and honed, and the really skillful have great prestige. Many leaders of gangs are more valued for smartness than toughness, but the ideal leader possesses both qualities.

4. *Excitement* refers to the lifestyle within the lower class that involves a constant search for thrills to offset an otherwise boring existence. Alcohol, sex, and gambling play large roles. The night on the town is a favorite pastime and involves alcohol, sex, and music. Fights are frequent, so "going to town" is an expression of actively seeking risk and danger, hence excitement. Most of the time between episodes of excitement is spent doing nothing or hanging around—common for gang members.

5. *Fate* involves luck and fortune. According to Miller, most members of the lower class believe that they have little or no control over their lives—that their destiny is predetermined. Much of what happens is determined by luck, so if one is lucky, life will be rewarding; if one is unlucky, then nothing one does will change one's fate; so why bother working toward goals?

6. *Autonomy* involves a contradiction. On the one hand, there is overt resentment of external authority and controls ("No one is going to tell me what to do!"). On the other hand, there are covert behaviors that show a desire for such control. External authority and controls provide a somewhat nurturing aspect. If one is imprisoned and subjected to rigid rules and regulations, one may overtly complain while locked up. However, behavior after release sometimes seems designed to ensure reimprisonment and a return to a controlled existence. Rebellion over rules is a test of the firmness of the rules and an attempt to seek reassurance that nurturing will occur. Youngsters often misbehave in school because they do not get such reassurance.

stream middle-class society. The one-sex peer group is important to Miller's theory in the sense that gangs provide male members opportunities to prove their masculinity in the absence of an adequate male role model within their family of origin. The principal unit in lower-class society is an age-graded, one-sex peer group constituting the major psychic focus and reference group for young people. The adolescent street-corner group is one variant of the lower-class structure, and the gang is a subtype distinguished by law-violating activities. For boys reared in female-headed households, the street-corner group provides the first real opportunity to learn essential aspects of the male role—by learning from other boys in the group with similar sex-role identification problems. The group also acts as a selection process in recruiting and retaining members.

Echoing Thrasher's work, Miller states that two central concerns of the adolescent street-corner group are belonging and status. One achieves belonging by adhering to the group's standards and values and continues to achieve belonging by demonstrating such characteristics as toughness, smartness, and autonomy. When there is conflict with middle-class norms, the norms of the group are far more compelling, because failure to conform means expulsion from the group. Status is achieved by demonstrating the qualities valued by lower-class culture. Status in the adolescent group requires *adultness*, that is, the material possessions and rights of adults (e.g., a car, the right to smoke and drink, etc.) but *not the responsibilities of adults*. The desire to act like an adult and avoid "kid stuff" results in gambling, drinking, and other deviant behaviors and compels the adolescent more than the adult to be smart, tough, and so on. He will seek out ways to demonstrate these qualities, even if they are illegal.

There is also a pecking order among different groups, defined by one's "rep" (reputation). Each group believes its safety depends on maintaining a solid rep for toughness compared with other groups. One's rep refers to both law-abiding and law-violating behavior. Which behavior will dominate depends on a complex set of factors, such as which community reference groups (criminals or police) are admired or respected or the individual needs of the gang members. Above all, having status is crucial and is far more important than the means selected to achieve it.

Violence is a learned behavior that can be unlearned. In desolate areas, pride becomes a fiercely guarded commodity and showing weakness invites trouble.[52] Deanna Wilkinson of Ohio State University researches urban youth violence and notes that if youths in some subcultures walk away from a fight, they fear losing whatever status they had. Gary Slutkin of Chicago's CeaseFire program said his group targets changing the social norms that feed violence. Experts believe many factors put children at risk of falling into a pattern of violent thinking and behavior: "growing up in poverty, living in violent circumstances, failing to read at grade level by third grade, not graduating high school, and not being surrounded by caring, protective adults."[53] Greg Boyle, a Jesuit priest in Los Angeles who runs Homeboy Industries (one of the nation's largest gang intervention programs) comments: "It's not about thinking or behavior. It's about infusing a sense of hope so the kid starts to care. No one scares them straight—you care them straight."[54]

In her dissertation, Margaret Hughes of CSU–San Bernardino focused on turning points in the lives of young men who abandoned destructive behaviors, who identified alternatives to crime, connections to neighborhoods, and understanding the damage they were causing in their communities as pivotal factors for change. Hughes notes that organizations can work on changing thinking and behavior, but unless they can offer employment, violence and crime will remain in the background as alternatives.[55]

Several recent studies have found that lower class offenders are often singled out for excessive punishments (especially minority males) by a court system that fails to take into account this subculture. Essentially, a mostly white, middle–class, bureaucratic subculture passes judgment on a very different subculture. Knowing that they will receive excessive punishment by the system, lower-class minority males are motivated not to get caught. At the same time they believe they must live up to, and integrate, these focal concerns into their everyday lives.[56]

Control/Social Bond Theory

The essence of *control theory* (sometimes called *social bond theory*) is that the weakening, breakdown, or absence of effective social control accounts for delinquency. A unique feature of this perspective is that instead of asking, "Why do they do it?" it asks, "Why *don't* they do it?" In other words, this theory wrestles with what it is that keeps or prevents people from committing crime. In this sense, control theory is really a theory of prevention. The basic assumption of control theory is that proper social behavior requires socialization. Thus, proper socialization leads to conformity, while improper socialization leads to nonconformity. Delinquency is one consequence of improper socialization. Carl Bell, director of the Institute for Juvenile Research at the University of Illinois at Chicago, says adults provide a protective shield in controlling youthful behavior. "To a great extent, children are all gasoline and no brakes. It's incumbent on parents, families, schools and society to provide them with those breaks—with expectations, rules, monitoring, and social-emotional skills."[57]

The essence of control theory is that delinquent behavior occurs because it is not prevented in the first place. There are several different versions of this theory. One states that the delinquent lacks either strong inner controls and/or strong outer controls.[58] The former refer to things such as a positive self-image or strong ego, while the latter refer to strong family controls, community controls, legal controls, etc. Another version maintains that many youths commit delinquent acts because they rationalize deviance before it occurs—that is, they neutralize (see discussion in section on social learning theory) the normal moral beliefs they have learned while growing up. For example, they deny that there is a victim by saying things like "He had it coming," or they deny that there was any real harm by saying something like "No one was really hurt" or "They won't miss it."[59]

Travis Hirschi's social bond theory conceives of all humans as basically antisocial; all are capable of committing a crime. What keeps most of us in check (i.e., prevents us from deviating) is what he calls the "social bond to society," especially the norms of society that we have internalized. There are four major elements of this bond, as shown in figure 7-5.

This theory is very popular (although many do not consider it a control theory). Most people accept the four social bonds as appropriate role behavior for young people. Juvenile justice workers daily try to *reattach* delinquents to family, school, and other primary social institutions; to get them to *commit* themselves to the demands of childhood; to *involve* them in conventional activities; and to help them acquire a *belief* and respect for the law. This theory becomes an important starting point for the social development model and the risk-focused approach to delinquency prevention.

John Johnstone suggests that purely ecological explanations of gangs are limited "and cannot account for why gangs influence only some of the boys who live in gang neighborhoods." He notes that the opportunity to join a gang

> is established by the external social environment, but the decision to do so is governed by social and institutional attachments and by definitions of self.... The transition from unaffiliated to gang-affiliated delinquency occurs at the point that a boy comes to believe that he has nothing further to gain by not joining a gang.[60]

Extensive studies of various ethnic gangs by Diego Vigil and Steve Yun led them to conclude that the common theme for all these gangs is that the weakening of the bonds identified by Hirschi frees them from social control and encourages deviant behavior. Interviews with 150 incarcerated gang members from four ethnic groups (Vietnamese, Chicano, African American, and Hispanic) confirmed the social control thesis.[61]

Figure 7-5   Hirschi's Four Elements of the Social Bond

1. *Attachment* refers to ties of affection and respect between kids and parents, teachers, and friends. Attachment to parents is most important because it is from them that they obtain the norms and values of the surrounding society and internalize them (very similar to Freud's superego but involving more conscious awareness).

2. *Commitment* is similar to Freud's concept of ego, except it is expressed in terms of the extent to which kids are committed to conventional childhood behavior, such as getting an education, postponing participation in adult activities (e.g., working full-time, living on your own, getting married), or dedication to long-term goals. If children develop a stake in conformity, then engaging in delinquent behavior would endanger their future.

3. *Involvement* is similar to the conventional belief that "idle hands are the devil's workshop." In other words, large amounts of unstructured time may decrease the ties to the social bond; those busy doing conventional things, such as chores at home, homework, sports, camping, working, or dating, do not have time for delinquency.

4. *Belief* refers simply to an acceptance of the law, especially the morality of the law (e.g., belief that stealing is just plain wrong).

Hirschi, T. (1969). *Causes of Delinquency*. Berkeley: University of California Press, pp. 16–34.

Informal social control networks within communities contribute to social bonding. Todd Clear notes that three levels of informal social control lessen the extent of crime: (1) what people do *privately* within their intimate relationships; (2) what people do *collectively* in their relationships with others in the community; and (3) people's attitudes toward criminal behavior. The most common forms of social control originate in the privacy of child rearing. Collective methods of social control extend the lessons through a variety of associations and groups. These include churches, businesses, social clubs, volunteer groups, youth groups, neighborhood associations and many more. Such social controls fall between the most formal controls (e.g., police) and family controls. Participation in these associations occupies a lot of free time for young people. This is one reason why after-school and summer activities are so important. In short, close bonding to these kinds of groups reduces the likelihood of delinquency.[62] One study verified the assertion that students with low commitments to education are more likely to become delinquent.[63] Another study found that youths who participated in structured activities with adult leaders became better adjusted and were less likely to engage in delinquent behavior. This relates to the "involvement" part of the social bond.[64]

One variation of this perspective centers on the issue of "self-control" or lack thereof. *Containment* theory argues that there are both internal and external forces that influence the lives and behavior of juveniles. By internal we mean personal factors such as anxiety, discontent, and hostility. By external factors we are referring to various social forces include significant others (especially the family) and the surrounding subculture. By developing both inner (e.g., self-control, positive self-concept) and outer (e.g., strong and supportive family) "containment" an individual will be able to resist involvement in delinquent behavior.[65] Several studies have supported this perspective, although most of them have focused on the individual delinquent's lack of self control and low self-concept, rather than the surrounding culture and economic system.[66]

Some have noted that parental criminality contributes to low self-esteem and in turn high levels of delinquency.[67] Parental involvement in various kinds of criminal behavior has consistently been correlated with delinquency. This has been especially underscored through longitudinal studies of delinquency.[68]

Social Learning Theory

According to this theory, people become delinquent or criminal through the same kind of process as learning to become anything else. One learns behavior through one's association with other human beings—just as one learns values, beliefs, and attitudes. (An example was noted in the section on "focal concerns" in the case of learning violence.) Edwin Sutherland developed the theory of *differential association*, one of the earliest variations of social learning theory that applies to delinquency.[69] According to this theory, one becomes a delinquent not only through contact with others who are delinquent but also through contact with various values, beliefs, and attitudes supportive of criminal/delinquent behavior. One of the central points of this theory is the proposition that one becomes a delinquent/criminal "because of an excess of definitions favorable to violation of law over definitions unfavorable [to violation] of law."[70] Social learning theory suggests that there are three related processes that lead one to become a delinquent or criminal: (1) acquisition, (2) instigation, and (3) maintenance.[71]

Acquisition refers to the original learning of behavior. The key to this process is that of reinforcement through the modeling influences of one's family, the immediate subculture (especially the peer subculture), and symbolic modeling (e.g., via television). In the case of learning aggression, a child who witnesses violence within the home is apt to engage in violence later in life. This is especially true if such violence within the home is rewarded or no sanctions are applied. Important here is the fact that children tend to acquire behaviors that they observe being rewarded by others.

Instigation refers to the process whereby once a person has acquired the behavior, certain factors work to cause or instigate a specific event—in this case, an act of delinquency. Learning theory suggests five key factors as major instigators:

1. *Aversive* events—situations marked by frustration, deprivation, verbal insults, and actual assaults. For those who are especially violent, threats to one's reputation and status, especially those occurring in public, are very important instigators of violent acts.

2. *Modeling influences*—actually observing delinquent or criminal behavior by someone who serves as a role model can be an immediate instigator.

3. *Incentive inducements*—anticipated rewards. One can be motivated to commit a crime by some perceived reward, usually monetary.

4. *Instructional control*—following orders from someone in authority. A gang member, for example, may obey a direct order from a leader of the gang.

5. *Environmental control*—factors in one's immediate environment, which include crowded conditions (including traffic), extreme heat, pollution, and noise.

Each of these can cause someone to "lose it" and act out, sometimes in a violent manner.[72] In order for delinquent or criminal behavior to persist, there needs to be consistent reinforcement or *maintenance*. Social learning theory suggests four specific kinds of reinforcement:

1. *Direct reinforcement* refers to extrinsic rewards that correspond to an act (e.g., money, or recognition).

2. *Vicarious reinforcement* includes seeing others get rewards and/or escape punishment for delinquent or criminal acts (e.g., a youth sees someone carrying a lot of money obtained by selling drugs).

3. *Self-reinforcement* happens if a person derives his or her self-worth or sense of pride from criminal acts.

4. *Neutralization of self-punishment* is the process whereby one justifies or rationalizes delinquent acts.

One long-standing sociological theory is commonly referred to as *techniques of neutralization*.[73] Gresham Sykes and David Matza suggest that delinquents often come up with rationalizations or excuses that absolve them of guilt. Thus, for example, a youth may say that no one was harmed or that the victim deserved it ("He had it coming to him"), or a youth may condemn those who condemn him or her (e.g., by saying that adults do these kinds of things, too), appeal to higher loyalties (e.g., "I'm doing it for the 'hood"), or merely put the blame on various external factors. Two significant outcomes of neutralization techniques is that the victim is dehumanized and there is a gradual desensitization to the use of violence or other means of force to get one's way.

Most of the perspectives summarized previously do not question the nature of the existing social order. Possible exceptions are social disorganization and strain theories, which to some extent provide at least an indirect critique of the existing order. Most of the theories focus on how offenders and at-risk youths can be made to accommodate to the existing social order. Beginning with the labeling perspective, theorists questioned the nature of the status quo, specifically the social order of advanced capitalism in the late twentieth century. The final two perspectives discussed in this chapter call for changing the nature of the existing social order so that fewer people will be drawn into criminal behavior.

The Labeling Perspective

The labeling perspective (also known as the *societal reaction* perspective) does not address in any direct way the causes of criminal/deviant behavior but rather focuses on three interrelated processes: (1) how and why certain behaviors are defined as criminal or deviant, (2) the response to crime or deviance on the part of authorities (e.g., the official processing of cases from arrest through sentencing), and (3) the effects of such definitions and official reactions on the person or persons so labeled.[74] Howard Becker summarizes the key to this perspective: "Social groups create deviance by making the rules whose infraction constitutes deviance, and by applying those rules to particular people and labeling them as outsiders."[75]

One key aspect of the labeling perspective is that the criminal justice system itself (including the legislation that creates laws and hence defines crime and criminals) helps to perpetuate crime and deviance. For example, several studies during the late 1960s and 1970s focused on the general issue of how agents of the criminal justice system (especially the police) helped to perpetuate certain kinds of criminal behavior (for example, how gangs and gang-related behavior may be perpetuated by the criminal justice system's attempts to control the problem).[76]

One of the most significant perspectives on crime and criminal behavior to emerge from the labeling tradition was Richard Quinney's theory of the *social reality of crime*. In a truly landmark textbook on crime and criminal justice, Quinney organized his theory around six interrelated propositions.[77]

1. Crime is a definition of human conduct that is created by authorized agents in a politically organized society.

2. Criminal definitions describe behaviors that conflict with the interests of the segments of society that have the power to shape public policy.

3. Criminal definitions are applied by the segments of society that have the power to shape the enforcement and administration of criminal law.

4. Behavior patterns are structured in segmentally organized society in relation to criminal definitions, and within this context persons engage in actions that have relative probabilities of being defined as criminal.

5. Conceptions of crime are constructed and diffused in the segments of society by various means of communication.

6. The social reality of crime is constructed by the formulation and application of criminal definitions, the development of behavior patterns related to criminal definitions, and the construction of criminal conceptions.

Key to Quinney's theory are four interrelated concepts: (1) process, (2) conflict, (3) power, and (4) action. By *process*, Quinney is referring to the fact that "all social phenomena . . . have duration and undergo change."[78] The *conflict* view of society and the law is that in any society "conflicts between persons, social units, or cultural elements are inevitable, the normal consequences of social life." Further, society "is held together by force and constraint and is characterized by ubiquitous conflicts that result in continuous change." *Power* is an elementary force in our society. Power, says Quinney, "is the ability of persons and groups to determine the conduct of other persons and groups. It is utilized not for its own sake, but is the vehicle for the enforcement of scarce values in society, whether the values are material, moral, or otherwise." Power is important if we are to understand public policy. Public policy, including crime-control policies, is shaped by groups with special interests. In a class society, some groups have more power than others and therefore are able to have their interests represented in policy decisions, often at the expense of less powerful groups. Thus, for example, white upper-class males have more power, and their interests are more likely to be represented than those of working- or lower-class minorities and women. Finally, by *social action*, Quinney is referring to the fact that human beings engage in voluntary behavior, which is not completely determined by forces outside of their control. From this perspective, human beings are "able to reason and choose courses of action" and are "changing and becoming, rather than merely being." It is true that humans are in fact shaped by their physical, social, and cultural experiences, but they also have the capacity to change and achieve maximum potential and fulfillment.

It is important to note the distinctions between primary and secondary deviance.[79] *Primary deviance* includes acts that the perpetrator and/or others consider alien (i.e., not indicative, incidental) to one's true identity or character. In other words, an act is "out of character" (commonly expressed by others as "this is not like you"). These acts have only marginal implications for one's status and psychic structure. They remain primary deviance as long as one can rationalize or otherwise deal with the behavior and still maintain an acceptable self-image and an image acceptable to others. *Secondary deviance,* on the other hand, refers to a process whereby the deviance takes on self-identifying features; that is, deviant acts begin to be considered as indicative of one's true self, the way one "really" is. Deviance becomes secondary "when a person begins to employ his deviant behavior or a role based upon it as a means of defense, attack, or adjustment to the overt and covert problems created by the consequent societal reaction to him."[80]

This perspective eventually led some scholars to question not only the criminal justice system but also the very social structure and institutions of society as a whole. In particular, some research in the labeling tradition directed attention to such factors as class, race, and sex in the formulation of criminal definitions and the major causes of crime itself.

Critical/Marxist Perspectives

Quinney and John Wildeman place the development of a critical/Marxist line of inquiry in the historical and social context of the late 1960s and early 1970s.

> It is not by chance that the 1970s saw the birth of critical thought in the ranks of American criminologists. Not only did critical criminology challenge old ideas, but it went on to introduce new and liberating ideas and interpretations of America and of what America could become. If social justice is not for all in a democratic society—and it was clear that it was not—then there must be something radically wrong with the way our basic institutions are structured.[81]

The critical perspective focuses on

> those social structures and forces that produce both the greed of the inside trader as well as the brutality of the rapist or the murderer. And it places those structures in their proper context: the material conditions of class struggle under a capitalist mode of production.[82]

The material conditions include the class and racial inequalities produced by the contradictions of capitalism (which produce economic changes that negatively affect the lives of so many people, especially the working class and the poor).

In *Class, State, and Crime,* Quinney linked crime and the reaction to crime to the modern capitalist political and economic system. He theorized that the capitalist system produces a number of problems because of attempts by the capitalist class to maintain the basic institutions of the capitalist order. In attempting to maintain the existing order, the powerful commit various crimes, which Quinney classified as crimes of control, crimes of economic domination, and crimes of government. At the same time, oppressed people engage in various kinds of crimes related to accommodation and resistance, including predatory crimes, personal crimes, and crimes of resistance.[83]

Much of what is known as criminal and delinquent behavior can therefore be understood as an attempt by oppressed people to accommodate and resist the problems created by capitalist institutions. Many gang members, for example, adapt to their disadvantaged positions by engaging in predatory and personal criminal behavior. Much of their behavior, moreover, is in many ways identical to normal capitalist entrepreneurial activity.[84]

According to Mark Lanier and Stuart Henry, there are six central ideas common to critical/Marxist theories of crime and criminal justice.[85]

1. *Capitalism shapes social institutions, social identities, and social action.* The mode of production in any given society determines many other areas of social life, including divisions based on race, class, and gender plus the manner in which people behave and act toward one another.

2. *Capitalism creates class conflict and contradictions.* Since a relatively small group (a "ruling class" consisting of perhaps 1–2% of the population) owns and/or controls the means of production, class divisions have resulted, as has the inevitable class conflict over control of resources. The contradiction is that workers need to consume the products of the capitalist system, but in order to do so they need to have sufficient income to spur the growth of the economy. However, too much growth may cut into profits. One result is the creation of a *surplus population*—a more or less steady supply of able workers who are permanently unemployed or underemployed (also called the "underclass").

3. *Crime is a response to capitalism and its contradictions.* This notion stems in part from the second theme in that the "surplus population" may commit crimes to survive. These can be described as crimes of *accommodation.*[86] Crimes among the more affluent can also result (see next point) in addition to crimes of *resistance* (e.g., sabotage and political violence).

4. *Capitalist law facilitates and conceals crimes of domination and repression.* The law and legal order can often be repressive toward certain groups and engage in the violation of human rights, which are referred to as *crimes of control and repression.* Crimes of *domination* also occur with great frequency as corporations and their representatives violate numerous laws (fraud, price-fixing, pollution, etc.) that cause widespread social harms but are virtually ignored by the criminal justice system.

5. *Crime is functional to capitalism.* There is a viable and fast-growing *crime control industry* that provides a sort of "Keynesian stimulus" to the economy by creating jobs and profits for corporations (e.g., building prisons; providing various products and services to police departments, courthouses, and detention centers).[87]

6. *Capitalism shapes society's response to crime by shaping law.* Those in power (especially legislators) define what a crime is and what constitutes a threat to the social order. Perhaps more importantly, they determine *who* constitutes such a threat—the answer is usually members of the underclass. Various problems that threaten the dominant mode of production become criminalized (e.g., the use of certain drugs used by minorities rather than drugs produced by corporations, such as cigarettes, prescription drugs, and alcohol).

The importance of the capitalist system in producing inequality and hence crime is apparent when examining recent economic changes in U.S. society and the effects of these changes. In recent years particularly, many scholars have begun to seek an explanation of crime and delinquency by examining changes in the economic structure of society and how such changes have contributed to the emergence of what some have called an "underclass," which in many ways represent what Marx called the "surplus population."[88] In many ways, this perspective is an extension of some of the basic assumptions and key concepts of social disorganization/ecology, strain, and cultural deviance theories in addition to critical/Marxist perspectives.

In 2008 the American economy began its downward slide toward the biggest crisis since the Great Depression of the 1930s. The results have been devastating, affecting not just the United States but the entire world. Many have begun to ask serious questions about the nature of capitalism and whether or not an alternative system can emerge.[89] Therefore, it seems that a critical/Marxist view of crime and justice is more relevant than ever before. In the next chapter, the recent economic crisis will be explored in more detail.

Summary

With few exceptions (e.g., social learning theory) the theories in this chapter stress the importance of the external socioeconomic environment in explaining delinquency. Beginning with social disorganization/ecology (especially the early work of Thrasher), these theories link delinquency to such environmental factors as poverty, social inequality, lack of community integration, and lack of meaningful employment and educational opportunities, along with the larger economic picture of a changing labor market and the corresponding emergence of a more or less permanent underclass mired in segregated communities.

A second theme is that adolescents who grow up in such environments face daily struggles for self-esteem, a sense of belonging, protection from outside threats, and some type of family structure. Primary social institutions such as the family, the school, the church, and the community are not meeting the basic human needs for significant numbers of youngsters.

A third theme developed in this chapter is that becoming a delinquent is a social process that involves learning various roles and social expectations within a given community. It involves the reinforcement of expectations through various rationalizations or techniques of neutralization in addition to the perpetuation of various lifestyles, attitudes, and behaviors modeled by significant others in the lives of these youths. Beginning at a very early age, a youth becomes embedded in his or her surrounding environment and cultural norms so that it becomes more and more difficult to leave the world of delinquency.

A fourth theme is that delinquency is shaped to a large degree by the societal reaction to such behavior and to the kinds of individuals who engage in such behavior. Such a response helps to perpetuate the very problem that the larger society is trying to solve.

A fifth and final theme is that one cannot possibly explain the phenomenon of delinquency without considering the economic context of capitalism. Much delinquency is consistent with basic capitalist values, such as the law of supply and demand, the need to make money (profit), and the desire to accumulate consumer goods.

Notes

[1] Lanier, M. M., and S. Henry (1998). *Essential Criminology.* Boulder, CO: Westview Press, ch. 9; Stark, R. (1987). "Deviant Places: A Theory of the Ecology of Crime." *Criminology* 25: 893–909.

[2] For a more detailed discussion of the work of Guerry and Quetelet, along with the "Chicago School," see Lanier and Henry, *Essential Criminology,* pp. 183–92; see also Quinney, R. and J. Wildeman (1991). *The Problem of Crime: A Peace and Social Justice Perspective* (3d ed.). Mountain View, CA: Mayfield, pp. 48–50.

[3] For documentation of this phenomenon, see Moore, J. (1991). *Going Down to the Barrio: Homeboys and Homegirls in Change.* Philadelphia: Temple University Press; and Moore, J. (1978). *Homeboys: Gangs, Drugs, and Prisons in the Barrio of Los Angeles.* Philadelphia: Temple University Press.

[4] Stark, "Deviant Places."

[5] Lanier and Henry, *Essential Criminology,* p. 182. Lanier and Henry also note that the term *social* or *human* ecology comes from the Greek word *oikos,* which translates roughly into "household" or "living space."

[6] Knupfer, A. M. (2001). *Reform and Resistance: Gender, Delinquency, and America's First Juvenile Court.* New York: Routledge, p. 25.

[7] Burgess, E. W. (1925). "The Growth of the City." In R. E. Park, E. W. Burgess, and R. D. McKenzie (Eds.), *The City.* Chicago: University of Chicago Press.

[8] Shaw, C. and H. D. McKay (1972). *Juvenile Delinquency in Urban Areas.* Chicago: University of Chicago Press (originally published in 1942).

[9] Thrasher, F. (1927). *The Gang.* Chicago: University of Chicago Press, pp. 32–33.

[10] Ibid., pp. 20–21.

[11] Ibid., p. 33.

[12] Ibid., pp. 228–31.

[13] Vigil, J. D. (1988). *Barrio Gangs.* Austin: University of Texas Press, pp. 89–90. Vigil concludes that the gang provides many of the functions of a family. "The gang has become a 'spontaneous' street social unit that fills a void left by families under stress. Parents and other family members are preoccupied with their own problems, and thus the street group has arisen as a source of familial compensation." Vigil notes that about half of those he interviewed mentioned how important the group was to them, that the gang was something they needed, and that it gave them something in return. Close friends become like family to the gang member, especially when support, love, and nurturance are missing from one's biological family.

[14] Spergel, I. A. (1964). *Racketville, Slumtown and Haulberg.* Chicago: University of Chicago Press.

[15] Sullivan, M. L. (1989). *Getting Paid: Youth Crime and Work in the Inner City.* Ithaca, NY: Cornell University Press.

[16] Ibid., p. 203.

[17] Ibid., p. 103.

[18] Ibid., p. 110.

[19] Stark, "Deviant Places."

[20] Ibid., pp. 896–97.

[21] Among others, see Sampson, R. J. (1985). "Neighborhood and Crime: The Structural Determinants of Personal Victimization." *Journal of Research in Crime and Delinquency* 22: 7–40; Sampson, R. J., S. W. Raudenbush, and F. Earls (1997). "Neighborhoods and Violent Crime: A Multilevel Study of Collective Efficacy." *Science* 277: 918–24; Laub, J. and R. J. Sampson (2006). *Shared Beginnings, Divergent Lives: Delinquent Boys to Age 70.* Cambridge, MA: Harvard University Press; Sampson, R. J. and J. Laub (1995). *Crime in the Making: Pathways and Turning Points through Life.* Cambridge, MA: Harvard University Press.

[22] Rubin, J. and A. Pesce (2010, January 26). "Within South L.A.'s Killing Zone, a Haven from Violence." *Los Angeles Times*. Retrieved from http://www.latimes.com/news/local/la-me-homicide26-2010jan26,0,7890734.story?track=rss&utm_source=feedburner&utm_medium=feed&utm_campaign=Feed%3A+latimes%2Fmostviewed+%28L.A.+Times+-+Most+Viewed+Stories%29

[23] Ibid.

[24] Ibid.

[25] See the following website: http://www.jfa-associates.com/publications/cjpm/JFA-JMC%20Mapping%20Gallery.pdf

[26] Retrieved from http://www.unlv.edu/centers/crimestats/CrimeMapping/

[27] The classic statement about anomie was made in Durkheim, E. (1951). *Suicide*. New York: Free Press.

[28] Merton, R. K. (1968). *Social Theory and Social Structure*. New York: Free Press.

[29] The reader is encouraged to browse through any introductory sociology textbook to find numerous references to these two terms. In fact, one definition of *sociology* itself could be "the study of culture and social structure."

[30] For an excellent discussion of the role of corporate propaganda see the following: Herman, E. and N. Chomsky (1988). *Manufacturing Consent: The Political Economy of the Mass Media*. New York: Pantheon; Fones-Wolf, E. (1994). *Selling Free Enterprise*. Indianapolis: University of Indiana Press; Carey, A. (1995). *Taking the Risk Out of Democracy*. Chicago: University of Illinois Press.

[31] For a quick and easy-to-read look at inequality see Teller-Elsberg, J., N. Folbre, J. Heintz, and the Center for Popular Economics (2006). *Field Guide to the U. S. Economy*. New York: The New Press.

[32] Messner, S. and R. Rosenfeld (2007). *Crime and the American Dream* (4th ed.). Belmont, CA: Thomson/Wadsworth.

[33] Ibid., p. 72.

[34] Chomsky, N. (1996). *Class Warfare*. Monroe, ME: Common Courage Press, p. 29.

[35] A good illustration of this dominance is shown in Derber, C. (1998). *Corporation Nation*. New York: St. Martin's Press.

[36] Messner and Rosenfeld note that the United States lags far behind other countries (whose economic institutions are not nearly as dominant) in paid family leave, p. 80.

[37] See this website: http://www.uwsc.wisc.edu/projects.php

[38] Eckholm, E. (2010, February 18). "A Sight All Too Familiar in Poor Neighborhoods." *New York Times*. Retrieved from http://www.nytimes.com/2010/02/19/us/19evict.html?scp=2&sq=evictions&st=cse

[39] Cloward, R. and L. Ohlin (1960). *Delinquency and Opportunity*. New York: Free Press.

[40] Ibid., p. 86.

[41] Hagan, J. (1993). "The Social Embeddedness of Crime and Unemployment." *Criminology* 31: 465–91.

[42] Granovetter, M. (1992). "The Sociological and Economic Approaches to Labour Market Analysis: A Social Structural View." In M. Granovetter and R. Swedberg (Eds.), *The Sociology of Economic Life*. Boulder, CO: Westview Press.

[43] Although not mentioned by Hagan, to become embedded in the labor market one also needs social or cultural capital. This term is discussed at length by MacLeod and is included in the next section. In summary, for those who lack the necessary social or cultural capital, being involved in the labor market with steady employment is quite difficult. See MacLeod, J. (1987). *Ain't No Makin' It: Leveled Aspirations in a Low-Income Neighborhood*. Boulder, CO: Westview.

[44] Hagan, "The Social Embeddedness of Crime and Unemployment," p. 469.

[45] Anderson, E. (1990). *Streetwise: Race, Class and Change in an Urban Community*. Chicago: University of Chicago Press, p. 244.

[46] Padilla, F. (1992). *The Gang as an American Enterprise*. New Brunswick, NJ: Rutgers University Press, pp. 101–2.

[47] Anderson, *Streetwise*; Hagedorn, J. M. (1998). *People and Folks: Gangs, Crime and the Underclass in a Rustbelt City* (2nd ed.). Chicago: Lakeview Press; Moore, *Going Down to the Barrio*; Padilla, *The Gang as an American Enterprise*.

[48] Cohen, A. (1955). *Delinquent Boys: The Culture of the Gang*. New York: Free Press.

[49] Copes, A. and J. P. Williams (2007). "Techniques of Alienation: Deviant Behavior, Moral Commitment, and Subcultural Identity." *Deviant Behavior* 28:247–72.

50 Empey, L. and J. Rabow (1961). "The Provo Experiment in Delinquency Rehabilitation." *American Sociological Review* 26: 679–95.

51 Miller, W. B. (1958). "Lower Class Culture as a Generating Milieu of Gang Delinquency." *Journal of Social Issues* 14: 5–19.

52 Ahmed, A. (2010, February 21). "No Backing Down." *Chicago Tribune*, pp. 1, 10.

53 Shelton, D. (2010, February 22). "Changing Violent Youths." *Chicago Tribune*, p. 4.

54 Ibid.

55 Ibid.

56 Hartley, R. D., S. Maddan, and C. C. Spohn (2007). "Concerning Conceptualization and Operationalization: Sentencing Data and the Focal Concerns Perspective." *Southwest Journal of Criminal Justice* 4: 58–78. Other studies addressing the same issue include: Steffensmeier, D. and S. Demuth (2000). "Ethnicity and Sentencing Outcomes in U.S. Federal Courts: Who Is Punished More Harshly?" *American Sociological Review* 65: 705–29; Steffensmeier, D. and S. Demuth (2001). "Ethnicity and Judges' Sentencing Decisions: Hispanic-Black-White Comparisons." *Criminology* 39: 145–78; and Steffensmeier, D., J. Ulmer, and J. Kramer (1998). "The Interaction of Race, Gender, and Age in Criminal Sentencing: The Punishment Cost of Being Young, Black, and Male." *Criminology* 36: 763–97.

57 Shelton, "Changing Violent Youths."

58 Reckless, W. (1961). *The Crime Problem* (3rd ed.). New York: Appleton-Century-Crofts.

59 Sykes, G. and D. Matza (1957). "Techniques of Neutralization." *American Journal of Sociology* 22: 664–70.

60 Johnstone, J. C. (1983). "Youth Gangs and Black Suburbs." *Pacific Sociological Review* 24: 297.

61 Vigil, J. D. and S. C. Yun (1996). "Southern California Gangs: Comparative Ethnicity and Social Control." In C. R. Huff (Ed.), *Gangs in America III*. Thousand Oaks, CA: Sage, pp. 139–56.

62 Clear, T. (2002). "Addition by Subtraction." In M. Mauer and M. Chesney-Lind (Eds.), *Invisible Punishment: The Collateral Consequences of Mass Imprisonment*. New York: New Press.

63 McCartan, L. K. and E. Gunnison (2007). "Examining the Origins and Influence of Low Self-Control." *Journal of Crime and Justice* 30: 35–62.

64 Persson, A., M. Kerr, and H. Stattin (2007). "Staying In or Moving Away from Structured Activities: Explanations Involving Parents and Peers." *Developmental Psychology* 43: 197–207.

65 This view was originally formulated by Reckless, W. C. (1952). "A New Theory of Delinquency and Crime." *Federal Probation* 24: 133–38.

66 Hay, C. and W. Forrest (2006). "The Development of Self-Control: Examining Self-Control Theory's Stability Thesis." *Criminology* 44: 739–74; Boutwell, B. B. and K. M. Beaver (2010). "The Intergenerational Transmission of Low Self-Control." *Journal of Research in Crime and Delinquency* 47(2): 174–209.

67 Higgins, G. E. (2009). "Parental Criminality and Low Self-Control: An Examination of Delinquency." *Criminal Justice Studies* 22: 141–52; Coleman, S. (2008, November 12). "The Impact of Parental Criminality on Individual Delinquency." Paper presented at the annual meeting of the ASC Annual Meeting, St. Louis, Missouri.

68 Wilson, H. (1975). "Juvenile Delinquency, Parental Criminality and Social Handicap." *British Journal of Criminology* 15: 241–50; see especially Farrington, D., R. Loeber, M. Stouthamer-Loeber, W. Van Kammen, and L. Schmidt (1996). "Self-Reported Delinquency and a Combined Delinquency Seriousness Scale Based on Boys, Mothers, and Teachers: Concurrent and Predictive Validity for African-Americans and Caucasians." *Criminology* 34: 501–25; a good review of this literature can be found in Dryfoos, J. G. (1990). *Adolescents at Risk: Prevalence and Prevention*. New York: Oxford University Press.

69 Sutherland, E. H. and D. R. Cressey (1970). *Criminology* (8th ed.). Philadelphia: Lippincott.

70 Shoemaker, D. J. (1996). *Theories of Delinquency* (3rd ed.). New York: Oxford University Press, pp. 152–53.

71 Goldstein, A. P. (1991). *Delinquent Gangs: A Psychological Perspective*. Champaign, IL: Research Press, pp. 55–61.

72 The movie *Falling Down* starring Michael Douglas illustrates how one can "lose it" because of some of these instigators.

73 Sykes and Matza, "Techniques of Neutralization."

[74] Schur, E. (1971). *Labeling Deviant Behavior.* New York: Harper & Row.

[75] Becker, H. S. (1963). *Outsiders: Studies in the Sociology of Deviance.* New York: Free Press, pp. 8–9.

[76] Examples can be cited endlessly. Two are: Chambliss, W. and R. Seidman (1971). *Law, Order, and Power.* Reading, MA: Addison-Wesley; and Werthman, C. and I. Piliavin (1967). "Gang Members and the Police." In D. Bordua (Ed.), *The Police: Six Sociological Essays.* New York: John Wiley, pp. 56–98.

[77] Quinney, R. (1970). *The Social Reality of Crime.* Boston: Little, Brown, pp. 15–25.

[78] All quotations in this paragraph are from Quinney, *The Social Reality of Crime*, pp. 8–15.

[79] Lemert, E. (1951). *Social Pathology.* New York: McGraw-Hill.

[80] Ibid., p. 76.

[81] Quinney and Wildeman, *The Problem of Crime*, p. 72.

[82] Ibid., p. 77.

[83] Quinney, R. (1977). *Class, State, and Crime: On the Theory and Practice of Criminal Justice.* New York: David McKay, pp. 33–62.

[84] Shelden, R. G., S. Tracy, and W. B. Brown (2004). *Youth Gangs in American Society* (3rd ed.). Belmont, CA: Wadsworth, ch. 4.

[85] Lanier and Henry, *Essential Criminology,* pp. 256–58.

[86] Quinney, *Class, State, and Crime.*

[87] Shelden, R. G. (2008). *Controlling the Dangerous Classes: A History of Criminal Justice in America* (2nd ed). Boston: Allyn & Bacon; Shelden, R. G. and W. B. Brown (2001). "The Crime Control Industry and the Management of the Surplus Population." *Critical Criminology* 9: 39–62.

[88] Marx distinguished between these two terms. The "lumpenproletariat" was seen by Marx as the bottom layer of society, the "social junk," "rotting scum," "rabble," and so on. In short, they were described as the "criminal class." The "surplus population" referred to working-class men and women who, because of various fluctuations in the market (caused chiefly by contradictions within the capitalist system), were excluded, either temporarily or permanently, from the labor market.

[89] Perhaps the most detailed exposition of this crisis and alternatives to capitalism is found in Wolff, R. D. (2010). *Capitalism Hits the Fan: The Global Economic Meltdown and What to do About It.* Northampton, MA: Olive Branch Press.

DELINQUENCY IN CONTEXT

In the previous chapter we reviewed some theories, such as strain and critical/ Marxist, that pointed to the role of the economic institution in generating crime and delinquency. In this chapter, we will briefly introduce concepts that define U.S. capitalism followed by a discussion of the changing economic structure of capitalism and how this relates to crime and delinquency.

As mentioned in chapter 7, the United States and the entire world in 2008 began to experience the worst economic crisis since the Great Depression of the 1930s. This crisis has impacted not just the underclass but the middle class too, as life savings for millions decreased significantly, millions of jobs were lost and, perhaps most devastating, the housing bubble burst and millions either lost or were close to losing their homes—arguably the bedrock of the "American Dream." It is hard to predict when things will begin to turn around. In March 2011, the latest economic figures were not optimistic. The unemployment rate was 8.8%—8.6% for adult men, 7.7% for adult women, 24.5% for teenagers, 7.9% for whites, 15.5% for blacks, and 11.3% for Hispanics.[1]

These are "official" unemployment figures, which leave out a lot.[2] There is also what is known as the "underemployment" rate, which is defined as the "unemployed; involuntarily part-time workers who want full-time work but have had to settle for part-time hours; and workers described as 'marginally attached,' who want and are available for a job, but have given up actively looking." In July 2010, underemployment was highest for young Americans (ages 18 to 29) at 28.4%. Among all adults in the workforce, a higher percentage of women were underemployed (21.6% versus 15.6% for men).[3]

The Bureau of Labor Statistics reports on "Alternative measures of labor underutilization." One measure of unemployment (labeled as "U6") is known as "Total unemployed, plus all persons marginally attached to the labor force, plus total employed part time for economic reasons, as a percent of the civilian labor force plus all persons marginally attached to the labor force." The percentage in February 2011 was: 15.9, down from 17.9 one year earlier.[4]

National unemployment rates report averages; individual states and specific neighborhoods have much higher unemployment. My own state of Nevada leads the nation with an unemployment rate of 14.0%.[5] In addition, Nevada has one of the highest foreclosure rates in the nation. The university system has already seen its budget cut by around 20%, and we expect more.[6] Universities in other states are experiencing the same problems.[7]

As we saw in chapter 3, cases of reported runaway youth have been rising, stemming directly from the current crisis. Children will be negatively affected by the recession as it will increase the likelihood that they will be living under the poverty level, which in turn may increase the likelihood of doing poorly in school and dropping out, which can lead to crime.

> Children who fall into poverty during a recession will fare far worse along a range of variables, even well into adulthood, than will their peers who avoided poverty despite the downturn in the economy. These children will live in households with lower overall incomes, they will earn less themselves, and they will have a greater chance of living in or near poverty. They will achieve lower levels of education and will be less likely to be gainfully employed. Children who experience recession-induced poverty will even report poorer health than their peers who did not fall into poverty during the recession. These differences will persist for decades into their adult lives.[8]

About 1 out of 9 children are living with an unemployed parent. "Children whose parents are unemployed are at increased risk for experiencing poverty, homelessness and child abuse."[9] Children represent 24.5% of the overall population and 35.5% of people in poverty—and 31.3% of people 50% below the poverty threshold (6.9 million children).[10]

> Half of the poor are now classified as in "extreme poverty"—described as living in families earning below 50 percent of the poverty line. The percent of children who are food insecure also increased to 18 percent in 2010. This growth translates into an additional 750,000 children nationwide who are malnourished.[11]

The 2010 Child and Youth Well-Being Index (CWI) created by the Foundation for Child Development (FCD) predicted that the effects of the recession will likely include: (1) a decline in pre-kindergarten enrollment; (2) an increase in the rate of those between the ages of 16 and 19 who are "detached" from mainstream institutions because they are not in school and do not have a job; and (3) an increase in "risky behavior" (violence, drugs, etc.).[12] The key finding here is the decline in pre-kindergarten enrollment as this is a leading predictor of child development in the early years, including delinquent behavior.

The Capitalist Economic System

Capitalism is one of several methods whereby societies attempt to meet the basic needs of citizens in terms of the production, distribution, and consumption of goods and services.[13] Often called the *mode of production*, this economic system consists of two essential parts: (1) the *forces (or means) of production* (the raw materials, tools, instruments, machines, buildings, etc., plus the current state of science and technology, and the skills, abilities, and knowledge of the people themselves) and (2) the *relations of production*, which can be defined as "the specific manner in which the surplus is produced and then appropriated from the direct producers."[14] These relations are essentially *class* relations, the most common of which are between the *owners/ managers* and the *workers* (salary and wage earners). The more popular term is that of *social class*, which may be defined as "a group of individuals or families who occupy a similar position in the economic system of production, distribution, and consumption of goods and services in industrial societies."[15]

The most common indicator of social class position is one's occupation. Indeed, it can be said that the work people engage in limits their financial status (income and wealth), their social status or prestige, the stability of their employment, the chances for upward social mobility, and their general health and longevity. It plays a key role in the way they think of themselves, places them within the larger systems of power and authority, and has significant implications for the future of their children. Erik Wright has written an entire book, *Class Counts*, on the topic.[16] There is probably no other social variable that has a more significant bearing on one's lifestyle, including the probability of becoming defined as a criminal or delinquent.[17]

Several key questions immediately arise when analyzing capitalism, such as who owns the means of production and who decides how the *surplus* is to be distributed. The term *surplus* refers to the "difference between the volume of production needed to maintain the workforce and the volume of production the workforce produces"—meaning, very generally, the margin over and above what is required to meet basic needs.[18]

Under most forms of capitalism in today's world, the relations of production are marked by an almost total separation of the workers (i.e., producers) from the means of production. One class (a small group, around 1–2% of the total population) owns most of the means of production—the factories, land, buildings, wealth, income, and other assets (see below for a discussion of the current distribution of wealth and income). This *capitalist class* or *ruling class* has an enormous amount of power in society. Wealth frequently is not an end in itself; rather, it is a *"means for gathering more wealth,"* which in turn serves "to augment the power of a dominant class."[19]

It is also important to note that inherent in this power relationship is the fact that the typical worker has little choice but to sell their labor to the capitalist. Possessing "capital" in all of its forms and owning the means of production leads very directly to the most important ingredient in the relations of production, namely *domination*. Unlike other forms of domination in history (like the domination of the army, church, etc.) this form involves the power *to refuse to sell commodities or buy labor power.*[20] A common example in recent years is the power the large corporations have to close production facilities in the United States and move to low-wage foreign countries.

Jeffrey Sachs, an economist and globalization expert at Columbia University notes: "Companies will go where there are fast-growing markets and big profits."[21] Sales in international markets for some companies are growing at least twice as fast as domestically, and half of the revenue for companies in the S&P 500 in recent years has come from outside the U.S. Corporations created 1.4 million jobs overseas in 2010, compared with fewer than 1 million in the

U.S., and they continue to build factories outside the U.S. to meet demand. According to Sachs, the U.S. is falling in most global rankings for higher education while others are rising—leaving multinational corporations little choice in their hiring decisions. "We are not fulfilling the educational needs of our young people. In a globalized world, there are serious consequences to that."[22]

One crucial difference between the capitalist system and other systems is the *drive for profit*, which can be almost an obsession. Robert Heilbroner aptly defines this unique feature of capitalism as "the restless and insatiable drive to accumulate capital." The possession of capital "confers on its owners the ability to direct and mobilize the activities of society." Control over capital gives people more than prestige and distinction; access to capital is power. Moreover, wealth itself becomes *a social category inseparable from power*. "Wherever there is great property, there is great inequality. For one rich man, there must be at least five hundred poor, and the affluence of the rich supposes the indigence of the many."[23]

Power and control are distinctive characteristics in a capitalist system. The desire to have power and control over others permeates throughout the society, whether we are talking about owners of large multinational corporations or leaders of drug gangs trying to maintain power and control over their local "drug markets." It is essentially the same phenomenon, although on much different scales. There seems to be an insatiable desire to continue "converting money into commodities and commodities into money." Everything is turned into a commodity—from the simplest products (e.g., paper and pencil) to human beings (e.g., women's bodies, slaves). More importantly, the size of one's wealth has no bounds. "Daily life is scanned for possibilities that can be brought within the circuit of accumulation," since any aspect of society that can produce a profit will be exploited, including the misery and suffering of people who have been victimized by crime.[24] Life itself has been "commodified."[25]

The accumulation of capital, and hence great wealth and inequality, would not be possible without the assistance of the state. Profits are secured with the assistance of the government, both state and local, in the form of tax loopholes, subsidies and other forms of what is essentially taxpayer assistance. Big business could not exist (and has never existed) without strong support from the government—and hence taxpayers. For example, the U.S. government helped enrich several U.S. corporations by awarding "more than $107 billion in contract payments, grants and other benefits over the past decade to foreign and multinational American companies while they were doing business in Iran, despite Washington's efforts to discourage investment there. That includes nearly $15 billion paid to companies that defied American sanctions by making large investments that helped Iran develop its vast oil and gas reserves." The CEOs of the top ten corporations that received funds distributed by the Troubled Asset Relief Program (TARP) earned a combined total of $242 million, which translates into about "$25 million per CEO to run companies that might have gone bankrupt if not for billions of dollars in taxpayer assistance."[26] Major banks in the U.S. paid employees a record amount in compensation and benefits—about $145.85 billion—a year after the government bailed out the U.S. financial system.[27] In the wake of the latest economic crisis, many commentators and scholars have documented the "myth of the free market" and have noted that literally billions of taxpayer dollars filters up to big business.[28]

The key point is that capitalism, while bringing about a virtual cornucopia of goods and a standard of living that is the envy of the world, has its negative effects—namely, it produces a tremendous amount of inequality. Within a capitalist system, especially that which exists in U.S. society, *such inequality is inevitable and a natural by-product of the system itself.* Despite the "economic boom" in the last decade of the twentieth century, inequality has become worse. This subject will be explored in more detail in the remainder of this chapter.

Class Distinctions

Karl Marx used the terms *reserve army* or *surplus population* to refer to a more or less chronically unemployed or underemployed segment of the population. The industrial revolution created the reserve workers who became "redundant" as mechanization increased. They were "superfluous" as far as producing profits were concerned. A closely related concept is what Marx and Engels called the *lumpenproletariat*. In the various English translations of *The Communist Manifesto* since the original publication in 1848, the term "dangerous class" has been used instead of "lumpenproletariat." In its original usage, Marx and Engels referred to this segment of society as "the social scum, that passively rotting mass thrown off by the lowest layers of old society."[29] Included in the *lumpenproletariat* were "thieves and criminals of all kinds, living on the crumbs of society, people without a definite trade, vagabonds, people without a hearth or home." Marx believed this segment of society was inevitable under capitalism because it was "not wholly integrated into the division of labor."[30]

There is, it should be noted, a "dual character" to the dangerous classes or surplus population. The surplus population has at times been viewed by those in power as a "threat" (viewed as social "junk" or "dynamite"—as was the case with almost the entire working class in the early years of the labor movement during the last half of the nineteenth century) or as a possible resource (e.g., a form of cheap labor or a group to exploit in order to keep wage levels down).[31] Moreover, the exact nature of this class has changed over the years, ranging from the working class in general in the nineteenth and early part of the twentieth centuries, to very specific categories in more recent years, such as racial minorities, the "underclass," and "gangs."

As Marx noted, the development of these class distinctions, especially the existence of a surplus population, is inevitable within a capitalist economic system. Capitalism produces several *contradictions*. One such contradiction occurs between capital and labor (owners and workers). Each group wants improved status. The owners want more profit, while workers want higher wages and/or more benefits (including better working conditions). This has been a continuous conflict throughout the history of capitalism; many believe *class conflict* is inevitable in capitalist societies. The battles have usually been won by the owners, although workers have made some very significant gains over the years (but not without constant struggles). The chief executive officers of large corporations have made the most gains. In 1980, the average CEO earned 42 times more than the average worker; in 1990, it was 107 times higher; in 2000 it was 525 times higher; and in 2010 it was 345 times higher.[32] Although the ratio has declined since 2000, the gap remains much higher than in other countries.

During the discussions of the emergence of the "underclass" that follow, keep in mind the comments about surplus population. It is my contention that the underclass, and especially those who belong to the "gangs" that flourish within this segment of the population, is an inevitable by-product of U.S. capitalism. I emphasize *American* capitalism for an important reason: other capitalist democracies (e.g., France, Germany, Japan, the Scandinavian countries, etc.) do not have the high degree of inequality and poverty—and hence the crime—that exist in the United States, mainly because of the existence of strong institutions like the family and the church that are able to offset the excesses of capitalism.

Barbara Ehrenreich titled her best-selling book *Nickel and Dimed: On (Not) Getting by in America*.[33] Ehrenreich spent the better part of a year working at six different low-paying jobs and trying to make ends meet with the minimal wages earned. The stories she tells of the lives of herself and coworkers reveal the underside of the American Dream and the failure of our so-called "market economy." The $6 or $8 an hour these workers earned put them all under the official poverty level. Most had to augment their meager wages with either a second job or depend on other workers in the household (usually a spouse, which in most cases was a husband, since most of the low-wage workers Ehrenreich worked with were women). Even with such additional help, they all struggled. In addition, their jobs required hard and rather boring labor.

If Ehrenreich's picture is gloomy, think for a moment that these are the *working poor*. The *nonworking poor* are among what William Julius Wilson has called the "truly disadvantaged" (see a discussion of his work later in this chapter). Moreover, the continuing economic woes facing the country, plus the growing deficits, impact millions of families, especially the nation's most marginalized populations. The spending on the "war on terrorism" and the continuing wars in Iraq and Afghanistan is estimated to be about $4 billion each month (the total defense budget is more than $533 billion, plus what is called "discretionary budget authority" which brings the total to $664 billion[34]). The inevitable cutbacks will have the most negative impact on the lives of ordinary people, but especially the poorest of our citizens. Inequality in the richest of all nations in the history of the world is astoundingly high. One percent of the population possesses almost half of all the financial wealth in the country. Meanwhile, social supports that might reduce poverty and inequality somewhat have been either eliminated altogether or reduced so much that they barely make a difference.

Changes in the U.S. Economy

We are presently in the midst of an important era in history, the last stage of the Industrial Revolution.[35] Several forces are producing this change: (1) technology, (2) the globalization of the economy, (3) the movement of capital, and (4) the overall shift of the economy away from manufacturing to information and services. Some have termed this stage *deindustrialization*.[36] Between 1998 and 2008, jobs in the production of goods sector declined from 17.3% to 14.2%; the projected percentage of manufacturing jobs in 2018 is 12.9. In contrast, the service providing sector increased from 72.8% in 1998 to 77.2% in 2008, with a projection of 78.8% in 2018.[37]

Cities like Rochester, Baltimore, Camden, Detroit, Memphis, and Richmond typify the deindustrialization process.[38] The movement of capital overseas, the relocation of plants to countries with lower wages, and mergers with other corporations have all had the effect of eliminating the jobs of many workers. In *The End of Work*, Jeremy Rifkin takes a close look at economic changes and how they have affected the African-American community in particular. After the end of World War II, millions of African Americans migrated to the North (as well as the West) in search of new job opportunities. Until 1954 the lot of the typical African-American worker steadily improved—until automation in the auto, steel, rubber, chemical, and other unskilled labor markets. Between 1953 and 1962, 1.6 million blue-collar jobs were lost in manufacturing industries. While unemployment among African-American workers never went higher than 8.5% between 1947 and 1953 (versus 4.6% for whites), by 1964 the rate was 12.4% (versus 5.9% for whites). Since this time the unemployment rate for African Americans has consistently been twice that for whites.[39]

A really significant change began in the 1950s with the growth of industrial parks in the suburbs. The first industry to feel the effects of these changes was the auto industry. The big Ford River Rouge plant in Detroit was the "flagship" of their operations and the location of the heaviest concentration of union power. Ford decided to move most of the production to the suburbs, where the new automated plants were located, even though there was plenty of room in the old site. Whereas in 1945 this plant had 85,000 workers, by 1960 it had just 30,000. GM and Chrysler made similar moves to the suburbs.

The many satellite businesses that served the auto industry (machine tools, tires, car parts, and so on) also began to move their operations to the suburbs. The bulk of the African-American population was left behind in the inner cities. Whereas in the 1950s African-American workers accounted for about one-fourth of the workers at GM and Chrysler, by 1960 there were 24 African-American workers in a workforce of 7,425 skilled workers at Chrysler; there were 67 African Americans among the 11,000 skilled workers at GM. In fact, between 1957 and 1964 the manufacturing output doubled, while the number of blue-collar workers declined by 3%.[40] As businesses flocked to the suburbs, millions of middle- and working-class families (mostly white) moved too, so that the inner cities became concentrated with poor, unemployed minorities.

The nature of work has changed. The proportion of workers (especially young workers) employed in high-paying manufacturing industries has declined. Meanwhile, the largest increases in the job market have been in the service industries of retail trade, finance, insurance, and real estate. There is increasing polarization into a low-wage/high-wage dichotomy. All of this has resulted in a drastic change in educational requirements for employment in industries paying the most money (job growth has generally been in areas requiring the most education).[41]

Young African Americans have found jobs in industries that generally pay the least. Those industries and occupations that pay the most require increasingly more education and skill levels (e.g., computer skills, knowledge of math and English).[42] Unemployment rates are consistently the highest for those who drop out of high school (see chapter 10).[43] The average earnings for blacks without a high school diploma are lower than the earnings for whites without a diploma.[44] As of December 2010, the unemployment rate for black males 20 years of age and older was 16.5% (8.5% for whites); for blacks of both sexes between 16 and 19, the rate was 44.2% (compared to 22.5% for whites).[45]

The average weekly wages ("real earnings" in 1982 dollars) in February 2011 were $351.89; the average hourly wage was $10.29.[46] Six percent of workers paid by the hour—4.4 million people—earn the minimum wage of $7.25 (or less).[47] Adjusted for inflation, the minimum wage is about $1.50 an hour lower than it was in 1968. Figure 8-1 illustrates the changing distribution of wealth and income. In the post-World War II growth period (1947–79) it was literally the case that a "rising tide lifts all boats." Since that time, it has been more like a "rising tide lifts all yachts."

The American dream generally holds out the promise that each generation will achieve more than the previous generation. "In the three decades following World War II, real earnings for workers grew by roughly 2 percent a year, nearly doubling incomes for each successive generation."[48] That has changed in recent decades—especially for men. Only 66% of men are employed full time versus 80% in 1970; in contrast, the proportion of women in the labor force increased from 34% to over 55%.[49] A portion of the gains for women are attributable to an increase in the proportion of workers employed as *temporary* workers. As of 2009, 26.5% of women workers worked part time, compared to 13.2% of the men; 19.5% of all workers were working part-time.[50] Temporary workers have been utilized more often in the last two decades, and the trend appears to be one that will continue.

For the less educated, the percentages are worse: 57% of high-school graduates have a full-time job today versus 79% in 1970. After adjusting for inflation, the median wage in 2009 was $49,777, which was roughly the same as in 1969. One analysis found that earnings have actually declined sharply, when adjusted for the fewer number of people working full time—finding that the median wage has effectively declined $13,000 (28%) since 1969.[51]

According to the latest census report, there are 249.4 million people living in families. Of those, 31.2 million (12.5%) live below the poverty level.[52] Female-headed households are the most likely to be living in poverty—sometimes described as the *feminization of poverty*. In 2009, 45.3 million lived in families with a female householder; 14.7 million (32.5%) lived below the poverty level. There were 14.5 million people living in black female-headed households; of those 39.8% lived under the poverty level, in comparison to 23.8% in families with a white female householder and 40.6% of families with a Hispanic householder.

Figure 8.1   Income and Wealth Inequality in the U.S.

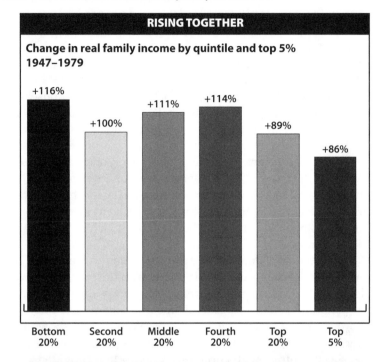

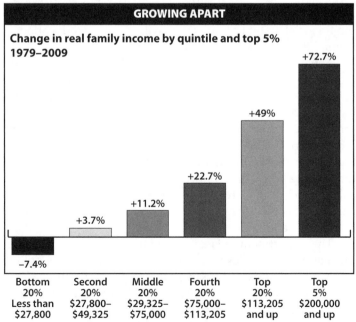

Source: Working Group on Extreme Wealth, "How Unequal Are We?" http://extremeinequality.org./page_id=8. Based on U.S. Census Bureau, Historical Income Tables, Table F-3 (for median income) and Table F-1 (for income ranges). Retrieved from http://www.census.gov/hhes/www/income/data/historical/inequality/index.html

In 2009, there were 78.9 million families; 10 million had incomes under $20,000 while 2 million earned more than $250,000.[53] Thirteen percent of all households earned under $15,000 per year while 3.8% earned more than $200,000.[54] The amount of household income of the top 5% of earners in 2009 increased 62.6% since 1979. For households in the lowest 20% of earnings, the amount increased by less than 5%.[55] In 1976 the percentage of total income that went to the top 1% of American households was about 9%; in 2008 the percentage had grown to 21. In 2009, the richest 1% of U.S. households owned more than one-third of all the private wealth in the nation, which was only slightly less than the wealth of the bottom 95% combined.[56]

Income inequality, measured by what is known as the *Gini Index of Inequality* (a value of 0 means perfect equality—everyone earns the same amount; and a value of 100 means perfect inequality—one person earns all), has gone up since the late 1960s. Whereas in 1970 the index for the United States was 35, in 2007 it was at 45, larger than any other industrialized nation (in contrast, the Gini for Canada is 31; the Netherlands is 31, while Sweden is the most equal with a score of 23).[57]

Over the last quarter of a century, many safeguards that people once counted on to shield them from financial harm have been weakened or completely lost. These include formal protections such as guaranteed corporate pensions and state and federal unemployment benefits. And they include informal ones, like the loyalty that employers once showed their workers by offering secure jobs with relatively little prospect of long-term layoff. The informal social contract with corporate America that provided workers benefits in exchange for their production is no longer there. Part of the American Dream is the financial stability that comes with a college education, which is too often beyond the reach of poor families today.

The proportion of people in the United States living in poverty has increased. As of 2009 14.3% of Americans lived under the official poverty level.[58] As inequality has grown, the social conditions of the most disadvantaged sectors of society have worsened. The poverty rate for African Americans was 25.8% and for those under 18 it was 35.7%; in contrast, the rates for whites were 11.5 and 18 respectively.[59] The Children's Defense Fund found that one in five children (15.5 million in 2009) lived in poverty—35% of black children and 12% of white children. Black were three times more likely than white children to live in extreme poverty; 40% of black children were born poor compared to 8% of white children, and black children were seven times more likely to be persistently poor.[60]

The Department of Health and Human Services has a complex formula for calculating poverty levels based on a subsistence level of living for individuals and families.[61] It is updated yearly and for 2009 it was $22, 050 for a family of four; in contrast it was $9,300 in 1982.[62] The minimal standard of living has been calculated on the same basis since the 1960s: the amount of money needed for a subsistence diet multiplied by 3, updated for inflation. As many critics point out, food costs now represent a much smaller share of family budgets, while rent and transportation costs have increased and now constitute a larger share of household expenditures. Ehrenreich notes that when the original method for defining the poverty line was devised, 24% of the typical family budget went for food, while housing constituted 29%. By 1999, the food portion had decreased to 16%, while the housing portion rose to 37%.[63] Most critics contend that the official poverty rate should be raised by at least 50%. The Census Bureau publishes income to poverty ratios of .5 (incomes 50% below the poverty level), 1.0 (incomes below poverty level) and 1.25 (incomes 25% higher than the poverty level) based on official poverty thresholds. In 2009, 19 million people—6.3% of the population—fell under the .5 ratio; 43.7% of people in poverty were 50% below the poverty threshold.[64]

The Economic Policy Institute, after careful review of dozens of studies, arrived at an estimated "living wage" for a family of one adult and two children of about $30,000 per year (which translates to a wage of $14 per hour, full time). The median weekly earnings in December 2010 were $751 per week ($39, 052 annually). The median earnings for black men were $629 (73.4% of the median earnings for white men), while the median earnings for black women were $605 (versus $695 for white women). The median earnings for employees without a high school diploma were $438, $637 for those with a diploma, and $1139 for those with a bachelor's degree.[65]

Michael Harrington wrote about the "invisible poor" in the early 1960s.[66] This underclass remains largely invisible today, unless they get "out of line." Plant closings, the movement of capital out of the central cities, the growth of suburbs, and many other changes have, in effect, made many youths "superfluous" within mainstream society. If underclass youth are unable to find jobs, they will not develop the work skills, attitudes, and habits that are appropriate and necessary in a competitive, highly technological economy. Without gainful employment, these youth are increasingly tempted to participate in the underground alternative economy of the urban ghettos—that is, the illegal system of barter in stolen goods, drugs, gambling, and prostitution.

The Development of the Underclass

The term *underclass* has been the subject of considerable debate. Herbert Gans refers to the term as an example of "new wine in old bottles." It has replaced terms such as "dangerous classes," the "undeserving poor," the "rabble," and so on. While it is synonymous with persistent and extreme poverty, it is also a "behavioral term invented by journalists and social scientists to describe poor people who are accused, rightly or wrongly, of failing to behave in the 'mainstream' ways of the numerically or culturally dominant American middle class."[67] The term essentially stigmatizes those who fall within the general category of the "underclass"—the homeless, those who live in "the projects," addicts, and young poor women with babies. The term is often used interchangeably with racial minorities. However, it is misleading to conclude that the "underclass" is synonymous with African Americans and other minorities. In sheer numbers, whites comprise the majority of the underclass and the poor in general. In 2009, there were 18.5 million whites below the poverty line compared to 9.9 million blacks and 12.4 million Hispanics.[68]

Inner cities have been the most negatively affected by the economic changes discussed earlier. The movement of capital out of the inner cities corresponded with the exodus of many middle-class minorities. The tax base declined while the concentration of the poor increased. Job opportunities disappeared. Federal funding for social programs, particularly those targeting the urban underclass, also decreased during the 1980s with the movement toward privatization—a system aimed at replacing federal assistance with private-sector methods of solving urban problems. Aid to disadvantaged school districts, housing assistance, financial aid to the poor, legal assistance to the poor, and social services in urban areas in general all declined.[69]

A commission that studied the "riots" (the term "riot" is used by the white majority, whereas minorities are more likely to describe such events as a "rebellion," "civil disobedience," or "legitimate protest"[70]) after the verdicts in the trials of the police officers who beat Rodney King noted the declining investments in the inner city on the part of the federal government. For example, between 1981 and 1992 the amount invested in job training fell from $23 billion to $8 billion, from $21 billion to $14 billion for local economic development, and from $6 billion to zero for "general revenue sharing"; federal support for housing was cut by 80%.[71]

The welfare reform movement of 1996 reduced the number of citizens on welfare from 12 million in 1996 to 7 million in 1999. Single mothers who left welfare often worked at poverty wages. More than one-fourth were working nights, while two-thirds had jobs without health insurance. More than half had trouble finding affordable child care and paying for such necessities as food and rent.[72]

The social and economic position of African Americans—especially young African-American males, whom one author in the 1980s called an "endangered species"—has been tenuous.[73] By the turn of the century, most young black men had become superfluous—part of the "surplus population." Although somewhat dated, William Julius Wilson's study of the black underclass in the late 1980s and mid-1990s is still relevant—in fact, the situation he reported on has grown worse (as noted above).

Wilson distinguished between inner-city ghettos of the 1980s and 90s and those of an earlier era. Until the 1960s, these areas were inhabited by *different classes* of African Americans (lower-class, working-class, and middle-class professionals), providing much stability and reinforcing dominant cultural norms and values (e.g., hard work, stability, importance of family, obeying the law). Youths growing up in these areas had a variety of stable role models:

> Even if the truly disadvantaged segments of an inner-city area experience a significant increase in long-term spells of joblessness, the basic institutions in that area (churches, schools, stores, recreational facilities, etc.) would remain viable if much of the base of their support comes from the more economically stable and secure families. Moreover, the very presence of these

families during such periods provides mainstream role models that help keep alive the perception that education is meaningful, that steady employ-ment is a viable alternative to welfare, and that family stability is the norm, not the exception.[74]

Wilson suggests that perceptive ghetto youngsters in a neighborhood that includes a good number of working and professional families may observe increasing joblessness and idleness but also witness many individuals regu-larly going to and from work; they may sense an increase in school dropouts but also see a connection between education and meaningful employment; they may detect a growth in single-parent families but also be aware of the presence of many married-couple families; they may notice an increase in wel-fare dependency but also see a significant number of families that are not on welfare; and they may be cognizant of an increase in crime but recognize that many residents in their neighborhood are not involved in criminal activity.

Unfortunately, this "social buffer" has practically disappeared, relocating to "better" neighborhoods. African Americans who are poor are far more likely than previously to live in areas where just about everyone else is poor. In con-trast, whites who are poor are far more likely to be surrounded by nonpoor, retaining the "social buffer." Inner-city residents have become more and more *isolated* from mainstream society. Such isolation includes being excluded from an informal job network that is found in other areas. One result of this is the growth of alternatives to the mainstream labor force, including welfare and crime, both of which have become more or less permanent alternatives in these areas. Wilson further notes that "the social transformation of the inner city has resulted in a disproportionate concentration of the most disadvantaged seg-ments of the urban African-American population, creating a social milieu sig-nificantly different from the environment that existed in these communities several decades ago."[75]

The relatively new social subgroup of the disadvantaged who interact and live only with similarly situated people can be distinguished from the tradi-tional "lower class" by its lack of mobility.[76] The individuals who make up the underclass are mostly "the sons and daughters of previous generations of the poor" whose own children will remain poor. Many of them have more or less permanently dropped out of the lower class and lack skills and education to ever "make it" in conventional society. They survive mainly through options "ranging from private entrepreneurial schemes to working the welfare system. Hustling, quasi-legitimate schemes, and outright deviant activity are also alter-natives to work."[77]

A somewhat different interpretation was offered by Douglas Massey and Nancy Denton in their 1990s study appropriately called *American Apartheid*. They linked the origins and perpetuation of the African-American urban underclass to specific patterns of *segregation*.

> Residential segregation has been instrumental in creating a structural niche within which a deleterious set of attitudes and behaviors—a culture of seg-regation—has arisen and flourished. Segregation created the structural con-

ditions for the emergence of an oppositional culture that devalues work, schooling, and marriage and that stresses attitudes and behaviors that are antithetical and often hostile to success in the larger economy.[78]

Because of segregation (especially within the housing market), African Americans have been far less able than other minorities (e.g., Mexican-Americans, Jews, Italians, Poles) to escape. Until about 1900 most African Americans lived in areas that were largely white. Massey and Denton document the changes since that time using five dimensions of segregation. *Unevenness* looks at overrepresentation and underrepresentation of African Americans in an urban area. *Isolation* refers to African Americans rarely sharing the same neighborhood with whites. *Clustering* occurs when African-American neighborhoods are grouped together so that they either form one continuous enclave (occupying a large area of land) or are scattered about the city. *Concentrated* describes a focus in one small area or sparsely settled throughout a city. *Centralization* measures location within the central core of a city versus spread out along the periphery. Massey and Denton conclude that

> a high score on any single dimension is serious because it removes blacks from full participation in urban society and limits their access to its benefits. . . . Blacks . . . are more segregated than other groups on any single dimension of segregation, but they are also more segregated on all dimensions simultaneously; and in an important subset of U.S. metropolitan areas, they are very highly segregated on at least four of the five dimensions at once, a pattern we call hypersegregation.[79]

About one-third of all African Americans currently live in *hypersegregated* areas. Massey and Denton conclude that quite often this isolation affects one's lifestyle and life chances:

> Typical inhabitants of one of these ghettos are not only unlikely to come into contact with whites within the particular neighborhood where they live; even if they traveled to the adjacent neighborhood they would still be unlikely to see a white face; and if they went to the next neighborhood beyond that, no whites would be there either. People growing up in such an environment have little direct experience with the white culture, norms, and behaviors of the rest of American society and few social contacts with members of other social groups. Ironically, within a large, diverse, and highly mobile post-industrial society such as the United States, blacks living in the heart of the ghetto are among the most isolated people on earth.[80]

Wilson noted that between 1960 and 1970 the number of inner-city African Americans aged 14 to 24 increased by 78% compared to a 23% increase among whites within this age-group. From 1970 to 1977, African Americans in this age group increased another 21%, but whites *decreased* by 4%. He also observed that the average age of metropolitan area populations was quite young. Generally speaking, the higher the median age of a group, the higher the income; since African Americans are on the average younger than whites, one finds higher unemployment rates, lower income, and higher crime rates (since crime is much higher among the younger age-groups).[81] As of 2008 most blacks are still concentrated in large urban areas, although an increasing number have been migrating elsewhere. The median age of blacks is about 31 compared to 37 for other races.[82]

Poverty and Family Structure

Nearly every criminologist agrees that the family is probably the most critical factor related to crime and delinquency (see chapter 9). For over 50 years, research has shown that three or four key family-related factors best distinguish the habitual delinquent from the rest of his or her peers. We have already noted that African-American families are far more likely to be headed by a female than are white families and that these families are far more likely to be living in poverty.

The percentage has increased for both racial groups since 1950; the gap between the two races has also increased. Wilson cited one major reason for the rise in African-American female-headed families was the "increasing difficulty of finding a marriage partner with stable employment." In other words, there is a "poor marriage market" for these young women. Wilson concludes that male unemployment is *the leading cause* of the rise in female-headed households.[83] In addition, there has been a dramatic rise in the percentage of African-American children living with their mother only: 30% in 1970 to 50% in 2009; the proportion of African-American children under 18 living with a mother who *has never been married* went from a mere 4% in 1970 to 32% in 2009.[84]

According to one recent report, educated black women are still finding it difficult to find a marriageable partner.[85] The reasons echo what Wilson said: unemployment, the drug war and the growing imprisonment rate for black males. More than 2% of men of prime employment age (25 to 54) live in institutions, primarily prisons.[86] One report concluded that a one percent increase in the male incarceration rate was associated with a 2.4% reduction in the proportion of women who would ever marry. "As incarceration rates exploded between 1970 and 2007, the proportion of US-born black women aged 30-44 who were married plunged from 62% to 33%."[87]

The effects on children have been devastating, contributing in large part to the increase in cases of abuse and neglect. Wilson found that by the time children born into single-parent families reach the age of 6, nearly two-thirds will have moved into different living arrangements. For African-American children, however, about two-thirds of these moves will be into female-headed families with no fathers; for white children, an almost identical percentage will move into families with two parents.[88]

Current research reinforces Wilson's findings. Female-householder families with no husband present have the highest poverty rate among all types of households. One study suggested that "as a response to their high risks of poverty, female-headed households with children are increasingly found to include a cohabiting partner, or to be headed by a grandmother caring for her grandchildren."[89] Families headed by a grandparent who is caring for a grandchild are becoming increasingly more common, often because of financial hardships, drug or alcohol abuse by the parents, or incarceration. This is especially the case for minority children. Another study attributed the high rate of poverty within female-headed households to the fact that the women who work in such families are more likely to work in low-wage occupations.[90] Although 22.8% of all families with children lived in households with the mother only, these households represented 47% of poor families.[91] "Children are the poorest age group in America—every fifth child is poor."[92]

In recent years, girls from single-parent households are far more likely than those from two-parent households to become unwed mothers. One recent study estimated that about 70% of black babies are born out of wedlock.[93] One of the main reasons for this is that it is more difficult to supervise the children's activities if there is only one parent in the household. Wilson's study in Chicago found that the highest rates of pregnancy among teens were in single-parent households living in very poor and highly segregated neighborhoods.[94] A study in London found that children living in single-parent families are far more likely to: (1) have more trouble in school; (2) be at risk of suffering physical, emotional, or sexual abuse; (3) run away from home; (4) become teenage parents; (5) drink and take drugs; (6) drop out of school; (7) get involved in criminal activities.[95]

Effects of Economic Changes on Delinquency

It would be misleading to conclude that the emergence of the underclass is the leading cause of crime. Some areas of the country have some of the economic changes described in this chapter but have not shown a significant rise in crime. Joan Moore refers to the U.S. labor market as *structurally segmented* based on factors such as job security, pay, and career opportunities. Jobs with good pay, security, and opportunities for advancement are relatively scarce. This is the *primary labor market.* Barrio and ghetto residents do not have ready access to these kinds of jobs. Instead, the majority are most likely to be found within the *secondary labor market,* which consists of unstable jobs with low wages (which are often only part-time jobs) and with little or no career advancement opportunities.[96]

One consequence of this system is the existence of *supplemental economic structures,* specifically a welfare economy and an illegal economy. These economic structures supplement the more marginal or peripheral sectors of the secondary labor market. Individuals may move back and forth between the secondary market and this peripheral market. In many instances the welfare and illegal economy "subsidizes" the marginal industries of the secondary labor market. These are "fall-back" sources of income since minimum wages are not enough to support a family.

> This is a world of limited opportunities, with legitimate jobs offering little prospect for lifetime satisfaction. In this respect, the segmented labor mar-

ket becomes an essential concept for understanding the structure and context of the Chicano gang, the use and marketing of illegal drugs and stolen merchandise, and the prison involvements of the residents of the Los Angeles barrios.[97]

The geographic distribution of jobs tends to eliminate many minorities, making them part of the "surplus population."[98] Most live within areas where industry has left; long commutes are required to try to find a job and to go to work if hired. High-tech jobs have replaced manufacturing jobs, leaving many minorities jobless. The good jobs of an earlier generation have been replaced by low-wage jobs with little security and no fringe benefits (the secondary labor market).

Urban decline contributes to social disorganization, weakening communities and lessening social control. The poor, the unemployed, and the unemployable are left behind while others leave the area for jobs, better schools, and better housing. Higher crime rates may be a by-product of the changing socioeconomic factors, since illegal activities are some of the only options that remain for the uneducated and underemployed.

The most recent data on poverty among children is not encouraging. Henry Giroux, a frequent writer on youth, tells the story in harsh but truthful words:

> The hard currency of human suffering that impacts children is evident in some astounding statistics that suggest a profound moral and political contradiction at the heart of our culture: for example, the rate of child poverty is currently at 17.4 percent, boosting the number of poor children to 13 million. In addition, about one in three severely poor people are under age 17. Moreover, children make up 26 percent of the total population but constitute an astounding 39 percent of the poor. Just as alarming as this is the fact that 9.4 million children in America lack health insurance and millions lack affordable child care and decent early childhood education. Sadly, the United States ranks first in billionaires and defense expenditures and yet ranks an appalling twenty-fifth in infant mortality. As we might expect, behind these grave statistics lies a series of decisions that favor economically those already advantaged at the expense of the young. Savage cuts to education, nutritional assistance for impoverished mothers, veterans' medical care, and basic scientific research, are often cynically administered to help fund tax cuts for the already inordinately rich.[99]

Another recent study, focusing on Chicago, found that black children suffer a great deal as a result of their exposure to "concentrated disadvantage" (living in extreme poverty, etc.) which has "had detrimental and long-lasting consequences for black children's cognitive ability, rivaling in magnitude the effects of missing 1 year of schooling."[100]

The correlation between economic conditions within urban areas and rates of delinquency has been noted for more than 150 years. Indeed, as the classic studies by Clifford Shaw and Henry McKay and others have noted (see chapter 7), delinquency and crime cannot be separated from surrounding economic conditions. Solutions that fail to address these variables are doomed to be little more than "band-aids."

The Death of Childhood in the Inner Cities

Children under the age of 18 constitute 39% of the homeless population—42% of the children are less than five years old.[101] The city of Los Angeles resembles many others in the United States; its "skid row" area is the largest in the United States. More than 11,000 adults and children are contained in its 55 square blocks. The failure of the American Dream to satisfy the needs and wants of people can be clearly seen in downtown Los Angeles, literally a stone's throw from many symbols of wealth. (The city of Las Vegas, where I live, is perhaps the most extreme expression of massive symbols of wealth juxtaposed with signs of poverty.)

The United Coalition East Prevention Project began working with young people in the skid row area of Los Angeles in 2003, attempting to improve their environment and to provide opportunities for the future before the children— "succumb to illness, crime, despair, and death."[102]

> They endure horrible living conditions, with no place to play, no sports, no chance for a good education. They have difficulty getting to school because of limited access to transportation, and once there, are often stigmatized by teachers and administrators. These young people are easy targets for the drug dealers and sexual predators. Yet the police rarely offer protection; instead they are quick to intimidate and cite these children for minor offenses like jaywalking.

The coalition reported that 45% of the youth on skid row had been cited by the police for jay walking, not having enough money for a bus or train, and "loitering." In essence, the citations criminalize poverty. The citations do not reduce crime, but they are disastrous for the families that do not have the financial resources to pay fines. If the citations become warrants, children already facing daunting challenges will have a record, which will add more complications to completing school and or finding a job. The report described the circumstances of children they have encountered. Michael and Jamaica are two of hundreds of examples:

> Michael is multiracial. He has moved repeatedly since he was three years old. He lived for several years in a dilapidated "skid row" hotel with his aunt. When she died suddenly, he was detained in juvenile hall. His "crime": being young and poor with no family to take him in. He is currently living in a group home.
>
> Jamaica is 16 years old and multiracial. Her family—mother and four siblings—also live in a "skid row" hotel. It takes her two hours to get to school each day, where she is taunted by her classmates and singled out by teachers for not wearing the appropriate clothes. She is currently on probation for defending her younger brother from a drunk, violent man.

We create and sustain social conditions that give rise to predictable responses like gangs and violence—and then blame those who exhibit the behavior. To paraphrase seventeenth-century poet John Milton (author of *Paradise Lost*) "We punch people's eyes out and then reproach them for their blindness."

Summary

There are many ways economic changes are related to delinquency and gang activity. Unemployment, poverty, and general despair lead young people to seek out economic opportunities in the growing illegal marketplace.

The "free market" is largely a myth, and a "surplus population" is constantly being created and reproduced. Most criminal activity is consistent with basic capitalist values, such as the law of supply and demand, the need to make money (profit), and the desire to accumulate consumer goods—and like the larger capitalist system, there are many failures in the world of crime and delinquency.

The term "underclass" has become a moral condemnation of various groups not falling within mainstream society. Closely correlated with this term is the "feminization of poverty" and the general economic decline of the inner cities. Labor market changes have propelled and perpetuated these problems, especially such processes as deindustrialization and capital flight. The increasing segregation of minorities isolates them from mainstream society and the contacts that lead to a good education and decent jobs.

NOTES

[1] Bureau of Labor Statistics (2011, January7). "News Release: The Employment Situation—December 2010." Retrieved from http://www.bls.gov/news.release/pdf/empsit.pdf

[2] Understanding unemployment statistics is a real challenge! A Google search found a variety of interpretations and also references to the "real" unemployment rate, which ranged from around 12% to more than 20% as of January 2010. For an overview see the Bureau of Labor Statistics, "How the Government Measures Unemployment." Retrieved from http://www.bls.gov/cps/cps_htgm.htm

[3] Jacobe, D. (2010, August). "U.S. Underemployment Steady at 18.4% in July." Retrieved from http://www.gallup.com/poll/141770/underemployment-steady-july.aspx

[4] Bureau of Labor Statistics (2011, January 7). "Alternative Measures of Labor Utilization," table A-15. Retrieved from http://www.bls.gov/news.release/empsit.t15.htm

[5] Aguero, J. (2010, August 6). "Nevada Employment: First to Worst." *Las Vegas Sun*. Retrieved from http://www.lasvegassun.com/news/2010/aug/06/nevada-employment-first-to-worst/; Bureau of Labor Statistics, "Metropolitan Area Employment and Unemployment."

[6] Schwartz, D. M. (2010, February 27). "State Legislative Leaders, Governor Reach Budget Deal." *Las Vegas Sun*. Retrieved from http://www.lasvegassun.com/news/2010/feb/27/state-legislative-leaders-governor-reach-budget-de/

[7] A Google search in March 2010 found hundreds of news stories on universities all over the country undergoing huge cuts to save money. For an overview see Lewin, M. (2009, March 16). "State Colleges Also Face Cuts in Ambitions." *New York Times*. Retrieved from http://www.nytimes.com/2009/03/17/us/17university.html?_r=2&emc=eta1

[8] First Focus (2009, May). "Turning Point: The Long-Term Effects of Recession-Induced Poverty," p. 1. Retrieved from http://www.firstfocus.net/sites/default/files/r.2009-5.12.ff_.pdf

[9] Isaacs, J. B. (2010, January 15). "The Recession's Impact on Children." The Brookings Institute. Retrieved from http://www.brookings.edu/opinions/2010/0115_recession_children_isaacs.aspx

[10] DeNavas-Walt, C., B. Proctor, and J. Smith (2010, September). *Income, Poverty, and Health Insurance Coverage in the United States: 2009*. U.S. Census Bureau, Current Population Reports, P60-238, p. 19. Retrieved from http://www.census.gov/prod/2010pubs/p60-238.pdf

[11] DiMaggio, A. (2010, July 7). "Forgotten Casualties of the Recession: Child Poverty in the Age of Neoliberalism." *Counterpunch*. Retrieved from http://www.counterpunch.org/dimaggio07072010.html

[12] Land, K. (2010). "The 2009 Foundation for Child Development and Youth Well-Being Index (CWI) Report." http://www.soc.duke.edu/~cwi/2009CWIReport.pdf

[13] Other modes of production have included mercantilism, feudalism, socialism, and communism. In primitive societies, the mode of production was hunting and gathering.

[14] Edwards, R. C., M. Reich, and T. E. Weisskopf (Eds.) (1986). *The Capitalist System* (2nd ed.). Englewood Cliffs, NJ: Prentice-Hall, pp. 7–8.

[15] Rothman, R. A. (1999). *Inequality and Stratification* (3rd ed.). Upper Saddle River, NJ: Prentice-Hall, p. 5.

[16] Wright, E. O. (2000). *Class Counts.* New York: Cambridge University Press.

[17] There is a wide body of literature documenting the relationship between social class and crime. Among other works, see Reiman, J., and P. Leighton (2010). *The Rich Get Richer and the Poor Get Prison* (9th ed.). Boston: Allyn & Bacon; Cole, D. (1999). *No Equal Justice: Race and Class in the American Criminal Justice System.* New York: The New Press.

[18] Heilbroner, R. L. (1985). *The Nature and Logic of Capitalism.* New York: W. W. Norton, p. 33.

[19] Ibid., p. 35.

[20] Ibid., pp. 39–40.

[21] Gogoi, P. (2010, December 28). "Job Market Booming Overseas for Many American Companies." *Associated Press.* Retrieved from http://www.huffingtonpost.com/2010/12/28/job-market-booming-overseas_n_801839.html

[22] Ibid.

[23] Heilbroner, *The Nature and Logic of Capitalism*, pp. 42–46. He is quoting from Adam Smith's famous *The Wealth of Nations* (1976). Oxford: Clarendon Press, pp. 709–10.

[24] Ibid., p. 60. Crime is indeed very profitable—for those who control it. It is not surprising that we have a multi-billion dollar "crime industry" which, like any other industry, seeks profits from crime in a variety of contexts—from those who build prisons, to those who supply an infinite variety of goods and services to the institutions, to those who write the news stories and sell books about crime and criminals. See Shelden, R. G., W. B. Brown, K. Miller, and R. Fritzler (2008). *Crime and Criminal Justice in American Society.* Long Grove, IL: Waveland Press, for a discussion of this "crime control industry."

[25] A fascinating slant on this process is described as the "McDonaldization" of U.S. society. This has been defined as "the process by which the principles of the fast-food restaurant are coming to dominate more and more sectors of American society as well as of the rest of the world." See Ritzer, G. (1996). *The McDonaldization of Society* (revised ed.). Thousand Oaks, CA: Pine Forge Press, p. 1.

[26] AFL/CIO (2009, March 26). "Runaway Executive Pay and the Wall Street Bailout." Retrieved from http://www.aflcio.org/corporatewatch/paywatch/tarp.cfm

[27] Grocer, S. (2010, January 14). "Banks Set for Record Pay." *Wall Street Journal.* Retrieved from http://online.wsj.com/article/SB10001424052748704281204575003351773983136.html?mod=djemalertNEWS; Baker, D. (2010, January/February). "The Big Bank Theory: How Government Helps Financial Giants Get Richer." *Boston Review.* Retrieved from http://bostonreview.net/BR35.1/baker.php

[28] See, for example, Baker, D. (2009, January 7). "Free Market Myth." Retrieved from http://www.zmag.org/znet/viewArticle/20181; Clarkson, C. A. (2009, March 26). "AIG Anger and the Free Market Myth." *Huffington Post.* Retrieved from http://www.huffingtonpost.com/charles-a-clarkson/aig-anger-and-the-free-ma_b_179632.html; Martens, P. (2008, January 3). "The Free Market Myth Dissolves into Chaos." Retrieved from http://www.counterpunch.org/martens01032008.html

[29] Eastman, M. (trans. and ed.) (1959). *Capital, The Communist Manifesto and Other Writings.* New York: The Modern Library, p. 332.

[30] Giddens, A. (1971). *Capitalism and Modern Social Theory.* New York: Cambridge University Press, p. 38.

[31] Spitzer, S. (1975). "Toward a Marxian Theory of Deviance." *Social Problems* 22: 638–51.

[32] AFL-CIO (2011). "Trends in Executive Pay." Retrieved from http://www.aflcio.org/corporatewatch/paywatch/ceopay.cfm; while the average pay for CEOs declined, retirement benefits increased 23%.

[33] Ehrenreich, B. (2001). *Nickel and Dimed: On (Not) Getting By in America.* New York: Henry Holt.

[34] Department of Defense (2010). Retrieved from http://www.whitehouse.gov/omb/assets/fy2010_new_era/Department_of_Defense.pdf. Another source puts the figure at about $965 billion, since it includes the military portion from other budgets, money spent on the "war on terror" and past military spending (e.g., benefits). See the following: http://www.warresisters.org/pages/piechart.htm

[35] Eitzen, D. S., M. B. Zinn, and K. E. Smith (2010). *In Conflict and Order: Understanding Society* (12th ed.). Boston: Allyn & Bacon.

[36] Bluestone, B. and B. Harrison (1982). *The Deindustrialization of America.* New York: Basic Books.

[37] Bureau of Labor Statistics (2010, December 8). "Employment by Major Industry Sector, 1998, 2008, and Projected 2018," table 2. Retrieved from http://www.bls.gov/news.release/ecopro.t02.htm

[38] The following article describes struggling former factory towns: Gonzales, J. M. (2009, June 16). "Ailing Factory Towns Face Tougher Recovery." Retrieved from http://www.manufacturing.net/Article-Ailing-Factory-Towns-Face-Tougher-Recovery-061609.aspx?menuid=242; Thomas Frank describes in some detail many once-thriving towns in Kansas now filled with many boarded-up former businesses in *What's the Matter with Kansas?* New York: Henry Holt and Company, 2004. See especially his description of Emporia (pp. 60–63).

[39] Rifkin, J. (1995). *The End of Work.* New York: G. P. Putnam, pp. 73–74.

[40] Ibid., p. 75.

[41] U.S. Department of Commerce, Bureau of the Census (2011). *Statistical Abstract of the United States, 2011.* Washington, DC: U.S. Government Printing Office, table 642. Retrieved from http://www.census.gov/compendia/statab/2011/tables/11s0642.pdf

[42] The latest figures show that more than a million students drop out of high school each year—about 71% finish high school on time with a regular diploma; about half of black and Hispanic students graduate on time. Alliance for Excellent Education (2009). "High School Dropouts in America." http://www.all4ed.org/files/GraduationRates_FactSheet.pdf

[43] Bureau of Labor Statistics (2011, January 6). "Employment Status of the Civilian Population 25 Years and Over by Educational Attainment," table A-4. Retrieved from http://www.bls.gov/news.release/empsit.t04.htm; Alliance for Excellent Education (2009, August). "The High Costs of High School Dropouts." http://www.all4ed.org/files/HighCost.pdf

[44] Bureau of the Census, *Statistical Abstract of the United States, 2011,* "Mean Earnings by Highest Degree Earned," table 228. Retrieved from http://www.census.gov/compendia/statab/2011/tables/11s0228.pdf

[45] Bureau of Labor Statistics (2011, January 7). "Employment Status of the Civilian Population by Race, Sex, and Age," table A-2. Retrieved from http://www.bls.gov/news.release/empsit.t02.htm

[46] Bureau of Labor Statistics (2011, March 17). "Real Earnings News Release," table A-1. Retrieved from http://www.bls.gov/news.release/realer.htm

[47] Editorial (2011, March 26). "A Minimum Wage Increase." *New York Times.* Retrieved from http://www.nytimes.com/2011/03/27/opinion/27sun2.html?src=twrhp

[48] Greenstone, M. and A. Looney (2011, March 4). "Have Earnings Actually Declined?" Retrieved from http://www.brookings.edu/opinions/2011/0304_jobs_greenstone_looney.aspx

[49] Bureau of Labor Statistics (2011). "Employment Situation Release," table A-1. Retrieved from http://www.bls.gov/news.release/empsit.t01.htm

[50] Bureau of Labor Statistics (2010, December 17). "Women in the Labor Force: A Databook (2010 edition)," table 20. Retrieved from http://www.bls.gov/cps/wlf-table20-2010.pdf

[51] Greenstone and Looney, "Have Earnings Actually Declined?"

[52] DeNavas-Walt et al., *Income, Poverty, and Health Insurance,* table B-1.

[53] U.S. Census Bureau (2010). "Income Distribution to $250,000 or More for Families: 2009." Current Population Survey, Annual Social and Economic Supplement, table FINC-07. Retrieved from http://www.census.gov/hhes/www/cpstables/032010/faminc/new07_000.htm

[54] U.S. Census Bureau (2010). "Households by Total Money Income, Race, and Hispanic Origin of Householder: 1967 to 2009," table H-17. Retrieved from http://www.census.gov/hhes/www/income/data/historical/household/index.html

55. U.S. Census Bureau (2010). "Mean Household Income Received by Each Fifth and Top 5 Percent," table H-3. Retrieved from http://www.census.gov/hhes/www/income/data/historical/household/index.html

56. Inequality.org (2010, October). "Inequality Data & Statistics." Retrieved from http://inequality.org/inequality-data-statistics/

57. This is taken from the CIA World Fact Book. Retrieved from https://www.cia.gov/library/publications/the-world-factbook/fields/2172.html

58. DeNavas-Walt et al., *Income, Poverty, and Health Insurance*, p. 14.

59. U.S Census Bureau (2010). "Annual Social and Economic (ASEC) Supplement." Retrieved from http://www.census.gov/hhes/www/cpstables/032010/pov/new01_100.htm

60. Children's Defense Fund (2011). "Portrait of Inequality 2011: Black Children in America." Retrieved from http://www.childrensdefense.org/programs-campaigns/black-community-crusade-for-children-II/bccc-assets/portrait-of-inequality.pdf

61. For details see the following website: http://aspe.hhs.gov/poverty/faq.shtml#differences

62. http://aspe.hhs.gov/poverty/figures-fed-reg.shtml

63. Ehrenreich, *Nickel and Dimed*, p. 200; she was citing an Economic Policy Institute Study—see Bernstein, J., C. Brocht, and M. Spade-Aguilar (2000). "How Much is Enough? Basic Family Budgets for Working Families." Washington, DC: Economic Policy Institute, p. 14.

64. DeNavas-Walt et al., *Income, Poverty, and Health Insurance*, p. 19.

65. Bureau of Labor Statistics (2011, January 20). "Usual Weekly Earnings of Wage and Salary Workers Fourth Quarter 2010." Retrieved from http://www.bls.gov/news.release/pdf/wkyeng.pdf

66. Harrington, M. (1962). *The Other America: Poverty in the United States.* Baltimore, MD: Penguin Books.

67. Gans, H. (1995). *The War Against the Poor: The Underclass and Antipoverty Policy.* New York: Basic Books, p. 2.

68. DeNavas-Walt et al., *Income, Poverty, and Health Insurance*, p. 16.

69. Cook, R. C. (2007). "Progressive Schemes to Reduce Poverty Will Fail without Monetary Reform." Center for Research on Globalization. http://www.globalresearch.ca/index.php?context=va&aid=5905

70. For an insightful analysis of the Watts riots, see Conot, R. (1967). *Rivers of Blood, Years of Darkness.* New York: Bantam; unfortunately, this work is rarely cited. For an exceptional and brilliant review of the Los Angeles Police Department's response to gangs and riots, see Davis, M. (1992). *City of Quartz.* New York: Vintage Books, especially chapter 5. The author regularly shows what he would describe as a very "disturbing" historical film contrasting the Rodney King "riots" with the Watts uprising 25 years earlier, called *The Fire This Time.* It is "disturbing" because it implicates the federal and local government, especially law enforcement, in perpetuating the conditions that lead to rebellion and even to create and sustain gangs.

71. Klein, M. (1995). *The American Street Gang.* New York: Oxford University Press, p. 196.

72. Associated Press (1999, March 30). "Whites Leaving Welfare Faster than Minorities, Survey Reveals"; Soss, J. (2002, January 15). "TANF Reauthorization: Where Is the Language of Racial Justice? Race and Welfare in the U.S." Presentation to the CHN Welfare Advocates Meeting, American University, p. 9.

73. Gibbs, J. T. (Ed.) (1988). *Young, Black, and Male in America: An Endangered Species.* Dover, MA: Andover House.

74. Wilson, W. J. (1987). *The Truly Disadvantaged: The Inner City, the Underclass, and Public Policy.* Chicago: University of Chicago Press, p. 56.

75. Ibid., p. 58.

76. Ibid., p. 8.

77. Glascow, D. C. (1981). *The Black Underclass.* New York: Vintage Books, pp. 8–9.

78. Massey, D. S., and N. A. Denton (1993). *American Apartheid: Segregation and the Making of the Underclass.* Cambridge, MA: Harvard University Press, p. 8.

79. Ibid., p. 74.

80. Ibid.

81. Wilson, *The Truly Disadvantaged*, ch. 2.

82. African American Population (2008). Retrieved from http://www.blackdemographics.com/

83. Wilson, W. J. (1996). *When Work Disappears.* New York: Knopf, pp. 72–75.

84 US Census (2010). "America's Families and Living Arrangements, 2009," table C3. Retrieved from http://www.census.gov/population/www/socdemo/hh-fam/cps2009.html; U.S. Department of Commerce, Bureau of the Census (1994). *Statistical Abstract of the United States: 1994.* Washington, DC: U.S. Government Printing Office, p. 52.

85 Alexander, B. (2009, August 13). "Marriage Eludes High-Achieving Black Women." MSNBC. Retrieved from http://www.msnbc.msn.com/id/32379727

86 Greenstone and Looney, "Have Earnings Actually Declined?"

87 "Sex and the Single Black Woman: How the Mass Incarceration of Black Men Hurts Black Women." (2010, April 8). *The Economist.* Retrieved from http://www.economist.com/world/united-states/displaystory.cfm?story_id=15867956

88 Wilson, *When Work Disappears,* p. 71.

89 Snyder, A. R., D. K. McLaughlin, and J. Findeis (2006). "Household Composition and Poverty among Female-Headed Households with Children: Differences by Race and Residence." *Rural Sociology* 71: 597–624. http://www.uwec.edu/bonstemj/GenderWork/women.bottom.pdf

90 Lichtenwalter, S. (2005, June). "Gender Poverty Disparity in US Cities: Evidence Exonerating Female-Headed Families." *Journal of Sociology and Social Welfare.* Retrieved from http://findarticles.com/p/articles/mi_m0CYZ/is_2_32/ai_n14711313/?tag=content;col1

91 U.S. Census Bureau (2010, March). "America's Families and Living Arrangements." Current Population Survey, table 3-C. Retrieved from http://www.census.gov/population/www/socdemo/hh-fam/cps2010.html

92 Children's Defense Fund (2010, December). "State of America's Children—2010," p. B-1. Retrieved from http://www.childrensdefense.org/child-research-data-publications/data/state-of-americas-children-2010-report-child-poverty.pdf

93 "Sex and the Single Black Woman."

94 Wilson, *When Work Disappears,* p. 75.

95 O'Neill, R. (2002, September). "Experiments in Living: The Fatherless Family." London: The Institute for the Study of Civil Society. http://www.civitas.org.uk/pdf/Experiments.pdf

96 Moore, J. W. (1978). *Homeboys: Gangs, Drugs, and Prisons in the Barrio of Los Angeles.* Philadelphia: Temple University Press.

97 Ibid., p. 33.

98 Shelden, R. G. (2008). *Controlling the Dangerous Classes: A History of Criminal Justice in America* (2nd ed). Boston: Allyn & Bacon; Shelden et al., *Crime and Criminal Justice in American Society.*

99 Giroux, H. A. (2008, November 28). "Disposable Youth in a Suspect Society: A Challenge for the Obama Administration." Retrieved from http://www.zcommunications.org/disposable-youth-in-a-suspect-society-a-challenge-for-the-obama-administration-by-henry-a-giroux

100 Sampson, R. J., P. Sharkey, and S. W. Raudenbush (2008). "Durable Effects of Concentrated Disadvantage on Verbal Ability among African-American Children." *National Academy of Sciences* 105(3): 845–52. Retrieved from http://www.pnas.org/content/105/3/845.full.pdf+html

101 National Law Center on Homelessness and Poverty (2009). "Children and Youth: Fact Sheets." http://www.nlchp.org/program_factsheets.cfm?prog=2

102 United Coalition East Prevention Project (2005). "Toxic Playground: Growing Up In Skid Row." Retrieved from http://www.socialmodelrecovery.org/sites/default/files/Toxic%20Playground.pdf

DELINQUENCY AND THE FAMILY

Contrary to popular belief, the traditional U.S. family is not always a very safe and secure institution. Consider some of the following numbers:

- 50%   Divorce rate in America;[1]
- 772,000   Number of children confirmed to have been abused or neglected;[2]
- 1,740   Number of children who died of abuse or neglect;[3]
- 35%   Proportion of children sexually assaulted by a family member;[4]
- 267,000   Number of children who were removed from their home because of abuse or neglect;[5]
- 24.2%   Proportion of homicides involving family members;[6]
- 4.8 million Estimated number of intimate partner related assaults on women each year (2,340 die).[7]

While there have been countless discussions about making schools (see next chapter) and streets safer, the home is usually assumed to be a safe haven. For some—especially women and children—the home can be a very dangerous place. Space does not permit a full discussion of domestic violence, but the institution of marriage and the family is sometimes troubled and has been for some time.[8] Listed below are five myths about families.[9]

Family Myths

1. *The myth of a stable and harmonious family in the past.* There has been no "golden age of the family," according to historians. There have always been divorces, desertions, and abuse. The main reasons for higher divorce rates today compared to earlier generations are the lessening of strong prohibitions against divorce and longer life spans.

2. *The myth of the family as a "haven in a heartless world."* The image of the family as a place of love and intimacy where people can escape the dehumanization of the external world is an unobtainable ideal. This myth ignores the reality of family life, which can be filled with physical and emotional aggression in addition to the difficulties of harsh economic conditions (poverty, inequality, unemployment, and underemployment).

3. *The myth of the monolithic family form.* From politicians, religious leaders, and television we often hear about the typical family—the man as

breadwinner, the woman as housewife, and two kids living in a home in the suburbs. The reality is that this kind of family constitutes about 7% of all families in America.

4. *The myth of an undifferentiated family experience.* There is often an assumption that everyone in a family experiences it the same way. The reverse is actually the case, as men and women experience family life differently (on most measures of mental and physical health, married men fare much better than married women, while single women fare much better than single men), as do each of the children. There are also noteworthy differences in experiences among children according to gender, which determines many of the differences in rates of delinquency between girls and boys.[10]

5. *The myth of family breakdown as the cause of social problems.* This myth, often illustrated with the popular phrase "family values," suggests that all sorts of social problems—poverty, crime, drugs, etc.—are the result of single-parent homes or women in the workplace. This ignores the important effects of economic conditions on families.

The Family in Contemporary Society

The history of the family in the United States has been closely connected to the development of capitalism. With the coming of the industrial age, work shifted from the home to the factory. Men went off to toil in low-wage, alienating work, while women were left in the home. While some men earned enough to support a family, others did not. For large numbers of immigrants and racial minorities, one-earner incomes were inadequate to provide the necessities. Many women also worked outside the home. In addition, many families grouped together in extended kinship groups. Starting in the twentieth century with the G.I. Bill (including VA loans for housing), some families received various kinds of social supports. Government funding of highways enabled millions of mostly white families to live in the suburbs and to commute to their jobs. These benefits were not as often available to minorities.[11]

As noted in the previous chapter, income/wealth inequality in U.S. society has grown in recent years. This has had a very negative impact on the family. Despite all the talk among conservative politicians about the importance of "family values," recent policies have done more harm than good for families. For instance, vacation time for workers has been reduced significantly in the United States (compared to a rise among workers in Europe).

> The United States is the only advanced economy in the world that does not guarantee its workers paid vacation. European countries establish legal rights to at least 20 days of paid vacation per year, with a legal requirement of 25 and even 30 or more days in some countries. Australia and New Zealand both require employers to grant at least 20 vacation days per year; Canada and Japan mandate at least 10 paid days off. The gap between paid

time off in the United States and the rest of the world is even larger if we include legally mandated paid holidays, where the United States offers none, but most of the rest of the world's rich countries offer between five and 13 paid holidays per year.[12]

Workers in the United States put in more hours per year than their European counterparts—on average, they work 350 more hours each year, which is about 9 weeks of additional labor.[13] In the United States maternity leave is almost nonexistent.[14] Most European countries provide a generous benefit package.

> The U.S. and Australia are the only developed economies in the world that provide no paid maternity leave. France, Singapore and Austria all offer four months' paid maternity leave benefits, and Germany offers 14 weeks. In the U.K., a woman receives 90% of her salary for up to a year off with her baby. Swedish mothers hit the jackpot with 480 days off at 80% of their salary, followed by their counterparts in Serbia and Denmark with a full year off at full pay. Even in Gambia, Somalia and Vietnam new mothers receive at least three months' paid maternity leave.[15]

Children's poverty has declined significantly in European countries, while remaining the highest in the U.S., at around 20% (as noted in the previous chapter).[16]

The growth of gangs within urban areas has been the direct result of changing economic conditions and how such conditions have affected the families living there.

> When family or other normative social forces and influences do not function as they should, street subcultures arise to fill the void. . . . The times in a person's life when these street processes occur, and the places and people with whom they unfold, are important because they almost predict that a gang member is in the making. Family strains and schooling problems erupt in the early childhood years, and street socialization gradually takes over at least by later childhood; when adolescence arrives, matters become more complicated. This time period leads to associations with a multiple-aged peer group of the streets that eventually dominates in the acquisition and retention of values and norms that contrast markedly with those accepted by the dominant society. Such social control breakdowns completely transform and undermine human development trajectories that affect cognitive, physical, social, and emotional needs and desires.[17]

Gang members tend to be drawn disproportionately from the poorest households within a community. More specifically, they come from households with incomes lower than other inner-city families and with a much higher incidence of *family stressors*, leading to *multiple marginality* (see chapter 4).

> The long history of racism and poverty has had lingering effects on a number of levels, such as where people live and what types of jobs are available to them, which in turn affects the extent to which their family life is structured and organized to effectively participate in society. Many people affected by racism and poverty live in deteriorating neighborhoods, crowded conditions, and their children attend schools that have crumbling infrastructures, insufficient staff, and no resources to fix these problems. These, and other deprivations, result in the marginalization of these populations. . . .

Ecological, socioeconomic, sociocultural, and sociopsychological marginality factors additively affect some members of particularly low-income,
ethnic minority groups. These factors all intersect with one another and
force some struggling families to adopt maladaptive, destructive behavior.[18]

The supervision of children can be seen not merely as an independent variable that causes delinquency but also as a *dependent variable*. Thus the degree to
which children are supervised may vary according to such factors as the number of children in the home, the number of rooms in the home, the type of residence (e.g., government housing project versus single-family residence), the
family income, and the presence of a father. In families experiencing multiple
stresses, especially those with many children, there is a loosening of control
networks. One result is that children spend more and more unsupervised time
in the streets with other similarly situated youths.

An individual's connections, or social bonds, with significant others ordi-
narily begin with the family and gradually extend to others outside kinship
networks starting mainly at school. However, multiple marginalization
erodes social bonds and contributes to the breakdown of family life and
schooling routines, resulting in a generally untethered existence for a youth,
which leads to more time spent on the streets. Outside the purview and
supervision of adult caretakers (in the home and school specifically), the
youth undergoes a socialization influenced and guided by a street-based
peer group—the resident gang. This street-based socialization becomes a
key factor in developing not only different social bonds but also different
aspirations for achievement, levels and intensities of participation, and
belief patterns.[19]

The idea that both the structure and internal dynamics of the family can be
a result of external causes needs to be kept in mind as we review some of the
research on the connection between family variables and delinquency. By
focusing too closely on a delinquent's family, we may lose sight of the external
causes of family dysfunction. For instance, the discussion of parenting styles as
they relate to delinquency could result in an inclination to blame the parents
(as people often do). The important question is why some parents engage in
negative parenting styles and others do not. The family does not exist in a
social vacuum.

Family Breakdown as a Cause of Delinquency

One of the most persistent explanations of delinquency is that of the "breakdown of the family." The kinds of family factors that have been cited involve
both the *structure* of the family and the *nature of relationships within the family*.
"Structure of the family" includes such variables as the "broken home" (a home
where one or both parents is absent because of death, desertion, or divorce), the
size of the family, family income, and other variables. The quality of relationships
within the family includes such factors as parental conflicts, parent–child relationships, criminality of parents, and methods of discipline and supervision.[20]

Broken Homes

Numerous studies, dating as far back as the 1920s and 1930s, have consistently shown that delinquents are far more likely than non-delinquents to come from broken homes. Sheldon and Eleanor Glueck began studying Boston delinquents in the 1930s. Their famous studies found that delinquents were about twice as likely as non-delinquents to come from broken homes (60% versus 35%).[21]

There are some criticisms of such studies, primarily because they focus on "official" delinquents. The relationship between broken homes and delinquency may thus be a function of the decisions of juvenile justice workers and police officers who believe there is a relationship and process such juveniles more than they do those from intact homes.[22] Self-report studies have shown only a minor relationship between delinquency and broken homes.[23] Joseph Rankin looked at self-reports of running away, truancy, and auto theft in the 1967 and 1972 National Surveys of Youth. He found that all the behaviors were strongly related to a broken home where *both biological parents are missing*. Such a relationship did not hold for homes in which only one parent is gone.[24]

A meta-analysis of 50 studies came to the following conclusions about the relationship between broken homes and delinquency.[25] First, delinquency in broken homes is 10%–15% higher than in intact homes. Second, the correlation is strongest for minor offenses. Third, the impact of broken homes is about the same for both males and females and black and white youths. Fourth, the influence of stepparents on rates of delinquency is negligible. In a longitudinal study of black families in a low-income area of Chicago, the researchers started with the first grade population in 1964 and 1966 and followed the children until 1975. Among the 1,387 first graders in 1966 there were *86 different family structures* based on the number and relation of adults in a household with children. The most common were as follows: (1) mother and father (40.6%); (2) mother only (37.2%); (3) mother and grandmother (5.4%); (4) mother and stepfather (4%); and (5) mother and "other" (5.7%). Living with mother alone was the most strongly related to the "social maladaptation" of the children (maladaptive behavior observed in school by teachers), while mother–father families *and* mother–grandmother families did equally well; mother–stepfather was about the same as mother alone. Three-quarters of mother-only families in 1966 remained in that status in 1975. These mothers usually had to raise their children without any outside help from other adults, and they were also far less likely to belong to any political or social organization, such as the church.[26]

Single-parent families confront a number of problems, and adolescents growing up in such families suffer from several disadvantages. One of the problems is poverty. Economic strain has been shown to have an adverse impact on families and "changes in income following a family disruption often place single-parents in a position where they cannot afford to offer extracurricular activities and other opportunities that might give youth less time to engage in delinquency. Loss of economic resources in single-parent families may also be associated with moves to lower-income neighborhoods which may, in turn, also place youth at higher risk for delinquent behavior."[27]

The research literature is quite clear on the effects of poverty; the strongest predictor of adolescent "outcomes" (e.g., overall well-being, school achievement, etc.) is that of family income.[28] Urie Bronfenbrenner, who has written a great deal about families, provides a succinct summary of the effects of poverty.

> The developmental risks associated with a one-parent family structure are relatively small . . . in comparison with those involved in two other types of environmental contexts. The first and most destructive of these is poverty. Because many single-parent families are also poor, parents and their children are in double jeopardy. But even when two parents are present, research in both developed and developing countries reveal that in households living under stressful economic and social conditions, processes of parent-child interaction and environmentally oriented child activity are more difficult to initiate and to sustain.[29]

If the head of a single-parent household is a woman, the chances are even greater that the family will be poor (see chapter 8). One study concluded that there were three "maternal factors" associated with the chance of a child living in poverty and a child being in the lower half of his or her class at school.[30] These factors were that the mother (1) never finished high school, (2) was not married to the child's father, and (3) had the child when she was a teenager. Among children between the ages of 7 and 12, the probability was that 79% would be living in poverty and that 58% would be in the bottom half of the class in school if all three factors were present. As the number of factors present decreased, so did the probabilities. Thus, among those with two of these factors present, the probability of being poor and in the bottom half of their school class was .48 and .53 respectively. For those with only one factor present, the percentages were .26 and .47. For those whose mothers finished high school, were married to the child's father, and gave birth at age 20 or older (i.e., zero factors were present), the percentages were .08 and .30. A more recent study, based on data from a large survey, confirms that attachment to the mother was the most important factor related to delinquency.[31]

To be sure, research indicates that when the mother, or some other adult committed to the child's well-being, does manage to establish and maintain a pattern of progressive reciprocal interaction, the disruptive impact of poverty on development is significantly reduced. Unfortunately, the proportion of parents who are able to provide quality care despite their stressful life circumstances is not very large. Even for those who are successful, the buffering effect of parents can decline sharply by the time children reach the ages of five or six and are exposed to impoverished and disruptive settings outside the home.

Family Relationships

The term "family relationships" usually refers to parental interaction, affection, supervision, and discipline. One of the original studies by the Gluecks found that four family factors strongly predicted, at an early age, which males would most likely become a delinquent, excluding the broken home factor.

1. Overly strict, erratic, threatening, or lax discipline by parents;

2. Low parental supervision;

3. Parental rejection/lack of affection toward the child;

4. Weak emotional attachment to the parents or the overall *cohesiveness* of the family.[32]

A reanalysis of the original statistics, using more modern statistical procedures, found that the variables that best explained delinquency were: erratic punishment by the father, erratic punishment by the mother, mother's supervision, parental rejection of the child, and the emotional attachment to the parent.[33]

A long-term study in St. Louis found that poor supervision and poor discipline were strong predictors of delinquency, in addition to antisocial or alcoholic parents.[34] The study also noted that if parents have criminal or juvenile delinquent records, the children usually will follow the same pattern. In London, a longitudinal study began in 1961 and 1962 with 411 boys between the ages of 8 and 9 and continued until they reached their 20s. The *best early-life predictors* included harsh or erratic discipline; a cruel, passive, or neglecting attitude on the part of the parents; poor supervision; and conflict within the family. Delinquents came from families where parenting skills were negligible. Low family income was the strongest predictor for the most frequent offenders (65% versus 18% of the non-offenders and 28% of the occasional offender).[35]

In a study that took place near Chicago, researchers conducted interviews with 2,000 parents of children around the age of 13. Parents' lack of knowledge about their children's friends and the use of physical punishment were strongly related to delinquency. However, the variable that was the most significantly related was the *attachment* between parent and child—the closer the reported relationship, the lower the delinquency.[36] Recall the importance of attachment in control/social bond theory discussed in chapter 7.

Joan McCord studied a sample of 250 delinquent and nondelinquent youth from the early 1940s through the 1970s.[37] She found that the best predictor for delinquency was *poor parental supervision*. Parental aggressiveness (e.g., harsh discipline) and conflict were found to be strong predictors of *violent crime*, but not property crime. Also, a passive or rejective attitude by the mother predicted property crime, but not violent crime. McCord also found that boys raised in a home without affectionate mothers and where there was conflict were more likely to have a record regardless of whether the home was "broken" (i.e., the incidence of delinquency is lower in broken homes with affectionate mothers than in intact homes that had conflict).

Rolf Loeber and Magda Stouthamer-Loeber identified four models of family functioning that relate to delinquency.[38]

1. *The neglect model* focuses on parent–child and child–parent involvement and parental supervision. Poor supervision and spending little time with children are the specific behaviors that *best* predict delinquency.

2. *The conflict model* focuses on discipline practices and parent–child and child–parent rejection. *Rejection* best predicts *serious* forms of delin-

quency, although inconsistent and overly strict physical discipline is strongly predictive of delinquency.

3. *The parental deviance and attitudes model* focuses on parental criminality and deviant attitudes and whether parents approve of, ignore, or encourage a child's deviance. *Parental criminality is one of the strongest predictors of serious delinquency.*

4. *The disruption model* focuses on marital conflict (including disagreements about how to raise the kids, thus resulting in inconsistent parenting) and the absence of one or both parents. Conflict is more strongly related to delinquency than a broken home per se.

In many families several of these models may be operating simultaneously (e.g., there could be both neglect and conflict), which is a stronger predictor of delinquency. These *interaction* variables increase over time in their capacity to predict persistent delinquency; in other words, the longer these problems persist and go untreated, the greater will be the likelihood of persistent delinquency.

A survey of over 900 youth in a Midwestern city concluded that there were several different patterns of family interaction that can have varying impacts on self-reported delinquency.[39] Indirect patterns include emotional and communicative factors, and direct problems include control and supervision. The most delinquent youths were those who had the most conflict with their parents. The conflicts often concerned the youths' choice of friends.

The research is firm on one point: the "socializing variables," such as lack of parental supervision, parental rejection, and parent–child involvement are the most powerful predictors. To be more specific, *affection, supervision*, and *discipline* are the three key variables that best predict delinquency. In general the parents of the most persistently delinquent youths have either (1) not cared or (2) even if they cared, did not have the time or energy to monitor the children's behavior, or (3) even if they cared and monitored, they did not see anything wrong with the deviant conduct, or (4) even if they did all of these, they may not have had the inclination or the means to apply sanctions to the behavior. Overall, weak family control over the behavior of children has been found to be the *most consistent* variable that distinguishes between delinquents and nondelinquents in countries as far ranging as the U.S., Japan, Sweden, and Ghana.[40]

Youths with the least amount of parental supervision during the after-school hours (police arrest data report the highest number of delinquent acts during these hours) have the highest rates of delinquency.[41] One study specifically found that low parental monitoring (supervision) of their children was associated with higher levels of delinquency, especially violent offenses, along with drug abuse and vulnerability to peer pressure.[42] The level of familial communication is also related to delinquency; families with the poorest level of communication produce the most delinquents.[43]

David Olson, Candyce Russell, and Douglas Sprenkle developed the circumplex model based on the assumption that cohesion and adaptability determine whether a family is "functional" or "dysfunctional."[44] Researchers designate families that have the greatest amount of affection toward their children and who have the highest degree of supervision and discipline as "cohesive" families.[45]

Monique Matherne summarizes cohesion and adaptability as follows:

> Cohesion refers to the level of attachment and emotional bonding between family members. There are four graded levels to the cohesion dimension: disengaged, separated, connected, and enmeshed. Families that are disengaged lack closeness and/or loyalty, and are characterized by high independence. At the other end of the scale of cohesion are families identified as enmeshed. These families are characterized by high levels of closeness, loyalty, and/or dependency. Adaptability is defined as the ability of the family to change in power structure, roles, and relationships in order to adjust to various situational stressors. It, too, has four graded levels: rigid, structured, flexible, and chaotic. Families with low levels of adaptability are considered rigid. Rigid family types are characterized by authoritarian leadership, infrequent role modification, strict negotiation, and lack of change. Families with high levels of adaptability are considered chaotic. Chaotic family types manifest a lack of leadership, dramatic role shifts, erratic negotiation, and are characterized by excessive change.[46]

Family cohesion is necessary for learning healthy social skills. Studies have consistently shown that attachment to one's parents is especially crucial; this affects the friendships formed by adolescents, which in turn relates to levels of delinquency. Even when adolescents are with their peers, those who are strongly attached to their parents often find that the parents are "psychologically present."[47] A balance between cohesion and adaptability creates more positive communication, which is characterized by empathy, supportiveness, and "reflective listening" among family members.[48] The lack of cohesiveness often leads to child abuse.[49]

Most of the family variables discussed impact delinquency rates for all racial groups. Within Hispanic families, there are two elements of family life that strongly relate to delinquency: family solidarity and familism (adherence to the *value and importance* of the family).

> The Hispanic family as a social organization wields a pattern of influence and control over its members which is effective in inhibiting delinquency among adolescents whose other background characteristics might predict delinquent involvement. Family solidarity implies the effectiveness of internal controls in creating patterns of conventional behavior. Deviations from conventional behavior toward delinquent acts activate the mechanism of influence in the high-solidarity family to bring the adolescent back to acceptable behavior.[50]

In his study of inner-city Puerto Rican youths in the South Bronx youths, Edward Pabon found that the least delinquent youths spent more time with family members in the evenings and on weekends. Consistent with Hirschi's control theory, Pabon concluded that "the more time the youth was preoccupied in activities (i.e., playing, talking, or working) with family members in the evening or on weekends, the less the opportunity for involvement in delinquency behavior."[51]

Parenting Styles

Researchers have identified four types of *parenting styles*. The *authoritarian* is characterized by high demands on children and low responsiveness to their needs. Authoritarian parents are very rigid and controlling with an emphasis on punishment or the threat of punishment to make children behave in a certain way. The *authoritative style* is characterized by high expectations, firm enforcement of rules and standards, and open communication with children. These parents do not constantly use punishment to achieve results, and they try to listen to their children and understand what is going on in their lives. The *permissive/indulgent style* is more of a "laissez faire" approach; rules are either nonexistent or inconsistently enforced. Methods of discipline are more passive, and parents make few demands on their children, giving them too much freedom to do as they please.[52] The *disengaged/indifferent style* involves parents who are unresponsive to their children and only minimally demanding of them. Children from such families are virtually ignored "except when they make demands, which are usually responded to with hostility and explosions."[53]

Children from families with authoritative styles are the least delinquent, and they do the best in school.[54] This style of parenting has been found to be associated with "better psychological development, school grades, greater self-reliance, and lower levels of delinquent behavior among adolescents."[55] Youths from authoritarian and permissive families tend to have the highest rate of delinquency. Social class affects the type of parenting style. In general, the lower the social class, the greater the likelihood of authoritarian styles.[56]

An interesting study was conducted in Chicago that focused on families and their children in ghetto areas.[57] The researchers compared mothers of children who were "high achievers" with the mothers of "low achievers." Mothers of high achievers emphasized developing their children's inner sense of self-direction, motivation, and trust in their own judgment, "rather than assuming that children are incapable of self-guidance and in need of unremitting control." They also emphasized "cooperation, consideration, and sharing responsibilities."[58] The mothers of the low achievers were concerned mostly with control and believed that the child should obey the authority of adults. They were overly protective about keeping their children out of trouble and shielding them from outside threats, rather than encouraging their children to strive for personal growth. Mothers of low achievers praised "constraint, withdrawal, non-engagement with others or, in some cases, aggregative alienation of others."[59] Their children tended to develop a hesitancy to take on difficult challenges, were easily discouraged, and tended to perform badly in school, all of which led to higher rates of delinquency. Elijah Anderson refers to the influences of two polar extremes of parenting as the "code of the streets" (see chapter 3).

The Social Context of the Family

What the majority of researchers have neglected to emphasize is that the family, including all that occurs within it, can be viewed as both an independent and dependent variable. By this we mean it is usually assumed that the family exists independently of the surrounding social, economic, and political environment. The ability of the family to function properly can certainly be a cause of delinquency, but it can also be the *result* of many factors outside of the family.

Conservative writers appear to see the material disadvantages suffered by a family and the quality of family life itself as mutually exclusive explanations.[60] In an earlier era the Gluecks believed that what went on within the family was more influential than what went on outside of the family. According to Elliott Currie this is the "fallacy of autonomy." By this he means that "what goes on inside the family can usefully be separated from the forces that affect it from the outside: the larger social context in which families are embedded for better or for worse."[61]

Beginning in the early 1800s writers and researchers have continuously placed the blame for delinquency on the family, which in the majority of instances has been the poor immigrant family or a minority family living in a depressed neighborhood. Parents in these families have always been viewed as "defective" or "unfit," as if the problems they had parenting were not at all shaped by outside forces, such as poverty, poor housing, lack of educational and work opportunities, etc. Even common sense would tell you that one's ability to be an effective parent depends on a number of outside factors. Can anyone argue that being a parent is just as easy for a single mother with three children living in public housing with a high crime rate as it is for a working mother living with her working husband in a middle-class suburb with a low crime rate?

While it is true that lax or overly harsh discipline and poor supervision are strongly predictive of delinquency, the question rarely asked is why do some parents employ harsh methods or ignore their children? The corollary question is whether social class affects such behaviors. A study in England compared a group of families in the inner city and a group in the suburbs. Those in the inner city had a higher level of what the author called "severe social handicaps." These included poor jobs, high rates of unemployment, large families, chronic stress, physical and mental disabilities among family members, and often permanent conditions of poverty. These parents were found to have "lax discipline" and "poor supervision." Blaming the parents for laxness and poor supervision without examining the social conditions does not provide insight into the problem.[62]

One study that did analyze environmental factors was a self-report instrument that focused on the family backgrounds of 98 violent delinquents in four major cities (Memphis, Boston, Newark, and Phoenix).[63] Most of these youths were black (73%), while 19% were white and 8% were Hispanic. In 42% of the families, there was violence between the parents; 32% of the parents hit the youths, mostly with some sort of object. About 40% of the parents had been arrested, 17% for a violent crime. In 44% of the cases, a sibling also had an arrest record, with 20% being arrested for a violent crime. Clearly violence was a pattern in these families.

Social environmental factors outside of the family were even stronger predictors than family factors, with delinquency among one's peers ranking first, followed by violence among peers, and property crimes by peers. Next in order came a youth's perceptions of work opportunities in the area, school integration (the extent of their bonds to the school), and whether or not they had committed a crime at school. Other factors correlated with delinquency were family physical health (the poorer the health, the higher the rate of delinquency), and whether or not the family was involved in cultural activities. The authors conclude that the role of the family as far as violent crime is concerned is not nearly as significant as what occurs outside of the family. Especially important are peer groups and the school. When violent or other antisocial acts are considered normal outside the family (e.g., among peers), families may not be able to prevent youths from being influenced.[64] The authors stress that most of these families live in high-crime neighborhoods where local institutions are weak. The fact that the majority of the families are poor means that they lack resources to be a positive force in preventing delinquency, especially violence.

Research has always documented the strong association between the behaviors of one's peer group and delinquency. As predicted by Sutherland's "differential association" theory (see chapter 7), strong and persistent association with delinquent peers will lead to greater delinquent involvement. However, this relationship can be mediated by strong family bonds and especially parental supervision.[65]

A unique study examined the relationship between delinquency and family poverty in connection with poverty rates within the surrounding community. The study found that delinquency rates were highest for families living in a communities with high rates of poverty and lower for families whose incomes were beneath the poverty level but living in communities with lower rate of poverty. Specifically, the study concluded that: "At high levels of community poverty (one standard deviation above the mean), the positive effect of family poverty on delinquency more than doubles; when community poverty is two standard deviation units above its mean, this effect more than quadruples."[66]

Discussions about the decline of "traditional family values" typically translate into: mom should stay home, dad should work, and the kids should receive the "proper" amount of "punishment" for their misdeeds. Some have even argued that working mothers are a major cause of crime, which is without any foundation in fact. The evidence strongly supports the opposite: children whose mothers work are *less* delinquent, *except in cases where wages are extremely low and low-cost child care is unavailable.* Children of working mothers are "not significantly different from those of children whose mothers are not in the labor force. Moreover, even when the experiences are different, their development and educational outcome do not seem to be."[67]

In a study that sampled 4,293 youths in Canada, 39% self-reported at least one delinquent act in the year prior to the survey. The study identified five core concepts consistent across different forms of delinquency for male and female youths: 1) inconsistent and inadequate parenting; 2) history of victimization; 3) anti-social peer involvement; 4) negative school attachment; and, 5) aggression.

> Since the seminal work of Glueck and Glueck, considerable research has been conducted in the social sciences to identify factors correlated with delinquency. One of the more important findings that has emerged is the

general understanding that such factors do not operate in isolation from one another. Rather, correlates of delinquency often have additive or interactive effects that increase the risk of delinquency for youth who experience multiple factors. Moreover, many factors tend to be involved in reciprocal relationships wherein delinquency leads to further deficits in the very factors most closely associated with it. Delinquency, therefore, may perpetuate its very existence.[68]

Girl Offenders and Their Families[69]

The experiences of 10 girls who were residents of a community residential treatment program in Honolulu provide insight into the links between family and delinquency. The girls ranged in age from 12 to 17. They were an ethnically diverse group, including Native American, African American, Puerto Rican, Hawaiian, Japanese, Filipino, and Chinese. Most were from working class and poor families and had committed a variety of crimes (primarily status offenses, petty theft, and the use of illegal drugs). These behaviors were often reactions to what was occurring at home. Eight of the girls came from extremely troubled and disruptive homes. Five sets of parents had divorced; one girl had been abandoned by her mother as a child; one mother had died during childbirth; and one parent had died when the daughter was 13. Most girls reported living in a variety of places—with one parent, then another, and often with an aunt, grandparents, or other extended family members.

All 10 of the girls suffered some form of abuse. Six were sexually abused, five by a family member and one by a police officer. Physical abuse was common, with one girl reporting that her father "broke the ukulele over my head." Another girl said her mother would "whack me all over. She used to break sticks over my leg." Seven of the girls reported being thrown against walls and whipped with belts and electric cords. One father cut off his daughter's hair.

The girls in this study were ambivalent about the physical abuse, feeling on the one hand that it was wrong and on the other that it was deserved. Four of girls said that they "asked for it"—the classic "blame the victim" response. Since violence is so common in the lives of girl offenders, it often becomes difficult for them to distinguish between punishment and abuse. Abuse and violence is so ingrained in their lives that they assume it is inevitable.

The girls acknowledged having trouble dealing with divorce, new partners of parents, deaths, and other changes in their families. These events were often cited as the cause of their personal problems and "bad" behavior. One of the girls, whose father died when she was five years old, had been living alone with her mother and younger brother until recently, when her mother entered a new relationship. Adjusting to "Mom's boyfriend" was not easy, and his presence had changed the atmosphere.

> Before I used to be good like that. Never get into trouble. But ever since she started going out with the boyfriend. . . . He the kind like boss us around and tryin' to make like he our father. And he started doing that and I got

mad and I never used to go home after school, just be with my friends then, get in trouble. Then I went run away.

A similar story was heard from another girl, whose parents divorced when she was 15. She had a long criminal record and admitted to stealing cars, purses, and money; beating others; and doing drugs. She explained her decision to be "bad" as follows: "When my mom then broke up I just said, 'Well, if they're gonna do that, then I'm gonna make my own life too, 'cuz they're changing their way of life.' I guess I was trying to be like them."

A 15-year-old explained how her father's death affected her and the family's "balance," saying that her father "passed away and that's when all the problems began. Cuz I got a sister, she's like four years older than me. So now my mom pets her, and I was pet by my dad. And now my dad is not here and I don't get pet by nobody."

Some of the girls told stories about family dysfunction that traced back to their births and early childhood years. The events were said to "haunt" them or to have "screwed them up" as they tried and were still trying to make peace with difficult pasts.

The mother of one of the girls abandoned her as a child, leaving her in the care of her natural father. The mother maintained only limited contact with her, and the father died in a car accident when she was nine. She reflected on her relationship with her mother:

> In a way I hate her, and then again I love her. But I think the hate takes over more so than the love because I always remember what she did to me when she left me and stuff. She left me with my father. . . . She was sending presents to my cousins which were in the same house but she wouldn't send me nothing. Then she lies and says she's my sister. You know, she never told me 'til I was fourteen [that she was my mother].

Nine of the girls had trouble getting along with one or both parents or stepparents. They spoke of strained relationships, inability to communicate, and general frustration about their deteriorating family life. Many felt isolated. One girl said of her mother, "She can't communicate with me and I can't communicate with her. . . . We cannot sit down and talk without yelling at each other."

Several of the girls felt unaccepted and unloved by various members of their families. One 14-year-old remarked:

> She [her mother] tries to ruin my life. She gets into my business, she's real nosey. . . . She can't accept me for what I am, for what I've done. She tells me to my face she can't accept me. . . . She wants to mold me into the child she always wanted. But it's too late to mold me, I'm already molded.

A 15-year-old also sensed that her mother wanted her to be someone other than who she is. She called herself the black sheep of the family because she was often compared unfavorably to her sister.

> We're different. I mean, I'm a smoker and she's not. And my mom can't face the fact that I'm different. I keep on telling her, you know, "Eh, I'm not your miss goody-two-shoes. . . . You can't change that."

A 16-year-old runaway said: "She caters to my brother because my brother looks like her and I look like my father. And she doesn't like my father so she doesn't like me."

Detailed stories about family relationships and family history were intensely emotional, with vivid descriptions of pain and loss. Most difficult was the inability to communicate their distress to other family members, leaving the girls to deal with their problems without family support. Asked what her life would be like if things went perfectly from now on, one girl fantasized: "Things will fall into place. . . . My mom would change her whole attitude and tell me that I can be the way I am."

The girls came from families characterized by divorce, abuse, abandonment, fighting, and general unrest; relationships were strained, deteriorating, or nonexistent. They had little or no security at home and believed that the lack of support pushed them into problems with authorities. In short, their families never resembled the idealized myths discussed at the start of this chapter.

Jean Bottcher, a researcher with the California Youth Authority (CYA), also studied the family backgrounds of ten girl offenders who were wards of the CYA.[70] She found three common themes: independence at an early age, extensive free time, and the inadvertence of their crimes. "An unusual riskiness pervaded their lives. On their own with little by way of plan or purpose, their daily lives seemed especially vulnerable to event, to association, and to personal need and feeling."[71]

As early as age 10 or 11 (but no later than 14 or 15), the girls spent most of their time on their own. As is true in the vast majority of both male and female delinquents, the parents were not available to provide guidance. The girls achieved their independence in one of two ways. Some of them lived in circumstances so grim (poverty, abandonment, violence in the family, etc.) that they had no choice but to leave—or they were "thrownaways." The second group had so little structure from their parents that they simply took their freedom, usually through some form of manipulation. In either case, they had limited choices. Diane ran away from home at the age of 12 and never went back. She had experienced a lot of abuse at home ("I really don't recall a day when I didn't get hit."); her mother "liked to go out and drink." An older brother and a sister had left home or were kicked out when they were teenagers, and Diane followed the same pattern.

When Perline was five years old, her mother ran off with a boyfriend. When she was in the sixth grade, Perline left her father and went to live with her mother and stepfather; she eventually dropped out of school in the tenth grade. At the age of 15, she asked her mother if she could live with her boyfriend. Her mother said no, but Perline defied her mother and left.

At a young age these women began to spend a lot of time on their own, without any sort of adult supervision. They began cutting school, usually beginning in junior high or middle school (the majority liked elementary school, but like most delinquents and many nondelinquents had trouble adjusting to junior high or middle school). They began to use school merely as a place to gather and plan the day's activities, which consisted mostly of just "having fun" and "hanging out," which eventually evolved into using drugs and consuming alcohol. Not surprisingly, most found school an alienating experience and were suspended at least once before dropping out. They were never alone, as they always gravitated toward a group of similarly situated friends, especially a boyfriend. In time, their friends became their home and family. Perline's case was typical.

Even though her respondents were doing time for kidnapping, forcible rape, murder, robbery, and assault with a deadly weapon, Bottcher reported that "for many of these young women, crime came as a shock to them. They seemed genuinely caught off guard by the event—totally surprised."[72] They seemed to drift into criminal behavior largely because their lives were falling apart; they had difficult home situations; or they had left home.

Another study looked at the influence of parents as important predictors of disruptive behavior among young girls (ages 8 and 9). The authors found two specific domains of parenting that contributed to early disruptive behavior— low parental warmth and harsh discipline.[73] The findings about girls' antisocial behavior were similar to the findings of previous studies about boys. Harsh treatment by parents contributes to coercive parent-child interactions and models aggressive behavior. Children internalize standards for behavior through exposure to harsh interactions with parents, such as yelling, arguing, and slapping. Punitive discipline by parents can lead to displays of anger and defiance by children. The failure of parents to form a warm, supportive relationship with their children impedes the development of emotional understanding and empathy. Children do not learn to consider the feelings of others. One additional contribution of this study was its examination of outcomes of parenting practices across ethnic groups—there were no variations between African-American and European-American girls.

As can be readily seen from these studies, the family situation of delinquents is an important component of their lives and a major causative factor in their delinquency. However, as we have already noted, we cannot focus exclusively on the family as if it exists in a social vacuum. Also, we cannot assume that the parents of all delinquents did not try to do right by their children. As we see in the next section, many of these parents struggle daily against incredible odds, as they cope with the fast-changing world around them.

Gang Members and Their Families

William Brown studied the complex world of gang members and their families, interviewing and observing 79 African-American gang members and 68 of their parents/guardians in Detroit.[74] Most of the participants in Brown's study lived in apartments (77%) and houses (18%) that would be condemned in many communities. Only 29% of the gang members lived in households where both parents were present. About 40% lived in family environments with a female single parent; 13% lived with their grandparent(s); the remainder lived either with their father, sister, brother, or friend. Four gang members lived, as one participant described, "wherever I can. Today a friend's house, and tomorrow a drug house."

In about three-fourths of the dual-parent households, both parents were employed. Part-time jobs paying minimum wages without benefits were common; 63% of the households in the study had only part-time jobs. They were what Michael Harrington called the "working poor" (see chapter 8).[75] Of the 31 female single-parent households, 58% of the women were unemployed. The father of three children (one was a gang member) had two full-time, minimum wage jobs and his wife worked part-time. "I've tried to get me a full-time job," she stated, "but they ain't none around here. We only got one car, and he's [husband] got to use it because his other job is a long way from the shop."

One mother of four, whose husband had abandoned her and the children several years earlier, lived in a deteriorating two-bedroom apartment with an inefficient heating system. During one visit Brown heard gunshots very close by and jerked his head toward the window. Obviously accustomed to the sound, the woman never moved.

> I used to think about the future all the time; that was before my husband lost his job. He started drinking heavy when he couldn't find no work. Then one day he just got up and left me and these kids. I used to think someday I'd have me a house and plant a garden. I love fresh tomatoes. I wanted my kids to get what I never got—a house of their own and a good education. Well, those times is gone now. I don't think much about what they ain't got because the biggest trouble is just feeding them mouths and having them a place to sleep. . . . We manage though, but it sure ain't easy none. I ask the Lord for some help everyday. Guess He is listening because we still got a roof over our head and something to eat.

There was a sense of resignation and a feeling that her life could be worse. When asked why she never left the neighborhood, she said:

> Where do you want me to go live? I ain't got no other place to live. I ain't got no skills to get no job—at least one that can pay the bills. The only real job I ever had was working downtown once, but downtown is all gone now. Do you know someone who's going to help some old black woman with no education and has four kids? I sure don't. I live here because this is all there is.

Ten gang members lived in households where a grandparent was the primary breadwinner. In eight of these cases, most of the family income was from social security and/or very modest retirement benefits. Rather than the elderly being assisted by their children, many grandparents found themselves in a position where they were raising a second family. One elderly woman, who had lived in the same neighborhood for more than 40 years, shared her two-bedroom house with her daughter-in-law and three grandchildren.

> Both my boys is in prison, and Bobby's[76] wife and kids stay here with me because they can't live no other place. What they going to do? I can't work no more because I got a bad leg, and besides, who's going to hire an old black woman anyhow? I get my check [social security]. Kathy gets some money from the state; it sure ain't much. She can't work because she's got

these kids to take care of. I help take care of them, but I'm old and can't do it by myself. Besides there ain't no jobs around here and we ain't got no car. We are doing the best we can do. I don't know what's going to happen to us. Engler [governor of Michigan] say he's going to cut welfare some more. If he do then I don't know what's going to happen. Sometimes I think that dying is about all that's left to do. But who is going to help Kathy with them kids if I ain't here? That oldest boy is a handful now. He's good to me and his mother though. He runs wild but I understand. He ain't got much else to do. There ain't no job for him. I worry about him all the time. He going to end up like his daddy—in prison some day. It's going to happen I tell you.

Bobby, who once was a member of a gang in this neighborhood, was prosecuted and convicted on auto theft and drug charges. He was sentenced to 5 years and 15 years (consecutively). In response to Brown's question about her husband, the woman replied:

Them boys' daddy was a good man. He bought this house for us when he worked at General Motors. We had a real good life then. Well, he killed himself off working all kinds of jobs when he got laid off from the plant. He managed to pay for this house before he died—God bless him. My boys was always mad about what happened to their daddy. Now I see Johnny mad about his daddy being taken away from him. He's running with the same crowd his daddy ran with.

All adult family members expressed concern about their children's, or grandchildren's, involvement in youth gangs. Most attempted to control their children's activities. "I tell him all the time to stay away from them kind of kids," said one mother. A father stated, "I don't like him running wild out there, but we [including his wife] both got jobs. We just can't watch him all the time." Another concerned parent said,

I do the best I can do to get him to stay in school. I work hard, but, as you can see, I don't seem to get nowhere. He's not dumb. He can see that this family is never going to get ahead. He respects me and his little sister, but he knows that what I am doing ain't getting his family nowhere.

One father admitted, "I beat the hell out of him when I found out he was banging. But he keeps right on doing it. I can't just keep beating him—then they'll come and arrest me." Another father stated, "I try to tell him that he's going to end up dead or in prison some day. He just won't listen. I want him to get a job, but there ain't none around. I'm lucky to be working myself." One grandmother said,

I know he is in a gang. I ain't dumb. But I also know that until all them kids lay down them guns then he's got to protect himself somehow. The police sure ain't going to protect him none. Those who is blaming the parents for these here gangs don't know much about life down here. We have to survive however we can. Them kids is surviving the only way they knows how to survive. They're just kids you know.

The parents and guardians who participated in Brown's study did not want their children to join youth gangs, nor did they encourage their children to sustain membership in the gang. Many parents actively attempted to discourage their children's gang involvement. They were, however, attempting to raise their children under conditions with gross limitations. Like their children, they too are realists. They realize their children's life chances outside the gang and outside the inner city are limited. This realization comes, in part, from their own futile attempts to forge a better life.

Children with Parents in Prison

Remember the reference above to the fact that a father of a child was in prison and that the grandmother was worried that the grandson was associating with the same type of acquaintances as his father had before him? This is an important point. One of the strongest predictors of whether or not a child will become a chronic delinquent is parental criminality, especially if a parent has spent time in jail or prison.[77] Almost 1,707,000 children (2.3% of the children in the United States) have a parent in prison.[78] There are racial disparities: one out of every 15 black children has a parent in prison compared to just one out of 110 white children and one in 41 Hispanic children.[79] The number of children with parents in prison severely underestimates the number of children facing problems because of parental involvement in the criminal justice system. On any given day, there are more than 7 million adults somewhere in the criminal justice system: prison, jail, on probation or parole.[80] Let us assume for the sake of argument that these individuals, on average, each have one child (some have more than one and others have none). This means that about 7 million children have witnessed a parent arrested and taken into custody at least once (i.e., placed in jail)—a very traumatic experience.[81]

The problem has grown worse because the population of women in prison has grown more rapidly than men in recent years. Their incarceration rate has increased by around 750% (from 8 per 100,000 to 68) during the past 30 years. The number of children under 18 with a mother in prison increased 131% since 1991, while the number with a father in prison increased 77%. In 2009 there were 113,462 women in prison.[82] Of the 147,400 children with mothers in prison, 45% had a white mother, 30% had a black mother, and 19% a Hispanic mother. Mothers most commonly (43%) identified the child's grandmother as the current caregiver, followed by the father (37% versus 88% of fathers who identified the child's mother), and other relatives (23%). Mothers were five times more likely to report that their children were in foster care, an agency, or an institution. Between 6% and 10% of women in prison are pregnant. Many of these women will lose custody of their children.[83]

While the numbers of incarcerated mothers are increasing, the fact remains that 92% of the parents in prison are male (40% black, 30% white, and 20% Hispanic). The nation's prisons held 744,200 fathers (compared with 65,600 mothers). The impacts are broad and long lasting. One study noted that there is an effect on gender norms in communities where the incarceration rates are extremely high, resulting in very skewed gender ratios of many more women than men. This in turn "produces an environment in which men and women are more likely to have children by multiple partners and children are less likely to live in households with their fathers present."[84]

One study suggests that parental incarceration, along with the crimes and arrests that precede it, "cause chaos in the lives of these children, including traumatic separations and erratic shifts from one caregiver to another. Most children with incarcerated parents live in poverty before, during, and after their parents' incarceration."[85] This in turn is an additional causative factor in delinquency. Children of incarcerated parents

> experience a broad range of emotions, including fear, anxiety, anger, sadness, loneliness, and guilt. They may exhibit low self-esteem, depression, and emotional withdrawal from friends and family. They may also begin to act out inappropriately, become disruptive in the classroom, or engage in other antisocial behaviors. Often, their academic performance deteriorates and they develop other school-related difficulties. These emotional and behavioral difficulties have been linked to a variety of factors, including the stress of parent-child separation, the child's identification with the incarcerated parent, social stigma, and attempts to deceive children about their parents' incarceration.[86]

Another study outlined additional problems for children whose parent is absent because of incarceration.

> While parental absences can occur through marital separation or even death, the removal of a parent through incarceration creates unique stressors in a child's life, many of which go unnoticed to the outside world. The stigma and shame associated with parental incarceration makes identifying children of incarcerated parents difficult for schools and social service agencies. Children of incarcerated parents are also subject to significant uncertainty and instability, as many incarcerated parents repeatedly cycle in and out of prison. Moreover, while most children have a means of personal contact with a parent who is absent because of marital separation, the barriers to communication between a child and his or her incarcerated parent are tremendous and are complicated by the fact that caregivers may be reluctant to facilitate such contact.[87]

It should be noted that it is hard to disentangle the effects of incarceration from other factors that existed long before a parent went to prison.

> One major challenge confronting researchers is disentangling the effects of parental incarceration from the effects of other factors that could have existed long before incarceration, such as child maltreatment, parental use of alcohol or drugs, parental mental illness, and domestic violence.[88]

The risk of child abuse and neglect may be exacerbated during and after the incarceration of parents.

> Prior to an incarceration, a parent's criminal justice involvement may be symptomatic of family problems or issues that prevent the parent from providing appropriate care. During a parent's incarceration, children may be at risk if placed with caregivers who are unwilling or unable to provide appro-

priate care. When a parent is released, the stresses associated with community and family reintegration may also increase the risk of abuse or neglect.[89]

As vital social services are cut in virtually every state, the juvenile justice system, along with the child welfare system, become the last resort—and often the first resort—in dealing with problems. This situation will continue to grow as the incarceration rates continue to rise.

Summary

The family is one of the most crucial institutions in human existence, but in U.S. society it is often troubled. High divorce rates and high rates of domestic violence provide the starkest evidence. Several myths about the U.S. family continue to survive, such as the myth of a harmonious unit and its breakup as one of the leading causes of most social problems in the country. In reality, the cause works in the opposite direction, as important social changes have had very negative impacts on the family, not the least of which is the growing inequality of wealth. Families at the bottom of the social class ladder are suffering from severe economic hardships.

Various problems associated with the family are linked to delinquency, as many years of social science research demonstrate. Both the structure of the family and the quality of relationships within the family are causative factors in delinquency. The authoritarian style of parenting is the most likely to cause high rates of delinquent behavior. Socializing variables, especially the degree of supervision and the extent of parental involvement, are the most powerful predictors of delinquency. The family should not be viewed as an "independent variable" causing delinquency; rather it is also a dependent variable affected by various outside forces. The family context looms as a crucial element for girls and gang members. A final critical factor in delinquency is having one or more parents involved in criminal activities, especially if sentenced to prison. Millions of children, particularly black children, are growing up with one or more parents (especially fathers) serving time in a jail or prison.

NOTES

[1] Based on census and other sources. There is some debate as to the accuracy of this figure, but the range is 35%–55%. The latest figures show the U.S. with the highest rate in the world at 49.5%: http://www.nationmaster.com/graph/peo_div_rat-people-divorce-rate. According to the National Vital Statistics System the divorce rate as of 2009 was 36%, but this excludes several states, such as California, which did not provide data.

[2] U.S. Department of Health and Human Services, Administration for Children and Families, Administration on Children, Youth and Families, Children's Bureau (2010). *Child Maltreatment, 2008*. Retrieved from http://www.acf.hhs.gov/programs/cb/stats_research/index.htm#can

[3] Ibid.

[4] Snyder, H. and M. Sickmund (2006, March). *Juvenile Offenders and Victims: 2006 National Report*. Washington, DC: Office of Juvenile Justice and Delinquency Prevention, p. 33. Retrieved from http://ojjdp.ncjrs.gov/ojstatbb/nr2006/downloads/NR2006.pdf

[5] *Child Maltreatment, 2008.*

[6] Federal Bureau of Investigation (2010, September). *Crime in the United States, 2009.* Retrieved from http://www2.fbi.gov/ucr/cius2009/offenses/expanded_information/homicide.html

[7] Centers for Disease Control and Prevention (2011). *Understanding Intimate Partner Violence: Fact Sheet.* http://www.cdc.gov/violenceprevention/pdf/IPV_factsheet-a.pdf

[8] See Coontz, S. (1992). *The Way We Never Were: American Families and the Nostalgia Trap.* New York: Basic Books.

[9] Eitzen, D. S., and M. B. Zinn (2004). *In Conflict and Order: Understanding Society* (10th ed.). Boston: Allyn & Bacon, pp. 428–29.

[10] Chesney-Lind, M. and R. G. Shelden (2004). *Girls, Delinquency and Juvenile Justice* (3rd ed.). Belmont, CA: Wadsworth.

[11] Eitzen and Zinn, *In Conflict and Order,* p. 430.

[12] Ray, R., and J. Schmitt (2007, May). "No-Vacation Nation." Center for Economic Policy Research. Retrieved from http://www.cepr.net/documents/publications/2007-05-no-vacation-nation.pdf

[13] Anderson, G. T. (2003, October 9). "Should America Be France?" Retrieved from http://money.cnn.com/2003/10/06/pf/work_less/

[14] Belkin, L. (2010, February 1). "The Fight for Paid Maternity Leave." Retrieved from http://parenting.blogs.nytimes.com/2010/02/01/the-fight-for-paid-maternity-leave/; see also Institute for Women's Policy Research (2007, August). "Maternity Leave in the United States." http://iwpr.org/pdf/parentalleaveA131.pdf

[15] Brown, H. (2009, May). "U.S. Maternity Leave Benefits Are Still Dismal." *Forbes.* Retrieved from http://www.forbes.com/2009/05/04/maternity-leave-laws-forbes-woman-wellbeing-pregnancy.html

[16] Chomsky, N. (2002). *Understanding Power.* New York: The New Press, pp. 363–64, plus footnotes found at: www.understandingpower.com

[17] Vigil, J. D. (2010). *Gang Redux: A Balanced Anti-Gang Strategy.* Long Grove, IL: Waveland Press, pp. 7–8.

[18] Ibid., pp. 99, 101.

[19] Ibid., p. 10.

[20] Farrington, D. P. (2010). "Crime and the Family." *The Criminologist* 35: 1–6; Ellis, L., K. Beaver, and J. Wright (2009). *Handbook of Crime Correlates.* San Diego: Academic Press; Farrington, D. P. and B. C. Welch (2007). *Saving Children from a Life of Crime: Early Risk Factors and Effective Interventions.* New York: Oxford University Press.

[21] Glueck, S., and E. Glueck (1950). *Unraveling Juvenile Delinquency.* Cambridge, MA: Harvard University Press. For an update on this study see Laub, J., and R. Sampson (1988). "Unraveling Families and Delinquency: A Reanalysis of the Gluecks' Data." *Criminology* 26: 355–80. See also: Loeber, R., and M. Stouthamer-Loeber (1986). "Family Factors as Correlates and Predictors of Juvenile Conduct Problems and Delinquency." In M. Tonry and N. Morris (Eds.), *Crime and Justice: An Annual Review of Research.* Chicago: University of Chicago Press.

[22] Fenwick, C. R. (1982). "Juvenile Court Intake Decision Making: The Importance of Family Affiliation." *Journal of Criminal Justice* 10: 443–53.

[23] Wilkinson, K. (1980). "The Broken Home and Delinquent Behavior: An Alternative Interpretation of Contradictory Findings." In T. Hirschi and M. Gottfredson (Eds.), *Understanding Crime: Current Theory and Research.* Beverly Hills, CA: Sage.

[24] Rankin, J. (1983). "The Family Context of Delinquency," *Social Problems* 30: 466–79.

[25] Wells, L. E. and J. H. Rankin (1991). "Families and Delinquency: A Meta-Analysis of the Impact of Broken Homes." *Social Problems* 38: 87–88. A "meta-analysis" is where a researcher examines a large number of studies in order to arrive at some general conclusions of what these studies, taken together, may tell us.

[26] Killian, S. (1977). "Family Structure and the Mental Health of Children." *Archives of General Psychiatry* 34: 1012–22; Killian, S. (1982). "The Long-term Evaluation of Family Structure of Teenage and Older Mothers," *Journal of Marriage and the Family* 44: 539–54.

[27] Mack, K. Y., M. J. Leiber, R. A. Featherstone, and M. A. Monserud (2007). "Reassessing the Family-Delinquency Association: Do Family Type, Family Processes, and Economic Factors Make a Difference?" *Journal of Criminal Justice* 35: 51–67.

[28] Commission on Behavioral and Social Sciences and Education. (1993). *Losing Generations: Adolescents in High-Risk Settings*. Washington, DC: National Academy Press, p. 48.

[29] Quoted in Ibid., pp. 49–50.

[30] Lerner, R. M. (1994). *America's Youth in Crisis*. Thousand Oaks, CA: Sage, p. 9.

[31] Mack et al., "Reassessing the Family-Delinquency Association," p. 53.

[32] Glueck and Glueck, *Unraveling Juvenile Delinquency*.

[33] Laub and Sampson, "Unraveling Families and Delinquency"; Sampson, R. J. and J. H. Laub (1994). "Urban Poverty and the Family Context of Delinquency: A New Look at Structure and Process in a Classic Study." *Child Development* 65: 523–40.

[34] Robins, L. N. (1966). *Deviant Children Grown Up*. Baltimore: Williams and Wilkins.

[35] West, D. and D. P. Farrington (1977). *The Delinquent Way of Life*. London: Heinemann; and West, D. and D. P. Farrington (1973). *Who Becomes Delinquent?* London: Heinemann.

[36] Rosenbaum, J. (1989). "Family Dysfunction and Delinquency." *Crime and Delinquency* 35: 31–44; Gove, W. R. and R. Crutchfield (1982). "The Family and Juvenile Delinquency," *Sociological Quarterly* 23: 301–19.

[37] McCord, J. (1983). "A Forty Year Perspective on Effects of Child Abuse and Neglect." *Child Abuse and Neglect* 7; and McCord, J. (1979). "Some Child-Rearing Antecedents of Criminal Behavior in Adult Men." *Journal of Personality and Social Psychology* 37: 1477–86.

[38] Loeber and Stouthamer-Loeber, "Family Factors as Correlates and Predictors."

[39] Cernkovich, S. and P. Giordano (1987). "Family Relationships and Delinquency." *Criminology* 16: 295–321.

[40] Ibid.; Commission on Behavioral and Social Sciences and Education, *Losing Generations*.

[41] Flannery, D. J., L. L. Williams, and A. T. Vazsony (1999). "Who Are They With and What Are They Doing? Delinquent Behavior, Substance Use, and Early Adolescents After School Time." *American Journal of Orthopsychiatry* 69: 247–53.

[42] Ibid.

[43] Clark, R. and G. Shields (1997). "Family Communication and Delinquency." *Adolescence* 32: 81–92.

[44] Olson, D., C. Russell, and D. Sprenkle (1979). "Circumplex Model of Marital and Family Systems II: Empirical Studies and Clinical Intervention." In J. Vincent (Ed.), *Advancement in Family Intervention, Assessment, and Theory*. Greenwich, CT: JAI Press, cited in Matherne, M. M. (2001). "Family Environment as a Predictor of Adolescent Delinquency." *Adolescence* (Winter). Retrieved from http://www.findarticles.com/p/articles/mi_m2248/is_144_36/ai_84722691

[45] Cashwell, C. S. and N. A. Vacc (1996). "Family Functioning and Risk Behaviors: Influences on Adolescent Delinquency." *School Counselor* 44: 105–14.

[46] Matherne, "Family Environment as a Predictor of Adolescent Delinquency."

[47] Warr, M. (1993). "Parents, Peers, and Delinquency." *Social Forces* 72: 247–64; Matlack, M. E., M. S. McGreevy, Jr., R. E. Rouse, C. Flatter, and R. F. Marcus (1994). "Family Correlates of Social Skill Deficits in Incarcerated and Nonincarcerated Adolescents." *Adolescence* 29: 117–32.

[48] Matlack et al., "Family Correlates of Social Skill Deficits."

[49] Mollerstrom, W. W., M. A. Patchner, and J. S. Milner (1992). "Family Functioning and Child Abuse Potential." *Journal of Clinical Psychology* 48: 45–54.

[50] Pabon, E. (1998). "Hispanic Adolescent Delinquency and the Family: A Discussion of Sociocultural Influences." *Adolescence*. Retrieved from http://www.findarticles.com/p/articles/mi_m2248/is_132_33/ai_53870308

[51] Ibid.

[52] Baumrind, D. (1991). "The Influence of Parenting Style on Adolescent Competence and Substance Use." *Journal of Early Adolescence* 11: 56–95.

[53] Commission on Behavioral and Social Sciences and Education, *Losing Generations*, p. 53.

[54] Dryfoos, J. G. (1990). *Adolescents at Risk: Prevalence and Prevention*. New York: Oxford University Press, p. 88.

[55] Commission on Behavioral and Social Sciences and Education, *Losing Generations*, p. 53.

[56] Loeber and Stouthamer-Loeber, "Family Factors as Correlates and Predictors." A more recent study found that a punishing style of parenting (which the authors placed under the category of "neglectful parenting") was more predictive of serious delinquency. Hoeve, M., A. Blokland, J. S.

Dubas, R. Loeber, J. R. M. Gerris, and P. H. van der Laan (2007). "Trajectories of Delinquency and Parenting Styles." *Journal of Abnormal Psychology* 36: 223–35.

[57] Scheinfeld, D. H. (1983). "Family Relationships and School Achievement among Boys of Lower-Income Black Families." *American Journal of Orthopsychiatry* 53, 1.

[58] Currie, E. (1985). *Confronting Crime.* New York: Pantheon, p. 201.

[59] Ibid., p. 202.

[60] Wilson, J. and R. Herrnstein (1985). *Crime and Human Nature: The Definitive Study of the Causes of Crime.* New York: Simon and Schuster; Wilson, J. and R. Herrnstein (1983). "Crime and the Family." In J. Q. Wilson (Ed.), *Crime and Public Policy.* San Francisco: Institute for Contemporary Studies.

[61] Currie, *Confronting Crime.*

[62] Wilson, H. (1980). "Parental Supervision: A Neglected Aspect of Delinquency." *British Journal of Criminology* (20) 3, quoted in Currie, *Confronting Crime*, p. 198.

[63] Elliott, D., D. Huizinga, and S. Ageton (1985). *Explaining Delinquency and Drug Use.* Beverly Hills, CA: Sage.

[64] Ibid.

[65] See, for example, the following: Dishion, T. J., D. Capaldia, K. M. Spracklena, and F. Lia (1995). "Peer Ecology of Male Adolescent Drug Use." *Development and Psychopathology* 7: 803–824; Stuart, J., M. Fondacaro, S. A. Miller, V. Brown, and E. M. Brank (2008). "Procedural Justice in Family Conflict Resolution and Deviant Peer Group Involvement among Adolescents: The Mediating Influence of Peer Conflict." *Journal of Youth and Adolescence* 37: 674–84; Reitz, E., P. Prinzie, M. Deković, and K. L. Buist (2007). "The Role of Peer Contacts in the Relationship between Parental Knowledge and Adolescents' Externalizing Behaviors: A Latent Growth Curve Modeling Approach." *Journal of Youth and Adolescence* 36: 623–34.

[66] Hay, C., E. N. Fortson, D. R. Hollist, I. Altheimer, and L. M. Schaible (2007). "Compounded Risk: The Implications for Delinquency of Coming from a Poor Family that Lives in a Poor Community." *Journal of Youth and Adolescence* 36: 593–605.

[67] Ibid., p. 191.

[68] Latimer, J., S. Kleinknecht, K. Hung, and T. Gabor (2003). "The Correlates of Self-reported Delinquency: Analysis of the National Longitudinal Survey of Children and Youth." Executive Summary. Department of Justice Canada, Research and Statistics Division. Ottawa, ON. Retrieved from http://www.justice.gc.ca/eng/pi/rs/rep-rap/2003/rr03_yj2-rr03_jj2/rr03_yj2.pdf

[69] The following section is based a case study from Chesney-Lind, M. and R. G. Shelden (1997). *Girls, Delinquency and Juvenile Justice* (2nd ed.). Belmont, CA: Wadsworth, pp. 200–1. A more recent study reaffirms these findings: Chesney-Lind, M. and K. Irwin (2008). *Beyond Bad Girls: Gender, Violence and Hype.* New York: Routledge. See also: Colman, R. A., D. H. Kim, S. Mitchell-Herzfeld, and T. A. Shady (2009). "Delinquent Girls Grown Up: Young Adult Offending Patterns and Their Relation to Early Legal, Individual, and Family Risk." *Journal of Youth and Adolescence* 38: 355–66; Miller, S., R. Loeber, and A. Hipwell (2009). "Peer Deviance, Parenting and Disruptive Behavior among Young Girls." *Journal of Abnormal Child Psychology* 37: 139–52; Stefuraka, T. and G. B. Calhoun (2007). "Subtypes of Female Juvenile Offenders: A Cluster Analysis of the Million Adolescent Clinical Inventory." *International Journal of Law and Psychiatry* 30: 95–111.

[70] Bottcher, J. (1986). *Risky Lives: Female Versions of Common Delinquent Life Patterns.* Sacramento: California Youth Authority.

[71] Ibid., p. 13.

[72] Ibid., p. 34.

[73] Miller et al., "Peer Deviance, Parenting and Disruptive Behavior." See also Bradley, R. and R. Corwin (2007). "Externalizing Problems in Fifth Grade: Relations with Productive Activity, Maternal Sensitivity, and Harsh Parenting from Infancy through Middle Childhood." *Developmental Psychology* 43(6): 1390–401.

[74] Brown, W. B. (1998). "The Fight for Survival: African-American Gang Members and Their Families in a Segregated Society." *Juvenile and Family Court Journal* 49: 1–14.

[75] Harrington, M. (1984). *The New American Poverty.* New York: Penguin Books. For a more current view of the "working poor" see Shipler, D. K. (2004). *The Working Poor: Invisible in America.* New York: Knopf. See also: Mishel, L., J. Bernstein, and J. Schmitt (1999). *The State of Working America, 1998–1999.* Ithaca: Cornell University Press. In 1996, almost three-fourths (72.6%) of those living

in poverty either worked (67%) or sought work (5.5%) during the year; in 1979 only 4.2% of the workforce were "very low earners" (wages that were 25% below the poverty level); in 1997 this percentage had risen to 28.6%. See Chomsky, *Understanding Power*, ch.10, footnote 14.

[76] All names of participants in Brown's study are pseudonyms to ensure confidentiality.

[77] See Dryfoos, *Adolescents at Risk*, for a summary of some of this research. See also Gabel, K. and D. Johnston (Eds.) (1995). *Children of Incarcerated Parents*. New York: Lexington Books; Gabel, S. (1992). "Children of Incarcerated and Criminal Parents: Adjustment, Behavior, and Prognosis." *Bulletin of the American Academy of Psychiatry Law* 20: 33–45; Gaudin, J. and R. Sutphen (1993). "Foster Care vs. Extended Family Care for Children of Incarcerated Mothers." *Journal of Offender Rehabilitation* 19: 129–47.

[78] Glaze, L. E. and Laura M. Maruschak (2008, August). "Parents in Prison and Their Minor Children." Retrieved from http://bjs.ojp.usdoj.gov/content/pub/pdf/pptmc.pdf

[79] Christian, S. (2009, March). "Children of Incarcerated Parents." National Conference of State Legislatures, p. 2. http://www.cga.ct.gov/COC/PDFs/fatherhood/NCSL_ ChildrenOfIncarceratedParents_0309.pdf

[80] Glaze, L. E. and T. P. Bonczar (2010, December). "Probation and Parole in the United States, 2009." Bureau of Justice Statistics. Retrieved from http://bjs.ojp.usdoj.gov/content/pub/pdf/ ppus09.pdf

[81] This is made poignantly clear in Bernstein, N. (2005). *All Alone in the World: Children of the Incarcerated*. New York: The New Press.

[82] Sabol, W. J., H. C. West, and M. Cooper (2010, December). "Prisoners in 2009." Bureau of Justice Statistics. Retrieved from http://bjs.ojp.usdoj.gov/content/pub/pdf/p09.pdf

[83] Richie, B. E. (2002). "The Social Impact of Mass Incarceration on Women." In M. Mauer and M. Chesney-Lind (Eds.), *Invisible Punishment: The Collateral Consequences of Mass Incarceration*. New York: New Press.

[84] Braman, D. (2002). "Families and Incarceration." In Mauer and Chesney-Lind, *Invisible Punishment*.

[85] Seymour, C. and C. F. Hairston (2001). "Children with Parents in Prison: Child Welfare Policy, Program and Practice Issues." The Child Welfare League of America, p. 2.

[86] Ibid., p. 4.

[87] La Vigne, N., E. Davies, and D. Brazzell (2008). "Broken Bonds: Understanding and Assessing the Needs of Children with Incarcerated Parents." Urban Institute, Justice Policy Center. Retrieved from http://www.urban.org/UploadedPDF/411616_incarcerated_parents.pdf

[88] Christian, "Children of Incarcerated Parents," p. 2.

[89] Seymour and Hairston, "Children with Parents in Prison."

SCHOOLS AND DELINQUENCY

Study after study shows a constant correlation between years of schooling and a number of positive social and personal indicators, ranging from where you work and how much money you will earn in your lifetime to how long you will live. Many studies show that the pathway to educational success starts early in life. Children from families in higher social classes are far more likely to have "a home environment that provides the intellectual skills they need to do well in school."[1]

Chapter 8 mentioned the growing impact of globalization on employment. While higher education has always promised a number of benefits, it is even more critical today when 60.1% of all new jobs require at least some college experience.

> The education premium—the payoff for earning a degree—will grow larger. . . . America is facing a bifurcated employment future. At the top end is a highly educated, technically competent workforce attuned to the demands of the global marketplace. At the other end is a willing but underskilled group that is seeing its prospects undermined by workers in countries like China in low-end manufacturing and by a skills mismatch in emerging industries.[2]

The job recovery will be "cruelly uneven. It will favor, more than ever, the college educated over blue collar workers."[3]

As we shall see in this chapter, both social class and race are closely related to educational achievement and, at least indirectly, to rates of delinquency.

> The repercussions from stressed families carry over onto learning and schooling. Schools are next in importance to the family in social control (i.e. societal equilibrium). They also usually represent society's first opportunity to participate in the socialization and development of its children. Where the family might fail or falter, somehow the public school must fill the void in fulfilling its obligatory role in socializing all youths.[4]

Schooling in a Class Society

As noted in chapter 7, we live in a highly stratified and unequal society. Given the class and racial inequalities that exist, it should come as no surprise that one of the most important social institutions of our society plays a key role in perpetuating these inequalities. One of the goals of our educational system is a conservative one, namely, to "preserve the culture" by indoctrinating students in culturally prescribed ways.[5]

We can clearly see this goal by tracing the historical origins of schooling in the United States. Starting with compulsory school laws in the nineteenth century, we see that one of the main goals of public schooling was not so much education as social control. As noted in chapter 1, the first compulsory school law was passed in Massachusetts in 1836—creating a new category of delinquent, the "truant," and a new method of controlling youths. New York passed a similar law in 1853. The objective of these laws was that of controlling rather than educating the children of the poor. Indeed, "mass education" was set up largely to train a mostly rural workforce for manufacturing plants in the cities. However, some of the public was against this because it removed children from the farms that needed their labor.

The business community was indeed keenly interested in public education, but not for "education" in the ideal sense of the word. As one writer noted, the leaders of the business world "encouraged schools to adopt a corporate model of organization and called for the education system to more explicitly prepare workers for the labor market through testing, vocational guidance, and vocational education."[6]

Businesses found it difficult to discipline industrial workers. Attendance was irregular and turnover was high, while the tolerance for the routinization and monotony of factory work was low. Both business leaders and social reformers became, in time, convinced that the adult population was "irredeemably unfit for factory work." Therefore, they looked to public schools to instill discipline in children that would "break" the working class and train them, in the words of a factory owner, for the "habits of work discipline now necessary for factory production." Forcing children to work long hours at school at subjects that were very dull was viewed as a positive, as it "habituated, not to say naturalized" children "to labor and fatigue."[7]

One of the famous social reformers of the era, Jane Addams, was up-front about the need to train children to be obedient. She stated in 1887 that:

> The businessman has, of course, not said to himself: "I will have the public school train office boys and clerks for me, so that I may have them cheap," but he has thought, and sometimes said, "Teach the children to write legibly, and to figure accurately and quickly; to acquire habits of punctuality and order; to be prompt to obey, and not question why; and you will fit them to make their way in the world as I have made mine!"[8]

As noted in chapter 1, it can be argued that the school system ultimately meant upward mobility for some (usually those already from privileged classes), but for the majority it meant remaining in their original class position. For African Americans and other minorities the situation was worse. This was especially the case in the public schools of the South, which were patterned after a social order based on caste and class and "separate but equal."[9] Race and class background play an important role in determining the degree of success a student has in the public school system. The school system is supposed to be the "great equalizer" by giving every child the same opportunities for an education, yet works like a sifter as it weeds out those from the lower classes.[10] Middle- and upper-class children are far more likely to have various toys and books in the home that better prepare them for success in school, plus the fact that their parents are more educated and engage in such activities as reading and writing that reinforce the importance of education in both direct and indirect ways.[11]

Lest the reader think that such practices are mere relics of a long-forgotten past, Jonathan Kozol's analysis of modern schooling informs us that it is not. He quotes a principal at one school who told top executives at a power breakfast: "I'm in the business of developing minds to meet a market demand."[12] Similarly, what children learn is referred to as a "product" of the school. Children are often "regarded as investments, assets, or productive units—or else, failing that, as pint-sized human deficits who threaten our competitive capacities."[13]

In another school, Kozol observed that children in the early grades are asked to list what kind of "managers" they want to be—a program created and financially backed by a businessman in Texas. Kozol quotes a teacher who said "We want to make them understand that, in this country, companies will give you opportunities to work, to prove yourself, no matter what you've done."[14] For minority children attending inner-city schools, instead of a "school-to-work pipeline" as per the propaganda of public school officials and corporations, there is a "school-to-prison pipeline" (see discussion below). The NAACP published a sobering report on the country's overfunding of prisons and underfunding of education—"depriving our schools of resources that would help children in some of our most distressed communities—children who, without an adequate education, are at the greatest risk of becoming the next generation of prisoners."[15]

Schools as "Day Prisons"

As the above discussion makes abundantly clear, schools perform a *social control* function. Schools resemble day prisons on two planes. First, many *look like prisons* with metal detectors in the corridors. Second, there is a preoccupation with order, control, and discipline. Schools do more than teach students to take their place in a class-based society. They warehouse students to prevent flooding the labor market while simultaneously "instilling the attitudes of passivity and apprehension, which in turn induce the fear of authority and the habits of obedience."[16] The rhetoric of zero tolerance shifted the emphasis in prison practices from rehabilitation to viewing prisoners as a threat to security—demanding control, surveillance, and punishment. That same rhetoric has been extended to schools. Henry Giroux notes that there has been a "dramatic shift away from civic education—the task and responsibility of which is to prepare students for shaping and actively participating in democratic public life—to models of training and regulation."[17]

Locke High School in South Central Los Angeles provides just one example.

> Once a beacon of hope in a neighborhood blighted by the Watts riots of 1965, for too many years now Locke has been a poster child for everything wrong with education in Los Angeles' poor neighborhoods. Its kids study behind prison-like gates on a litter-strewn campus that serves as an inviting canvas for competing tagging crews. The school doesn't offer much in the way of extracurricular activities beyond its sports teams, but it is host to an on-site police station with two officers and a fully utilized open-air space for all the kids caught in its daily truancy sweeps. Reforms and programs have come and gone as quickly as the teachers and administrators assigned to implement them. The only constant has been low academic achievement.[18]

Donna Foote spent a year at Locke researching her book on Teach for America.[19] She said she never met a student who didn't want to learn, but only 2% of ninth-graders were proficient in algebra, and only 11% could read at grade level. There were 1,000 students in the class of 2005—240 graduated; only 30 were eligible to apply to a California state university.

> For every 100 students who entered the ninth grade in 2001, three graduated with what they needed to go to college. Figuring out what happened to their classmates doesn't require a high school diploma. An unacceptably high number are dead or in prison. The fact that kids at Locke—and schools like it in poor minority neighborhoods—are being denied access to a quality education is old hat to anyone familiar with the history of urban education in America.[20]

"Zero-Tolerance" Policies

Fueled by moral panics about drugs, violence, and gangs, "A national mood of fear provided legitimacy for zero-tolerance policies in the schools."[21]

> The growth and popularity of zero-tolerance policies within public schools have to be understood as part of a broader educational reform movement in which the market is now seen as the master design for all pedagogical encounters. . . . As the state is downsized and support services dry up, containment policies become the principal means to discipline youth and restrict dissent. Within this context, zero-tolerance legislation within the schools simply extends to young people elements of harsh control and administration implemented in other public spheres where inequalities breed the conditions for dissent and resistance.[22]

The Gun Free Schools Act was signed into law on October 22, 1994, as part of the Elementary and Secondary Education Act of 1994. It required school districts that receive federal funds to adopt a gun-free school policy and to expel students who carry a gun to school for one year. Many states followed that legislation with more stringent policies.

> The failure of this idea [that courts are the best place for disciplining children] is clear in New York, where zero-tolerance policies have led to arrests for gun possession on school grounds, but also for relatively minor offenses like shoving. Even nonviolent incidents—doodling, throwing food, back-

talking—have landed kids in court, where last year [2009] New York sent more than 1,400 minors (average age: less than 16) to correctional facilities. According to a series of recent reports by the Justice Department and the state Office of Children and Family Services—the institutions don't help. Nearly nine of 10 occupants commit additional crimes. It's a "school-to-prison pipeline," says Judith S. Kaye, the state's former chief judge.[23]

Many high school students walk by numerous hidden cameras and through metal detectors manned by guards when they arrive at school each morning. Once there, students are subject to random searches of their bodies and belongings. Lockers can be searched without warning with or without the student present, and in many places police will use drug-sniffing dogs during raids where they search lockers and even students' parked cars.[24]

A student who was the editor-in-chief of *Gumbo Magazine*, a youth-run publication in Milwaukee, talked about the effect of searches on students. "It violates us. Some days you'll come to school and they'll just be like, 'Take your purse off, your jacket, your backpack,' and search everything." Another student said: "I can see why they needed security, but personally I hated it. I knew I wasn't doing anything wrong, but they treat you like you are. And they don't search everybody, so it's like profiling who they pick to search."[25] Sometimes the searches are done by school staff or hired guards, other times by local police. Usually the contraband found hardly justifies the expenditure of resources. Another student complained that they "only found cell phones and pagers, never guns, maybe a few drugs here and there."

On June 16, 2011, the Supreme Court addressed protections for youths in *J.D.B. v. North Carolina*.[26] The police suspected that a 13-year-old special education student had committed neighborhood burglaries and arrived at school to question him. He was interrogated in a school conference room in the presence of school officials, but his parents were not contacted. He confessed to the crimes. Arguing that the boy was effectively in police custody when he incriminated himself, the family sought to have his confession suppressed because he was never read his Miranda rights. In December 2009, the North Carolina Supreme Court determined that he was not in custody and therefore was not entitled to Miranda warnings. The Supreme Court did not set a strict rule for what qualifies as "in custody" in a school setting. The Court did, however, say age was a critical factor in determining whether an adolescent would feel free to leave an interrogation.

Jorge Rodriguez, who was a juvenile public defender for thirteen years in Indianapolis, calls the nexus of school and law enforcement a serious gray area. He believes interrogations of juveniles in school are "frequent enough that it doesn't surprise me when it happens. We see the police using the school as an access avenue to a kid without their parents." Indiana requires a parent to be present in order for anything a juvenile says to be admissible in a court proceeding. Rodriguez says that typically the police officer will sit in the corner while the principal questions the student. Having confessed once, he or she will often repeat the confession with parents in the room—not understanding that the first confession could not be used against them in a court proceeding.

"I've seen situations where, clearly to me, [law enforcement] are using school officials and setting to circumvent the law, knowing they can't do it directly."[27]

Public schools more and more resemble "Big Brother" watching every movement. Monitoring devices have become a big business. Numerous companies have entered the market, including many that sold surveillance equipment to private prisons or GPS monitoring devices to state agencies for probationers and parolees. The use of GPS devices has been extended to schools to monitor truants. Students punch in an identification code into the GPS device. Supporters claim that the devices have helped reduce truancy. While the long-term effects are unknown, use of the technology represents another potential entry into the school-to-prison pipeline (see discussion below). If truants fail the monitoring program, they will probably be referred to juvenile court.[28] The vice president of one company said "We have so much business that we can hardly keep up with manufacturing. We're exploding."[29] In a brief Google search, the author found several companies engaging in the business of surveillance. One was called "KeepnTrack," with the motto "School Safety. Serious Business." Their website is filled with "school security solutions" such as "visitor tracking," "student tracking," "staff tracking," and "vendor tracking." The company sells a variety of accessories such as an ID scan, a laser scanner, and a "Verifi Fingerprint Reader."[30]

In addition to the cost of surveillance systems, there are concerns that security devices may be ineffective and create more problems—not the least of which is the invasion of privacy.[31] For example, the Boston suburb of Lexington installed its third security system in a middle school. The cost was $46,750, funded by a federal grant to the Lexington Police department; upkeep was projected as $5–10,000 annually.[32] Concerns about the cost of replacing property damaged by vandalism and graffiti seem to outweigh concerns about privacy. Many schools throughout the Boston area have security devices automatically installed as part of the architectural design of the schools. A staff attorney for the ACLU said government should not be watching people all of the time. "The more we make our schools like a prison, the more we get away from what I consider good education."[33]

The Nashville school system became the first in the nation to install security cameras using face-recognition technology in December 2007. Digital photos of students enrolled at the school are stored in the system. The cameras alert security when they detect a face that does not match a stored photo, including expelled or suspended students. The ACLU warned that widespread use of the devices would result in authorities being able to track movements throughout the day, and a representative of the Electronic Privacy Information Center stated "Schools should not feel like some sort of prison."[34]

The Office of Community Oriented Policing Services (COPS Office) has granted $900 million through programs like Secure Our Schools (SOS), COPS in Schools, School-Based Partnerships, and the Safe Schools Initiative. In 2010, almost $16 million in SOS grant funding was awarded to 167 law enforcement agencies "to help schools respond to growing school safety and security concerns."[35] The announcement of the availability of approximately $13 million in SOS funds in 2011 included the following:

Specifically, this program will fund up to 50% of the total cost to implement one or more of the following options: placement and use of metal detectors, locks, lighting, and other deterrent measures; security assessments; anti-violence initiatives; security training of personnel and students; coordination with local law enforcement; and/or any other measure that may provide a significant improvement in security. Applicants will be required to demonstrate a comprehensive approach to preventing school violence.[36]

Since the institution of strict zero-tolerance policies at schools around the country, students are regularly suspended or even expelled for offenses that range from the relatively minor, like minimal marijuana possession, to the truly ridiculous, like possession of a dull table knife to cut a grapefruit at lunch or taking Tylenol for a headache. Paranoid school officials and parents look for tell-tale signs of potentially violent students, including turning to an FBI "profiling software" that suggests that the following are "signs for potential shooters": "having parental troubles, disliking popular students, experiencing a failed romance, and listening to songs with violent lyrics."[37] These clues should narrow it down to around 90% of all students!

Earlier in this section, we mentioned the problems in New York. Many nonviolent offenses have resulted in custodial actions. In March 2009, a boy and a girl in sixth grade drew a line on each other's desk with an erasable marker. The teacher told them to erase the lines, and the students went to get tissues. Then security was called, and two "peace officers" (police officers assigned to the elementary school) placed handcuffs on the two children before taking them to the local precinct station. In February 2010, a 12-year-old girl at a junior high school in Queens was arrested for doodling on her desk with an erasable marker. She also was handcuffed at the school and then taken to a precinct station house. In January 2008, a 5-year-old kindergarten pupil became unruly at a public school in Queens. A public safety officer handcuffed the boy and sent him to a hospital psychiatric ward.[38] The New York Civil Liberties Union filed a suit alleging widespread mistreatment of public school students by safety officers and the police. New York City schoolchildren are often arrested, the suit charges, for minor misbehavior that might be a violation of school rules but is in no way a violation of law.

In Delaware in 2009, Zachary (6 years old) took his Cub Scout camp knife to school—something millions of kids have done over the past 100 years or so (including the author). The school disciplinary committee decided he violated their zero-tolerance policy on weapons and suspended him.[39] School officials claimed they had no choice because the policy bans all knives. Because of an increase in expulsions, state lawmakers in Delaware had tried to make disciplinary rules more flexible by giving local boards authority to decide on a case-by-case basis. "The law was introduced after a third-grade girl was expelled for a year because her grandmother had sent a birthday cake to school, along with a knife to cut it. The teacher called the principal—but not before using the knife to cut and serve the cake." Because the law mentioned only expulsions and he was suspended, Zachary was not eligible for the more flexible rules.

Nick Stuban, 15 years old, played football for Woodson High School in Fairfax County, Virginia. He helped care for his mother, who had Lou Gehrig's disease. On November 3, 2010, he purchased at school a single capsule of a legal synthetic compound that acts like marijuana. Someone told school officials, and Nick confessed. The Student Responsibilities and Rights handbook states that a first offender under the influence of cocaine or Ecstasy or alcohol at school would receive a suspension of 5 to 10 days—no expulsion, no hearing process, no school transfer. The hearing officer in Nick's case explained that under the influence is different because "that student hasn't brought anything on school grounds" that endangers others.[40] Nick was suspended immediately. He was banned from Woodson and from the weekly Boy Scout meetings, sports events, and driver's education sessions, which were held on school grounds. The rumor mill generated exaggerated versions of why he'd been suspended. The hearing took place two weeks later. Nick's parents did not hire a lawyer on the advice of a school administrator, who counseled that doing so might create a confrontational climate. The ruling of transfer to another school was issued December 14—six weeks after the incident, right before winter break.

> Over the next 11 weeks, his mistake unraveled much of what Nick held close—his life at school, his sense of identity, his connection to the second family he'd found in his football team. Nick's emotional descent was steeper than anyone imagined, and its painful finality brought light to a discipline system that many Fairfax families call too lengthy, too rigid and too hostile.[41]

Nick committed suicide on January 20, 2011.

Nancy Gibbs commented on the tragedy.

> Thus has Fairfax County become the latest to reconsider whether the edicts born of fear and Columbine actually make any sense or keep anyone safe. The original rules against drugs and knives soon swelled, with schools that once called parents now calling the police. Suddenly middle schoolers were being suspended for puddle stomping and Alka-Seltzer possession or referred to a drug awareness program for accepting a breath mint. . . . A 9-year-old perp was questioned by police about a plan to launch a spitball with a rubber band; he had to undergo psychological counseling before he could go back to class. . . . A high school sophomore was suspended for breaking the no-cell-phone rule when he took a call from his father who was serving in Iraq. A Florida honor student faced felony charges when a dinner knife—not a steak knife or a butcher knife—was found on the floor of her car, which she had parked at school. "A weapon is a weapon is a weapon," the principal said.
>
> Except it's so obviously not. Sometimes a weapon is just a dinner knife. Making distinctions is part of learning. So is making mistakes. When authorities confuse intent and accident, when rules are seen as more sacred than sense, when a contrite first-time offender is treated no differently from a serial classroom menace, we teach children that authority is deaf and dumb, that there is no judgment in justice. It undermines respect for discipline at a stage when we want kids to internalize it.[42]

Reaction to Excess

Cases like those mentioned above have convinced some parents and lawmakers that the policies have gone too far. Fred Hink founded Texas Zero Tolerance, a parents' group that urges school administrators to use common sense in disciplinary cases. Referring to Zachary's case, he said "It's almost like taking a jaywalker and throwing him into a maximum-security prison." State lawmakers in Texas in 2009 required school officials to consider intent, self-defense, past disciplinary history, and whether a child has special needs before expelling or suspending students. The state legislature in Florida prohibited school boards from expelling students or referring them to law enforcement for petty misconduct; those sanctions were reserved only for students posing a serious threat. The ACLU of Michigan criticized the state's zero-tolerance expulsion law for creating a school-to-prison pipeline. Expelled students often do not return to school, and 68% of Michigan prisoners are high school dropouts.[43]

In Georgia, students had been suspended for "kissing a girl on the forehead, wearing a studded belt, bringing a French teacher a gift-wrapped bottle of wine and carrying a Tweety Bird wallet with a chain on it." Clayton County Juvenile Judge Steve Teske said, "I don't call it 'zero tolerance,' I call it 'zero intelligence.'"[44] In 2010, the plight of one Georgia 14-year-old prompted a state senator to take action. Amanda Hensler was trying to speed the process of getting her 14-year-old son, Eli, to school on time. She threw his books into a bag on his dresser. Eli had used the bag a few days earlier to go fishing, and his 2.5-inch fishing knife was in it. Eli discovered the knife about 30 minutes after school started, and he turned it in to the principal, who called the police. The Sheriff's Office phoned Hensler and told her that she could either bring her son, Eli, to the office to surrender or they would come to get him. She drove her son to the office, where he was handcuffed, placed in the back of a patrol car, and driven 90 minutes to the Sandersville Regional Youth Detention Center. He spent the night in the detention center. Eli, who had never been in trouble before, spent the remainder of the first semester in alternative school. When he returned to his regular school the following semester, he could no longer be the water boy on the basketball team, had lost his position in the band, and could not try out for the wrestling team. He had to sign a contract that indicated any infraction could send him back to the alternative school or to the detention center.

Because of Eli's case, Senator Emanuel Jones drafted a bill to ease the zero-tolerance policy, including a requirement that a judge must hold a hearing before a student is taken into custody. "The schools turn these kids over to the judiciary and let the courts figure it out. The message must be sent: Don't be sending our kids through the judicial system for minor offenses." Teske reinforced that approach: "When I am dealing with gangbangers and kids who are breaking into homes—you're gonna ask me to worry about your school fight when I need to use my time to deal with kids who are actually scary? We need to deal with the kids we are scared of, not the kids we are mad at."[45] The bill has found bipartisan support, including the lieutenant governor who applauded its common-sense approach.

The U.S. Supreme Court also curtailed one of the most egregious zero-tolerance policies. Savana Redding was an eighth-grader in Safford, Arizona, in 2003. At the beginning of the school year, a boy became violently ill after taking pills at school. When another girl was found with several white pills in a folder, she told the vice principal that Savana gave her the pills, which were prescription-strength ibuprofen (equivalent to two Advil tablets). Savana denied giving the pills to the girl. The vice principal searched her backpack. When no pills were found, he sent her to a nurse's office. Savana was told to remove her outer clothes and to pull out her bra and underwear to check for hidden pills. Nothing was found, and the school officials did not apologize when Savana's mother confronted them about the strip search. The Reddings then filed suit, alleging a violation of Savana's rights under the Fourth Amendment, which forbids unreasonable searches by the government.[46]

Supreme Court Justice David Souter wrote:

> Savana's subjective expectation of privacy against such a search is inherent in her account of it as embarrassing, frightening, and humiliating. The reasonableness of her expectation (required by the Fourth Amendment standard) is indicated by the consistent experiences of other young people similarly searched, whose adolescent vulnerability intensifies the patent intrusiveness of the exposure. . . . The common reaction of these adolescents simply registers the obviously different meaning of a search exposing the body from the experience of nakedness or near undress in other school circumstances. Changing for gym is getting ready for play; exposing for a search is responding to an accusation reserved for suspected wrongdoers and fairly understood as so degrading that a number of communities have decided that strip searches in schools are never reasonable and have banned them no matter what the facts may be.[47]

The School-to-Prison Pipeline: Suspension and Expulsion

The examples in the previous section highlight multiple disturbing situations of zero-tolerance policies in the schools. The ACLU summarizes the potential outcomes of such policies.

> The School to Prison Pipeline is a nationwide system of local, state, and federal education and public safety policies that pushes students out of school and into the criminal justice system. This system disproportionately targets youth of color and youth with disabilities. The School to Prison Pipeline operates directly and indirectly. Schools directly send students into the pipeline through zero-tolerance policies that involve the police in minor incidents and often lead to arrests, juvenile detention referrals, and even criminal charges and incarceration. Schools indirectly push students towards the criminal justice system by excluding them from school through suspension, expulsion, and discouragement.[48]

Zero-tolerance policies are the beginning of the pipeline, as they represent a shift away from informal methods of discipline that were prevalent until very recently. Instead of being called into the principal's office, schools now rely on suspensions, citations, and arrests to maintain order; as a result, the police are often called in and charges are filed. The presumption is that suspension is reserved for serious offenses, but data reveal that suspension from school is used in response to a wide range of behavior from fighting to insubordination. Only a small percentage of suspensions are for behavior that threatens the safety or security of schools.[49]

> In response to a widespread perception that school violence was increasing dramatically, the policy of zero tolerance, mandating harsher consequences for both major and minor violations, began to be widely implemented in schools and school districts. Although subsequent data demonstrated that school violence had in fact remained stable over a twenty year period, the implementation of zero-tolerance policies led to substantial increases in the rates of out-of-school suspension and expulsion. Two categories of suspensions and expulsions have caused particular controversy at the local level: those in which students have been suspended or expelled for what seem to be trivial infractions (e.g., making a paper gun) and those where racial disparities in suspension and expulsion are clearly evident.[50]

Of the approximately 38,500 public schools, 46% invoked at least one serious disciplinary action during the 2007–2008 school year against a student. There were 767,900 serious disciplinary actions; 76% were suspensions for 5 days or more; 19% were transfers to specialized schools; and 5 percent were expulsions. The two largest categories for suspensions were insubordination (327,100 actions) and physical attacks or fights (271,800 actions).[51]

Daniel Losen and Russell Skiba researched the question of how frequently suspension is used in schools and whether there are significant differences in the frequency of suspension depending on race/ethnicity/gender. African-American children are suspended far more frequently than white children, with especially high racial differences in middle school. During a critical period in academic and social development, middle-school students are missing valuable class time. The study included a national sample of more than 9,000 middle schools; 28.3% of black males were suspended at least once during a school year—nearly three times the 10% rate for white males—and 16.3% of Hispanic males were suspended. Four percent of white females were suspended versus 18% of black females. The suspension rate for all middle-school students was 11.2%. Ninety-five percent of suspensions were for "disruptive behavior" or "other"; 5% involved weapons or drugs.[52]

> Research on student behavior, race, and discipline has found no evidence that African-American overrepresentation in school suspension is due to higher rates of misbehavior. . . . White students were referred to the office significantly more frequently for offenses that appear more capable of objective documentation (e.g., smoking, vandalism, leaving without permission, and obscene language). African-American students, however, were referred more often for disrespect, excessive noise, threat, and loitering—behaviors that would seem to require more subjective judgment.[53]

Anne-Marie Iselin reviewed the literature on suspensions and came to the same conclusions.[54] Zero-tolerance policies frequently are implemented arbitrarily and are often used to discipline minor misconduct. There is no support for the claim that suspensions improve overall school safety, but there are indications that suspensions are associated with lower academic performance, increased academic disengagement, failure to graduate on time, and higher dropout rates—as well as higher rates of antisocial behaviors and involvement in the juvenile justice system. African-American students are more likely to be disciplined more severely for minor misconduct and suspensions are often used subjectively as disciplinary actions. There is no conclusive evidence African-American students engage in more school misconduct or violent behaviors.

Nationwide, less than half of black students graduate compared to 75% of white students; this is largely attributable to being expelled and/or suspended.[55] Research on specific cities and states also reveals very high rates of suspensions and expulsions for black males. In Chicago, for instance, almost one out of every four black male students was suspended at least once during the 2008 school year, double the district average.[56] In the state of Maryland, 60% of the 72,683 students suspended were black.[57] A report called "Education on Lockdown: The Schoolhouse to Jailhouse Track" found that in three areas studied (Denver, Chicago and Palm Beach County, Florida) black and Latino students were far more likely to be suspended and expelled, regardless of other variables. In Denver, for instance, "Black and Latino students are 70% more likely to be disciplined (suspended, expelled, or ticketed) than their White peers."[58] Many other studies have arrived at similar results.[59] All of these reports cite various kinds of zero-tolerance policies in addition to subtle and not-so-subtle racism on the part of white teachers and administrators.

Texas Appleseed, a group of volunteer lawyers and other professionals, conducted a multi-year study about the intersection of school discipline and gateways to the juvenile justice system. The second of their reports, *Texas' School-to-Prison Pipeline: School Expulsion—The Path from Lockout to Dropout*, found that African Americans were disproportionately expelled. Fourteen percent of Texas public school students are African American, but 25% of expelled students are black. In comparison, whites represent 35% of public school students but only 21% of those expelled.[60] Depending on the school district in Texas, African Americans are 2 to 54 times more likely to be expelled. Seventy-one percent of all expulsions and 62% of expulsions to a Juvenile Justice Alternative Education Program (JJAEP) are discretionary. JJAEP programs are an entry into the juvenile justice system; they are operated by juvenile boards and overseen by the Texas Juvenile Probation Commission. They were originally designed for students who committed a criminal offense—not for low-level behavior problems.

Discretionary expulsion of students for nonviolent, noncriminal misbehavior puts students at risk. Expulsion may introduce students to the justice system when they have broken no laws, and it may push them into dropping out of school. Modifying school policies to address behavior problems without resorting to expulsion would allow students to remain in school—and break the potential school-to-prison pipeline. "Numerous studies by national experts in the fields of education, criminal justice, and mental health have established a link between school discipline, school dropout rates, and incarceration."[61] The study notes that more than 80 percent of Texas adult prison inmates are school dropouts.

The Southern Poverty Law Center also addresses the school-to-prison pipeline and has created a school-to-prison reform project to "stem the flow of children from schools to jails by reforming punitive school discipline practices and ensuring that youth most likely to be pushed out of school receive individualized support to increase their chances of graduating." They help implement a change in school cultures through Positive Behavioral Interventions and Supports (PBIS), a research-based alternative to destructive discipline policies like zero tolerance. Linked with that project are class action lawsuits to stop the practice of overusing suspensions and expulsions. After a successful settlement in Jefferson Parish in Louisiana, a special master was appointed to oversee a corrective action plan. From 2007–2009, the number of students referred to the juvenile justice system was reduced by 35%, and the number of students suspended for longer than 10 days was reduced from 235 for the 2005–2006 school year to 13 in 2008–2009.[62] Two other class action suits against Louisiana parishes were settled; all three districts (the largest in Louisiana) had routinely suspended or expelled students for minor offenses.

Zero-tolerance laws make it easier for administrators to expel students so that they won't have to do the hard work of dealing "with parents, community justice programs, religious organizations, and social service agencies."[63] Administrators may attempt to improve the learning environment for others by removing troublesome students through suspension and expulsion, but disciplinary exclusion raises thorny questions.

> Given that educational research has consistently shown that the strongest predictor of academic achievement is active academic engagement, strategies such as suspension and expulsion pose a dilemma for administrators by removing students from the opportunity to learn. The use of suspension and expulsion has also raised civil rights concerns due to strong and consistent evidence that students of color are over-represented among those who are so disciplined. A number of authors have argued that the increased use of zero tolerance is directly responsible for increasing racial and ethnic disparities in school discipline.[64]

One negative consequence of suspending or expelling students, often unrecognized by school officials, is an increase in delinquent behavior and also the attractiveness of gangs. One gang member suggested that expelling students added to the pool of potential gang members.[65] A recent study notes that there is a close correlation between suspensions—and truancy in general—and violence. A study in Baltimore found that two-thirds of the victims of homicide or some other shooting had been suspended.[66] Lack of attachment to schools is one of the key predictors of delinquency.

Losen and Skiba emphasize both racial and gender disparity and the lost opportunity that suspensions and expulsions create.

> One of the goals of public schooling is to prepare children to participate in our democracy, and become productive law-abiding citizens. Disciplinary

> tactics that respond to typical adolescent behavior by removing students from school do not better prepare students for adulthood. Instead, they increase their risk of educational failure and dropout.[67]

The American Psychological Association convened a task force to examine the effectiveness of zero-tolerance policies.

> Zero tolerance has not been shown to improve school climate or school safety. Its application in suspension and expulsion has not proven an effective means of improving student behavior. It has not resolved, and indeed may have exacerbated, minority overrepresentation in school punishments. Zero-tolerance policies as applied appear to run counter to our best knowledge of child development. By changing the relationship of education and juvenile justice, zero tolerance may shift the locus of discipline from relatively inexpensive actions in the school setting to the highly costly processes of arrest and incarceration. In so doing, zero-tolerance policies have created unintended consequences for students, families, and communities.[68]

How Safe Are Schools?

The previous section described conditions that many might consider unsafe to civil liberties. As mentioned earlier, panic about school safety pushed such concerns aside. Following the killings at Columbine and other schools around the country in the late 1990s, public officials reacted with a frenzy. It was a classic case of exception-based policies: a few, isolated cases that were clearly the exception rather than the rule became the basis for wide-ranging policies. "A moral panic swept the country as parents and children suddenly feared for their safety at school."[69] One middle-school principal claimed school shootings could happen anywhere—yet in his community there had been a 26% drop in juvenile crime in the past several years and no murders had been committed.

Statistics versus Fears

In the years preceding Columbine, juvenile violence had been on a significant decline. Most citizens believed, however, that crime was out of control. Despite a 13% drop in homicides between 1990 and 1995, the coverage of homicides on the three major television networks went up by 240%.[70] There was a 27% drop in school-associated violent deaths (including suicides) between 1992 and 1998, but the public believed schools were no longer safe. Between the 1997–1998 and the 1998–1999 school years (8 school shootings including Columbine and Jonesboro occurred during those years), there was a 40% *decrease* in school-associated violent deaths (from 43 to 26).[71] The number of people in the United States who reported being fearful of their schools rose nearly 50% during that same period. Students who experienced the results of policies enacted because of fear had far different concerns: "Too much security makes you wonder whether it is safe"; "When I get up to go to school in the morning, I don't want to feel like I'm going to a correctional facility."[72]

In the school year 1998–1999, there were 26 student deaths on school grounds (including 14 at Columbine). Based on the number of violent deaths on school grounds, the likelihood of a child being killed at school during that year was one in two million.[73] In contrast, 71% of parents polled thought that a school shooting was "likely" to happen in their community. Similarly, despite the fact that juvenile homicide arrests had declined by 56% between 1993 and 1998, 62% of those polled believed that juvenile crime was increasing. While 4% of all juvenile homicides occur in rural areas, 54% of rural parents feared for their children's safety in schools versus 46% for urban and 44% for suburban parents.

Student self-reports and opinions about their safety at school should have reassured their parents. Student reports of fights on and off school grounds declined by 14%, with a 9% decline in fights on school grounds during this same period of time. Only 3.5% of students reported being injured in a fight (down from 4.4%); self-reports of carrying a weapon declined from 26% to 18%; there was a 25% decline in the number of students who reported carrying a gun to school in the previous 30 days (from 7.9% to 5.9%).[74] The percentage of youths who said they were afraid of being the victim of a serious crime either inside or outside school was 24, down from 40% in 1994; 87% thought their schools were safe.[75]

Publications like the 1999 *Juvenile Offenders and Victims National Report* and the *2000 Annual Report on School Safety* reinforced the fact that serious (especially violent) crime within the public schools was a relatively rare event.[76] The former report noted that: "Serious violent crime appears to be prevalent in only a minority of the Nation's public schools."[77] Less than 15% of high schools and middle schools contacted police about violent incidents. The percentage of students reporting *any* type of victimization remained the same in 1989 and 1995 (15%). Echoing numerous studies conducted over many years, the report noted that there is a much greater risk of being the victim of a serious crime in places other than at school. The *2000 Annual Report on School Safety* essentially said the same thing. The report noted that in 1999, about 8% of students nationwide reported being threatened or injured with a weapon at school, about the same percentage as in 1993.[78]

Despite substantial data about the reality of school safety, public officials continue to exaggerate the danger. After three students were killed and five wounded at Heath High School in Paducah, Kentucky, a civil complaint included this description.

> Our schools have become killing fields. Our children are no longer safe because other children prey upon them. Murder has become the preferred method of settling the schoolyard dispute. The epidemic of school violence has reached into the very heart of America. It is no longer the story of the big city or the ghetto. The infection of violence has found its way into our small towns and rural communities. It is everywhere in our country.[79]

Has anything changed during the decade since these reports were issued and the claims that schools were "killing fields"? A report on school safety found that during the school year 2008–2009 there were 38 school-associated violent deaths—in a population of about 55.6 million students in grades pre-kindergarten through 12. There were 15 homicides and 7 suicides of school-age youth. There were 1.2 million victims of nonfatal crimes at school, including 619,000 thefts and 743,100 violent crimes (which include simple assault). The report noted that victimization surveys revealed that only 4% of students between the ages of 12–18 said they were victims at school during the past 6 months: 3% reported a theft and 2% reported a "violent victimization"—but less than .5% reported that this was a "serious violent victimization."[80]

Eighty-three percent of public schools reported no serious violent crime; 13% of public schools reported at least one violent incident to the police. The *rate* of serious violent crime at school was 4 (per 1,000 students) compared to a rate of 8 away from school. Of the students in grades 9–12, 8% reported being threatened or injured with a weapon on school property. Ten percent of males and 5% of females reported an incident with a weapon. Between 1993 and 2009, the percentages of students carrying a weapon at least one day onto school property declined from 12% to 6%. Almost a third (31%) of the students reporting being in a physical fight sometime during the previous year versus 11% who reported being in a physical fight on school property.[81] Within city schools only 10% of teachers reported being threatened with injury (5% said they had been attacked by a student), compared to just 6% in rural or suburban schools.[82]

These numbers completely contradict the beliefs among the general population, law enforcement, and politicians that public schools have become "war zones" or anything approaching that description. Some schools do have higher rates of criminal conduct than others, particularly in the poorest (and lowest funded) schools in the inner cities. The Consortium on Chicago School Research at the University of Chicago conducted a two-year study and found that building strong relationships between teachers and students can foster safe environments even in crime-ridden neighborhoods.[83] The report also found that schools with higher suspension rates were less safe than schools with lower rates. Students across the Chicago Public Schools felt safer inside their classrooms than in areas with little adult supervision.

Bullying

Another behavior that takes place frequently at school has garnered headlines—fueled by tragic cases and new technologies. The behavior isn't new, but the coverage by the media has intensified. Bullying has been labeled a "pandemic," even though social scientists say it is no more prevalent—and no more extreme—than it was fifty years ago.[84]

> Bullies can be anywhere, but there's no place they show up more than in schools, and no time more than in September. Once the academic year starts, the complicated social hierarchy of a campus—popular kids, nerdy kids, ADHD kids, nerdy ADHD kids who are popular because they sell Adderall—gets reinvented. But this fall [2010] the casual brutality of the schoolyard seems particularly bitter. In the past few weeks, at least three teenage boys . . . have committed suicide after being bullied.[85]

Asher + was 13 and was bullied about his assumed homosexuality and his inability to afford nice clothes; Seth Walsh, also 13, was bullied for being homosexual and not fitting in; William Lucas, 15, was bullied repeatedly at school. A fourth teen, Tyler Clementi, was a freshman at Rutgers and jumped off the George Washington Bridge after his roommate streamed a video of him in a romantic encounter with a man. "Cases like these are being invoked as potent symbols for why, in the digital age, schools need strong bullying policies and states need stronger legislation."[86]

Where is the line between behavior that is cruel and behavior that is criminal? In the age of Facebook, YouTube, and ubiquitous cell phones with cameras, embarrassing photos and public humiliation spread virally. Bullying behavior today reaches far more people and is visually more potent than older behaviors like comments scrawled on bathroom walls. Home was once a potential respite from taunts and insults, but electronic postings remove that safe harbor unless teens resist visiting the sites.

Fifteen-year-old Phoebe Prince committed suicide in January 2010 after three months of orchestrated, relentless harassment that included slurs about her Irish heritage, insults on Facebook, and physical threats. Soon after Phoebe's death, Massachusetts passed a bill that defines bullying as "the repeated use by a perpetrator of a written, verbal, or electronic expression, or physical act or gesture . . . directed at a victim that causes physical or emotional harm or damage to the victim's property; places the victim in reasonable fear or harm to himself or of damage to his property; [or] creates a hostile environment at school."[87] The law in Massachusetts is one of the strictest of the forty-five states that have anti-bullying laws. It mandates anti-bullying programs in schools and outlines criminal punishment.

Phoebe's family had moved to South Hadley, Massachusetts (100 miles west of Boston), from Ireland. Phoebe had dated two popular boys at the school, including the captain of the football team, Sean Mulveyhill. Four girls were angry about the relationships, including Kayla Narey. Mulveyhill encouraged the girls to harass Phoebe after he broke up with her. The district attorney charged the two boys with statutory rape, two of the six defendants with stalking, two with criminal harassment, and five with civil-rights violations resulting in bodily injury. The students were suspended from March 2010 until resolution of the case in court. The superintendent in South Hadley noted that the six had been in good academic standing and were headed to college. "Now, in addition to losing Phoebe, we're losing [them] too."[88]

Phoebe's family agreed to a plea deal in 2011 that required the teens to admit that their threats, insults, and slurs were criminal acts. Mulveyhill agreed to a single count of misdemeanor criminal harassment; Narey's record will be erased if she successfully completes one year of probation; the three other girls agreed to similar resolutions. The single charge of statutory rape against Austin Renaud was dropped at the request of Phoebe's parents. After the pleadings, the district attorney announced: "Today's proceedings signify that bullying and harassment will not be tolerated in our schools and when it rises to the level of criminal conduct . . . those responsible will be prosecuted."[89]

One of the 21 indicators in the School Crime and Safety annual report is "Bullying at School and Cyber-Bullying Anywhere."[90] Thirty-two percent of students reported having been bullied at school—79% inside the school, 23% on school grounds, 8% on the school bus. Twenty-one percent said that bullying consisted of being made fun of; 18% said they were the subject of rumors; 11% said that they were pushed, shoved, tripped, or spit on (19% reported being injured); 6% said they were threatened with harm; 5% said they were excluded from activities; and 4% said that someone tried to make them do things they did not want to do and that their property was destroyed intentionally. The frequency of bullying was once or twice during the school year for 63% of those reporting; 21% reported being bullied once or twice a month; 10% reported a frequency of once or twice a week; and 7% said they were bullied almost daily. Thirty-six percent notified a teacher or adult about the bullying. There were no significant racial differences, although whites were slightly more likely to report being bullied. Males and females were almost equally (30% and 33%, respectively) as likely to be bullied.[91]

The media compounds the problem of bullying by running headlines like "Bullied to Death." While bullies should be accountable for their own behavior, can they be liable for the chain of events that follow?[92] In the Phoebe Prince tragedy, other contributing factors to her suicide might have been her medication for depression, a prior attempt to kill herself, and struggling with her parents' separation.

Dharun Ravi and Molly Wei were charged with two counts each of invasion of privacy, which carries a maximum penalty of five years in prison, for streaming the video of Tyler Clementi (the Rutgers student who committed suicide). In April 2011, Ravi was indicted by a New Jersey grand jury on hate-crime charges, which could double the penalty. Wei was admitted to a pretrial-intervention program in May 2011; over the next three years (the longest term that can be imposed for a pretrial intervention), she must hold a job, perform 300 hours of community service, participate in counseling to deter cyber bullying, cooperate with authorities, and testify at any proceedings. If she complies, the charges of invasion-of-privacy (for using a camera to view and transmit a live image) will be dropped.[93] Clementi's parents approved of the agreement with Wei but favored harsher treatment of Ravi.

After Clementi's suicide, some people wanted charges of manslaughter, but a guilty verdict would require that the jury find that suicide was a foreseeable outcome. Orin Kerr, a law professor at George Washington University who specializes in cyber crime, observed: "There's an understandable wish by prosecutors to respond to the moral outrage of society, but the important thing is for the prosecution to follow the law."[94] The punishment must fit the crime, not the sense of outrage over it. Kerr warns that society should be alarmed if the government prosecutes a person for the response of the victim rather than the action of the person her- or himself. There are laws against invading someone's privacy, and perpetrators should be punished for those violations.

Society also needs to be aware of the environment it creates. Facebook and Twitter, which are immensely popular, encourage participants to record every thought and moment online. When teens willingly sacrifice their own privacy to be connected on popular sites, they are less likely to worry about the privacy of others. Nancy Willard, a lawyer and founder of the Center for Safe and Responsible Internet Use, says impulsiveness, immaturity, and immense publishing power can be a dangerous mix: "With increased power to do things comes increased responsibility to make sure that what you're doing is O.K."[95] Daniel Solove, author of *The Future of Reputation: Gossip, Rumor and Privacy on the Internet*, says society needs to work on educating students about the consequences of their actions.

Anti-bullying programs are mandated in a number of schools, and prevention programs can reduce school bullying by as much as 50%.[96] Kids who are bullied, which includes an alarming 9 in 10 gay students, are more likely to be depressed. Almost 160,000 students skip school each day because they are afraid of or intimidated by their peers. The outlook isn't brighter for the other side of the equation; one study found that 60% of boys who bullied others in middle school would be convicted of at least one crime by the time they were 24. Another study found that 27% of girls who were bullied online became bullies themselves.[97] Bullying can leave scars that last a lifetime—for both the victims and the perpetrators who have to live with what they have done.[98]

Bullying is a behavior that has existed for decades, but the reaction to it has changed. Parents are particularly fearful about cyber bullying—reported by only 4% of children in the Indicators of School Crime and Safety Report (2% reported another student posting hurtful information on the Internet, and 2% reported unwanted contact).[99] The parent of one of the defendants in the Phoebe Prince case said the family received death threats, prank calls, a rock through a window, media cameras, and other forms of harassment—ironically similar to what Phoebe endured.

> Bullying is not just a social ill; it's a "cottage industry," says Suffolk Law School's David Yamada—complete with commentators and prevention experts and a new breed of legal scholars, all preparing to take on an enemy that's always been there. None of this is to say that bullying is not a serious problem, or that tackling it is not important. But like a stereo with the volume turned too high, all the noise distorts the facts, making it nearly impossible to judge when a case is somehow criminal, or merely cruel.[100]

Research has shown that legal prohibitions do not deter kids who respond emotionally to their surroundings. "Ultimately, labeling a group of raucous teens as 'criminals' will only make it harder for them to engage with society when they return."[101] As Nancy Gibbs advises, "Adolescence, that swampy zone between safety and power, is best patrolled by adults armed with sense and mercy, not guns and a badge."[102]

Reinforcing Class and Race Inequality

Starting in the nineteenth century, the school system began to focus on a two-tiered system of education: vocational training for the working and lower class; college preparation for the middle and upper-middle class. The stated goal was to cater to individual needs, but the result was a stratified public educational system. Children from upper-class families were already in a different stratum; they went to expensive private schools.[103]

Follow the Money

If we look at school funding, we obtain an overview of the many direct and indirect ways public schooling perpetuates class and racial inequalities.[104] Students from privileged backgrounds begin their quest for success substantially ahead of students from the bottom of the social order. The initial advantage compounds—all the way to the best colleges.[105] The college admissions process favors the privileged and undermines professed commitments to diversity. Affirmative action, originally intended as a tool to promote social justice, has morphed into a tool that colleges use to sell themselves and to attract corporate support. Children of the privileged are on track for admission; lower and middle-class students of all races find the deck stacked against them. Money and connections influence college admissions, reinforcing wealth and privilege. Schools reward donors and alumni—increasing their endowments and reinforcing wealth and privilege.

Since public schools depend on tax dollars for financing, the fact that we live in a highly stratified and unequal society results in unequal financing of public schools. Schools in wealthier areas of the state get more money than schools in areas where residents make less money. Whether we compare public school financing on a state-by-state basis or within local school districts, the disparities are enormous. For instance, traditionally Southern states have spent on average considerably less than northeastern states in terms of per-pupil spending. New York, for example, spent $17,173 per student (the highest amount in the United States), while Tennessee spent $7,739 (only four states ranked lower).[106] The U.S. average was $10,259, and all Southern states spent less than the average. Utah spent the least per student—$5,765.

A national study conducted by Rutgers University researchers and the Education Law Center in Newark, New Jersey, ranks states and the District of Columbia on how fairly they fund public schools. The researchers note that how we fund public schools is fundamental to creating equal access to high quality educational opportunities that prepare students to succeed. Fairness depends on a sufficient level of funding for all students, which means providing additional resources to districts where there are more students with greater needs. Many states do not fairly allocate education funding to address the needs of the most disadvantaged students. The study looks at four interrelated fairness indicators: funding level, funding distribution, state fiscal effort, and public school coverage. Key findings include:

- Six states do relatively well on all four indicators (NJ, CT, MA, VT, IA, and WY);
- Four states are below average on all the indicators (IL, LA, MO, and NC);
- Several states have high levels of education spending but allocate less funding to higher poverty districts (e.g., NY, ME, NH, MI);

- Most states need improvement in at least one area, and many do poorly on the indicators most influenced by policy decisions.[107]

One additional point about funding needs to be underscored. Most public schools depend on property taxes: as property values go up, so does the funding for public schools. Homeowners receive a tax deduction for these property taxes. In effect, this is a "federal subsidy for an unequal education."[108] While homeowners in poorer districts also receive a subsidy, the amounts of the taxes (and therefore the deductions) are less than in the wealthier areas. The mortgage deduction is another indirect subsidy. Federal tax policies exacerbate the gulf between funding for the richest and the poorest schools. Federal grants to public schools in poorer districts somewhat offset the disparity in available funds, but not by much since federal revenues account for less than 10% of all school revenues.

Congress mandates that The National Center for Education Statistics report annually on the condition of education in the United States. In 2010, the report included a section that compared high-poverty schools and their students to low-poverty schools and their students. The poverty measure is based on the percentage of a school's enrollment that is eligible for free or reduced-price lunches through the National School Lunch Program. High-poverty schools are those where at least 76% of the students qualify for the program; in low-poverty schools, less than 25% of the students are eligible.

In 2008, 17% (16,122) of all public schools were in the high-poverty category—20% (12,971) of all public elementary schools; 9% (2,142) of all secondary schools; and 18% (1,009) of combined schools. In 2000, the percentage of high-poverty schools was 12%. High-poverty schools enrolled 20% of all public-school elementary students and 6% of secondary students. Cities have the highest concentration of high-poverty elementary schools (40%) and secondary schools (20%). The states with the highest percentages of high-poverty elementary and secondary public schools were Mississippi (53%, 43%), Louisiana (52%, 27%) and New Mexico (46%, 34%). About 42% of Hispanic, 40% of black, and 5% of white elementary school students attended high-poverty schools. At the secondary level, the percentages were: 15% of black students, 15% of Hispanic, and 1% of white. High-poverty public schools have more students who are learning English—about 25% of students in high-poverty elementary schools and 16% of students in high-poverty secondary schools were limited-English proficient, compared to 4% of students at low-poverty elementary schools and 2% of students at low-poverty secondary schools. There are persistent achievement gaps between students at high-poverty schools and those at low-poverty schools. The average reading-assessment score for 8th-graders at high-poverty schools was 34 points lower than the score for 8th-graders at low-poverty schools. The average math-assessment score for 8th-graders at high-poverty schools was 38 points lower than the score for those at low-poverty schools. At high-poverty secondary schools, 68% graduated versus 91% at low-poverty schools. The percentage of students at high-poverty public high schools who immediately attended a 4-year college after graduation was 28% versus 52% at low-poverty schools.[109]

In most public schools the children of the poor start at a terrible disadvantage, especially those for whom English is a second language. The children in wealthier schools come from neighborhoods with good housing, reliable transportation, parks, and good public libraries. One or both parents are often professionals. Children from poorer districts face a very different reality: drug dealers on street corners; police and ambulance sirens almost nightly; many (if not most) of the men either unemployed or underemployed; and neighbors in jail or prison. As noted at the beginning of this section, children from such disparate backgrounds do not begin their education from equivalent starting points. Should we be surprised that so many children, acutely aware of the huge differences between their schools and those of the more affluent, simply give up very early in life?

Apartheid Schooling

Kozol has studied educational and social inequalities in the United States for 40 years and finds that they are more segregated than ever, as reflected in the subtitle of one of his books: *The Restoration of Apartheid Schooling in America*.[110] He deplores widespread acceptance of the idea that schools in poverty-stricken areas must accept different academic and career goals than the goals of schools in middle-class neighborhoods. Tolerating separate schools and their unequal opportunities for offering alternatives to one's current socioeconomic status means society is confining poor, minority children to spend their lives in poverty.

Tracking

A common feature of U.S. schools is the placement of students into different classes or groups of perceived intellectual ability based on the scores on standardized tests. Jeannie Oakes defines tracking as "the process whereby students are divided into categories so that they can be assigned in groups to various kinds of classes. Sometimes students are classified as fast, average, or slow learners." In essence, Oakes notes, tracking is a "sorting of students that has certain predictable characteristics."[111] Tracking goes on in at least 80% of the secondary schools and 60% of all elementary schools in the country—and has serious consequences. As Oakes notes, "Those at the bottom of the social and economic ladder climb up through twelve years of the 'great equalizer,' Horace Mann's famous description of public schools, and end up still at the bottom rung."[112]

Stamford, Connecticut, has used rigid educational tracking for years. Tracking children by academic ability for more effective teaching had evolved into a caste system, segregating students by race and socioeconomic background—both inside and outside classrooms. The principal at one school said parents have consistently complained that the tracking numbers assigned to students dictate friends and cafeteria cliques as well as classes. Parents lobby to move their children to the highest track—for higher status. Students know their own levels and those of their classmates. One girl said, "I don't like being classified because it makes you feel like you're not smart."[113]

Black and Hispanic students made up 46% of the 2009 sixth-grade class, but they comprised 78% of the lowest track and only 7% of the highest. One of the schools decided to test mixed-ability classes for science and social studies. There were fewer behavior problems and better grades for struggling students. Some high-performing students complained that they were not learning as much. The superintendent, Joshua Starr, said the tracking system has failed to prepare lower-track children for high school and college. "There are certainly people who want to maintain the status quo because some people have benefited from the status quo. I know that we cannot afford that anymore. It's not fair to too many kids."[114]

Deborah Kasak, executive director of a national group for middle grades reform, said research shows that all students benefit from mixed-ability classes. "We see improvements in student behavior, academic performance and teaching, and all that positively affects school culture."[115] Daria Hall, a director of an advocacy group, said that tracking funnels poor and minority students into low-level and watered-down courses. "If all we expect of students is for them to watch movies and fill out worksheets, then that's what they will give us."[116] Black and Hispanic performance on state tests trails that of whites. Of the white students in grades three to eight, 92% passed math and 88% passed reading; the percentages for blacks were 63% for math and 56% for reading; for Hispanic students, 74% passed math and 60% reading.

Students in lower tracks become discouraged and often give up. They have been labeled as "low-ability," and a self-fulfilling prophecy sets in. One critic argues that instead of viewing these students as placed in a track where they will have the opportunity to catch up with others, many teachers see them as kids who can't make it and therefore need to be "weeded out" of the system.[117] Students placed in the lower tracks are, in effect, "tracked to fail." And they fail at a far greater rate than students in higher tracks. Students in upper tracks begin to see themselves as superior, while those in the bottom tracks see themselves as inferior. The self-fulfilling prophecies take two very divergent paths. Tracking is linked to both class and race, as a disproportionate number of lower-class and minority students are placed into the lower tracks. Critics have noted that even if test scores are roughly the same, kids from the lower class are more likely to be placed in a low track class.[118]

Finally, tracking has been found to have very little educational value. In one of the most comprehensive examinations of school tracking, Oakes provides abundant evidence of how it perpetuates inequality.[119] Kozol's analysis of the New York public school system found that tracks for "emotionally handicapped," the "learning disabled" and the "educable mentally retarded" are populated by African-American students. Tracks for "speech, language, and hearing impaired" are mostly Latino students. Moreover, these are not routes for improvement or to achieve parity, rather, they are *tracks for failure*. "Fewer than 10% of children slotted in these special tracks will graduate from school." Kozol also reports that nationwide "black children are three times as likely as white children to be placed in classes for the mentally retarded but only half as likely to be placed in classes for the gifted."[120]

Numerous studies dating back more than 40 years have demonstrated the negative impact of such tracking practices. Students placed in the lowest tracks fared far worse than those in the higher tracks, even when controlling for the father's occupation, student's IQ scores, and other variables. More importantly, assignment into the lowest track was strongly correlated with dropping out, lack of participating in school activities, and (not surprisingly) delinquency.[121] Another study found that track position was a better predictor than gender and social class for about 25 different types of delinquency (left unsaid was the fact that class background is correlated with track position).[122] Oakes researched tracking over a 20-year period and concluded that the curriculum of the lower track retards academic development, lowers self-esteem and career aspirations, and in many ways encourages racial segregation.[123] She found that lower-track students are taught how to fill out forms and write checks, while their upper-track counterparts are reading Shakespeare. The author's conclusion is that we may be teaching behaviors to children in the lower tracks that will guarantee they fit well into the lowest levels of the class system, while simultaneously teaching those in the upper tracks to take their place within the world of big business and the professions.

Several other authors reaffirm the negative effects of tracking and how it perpetuates class and racial inequality. Jay Macleod discusses how social inequality is reproduced generation after generation.

> Observed classroom phenomena—the different expectations teachers hold for students of different social origins, the determination of what counts as knowledge, teacher-student interaction, the tracking of courses—serves to handicap the performance of the lower classes.[124]

Peter Sacks discusses the reasons why some parents continue to support tracking and the reasons why it is inequitable.

> American elites vigorously promote and defend their positions in the high-stakes game of educational opportunity for their children. From tracking policies that largely benefit white and upper-middle-class kids in public schools to strategies for admission to prestigious private colleges, the privileged and well-educated inhabit an information-rich web of connections and access, in which they and their appointed agents can work closely with schools to perpetuate their advantages.[125]
>
> Middle-class teaching methods, testing, tracking, and other sorting systems distinguish the children of affluence as gifted, talented, and meritorious, thus deserving the most challenging and enriched learning environments, under the guidance of the best teachers. These same methods often label lower-class children as academically deficient misfits who are in need of remediation in order to fill even the most basic societal needs.[126]

School Failure and Delinquency

Criminologists have consistently reported a close connection between such variables as grades, tracking, falling behind in school, attending inferior schools, being suspended or expelled, and rates of delinquency. School failure results in a delinquency rate that may be as much as seven times greater than the rates for those who do not fail. It is one of the strongest predictors of whether or not a youth will be referred to juvenile court.[127]

The process is easy to understand. We begin with class and racial background, which puts students at increased risk of school failure.[128] We then add school tracking that exacerbates the situation. Then we consider how the youth responds to his or her lowly status, which is usually by hating the school system, while rejecting the school's authority. As young people continue to fail (especially when falling behind at least one grade), they naturally seek out other, similarly situated students and start to "hang out" with them, forming one among many student subcultures.[129] They begin to get into trouble, both at school and off school property, especially as they become frequent truants or spend their afternoons engaging in various forms of delinquency. Eventually, such students begin to miss more school, develop arrest records, spend time within the juvenile justice system, become further enmeshed within a delinquent subculture, and/or join a gang.[130]

> Tracking low-achieving students by placing them in learning groups is a common practice among educators. However, this technique should be avoided because it reinforces the "grouping tendency and pattern generally common to gang formation. . . .
> Unfortunately, the grouping and tracking phenomena in the early grades are further strengthened when a student reaches an alternative or continuation high school. Here, putting all the students with serious problems together reaches a critical mass and generates a state of additional cohesion.[131]

Falling Behind and Dropping Out

Falling behind in school and dropping out should be seen as a *process* rather than a *single event* in the life course of students. Theodore Wagenaar notes: "The precursors to dropping out, the decision to drop out, the process of dropping out, the responses to dropping out and the consequences of dropping out all result from a complex interplay of personal, social, situational and contextual factors."[132]

One group of researchers identified four types of students who drop out:

- maladjusted; these students have poor grades and behave poorly at school;
- underachievers; students who have poor grades;
- disengaged; students who perform better than the maladjusted and the underachievers, but simply do not like school;
- quiets; students who, other than having slightly lower grades, resemble graduates more than dropouts.[133]

A vast amount of research suggests that youths are more likely to drop out of school if they: (1) are doing poorly academically, especially those in lower academic tracks; (2) have lower levels of self-esteem and a poor sense of control over their lives; (3) are less interested in school and experience feelings of alien-

ation; (4) work excessive hours in part-time employment; and/or are frequently truant, and generally have a poor attitude towards school. Studies
have shown that "grade retention" (holding back a child one grade level) may
increase the likelihood of dropping out and hence delinquency.[134]

Ninth grade is often the bottleneck for many students who find that their
academic skills are insufficient for high school. Up to 40% of ninth grade students in cities with the highest dropout rates repeat ninth grade—only 10–15%
of those students will graduate. Academic success in ninth grade course work
is more important than demographic characteristics or prior academic achievement in predicting who will graduate. Ninth grade is the crunch point for more
than 33% of dropouts.[135]

As noted in chapter 7, Hirschi's "social bond" theory suggests that those
youths who are closely bonded to school, among other attachments, are less
likely to be delinquent. Some researchers are using the term *engagement* to refer
to the extent to which students participate in academic and nonacademic
school activities and identify and value schooling outcomes. Engagement
includes both a *participation* and a *psychological* component. The participation
component refers to such factors as class attendance, being prepared for class,
completing homework, and being involved in extracurricular activities. The
psychological engagement component includes a sense of belonging, social ties,
and bonds with other students and teachers, a feeling of safety and security at
school, and valuing school success.[136] The lowest 25 percent of secondary students in terms of achievement are twenty times more likely to drop out of high
school than students who rank in the highest 25% for achievement. Research
indicates that a lack of engagement is an important predictor for dropping out,
even after controlling for academic achievement and student background.[137]

Quite often a youngster will become increasingly frustrated and self-con-
scious about his or her failure in school, which often leads directly to various
forms of acting out, including delinquency. More often than not, the official
response is to try to *control* the behavior, rather than finding out *why* a student
is acting out and then providing a solution to the behavior. This eventually
leads to the student getting more and more frustrated and embarrassed (which
can be especially painful in front of peers), which in turn leads to getting suspended or expelled from school, and ultimately dropping out entirely.

Peers are an important component affecting the decision to drop out. Kids
who fall behind and eventually drop out have friends who are in exactly the
same situation. Rejected by peers with more academic success, these youths are
not well integrated into the peer social network at school. Researchers in one
study examined how peer networks differ between dropouts and those who
remain in school. The researchers used a peer-report technique that asked students to identify the three classmates with whom they would most likely participate in an activity and the three with whom they would be least likely to
participate. Dropouts had more friends in a similar situation and had those
friends at the end of the ninth grade. They were the most likely to have at least
one friend who was not in school and to have fewer friends in general than
their graduating counterparts. At-risk youths were also more likely to have at

least one dropout friend, to have fewer same-sex friends, and were the most likely to be rejected by their peers at the end of the ninth grade (a crucial turning point, as noted above). There was an important gender difference, as the rejected girls were less likely than boys to have same-sex friends.[138]

There are multiple factors in the process of dropping out. Researchers attribute approximately half of the variation in dropout behavior to the individual and the family—and the remaining half to the schools themselves. School resources, school structure and school processes affect the dropout rate. Particularly important are: student-teacher ratio, school control, size, and average daily attendance.[139]

Among the proposals to reform public schools, the most prominent are "choice" (e.g., school vouchers and charter schools) and "standardized tests." Both of these reforms have just been given a grade of "F" by noted critic Diane Ravitch in her latest book *The Death and Life of the Great American School System*.[140] Her conclusions are based on a thorough analysis of research on these proposals. Charter schools and vouchers generally have not provided significant gains for students. Testing has resulted in teachers "teaching to the test," with little improvement in learning. Indeed, the Los Angeles school board shut down six schools where principals and teachers were ordered "to prepare students for last year's exams with the actual test questions. Several teachers at the schools alerted the district about the cheating."[141]

Consequences of Dropping Out

Of the 4 million students who enter high school each year, one million will drop out. In large cities, the problem is even more severe. Almost half of all students in the country's 50 largest school districts fail to get a high school diploma. The United States ranks eighteenth among industrial nations—compared to first thirty years ago.[142] Approximately 12% of the nation's high schools produce more than half of the nation's dropouts. In these "dropout factories," the number of seniors enrolled is routinely 60% less than the number of freshmen three years earlier. Thirty-five percent of African-American students attend one of these schools versus 8% of white students.[143] Eighty percent of the high schools that produce the most dropouts are found in fifteen states, primarily in northern and western cities and throughout the South.[144] About half of African-American and Hispanic students graduate with their peers. In many states, white and minority graduation rates differ by as much as 40–50%. Students whose families are in the highest quartile of income are about seven times as likely to graduate as those whose family incomes are in the lowest quartile.

In addition to the cost to individuals of failing to graduate, there is also a cost to society. Dropouts cost taxpayers more than $8 billion annually in public assistance programs like food stamps and Medicare. High school dropouts earn about $10 thousand less a year than workers with diplomas—about $300 billion in lost earnings and taxes every year. Dropouts are more likely to be unemployed (15% compared to the already high average of 9.4% caused by the recession).[145] If the graduation rates of Hispanic, African American, and Native

American students were to reach the levels of white students by 2020, the potential increase in personal income would add more than $310 billion to the U.S. economy. Increasing the college graduation of male students in the United States by 5% could lead to combined savings and revenue of almost $8 billion each year by reducing crime-related costs.[146] Researchers at the California Dropout Research Project at the University of California-Santa Barbara found that students dropping out of school was costing the state of California about $1.1 billion annually in terms of increasing. One of their conclusions was that "cutting the dropout rate in half would prevent 30,000 juvenile crimes and save $550 million every year."[147]

Dropping out increases the probability of adult criminality and imprisonment. A study that examined nationwide data found that almost 1 of every 10 male, 16–24-year-old high school dropouts was institutionalized versus fewer than 1 of 33 high school graduates, 1 of 100 of those who completed 1–3 years of post-secondary schooling, and only 1 of 500 men who held a bachelor's or higher degree.[148] For black youths the ratios were even worse. Approximately 23 of every 100 black male dropouts were institutionalized versus only 6 to 7 of every 100 Asians, Hispanics, and Whites. Sixty percent of federal inmates are high school dropouts. As an educator in California noted, "You have high schools in Los Angeles that send more kids to prison, than they graduate from college. It's time for a radical, radical change."

Gangs and Schools

As noted in chapter 4, gangs have become a hot issue over the past couple of decades, and the very terms "gang" and "gang member" are subject to gross misinterpretation. Twenty-three percent of students report the presence of gangs in their schools.[149] The percentage has fluctuated from 28% in the mid-1990s, then dropping to 17% in 1999, before rising again.[150] The fluctuations can be the result of the definitions used for "gang."[151] Gangs are most likely to be found within urban schools.

A longitudinal study tracked 4,000 young people in Rochester, New York, for ten years and found that 30% of the sample joined a gang at some point before the end of high school.

> The gang-involved youth, about a third of the sample, accounted for the vast share of self-reported delinquency committed—65% of the delinquent acts, 86% of the serious delinquent acts, 69% of the violent delinquent acts, 70% of the drug sales, and 63% of the reported drug use. In addition, compared with youth who never joined a gang, the gang members were significantly more likely to drop out of school, become teenage parents, and have unstable employment.[152]

Gang involvement has been linked to low levels of attachment to school and teachers, poor school performance, and low expectations for educational success.

Youths are more likely to join gangs if they come from families that are poor, are structurally unstable, lack parental supervision, have low levels of communication between parents and children, or are dysfunctional in certain other ways (e.g., parents are accepting of violence and exhibit low levels of attachment to children, siblings exhibit antisocial behavior).[153]

In many parts of the country we can trace the development of "gangs" directly to various conflicts on or near public schools. Los Angeles is a case in point. There were reported "racial wars" on several Los Angeles area high schools during the late 1940s and early 1950s. African-American "gangs" emerged as a *defensive* response, defined mostly in terms of school-based turfs.[154] As several researchers have noted, school desegregation ironically contributed to the growth of the gang problem by placing rival gang members in the same schools and in the process destroying some of the turf connections of these gangs.[155]

School involves several important risk factors for gang membership. One study found that "low academic achievement" was among the top predictors of gang involvement.[156] Other factors include: frequent truancy/absences/suspensions/expulsions; learning disabilities; low school engagement; poor school performance; poorly functioning schools; negative labeling by teachers; low academic aspirations; low attachment to teachers; low parent college expectations for child; low math achievement test score for males.[157]

School became a serious problem for many second-generation Latinos in Southern California, a key element in the development of Latino gangs. School failure is one of the key variables distinguishing gang members from other youths from similar backgrounds. The high incidence of dropping out and/or exclusion or expulsion from school resulted in significant numbers of barrio youngsters being socialized in the streets, as discussed in chapter 4. The majority of the gang youths Diego Vigil studied began to withdraw from school life by the third or fourth grade. For many, their "school careers began with skepticism, limited parental encouragement, and early exposure to street experiences that did little to promote self-discipline. It is clear that by the third or fourth grade they had not effectively adapted to the school situation."[158] Long before they officially dropped out (usually around age 16), they had been turned off by school. "Schooling for children in these neighborhoods has often been a process of disengagement and dropping out. More time is spent out of school, as the outside street world takes over."[159] Some began to have problems as early as kindergarten, with the language barrier being the predominant cause. Many had experienced a great deal of prejudice and discrimination. Most of the problems at school began long before any involvement with a gang.

Felix Padilla found that the gang members he studied in Chicago had been labeled deviants and troublemakers by school officials, usually during their elementary school years—long before they joined the gang. These youths responded "by joining with others so labeled and engaging in corresponding behavior."[160] They developed various forms of oppositional behavior (fighting, cutting classes, and not doing homework) and a distinctive subculture—thus responding very early in their lives in ways that were almost identical to gang behavior. In effect, says Padilla, "They were undergoing early preparation for a later stage in their teenage years (during high school) when they would finally join the gang."[161] The youths experienced a form of public humiliation from some of their teachers and from some of their peers—painful experiences that influenced them to seek out others who had been similarly branded.

> If the teachers and everyone else thought that we were bad, we started to show that we were. So, we started doing a lot of bad things, like hitting some kids and even talking back to the teacher and laughing at her. In a way, it was kind of fun, because here are these teachers thinking we were nuts and we would act nuts. That made them feel good.[162]

Rather than suffer additional humiliation, many youths skipped school to avoid verbal abuse, even as early as elementary school. Padilla observes that "during their adolescent years the institution of education and its agents, the administrators and teachers, were already experienced as antagonistic elements in their socialization rather than as facilitators of their goals."[163] Padilla's Chicago gang members indicate that one of the turning points in their lives came during high school. Prior to this time most of these youths were marginal members of the gang, engaged mostly in hanging out on the street corners or at school; "turning" (becoming regular and committed gang members) came during their early high school years.

School problems figure prominently in the lives of girl gang members. Many have had very negative reactions toward the school system. One study found that even though seven of ten girl subjects graduated from high school, they all felt unprepared to compete in the legitimate economy. A typical response was: "Mostly school is a waste. The teachers don't care nothing about us. . . . It has nothing to do with the real world." Another said, "School doesn't teach you about real life. All it prepares you for is a minimum wage job."[164] Most girl gang members are highly likely to drop out of school. A study of San Francisco gangs found that the median number of years of education was 10, and only about one-third of the gang members were actually in school at the time of the interviews.[165] Laura Fishman's study of the Vice Queens in Chicago found that most attended school only sporadically because of conflict with school officials. Most eventually dropped out of school.[166]

Many have noted that school is often deemed totally irrelevant to the lives of gang members. Being bored at school and believing that gang life is exciting are motivations to drop out and join a gang. Nanette Davis summarized the dismal prospects for many girl gang members: "School is a road that leads to nowhere, and emancipation and independence are out of reach, given their limited family and community networks . . . avenues of opportunity for urban underclass girls are blocked by several sobering realities."[167] These include lack of education, training, access to meaningful employment, and few, if any, career possibilities.

Mary Harris found that the bonds to both family and to school were weak for many girls; none of the females in her study completed high school. Their source of status and identity was the gang—"the most prevalent peer group association in the barrio, the one most readily available and [that] provides a strong substitute for weak family and lack of conventional school ties."[168]

Victimization is a critical issue for youth who are in gangs. Studies have shown that a key reason youth join gangs is for safety or protection. The percentage of gang-involved youths who report feeling safe at school is 53% versus 71% of nongang youths.[169] Researchers also have found that a large percentage of adolescents who committed a property or violent offense had themselves been victimized previously. Gang-involved youths engage in a higher proportion of delinquency than their nongang peers—and also experience considerably higher levels of victimization.[170] In California, 26% of gang members reported being threatened or injured with a weapon at school versus 7% of nongang members. The percentages for being pushed, shoved, or hit were 43% for gang members versus 32% for nongang members. Of those reporting harassment due to ethnicity, 29% were gang members versus 16% nongang members.[171]

Youth who are at risk of gang membership or who have joined gangs face a variety of challenges. Zero-tolerance policies at schools may exacerbate the gang problem. "Suspensions and expulsions force already marginalized youth onto the streets and away from prosocial connections at school."[172]

Summary

Schools are some of the most important U.S. social institutions, providing building blocks for a better life. Money spent on public schooling pays enormous returns down the road. Likewise, failure at this stage of one's life results in a heavy toll for all of us.

Before the average citizen reaches the age of 18, about three-fourths of his or her life has been spent in the public school system, at least for nine months out of every year. Schooling has always been closely related to social class and often perpetuates class differences. Rather than equalizing differences through education, public schools sometimes seem only to perform the function of social control. In the modern era, "zero tolerance" has often led to policies that create a resemblance to "day prisons." Virtually every school district in large urban areas now has police officers either inside or nearby schools.

The public school experience is closely related to delinquency and juvenile justice. Problems at school have a tendency to escalate and eventually reach the juvenile court. A great amount of delinquent behavior is directly related to a youth's performance in school. Below-average grades, suspension, and expulsion lead to dropping out. One of the key variables in explaining membership in a gang is what occurs within the school context, especially in junior high or middle schools.

NOTES

[1] Kerbo, H. R. (2003). *Social Stratification and Inequality* (5th ed.). New York: McGraw-Hill, p. 404. Kerbo provides a good brief summary of the literature on education and achievement.

[2] Saporito, B. (2011, January 17). "Where the Jobs Are." *Time* 177(2), pp. 32, 35.

[3] Ibid., p. 31.

[4] Vigil, J. D. (2010). *Gang Redux: A Balanced Anti-Gang Strategy.* Long Grove, IL: Waveland Press, p. 47.

[5] Cooley, A. (2010). "Failed States in Education: Chomsky on Dissent, Propaganda, and Reclaiming Democracy in the Media Spectacle." *Educational Studies* 46: 579–605.

[6] Fones-Wolf, E. (1992). *Selling Free Enterprise: The Business Assault on Labor and Liberalism, 1945–1960.* Urbana: University of Illinois Press, p. 190.

[7] Schor, J. (1991). *The Overworked American: The Unexpected Decline of Leisure.* New York: Basic Books, pp. 60–61.

[8] Quoted in Curti, M. (1959). *The Social Ideas of American Educators.* Totowa, NJ: Littlefield, Adams, p. 203.

[9] Shelden, R. G. (1976). "Rescued from Evil; Origins of the Juvenile Justice System in Memphis, Tennessee, 1900–1917." Ph.D. dissertation, Southern Illinois University, Carbondale; see also Shelden, R. G. (2008). *Controlling the Dangerous Classes: A History of Criminal Justice in America* (2nd ed). Boston: Allyn & Bacon.

[10] This idea is documented in Kozol, J. (2005). *The Shame of the Nation: The Restoration of Apartheid Schooling in America.* New York: Broadway Books.

[11] Kerbo, *Social Stratification and Inequality*, p. 404.

[12] Kozol, *The Shame of the Nation*, p. 96.

[13] Ibid., p. 94.

[14] Ibid., p. 93.

[15] Jealous, B. T., R. M. Brock, and A. Huffman (2011, April). "Misplaced Priorities: Over Incarcerate, Under Educate." NAACP Smart and Safe Campaign. Retrieved from http://naacp.3cdn.net/01d6f368edbe135234_bq0m68x5h.pdf

[16] Lapham, L. (2000, August). "School Bells." *Harper's Magazine*, p. 9.

[17] Giroux, H. (2001). *Public Spaces, Private Lives: Beyond the Culture of Cynicism.* Lanham, MD: Rowman & Littlefield, p. 47.

[18] Foote, D. (2008, May 20). "Rewriting the Locke Story." *Los Angeles Times.* Retrieved from http://articles.latimes.com/2008/may/20/opinion/oe-foote20

[19] Foote, D. (2008). *Relentless Pursuit: A Year in the Trenches with Teach for America.* New York: Vintage Books.

[20] Foote, "Rewriting the Locke Story." There is hope that students at Locke will have a better chance. Green Dot Public Schools, an organization that operates 18 public charter high schools in Los Angeles and one in the Bronx, took control of Locke for the 2008–2009 school year. It created seven smaller learning communities and emphasized parental participation and a curriculum that would prepare students for college. At the end of Green Dot's second year of running the school, the retention rate had increased 36%. Green Dot Public Schools (2010, August 11). "Transformation of Locke High School." Retrieved from http://www.greendot.org/green_dot039s_transformation_of_locke_high_school_yields_impressive_retention_and_enrollment_rates

[21] Ibid.

[22] Ibid., p. 46.

[23] Dokoupil, T. (2010, June 7). "'Zero Tolerance' Trouble in New York." *Newsweek*, p. 6.

[24] Lydersen, K. (2003, July 1). "Zero Tolerance for Teens." *AlterNet.* Retrieved from http://www.alternet.org/story/16305/

[25] Lydersen, "Zero Tolerance."

[26] *J. D. B. v. North Carolina* No. 09-11121. Argued March 23, 2011. Retrieved from http://www.supremecourt.gov/oral_arguments/argument_transcripts/09-11121.pdf; Savage, D. (2010, November 2). "Justices Take Up Kids' Rights." *Chicago Tribune*, p. 13.

[27] Kelly, J. (2010, November 12). "Weekly Notes." Youth Today. Retrieved from http://www.youthtoday.org/view_blog.cfm?blog_id=420

[28] Santa Cruz, N. (2011, February 25). "For Chronic Truants, a GPS Program Can Help Them Make the Grade." *Los Angeles Times.* Retrieved from http://www.latimes.com/news/local/la-me-0225-gps-kids-20110225,0,5243827.story

[29] Quoted in Selmon, D. and P. Leighton (2010). *Punishment for Sale: Private Prisons, Big Business, and the Incarceration Binge*. Lanham, MD: Rowman & Littlefield, p. 171.

[30] The website is: http://www.keepntrack.com/

[31] Warnick, B. R. (2008). "Surveillance Cameras in Schools: An Ethical Analysis." *Harvard Educational Review* 77: 317–43.

[32] Paige, C. (2008, October 19). "'Big Brother' Concerns over School Cameras." *Boston Globe*. Retrieved from http://www.boston.com/news/local/articles/2008/10/19/big_brother_concerns_over_school_cameras/

[33] Parker, B. (2009, October 22). "High School Tightens Security." *Boston Globe*. Retrieved from http://www.boston.com/news/local/articles/2009/10/22/lexington_high_school_to_install_125_surveillance_cameras/

[34] Frank, T. (2007, November 1). "School Security Cameras Go Cutting Edge." *USA Today*. Retrieved from http://www.usatoday.com/news/nation/2007-11-01-school-cameras_n.htm

[35] COPS (2010, September). "Secure Our Schools." Retrieved from http://www.cops.usdoj.gov/pdf/fact_sheets/e091028312-SOS-FactSheet_093010.pdf

[36] COPS (n.d.). "FY2011 Secure Our Schools Program." Retrieved from http://www.cops.usdoj.gov/Default.asp?Item=2368

[37] Lydersen, p. 3.

[38] Herbert, B. (2010, March 5). "Cops vs. Kids." *New York Times*. Retrieved from http://www.nytimes.com/2010/03/06/opinion/06herbert.html

[39] Urbina, I. (2009, October 12). "It's a Fork, It's a Spoon, It's a . . . Weapon?" *New York Times*. Retrieved from http://www.nytimes.com/2009/10/12/education/12discipline.html

[40] St. George, D. (2011, February 20). "Suicide Turns Attention to Fairfax Discipline Procedures." *Washington Post*. Retrieved from http://www.washingtonpost.com/wp-dyn/content/article/2011/02/19/AR2011021904528.html?sid=ST2011021904571

[41] Ibid.

[42] Gibbs, N. (2011, March 21). "Zero Tolerance, Zero Sense." *Time* 177, pp. 11, 62.

[43] Dorell, O. (2009, November 2). "Schools' Zero-tolerance Policies Tested." *USA Today*. Retrieved from http://www.usatoday.com/news/nation/2009-11-01-zero-tolerance_N.htm

[44] Suggs, E. (2010, February 13). "Zero Tolerance in Schools to Be Challenged under New Senate Bill." *The Atlanta Journal-Constitution*. Retrieved from http://www.ajc.com/news/georgia-politics-elections/zero-tolerance-in-schools-301284.html

[45] Ibid.

[46] Savage, D. G. (2009, June 26). "Supreme Court Declares Strip-Search of Student Unconstitutional." *Los Angeles Times*. Retrieved from http://www.latimes.com/news/nationworld/nation/la-na-court-strip-search26-2009jun26,0,5149828.story

[47] *Safford Unified School District v. Redding*, 557 U.S. __ (2009) (docket no. 08-479). Retrieved from http://www.law.cornell.edu/supct/pdf/08-479P.ZO

[48] NYCLU (n.d.). "School to Prison Pipeline." Retrieved from http://www.nyclu.org/issues/racial-justice/school-prison-pipeline

[49] Skiba, R. J., S. E. Eckes, and K. Brown (2009/10). "African American Disproportionality in School Discipline: The Divide Between Best Evidence and Legal Remedy." *New York Law School Law Review*, 54: 1076. Retrieved from http://www.nyls.edu/user_files/1/3/4/17/49/1001/Skiba%20et%20al%2054.4.pdf

[50] Ibid., p. 1072.

[51] Robers, S., J. Zhang, and J. Truman (2010, November). *Indicators of School Crime and Safety: 2010*. National Center for Education Statistics, p. 72. Retrieved from http://nces.ed.gov/pubs2011/2011002.pdf

[52] Losen, D. J. and R. J. Skiba (2010, September). "Suspended Education: Urban Middle Schools in Crisis." Southern Poverty Law Center, pp. 5, 9. Retrieved from http://www.splcenter.org/get-informed/publications/suspended-education

[53] Ibid., pp. 10–11.

[54] Iselin, A. (2010, April 27). "Research on School Suspension." Center for Child and Family Policy. Retrieved from http://www.childandfamilypolicy.duke.edu/pdfs/familyimpact/2010/Suspension_Research_Brief_2010-04-27.pdf

[55] The Schott 50 State Report (2008). Retrieved from http://blackboysreport.org/node/9

[56] Carp, S. (2009, June). "Black Male Conundrum." Catalyst Chicago. Retrieved from http://www.catalyst-chicago.org/news/index.php?item=2593&cat=23

[57] Moore, M. (2007, May 23). "Blacks and Latinos Are Suspended More Often." Retrieved from http://www.gazette.net/stories/052307/montnew221126_32333.shtml

[58] Children & Family Justice Center of Northwestern University School of Law (2005, March 24). *Education on Lockdown: The Schoolhouse to Jailhouse Track*. Retrieved from http://www.mindfully.org/Reform/2005/Schoolhouse-Jailhouse-Track24mar05.htm

[59] Sullivan, E. L. (2007). "A Critical Policy Analysis: The Impact of Zero Tolerance on Out-of-School Suspensions and Expulsions of Students of Color in the State of Texas by Gender and School Level." Doctoral dissertation, Texas A&M University. See also the following: Taylor, M. C. and G. A. Foster (2007)." Bad Boys and School Suspensions: Public Policy Implications for Black Males." *Sociological Inquiry* 56: 498–506; Wallace, J. M. Jr., S. Goodkind, C. M. Wallace, and J. G. Bachman (2008). "Racial, Ethnic, and Gender Differences in School Discipline among U.S. High School Students: 1991–2005." *Negro Educational Review* 59: 47–62, a study that found that while school discipline rates declined during the period studied, they increased among black students; Hornera, S. B., G. D. Firemana, and E. W. Wang (2010). "The Relation of Student Behavior, Peer Status, Race, and Gender to Decisions about School Discipline Using CHAID Decision Trees and Regression Modeling." *Journal of School Psychology* 48: 135–61; Drakeford, W. (2004). "Racial Disproportionality in School Disciplinary Practices." Denver: National Center for Culturally Responsive Educational Systems. Retrieved from http://www.nkces.org/139810101914247170/lib/139810101914247170/DoSE/Disproportionality/07_-_Disproportionality_-_Discipline.pdf; Arcia, E. (2007). "A Comparison of Elementary/K–8 and Middle Schools' Suspension Rates." *Urban Education* 42: 456–69.

[60] Texas Appleseed (2010). *Texas' School-to-Prison Pipeline: School Expulsion—The Path from Lockout to Dropout*. Austin, TX. Retrieved from http://www.texasappleseed.net/index.php?option=com_docman&task=doc_download&gid=309&Itemid=

[61] Ibid.

[62] Southern Poverty Law Center (n.d.). "School-to-Prison Pipeline." Retrieved from http://www.splcenter.org/what-we-do/children-at-risk/school-to-prison-pipeline

[63] Giroux, *Public Spaces*, p. 48.

[64] Skiba et al., "African American Disproportionality in School Discipline," p. 1074.

[65] Shelden, R. G., S. Tracy, and W. B. Brown (2004). *Youth Gangs in American Society* (3rd ed.). Belmont, CA: Wadsworth.

[66] Neufeld, S. and A. Linskey (2008, May 9). "Baltimore Study Links Truancy and Street Violence." *Baltimore Sun*. Retrieved from http://www.latimes.com/news/nationworld/nation/la-na-skippingschool9-2008may09,0,3627757.story

[67] Losen and Skiba, "Suspended Education," p. 11.

[68] American Psychological Association Zero Tolerance Task Force (2008, December). "Are Zero Tolerance Policies Effective in the Schools? An Evidentiary Review and Recommendations." *American Psychologist*, p. 860. Retrieved from http://www.apa.org/pubs/info/reports/zero-tolerance.pdf

[69] Donohue, E., V. Schiraldi, and J. Ziedenberg (1998). *School House Hype: School Shootings and the Real Risks Kids Face in America*. Washington, DC: Justice Policy Institute, p. 1. Retrieved from http://www.prisonpolicy.org/scans/jpi/schoolhouse.pdf

[70] Ibid., p. 4.

[71] Brooks, K., V. Schiraldi, and J. Ziedenberg (2000). *School House Hype: Two Years Later*. Washington, DC: Justice Policy Institute, p. 3. Retrieved from http://www.justicepolicy.org/uploads/justicepolicy/documents/school_house_hype.pdf

[72] Bayles, F. (1999). "Students Say They Feel Safe." *USA Today*, October 29, quoted in Ibid, p. 3.

[73] Brooks et al., *School House Hype: Two Years Later*, p. 31.

[74] Ibid., p. 8.

[75] Ibid., p. 11.

[76] Snyder, H. N. and M. Sickmund (1999). *Juvenile Offenders and Victims: 1999 National Report*. Washington, DC: Office of Juvenile Justice and Delinquency Prevention. Retrieved from http://

www.ncjrs.gov/html/ojjdp/nationalreport99/chapter2.pdf; U.S. Department of Education (2000). *2000 Annual Report on School Safety.* Retrieved from http://www.ncjrs.gov/pdffiles1/ojjdp/193163.pdf

[77] Snyder and Sickmund, *Juvenile Offenders and Victims,* p. 33.

[78] U.S. Department of Education, *2000 Annual Report on School Safety,* p. 11.

[79] *James v. Carneal,* 1998, quoted in Brooks et al., *School House Hype: Two Years Later,* p. 12.

[80] Robers et al., *Indicators of School Crime and Safety.*

[81] Ibid, p. v.

[82] Ibid, p. 20.

[83] Hood, J. (2011, May 10). "School-Safety Solutions Shared." *Chicago Tribune,* p. 13.

[84] Bennett, J. (2010, October 11). "From Lockers to Lockup." *Newsweek,* p. 38.

[85] Cloud, J. (2010, October). "Bullied to Death?" *Time* 176(160): 61–63.

[86] Bennett, "From Lockers to Lockup."

[87] Abel, D. (2010, March 19). "Bullying Bill OK'd in House, 148 to 0." *Boston Globe.* Retrieved from http://www.boston.com/community/moms/articles/2010/03/19/bullying_bill_okd_in_house_148_to_0/

[88] Bennett, "From Lockers to Lockup."

[89] Associated Press (2011, May 4). "Two Teens in South Hadley Bullying Case Get Probation." Retrieved from http://www.wbur.org/2011/05/04/bullying-case-guilty

[90] Robers et al., *Indicators of School Crime and Safety,* Indicator 11, pp. 42–44.

[91] Ibid., pp. 42–43.

[92] Bennett, "From Lockers to Lockup."

[93] Schweber, N. (2011, May 6). "In Fallout of Suicide by Student, a Plea Deal." *New York Times.* Retrieved from http://www.nytimes.com/2011/05/07/nyregion/in-rutgers-suicide-case-ex-student-gets-plea-deal.html?_r=1&ref=mollywei

[94] Schwartz, J. (2010, October 2). "Bullying, Suicide, Punishment." *New York Times.* Retrieved from http://www.nytimes.com/2010/10/03/weekinreview/03schwartz.html

[95] Ibid.

[96] Burrows, "From Lockers to Lockup."

[97] Gibbs, N. (2010, April 19). "Sticks and Stones: When Does Bullying Cross the Line from Cruel to Criminal?" *Time* 175(15): 64.

[98] Editorial (2010, April 1). "Remember Phoebe." *Chicago Tribune,* p. 16.

[99] Robers et al., *Indicators of School Crime and Safety,* p. 42.

[100] Bennett, "From Lockers to Lockup."

[101] Ibid.

[102] Gibbs, "Sticks and Stones."

[103] Katz, J. (1988). *Seductions of Crime: Moral and Sensual Attractions in Doing Evil.* New York: Basic Books.

[104] For a more detailed analysis, see the following: Carnoy, M. (Ed.). (1975). *Schooling in a Corporate Society.* New York: David McKay; Bowles, S. and H. Ginitz (1976). *Schooling in Capitalist America.* New York: Basic Books; Jenks, C. (1979). *Who Gets Ahead? The Determinants of Economic Success in America.* New York: Basic Books; Kozol, J. (1985). *Illiterate America.* New York: New American Library; Kozol, J. (1991). *Savage Inequalities.* New York: Crown.

[105] Schmidt, P. G. (2007). *Color and Money: How Rich White Kids Are Winning the War over College Affirmative Action.* New York: Palgrave Macmillan; Golden, D. (2007). *The Price of Admission: How America's Ruling Class Buys Its Way into Elite Colleges—and Who Gets Left Outside the Gates.* New York: Three Rivers Press; Katznelson, I. (2005). *When Affirmative Action Was White.* New York: W. W. Norton.

[106] U.S. Census Bureau (2010, June). "Public Education Finances 2008." Figure 4, p. xiii. Retrieved from http://www2.census.gov/govs/school/08f33pub.pdf

[107] Baker, B., D. Sciarra, and D. Farrie (2010, September). *Is School Funding Fair? A National Report Card.* Newark, NJ: Education Law Center. Retrieved from http://www.schoolfundingfairness.org/National_Report_Card.pdf

[108] Kozol, *Savage Inequalities,* p. 55.

[109] National Center for Education Statistics (2010, May 27). *Condition of Education 2010.* Retrieved from http://nces.ed.gov/whatsnew/commissioner/remarks2010/5_27_2010.asp

[110] Kozol, *The Shame of the Nation*.

[111] Oakes, J. (2005). *Keeping Track: How Schools Structure Inequality* (2nd ed.). New Haven, CT: Yale University Press, p. 4.

[112] Ibid.

[113] Hu, W. (2009, June 14). "No Longer Letting Scores Separate Students." *New York Times*. Retrieved from http://www.nytimes.com/2009/06/15/education/15stamford.html?pagewanted=1

[114] Ibid.

[115] Ibid.

[116] Ibid.

[117] Rachlin, J. (1989, July 3). "The Label that Sticks." *U.S. News & World Report*, pp. 51–52.

[118] Kelly, S. P. (2007). "Social Class and Tracking within Schools." In L. Weis (Ed.), *The Way Class Works: Readings on School, Family and Economy*. New York: Routledge, pp. 210–24.

[119] Oakes, *Keeping Track*; see also Oakes, J. and M. Saunders (Eds.) (2008). *Beyond Tracking: Multiple Pathways to College, Career, and Civic Participation*. Cambridge, MA: Harvard Educational Press.

[120] Kozol, *Savage Inequalities*, p. 119.

[121] Schafer, W. E., C. Olexa, and K. Polk (1970, October). "Programmed for Social Class Tracking in High School." *Transaction* 7: 39–46. Shelden once examined the school records for a group of gang members and compared them with a group of non-gang members and found that literally *none* of the gang members had any extracurricular activities noted in their transcripts, while most of the non-gang members did. Shelden, R. G., T. Snodgrass, and P. Snodgrass (1992). "Comparing Gang and Non-Gang Offenders: Some Tentative Findings." *Gang Journal* 1: 73–85.

[122] Kelly, D. H. (1974). "Track Position and Delinquency Involvement: A Preliminary Analysis." *Sociology and Social Research* 58: 380–86.

[123] Oakes, *Keeping Track*; see also Oakes and Saunders, *Beyond Tracking*.

[124] Macleod, J. (2008). *Ain't No Makin' It: Aspirations and Attainment in a Low-Income Neighborhood* (3rd ed.). Denver: Westview Press, p. 101.

[125] Sacks, P. (2009). *Tearing Down the Gates: Confronting the Class Divide in American Education*. Berkeley: University of California Press, p. 93.

[126] Ibid., p. 195.

[127] President's Commission on Law Enforcement and Administration of Justice (1967). *Task Force Report on Juvenile Delinquency and Youth Crime*. Washington, DC: U.S. Government Printing Office; Cernkovich, S. and P. Giordano (1992). "School Bonding, Race, and Delinquency." *Criminology* 30: 261–91; Liska, A. E. and M. D. Reed (1985). "Ties to Conventional Institutions and Delinquency: Estimating Reciprocal Effects." *American Sociological Review* 50: 547–60.

[128] Dryfoos, J. G. (1990). *Adolescents at Risk: Prevalence and Prevention*. New York: Oxford University Press.

[129] Schwendinger, H. and J. Schwendinger (1976). "Delinquency and the Collective Varieties of Youth." *Crime and Social Justice* 5 (Spring–Summer).

[130] Shelden et al., *Youth Gangs in American Society*.

[131] Vigil, *Gang Redux*, pp. 48–49.

[132] Quoted in Audas, R. and J. D. Willms (2001, February). "Engagement and Dropping Out of School: A Life-Course Perspective." Applied Research Branch of Strategic Policy, p. 1. Retrieved from http://www.hrsdc.gc.ca/eng/cs/sp/hrsd/prc/publications/research/2001-000175/SP-483-01-02E.pdf

[133] Janosz, M., M. LeBlanc, B. Boulerice, and R. E. Tremblay (1997). "Disentangling the Weight of School Dropout Predictors: A Test on Two Longitudinal Samples." *Journal of Youth and Adolescence* 26: 733–62.

[134] Jimerson, S. R., G. E. Anderson, and A. D. Whipple (2002). "Winning the Battle and Losing the War: Examining the Relation between Grade Retention and Dropping Out of High School." *Psychology in the Schools* 39 (July).

[135] Alliance for Excellence in Education (2009). "High School Dropouts in America." Retrieved from http://www.all4ed.org/files/GraduationRates_FactSheet.pdf

[136] Audas and Willms, "Engagement and Dropping Out of School," pp. 12–13.

[137] Alliance for Excellence in Education, "High School Dropouts in America."

[138] Ellenbogen, S. and C. Chamberland (1997). "The Peer Relations of Dropouts: A Comparative Study of At-Risk and Not At-Risk Youths." *Journal of Adolescence* 20: 355–67.

[139] Audas and Willms, "Engagement and Dropping Out of School," p. 26.

[140] Ravitch, D. (2010). *The Death and Life of the Great American School System: How Testing and Choice Are Undermining Education.* New York: Basic Books.

[141] Blume, H. (2011, March 2). "L.A. School Board to Close Six Charter Schools Caught Cheating." *Los Angeles Times.* Retrieved from http://www.latimes.com/news/local/la-me-0302-lausd-charters-20110302,0,1573991.story

[142] Whitaker, B. (2010, May 28). "High School Dropouts Costly for U.S. Economy." CBS News. Retrieved from http://www.cbsnews.com/stories/2010/05/28/eveningnews/main6528227.shtml

[143] Children's Defense Fund (2011). *Portrait of Inequality 2011: Black Children in America,* p. 4. Retrieved from http://www.childrensdefense.org/programs-campaigns/black-community-crusade-for-children-II/bccc-assets/portrait-of-inequality.pdf

[144] Alliance for Excellence in Education, "High School Dropouts in America."

[145] Whitaker, "High School Dropouts."

[146] Alliance for Excellence in Education, "High School Dropouts in America."

[147] Seema Mehta, S. (2009, September 24). "Dropouts Costing California $1.1 Billion Annually in Juvenile Crime Costs." *Los Angeles Times.* For the complete report see Belfield, C. (2009). "High School Dropouts and the Economic Losses from Juvenile Crime in California." Retrieved from http://cdrp.ucsb.edu/dropouts/pubs_reports.htm

[148] Sum, A., I. Khatiwada, and J. McLaughlin (2009, October). *The Consequences of Dropping Out of High School.* Boston: Center for Labor Market Studies, Northeastern University. http://www.clms.neu.edu/publication/documents/The_Consequences_of_Dropping_Out_of_High_School.pdf

[149] Glesmann, C., B. Krisberg, and S. Marchionna (2009, July). "Youth in Gangs: Who Is at Risk?" National Council on Crime and Delinquency, p. 1. Retrieved from http://www.nccd-crc.org/nccd/pdf/Youth_gangs_final.pdf

[150] Office of Juvenile Justice and Delinquency Prevention (2009, May). *Comprehensive Gang Model: A Guide to Assessing Your Community's Youth Gang Problem.* "Student and School Data," p. 49. Retrieved from http://www.nationalgangcenter.gov/Content/Documents/Assessment-Guide/Assessment-Guide.pdf

[151] Naber, P. A., D. C. May, S. H. Decker, K. L Minor, and J. B. Wells (2006). "Are There Gangs in Schools? It Depends upon Whom You Ask." *Journal of School Violence* 5: 53–72.

[152] Urban Institute Policy Center (2008, May). *Community Collaboratives Addressing Youth Gangs: Interim Findings from the Gang Reduction Program,* p. 5. Retrieved from http://www.urban.org/UploadedPDF/411692_communitycollaboratives.pdf

[153] Ibid., p. 6.

[154] Howell, J. O. and J. P. Moore (2010, May). "History of Street Gangs in the United States." National Gang Center Bulletin, No. 4, p. 11. Retrieved from http://www.nationalgangcenter.gov/Content/Documents/History-of-Street-Gangs.pdf

[155] Shelden et al., *Youth Gangs in American Society.*

[156] Hill, K. G., C. Lui, and J. D. Hawkins (2001). "Early Precursors of Gang Membership: A Study of Seattle Youth." Bureau of Justice Statistics. Retrieved from http://www.ncjrs.gov/pdffiles1/ojjdp/190106.pdf

[157] Glesmann et al., "Youth in Gangs," p. 2.

[158] Vigil, J. D. (1988). *Barrio Gangs.* Austin: University of Texas Press, p. 37.

[159] Vigil, *Gang Redux,* p. 46.

[160] Padilla, F. (1992). *The Gang as an American Enterprise.* Piscataway, NJ: Rutgers University Press, p. 69.

[161] Ibid.

[162] Ibid., p. 74.

[163] Ibid., p. 78.

[164] Kitchen, D. B. (1995). "Sisters in the Hood." Unpublished Ph.D. dissertation, Western Michigan University, pp. 119–20.

[165] Lauderback, D., J. Hansen, and D. Waldorf (1992). "'Sisters Are Doin' It for Themselves': A Black Female Gang in San Francisco." *The Gang Journal* 1: 70.

[166] Fishman, L. T. (1995). "The Vice Queens: An Ethnographic Study of Black Female Gang Behavior." In M. Klein, C. Maxson, and J. Miller (Eds.), *The Modern Gang Reader.* Los Angeles: Roxbury, pp. 83–92.

[167] Davis, N. (1999). *Youth Crisis: Growing Up in the High Risk Society.* Westport, CT: Praeger, p. 257.

[168] Harris, M. G. (1997). "Cholas, Mexican-American Girls, and Gangs." In L. G. Mays (Ed.), *Gangs and Gang Behavior.* Chicago: Nelson-Hall, p. 156.

[169] Glesmann et al., "Youth in Gangs," p. 6.

[170] Ibid., p. 5.

[171] Ibid.

[172] Ibid., p. 8.

PART III

RESPONSES TO DELINQUENCY

PROCESSING OFFENDERS THROUGH THE JUVENILE JUSTICE SYSTEM

This chapter focuses on the four major topics of the modern juvenile justice system: (1) juvenile laws, (2) the rights of juveniles, (3) the structure of the juvenile court, and (4) the processing of youths through the court system.

Juvenile Laws

The juvenile court today has jurisdiction over youths under a certain age who (1) violate laws applicable to adults, (2) commit *status offenses*, and (3) are dependent or neglected. The upper age of juvenile court *jurisdiction* in most states is 17. In 10 states, the upper age limit is 16; in three states it is 15.[1] In a growing number of states youths who commit certain offenses are transferred to the adult system, a process known as *certification* or *waiver* (discussed later in this chapter).

As discussed in previous chapters, one of the most controversial aspects of the juvenile law involves *status offenses*. The distinguishing characteristic of juvenile law is that youths under a certain age may be arrested and processed for behavior in which adults are free to engage. Most of the controversy stems from the vagueness of the statutes; some of it stems from the *parens patriae* justification for state intervention; and much of it stems from differential application. The double standard treatment of males and females will be discussed in more detail in the next chapter. Chapter 1 described the application of many of these offenses primarily to children of immigrant parents. After more than 150 years these laws are still being applied more vigorously against the children of the poor, and they are just as vague as they have always been. The ambiguity of the statutes gives those in authority a tremendous amount of discretionary power and often leads to arbitrary decisions based on subjective value judgments colored by class, race, and sexual biases.

The Rights of Juveniles

During the past four decades there has been an increase in the use of attorneys in juvenile court cases and a greater emphasis on procedural rights, at least in the courts in major metropolitan areas. One reason for this change can be attributed to several important Supreme Court decisions beginning in the late 1960s that extended due process rights to juveniles. The first case was *Kent v. United States*, decided in 1966.[2] The case presented important challenges to the procedures of the police and juvenile court officials in cases where juveniles commit an offense that would be a major felony if committed by an adult. In September 1961, Morris Kent (age 16 and on probation) was charged with raping a woman and stealing her wallet. He confessed to the crime, and his lawyer filed a motion requesting a hearing on jurisdiction. The juvenile court judge waived Kent to the jurisdiction of the adult court—without having talked with Kent's lawyer, without ruling on the lawyer's motion, and without a written statement of the reasons for the waiver. Kent was convicted and sentenced in adult court to a term of 30 to 90 years in prison.

The Supreme Court ruled that when a judge considers whether to transfer a case from the juvenile court to an adult court, a juvenile is entitled to a hearing and has the right to counsel. The court must provide a written statement giving the reasons for the waiver, and the defense counsel must be given access to all records and reports used in reaching the decision to waive. Justice Abe Fortas wrote the opinion and issued one of the strongest indictments of the juvenile court ever:

> There is no place in our system of law for reaching a result of such tremendous consequences without ceremony—without hearing, without effective assistance of counsel, without a statement of reasons. It is inconceivable that a court of justice dealing with adults, with respect to a similar issue, would proceed in this manner. . . . There is much evidence that some juvenile courts . . . [lack] the personnel, facilities and techniques to perform adequately as representatives of the State in a *parens patriae* capacity, at least with respect to children charged with law violation. There is evidence, in fact, that there may be grounds for concern that the child receives the worst of both worlds; that he gets neither the protection accorded to adults nor the solicitous care and regenerative treatment postulated for children.[3]

The Court reversed the conviction.

Perhaps the most significant case regarding juvenile court procedures was *In re Gault* decided in 1967.[4] The sheriff placed fifteen-year-old Gerald Gault in a detention home without notifying his parents after a neighbor complained about receiving a lewd telephone call that she believed had been made by Gault. At the time, Gault was on six months probation after having been found delinquent for being in the company of a boy who had stolen a wallet. He was not given adequate notification of the charges and not advised that he could be represented by counsel—nor did his accuser appear in court. He was convicted and sentenced to the State Industrial School until the age of 21. Gault's attorneys filed a writ of habeas corpus in the Superior Court of Arizona, which was denied.

On appeal to the U.S. Supreme Court, Gault's attorneys argued that the juvenile code of Arizona was unconstitutional. The justices found in favor of Gault and held that at the adjudicatory hearing stage, juvenile court procedures must include (1) adequate written notice of charges, (2) the right to counsel, (3) privilege against self-incrimination, (4) the right to cross-examine accusers, (5) a transcript of the proceedings, and (6) the right to appellate review. Justice Fortas again wrote the decision, very revealing of actual juvenile court procedures.

> A boy is charged with misconduct. The boy is committed to an institution where he may be restrained of liberty for years. It is of no constitutional consequence *and of limited practical meaning* that the institution to which he is committed is called an Industrial School. The fact of the matter is that, however euphemistic the title, a "receiving home" or an "industrial school" for juveniles is an institution of confinement in which the child is incarcerated for a greater or lesser time. His world becomes "a building with whitewashed walls, regimented routine and institutional hours. Instead of mother and father and sisters and brothers and friends and classmates, his world is peopled by guards, custodians, state employees, and "delinquents" confined with him for anything from waywardness to rape and homicide.
>
> In view of this, it would be extraordinary if our Constitution did not require the procedural regularity and the exercise of care implied in the phrase "due process." Under our Constitution, the condition of being a boy does not justify a kangaroo court. . . .
>
> The essential difference between Gerald's case and a normal criminal case is that safeguards available to adults were discarded in Gerald's case. The summary procedure as well as the long commitment was possible because Gerald was 15 years of age instead of over 18. . . . For the particular offense immediately involved, the maximum punishment would have been a fine of $5 to $50, or imprisonment in jail for not more than two months. Instead, he was committed to custody for a maximum of six years. If he had been over 18 and had committed an offense to which such a sentence might apply, he would have been entitled to substantial rights under the Constitution of the United States as well as under Arizona's laws and constitution. . . . So wide a gulf between the State's treatment of the adult and of the child requires a bridge sturdier than mere verbiage, and reasons more persuasive than cliché can provide.[5]

The Court essentially found that Gault was being punished for his youth rather than being helped by the juvenile court. As in the *Kent* decision, the Court questioned *parens patriae* as the founding principle of juvenile justice. It criticized the fiction created by the progressive reformers—that juveniles could only be entitled to custody, rather than liberty—which made the juvenile proceedings civil in nature and not subject to constitutional safeguards.[6] "Juvenile court history has again demonstrated that unbridled discretion, however benevolently motivated, is frequently a poor substitute for principle and procedure."[7]

Another significant case was *In re Winship*, decided in 1970.[8] Justice Brennan wrote the decision, which addressed how much proof is necessary to support a finding of delinquency. Again rejecting the idea that the juvenile justice system was a civil system, the Supreme Court held that the due process clause of the Fourteenth Amendment required that delinquency charges in the juvenile system have to meet the same standard of "beyond a reasonable doubt" required in the adult system.

> In sum, the constitutional safeguard of proof beyond a reasonable doubt is as much required during the adjudicatory stage of a delinquency proceeding as are those constitutional safeguards applied in *Gault*—notice of charges, right to counsel, the rights of confrontation and examination, and the privilege against self-incrimination. . . . Where a 12-year-old child is charged with an act of stealing which renders him liable to confinement for as long as six years, then, as a matter of due process the case against him must be proved beyond a reasonable doubt.

The Court noted that the New York Court of Appeals had attempted to justify a preponderance-of-evidence standard based on the grounds that juvenile proceedings are designed to save the child rather than to punish. It also noted that *Gault* rejected such justifications. "Good intentions do not themselves obviate the need for criminal due process safeguards in juvenile courts."[9]

In *McKeiver v. Pennsylvania* the Court dealt with the right of trial by jury, normally guaranteed to adults but traditionally denied to juveniles.[10] The Court ruled in 1971 that jury trials were admissible but not mandatory within the juvenile court. (Ten states currently allow jury trials for juveniles.)

> We must recognize, as the Court has recognized before, that the fond and idealistic hopes of the juvenile court proponents and early reformers of three generations ago have not been realized. . . . Too often the juvenile court judge falls far short of that stalwart, protective, and communicating figure the system envisaged. The community's unwillingness to provide people and facilities and to be concerned, the insufficiency of time devoted, the scarcity of professional help, the inadequacy of dispositional alternatives, and our general lack of knowledge all contribute to dissatisfaction with the experiment. . . . Despite all these disappointments, all these failures, and all these shortcomings, we conclude that trial by jury in the juvenile court's adjudicative stage is not a constitutional requirement. . . . If the formalities of the criminal adjudicative process are to be superimposed upon the juvenile court system, there is little need for its separate existence. Perhaps that ultimate disillusionment will come one day, but for the moment we are disinclined to give impetus to it.

The Court's decisions in *Gault* and *Winship* directed juvenile courts to insure the accuracy of the fact-finding stage. In *McKeiver*, the Court considered whether a jury is a necessary component to accurate fact finding in juvenile adjudications. It decided that juries are not more accurate than judges in the adjudication stage; moreover it expressed concerns that juries could be disruptive to the informal atmosphere of the juvenile court and could make the process more adversarial.[11] The Court reasoned that mandatory jury trials could create problems for juveniles, including publicity that would be contrary to the confidentiality usually linked with juvenile justice.

Since this ruling several states have allowed juveniles to have jury trials. Some allow them under some special circumstances (e.g., Colorado) and some under no circumstances (e.g., California). The impact of these decisions has been minimal since only a small number of juveniles end up in front of a jury. One study found that only 94 cases out of 710 petitioned to court were set for trial, and only 7 actually went to trial.[12]

Breed v. Jones was decided in 1975, nine years after *Kent*.[13] It involved essentially the same issue—waiver to the adult court. However, in this case, Jones' lawyer argued that his client had been subjected to "double jeopardy" since he was adjudicated in juvenile court (tantamount to a conviction in an adult court) and then tried again in an adult court for the same crime. The Court ruled that an adjudication in juvenile court involving a violation of a criminal statute is equivalent to a trial in criminal court. The Court also specified that jeopardy applies at the adjudication hearing when evidence is first presented. Waiver cannot occur after jeopardy attaches; juvenile courts must hold transfer hearings prior to adjudication.

In 1984, the Supreme Court issued a ruling in *Schall v. Martin* that most consider to be a setback to juvenile rights. It ruled that the courts have a right to hold youths in preventive detention if judges determine the youths pose a danger to the community. Fourteen-year-old Gregory Martin was arrested in 1977 and charged with robbery, assault, and possession of a weapon. He was detained pending adjudication because the court found there was a serious risk that he would commit another crime if released. Martin's attorney filed a habeas corpus action challenging the fairness of preventive detention. The lower appellate courts reversed the juvenile court's detention order. The Supreme Court upheld the constitutionality of the preventive detention statute, ruling that preventive detention serves a legitimate objective to protect both the juvenile and society from pretrial crime and is not intended as punishment. The Court found that there were enough procedures in place to protect juveniles from wrongful deprivation of liberty: namely, a notice, a statement of the facts and reasons for detention, and a probable cause hearing within a short time. In *Schall v. Martin*, the Court confirmed *parens patriae* in promoting the welfare of children.[14]

In his dissent, Justice Marshall (joined by Justices Brennan and Stevens) emphasized the lack of adequate criteria at a judge's disposal to determine whether or not a juvenile may, after release, commit a crime. He also noted that "Family Court judges are incapable of determining which of the juveniles who appear before them would commit offenses before their trials if left at large and which would not."[15] The district court's ruling that prompted the appeal had noted that there were no diagnostic tools that enable even highly trained criminologists to predict reliably which juveniles will engage in violent crime. Brennan also pointed to the minimal amount of data available to a judge at a youth's initial appearance, yet the judge "must make his decision whether to detain a juvenile on the basis of a set of allegations regarding the child's alleged offense, a cursory review of his background and criminal record, and the recommendation of a probation officer who, in the typical case, has seen the child only once."[16]

Even after the decision in *Gault*, the vast majority of juveniles have waived their rights to counsel in juvenile court (recall the example of Nick Stuban in chapter 10).

> In the years following *Gault*, states moved to implement the right to counsel, but few have defined it as an absolute right by requiring that the juve-

nile have the advice of an attorney before the right to counsel can be waived, or by prescribing an "unwaivable" right to counsel.[17]

Studies by Barry Feld and the Government Accounting Office reveal that many juveniles waive their right to a lawyer.[18] The American Bar Association (ABA) estimated that "as many 90% of the children waive counsel in delinquency proceedings, almost always without the benefit of consulting with a lawyer beforehand and no warning of the dangers of proceeding without a lawyer."[19] The ABA also discussed the excessive caseloads of lawyers representing juveniles—as many as 900 a year—resulting in minimal contact with clients and often meeting for the first time when they appear in court. Many juveniles are poor, and the problems are especially acute when it comes to indigent defense. Some courts have operated on the assumption that lawyers are not really needed and that they are impediments to the court's philosophy of acting in the best interest of the child. Another study examined the effects of *Gault* in Minnesota and found that after three decades of resistance on the part of judges a law was passed in 1995 forcing them to appoint counsel in all delinquency cases. Four years later it was found that there were still inconsistencies in the appointment of counsel.[20] In sum, the fact that juveniles have various rights approaching those of adults may be meaningless in the daily reality of juvenile court procedures.

Courts have also determined that juveniles adjudicated and committed to correctional facilities have a *right to treatment*. A case decided in 1954 ruled that juveniles could not be held in institutions that did not provide any form of rehabilitation.[21] In a 1972 case, *Inmates of the Boys' Training School v. Affleck*, a federal court ruled that since the purpose of the juvenile court is rehabilitation, youths have a right to treatment if committed to an institution.[22] This case established certain minimal standards, such as sufficient clothing to meet seasonal needs, proper bedding (sheets, pillow cases, etc.), daily showers, personal hygiene supplies, minimal writing materials, and access to books and other reading materials. It "shocks the conscience" that some jurisdictions did not follow such standards until this ruling.

The Violent Crime Control and Law Enforcement Act of 1994 gave the Attorney General the authority to investigate and to seek judicial remedies when the practices of administrators of juvenile justice systems violate the federal rights of incarcerated juveniles. The Special Litigation Section has investigated conditions of confinement in more than 100 juvenile facilities in 16 states. It currently monitors conditions in more than 65 facilities that operate under settlement agreements with the United States. The cases involved both publicly and privately operated facilities, as well as conditions for youths being held prior to their juvenile court adjudication and those placed in facilities as a result of being adjudicated delinquent. The investigations and subsequent settlements focused on constitutional rights to reasonable safety, adequate medical and mental health care, rehabilitative treatment, and education. Several of the cases involved allegations of staff abuse, preventable youth-on-youth violence, excessive use of restraints and isolation, and the problems of overcrowding.[23] Despite such intervention and investigation, abuses continue within juvenile institutions, a subject to be discussed in more detail in the next chapter.

The Eighth Amendment Protection

Prior to 2005, about one in every 50 individuals on death row was a juvenile offender. Victor Streib found that executions for crimes committed by youths younger than 18 accounted for 1.8% of all confirmed legal executions carried out between 1642 and 2004—the 366 executions equaled about one per year.[24] Between January 1, 1973 and April 30, 2004, 22 juvenile offender executions (2.4% of the 909 executions during those years) were carried out in the United States. One of the juveniles executed was 16 at the time of his crime; the others were all 17. Ten were white; 11 were black; one was Latino.[25] Imposing the death penalty for crimes committed at 16 or 17 violated the social construction of adolescence and the idea that juveniles are less criminally responsible than adults.[26]

In 1955, the United States ratified Article 68 of the Fourth Geneva Convention (1949), which states "the death penalty may not be pronounced on a protected person who was under 18 years of age at the time of the offense."[27] Thus, for five decades, the U.S. protected youthful offenders in other countries from the death penalty during war or armed conflict but did not offer the youth in this country the same protections during peace. The International Covenant on Civil and Political Rights was signed by the U.S. in 1977 and ratified in 1992.[28] The provisions in this covenant include that youths should be separated from incarcerated adults and receive appropriate treatment, and the death penalty must not be imposed for crimes committed by juvenile offenders. The U.S. government stated:

> The policy and practice of the United States are generally in compliance with and supportive of the Covenant's provisions regarding treatment of juveniles in the criminal justice system. Nevertheless, the United States reserves the right in exceptional circumstances to treat juveniles as adults.[29]

The vast majority of juvenile offenders executed in the U.S. before 1972 were sentenced to death and executed while still teenagers. After the death penalty was reinstated in 1976, the delay between sentencing and execution increased substantially. Of the 22 juveniles discussed earlier, the youngest at the age of execution was 24 and the oldest was 38. Perhaps the fact that it was not actually a child strapped down and killed made it easier for society to allow such sentences. The fact remains, however, these people were executed for crimes they committed as juveniles. Many had been sentenced to death by juries ill informed about any mitigating facts.

For instance, Dwayne Allen Wright was sentenced to death for murder in Virginia. Dwayne grew up in a poor family in a neighborhood characterized by illegal drug activity, gun violence, and homicides. At the age of four, Dwayne's father was incarcerated. His mother, suffering from mental illness, was unemployed for most of his life. When he was 10, his older brother was murdered, after which Dwayne developed serious mental problems. He did poorly at school, and for the next seven years spent time in hospitals and juvenile detention facilities. He was treated for major depression with psychotic episodes; his mental capacity was evaluated as borderline retarded, his verbal ability retarded, and doctors found signs of organic brain damage.[30] In their request for clemency from the governor, Dwayne's attorneys obtained affidavits from two jurors in his 1991 capital trial who stated that they would not have sentenced him to death had they known of brain damage suffered at birth, which left Dwayne prone to violent outbursts. Clemency was denied, and Dwayne was executed on October 14, 1998, for a crime he committed when he was 17.

Thompson v. Oklahoma

In 1983, when he was 15 years old, William Wayne Thompson and three accomplices (who were older than 18) murdered his sister's abusive ex-husband and dumped his body in a river. Thompson was waived to adult court and all 4 defendants were sentenced to death. The Supreme Court ruled in *Thompson v. Oklahoma* that the "cruel and unusual punishments" provision of the Eighth Amendment prohibits the execution of a person who was under 16 years of age at the time of his or her offense.[31]

> This Court has already endorsed the proposition that less culpability should attach to a crime committed by a juvenile than to a comparable crime committed by an adult, since inexperience, less education, and less intelligence make the teenager less able to evaluate the consequences of his or her conduct while at the same time he or she is much more apt to be motivated by mere emotion or peer pressure than is an adult. Given this lesser culpability, as well as the teenager's capacity for growth and society's fiduciary obligations to its children, the retributive purpose underlying the death penalty is simply inapplicable to the execution of a 15-year-old offender. Moreover, the deterrence rationale for the penalty is equally unacceptable with respect to such offenders, since statistics demonstrate that the vast majority of persons arrested for willful homicide are over 16 at the time of the offense, since the likelihood that the teenage offender has made the kind of cold-blooded, cost-benefit analysis that attaches any weight to the possibility of execution is virtually nonexistent, and since it is fanciful to believe that a 15-year-old would be deterred by the knowledge that a small number of persons his age have been executed during the 20th century.[32]

Extending Eighth Amendment protections for juveniles was halted for a number of years. In 1989 the Court ruled in *Stanford v. Kentucky* that the Constitution did not prohibit the execution of 16- and 17-year-old offenders.[33]

Roper v. Simmons

Christopher Simmons was 17 years old when he murdered Shirley Crook in Missouri in 1993; he was sentenced to death. After the Supreme Court ruled in *Atkins v. Virginia* that the Constitution prohibits the execution of mentally retarded people, Simmons filed a new petition arguing that the Constitution prohibits the execution of people who were younger than 18 at the time of the crime. In 2003, the Missouri Supreme Court reviewed his case. The court determined that juvenile executions violated the Eighth Amendment's provision against cruel and unusual punishment under the "evolving standards of decency" test. Simmons' death sentence was vacated, and he was sentenced to life without parole.[34]

In their decision to overturn the death penalty, the Missouri Supreme Court cited *Atkins v. Virginia*. The court stated that although they often know the difference between right and wrong, mentally retarded people "have diminished capacities to understand and process mistakes and learn from experience, to engage in logical reasoning, to control impulses, and to understand the reactions of others." The court also said that "while such deficiencies do not warrant an exemption from criminal sanctions . . . they do diminish their personal culpability."[35]

The state of Missouri appealed the case to the Supreme Court in July 2004. The Court heard arguments in October 2004. Defense lawyers cited the research on brain development during adolescence. Briefs filed jointly by eight medical and mental health associations cited numerous studies in the developmental biology and behavioral literature to support the argument that the areas of the adolescent brain that relate to criminal responsibility do not develop until after the age of 18. While this does not excuse the behavior, it is a mitigating factor that should be considered when deciding on the punishment.[36]

An amicus curiae brief filed jointly by several prominent organizations (including the American Medical Association, American Psychiatric Association, American Society for Adolescent Behavior, and National Mental Health Association) stated:

> Adolescents as a group, even at the age of 16 or 17, are more impulsive than adults. They underestimate risks and overvalue short-term benefits. They are more susceptible to stress, more emotionally volatile, and less capable of controlling their emotions than adults. In short, the average adolescent cannot be expected to act with the same control or foresight as a mature adult. . . . Cutting-edge brain imaging technology reveals that regions of the adolescent brain do not reach a fully mature state until after the age of 18. These regions are precisely those associated with impulse control, regulation of emotions, risk assessment, and moral reasoning. Critical developmental changes in these regions occur only after late adolescence.[37]

Additionally there are often dramatic hormonal and emotional changes. Especially relevant here would be testosterone, which relates to aggression.

The decision in *Roper v. Simmons* clearly represents a turning point in the history of juvenile justice, as did *In re Gault* and *Kent*.

> The Eighth Amendment's prohibition against "cruel and unusual punishments" must be interpreted according to its text, by considering history, tradition, and precedent, and with due regard for its purpose and function in the constitutional design. To implement this framework this Court has established the propriety and affirmed the necessity of referring to "the evolving standards of decency that mark the progress of a maturing society" to determine which punishments are so disproportionate as to be "cruel and unusual."[38]

The Court specifically reasoned that a majority of states (31) had rejected the death penalty for juveniles (and 12 outlawed the death penalty for any offender), that execution was infrequent even in the states where it was allowed (no juveniles had been executed since 1976 in 43 states), and that there was a consistent trend toward abolition of the juvenile death penalty (no juveniles were on death row in 38 states). These facts demonstrated a national consensus against the practice. Sixteen years after *Stanford v. Kentucky*, the court found that evolving standards of decency had formed a national consensus against the execution of juvenile offenders. Justice Kennedy wrote: "The age of 18 is the point where society draws the line for many purposes between childhood and adulthood. It is, we conclude, the age at which the line for death eligibility ought to rest. *Stanford* should be deemed no longer controlling on this issue."[39]

The ruling also made reference to the fact that juveniles are vulnerable to influence and that they are inclined toward immature and irresponsible behavior. Given their diminished culpability, retribution or deterrence does not provide adequate justification for the death penalty. The Court also noted that the execution of juvenile offenders violated several international treaties, including the United Nations Convention on the Rights of the Child and the International Covenant on Civil and Political Rights. The ruling stated that the overwhelming weight of international opinion against the juvenile death penalty confirms the conclusion of the Court that the death penalty is a cruel and unusual punishment for offenders under 18.

Four justices dissented (O'Connor, Rehnquist, Scalia, and Thomas). O'Connor argued that the difference in maturity between adults and juveniles was neither universal nor significant enough to justify a rule excluding juveniles from the death penalty. Scalia argued that the Court improperly substituted its own judgment for that of the people in outlawing juvenile executions. He criticized the majority for counting non-death penalty states toward a national consensus against juvenile executions, and he stated that acknowledgement of foreign approval had no place in the legal opinion of the Supreme Court.

Life without Parole

On May 17, 2010, the Supreme Court ruled that juveniles who commit crimes in which no one is killed may not be sentenced to life without parole.[40] The court found that such sentences violate the Eighth Amendment prohibition against cruel and unusual punishment.

> The inadequacy of penological theory to justify life without parole sentences for juvenile nonhomicide offenders, the limited culpability of such offenders, and the severity of these sentences all lead the Court to conclude that the sentencing practice at issue is cruel and unusual. No recent data provide reason to reconsider *Roper*'s holding that because juveniles have lessened culpability they are less deserving of the most serious forms of punishment.[41]

Justice Kennedy wrote the majority opinion and explained that the State had denied Graham "any chance to later demonstrate that he is fit to rejoin society based solely on a nonhomicide crime that he committed while he was a child in the eyes of the law. This the Eighth Amendment does not permit." Bryan Stevenson, Executive Director of the Equal Justice Initiative, represented Graham and stated:

> This is a significant victory for children. The Court recognized that it is cruel to pass a final judgment on children, who have an enormous capacity for change and rehabilitation compared to adults. I am very encouraged by the Court's ruling. It's an important win not only for kids who have been condemned to die in prison but for all children who need additional protection and recognition in the criminal justice system.[42]

Terrence Graham, age 16, and three accomplices robbed a restaurant in Jacksonville. He was sentenced to one year in jail and three years probation. The next year, he and two accomplices were involved in a home invasion. The judge sentenced him to life without parole for violating his probation.[43] *Graham v. Florida* entitles Graham to a resentencing hearing (which had not been set by May 2011). The ruling affects 129 inmates, 77 in Florida.[44] Included among those inmates is Joe Sullivan, now 33, although the Court declined to hear his companion case (*Sullivan v. Florida*) on the grounds that it was "improvidently granted" (probably because of procedural difficulties).[45]

Joe Sullivan is 1 of only 2 people in the United States sentenced to life without parole for a nonhomicide offense committed at the age of 13. In 1989, Joe was mentally disabled and living in a home where he was physically and sexually abused. Two older boys convinced Joe to participate in a burglary. The three boys entered an empty home, and one older boy took some money and jewelry. That afternoon, the elderly homeowner was sexually assaulted in her home but never saw her attacker. One of the older boys accused Joe of the sexual battery. Both older boys received short sentences in juvenile detention; Joe was charged and tried in adult court by a six-person jury in a one-day proceeding. During the trial, the prosecutor and witnesses repeatedly noted that Joe was African American and the victim was white. Joe was sent to an adult prison at age fourteen, where he was victimized by older inmates. Now 33, he has multiple sclerosis and uses a wheelchair.[46]

As of 2004, Human Rights Watch identified 2,225 inmates who were serving life without parole for crimes committed as juveniles.[47] Most of the sentences were for homicides, which includes felony murder (participation in a crime in which another participant commits murder). By 2009, the number was 2,574.[48] Some of the sentences were unjust beyond the age at which the crime was committed. For example, a 16-year-old girl killed her pimp after three years of brutal treatment. She was arrested and convicted of first-degree murder, despite attempts by her lawyer to have her sentenced as a juvenile. The judge decided she lacked moral scruples and described her crime as well planned; he sentenced her to life without parole. She is now 32 years old. A report by the Equal Justice Initiative found that of the juveniles sentenced to life without parole, at least 73 were 14 or younger when they committed their crimes.[49]

As noted above, 60% of the juveniles serving a sentence of life without parole in the United States are in the state of Florida; 75% are in the South. The rate of such sentences for black juveniles is about 10 times higher than for whites.[50] Why does Florida have such a high concentration of juvenile-life-without-parole cases? Part of the answer comes from an unusual series of events. Nine foreign tourists were killed during an 11-month period from 1992 to 1993. Fears about violent crime and threats to tourism (a significant part of Florida's economy) created an atmosphere ripe for severe penalties. Judge Thomas K. Petersen said: "Florida, probably more than other places because of that rash of crimes, overreacted. It was a hysterical reaction." Former prosecutor Shay Bilchik observed: "My biggest regret is that during the time I was in the prosecutor's office, we were under the false impression that we were insuring greater public safety when we were not."[51]

Juvenile Court: The Structure

The centerpiece of the juvenile justice system is the juvenile court. The size and functions of these courts vary from one jurisdiction to another. Some jurisdictions hear cases on special days in other courts. Other jurisdictions have facilities that range from a small courthouse with a skeleton staff to a large, bureaucratic complex with many separate divisions (often occupying different buildings over several acres of land) and employing over 100 personnel. Some juvenile courts (e.g., Honolulu, New York City, Las Vegas) are called *family courts* and handle a wide variety of family-related problems (e.g., child custody, child support, etc.).

Typically, juvenile courts are part of municipal courts, county courts, or other types of court systems, depending on an area's governmental structure. Most of the courts have the following divisions: (1) intake and detention, (2) probation, (3) records, (4) psychological services, (5) judges and personnel staff, (6) medical services (doctor and nurses), and (7) volunteer services.

Among the most important juvenile court personnel are the judges, referees, probation and parole officers, and the defense and prosecuting attorneys. Judges are usually elected officials and have a wide variety of duties, not unlike judges in the adult system. Referees (sometimes called "masters") are typically lawyers who perform some of the same functions as judges and supplement the roster of juvenile court judges.

Defense attorneys have become more common in juvenile court since *Gault* and are usually part of the public defender system. As noted above, however, many youths who appear in juvenile court are still not represented by an attorney.

The prosecutor is generally a member of the local district attorney's office assigned to the juvenile court (other district attorneys may be assigned to areas like domestic violence, gang prosecution, appeals, etc.). Like their criminal court counterparts, they are involved in every stage of the process, including such important decisions as whether or not to charge, what to charge, whether or not to detain, whether or not to certify a youth as an adult.

There are several other important personnel within a juvenile court, many of whom make some very important decisions. These include intake workers (who are generally the first personnel a youth actually sees when taken into custody and who often decide whether or not to detain), detention workers (who supervise youths who are detained), and probation and parole officers (who supervise youth placed on probation and those released from institutional care, respectively).

While the juvenile court differs in many significant ways from the adult system, there are also numerous similarities. For instance, cases proceed generally from arrest through pretrial hearings through the actual court process to disposition and finally to some form of punishment and/or treatment in a "correctional institution." The juvenile court, however, has different terminology for the stages in the process. For instance, in the juvenile court a *petition* is the equivalent to an indictment, a trial is called an *adjudicatory hearing*, which is often followed by a *dispositional hearing*, roughly the equivalent of a sentencing hearing in the adult system. Parole is known as *aftercare*, while a sentence is called a *commitment*. The term *detention* is the equivalent of jailing, while *taking into custody* is the same as being arrested.[52] Figure 11-1 illustrates the various stages within the typical juvenile court, along with standard definitions.

Figure 11-1   The Juvenile Court Process

Arrest

When a juvenile is arrested by the police, one of three options is usually available: they can release the youth with a simple warning, issue a misdemeanor citation (like a traffic ticket, ordering the youth to appear in court on a certain date), or physically take the youth to the juvenile court and the intake division, where he or she is booked.

Intake

This is the first step following the police decision to take the youth to court. The intake process is an initial screening of the case by staff members. Normally there are also probation officers (sometimes called "intake officers") who review the forms filled out by a staff member who collects some preliminary information (e.g., the alleged offense, various personal information about the youth, such as name, address, phone, names of the parents, etc.). During this stage, a decision is made as to whether to file a *petition* to appear in court on the charges, to drop the charges altogether (e.g., for lack of evidence), or to handle the case informally.

Diversion

In the event that the intake decision is to handle informally, probation staff, usually in cooperation with the prosecutor's office, will either release the youth without any further action or propose a diversion alternative. Diversion entails having the youth and his or her parent or guardian agree to complete certain requirements instead of going to court. This may include supervision by the probation department, plus satisfying certain requirements (e.g., curfew, restitution, community service, substance–abuse treatment, etc.). After a certain length of time, if the youth successfully completes the program, the charges are usually dropped; if not, the youth is brought back to court via a formal petition.

Detention

If the case is petitioned to court, the next major decision is whether to detain the youth or release him or her to a parent or guardian, pending a court appearance. The reasons for

(continued)

detaining a youth usually include: (1) safety (does the youth pose a danger to himself or to others) or (2) flight risk (does the youth pose a risk to flee or not appear in court). If the youth is detained, then a hearing must be held (called a "detention hearing") within a certain period of time (normally 24 to 72 hours), in order for a judge to hear arguments as to whether the youth should be detained any longer. Bail is not generally guaranteed.

Transfer/Waiver
In rare cases, a youth may be transferred or "waived" to the adult system. This is usually (but not always) done only in the case of extremely serious crimes or when the youth is a "chronic" offender.

Adjudication
The juvenile court equivalent of a trial in the adult system is called an *adjudication hearing*. Rather than a jury hearing the case, the final decision rests with a judge or referee. Both defense and prosecuting attorneys present their cases if the youth denies the petition (i.e., pleads not guilty). If a youth admits to the charges (which happens in the majority of all cases), the case proceeds to the next stage.

Disposition
The *disposition hearing* is the equivalent of the sentencing stage in the adult system. Numerous alternatives are available at this stage, including outright dismissal, probation, placement in a community–based program (e.g., "boot camp," wilderness programs, group homes, substance abuse facility, etc.) or incarceration in a secure facility (e.g., "training school").

Aftercare
This stage occurs after a youth has served his or her sentence. It is the equivalent to "parole" in the adult system and, in fact, is often called "youth parole."

Juvenile Justice: The Process

The first stage of the juvenile justice system begins when the police apprehend a youngster for an alleged offense.

Initial Contact: The Police

Given the fact that the police make so many arrests of persons under the age of 18, it should come as no surprise that the largest percentage of referrals to the juvenile court come from the police (over 80%). In most jurisdictions, the police have several options when contact with a juvenile is made (either because of a citizen complaint or an on-site observation of an alleged offense). First, they can, and often do, simply warn and release (for instance, telling a group of young people hanging around a street corner to "move along" or "go home"). Second, they can release after filling out an interview card ("field investigation card" or "field contact card"). Third, they can make a "station adjustment" where a youth is brought to the police station and then either (1) released to a parent or guardian, or (2) released with a referral to some community agency. Fourth, they can issue a misdemeanor citation, which will require the youth and a parent or guardian to appear in juvenile court at some future date (not unlike a traffic ticket). Fifth, they can transport a youth to the juvenile court after making a formal arrest.

One of the most revealing statistics is the number of times the police use a particular option. Police today are far more likely to refer a youth to the juvenile court. In 1974, less than half (47%) of the cases where a juvenile was taken into custody by the police resulted in a referral to juvenile court; most cases (44%) were handled informally within the department.[53] In 2008, the vast majority (66%) were referred to the juvenile court, while 20% were handled within the department.[54] This reflects the general trend toward increasing formality in our response to human problems. Schools used to handle minor conflicts such as fights; now we have literally thousands of "assaults" processed through the juvenile courts. Parents and community groups (mental health workers, counselors, youth leaders, sports coaches, etc.) used to handle various other youth problems.

Does this mean that the offenses committed by youths are getting more serious and thus require more formal processing? No. The offenses for which the majority of youths are charged remain minor—as they always have been. It should be emphasized that the majority of times that the police interact in some way with juveniles, nothing "official" happens—that is, the encounter is not recorded anywhere.[55] One study found that 22% of police encounters with juveniles resulted in an arrest.[56]

Police Discretion and Juveniles

The police have a great deal of *discretion* as to what courses of action to take when dealing with juveniles (or any other member of the public). Decades ago Joseph Goldstein observed that police decision making represents "low visibility decisions in the administration of justice."[57] Police officers make decisions largely out of public view with little public scrutiny—discretion is inherent in the job. Officers can use their discretion to detour juveniles from the juvenile justice system or to involve them with it.

As described above, the police have several alternatives available when they encounter delinquent behavior. They can release with a warning, or they can release after filling out a report that does not constitute an arrest but is an official record of deviant behavior. It is important to note that this information may be used against the youth at a later date. The youth, however, does not have the opportunity to review or contest the charges in the report, a problem that has yet to be dealt with by the courts. After taking the youth to the police station, officers can decide to release him or her to a parent or guardian or release with a referral to a community agency, or to a mental health or social welfare agency. The last option is to decide to start the intake process.

The police are provided with few guidelines about how to determine what action to take. In most states the police are empowered to arrest juveniles without a warrant if there is "reasonable grounds" to believe that the child (1) has committed a delinquent act, (2) is "unruly," (3) is "in immediate danger from his surroundings," or (4) has run away from home. The following factors seem to be the most influential in determining the course of action the police take when confronting a juvenile who may be in violation of the law.

1. *The nature of the offense.* The more serious the offense, the more likely formal action will be taken.

2. *Citizen complainants.* If a citizen has made a complaint and remains on the scene demanding that an arrest be made, the police will comply.

3. *Gender.* Males are far more likely than females to be referred to court, since their offenses are typically more serious. There are some exceptions, such as when girls act contrary to role expectations and the complainant is a parent.[58]

4. *Race* (this is such an important issue that a separate section will be devoted to it later in this chapter). Studies have concluded that race is the most critical variable in determining how far into the system a youth is processed.[59]

5. *Social class.* In general, the lower the social class, the more likely a youth will be formally processed. Police often believe that kids from wealthier neighborhoods have parents who can handle the problem.

6. *Individual factors related to the offender.* Factors such as prior record, age, the context of the offense, the offender's family, etc. influence arrest decisions.

7. *The nature of police–youth encounters.* Much research has focused on the *demeanor* or attitude of the youth. If the youth appears cooperative and respectful, no formal action will be taken. All other things being equal, if the youth is hostile or, in police parlance, "flunks the attitude test," formal action generally follows. Race, class, and gender play a role here; lower class and minority males are far more likely than white males and females to flunk the attitude test.[60]

8. *Departmental policies.* Police departments vary with regard to policies about how to handle juveniles. Some emphasize formal handling, and others stress informal handling, with predictable results that some have much higher referral rates than others.[61]

9. *External pressures in the community.* The attitudes of the local media and the public, the social status of the complainant or victim, and the extent to which local resources are available to provide alternative service affect the decisions made.[62]

Youths who "smart off" or otherwise do not display the "proper" deference are usually the most likely to be processed formally. This is especially the case with minor offenses and even when there is little or no evidence that a crime has been committed. As with social class, race will figure into this equation because so many African-American youths are angry at the white establishment and especially at their representatives in authority like the police. Many minority youths, especially gang members, display a defiance that is interpreted as a challenge to the police.[63]

Departmental policies and external pressures are particularly important when the delinquent behavior involves drugs. Indeed, drug arrests and subsequent referrals to court for these charges have had an enormous impact on the juvenile justice system and have in turn been strongly related to race (see section below).

Juvenile Court Processing

Table 11-1 presents a breakdown of all juvenile court referrals for delinquent offenses in 2007 and compares them with two previous years, 1998 and 2003 (no comparable data are available for status offenses, except those that are petitioned to court). The most obvious thing about these figures is the minor nature of the majority of the referrals. For instance, the second largest category of offenses is "public order" (28% of all cases); the most common of these is "obstruction of justice"[64] (45% of all public order offenses). Note that between 1998 and 2007 referrals for public order offenses increased more than any other category (13%). While "person offenses" comprised one-fourth of all referrals,

Table 11-1   Referrals to Juvenile Court, 1998–2007

Most serious offense	Number of cases (2007)	Percent change	
		1998–2007	2003–2007
Total delinquency	**1,666,100**	**–7%**	**–2%**
Person offenses	**409,200**	**1**	**0**
Criminal homicide	1,400	–31	5
Forcible rape	4,300	–10	–3
Robbery	31,000	4	45
Aggravated assault	49,600	–16	1
Simple assault	274,900	4	–4
Other violent sex offenses	15,700	20	–3
Other person offenses	32,300	3	5
Property offenses	**594,500**	**–24**	**–6**
Burglary	105,300	–22	0
Larceny–theft	255,500	–28	–11
Motor vehicle theft	26,600	–39	–29
Arson	8,100	–5	–1
Vandalism	108,800	–2	+11
Trespassing	54,300	–14	6
Stolen property offenses	17,900	–43	–14
Other property offenses	18,000	–38	–16
Drug law violations	**190,100**	**–2**	**1**
Public order offenses	**472,300**	**13**	**2**
Obstruction of justice	214,700	2	–2
Disorderly conduct	124,600	39	7
Weapons offenses	40,900	–3	11
Liquor–law violations	36,600	76	4
Nonviolent sex offenses	11,400	–1	–15
Other public order offenses	44,400	–3	0

Note: Detail may not add to totals because of rounding. Percent change calculations are based on unrounded numbers.

Source: Knoll, C. and M. Sickmund (2010, June). "Delinquency Cases in Juvenile Court, 2007," p. 2. Bureau of Justice Statistics. Retrieved from http://www.ncjrs.gov/pdffiles1/ojjdp/230168.pdf

the bulk of these were "simple assaults" (67% of all person offenses and 16% of all referrals). Property offenses were the largest category of referrals (36%), with larceny-theft leading the way (43% of all property offenses and 15% of all referrals).[65] For the first time ever, vandalism passed burglary as the second most common property offenses; burglary has been declining steadily for the past couple of decades. It should be emphasized that these are "delinquency cases" and do not include several thousand cases classified as "status," "dependency" and "abuse and neglect" (see chapter 2). Also, it should be noted that the past ten years represent a notable drop in juvenile court referrals, after they went up by about 60% from 1985 to 1997.

Race, the "War on Drugs," and Referrals to Juvenile Court

It is impossible to talk about juvenile court processing without reference to race and drug offenses. Race often plays an indirect role in that race relates to offense, which in turn affects the police decision to arrest. Race relates to the *visibility* of the offense. This is especially the case with regard to drugs. There is abundant evidence that the "war on drugs" has, in effect, resulted in a targeting of African Americans on a scale that is unprecedented in U.S. history. As the research by Jerome Miller has shown, young African-American males have received the brunt of law enforcement efforts to "crack down on drugs." He notes that in Baltimore, for example, African Americans were arrested at a rate six times that of whites; more than 90% of the arrests were for possession.[66]

The juvenile arrest rate for both races for heroin and cocaine possession was virtually the same in 1965. By the 1970s, the gap began to widen; by 1990, the arrest rate for African Americans stood at 766, compared to only 68 for whites. By 2008 the arrest rate for black juveniles stood at 921, compared to 503 for whites (see chapter 2). Between 1985 and 2007, referrals for drug offenses for black youths increased by 223% compared to a 127% increase for whites (table 11-2).[67] (It is worth noting once again how little whites and blacks differ when it comes to actual use of illegal drugs and the fact that some studies find white youths are more likely to use drugs.)

A study by Edmund McGarrell found evidence of substantial increases in minority youths being referred to juvenile court during late 1980s when the war on drugs really took off, thus increasing the likelihood of being detained.

Table 11-2   Percent Change in Number of Cases by Race, 1985–2007

Most Serious Offense	White	Black
Total	26%	94%
Person	114	131
Property	−25	13
Drugs	127	223
Public order	98	297

Source: C. Puzzanchera, B. Adams, and M. Sickmund (2010). "Juvenile Court Statistics 2006–2007," p. 18. http://www.ncjjservehttp.org/ncjjwebsite/pdf/jcsreports/jcs2007.pdf

The detention, petition, and placement of minorities, however, exceeded what would have been expected given the increases in referrals. The increase in formal handling of drug cases has been devastating to minorities. "Given the proactive nature of drug enforcement, these findings raise fundamental questions about the targets of investigation and apprehension under the recent war on drugs."[68] As noted in a study of Georgia's crackdown on drugs, the higher arrest rate for African Americans was attributed to one single factor.

> It is easier to make drug arrests in low-income neighborhoods. . . . Most drug arrests in Georgia are of lower-level dealers and buyers and occur in low-income minority areas. Retail drug sales in these neighborhoods frequently occur on the streets and between sellers and buyers who do not know each other. Most of these sellers are black. In contrast, white drug sellers tend to sell indoors, in bars and clubs and within private homes, and to more affluent purchasers, also primarily white.[69]

Regardless of whether race, class, or demeanor is statistically more relevant, one fact remains: growing numbers of African-American youths are finding themselves within the juvenile justice system. They are more likely to be detained, more likely to have their cases petitioned to go before a judge, more likely to be waived to the adult system, and more likely to be institutionalized than their white counterparts.[70] "At each stage, there's a slight empirical bias, which compounds with every stage of the process. By the time you reach the end, you have all minorities in the deep end of the system."[71] African-American youths constitute only 13% of the total population, but they are 31% of those arrested, 42% of those detained, 35% of those adjudicated, 39% of those placed in a residential facility, and 58% of those who end up in state prison (see figure 11-2).[72] In Ohio, blacks are 2–3 times more likely than whites to be detained.[73]

Figure 11-2   Percentage of African-American Youth at Each Stage of the Juvenile Justice Process

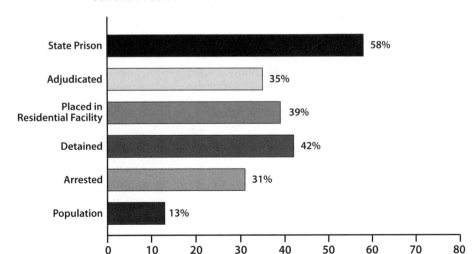

On the bright side, there has been some progress in decreasing disproportion-ate minority representation within the juvenile justice system nationally.[74]

One often overlooked source of racial bias is in child welfare case process-ing and how it relates to juvenile justice processing. One study examined data on child maltreatment cases covering a 30-year period in Los Angeles and found that the child welfare system is a major source of African-American overrepresentation in the juvenile justice system. Delinquency cases that began within the child welfare system were found to be far less likely to receive pro-bation or other alternatives to incarceration.[75]

Some believe that the overrepresentation of minority youth is a result of their committing more crimes than whites. However, self-report surveys and surveys on drug use (see chapter 2) contradict that belief. The differential is more likely the result of police policies (e.g., targeting low-income, mostly minority neighborhoods) or the location of some offenses (especially drug use) in more visible places. A study in Kentucky found that at each stage of the process whites were treated more leniently than minorities.[76] As cases move further and further into the system, the disadvantages of minority sta-tus increase.

Racial bias is cumulative, starting long before a youth is ever contacted by the police. It is not being suggested that everyone connected with the juvenile justice system is a racist and practices discrimination, although stereotypes about youth from certain race or class backgrounds definitely exist. Cultural biases that affect police practices (especially drug cases) and the existence of various forms of racial profiling contribute to disproportionality.[77] Part of the problem is institutional in that such negative stereotypes are deeply imbedded in our culture. Juvenile courts and police departments are largely staffed by whites. The widespread poverty and joblessness affecting minority communi-ties result in the lack of available resources (e.g., alternatives to formal court processing) to deal with crime-related issues and the general failure of schools.

The Influence of Social Class

Social class is another important factor. While juvenile court and arrest sta-tistics do not give any indication of the class backgrounds of youths, studies over the years have documented the class bias at each stage of the process. A longitudinal study of over 10,000 cases in Philadelphia determined that at every step, minorities and youths from the lowest socioeconomic backgrounds were processed further into the system than whites and those from higher-class backgrounds.[78] Some studies have suggested that social class, rather than race per se, best predicted police decisions.[79] For instance, research by Sampson found that the overall socioeconomic status of a *community* was more important than other variables, although race figured prominently.[80] In general, the lower the socioeconomic standing of the community as a whole, the greater will be the tendency for formal processing of youths encountered by the police.[81]

Forty years ago, William Chambliss researched the relevance of social class in his study of the "Saints" and the "Roughnecks."[82] The Saints were eight white boys from upper-middle-class backgrounds, and the Roughnecks were six white boys from lower-class backgrounds. Each of the two groups engaged in a variety of mostly minor delinquencies, typical of American teenagers. The "Saints" however were viewed by teachers and the police as "good kids" engaging in pranks while the "Roughnecks" were seen as "bad kids," proving through their actions that they were headed for trouble. The differential treatment, suggests Chambliss, stemmed in part from the greater *visibility* of the Roughnecks, as they committed their acts mostly in public, while the Saints were able to drive to neighboring communities in their cars to commit delinquent acts and/or offend discretely in their private backyards in the suburbs. The two groups had predictable careers, with two of the Roughnecks ending up in prison and all but one of the Saints going to college and pursuing respectable careers.

By defining certain acts as delinquent, the juvenile justice system (at least in effect), helps prevent upward mobility for the majority of lower-class youths. Chambliss concluded that the juvenile justice system and other control/processing institutions (e.g., schools) help maintain the class structure by channeling youth in directions appropriate to their class background.

> The answer lies in the class structure of American society and the control of legal institutions by those at the top of the class structure. Obviously, no representative of the upper class drew up the operational chart for the police which led them to look in the ghettoes and on street-corners—which led them to see the demeanor of lower-class youth as troublesome and that of upper-middle-class youth as tolerable. Rather, the procedures simply developed from experience—experience with irate and influential upper-middle-class parents insisting that their son's vandalism was simply a prank and his drunkenness only a momentary "sowing of wild oats"— experience with cooperative or indifferent, powerless, lower-class parents who acquiesced to the law's definition of their son's behavior.[83]

Social class helps determine many, if not most, of the life chances of people in the United States.[84] When combined with race, the restrictions can be truly devastating. Take, for instance, decisions made by the police and courts. Members of racial minorities and the lower classes tend to have their behaviors defined as felonies, while whites and more privileged youths are far more likely to be charged with misdemeanors, if charged at all. In juvenile courts all over the country, minorities and lower class youth will be processed further into the system than their more privileged and white counterparts. Even when out-of-home "placements" are ordered, the more privileged youth are sent to group homes or well-funded drug treatment programs paid for by insurance, while their lower class and minority counterparts are sent to public facilities.

The Intake Process and the Decision to Detain

Juveniles enter the juvenile court after having been referred to it by a law enforcement agency or a parent or guardian. Sometimes a young person may receive a misdemeanor citation (not unlike a traffic citation) that informs the individual that he or she must appear in court on or before a certain date.

Upon arrival, the juvenile faces *intake screening*, another unique feature of the juvenile court. This division is staffed by full-time employees of the court (normally probation officers), who are usually college graduates with majors such as social work, sociology, or criminal justice. One of the first decisions made is whether or not the case falls within the jurisdiction of the court. It then must be determined whether the youth will be detained before the hearing and whether to file a petition requiring a formal court appearance before a judge. Customarily, the youth and a parent or guardian are interviewed at intake.

The options available to the court representative at this stage vary somewhat among jurisdictions but fall into four categories: (1) dismissal, (2) informal supervision, or "informal probation," (3) referral to another agency, and (4) formal petition to the court.

The decision about whether the youth needs to be placed in detention is usually based on written court policies. The three typical reasons for detention are (1) the youth may harm others or himself or herself or be subject to injury by others if not detained; (2) the youth has no parent, guardian, or other person able to provide adequate care and supervision, is homeless, or is a runaway; and (3) it is believed that if not detained the youth will leave the jurisdiction and not appear for court proceedings. The intake staff is usually instructed to consider the nature and severity of the current offense and previous offenses (if any), the youth's age, the youth's conduct within the home and at school, ability of the parents or guardians to supervise the youth, whether the current offense is a continuation of a pattern of delinquent behavior, and the willingness of the parents or guardian to cooperate with the court.

These criteria are usually measured through the use of a *risk assessment instrument* (see figure 11-3) devised as a method to determine the likelihood of appearance in court and whether the youth presents a danger to self or others. However, the theory behind the analysis is seriously flawed; it assumes that there is a valid method of predicting who is most likely to commit a crime if released. Risk assessment instruments can be misused, and their predictive accuracy has been questioned.[85] One study found that probation officers used their own set of criteria (revolving around respect for and compliance with legal institutions) that had little or nothing to do with predicting recidivism.[86] On the other hand, some instruments have been proven to be of value in predicting recidivism among offenders following release from incarceration.[87]

It could be argued that detention should be reserved for youths who are charged with serious crimes. This is not the case, however. In 2007, 21% of youths detained nationwide were charged with a serious violent crime, while 25% were charged with a technical violation (violation of a court order or violation of probation or parole, which does not include a new offense); the next largest category was property index crimes at 18% (see table 11-3).[88]

After the decision to detain has been made, the intake officer has several options. These include: (1) counsel, warn, and release, sometimes called *informal adjustment*; (2) *informal probation* (release under certain conditions, with

Figure 11-3   State of Virginia Risk Assessment Instrument

VIRGINIA DEPARTMENT OF JUVENILE JUSTICE
DETENTION ASSESSMENT INSTRUMENT (Rev. 8/15/05)

Juvenile Name: _____ DOB: _____/_____/_____   Juvenile #: _____ ICN#

Intake Date: _____/_____/_____   Time: ____:____ ☐AM ☐PM   Worker Name: _____ CSU #:

Completed as Part of Detention Decision: ☐   Completed as Follow-Up (On-Call Intake): ☐

	Score

1. **Most Serious Alleged Offense (see reverse for examples of offenses in each category)**
   Category A: Felonies against persons. 15
   Category B: Felony weapons and felony narcotics distribution. 12
   Category C: Other felonies. 7
   Category D: Class 1 misdemeanors against persons. 5
   Category E: Other Class 1 misdemeanors. 3
   Category F: Violations of probation/parole... 2   _____

2. **Additional Charges in this Referral**
   Two or more additional current felony offenses.. 3
   One additional current felony offense 2
   One or more additional misdemeanor **OR** violation of probation/parole offenses................. 1
   One or more status offenses **OR** No additional current offenses 0   _____

3. **Prior Adjudications of Guilt (includes continued adjudications with "evidence sufficient to finding of guilt")**
   Two or more prior adjudications of guilt for felony offenses.. 6
   One prior adjudication of guilt for a felony offense.. 4
   Two or more prior adjudications of guilt for misdemeanor offenses..................................... 3
   Two or more prior adjudications of guilt for probation/parole violations.............................. 2
   One prior adjudication of guilt for any misdemeanor or status offense 1
   No prior adjudications of guilt.. 0   _____

4. **Petitions Pending Adjudication or Disposition** (exclude deferred adjudications)
   One or more pending petitions/dispositions for a felony offense 8
   Two or more pending petitions/dispositions for other offenses... 5
   One pending petition/disposition for an other offense 2
   No pending petitions/dispositions.. 0   _____

5. **Supervision Status**
   Parole 4
   Probation based on a Felony or Class 1 misdemeanor 3
   Probation based on other offenses **OR** CHINSup **OR** Deferred disposition with conditions .. 2
   Informal Supervision **OR** Intake Diversion 1
   None 0   _____

6. **History of Failure to Appear** (within past 12 months)
   Two or more petitions/warrants/detention orders for FTA in past 12 months 3
   One petition/warrant/detention order for FTA in past 12 months 1
   No petition/warrant/detention order for FTA in past 12 months.. 0   _____

7. **History of Escape/ Runaways** (within past 12 months)
   One or more escapes from secure confinement or custody 4
   One or more instances of absconding from non-secure, court-ordered placements 3
   One or more runaways from home.. 1
   No escapes or runaways w/in past 12 months 0   _____

8. **TOTAL SCORE**..   _____

Indicated Decision:_____ **0 - 9 Release** _____ **10 - 14 Detention Alternative** _____ **15+ Secure Detention**

Mandatory Overrides: ☐ 1. Use of firearm in current offense
(must be detained)   ☐ 2. Escapee from a secure placement
                             ☐ 3. Local court policy (indicate applicable policy) _____

Discretionary Override: ☐ 1. Aggravating factors (override to more restrictive placement than indicated by guidelines)
                             ☐ 2. Mitigating factors (override to less restrictive placement than indicated by guidelines)
                             ☐ 3. Approved local graduated sanction for probation/parole violation

Actual Decision / Recommendation: _____ **Release** _____ **Alternative** _____ **Secure Detention**

Table 11-3   Offense Profile of Detained Residents by Sex and Race/Ethnicity for United States, 2007 (percent)

Most Serious Offense	Total	Sex		Race		
		Male	Female	White	Black	Hispanic
Total	**100%**	**100%**	**100%**	**100%**	**100%**	**100%**
Violent Index	22	24	13	14	26	26
Other person	11	10	16	13	10	10
Property Index	16	17	12	19	16	13
Other property	5	5	4	6	4	5
Drug	7	8	5	7	8	7
Public order	12	12	13	11	12	13
Technical violation	23	22	30	25	20	26
Status offense	3	2	6	4	3	1

Source: Sickmund, M., T. J. Sladky, and W. Kang (2011). "Census of Juveniles in Residential Placement Databook." Retrieved from http://www.ojjdp.gov/ojstatbb/ezacjrp/asp/Offense_Detained.asp?state=0&topic=Offense_Detained&year=2007&percent=column

supervision by a volunteer or a regular probation officer; after a certain period of time if no new offense is committed, the case is dismissed); (3) referral to another agency; (4) outright dismissal; (5) file a *consent decree* (somewhat more restrictive than informal probation); or (6) file a petition to have the youth appear in court for a formal *adjudicatory hearing*.

As mentioned earlier, race figures prominently in the decision to detain. Table 11-4 presents the rates per 100,000 juveniles. Here we clearly see the racial discrepancies. Regardless of offense, African-American youths are far more likely to be detained than their white counterparts. Indeed, for all delinquent offenses, black youths are 5.5 times more likely to be detained (a rate of 216 versus 39); they are 6 times more likely to be detained for a drug offense and 9.67 times more likely to be detained for a violent index crime. Many studies have documented the higher rates of detention for black and other minority youth.[89] A study in Iowa found that although minority youths were only 18% of the youth population, they were 50% of the youth placed in detention in 2007. These differences existed regardless of other variables, such as the nature of the offense.[90]

After the decisions in the *Kent* and *Gault* cases, there was a movement to try to keep young offenders out of juvenile court. If they were processed, the goal was to *divert* them out of the system as quickly as possible. The research that was done in conjunction with the two court decisions (and a great deal of research immediately following them) demonstrated the need for some type of diversion. If youths are not diverted from further processing, they move to the adjudication stage of the juvenile court process.

Adjudication

Adjudication is the juvenile court counterpart to trial in adult court, but it has some significant differences. Very often the hearings are rather informal

Table 11-4   Offense Profile of Detained Residents by Sex and Race/Ethnicity for United States, 2007 (rate per 100,000 juveniles)

Most Serious Offense	Total	Sex		Race		
		Male	**Female**	**White**	**Black**	**Hispanic**
Total	**80**	**130**	**27**	**41**	**222**	**97**
Violent Index	18	31	4	6	58	25
Other person	9	13	4	5	23	9
Property Index	13	22	3	8	36	12
Other property	4	6	1	2	9	5
Drug	6	10	1	3	18	6
Public order	10	16	3	5	27	13
Technical violation	19	28	8	10	45	25
Status offense	2	3	2	2	6	1

Source: Sickmund, M., T. J. Sladky, and W. Kang (2011). "Census of Juveniles in Residential Placement Databook." Retrieved from http://www.ojjdp.gov/ojstatbb/ezacjrp/asp/Offense_Detained.asp?state=0&topic=Offense_Detained&year=2007&percent=rate

(sometimes they are merely conversations between a judge, parents, and the child), and they are closed to the public and to reporters. In recent years the procedures have become more formal, especially in large metropolitan courts—almost as formal as an adult court.

There are two types of hearings. The *adjudicatory hearing* is the fact-finding stage of the juvenile court process, which is followed by the *dispositional hearing*. These two stages are roughly the equivalent of the trial and sentencing stages of the adult system. In most urban courts, both the defense and the prosecutor present the evidence of the case. Like the adult counterpart, hearsay evidence is inadmissible; the defendant has the right to cross-examine a witness; he or she is protected against self-incrimination; and a youth's guilt must be proven beyond a reasonable doubt.

In the majority of juvenile courts, the dispositional hearing is a separate hearing altogether, part of what is often referred to as a *bifurcated* system. During this hearing, the judge relies heavily on two important court documents, usually prepared by the probation department of the court. One document is the *legal* file that contains a complete referral history, including the nature of all the offenses that brought the youth into court prior to the current offense, along with prior dispositions. The other document is probably the most important; it contains a wide range of personal information about the juvenile. This is known as the *social* file, which contains such information as family background, school records, psychological profile, and the like. Together these two documents aid the probation department in preparing what is known as the *presentence report*, roughly the equivalent of the one prepared in the adult system. Perhaps the most important part of the presentence report is the recommendation. Typically some sort of a "treatment plan" is prepared for the case, along with the actual sentence. More often than not, the judge agrees to the recommendation.

There are several alternative dispositions available to juvenile court judges. These alternatives can be grouped into four major categories: (1) dismissal, (2) probation, (3) commitment to an institution or "out-of-home placement" (with several different types, according to level of security, ranging from group homes to training schools), and (4) waiver to an adult court.

What are the final decisions at this stage? Table 11-5 shows the outcome of 1,666,100 juvenile court cases handled in 2007. A slight majority of all referrals result in a petition to court (56%). Of those cases that do not result in a petition, the most common outcome is dismissal (42%) followed by other sanctions (34%; includes community service, restitution, and fines) and probation (23%). Of those petitioned to court, 63% are adjudicated as delinquent, usually as the result of a guilty plea; 56% are granted probation; 25% are placed in a confinement facility. Of the petitioned cases not adjudicated delinquent, 67% are dismissed.

Each decision point as youths move through the court system contributes differently to the overall disparity in the system. Black youths are referred to juvenile court for a delinquency offense at a rate that is 140% greater than the rate for white youths. The rate for cases petitioned for formal processing was 12% greater for blacks than for whites. One decision point at which the rate for blacks was somewhat less than the rate for whites (8% less) was petitioned cases that were adjudicated. The rate at which petitioned cases were waived to criminal court was 9% greater for black youths than the rate for white youths. The rate at which youth in adjudicated cases were ordered to residential placement was 27% greater for black youths than for white youth. The second decision point where the rate for black youths was less than the rate for white youths was probation—14% less.[91]

Table 11-5   Juvenile Court Processing, 2007 (n = 1,666,100 Estimated Cases)

Total		**100%**
Petitioned		56%
Non-petitioned		44%
Probation	23%	
Other Sanction	34	
Dismissed	42	
Judicial Decision of Petitioned Cases		
Waived*		
Adjudicated		63%
Placed	25%	
Probation	56	
Other	19	
Non-adjudicated		36%
Probation	18%	
Dismissed	67	
Other	15	

*Less than .1%.

Source: Knoll, C. and M. Sickmund (2010, June). "Delinquency Cases in Juvenile Court, 2007." Bureau of Justice Statistics, p. 4. Retrieved from http://www.ncjrs.gov/pdffiles1/ojjdp/230168.pdf

In 2006, there were 92,854 juveniles in residential placements—a rate of 295 per 100,000. Most were male (85%). Of those, 34% were white (rate of 270); 41% were black (rate of 1,317), and 21% were Hispanic (rate of 560).[92]

> Juvenile delinquency has potentially high stakes for both individuals and society as a whole. Delinquency is linked to higher crime rates in adulthood and other negative outcomes.   One estimate suggests that between 50 and 75 percent of adolescents who have spent time in juvenile detention centers are incarcerated later in life.[93]

Juveniles tried as adults and committed to adult facilities face higher risks of rape, assault, and suicide. Even in juvenile facilities, children may be victimized by staff members. Twelve percent of young people in juvenile facilities reported sexual victimization by staff members or a peer.[94] Many have mental health needs; suicide rates in juvenile detention facilities are more than four times higher than for adolescents overall.

Keeping Offenders from Further Penetration

It has long been recognized that the juvenile court can and often does have a negative impact on youths who are referred. Indeed, there have been a plethora of studies documenting this, starting with the President's Commission report on juvenile delinquency in 1967.[95] A meta-analysis of 29 different studies covering a period of 35 years concluded that with few exceptions "juvenile system processing appears to not have a crime control effect, and across all measures appears to increase delinquency."[96]

Diversion

Diversionary tactics have a strong theoretical background (see the discussion on labeling in chapter 7). Legal interaction by the juvenile justice system may actually perpetuate delinquency by processing the cases of children and youths whose problems might be better ignored, normalized in their original settings, or dealt with in more informal settings within the community. Courts may inadvertently stigmatize some youths for relatively petty acts.

Diversion programs are designed, in part, to deal with the problem of overcrowded juvenile courts and correctional institutions (including detention), so that greater attention can be devoted to more serious offenders. The President's Commission called for the creation of youth services bureaus to develop alternative programs for juvenile offenders in local communities. The establishment of these bureaus initiated a move toward diverting youths, especially status offenders and other nonserious delinquents, from the juvenile court. These bureaus were quickly established in virtually every community regardless of size. Unfortunately, the youth services bureau concept was far from clear and unambiguous.

> The recommendation that community services be coordinated by the bureau assumed that there was a wealth of services to be coordinated when,

in fact, the lack of such agencies and services had been an impediment to successful juvenile court work.[97]

There are many different types of programs that come under the general heading of "diversion." These include teen courts, drug courts, mental health programs, cultural programs, mentoring programs, truancy courts and law-related education (LRE), among others. Like many other programs for young offenders, few have been evaluated, and there is relatively little systematic data available.[98] One evaluation of a teen court found that it had little impact on recidivism.[99] A comprehensive evaluation of 18 mentoring programs in England found that seven had a positive impact. Those that were the most effective were usually one of a number of interventions applied and were programs in which mentors spent the most amount of time with offenders.[100]

Conflicting expectations, findings, and conclusions emerged from the widespread, disjointed, and complicated experiment with diversion. Although many studies found diversion programs to be successful in reducing subsequent deviance, there were an equal number that found no impact. One of the problems with assessing diversion programs is the fact that so many deal with very minor (or first-time) offenders. In such cases, the offenders might never commit another delinquent act even if no action were taken—which explains why many studies find little or no differences between those placed in diversion programs and those not placed.[101] A comprehensive meta-analysis of many diversion and similar alternative programs found that only three factors predicted program effectiveness: (1) a "therapeutic" intervention philosophy, (2) a program that served high-risk offenders and (3) the quality of implementation of the program.[102] A recent evaluation of a diversion program in Florida found that the use of experienced youth workers had a positive impact on recidivism rates.[103]

Widening the Net or True Alternatives?

The process of "diverting" youth away from existing institutions and into new, theoretically more humane alternatives is not as new as we might like to think. The process began when the New York House of Refuge opened in 1824 to divert youth from adult institutions (although the word "diversion" was not used). In time, as we saw in chapter 1, it became like its adult counterparts. Over the next century, new institutions emerged to take its place. With each new institution or alternative, the number of youths being processed in a formal manner increased.

Diversion has created concern over such issues as prejudice, discrimination, civil rights violations, and net widening. The latter issue has received the most attention. Ideally, a true diversion program (and the original concept behind diversion) would remove youths from the juvenile justice system. So, for example, if 1,000 youths would previously have been processed through the system, a true diversion would be to take, say, 300 of those youths and place them in some alternative program. Essentially, net widening would occur if instead of reducing the number in the juvenile justice system to 700, diversion resulted in the same 1,000 being processed plus 300 more youths placed in diversion programs. In this example, the "net" would have been extended to envelope 1,300 youths. Part of the net-widening problem stems from the fact that as many as half of all referrals come from schools, parents and welfare agencies—not from the police and juvenile court intake officers. Ironically, these are the people and local agencies who were supposed to keep youths away from legal processing.[104]

For the most part, a variety of programs within the community serve more or less independently of any formal bureaucracy. One example is the Detention Diversion Advocacy Project in San Francisco (DDAP). Youths who would normally be placed in detention receive intensive supervision while participating in one or more community-based programs (e.g., drug counseling, tutoring, job training). An evaluation of this program by the author found it to be highly successful (see chapter 15).[105]

Relative Rate Index (RRI)

In 1988 Congress amended the Juvenile Justice and Delinquency Prevention (JJDP) Act of 1974 (see chapter 3) to require states to address disproportionate minority confinement (DMC). If the proportion of minority group youths detained in any secure detention facility exceeded the proportion of such groups in the general population, the state was required to reduce the number of minorities confined or lose a portion of its federal funds. In November 2002, the DMC requirements were amended again—broadening the requirements to disproportionate minority *contact*. States were now required to examine representation of minority youth at *all* decision points along the juvenile justice system continuum—arrest, referral to juvenile court, detention, petitioning, transfer to criminal court, adjudication, and out-of-home placement following adjudication—to be eligible for federal funds. In 2003, the Relative Rate Index (RRI) was introduced as the method to calculate proportionality, replacing the previous index.[106]

Despite the federal guidelines, studies continue to reveal disparate outcomes in juvenile court processing for juveniles. In Arizona, blacks, Hispanics and Native Americans were treated more harshly than whites, and whites were most likely to be placed in diversion programs, regardless of other variables.[107] Another study looked at relative rate indices in 2005 (the indices are always relative to whites). For blacks, the greatest disparity in arrests was for person offenses (3.6) and drug law violations (1.4). African Americans were 40% more likely to be petitioned (relative rate index of 1.4), and whites were twice as likely as blacks to have their drug cases diverted. The RRI for blacks for detention in drug cases was 2.1.[108] The National Disproportionate Minority Contact Databook compiles counts, rates, and RRIs back to 1990. In 2007, the RRIs for blacks were again 3.6 for person-offense arrests and rose to 2.0 for arrests for drug violations; the RRI for drug cases petitioned declined slightly to 1.3; the diversion rate remained the same at .5; and detention increased to 2.3.[109]

Probation

Probation, from the Latin verb *probare*—to prove, to test—began in the mid-nineteenth century with the efforts of John Augustus. In 1841 he persuaded the Boston Police Court to release an adult drunkard into his custody rather than sending him to prison (which was the most common disposition at the time). In 1843, he expanded his efforts to include children. By 1846 he was managing the cases of about 30 children ranging from 9 to 16 years old.[110] By 1869, the Massachusetts legislature required that an agent of the state be present if court actions might result in the placement of a child in a reformatory. These agents were to search for other placement, protect the child's interests, investigate the case before trial, and supervise the plan for the child after disposition. In every respect it was a social work role before the coming of "social work" as a profession. In 1878 Massachusetts passed the first probation statute creating the first official state probation system with salaried probation officers. Other states quickly followed suit, and by 1900 Vermont, Rhode Island, New Jersey, New York, Minnesota, and Illinois had created probation systems. By 1930 probation was established in every state except Wyoming.[111]

Social Work or Law Enforcement?

Augustus was a *volunteer*, rather than a salaried bureaucrat. What began as a true alternative to the justice process became *bureaucratized* (or what Weber called *rationalized*).[112] The humane gesture of an individual to help the unfortunate morphed over time into a huge, often impersonal, bureaucracy encompassing the conflicting roles of law enforcement and social work. It did not take long for this to happen. By the second decade of the twentieth century, probation was an established part of the juvenile court system. Probation became even more institutionalized with the founding, in 1907, of the National Association of Probation Officers (eventually renamed the National Probation Association in 1911). Many of the first probation officers were former policemen.[113]

As more and more people with social work degrees and licenses began working in probation, the social work functions evolved but the law enforcement aspect persisted. In many states, both probation and parole officers are designated as "peace officers"—yet many carry both a badge and a gun.[114] The author has met many who seem to be "frustrated cop wannabes." Jerome Miller found a sign on the office wall of the chief probation officer in California that read: "Trail 'em, "Surveil 'em, Nail 'em, and Jail 'em."[115] There seems to be a general attitude that social work solutions are not sufficiently punitive and that probation should be a "tough" test.

Should Probation Officers Be Armed?

The subject of probation officer safety has prompted decisions about the need to carry weapons.[116] As of 2002, 41 states allowed parole officers to be armed and 38 states allowed it for probation officers.[117] In South Dakota after an increase in the number of serious offenders placed on probation, many probation departments revised their mission statements to "depict the tasks associated with their new role definition, which traditionally are associated more with law enforcement activities."[118] In Santa Clara County, California, probation officers have the power to arrest, make unannounced home visits, administer drug tests, and execute searches. The decision to allow some probation officers to carry arms resulted in a great deal of controversy. Barry Krisberg called the proposal worrisome and inconsistent with the traditional role of probation officer. "You can't be delivering cognitive behavioral therapy with a gun strapped to your waist. The therapeutic relationship is inhibited and destroyed by someone carrying a gun openly."[119] Dan Macallair echoed Krisberg's concerns, saying the decision was an indication of why probation officers have become so woefully ineffective. He questioned the necessity for probation officers if they are armed and suggested simply hiring more police officers.

The question that needs to be asked is this: do juvenile probation officers face more dangers than before? Have there been any significant increases in actual attacks on them in recent years? While information on law enforcement officers killed is compiled and published annually by the FBI (in 2009 a total of 48 were feloniously killed in the line of duty, 47 were accidentally killed in the line of duty, and 1 federal officer was killed in the line of duty),[120] there is no comparable national compilation of probation or parole officers killed in the line of duty. The Bureau of Labor Statistics reports annually on fatal work injuries. In 2009, the rate of occupation-related death was 3.3 per 100,000 full-time equivalent workers. Agriculture, mining, construction, and transportation workers had the highest death rates; the rate for government workers was 1.9 per 100,000.[121]

The Functions of Probation

Probation officers serve three important functions. The officers perform the *intake* function, providing a preliminary investigation of cases as they first come into the system. The second major function is that of *investigation*, which produces the *social history report* presented to the judge. The social history report summarizes a wide variety of facts pertaining to the youth's background (e.g., school record, family history, prior record, drug use, etc.). Finally, perhaps the most important function is *supervision.* Youths are assigned to a probation officer who performs multiple duties related to supervision, such as surveillance, casework services, counseling, etc.

Probation officer caseloads range from a low of around 20 to as high as 200 in large urban areas. The ideal caseload, according to experts, is around 35.[122] The number of cases placed on probation increased 34% between 1985 and 2007; the overall delinquency caseload increased 44%.[123] The additional pressure on individual probation officers has shifted the emphasis from a social work orientation to law enforcement. In Las Vegas where the author lives the average caseload of a juvenile probation officer went from about 39 to 56 between 2003 and 2007, with many officers having caseloads of 70 or 80.[124] Consequently, probation officers have less time to spend with offenders.

Probation departments have become huge entities within the juvenile justice system. In large urban areas it is not uncommon to employ thousands of people and to have large budgets. The budget of the Los Angeles County Probation Department is in excess of $700 million. A series of investigative reports revealed serious problems. "At least 11 Los Angeles County juvenile probation officers have been convicted of crimes or disciplined in recent years for inappropriate conduct involving current or former probationers, including several cases of molesting or beating youths in their care."[125] Recently, the department was the subject of federal investigations for failing to prevent, report and document child abuse. In fact, there were 102 allegations of officer misconduct involving youths over the last three years. "At least 170 Los Angeles County Probation Department employees have committed misconduct—including cases of excessive force and abuse—but have so far escaped punishment because there is not enough staff to mete out discipline."[126]

Part of the bureaucratic nature of probation is the number of rules and regulations to which the probationer must adhere, such as going to school and/or work, obeying all laws, not associating with other delinquents, obeying the lawful demands of his or her parents, contacting the probation officer periodically, etc. With varying caseloads, officers cannot provide the same services for all youths; in larger urban areas, probation officers may not be able to schedule more than a perfunctory phone call once a month. It is often difficult for officials to know exactly what is going on between probation officers and juveniles when the caseloads are large.

Recent evaluations of "intensive supervision" have arrived at negative results. Researchers in one five-year study found mixed results.[127] Another study also found no evidence that offenders given intensive probation supervision demonstrated a decrease in offending.[128]

House arrest is similar to "grounding." The only difference is that it is imposed by the court. It is much better than being locked up in detention or some other form of official confinement, but its effectiveness has not been demonstrated. House arrest is often used in conjunction with *electronic monitoring*, a punishment originally inspired by a *Spiderman* comic strip where someone was tracked by a transmitter attached to his wrist. For juveniles (and adults too), an electronic bracelet is attached to the offender (usually on the ankle) that signals when the probationer travels a certain distance (usually meaning a violation of probation by leaving the home). While electronic monitoring has been a boon to various businesses that produce these products (see discussion in chapter 10), the effectiveness for juveniles, as with house arrest, has not been demonstrated. Some studies find that recidivism is reduced if a variety of alternatives are used in combination with electronic monitoring.[129] Using house arrest (with or without the bracelets) is considerably less expensive than detention.[130]

The philosophy of the juvenile court and the theoretical perspective on delinquency assume that delinquency is a symptom of a problem and that the court should protect children (*parens patriae*) who come to its attention or otherwise treat the problem. Yet the court dismisses two-thirds of the cases that come through its doors or places youths on probation, where they get very little supervision.

Jerome Miller, reflecting on his own 30-plus years of working with youthful offenders, notes that one of the problems within the modern juvenile justice system is the method of diagnosing youth and recommending appropriate dispositions. He notes that the treatment options that the diagnostician has in mind helps to determine the actual diagnosis of the youth, rather than the other way around.

> The theory-diagnosis-treatment flow runs backward. The diagnostician looks first to the means available for handling the client, then labels the client, and finally justifies the label with psychiatric or sociological theory. Diagnosis virtually never determines treatment; treatment dictates diagnosis.[131]

Perhaps giving in to the "law and order" rhetoric of the past two decades, the juvenile courts have begun to rely increasingly on one of the most extreme dispositions within the juvenile justice system—certifying a youth as an adult. It is as if they have said: "We give up! We have done everything we can think of to help you." Yet, as will be shown in the next section, those the juvenile court has "given up on" are disproportionately African-American youths. They are, in effect, disposable children.

Giving Up on Delinquent Youth: Transfer to Adult Court

One of the most talked-about issues in juvenile justice in recent years is that of treating children as adults when certain crimes are committed. Indeed, given the extensive news coverage of the small number of cases, one would think there is an epidemic of kids committing murder! Sample headlines include:

"Boy, 13, Charged with Killing Father."
"Boy, 12, Will Be Tried as Adult in Double Homicide"
"Florida Teens Accused of Burning Boy Plead Not Guilty"
"Boy, 14, Charged as Adult in Clothes-Dryer Murder of 4-Year-Old"[132]

Moving the cases of juveniles to adult court is technically known as *waiver* or *certification*. If a juvenile court believes that an offender is too dangerous or not amenable to treatment, the court transfers (i.e., waives) its jurisdiction to the adult system by, legally speaking, making the youth an adult.[133]

In 1938, the Federal Juvenile Delinquency Act (FJDA) separated juveniles from adults for federal crimes. The FJDA provided a procedural device for juveniles (under age 18 when the crime was committed and under 21 when the case was tried) to be adjudicated outside of adult criminal courts. When originally passed, the Attorney General could decide to waive the case; now the district court decides based on six factors outlined in the Act: the age and social background of the juvenile; the nature of the alleged offense; the extent and nature of the juvenile's prior delinquency record; the juvenile's present intellectual development and psychological maturity; the nature of past treatment efforts and the juvenile's response to such efforts; the availability of programs designed to treat the juvenile's behavioral problems.[134] The court has the discretion to weigh each factor as it determines appropriate and is not required to give the same weight to each factor.

Every state has some provisions for transferring offenders to adult courts. While state laws differ, most states have a variation or combination of requirements from *Kent v. United States* that must meet a minimum age, a specified type or level of offense, a serious record of previous delinquency, or a combination of these three criteria. The crime must be serious, aggressive, violent, and premeditated. Further, the crime must be against persons, resulting in serious personal injury. The sophistication and maturity of juveniles are evaluated using external factors, such as emotional attitude and the juvenile's record and history. The evaluation must conclude that if the juvenile is not treated and punished as an adult, the public will not be protected from future victimizations.

States establish the ages of offenders for cases to be adjudicated in juvenile courts (generally 15, 16, or 17). However, states also have laws that allow juveniles younger than the upper age limits to be tried as adults. There are three types of transfer laws. Concurrent jurisdiction laws allow prosecutors the discretion to file a case in juvenile or criminal court. Statutory exclusion laws grant criminal courts jurisdiction over certain classes of cases involving juveniles. Judicial waiver laws authorize or require juvenile court judges to remove certain youths from juvenile court jurisdiction and to try them as adults in criminal court.[135]

Judicial waiver includes three categories: discretionary, presumptive, and mandatory. Forty-five states have discretionary waiver provisions, meaning juvenile court judges decide whether individual juveniles will be prosecuted in adult criminal court. Fifteen states have presumptive waiver laws, which designate specific crimes for which waiver to criminal court is presumed to be appropriate. Juveniles who meet the age, offense, or other statutory criteria will be transferred to criminal court unless they can make an adequate argument against transfer. Fifteen other states have mandatory waiver provisions for specific offenses. Although the proceedings begin in juvenile court, the only role for the court is to confirm that the case meets statutory requirements for mandatory waiver.[136]

Judicial waiver and transfer laws proliferated dramatically during the 1980s and 1990s. Between 1992 and 1999, Nebraska was the only state that did not expand the scope of waiver laws—whether by lowering age and/or offense thresholds or shifting discretionary decisions from judges to prosecutors. Thirteen states enacted presumptive waiver laws, and 9 states expanded or enacted mandatory waiver laws.[137] Nonwaiver transfer mechanisms had been relatively rare, but 22 states created or expanded statutory exclusion laws that required specific offenses to be excluded from juvenile court and filed in criminal court; 11 states enacted or expanded concurrent jurisdiction laws allowing prosecutors to choose. In 34 states, juveniles who have been convicted as adults must be prosecuted in criminal court for any subsequent offenses ("once an adult, always an adult").[138] There is no minimum age for transfer specified in 23 states; the minimum age is 10 in Kansas and Vermont.

Judicial waivers and prosecutorial discretion are often arbitrary, fluctuating from judge to judge and jurisdiction to jurisdiction; they follow no consistent pattern.[139] One survey found there are three factors judges use to consider whether or not to grant a waiver: (1) potential risk of dangerousness, (2) level of sophistication–maturity, and (3) treatment amenability. Despite the importance of these concepts, "virtually no information or guidelines exist describing how juvenile court judges or mental health professionals should weigh these constructs when making vivid line distinctions with respect to transfer." According to this survey, judges most often weigh the first two factors, but not the third.[140] Legislative waivers reflect perceived public opinion, changing values and norms, and a "get tough" attitude on juvenile crime. Legislative waiver strategies attempt to reconcile the cultural conceptions of youth and choose between the boundaries of criminal activities and criminal responsibility of youth.[141]

In 2007, there were 1.7 million delinquency cases; 56% were petitioned, and less than 1% were waived. In 1985 there were 7,200 cases waived versus 13,100 in 1994 and 8,500 in 2007. However, nonjudicial transfer laws could have automatically transferred cases directly to adult court, bypassing the juvenile justice system and skewing comparisons with previous years.[142] In 2007, 90% of the juvenile cases waived were males and 10% were females. The percentages of waived cases involving white youths were the same in 1984 and 2007—59%—after a dip to 53% in 1994. The waived cases involving black youths rose from 40% in 1984 to 44% in 1994 and dropped to 37% in 2007. Judicial waivers declined for both white and black youths, but the decline was greater for blacks. In 1993, person offenses were twice as likely to be waived for blacks as whites, and drug offenses were three times as likely. While both offenses were more likely to be waived for blacks in 2007, the reverse was true for property and public order offenses. The overall likelihood of delinquency cases being waived was approximately the same for blacks and whites in 2007—1% and .9% respectively.

What is the result of waiving a youth to the adult system? Sadly, it has not been the cure-all proponents have hoped for. In the mid-1990s many law enforcement officials began to question this method of responding to youth crime. In response to a proposed juvenile crime bill before Congress in 1997, they said it would make their jobs more difficult: "lock up a 13-year-old with murderers, rapists and robbers, and guess what he'll want to be when he grows up?"[143] Even the normally conservative criminologist John DiIulio warned: "Most kids who get into serious trouble with the law need adult guidance. And they won't find suitable role models in prison. Jailing youth with adult felons under Spartan conditions will merely produce more street gladiators."

Adults receive different sentences even when the offenses caused the same harm because defendants differ in culpability. Such differences are even more pronounced during adolescence with its undeveloped decision-making abilities, impulsiveness, lack of future orientation, and susceptibility to negative peer pressure. Brain imaging technology reveals that the teenage brain undergoes dramatic changes during adolescence. These changes affect the ability of teens "to reason, to weigh consequences for their decisions, and to delay gratification long enough to make careful short- and long-term choices."[144]

Laurence Steinberg and Elizabeth Scott, leading scholars in law and adolescent development, have concluded that people younger than 15 should never be tried as adults. They also note that trying youths in juvenile court is not the equivalent of absolving them of responsibility and that age as a mitigating factor is not the equivalent of an excuse. Youths should be punished for their crimes, but the punishment should be developmentally appropriate. "Any parent would know that it makes little sense to punish a 10-year-old the same as a 17-year-old."[145]

Young adolescents are not competent enough to be defendants; they lack the skills to consult with their lawyers and to shape trial strategy. Recall the case of Jordan Brown from the introduction, who was 11 when he committed murder. Imagine him trying to balance the positives and negatives of pleading guilty or helping his lawyer with questions for cross-examination of witnesses. If Jordan is adjudicated delinquent, the juvenile justice system can keep him until his 21st birthday—a sufficient amount of time to address public safety concerns, to hold the young offender accountable, and to rehabilitate him. Studies routinely show that in such cases, the juvenile justice system protects the public better than the criminal justice system.[146]

Jeffrey Fagan summarizes the literature on the deterrent effect of certification as follows:

> Most of the evidence on general deterrence suggests that laws that increase the threat of sentencing and incarceration as an adult have no effect on youth crime rates. Research on specific deterrence consistently finds that adolescent offenders transferred to criminal court have higher rates of re-offending than do those retained in juvenile court. Rarely do social scientists or policy analysts report such consistency and agreement under such widely varying sampling, measurement, and analytic conditions.[147]

Another study found that transferring juveniles to adult court *does not result in a reduction of crime and may even contribute to at least a short-term increase in crime*.[148] Other researchers came to the same conclusion, finding that certifying young offenders as adults "decreases community risk through lengthy incapacitation of violent youngsters . . . the social costs of imprisoning young offenders in adult facilities may be paid in later crime and violence upon their release."[149]

Summary

The processing of cases through the various stages of the juvenile justice system begins with juvenile laws, which address both criminal and misdemeanor behavior—including behavior that would not be unlawful for an adult (status offenses). More than 60 years elapsed before the Supreme Court took a serious look at the possible violation of rights for juveniles processed through the system. Despite the rulings in *Kent, Gault, Winship, McKeiver, Breed, Thompson, Roper,* and *Graham,* juvenile rights are still restricted.

Juvenile (or family) courts are found in most large and medium cities, with some consisting of rather elaborate and very bureaucratic organizations. Thousands of cases are processed through these courts every year, usually referred by the police, who have a great deal of discretion as to what course of action to take. Class and race are significant predictors to how juveniles will be processed. The case study of the "saints and roughnecks" illustrates the cultural biases.

Intake screening is the first step into the court system. At this point, a decision with important consequences is made: the decision to detain. Race again plays a key role. Minorities are far more likely to be detained, no matter the offense. This in turn affects other stages within the court process, such as adjudication and the final disposition. It was noted that at each stage of the process there are several dispositional options. The final disposition following adjudication may involve commitment to a juvenile institution. As noted, minorities receive the harshest dispositions.

The juvenile court, in spite of the promises of a century ago, has not had a very positive record of achievement. In fact, dissatisfaction with the court (accusations of being too lenient leading the way) has resulted in a movement to certify youths as adults. The results have been far from promising.

NOTES

[1] Kappeler, V. E. and G. W. Potter (2005). *The Mythology of Crime and Criminal Justice* (4th ed.). Long Grove, IL: Waveland Press, p. 221.

[2] *Kent v. United States* (383 U.S. 541, 1966). Retrieved from http://caselaw.lp.findlaw.com/cgi-bin/getcase.pl?court=US&vol=383&invol=541

[3] Ibid.

[4] *In re Gault* (387 U.S. 1, 1967). Retrieved from http://caselaw.lp.findlaw.com/cgi-bin/getcase.pl?navby=volpage&court=us&vol=387&page=21

[5] Ibid.

[6] Treaster, A. (2009, April). "Juveniles in Kansas Have a Constitutional Right to a Jury Trial. Now What? Making Sense of *In re L.M.*" *Kansas Law Review* 57: 1275–1303. Retrieved from http://www.law.ku.edu/publications/lawreview/pdf/07-Treaster_Final.pdf

[7] *In re Gault* quoted in *Juvenile Justice Bulletin* (1999). "Juvenile Justice: A Century of Change." Retrieved from http://www.ncjrs.gov/html/ojjdp/9912_2/juv2.html

[8] *In re Winship* (397 U.S. 358, 1970). Retrieved from http://caselaw.lp.findlaw.com/cgi-bin/getcase.pl?court=US&vol=397&invol=358

[9] Ibid.

[10] *McKeiver v. Pennsylvania* (403 U.S. 528, 1971). Retrieved from http://www.oyez.org/cases/1970-1979/1970/1970_322; there were two other cases heard at the same time: *In re Terry* (438 Pa., 339, 265A.2d 350, 1970) and *In re Barbara Burris* (275 N.C. 517, 169 Sk. E. 2d 879, 1969k). The major decision for all three cases was issued in *McKeiver.*

[11] *Juvenile Justice Bulletin*, "Juvenile Justice."

[12] Mahoney, A. R. (1985). "Jury Trial for Juveniles: Right or Ritual?" *Justice Quarterly* 2: 553–65.

[13] *Breed v. Jones* (421 U.S. 519, 1975). Retrieved from http://caselaw.lp.findlaw.com/scripts/getcase.pl?court=us&vol=421&invol=519

[14] *Juvenile Justice Bulletin*, "Juvenile Justice."

[15] J. Marshall Dissenting Opinion in *Schall v. Martin* (467 U.S. 253, 1984). Retrieved from http://www.law.cornell.edu/supct/html/historics/USSC_CR_0467_0253_ZD.html

[16] Ibid.

[17] Shepherd, R. E. (2007). "*In re Gault* at 40: Still Seeking the Promise." *Criminal Justice* 22(3). Retrieved from http://www.americanbar.org/content/dam/aba/publishing/criminal_justice_section_newsletter/crimjust_cjmag_22_3_juvenilejustice.authcheckdam.pdf

[18] Ibid.

[19] American Bar Association (2001). An Assessment of Access to Counsel and Quality of Representation in Delinquency Proceedings. Retrieved from http://www.schr.org/files/resources/aaa.pdf

[20] Feld, B. and S. Schaefer (2009). "The Right to Counsel in Juvenile Court: The Conundrum of Attorneys as an Aggravating Factor at Disposition." *Justice Quarterly* 27: 713–41.

[21] *White v. Reid*, 125 F. Supp. 647, D.D.C., 1954.

[22] 346 F. Supp. 1354 D.R.I., 1972. An identical conclusion was rendered in *Nelson v. Heyne* concerning an Indiana training school (355 F. Supp. 451 N.D. Ind. 1973). Finally, in *Morales v. Turman* (364 F. Supp. 166 E.D. Tex. 1973) the U.S. District Court for the Eastern District of Texas made this right more specific, saying a number of criteria had to be followed to insure that youths received proper treatment, such as establishing certain minimal standards.

[23] U.S. Department of Justice, Civil Rights Division, Special Litigation Section. Retrieved from http://www.justice.gov/crt/about/spl/cripa.php

[24] Streib, V. L. (2004, May). "The Juvenile Death Penalty Today: Death Sentences and Executions for Juvenile Crimes, January 1, 1973–April 30, 2004," p. 4. Retrieved from http://www.internationaljusticeproject.org/pdfs/JuvDeathApril2004.pdf

[25] Ibid., Table 1. "Cruel and Unusual Punishment."

[26] Feld, B. C. (1999). *Bad Kids: Race and the Transformation of the Juvenile Court*. New York: Oxford University Press, p. 236.

[27] Amnesty International (1998, October). *On the Wrong Side of History: Children and the Death Penalty in the USA*, p. 7. Retrieved from http://www.amnesty.org/en/library/asset/AMR51/058/1998/en/7a64e938-d9be-11dd-af2b-b1f6023af0c5/amr510581998en.pdf

[28] United Nations (1997). *International Covenant on Civil and Political Rights*. Geneva, Switzerland: Office of the United Nations Commissioner for Human Rights.

[29] Ibid., p. 28.

[30] Amnesty International, *On the Wrong Side of History*.

[31] *Thompson v. Oklahoma*, 487 U.S. 815 (1988).

[32] Ibid.

[33] *Stanford v. Kentucky*, 492 U.S. 361 (1989).

[34] The Death Penalty Information Center provides complete coverage of this case. See the following website: http://www.deathpenaltyinfo.org/article.php?scid=38&did=885

[35] *Atkins v. Virginia*, 536 U.S. 304, 318, 122 S. Ct. 2242, 2250 (2002).

[36] Beckman, M. (2004). "Crime, Culpability and the Adolescent Brain." *Science Magazine* 305(5684): 596–99.

[37] Amici curiae in support of respondent, filed with the U.S. Supreme Court in *Roper v. Simmons*, p. 2. Retrieved from http://www.ama-assn.org/ama1/pub/upload/mm/395/roper-v-simmons.pdf

[38] *Roper, Superintendent, Potosi Correctional Center v. Simmons* (No. 03-633, 2005). Retrieved from http://caselaw.lp.findlaw.com/scripts/getcase.pl?court=us&vol=000&invol=03-633

[39] Ibid.

[40] Liptak, A. (2010, May 17). "Justices Bar Life Terms for Youths Who Haven't Killed." *New York Times*. Retrieved from http://www.nytimes.com/2010/05/18/us/politics/18court.html?hp

[41] *Graham v. Florida*, No. 08-7142; decided May 17, 2010. Retrieved from http://www.law.cornell.edu/supct/html/08-7412.ZS.html

[42] Equal Justice Initiative (n.d.). *Sullivan v. Florida/Graham v. Florida*. Retrieved from http://eji.org/eji/childrenprison/deathinprison/sullivan.graham

[43] Savage, D. G. (2010, May 17). "Supreme Court Limits Life Sentences without Parole for Young Criminals." *Los Angeles Times*. Retrieved from http://www.latimes.com/news/nationworld/nation/la-na-court-juveniles-20100518,0,276108.story

[44] Chen, S. (2010, May 19). "Battle for a Second Chance Leads to a Landmark Ruling." Retrieved from http://articles.cnn.com/2010-05-19/justice/terrance.graham.teen.lifer_1_court-s-majority-sentences-high-court?_s=PM:CRIME

[45] Liptak, "Justices Bar Life Terms."

[46] Ibid.

[47] Ibid.

[48] Segura, L. (2009, October 31). "16-Year-Old Got Life without Parole for Killing Her Abusive Pimp—Should Teens Be Condemned to Die in Jail?" AlterNet. Retrieved from http://www.alternet.org/story/143635/

[49] Equal Justice Initiative (2007, November). "Cruel and Unusual: Sentencing 13 and 14 Year Old Children to Die in Prison." Retrieved from http://eji.org/eji/files/20071017cruelandunusual.pdf

[50] Human Rights Watch (2005). "The Rest of Their Lives: Life without Parole for Child Offenders in the United States." Retrieved from http://www.hrw.org/reports/2005/us1005/index.htm

[51] Liptak, A. (2009, November 7). "Weighing Life in Prison for Youths Who Didn't Kill." *New York Times*. Retrieved from http://www.nytimes.com/2009/11/08/us/08juveniles.html?_r=1&ref=us

[52] A Glossary of Juvenile Justice terms is found at the end of the text.

[53] Monahan, T. P. (1970). "Police Dispositions of Juvenile Offenders." *Phylon* 31: 91–107.

[54] Puzzanchera, C. (2009, December). *Juvenile Arrests 2008*. Washington, DC: Office of Juvenile Justice and Delinquency Prevention, p. 5. Retrieved from http://www.ncjrs.gov/pdffiles1/ojjdp/228479.pdf

[55] Myers, S. (2004). *Police Encounters with Juvenile Suspects: Explaining the Use of Authority and Provision of Support*. Washington, DC: National Institute of Justice.

[56] Brown, R. A., K. J. Novak, and J. Frank (2009). "Identifying Variation in Police Officer Behavior between Juveniles and Adults." *Journal of Criminal Justice* 37: 200–08; Terrill, W. and E. A. Paoline, III (2007). "Nonarrest Decision Making in Police–Citizen Encounters." *Police Quarterly* 10: 308–33.

[57] Goldstein, J. (1960). "Police Discretion Not to Invoke the Criminal Process: Low Visibility Decisions in the Administration of Justice." *Yale Law Journal* 69: 543–94.

[58] Chesney-Lind, M. R. and R. G. Shelden (2004). *Girls, Delinquency and Juvenile Justice* (3rd ed.). Belmont, CA: Wadsworth, chs. 7 and 8; 12 continues the discussion of gender issues.

[59] Bishop, D. and C. E. Frazier (1988). "The Influence of Race in Juvenile Justice Processing." *Journal of Research in Crime and Delinquency* 25: 242–63; Wolfgang, M. E., R. Figlio, and T. Sellin (1972). *Delinquency in a Birth Cohort*. Chicago: Aldine.

[60] See for instance: Dunham, R. G. and G. P. Alpert (2009). "Officer and Suspect Demeanor: A Qualitative Analysis of Change." *Police Quarterly* 12(1): 6–21; Tapia, M. A. (2008). "Extralegal Determinants of Juvenile Arrests." PhD dissertation, Ohio State University. Retrieved from http://etd.ohiolink.edu/send-pdf.cgi/Tapia%20Michael%20A.pdf?osu1218995526; Worden, R. E. and R. L. Shepard (1996). "Demeanor, Crime and Police Behavior: A Reexamination of the Police Services Study Data." *Criminology* 34: 61–82; Lundman, R. (1996). "Demeanor and Arrest: Additional Evidence from Previously Unpublished Data." *Journal of Research on Crime and Delinquency* 33: 306–23; Klinger, D. A. (1994). "Demeanor or Crime? Why 'Hostile' Citizens Are More Likely to Be Arrested." *Criminology* 32: 475–93; Werthman, C. and I. Piliavin (1975). "Gang Members and the Police." In J. Skolnick and T. C. Gray (Eds.), *Police in America*. Boston: Little, Brown; Piliavin, I. and S. Briar (1964). "Police Encounters with Juveniles." *American Journal of Sociology* 70: 206–14.

[61] Uchida, C. D., M. Wells, and S. E. Solomon (2009, August). *Assessing the Las Cruces Police Department: A Review of Community Perceptions and Police Operations and Procedures*. Las Cruces, NM: Justice & Security Strategies, Inc. Retrieved from http://extras.mnginteractive.com/live/media/site557/2009/0914/20090914_113454_Final_police_report.pdf; Cabanissa, E. R., J. M. Frabutta, M. H. Kendricka, and M. B. Arbuckle (2007). "Reducing Disproportionate Minority Contact in the Juvenile Justice System: Promising Practices." *Aggression and Violent Behavior* 12: 393–401; Feld, B. C. (2006). "Police Interrogation of Juveniles: An Empirical Study of Policy and Practice." *Journal of Criminal Law and Criminology* 97: 219.

[62] Weitzer, R., S. A. Tuch, and W. G. Skogan (2008). "Police–Community Relations in a Majority-Black City." *Journal of Research in Crime and Delinquency* 45: 398–428; Bazemore, G. and S. Senjo (1997). "Police Encounters with Juveniles Revisited: An Exploratory Study of Themes and Styles in Community Policing." *Policing: An International Journal of Police Strategy and Management* 20: 60–82; see also Pope, C. and W. Feyerherm (1990). "Minority Status and Juvenile Justice Processing: An Assessment of the Research Literature" (Parts I and II). *Criminal Justice Abstracts* 22(2, 3).

[63] Durán, R. J. (2009). "Legitimated Oppression: Inner-City Mexican American Experiences with Police Gang Enforcement." *Journal of Contemporary Ethnography* 38: 143–68; Lurigio, A. J., J. L.

Flexon, and R. G. Greenleaf (2008). "Antecedents to Gang Membership: Attachments, Beliefs, and Street Encounters with the Police." *Journal of Gang Research* 15: 15–33; Jankowski, M. S. (1990). *Islands in the Street: Gangs and American Urban Society.* Berkeley: University of California Press.

[64] This term seems to be a catchall of several different offenses, including "intentionally obstructing court or law enforcement efforts in the administration of justice, acting in a way calculated to lessen the authority or dignity of the court, failing to obey the lawful order of a court, escaping from confinement, and violating probation or parole." Also included is "contempt, perjury, bribery of witnesses, failure to report a crime, and nonviolent resistance of arrest." These definitions are found in the appendix of the annual *Juvenile Court Statistics* (OJJDP).

[65] Knoll, C. and M. Sickmund (2010, June). "Delinquency Cases in Juvenile Court, 2007." Bureau of Justice Statistics. Retrieved from http://www.ncjrs.gov/pdffiles1/ojjdp/230168.pdf

[66] Miller, J. G. (1996). *Search and Destroy: African-Americans Males in the Criminal Justice System.* New York: Cambridge University Press, p. 8; similar documentation can be found in the following studies: Tonry, M. (1995). *Malign Neglect: Race, Crime, and Punishment in America.* New York: Oxford University Press; Lockwood, D., A. E. Pottieger, and J. A. Inciardi (1995). "Crack Use, Crime by Crack Users, and Ethnicity." In D. F. Hawkins (Ed.), *Ethnicity, Race, and Crime.* Albany: State University of New York Press; Currie, E. (1993). *Reckoning: Drugs, the Cities, and the American Future.* New York: Hill and Wang.

[67] Puzzanchera, C., B. Adams, and M. Sickmund (2010). "Juvenile Court Statistics 2006–2007," p. 18. http://www.ncjjservehttp.org/ncjjwebsite/pdf/jcsreports/jcs2007.pdf

[68] McGarrell, E. (1993). "Trends in Racial Disproportionality in Juvenile Court Processing: 1985–1989." *Crime and Delinquency* 39: 29–48.

[69] Fellner, J. (1996, October). "Stark Racial Disparities Found in Georgia Drug Law Enforcement." *Overcrowded Times* 7(5): 11.

[70] Walker, S., C. Spohn, and M. DeLone (2007). *The Color of Justice: Race, Ethnicity, and Crime in America* (4th ed.). Belmont, CA: Cengage, p. 144.

[71] Center on Juvenile and Criminal Justice (2004). "Race and Juvenile Justice." http://cjcj.org/jjic/race_jj.php (emphasis in the original).

[72] Annie E. Casey Foundation (2009). Detention Reform Brief. Retrieved from http://www.aecf.org/~/media/Pubs/Initiatives/Juvenile%20Detention%20Alternatives%20Initiative/DetentionReformAnEffectiveApproachtoReduceRac/JDAI_factsheet_3.pdf; the following are among the studies documenting the importance of race: Leiber, M. J. (2009). "Race, Pre-and Post Detention, and Juvenile Decision Making." *Crime and Delinquency.* doi:10.1177/0011128709345970; Leiber, M. J., S. J. Brubaker, and K. C. Fox (2009). "A Closer Look at the Individual and Joint Effects of Gender and Race on Juvenile Justice Decision Making." *Feminist Criminology* 4: 333–58; Shook, J. J. and S. A. Goodkind (2009). "Racial Disproportionality in Juvenile Justice: The Interaction of Race and Geography in Pretrial Detention for Violent and Serious Offenses." *Race and Social Problems* 1: 257–66; Guevara, L., D. Herz, and C. Spohn (2008). "Race, Gender, and Legal Counsel: Differential Outcomes in Two Juvenile Courts." *Youth Violence and Juvenile Justice* 6: 83–104; Leiber, M. J. and J. D. Johnson (2008). "Being Young and Black: What Are Their Effects on Juvenile Justice Decision Making?" *Crime & Delinquency* 54: 560–81; Kempf-Leonard, K. (2007). "Minority Youths and Juvenile Justice Disproportionate Minority Contact after Nearly 20 Years of Reform Efforts." *Youth Violence and Juvenile Justice* 5: 71–87.

[73] Stewart, M. J. (2008, May). "An Outcomes Study of Juvenile Diversions Programs on Non-Serious Delinquent and Status Offenders." PhD dissertation, Case Western University.

[74] Davis, J. and J. R. Sorensen (2010). "Disproportionate Minority Confinement of Juveniles: A National Examination of Black-White Disparity in Placements." *Crime & Delinquency.* doi:10.1177/0011128709359653.

[75] Ryan, J. P., D. Herzb, P. M. Hernandeza, and J. M. Marshall (2007). "Maltreatment and Delinquency: Investigating Child Welfare Bias in Juvenile Justice Processing." *Children and Youth Services Review* 29: 1035–50.

[76] Colwell, P., T. Grieshop-Goodwin, and A. Swann (2009). "Opportunities Lost: Racial Disparities in Juvenile Justice in Kentucky and Identified Needs for System Change." Jeffersontown, KY: Kentucky Youth Advocates. Retrieved from http://www.kyyouth.org/documents/09brief_DMC_EMBARGOED.pdf

[77] Chambliss, W. J. (1999). *Power, Politics, and Crime.* Boulder, CO: Westview; Cole, D. (1999). *No Equal Justice: Race and Class in the American Criminal Justice System.* New York: The New Press; Chambliss, W. J. (1995). "Crime Control and Ethnic Minorities: Legitimizing Racial Oppression by Creating Moral Panics." In D. F. Hawkins (Ed.), *Ethnicity, Race, and Crime.* Albany: State University of New York Press.

[78] Wolfgang et al., *Delinquency in a Birth Cohort.*

[79] Interested readers should start with Reiman, J. and P. Leighton (2010). *The Rich Get Richer and the Poor Get Prison* (9th ed.). Boston: Allyn & Bacon. Looking at case files in just about any juvenile court—from one end of the country to the next—will reveal that kids from privileged environments, with intact families and many resources available, will be far more likely to avoid a court appearance in the first place, since their cases will be settled at intake. The author has personally examined in detail more than 1,000 such cases in Las Vegas. Sitting in the waiting areas just outside courtrooms, he has observed that the only people dressed in clothing that would indicate a higher social class are court probation officers, judges, and lawyers.

[80] Sampson, R. J. (1986). "SES and Official Reaction to Delinquency." *American Sociological Review* 51: 876–85.

[81] Brown, S. E. (2007). "The Class-Delinquency Hypothesis and Juvenile Justice System Bias." *Sociological Inquiry* 55: 212–23; Bishop, D. (2005). "The Role of Race and Ethnicity in Juvenile Justice Processing." In D. F. Hawkins and K. Kempf-Leonard (Eds.), *Our Children, Their Children: Confronting Racial and Ethnic Differences in American Juvenile Justice.* Chicago: University of Chicago Press.

[82] Chambliss, W. (1975). "The Saints and the Roughnecks." In W. J. Chambliss (Ed.), *Criminal Law in Action.* New York: John Wiley.

[83] Ibid., p. 78.

[84] For good summaries of this literature see: Gilbert, D. (2008). *The American Class Structure* (7th ed.). Thousand Oaks, CA: Pine Forge Press; Macleod, J. (2008). *Ain't No Makin' It: Aspirations and Attainment in a Low-Income Neighborhood* (3rd ed.). Denver, CO: Westview Press; Marger, M. N. (2007). *Social Inequality: Patterns and Processes* (4th ed.). New York: McGraw-Hill; Lareau, A. (2003). *Unequal Childhoods: Class, Race, and Family Life.* Berkeley: University of California Press.

[85] See, for example: Elkovitch, N., J. L. Viljoen, M. J. Scalora, and D. Ullman (2008). "Assessing Risk of Reoffending in Adolescents Who Have Committed a Sexual Offense: The Accuracy of Clinical Judgments after Completion of Risk Assessment Instruments." *Behavioral Sciences and the Law* 28: 511–28; Shook, J. J. and R. C. Sarri (2007). "Structured Decision Making in Juvenile Justice: Judges' and Probation Officers' Perceptions and Use." *Children and Youth Services Review* 29: 1335–51; Miller, J. and J. Lin (2007). "Applying a Generic Juvenile Risk Assessment Instrument to a Local Context: Some Practical and Theoretical Lessons." *Crime & Delinquency* 53: 552–80; Mills, J. F., D. G. Kroner, and T. Hemmati (2007). "The Validity of Violence Risk Estimates: An Issue of Item Performance." *Psychological Services* 4: 1–12; Shelden, R. G. (1999). "Detention Diversion Advocacy: An Evaluation." *OJJDP Juvenile Justice Bulletin* (September); Brown, W. B. (1992). "The Presentence Report and Risk Assessment." Unpublished doctoral dissertation, University of Nevada–Las Vegas, Department of Sociology.

[86] Lin, J., J. Miller, and M. Fukushima (2008). "Juvenile Probation Officers' Disposition Recommendations: Predictive Factors and Their Alignment with Predictors of Recidivism." *Journal of Crime and Justice* 31: 1–34.

[87] Bechtel, K., C. T. Lowenkamp, and E. Latessa (2007). "Assessing the Risk of Re-offending for Juvenile Offenders Using the Youth-Level of Service/Case Management Inventory." *Journal of Offender Rehabilitation* 45: 85–108.

[88] Sickmund, M., T. J. Sladky, and W. Kang (2011). "Census of Juveniles in Residential Placement Databook." Retrieved from http://www.ojjdp.gov/ojstatbb/ezacjrp/asp/Offense_Detained.asp?state=0&topic=Offense_Detained&year=2007&percent=column

[89] A sample of this research includes: Farrington, D. (2007). "Disproportionate Minority Contact in the Juvenile Justice System: A Study of Differential Minority Arrest/Referral to Court in Three Cities." Washington, DC: Office of Juvenile Justice and Delinquency Prevention; Holman, B. and J. Zeidenberg (2006). "The Dangers of Detention." Washington, DC: Justice Policy Institute. Retrieved from http://www.justicepolicy.org/content-hmID=1811&smID=1581&ssmID=25.htm; Bishop, "The Role of Race and Ethnicity in Juvenile Justice Processing"; Leiber, M. (2003). *The*

Contexts of Juvenile Justice Decision Making: When Race Matters. Albany: State University of New York Press; Engen, R., S. Steen, and G. Bridges (2002). "Racial Disparities in the Punishment of Youth: A Theoretical and Empirical Assessment of the Literature." *Social Problems* 49: 194–220.

⁹⁰ Leiber, M. J., K. Fox, and R. Lacks (2007). "Race and Detention Decision Making and the Impact on Juvenile Court Outcomes in Black Hawk County, Iowa." Retrieved from http://fog.its.uiowa.edu/~nrcfcp/dmcrc/documents/DetentionFinalLeiberReport.pdf

⁹¹ Knoll and Sickmund, "Delinquency Cases in Juvenile Court 2007," p. 2.

⁹² Child Trends (2011). *Juvenile Detention,* Table 1. Retrieved from www.childtrendsdatabank.org/?q=node/129

⁹³ Ibid.

⁹⁴ Beck, A., P. Harrison, and P. Guerino (2010, January). "Sexual Victimization in Juvenile Facilities Reported by Youth, 2008–09." Retrieved from http://bjs.ojp.usdoj.gov/content/pub/pdf/svjfry09.pdf

⁹⁵ President's Commission on Law and Administration of Justice (1967). *Task Force Report: Juvenile Delinquency and Youth Crime.* Washington, DC: U.S. Government Printing Office; two of the earlier studies are: Bortner, M. A. (1982). *Inside a Juvenile Court: The Tarnished Idea of Individualized Justice.* New York: New York University Press; and Sarri, R. C. and Y. Hasenfeld (Eds.). (1976). *Brought to Justice? Juveniles, the Courts, and the Law.* Ann Arbor, MI: National Assessment of Juvenile Corrections.

⁹⁶ Petrosino, A., C. Turpin-Petrosino, and S. Guckenburg (2010). *Formal System Processing of Juveniles: Effects on Delinquency.* Woburn, MA: The Campbell Collaboration (Campbell Systematic Reviews). Retrieved from http://www.campbellcollaboration.org/news_/formal_processing_reduce_juvenile_delinquency.php

⁹⁷ Gibbons, D. C. and M. D. Krohn (1991). *Delinquent Behavior* (5th ed.). Englewood Cliffs, NJ: Prentice-Hall, p. 313.

⁹⁸ The author has personally observed many such programs where he lives and teaches (Las Vegas) and most are positively promoted by those who operate them, but can rarely offer any data. Many persist because they "make sense" or someone has a "gut feeling" that it works. This assessment is very common. Walker makes the point that many programs are based more upon "faith" than evidence: Walker, S. (2011). *Sense and Nonsense about Crime and Drugs* (7th ed.). Belmont, CA: Cengage.

⁹⁹ Norris, M., S. Twill, and C. Kim (2011, March). "Smells Like Teen Spirit: Evaluating a Midwestern Teen Court." *Crime and Delinquency* 57(2): 199–221.

¹⁰⁰ Jolliffe, D. and D. P. Farrington (2007). "A Rapid Evidence Assessment of the Impact of Mentoring on Re-Offending: A Summary." Cambridge, UK: Home Office Online Report. Retrieved from http://www.youthmentoring.org.nz/content/docs/Home_Office_Impact_of_mentoring.pdf

¹⁰¹ Garcia, V. M. (2009). "An Examination of Net Widening and Discrimination in Juvenile Diversion Programming." PhD dissertation, Long Beach State University; Jaffe, P. H., B. J. Kroeker, C. Hyatt, M. Miscevick, A. Telford, R. Chandler, C. Shanahan, and B. Sokoloff (2009). "Diversion in the Canadian Juvenile Justice System: A Tale of Two Cities." *Juvenile and Family Court Journal* 37: 59–66.

¹⁰² Lipsey, M. W. (2009). "The Primary Factors that Characterize Effective Interventions with Juvenile Offenders: A Meta-Analytic Overview." *Victims and Offenders* 4: 124–47.

¹⁰³ Dembo, R., W. Walters, J. Wareham, C. Burgos, J. Schmeidler, R. Hoge, and L. Underwood (2008). "Evaluation of an Innovative Post-Arrest Diversion Program: 12-Month Recidivism Analysis." *Journal of Offender Rehabilitation* 47: 356–84.

¹⁰⁴ Polk, K. (1995). "Juvenile Diversion: A Look at the Record." In P. M. Sharp and B. W. Hancock (Eds.), *Juvenile Delinquency.* Englewood Cliffs, NJ: Prentice-Hall, p. 372.

¹⁰⁵ Shelden, "Detention Diversion Advocacy."

¹⁰⁶ Coleman, A. R. (2010). A Disproportionate Minority Contact (DMC) Chronology: 1988 to Date. Retrieved from http://www.ojjdp.gov/dmc/chronology.html

¹⁰⁷ Rodriguez, N. (2008, July). "A Multilevel Analysis of Juvenile Court Processes: The Importance of Community Characteristics." Washington, DC: National Institute of Justice. Retrieved from http://www.ncjrs.gov/pdffiles1/nij/grants/223465.pdf; see also Leiber, M. J. and J. D. Johnson (2008). "Being Young and Black: What Are Their Effects on Juvenile Justice Decision Making?" *Crime & Delinquency* 54(4): 560–81; Kempf-Leonard, "Minority Youths and Juvenile

Justice Disproportionate Minority Contact"; Shook and Goodkind, "Racial Disproportionality in Juvenile Justice."

[108] Arya, N. and I. Augarten (2009). *Critical Condition: African-American Youth in the Justice System.* Washington, DC: Campaign for Youth and Justice, p. 19. Retrieved from http://www.campaignforyouthjustice.org/documents/AfricanAmericanBrief.pdf; see also National Disproportionate Minority Contact Databook available at http://ojjdp.ncjrs.gov/ojstatbb/dmcdb/index.html

[109] Puzzanchera, C. and B. Adams (2010). National Disproportionate Minority Contact Databook. Retrieved from http://www.ojjdp.gov/ojstatbb/dmcdb/asp/display.asp?year=2007&offense=4&displaytype=rri&cmdRun=Show+Table; national RRIs are available at http://www.ojjdp.gov/ojstatbb/dmcdb/asp/display.asp

[110] Binder, A., G. Geis, and D. D. Bruce (1997). *Juvenile Delinquency: Historical, Cultural and Legal Perspectives.* Cincinnati, OH: Anderson.

[111] National Center for Juvenile Justice. (1991). *Desktop Guide to Good Juvenile Probation Practice.* Pittsburgh, PA: National Center for Juvenile Justice.

[112] Giddens, A. (1971). *Capitalism and Modern Social Theory.* London: Cambridge University Press, pp. 178–84.

[113] I found this to be the case in my study of the early years of the juvenile court in Memphis. Shelden, R. G. (1976). "Rescued from Evil: Origins of Juvenile Justice in Memphis, Tennessee, 1900–1917." PhD dissertation, Southern Illinois University, Carbondale.

[114] Murphya, D. and F. Lutze (2009). "Police-Probation Partnerships: Professional Identity and the Sharing of Coercive Power." *Journal of Criminal Justice* 37: 65–76.

[115] Miller, *Search and Destroy,* p. 131. The former chief of probation for Los Angeles County once stated: "Probation should be a form of punishment. If we can help [offenders] along the way, fine. But primarily the client has to be the community rather than the probationer." Rourke, M. (2004, December 17). "Barry J. Nidorf: Ex-Chief of L. A. County Probation." *Los Angeles Times.*

[116] de Sá, K. (2010, January 30). "Santa Clara County Seeks to Arm Some Probation Officers." *San Jose Mercury News.* Retrieved from http://celebrifi.com/gossip/Santa-Clara-County-seeks-to-arm-some-probation-officers-2589091.html; Gregory, L. (2008, October 5). "Tennessee: State Considers Arming Probation, Parole Officers." *Chattanooga Times Free Press.* Retrieved from http://www.timesfreepress.com/news/2008/oct/05/tennessee-state-considers-arming-probation-parole-/; Roscoe, T., D. E. Duffee, C. Rivera, and T. R. Smith (2007). "Arming Probation Officers: Correlates of the Decision to Arm at the Departmental Level." *Criminal Justice Studies* 20: 43–63; Von Zeilbauer, P. (2003, August 7). "Probation Dept. Is Now Arming Officers Supervising Criminals." *New York Times.* Retrieved from http://www.nytimes.com/2003/08/07/nyregion/07GUNS.html

[117] Taxman, F. S. (2006, January). "A Behavioral Management Approach to Supervision: Preliminary Findings from Maryland's Proactive Community Supervision (PCS) Pilot Program." Commissioned paper. Irvine, CA: National Research Council. Retrieved from http://www.fedcure.org/information/USSC-Symposium-0708/dir_02/Taxman_BehaviorMgmtApproach.pdf

[118] Allard, N. J. (2009). "Assessing the Need and Feasibility of Expanding and Standardizing a Safety Protocol and Training Program for Probation Officers in South Dakota." Pierre, SD: Institute for Court Management. Retrieved from https://www.ncsconline.org/D_ICM/programs/cedp/papers/Research_Papers_2009/Allard_AssessingTheNeed.pdf

[119] de Sá, "Santa Clara County Seeks to Arm Some Probation Officers."

[120] FBI (2010, October) "Law Enforcement Officers Killed and Assaulted," Tables 1, 48, and 75. Retrieved from http://www2.fbi.gov/ucr/killed/2009/aboutleoka.html

[121] Bureau of Labor Statistics (2010, August). "National Census of Fatal Occupational Injuries in 2009." Retrieved from http://www.bls.gov/news.release/pdf/cfoi.pdf

[122] Hurst, H. (1999, November). "Workload Measurement for Juvenile Justice System Personnel: Practices and Needs." Washington, DC: Office of Juvenile Justice and Delinquency Prevention. Retrieved from http://www.ncjrs.gov/pdffiles1/ojjdp/178895.pdf

[123] Livsey, S. (2010, June). "Juvenile Delinquency Probation Caseload, 2007." Washington, DC: Office of Juvenile Justice and Delinquency Prevention. Retrieved from http://www.ncjrs.gov/pdffiles1/ojjdp/230170.pdf

124 Cook, T. (2008, April 27). "Rising Caseloads Keep Probation Officers from Involvement in Children's Lives." *Las Vegas Sun*. Retrieved from http://www.lasvegassun.com/news/2008/apr/27/rising-caseloads-keep-probation-officers-involveme/

125 Hennessy-Fiske, M. and R. Winton (2010, February 21). "Records Reveal Problems in L.A. County Juvenile Probation Office." *Los Angeles Times*. Retrieved from http://www.latimes.com/news/local/la-me-probation21-2010feb21,0,2787011.story

126 Hennessy-Fiske, M. and R. Winton (2010, March 3). "L.A. County Probation Workers Elude Punishment for Misdeeds." *Los Angeles Times*. Retrieved from http://www.latimes.com/news/local/la-me-probation3-2010mar03,0,4830157.story; additional reports have discovered numerous other violations, including illegal use of county credit cards to purchase personal items. Lopez, S. (2010, June 16). "Credit Card Caper Is L.A. County's Next Bombshell." *Los Angeles Times*. Retrieved from http://www.latimes.com/news/local/la-me-lopezcolumn-20100616,0,472543.column; an independent review provides further documentation, including the fact that investigators took so long that the statute of limitations has expired and most will escape any kind of sanctions. Among other violations, the investigation found that 31 probation officers committed such acts as theft and sexual assault. Office of Independent Review, County of Los Angeles (2010, June 2). "Evaluation and Recommendations Concerning Internal Investigations at the Los Angeles County Probation Department." Retrieved from http://file.lacounty.gov/bc/q2_2010/cms1_147294.pdf

127 Hennigan, K., K. Kolnick, T. S. Tian, C. Maxson, and J. Poplawski (2010). "Five-Year Outcomes in a Randomized Trial of a Community-Based Multi-Agency Intensive Supervision Juvenile Probation Program." Washington, DC: U.S. Department of Justice.

128 MacKenzie, D. L. (2006). *What Works in Corrections: Reducing the Criminal Activities of Offenders and Delinquents*. New York: Cambridge University Press.

129 Gedeon, M. (2000). "Annie E. Casey Foundation: Reduce Inappropriate Detention of Youth Awaiting Trial or Placement." Retrieved from http://www.aypf.org/publications/lesscost/pages/10.pdf

130 Grieshop-Goodwin, T. and A. Swann (2009). "Reducing the Use of Detention for Status Offenses in Kentucky." Blueprint for Kentucky's Children. Retrieved from http://www.kyyouth.org/documents/09brief_StatusOffenses.pdf

131 Miller, J. (1998). *Last One Over the Wall: The Massachusetts Experiment in Closing Reform Schools* (2nd ed.). Columbus: Ohio State University Press, p. 232.

132 Adams, B. (2010, January 21). "Boy, 13, Charged with Killing Father." *Wisconsin State Journal*. Retrieved from http://host.madison.com/wsj/news/local/crime_and_courts/article_e6a0cf7c-05e1-11df-b8b7-001cc4c002e0.html; CNN (2010, March 29). "Judge: Boy, 12, Will Be Tried as Adult in Double Homicide." Retrieved from http://www.cnn.com/2010/CRIME/03/29/boy.homicide/index.html; Phillips, R. (2009, November 19). "Florida Teens Accused of Burning Boy Plead Not Guilty." CNN. Retrieved from http://www.cnn.com/2009/CRIME/11/19/florida.burned.boy/index.html#cnnSTCText; CNN (2009, November 3). "Boy, 14, Charged as Adult in Clothes-Dryer Murder of 4-year-old." Retrieved from http://www.cnn.com/2009/CRIME/11/03/california.boy.murder/index.html#cnnSTCText

133 Rarely discussed is the logical extension of declaring a minor an adult. If a 15-year-old youth is certified as an adult, does that mean he or she can vote, drop out of school, buy cigarettes, purchase alcohol, leave home, or do anything an adult can do? In actual fact they cannot, even if they are placed on probation by the adult court and are still under 18.

134 Lewis, M. E. (2009). "Lessening the Rehabilitative Focus of the Federal Juvenile Delinquency Act: A Trend towards Punitive Juvenile Dispositions." *Missouri Law Review* 74: 193. Retrieved from http://law.missouri.edu/lawreview/docs/74-1/Lewis.pdf

135 Adams, B. and S. Addie (2010, June). "Delinquency Cases Waived to Criminal Court, 2007," p. 1. Retrieved from http://www.ncjrs.gov/pdffiles1/ojjdp/230167.pdf

136 Ibid., p. 1.

137 Ibid., p. 2.

138 Sickmund, M. (2003, June). *Juveniles in Court*. Retrieved from http://www.ncjrs.gov/html/ojjdp/195420/page4.html.

139 Bishop, D., C. E. Frazier, L. Lanza-Kaduce, and L. Winner (1996). "The Transfer of Juveniles to Criminal Court: Does It Make a Difference?" *Crime and Delinquency* 42: 187–202; Podkopacz, M.

R. and B. C. Feld (1996). "The End of the Line: An Empirical Study of Judicial Waiver." *Journal of Criminal Law and Criminology* 86: 449–92; Feld, B. C. (1999). "Criminalizing the American Juvenile Court." In B. C. Feld (Ed.), *Readings in Juvenile Justice Administration*. New York: Oxford University Press.

[140] Brannena, D. N., R. T. Salekina, P. A. Zapf, K. L. Salekina, F. A. Kubaka, and J. DeCoster (2006). "Transfer to Adult Court: A National Study of How Juvenile Court Judges Weigh Pertinent Kent Criteria." *Psychology, Public Policy and Law* 12: 332–55; similar findings were reported in Sridharan, S., L. Greenfield, and B. Blakley (2006). "A Study of Prosecutorial Certification Practice in Virginia." *Criminology and Public Policy* 3: 605–32.

[141] Feld, *Bad Kids*, p. 190.

[142] Adams and Addie, "Delinquency Cases Waived to Criminal Court, 2007," p. 1.

[143] Schiraldi, V. and J. Zeidenberg (1997) The Risks Juveniles Face When They Are Incarcerated with Adults. Retrieved from http://www.justicepolicy.org/images/upload/97-02_REP_RiskJuvenilesFace_JJ.pdf

[144] Schwartz, R. (2010, February 18). "Kids Should Never Be Tried as Adults." CNN. http://www.cnn.com/2010/OPINION/02/18/schwartz.kids.trials/index.html

[145] Ibid.

[146] Ibid.

[147] Fagan, J. (2008, Fall). "Juvenile Crime and Criminal Justice: Resolving Border Disputes." *Juvenile Justice* 18(2): 101. Retrieved from http://www.princeton.edu/futureofchildren/publications/docs/18_02_05.pdf

[148] Bishop et al., "The Transfer of Juveniles to Criminal Court."

[149] Fagan, J., M. Forst, and T. S. Vivona (1989). "Youth in Prisons and Training Schools: Perceptions and Consequences of the Treatment-Custody Dichotomy." *Juvenile and Family Court Journal* 2.

PRISONS OR "CORRECTIONAL" INSTITUTIONS
WHAT'S IN A NAME?

Within the formal juvenile justice system, the most severe disposition has always been commitment to some form of secure facility, today commonly known as a "juvenile correctional institution." As we saw in chapter 1, other terms have been used throughout the past 180 years: houses of refuge, reform schools, industrial and training schools, and just plain training schools. Notice that none of these names include the word "prison." However, when one cannot leave and there are walls or fences surrounding the place you are in, you are, in fact, "imprisoned." Nothing could be simpler than that. (In an article about detention, Christopher Bickel uses the term "captivity" to describe these and other institutions.)[1] Americans have a hard time admitting what we do with young offenders, and in Orwellian fashion we hide what is going on by using "nice" terminology.[2] The plain and simple truth is that these institutions are prisons.[3]

> For more than a century, the predominant model for the treatment, punishment, and rehabilitation of serious youthful offenders has been confinement in a large, congregate-care correctional facility. In most states, these institutions still house the bulk of all incarcerated youth and still consume the lion's share of taxpayer spending on juvenile justice.
>
> Unfortunately, the record of large juvenile corrections facilities is dismal. Though many youth confined in these training schools are not serious or chronic offenders, recidivism rates are uniformly high. Violence and abuse inside the facilities are alarmingly commonplace. The costs of correctional incarceration vastly exceed those of other approaches to delinquency treatment with equal or better outcomes, and the evidence shows that incarceration in juvenile facilities has serious and lifelong negative impacts on confined youth.[4]

Commitment to an Institution

Commitment to a juvenile prison often represents the "end of the line" for some youthful offenders. Starting with houses of refuge, these institutions have not had a very positive history. Barry Feld notes that research indicates incarcerating young offenders in large juvenile institutions is not rehabilitative and may actually be harmful. "A century of experience with training schools and youth prisons demonstrates that they constitute the one extensively evaluated and clearly ineffective method to treat delinquents."[5] Conditions in many of these institutions have not improved much over the years. Any "treatment" that goes on is the exception rather than the rule.

Individual states vary a great deal in where they place the juvenile, the length of stay, and the conditions of release. The most common arrangement (27 states) is that the delinquency agency that administers a state's institutions makes decisions as to where juveniles will be committed. In 23 states, the juvenile court takes a significant role in the determination of placement specifics. In some states the court literally chooses the exact location where the juvenile will be sent. Most commonly, the court orders that the juvenile be committed somewhere.[6]

As far as the actual time a juvenile will spend in an institution, there are six variations.[7]

1. *Indeterminate only:* This is the norm in 20 states. Regardless of the adjudicated offenses, the commitment is for an indefinite period of time, which could theoretically last until juveniles reach the age of majority. The exact length of stay is at the discretion of the releasing authority.

2. *Indeterminate with a minimum:* Five states add a minimum period of time that must be served to the indeterminate commitment.

3. *Indeterminate up to a maximum.* Six states specify that a youth cannot be confined for more than a certain period. An example would be California, where a juvenile cannot be confined longer than the maximum sentence that could have been imposed if the crime were committed by an adult.

4. *Indeterminate with minimums and maximums:* This exists in just one state, Pennsylvania, where the court determines the minimum period of the sentence "that is consistent with the protection of the public and the rehabilitative needs of the juvenile," but then "reviews the commitment periodically thereafter." Also, the maximum time served cannot exceed four years or the maximum time if convicted as an adult.

5. *Determinate and indeterminate:* A total of 13 states authorizes courts to fix an exact period of confinement but also permits them to order indeterminate commitments as well.

6. *Determinate only:* In six states, the commitment is for a period of time set by the court.

The decision to release a youth from confinement is made by the institution where the youth is confined, the original court, a *youth parole board*, or some combination of these authorities. In 23 states and the District of Columbia the decision is with the institution; in 10 states it lies with the committing court; in 7 states a parole board makes this decision; and in 10 states the decision is made by a combination of the agencies.[8]

There are several different prisons to which a youth can be committed. Some of these institutions are public (i.e., run by state or local governments); others are privately funded. Prisons for young offenders can be further subdivided into short-term (usually ranging from a few days to a couple of months) and long-term (ranging from three or four months to one or two years) confinement.

Short-Term Facilities

During the 1970s excessively large numbers of young offenders—up to one million per year—were incarcerated in the same facilities as adults under horrible conditions.

Adult Jails

Revelations about the physical conditions, the high number of suicides, and numerous sexual assaults caused a number of scandals. The Juvenile Justice and Delinquency Prevention Act (JJDPA) in 1974 mandated that states remove juveniles from such facilities and create alternatives or be subject to a loss of federal funding. Many states dragged their feet and Congress extended deadlines. After constant criticism, JJDPA was revised in 2002 (see summary in figure 12-1). The Act prohibits states receiving federal funds from detaining juveniles for more than six hours (24 hours in rural areas) in facilities that hold adults. Advocates are adamant that juveniles should never be held in adult facilities, even for fewer than six hours. According to ACT4 Juvenile Justice, youths incarcerated with adults are in danger of sexual and physical assault and are 36 times more likely to commit suicide than their counterparts in juvenile detention.[9] They also have a high rate of recidivism.

As of 2009, several states were still not in full compliance, including Maryland. Non-compliance can cost the state up to 20% of its federal grant allocation (approximately $170,000). In 2008, Maryland had a rate of 43.48 juveniles per 100,000 juvenile population of the state held with adults for more than six hours—almost five times the permitted rate of 9 per 100,000. In 2009, the rate had fallen to 19.13 juveniles per 100,000, and preliminary 2010 numbers indicated a rate of 6.07 per 100,000, which was within federal guidelines.[10]

Regardless of the intentions of the Act, a large number of juveniles are found in adult facilities. A recent report from the Bureau of Justice Statistics notes that in 2010 there were 7,560 juveniles in adult jails (most of them held as adults following certification), a slight decrease from 7,615 in 2000.[11] As noted in chapter 3, an amendment to JJDPA in 1980 created an exception to the rule that status offenders were not to be placed in detention. The amendment allowed for the detention of status offenders for violations of a valid court order (VCO). Court orders include requiring a juvenile to stop engaging in certain noncriminal behaviors. An example might be "a foster youth may be ordered at a dependency review hearing to stop running away from placement, or a truant may be ordered to stop skipping school. If the juvenile continues the prohibited behavior, he or she may be incarcerated for violating the court's order."[12]

One detailed study found that as of 2005, only four jurisdictions had not violated the rule prohibiting the detention of status offenders (American Samoa, Delaware, Montana, and New Mexico). Forty-eight other jurisdictions were in compliance only by virtue of not having exceeded the "de minimis" exceptions level of violations.[13] Three states were not in compliance at all

---

Figure 12-1   Summary of the Juvenile Justice and Delinquency Prevention Act of 2002

Federal Activities
- Reauthorizes the U.S. Department of Justice's Office of Juvenile Justice and Delinquency Prevention and designates an Administrator, nominated by the President and confirmed by the Senate, to head up this Office.
- Requires the Administrator to develop model mental health care standards for juveniles.
- Establishes programs for developing, testing, and demonstrating promising new initiatives and programs aimed at preventing and reducing juvenile delinquency.
- Establishes research and evaluation, statistical analyses, and information dissemination activities. Stipulates that within a year of enactment a study will be conducted of juveniles who were under the care or custody of the child welfare system or who are unable to return to their family after completing their disposition in the juvenile justice system.

Core Protections for Juveniles
- Deinstitutionalization of Status Offenders (DSO). Retains current prohibition on detaining status offenders in secure facilities.
- Separation of Juveniles from Adults in Institutions (Sight and Sound). Revises mandate to reflect current regulations which disallow contact between juvenile offenders in a secure custody status and incarcerated adults.
- Removal of Juveniles from Jails and Adult Facilities. Provides additional flexibility for rural areas by extending the period of time from 24 to 48 hours for which juveniles can be held in a jail or adult facility. Rural jurisdictions are allowed to place juveniles in adult facilities for a longer period of time, however strict "sight and sound" separation continues to apply.
- The law does not include the "parental consent rural exception" provision that had been included in the House passed bill that allowed youths to be held in adult facilities for up to 20 days when the court, parents or legal guardian, in consultation with counsel, agreed.
- Disproportionate Minority Confinement (DMC). Requires states to address prevention efforts and systemic efforts to reduce the disproportionate representation of minorities that come into contact with the juvenile justice system.

Compliance with Core Requirements
Current law ties 100% of a state's formula grant to compliance with the four core requirements. If a state fails to comply with any requirement, the state forfeits 25% of the allocation and must use the remainder of funds to come back into compliance with the core requirement. In the new law, a state that fails to comply with a core requirement will be penalized by 20% and must use 50% of the remaining funds to come back into compliance.

Source: Child Welfare League of America. Retrieved from http://www.cwla.org/advocacy/jjpnjja.htm

(Mississippi, Washington, and Virgin Islands; Wyoming did not participate in the grant program in fiscal year 2005). A total of eighteen states have posted either their three-year plan or an annual report on JJDPA compliance; of these, only four (Indiana, Iowa, Massachusetts, and Maine) have reported that they were in compliance with the no status offenders in detention rule. Fourteen states reported that they had violations of the act's requirement, the number ranging from three to 748. Between 2004 and 2007, three states (Washington, Wisconsin, and Wyoming) reported being totally out of compliance.

Detention Centers

Detention, briefly discussed in the previous chapter, is primarily a temporary holding facility that functions like a jail. Youths are placed in these centers pending a court hearing to determine whether or not they should be released. It has been repeatedly determined that most youths do not need to be placed in detention, that far too many have been charged with minor offenses (including status offenses), and that there are many negative consequences of being in detention, which:

- promotes further delinquency through association with delinquent peers;
- stigmatizes and reinforces a delinquent identity;
- results in harsher treatment by decision makers throughout the process;
- accelerates further involvement in the juvenile justice system;
- diverts resources from comprehensive community-based interventions;
- reduces involvement and interaction with community-based services;
- increases rejection by local public institutions such as schools;
- promotes isolation, lethargy, and ineffectiveness;
- results in overcrowding, punitive custody, and abusive conditions.[14]

The ultimate negative consequence is that youths in custody are at greater risk of death. A study published in *Pediatrics* documents that youths entering the juvenile justice system are four times more likely than the general population to die, with 90% of the deaths attributed to homicide. The researchers also noted that the "mortality rate among female youth was nearly 8 times the general-population rate." Researchers tracked a sample of 1,829 youths processed through the Cook County Juvenile Court starting in 1995, with a 3-year follow-up period. The death rate for black youths was the highest, followed closely by Hispanics (of the 65 who died, 23 were black and 21 were Hispanic).[15]

A particularly horrifying scandal about detention centers involved two Pennsylvania judges who were convicted of sending more than 5,000 children to one of two privately operated detention centers in return for kickbacks that amounted to more than $2.6 million. The judges had helped the detention centers obtain a county contract worth $58 million. They then guaranteed the operators a steady income by providing a steady stream of juveniles, mostly for very minor offenses.[16]

In October of 2009 the Southern Poverty Law Center (SPLC) filed a suit concerning conditions at the Lauderdale County Juvenile Detention Center in Mississippi.

> Youths endured physical and mental abuse as they were crammed into small, filthy cells and tormented with pepper spray for even minor infractions. Many of the youths had mental illnesses or learning disabilities. They were either awaiting court hearings or serving sentences for mostly nonviolent offenses. During one three-week stretch, a 17-year-old girl, identified in the suit as J.A., languished in her small cell for 23 hours a day. Most of the children were allowed to leave their cells for only one to two hours a day.[17]

One of the most problematic features of detention centers is the large number of youths with serious mental health problems. Estimates have found that from 67% to 70% of youths in all juvenile facilities (detention and juvenile prisons) have at least one mental health disorder and that 79% of those youths met criteria for two or more diagnoses; over 60% were diagnosed with three or more mental health disorders.[18] Another survey found that more than one third of juveniles in detention and almost half of females "had felt hopeless or thought about death in the 6 months before detention," while about 10% had thought about suicide and the same percentage actually attempted suicide.[19] Another survey found that about 11% of the males and 30% of the girls were diagnosed with major depression and just over half of both males and females were diagnosed with "conduct disorders."[20] Solomon Moore of the *New York Times* says that "jails and juvenile justice facilities are the new asylums."[21]

The costs to keep youths with mental health problems in detention are greater than the costs for other youths. One California study of 18 counties found an additional cost of $18,000 per juvenile; the study also noted that the costs of drugs administered to such youths amounted to an average of $4,387 per month.[22]

One of the worst states (and there are many) is Mississippi. In March of 2010 the Southern Poverty Law Center filed another suit against the state (*J.B., et al. v. Barbour, et al.*) charging that:

> (1) Mississippi discriminates against children with mental illness by unlawfully separating them from their families and communities and by forcing them to cycle through psychiatric institutions that fail to provide adequate services; (2) The state ignores the ongoing needs of children with mental illness by failing to provide federally mandated and medically necessary home- and community-based mental health services.[23]

Local Facilities

Status offenders and dependent, neglected, and abused children are housed in local facilities, which may include foster homes and other group homes.

- *Foster home:* the private home of foster parents providing twenty-four-hour care to one to three children unrelated to the foster parents by blood, marriage, or adoption;

- *Group foster home:* the private home of foster parents providing twenty-four-hour care to no more than six children unrelated to the foster parents by blood, marriage, or adoption;

- *Group home:* a child care facility that approximates a family setting, provides access to community activities and resources, and provides care to no more than twelve children.[24]

Foster care programs have been plagued with scandals over the years. Officials in New York City cancelled all contracts with one of the oldest foster care agencies, St. Christopher's Inc., founded in 1881, after an investigation revealed that it systematically falsified case records for children in its care.

> St. Christopher's has been under investigation for almost a year since former employees came forward to city officials to complain that superiors had urged them to invent records of home visits and to forge signatures. The city's Department of Investigation reviewed 50 case files provided by St. Christopher's, and officials said that all of the files held evidence that the agency tried to cover up its neglect of the foster children's needs.[25]

These problems are not limited to New York. The *Los Angeles Times* documented 98 deaths in 2009 of children who had at one time or another been under the supervision of the county's child welfare system, many of whom had been assigned to foster parents.[26] Another investigation found abuse, neglect, and deaths of children over a period of 12 years.[27] "United Care, which oversaw 88 homes with 216 foster children under contract with the county, had been repeatedly cited in recent years after caregivers choked, hit or whipped their charges with a belt."[28] A two-year-old child died at the hands of a person certified as a foster parent despite having an arrest record and being "the subject of five child abuse complaints, including one substantiated case involving her biological child."[29] These types of abuses have been known for more than a decade, yet little has been done to change the situation. Virtually every case involved kids who were racial minorities and/or from extremely poor families.

Boys Town: A Unique Case

Boys Town was founded by Father Edward Flanagan in 1917 in Nebraska. There are now 12 locations throughout the United States that provide care and shelter for abused, abandoned, neglected, handicapped, or otherwise troubled children. The Las Vegas location opened in 1991. The website refers to services and programs that touch the lives of 20,000 children and families in Nevada each year.[30] Various kinds of treatment programs are provided at the temporary shelter facility. The author has personally visited some of the facilities in the area, which provide a home-like environment, with no walls or bars.

Boys Town operates more than a hundred long-term, residential-care homes with family-style living in the least restrictive environment. In each home, a married couple lives with six to eight youths. Couples are trained to teach youths how to build positive relationships with others, to reinforce appropriate behavior, to apply consequences to inappropriate behavior, and to empower youths to make responsible and meaningful decisions.[31]

The Emergency Shelter Program provides short-term living arrangements for certain youths referred by the local juvenile court, family services, police agencies, school counselors, homeless shelters, and other local agencies. The shelter in Las Vegas has two eight-bed units, one for boys and one for girls. A certified schoolteacher designs and teaches the education curriculum and several full- and part-time counselors are on staff. The overall goal of the program is to provide temporary care for youths facing some kind of crisis in their life until a long-term placement can be arranged.

Long-Term Facilities

Juvenile prisons can be classified as "long-term facilities" since the stay is generally three to six months or more.

Reception and Diagnostic Centers

Prior to starting their sentence, offenders are evaluated by a psychologist or social worker to determine what sort of treatment will be required. These facilities are usually attached to a juvenile prison, and the stay is normally no more than a month. Various tests are given to assess the youth's level of intelligence, attitudes, degree of maturity, emotional problems, academic problems, and the like. Those in charge of the dormitories or cottages where the youths live are also involved in the assessment, helping to determine what problems, if any, the youth will have.

Some of these facilities do not in any way fit the image of a reception and diagnostic center. Some resemble warehouses—large, impersonal institutions. The Logansport Juvenile/Intake Diagnostic Center in Logansport, Indiana (a small town of just under 20,000 in the middle of Indiana about 60 miles north of Indianapolis) was established in 1995. "The Intake Unit is an 84 bed maximum security facility serving as the intake facility for all male juveniles between the ages of 12 and 18 who have been committed to the Indiana Department of Correction or have been ordered by the court for a pre-dispositional diagnostic evaluation."[32] The state of Virginia describes its Reception and Diagnostic Center as a processing center for any child found guilty in juvenile court in the state. It confines all juveniles "while they undergo academic, medical, psychological, behavioral, and sociological evaluation and classification to determine appropriate treatment needs, institutional placement recommendation, and a length of stay project."[33]

The state of Oklahoma describes its Reception and Orientation Center (ROC) as a place where "residents" (the euphemistic terminology used in place of "prisoners" or "inmates") are first admitted to the Southwest Oklahoma Juvenile Center. The website states that the goal of the staff is to gain control of the resident's behavior by having them memorize 18 rules of appropriate behavior and how they apply to the crimes committed before entering the ROC. Residents ask permission to speak and permission to enter and exit certain areas. There are no televisions or radios. Residents take classes in the unit, eat on the premises, and exit the unit only one hour a day for outside recreation.[34] The military model of discipline is readily apparent. Whether this description translates into success after release is doubtful given the high rates of recidivism among graduates of juvenile institutions (see discussion later in this chapter).

Ranches and Forestry Camps

Usually located near state parks and/or in rural areas, these are small facilities where the residents do conservation work or various sorts of farm/ranching type work. In 2003, California had 10 camps; there are now 2 facilities. Crews work in state and county parks clearing streams and performing fire prevention tasks under the direction of California fire officers. The emphasis in the programs is on work habits and employability skills.[35]

Boot Camps

Boot camps operate somewhat like their military counterparts. The drumbeat for zero tolerance, the criminalization of minor offenses, and the emphasis on respecting authority and learning responsibility coalesced into a culture ripe to embrace a militaristic approach to delinquency. The first adult prison boot camps opened in 1983. By 1995, 15,000 offenders had been sentenced to boot camps. All studies showed that boot camps had zero effect on recidivism.[36] Yet when juvenile crime spiked in the early 1990s, politicians decided boot camps would be a solution for juvenile offenders, despite no proven success.

> The use of these programs has always followed a pattern: Fear of growing youth crime fuels widespread skepticism about existing public policies. Seeking to quell criticism, public officials introduce military training as a quick fix. Military training as a treatment for adolescent problems is founded on the popular notion that adolescent problems result from inadequate discipline and structure.[37]

The first juvenile boot camp opened in 1985 in Orleans Parish, Louisiana; by 1995 state and local agencies operated 30 boot camps.[38] The federal government funded three programs in 1992 (in Cleveland, Denver, and Mobile, Alabama). The Mobile program was forced to shut down for three months in its first year after allegations of abuse by staff members. Brutality-related criminal charges or lawsuits surfaced in a number of states, including Alabama, Arizona, Florida, Louisiana, and Texas. Evaluations in California, Indiana and a multisite evaluation sponsored by the Office of Juvenile Justice and Delinquency Prevention (OJJDP) found no significant differences in recidivism rates between boot camp participants and comparison groups; in some cases, boot camp graduates had higher rates of recidivism.[39]

Several aspects of boot camps contribute to the poor results. There are few, if any, follow-up services to prepare youths for reentry into the community. Unlike boot camps for the armed services, no career awaits the graduates of juvenile boot camps. Several boot camps have been modified to provide more counseling and education, rather than the strict military model, but the length of stay (average 90 to 120 days) is too brief to provide adequate services to effect change. Samuel Walker has referred to the effectiveness of boot camp lasting about as long as the haircut.[40] The goals of treatment often conflict with the unrealistic goals of state legislatures that want to save money and to appear tough on crime. The confrontational environment and degrading tactics do not foster positive interpersonal relationships. The atmosphere is one of strict control, intimidation, and humiliation, sometimes leading to abuse of juveniles by those in charge. In addition to physical abuse, aggressive interactions can damage youths with emotional, behavioral, or learning problems.

In 1999 a *Baltimore Sun* reporter planned to write a story about troubled teenagers in boot camps. When he and his photographer witnessed repeated instances of brutality, the story turned into an investigative report about Maryland's three juvenile boot camps. The articles described beatings inflicted by guards, sometimes while youths were handcuffed and shackled. After publication of the articles, the governor closed the camps (two later reopened with fewer military trappings). In 2002, the state approved $4.6 million to settle claims by former inmates of the boot camps. About 890 youths went through the camps from 1996 when they opened until they were closed in 2000. The settlement included $2.1 million in education funds; about 350 former inmates applied for a portion of those funds.[41]

The Government Accountability Office (GAO) investigated boot camps and wilderness programs. "We found thousands of allegations of abuse, some of which involved death, at public and private residential treatment programs across the country between the years 1990 and 2007."[42] In 2005 alone, 33 states reported 1,619 staff members involved in incidents of abuse in residential programs. GAO investigated ten deaths at boot camps from 1990 through 2004. It found significant evidence of ineffective management playing a significant role in the deaths, including the hiring of untrained staff, a lack of adequate nourishment, and reckless or negligent operating practices, including a lack of adequate equipment.[43]

Georgia is phasing out its boot camp program, which had a 73% recidivism rate. Physical abuse by guards and inadequate care for mentally ill or disabled juveniles created ineffective and harmful conditions. Six counselors at a state-run wilderness camp in Cleveland, Georgia, were charged with murder, child cruelty, and involuntary manslaughter. Travis Parker, a 13-year-old asthmatic boy, had angrily confronted one of the counselors after they punished him by withholding food. The counselors restrained him by holding him face down for more than an hour and refused to give him his inhaler. He died the next day.[44]

In May 2006 the Florida legislature passed the Martin Lee Anderson Act, which eliminated the five boot camps in Florida.[45] Anderson was a good student serving probation for taking his grandmother's car from a church parking lot. He violated the probation by trespassing at school and was sent to boot camp. He died at age 14 the "day after guards were videotaped kicking, kneeing, and dragging him."[46] Other states have been phasing out boot camps or cutting them back (e.g., Colorado, North Dakota, Arizona, and California).[47]

Training Schools

In 2002 the SPLC investigated conditions inside the Oakley Training School in Raymond, Mississippi and the Columbia Training School in Columbia, Mississippi and filed a lawsuit. Oakley sits on approximately 1,068 acres of land surrounded by agricultural fields approximately 30 minutes outside of Jackson, Mississippi. It was designed to function as a paramilitary program for delinquent boys and imposes a military style discipline and a self-described vigorous physical fitness training program.[48] The SPLC report concluded: "We find that conditions at Oakley and Columbia violate the constitutional and statutory rights of juveniles. Youth confined at Oakley and Columbia suffer harm or the risk of harm from deficiencies in the facilities' provision of mental health and medical care, protection of juveniles from harm, and juvenile justice management. There are also sanitation deficiencies at Oakley. In addition, both facilities fail to provide required general education services as well as education to eligible youth."[49]

The state settled the suit and promised to make changes, but in 2006 a federal court monitor noted that few if any changes had been made "In addition to being hog-tied and left for days in pitch-black cells, children ages 10 to 17 were sometimes sprayed with chemicals during mandatory exercises and forced to eat their own vomit. Other youth were forced to run with automobile tires around their necks or mattresses on their backs." Mississippi Youth Justice Project (MYJP) co-director Ellen Reddy stated that: "At best, the training schools do nothing but warehouse children. At worst, our children experience gross abuse and neglect when sent away from their home communities."[50] Rhonda Brownstein, the Legal Director of SPLC stated: "These abuses are the kind of things you would hear about in some torture chamber in a Third World country. This is not how we treat our children in the United States."[51]

A website called "Boot Camp for Kids: Torturing Teens for Fun and Profit" provides links to 209 news reports from 1992 to 2011 on "cruelty, sadism, injury, and death in locked residential facilities for troubled youth."[52] One story was about the Florida School for Boys. In 2009, a group of men in their 50s came forward to tell of the abuse they had suffered that affected the course of their lives. The article details repeated investigations of abuse. In 1903 a Florida senate committee said: "We have no hesitancy in saying, under its present management it is nothing more nor less than a prison, where juvenile prisoners are confined." Sixty-five years later, the institution was renamed the Arthur G. Dozier School for Boys, and another investigation called it "Hell's 1,400 Acres."[53] Thirty-nine years later, state officials fired the school's superintendent and a guard after a violent incident, saying operational problems at the school spanned the chain of command from top to bottom.

These abuses are only a tiny portion of the many examples that date back to houses of refuge in the early nineteenth century. Developments discussed later in the chapter offer some hope that long-term juvenile prisons will be replaced by more effective, local facilities.

Institutional Populations

Table 12-1 presents data on the offense profile of juveniles in custody in 2007. A total of 86,927 were in a correctional institution or a local detention center. This represents a drop of about 20% since 1997, when there were 105,055 juveniles in custody. A much smaller number (1,498) were in some form of diversion program. Of the 60,426 youths committed, 16% were in for either a technical violation or a status offense. Most of the remainder were charged with a property, public order, or drug offense. As for the 24,958 detained youths, 26% were charged with a technical violation or status offense.

Table 12-2 (on p. 412) shows the number of juveniles detained in public or private facilities and the most serious offense for which they were detained. Public facilities are operated by state or local government agencies, and employees are state or local government employees. Private facilities are operated by private for-profit corporations or nonprofit organizations; employees are hired by the private corporations or organizations.[54] Although most facilities are small and private, most offenders are held in large public facilities. In October 2004, 42% of juvenile facilities were publically operated and held 69% of the juvenile population.[55] Training schools tend to be state facilities; detention centers are usually local facilities; group homes tend to be private. Boot camps and reception centers are generally public, but a substantial number are private. Most shelters and ranch/wilderness camps are private. Public facilities were more likely to be crowded.

Note that a larger percentage of juveniles in private facilities are status offenders (9% versus 2% in public facilities). The most common offense in both kinds of facilities is a personal crime, followed by property offenses. Note also that those adjudicated for technical offenses (mostly violation of probation or parole or various court orders) constitute a sizeable proportion (15% for all institutions). For person crimes, 25% were charged with an index crime, with 11% confined for either simple assault or other person crime.

The most recent survey of those in juvenile prisons reveals what everyone has known for years, namely that most had experienced some kind of abuse prior to being committed. In fact, the survey found that 70% had experienced some type of past traumatic experience, much of it related to physical or sexual abuse. About one-fifth (22%) attempted suicide.[56]

Racial Composition of Juvenile Institutions

The percentage of incarcerated youth who are racial minorities has risen steadily over the years. The national percentage of minorities in training schools was 23% in 1950, 32% in 1960, 40% in 1970, 60% in 1989, and 66% in 1997, then dropping to 63% in 2006. In contrast, the majority of youths confined in *private* facilities are white. This is no doubt because most of the costs are paid for by family members, usually through their insurance.

Table 12-1   Detailed Offense Profile by Placement Status for United States, 2007 (Column Percent)

Most serious offense	Placement Status			
	Total	**Committed**	**Detained**	**Diversion**
Total	**100%**	**100%**	**100%**	**100%**
Delinquency	96%	96%	97%	86%
Person	**36%**	**37%**	**33%**	**36%**
Criminal homicide	1%	1%	2%	1%
Sexual assault	7%	8%	3%	10%
Robbery	9%	9%	9%	8%
Aggravated assault	8%	9%	8%	7%
Simple assault	8%	8%	7%	7%
Other person	3%	3%	4%	1%
Property	**24%**	**26%**	**21%**	**13%**
Burglary	10%	11%	8%	6%
Theft	5%	5%	4%	3%
Auto theft	4%	5%	3%	2%
Arson	1%	1%	1%	0%
Other property	5%	4%	5%	2%
Drug	**8%**	**9%**	**7%**	**6%**
Trafficking	2%	2%	2%	1%
Other drug	6%	7%	6%	5%
Public order	**13%**	**13%**	**12%**	**14%**
Weapons	5%	5%	5%	2%
Alcohol	0%	0%	0%	0%
Other public order	8%	8%	7%	12%
Technical violation	**15%**	**12%**	**23%**	**17%**
Violent Crime Index*	**25%**	**26%**	**22%**	**27%**
Property Crime Index**	**20%**	**21%**	**16%**	**11%**
Status offense	**4%**	**4%**	**3%**	**14%**
Running away	1%	1%	1%	4%
Truancy	1%	1%	0%	1%
Incorrigibility	1%	2%	1%	5%
Curfew violation	0%	0%	0%	0%
Underage drinking	1%	1%	0%	2%
Other status offense	0%	0%	0%	1%

* Includes criminal homicide, violent sexual assault, robbery, and aggravated assault.
** Includes burglary, theft, auto theft, and arson.

Note: U.S. total includes 1,466 juvenile offenders in private facilities for whom state of offense was not reported and 124 juvenile offenders in tribal facilities.

Note: Committed juveniles include those placed in the facility as part of a court ordered disposition. Detained juveniles include those held awaiting a court hearing, adjudication, disposition or placement elsewhere. Diverted juveniles include those voluntarily admitted to the facility in lieu of adjudication as part of a diversion agreement. Totals include juveniles for whom placement status was reported as unknown or "other."

Source: Sickmund, M., T. J. Sladky, and W. Kang (2011). "Census of Juveniles in Residential Placement Databook." Retrieved from http://www.ojjdp.gov/ojstatbb/ezacjrp/asp/Offense_Adj.asp?state=0&topic=Offense_Adj&year=2007&percent=column

The overall rate of incarceration of juveniles in the United States was 279 in 2007 (738 for blacks, 305 for Hispanics, and 157 for whites).[57] Table 12-3 reveals stark contrasts in the rates for committed youths. The rate for blacks was 499,

Table 12-2   Juvenile Offenders in Residential Placement, in Public and Private Facilities, 2007 (Column Percent)

	Facility Type		
Most serious offense	**All Facilities**	**Public**	**Private**
Total	**100%**	**100%**	**100%**
Delinquency	96%	98%	91%
Person	**36%**	**38%**	**31%**
Criminal homicide	1%	2%	0%
Sexual assault	7%	6%	8%
Robbery	9%	10%	5%
Aggravated assault	8%	9%	6%
Simple assault	8%	7%	9%
Other person	3%	3%	3%
Property	**24%**	**24%**	**24%**
Burglary	10%	10%	10%
Theft	5%	5%	5%
Auto theft	4%	4%	4%
Arson	1%	1%	1%
Other property	5%	5%	4%
Drug	**8%**	**7%**	**11%**
Trafficking	2%	2%	2%
Other drug	6%	5%	9%
Public order	**13%**	**13%**	**13%**
Weapons	5%	5%	4%
Alcohol	0%	0%	0%
Other public order	8%	7%	9%
Technical violation	**15%**	**17%**	**12%**
Violent Crime Index*	**25%**	**28%**	**19%**
Property Crime Index**	**20%**	**20%**	**20%**
Status offense	**4%**	**2%**	**9%**
Running away	1%	0%	2%
Truancy	1%	0%	2%
Incorrigibility	1%	0%	4%
Curfew violation	0%	0%	0%
Underage drinking	1%	0%	1%
Other status offense	0%	0%	1%

* Includes criminal homicide, violent sexual assault, robbery, and aggravated assault.
** Includes burglary, theft, auto theft, and arson.

Note: U.S. total includes 1,466 juvenile offenders in private facilities for whom state of offense was not reported and 124 juvenile offenders in tribal facilities.

Source: Sickmund, M., T. J. Sladky, and W. Kang (2011). "Census of Juveniles in Residential Placement Databook." Retrieved from http://www.ojjdp.gov/ojstatbb/ezacjrp/asp/Offense_Facility.asp?state=0&topic= Offense_Facility&year=2007&percent=column

compared to 206 for Hispanics, and 114 for whites. Even when considering the most serious offense charged, commitment rates for minorities far exceeded those of whites. For example, the black rate for person crimes was 199 compared to 76 for Hispanics and 39 for whites. *For drug offenses, the black rate was five times the rate for whites.* In fact, for every offense category, whites had the lowest rate, blacks had the highest, and Hispanics were in the middle. As Christopher Bickel notes: "Not since slavery have we seen the rise of an institution that so fundamentally perpetuates and legitimates massive inequality, especially for inner city children of color."[58] The sad fact is that incarceration has become part of the life course for the urban poor.

Studies in individual states are also revealing.[59] The seven highest state rates for blacks in 2007 were: 3,956 (SD), 2,612 (MT), 1,868 (NE), 1,690 (ND),

Table 12-3   Offense Profile of Committed Residents by Sex and Race/Ethnicity, 2007 (rate per 100,000 juveniles)

| | Committed | | | | | | | |
| | | Sex | | Race/Ethnicity | | | | |
Most serious offense	Total	Male	Female	White	Black	Hispanic	American Indian	Asian
Total	194	332	48	114	499	206	341	53
Delinquency	186	323	42	107	482	203	306	52
Person	72	125	16	39	199	76	111	21
Violent Crime Index*	50	92	7	25	145	56	65	15
Other Person	21	33	9	13	54	20	46	6
Property	50	88	11	32	119	52	88	16
Property Crime Index**	41	73	9	27	100	41	73	14
Other Property	9	15	2	5	19	11	15	2
Drug	17	29	4	9	49	16	23	3
Public order	25	45	4	14	63	30	42	5
Technical violation	23	37	8	13	52	29	43	7
Status offense	8	10	6	7	16	4	35	1

* Includes criminal homicide, violent sexual assault, robbery, and aggravated assault.

** Includes burglary, theft, auto theft, and arson.

Note: The rate is the number of juvenile offenders in residential placement per 100,000 juveniles ages 10 through the upper age of original juvenile court jurisdiction in each State.

Note: U.S. total includes 1,466 juvenile offenders in private facilities for whom state of offense was not reported and 124 juvenile offenders in tribal facilities.

Rates for "All racial/ethnic groups" include juveniles identified in the CJRP as "Other" race, most of whom were individuals with multiple race identification. Rates are not presented separately for these "Other" race juveniles because there is no comparable reference population available.

Note: Committed juveniles include those placed in the facility as part of a court ordered disposition.

Note: The "Hispanic" category includes persons of Latin American or other Spanish culture or origin regardless of race. These persons are not included in the other race/ethnicity categories.

Source: Sickmund, M., T. J. Sladky, and W. Kang (2011). "Census of Juveniles in Residential Placement Databook." Retrieved from http://www.ojjdp.gov/ojstatbb/ezacjrp/asp/Offense_Committed.asp?state=0&topic=Offense_Committed&year=2007&percent=rate

1,575 (CO), 1,527 (UT), and 1,413 (PA). In California, minority youths constituted the overwhelming majority of committed juveniles, with Hispanics
accounting for more than half (54%) and blacks constituting another 27%;
whites were only 15% of the totals.[60]

Commitment rates in Nevada are far higher for blacks (1,121) than for
whites (250).[61] In 1999 a new "super-max" youth prison opened in North Las
Vegas to house offenders classified as "Level IV," the highest classification in
the state based on alleged degree of dangerousness. This new category was
determined by a point system, which involved assigning a numerical value to
previous offenses. Careful investigation by the author discovered that there
was no scientific rationale for the point system and no research cited to justify
the system. Summit View Correctional Center cost the state $15 million ($1.2
million annual bond payments); originally it was operated by a private company until the state took over in 2004. Within one year of opening, the prison
was beset by a number of problems—including too many empty beds (the
facility was built to house 96 offenders). The state could not find enough "dangerous" youth to qualify for Level IV (in fact, for a time the prison "borrowed"
a few "Level III" youths from the detention center at the juvenile court in Las
Vegas). They did, however, find a large number of minority youths to house in
this prison; 80% of the youths were minorities.[62]

Juveniles Incarcerated in Adult Prisons

As noted in chapter 11, there are 2,574 people serving sentences of life
without the possibility of parole for crimes committed when they were under
18. As one report noted, these children effectively have been sentenced to die in
prison. The particulars in many of the cases are heartbreaking.

> Ashley Jones is the only girl in Alabama sentenced to death in prison for an
> offense when she was 14 years old. From the time she was an infant, Ashley
> was terrorized by abusive and violent adults. Her addicted mother aban-
> doned Ashley in crack houses while she was still in diapers and on several
> occasions threatened her at gunpoint. Her father assaulted her, resulting in a
> hospitalization. Her stepfather sexually assaulted her when she was 11.
> Relentless violence in her home left Ashley depressed, traumatized, and sui-
> cidal. At 14, Ashley tried to escape the violence and abuse by running away
> with an older boyfriend who shot and killed her grandfather and aunt. Her
> grandmother and sister, who were injured during the offense, want Ashley
> to come home. But Alabama's mandatory sentencing law does not recognize
> mitigation, mercy, or the abusive dysfunction that lead to her crime.[63]

The average prison sentence for juvenile offenders convicted as an adult is
89 months; for violent offenses, the average is 106 months.[64] In 1998 there were
about 14,500 juveniles in adult prisons and jails, with the largest number (about
9,100) in local jails.[65] A total of 44 states have juveniles in adult jails and prisons, and 18 of those states have youthful offender housing units. Most (79%) of
the youths were 17 (18% were 16); 75% had been sentenced as adults, while

21% were adjudicated as juvenile offenders or pretrial detainees. More than half (55%) of the juveniles held in adult facilities were black and had been convicted of crime against persons. Dormitory settings house 51% of the population; 30% are in single cells and 19% in double cells. While the number of youths in adult prisons has leveled off, the number in local jails has increased.

Get tough policies for juvenile offenders are viewed as a deterrent for "out of control" juveniles and to protect society, yet in reality incarcerating juveniles in adult facilities is detrimental. Failure to separate juveniles from adults leads to exposure to people with extensive criminal records; it also places juveniles at risk for sexual or physical assault.[66] Juveniles housed in adult penitentiaries and jails commit suicide at a far higher rate. Studies have found that juveniles who are prosecuted and punished as adults are more likely to re-offend and to do so more quickly, compared to juveniles who are dealt with by the juvenile justice system.

The Inmate Social System and Victimization

Erving Goffman offered excellent insight into the lives of people confined in what he termed *total institutions*.[67] Captives are subjected to various forms of "status degradation"; their movements are restricted; they are severed totally from the outside world—and they are reduced to a state of almost total dependency. Bickel describes a juvenile detention center he studied—which resembled an adult prison—from the standpoint of the architecture itself: "the thick steel doors, the countless locks on every door and every drawer, and the numerous gazing security cameras."[68] An expert on trauma observed that these institutions destroy the ability to cope in the free world through:

> a lack of rehabilitation opportunities, excessive reliance on isolation as punishment, the restriction of visits and contacts with the outside world, the pervasiveness of sexual abuse, disrespect at every turn, the failure of pre-planning release—all these things add up to throwing the prisoner who completes a term out into the world broken, with no skills, and a very high risk of recidivism.[69]

Several studies covering a period of around 30 years document the abuses within these institutions.[70] The National Assessment of Juvenile Corrections surveyed 42 juvenile prisons in the 1970s.[71] The study focused on the effects on youths of being institutionalized. "Newcomers," those who had been at the facility two months or less, were distinguished from "veterans," those who had been incarcerated nine months or more. The survey found significant differences between programs having large proportions of veterans and those having relatively few veterans. Generally, veterans were significantly more likely than newcomers to: (1) commit more offenses and have friends who had committed offenses while incarcerated; (2) have learned more ways to break the law while incarcerated (46% of the veterans, compared to 20% of the newcomers); and (3) become "hardened" (measured in several ways, such as being critical of the staff, previous encounters with institutions, number and seriousness of offenses while incarcerated, and other indicators) over time. The longer a youth remained in the institution, the more the youth would: (1) fight with other youths, (2) use drugs, (3) steal something, (4) run away, and (5) hit a staff member. These problems were more apparent in the larger institutions and were most acute when there was a critical mass of veterans.

John Irwin studied adult felons and found that a significant number were what he termed *state-raised youths*—offenders who more or less "grew up" in various institutions (such as juvenile detention centers, foster care, group homes, and the like). They had rarely spent any significant amounts of time in free society. Irwin described the worldview of state-raised youths as distorted, stunted, and incoherent. The prison world became their only meaningful world.[72] Juvenile institutions have a very potent *inmate subculture*. In most of the larger institutions there is a hierarchy within a strongly defined peer subculture.

A very detailed study in the 1970s by three criminologists of an institution in Columbus, Ohio, focused on the extent of victimization in institutions. It described a brutal social system. Within the "jungle" (the term the inmates themselves used), the powerful preyed on the weak.[73] The researchers identified a number of *social roles* that have existed in the inmate subculture since the earliest institutions in the nineteenth century. Some youths are aggressive; others are manipulative; and some are passive. The aggressors are the leaders and often have crew members who might be referred to by military or organized crime terms, such as "lieutenants" or "wise guys." Manipulators do what is necessary to survive and make their stay easier. Some might engage in various businesses and become known as "peddlers" or "merchants." Passive youth are not deeply involved in the inmate social system and generally try to please the staff.

The researchers returned 15 years later; what they found was not encouraging.[74] They discovered that the youth culture still existed and victimized the weak, although less for sex than for food, clothing, and toiletries. Consensual sexual behavior seemed to be more prevalent, while the violent youths were in the minority; the majority consisted of drug dealers, addicts, and users of drugs. Gangs did not dominate within the institution, as popularly believed. Most discouraging was the fact that there were almost no treatment programs, with the lone exception of a drug abuse program. Social workers said they didn't do anything for the youths and that the institution was a warehouse for children.

Youths in institutions are at risk for sexual victimization. The Prison Rape Elimination Act of 2003 mandated a comprehensive study of the problem. The Bureau of Justice Statistics conducted the first National Survey of Youth in Custody at large facilities that included youths held at least 90 days (26,550 youths). However, there are almost 93,000 youths in juvenile detention each day—many held for shorter periods of time or in smaller facilities.[75] Thus the 3,220 juveniles who reported sexual abuse (12.1% of juveniles in such facilities) probably underrepresent the problem. On any given day, approximately 8,500 kids under 18 are confined in adult prisons and jails. Although probably at greater risk of sexual abuse than any other detained population, they were not included in the BJS study.

More than 10% (2,730) of the juveniles reported victimization by a facility staff member, and 95% of the youths said they were victimized by female staff. In 2008, 42% of the staff in juvenile institutions was female.[76] Although 63% of the juveniles reported at least one incident in which there was no explicit coercion, claims of consensual sex in circumstances where one party has control over another are suspect. Staff can grant privileges or decide punishment, including solitary confinement and extended sentences. "The notion of a truly consensual relationship in such circumstances is grotesque even when the inmate is not a child."[77]

Female only institutions had the highest rates of youth-on-youth victimization; male only institutions had the highest rates of staff-on-youth sexual victimization.[78] Unwanted sex with another youth was reported by 9.1% of females and 2% of males. Unwanted sex with staff was reported by 10.8% of males and 4.7% of females. White youths (4.4%) were more likely than blacks (2.1%) or Hispanics (.9%) to report youth-on-youth victimization. The percentages were more similar for staff-on-youth victimization: 11.9% of blacks, 9.7% of whites, and 8.1% of Hispanics. Staff-on-youth victimizations increased with the length of time spent at the facility.[79]

The biggest risk factor found in the study was prior abuse; 81% of those sexually abused by other inmates were victimized more than once, 32% more than ten times, and 42% were assaulted by more than one perpetrator. Of those victimized by staff, 88% had been abused repeatedly, 27% more than ten times, and 33% by more than one facility employee. Survey respondents had been in their facilities for an average of half a year. "In essence, the survey shows that thousands of children are raped and molested every year while in the government's care—most often, by the very corrections officials charged with their rehabilitation and protection."[80]

Will Budget Necessities Lead to Improvement?

California has a $26 billion deficit; New York has a $10 billion deficit.[81] Both states are moving toward permanently closing state youth prisons. Juvenile prisons are expensive and ineffective, if not detrimental. Other states have not yet decided to eliminate the state role, but they are reducing the numbers of juveniles held in state institutions. Texas and California—the two largest state systems—reduced the numbers of youths held in long-term confinement by moving low-level offenders to detention halls in counties. Texas previously confined 5,000 youths and reduced that population by half within two years. In 1996, California confined 10,000 juveniles; the number was 1,300 in 2011.[82] Ohio has reduced the number of incarcerated juveniles from 1,800 in 2007 to 736 in 2011. Illinois and Pennsylvania have reduced the number of their incarcerated youths by offering financial incentives to counties to keep youthful offenders in local programs.

California

Farrell v. Harper was filed as a taxpayer action suit in California in 2003. When it became apparent that fighting the suit in court would be a costly and losing battle, California agreed to allow jointly selected national experts to determine the nature and extent of the system's problems. The reports (in what had now become *Farrell v. Hickman*) were released in January 2004.

> They confirmed horrible abuses and major deficiencies in almost every aspect of institutional operation, and blasted the agency for utterly failing in its rehabilitative and public safety mission. The CYA was found to be shockingly incompetent in every area reviewed: the safety of the facilities; the quality of the school and health care systems; and the efficacy of the mental health, substance abuse and other treatment programs. The system was not simply failing to rehabilitate. It was affirmatively damaging its youthful population, who often were discharged with increased criminal sophistication, entrenched gang involvement and exacerbated mental illness.[83]

After the reports, many counties sent representatives to visit the youths from their area who had been committed to the CYA; some declared a moratorium on new CYA commitments. Families of wards organized protests. The attorney general and the CYA acknowledged the accuracy of the reports and agreed to working with the Farrell lawyers to improve conditions.

The court agreement listed a number of required changes.

- Shift to an "open programming" model, as opposed to one that confines inmates in their cells for long stretches at a time, at all prisons by May 2. Under the change, inmates must be released for education, meals, treatment and recreation on a daily basis, and dangerous youths would be separated from those considered vulnerable.

- House youths in the facility closest to their homes. This addresses a chief complaint of families, who often live hundreds of miles from their incarcerated children, making visits difficult.

- Involve families in the therapy provided to youths, unless it would be considered detrimental to the inmate.

- Emphasize "positive reinforcement rather than punitive disciplinary methods" to encourage good behavior.

- Require all staff who work with youths to be trained in rehabilitative and treatment services.[84]

Four years after the settlement, Krisberg found that the rate of violence within the existing facilities had actually increased slightly (from a rate of 74 per 100 youth to 82) and the rate of the use of force against youth remained unchanged.[85]

> First, youth are frightened about the prospects of their return home and do not believe that DJJ is offering them the life skills to succeed on the outside. Aftercare and reentry services remain in need of stronger internal leadership and much greater attention. Therapy behind "razor wire" has not proven to be an effective method of reducing recidivism rates. Second, youth feel disconnected from staff. When they are feeling anxious, stressed,

troubled, or threatened by other youth, DJJ residents do not generally feel that they can talk with DJJ staff. The youth report that mental health clinicians are often detached and less than fully available to them and living unit staff still communicate that they are "too busy."[86]

After almost four years and hundreds of millions of dollars, the state had still not implemented the required reforms. In 2007, the state passed legislation that shifted responsibility to the counties for all but the most serious youth offenders and committed funds to help local areas pay for the necessary programs and services.[87]

One Fresno youth spent two years in California's juvenile prison system. Rather than rehabilitating young offenders, correctional officers spent most of their time separating rival gangs. He said the situation was no better than the streets he came from—violence was so pervasive that he kept his gang affiliation to protect himself.[88] The Preston Youth Correctional Facility was shut down in June 2011. It was the ninth state youth detention facility to close since 2002, leaving four facilities. The population of young offenders in state care has plummeted from 10,000 in 1996 to 1,300 in 2011 because of lower crime rates and laws mandating that only the most serious offenders remain in state custody. The vast majority of young offenders are held at county facilities.

In January 2011, Governor Jerry Brown called for the elimination of the youth prison system—his proposal would have made California the first state to follow that path. The state's 58 county probation departments would split the annual $242 million budget for DJJ. Joan Petersilia called it "an incredibly massive shift for a state system that was sending everybody and their brother to prison" (referring to both juveniles and adults). She also cautioned against naively thinking the process would be inexpensive because the offenders have serious needs.[89] Donna Hitchens, a retired San Francisco judge who had tried to avoid sending young offenders to state institutions, said: "On a policy level, it's a great idea. But long-term treatment requires really strong programs in a secure setting, and a campus environment since they're going to be there for so long." If the counties are going to do better than the state, they will need more money and rehabilitation services to deal with young people for whom violence is common.

While critics had long deplored the violent, abusive, and decaying facilities, they were also cautious about the proposed elimination of the state system in favor of confining the most violent young offenders at the local level. Critics were concerned that counties are not prepared to handle an influx of severely troubled young people. Sue Burrell, a lawyer at the Youth Law Center in San Francisco, said: I'm disgusted with myself to think of defending DJJ with all the things that have happened over the years, but if you ask me right now, I would opt for keeping a very, very small DJJ open and not throwing the kids to the wolves." She was concerned that prosecutors might view counties as incapable of handling serious offenders and would try the juveniles as adults—meaning they would face adult prison if convicted. Dan Macallair, who has referred to state institutions as relics of the nineteenth century, said that the proposed state closings did present challenges. However, he also noted that young offenders

---

Figure 12.2   The Demise of the California Youth Authority

The Youth Corrections Authority Act of 1941 created The California Youth Authority (CYA). The law mandated the acceptance of all youths under the age of 23 who had been committed to various prisons and already existing youth facilities. Its stated mission was to provide education, training, and treatment services for youthful offenders.

Forty years later, the reality differed dramatically from the stated mission. Reports documented extreme brutality and the lack of meaningful treatment. CYA institutions were described as "seriously overcrowded, offer minimal treatment value despite their high expense, and are ineffective in long-term protection of public safety."[1] In the 1980s, the CYA housed over 7,000 wards in institutions designed for 5,840. Life in these youth prisons was violent and harsh. Thousands spent their adolescence in an institution where their physical and emotional safety was threatened daily.[2]

The Preston School of Industry was a prime example of a failed California institution. It opened in 1894 and closed in 2011, leaving a 117-year "legacy of maltreatment."[3] Marked by appalling physical conditions and extreme brutality, the overcrowded facility had a history of sexual abuse, violent assaults, and suicides. Inmates were sometimes confined in dungeon-like, isolated, deplorable conditions for 23 hours a day, released only for an hour of exercise—shackled in a cage.

In 1998 the CYA decided to use cages in classrooms at the four highest security youth prisons. The cages, called "secure program areas," were constructed of metal mesh or chain link fencing and contained a chair and a desk. The cages were arranged in a semicircle around a teacher's desk. Critics were outraged at the practice; one stated that "If the only place a ward feels safe is in a cage, what kind of system is that?"[4] Another called the CYA system "a very dangerous place" with "an intense climate of fear."[5]

In 2004, correctional officers and counselors were captured on videotape twice in four months. In the first incident, a canine officer allowed his German shepherd to attack a prisoner, even though the inmate was following orders and lying on the floor. The other incident showed two counselors punching and kicking two inmates. The FBI opened an investigation after the videotape was released by a state senator, and the beatings were televised nationally.[6] In January 2004, two cellmates committed a double suicide. The reporter covering the story detailed appalling conditions in CYA facilities: "Excessive rates of violence; inadequate mental health care and educational services; overuse of isolation cells; and deplorable conditions, including feces spread all over some of the cells."[7]

A class action lawsuit (*Farrell v. Cate*) was filed in 2002 alleging unconstitutional treatment of inmates.[8] The plaintiff was Margaret Farrell of Reseda, "whose nephew, mentally ill inmate Edward Jermaine Brown, was locked in a filthy isolation cell for 23 hours a day for seven months. . . . The toilet in the cell often did not function and Brown was fed 'blender meals,' a whipped mix of food groups, through a straw pushed through his cell door."[9] The CYA closed the Tamarack Lodge at Preston where Brown was locked up in March 2004.[10]

Part of the settlement required that independent experts evaluate the CYA.[11] An audit in 2004 found that the CYA failed to comply with minimum standards for education and failed to meet mandated treatment services. The audit showed that the CYA had complied with only

57% of the 241 recommendations in the 9 reviews over the previous 4 years.[12] It failed to address gang management and suicide prevention; violence was "off the charts."[13] The CYA "agreed to develop a system to separate vulnerable inmates from dangerous ones, to reduce the time prisoners spend in isolation cells, and to make improvements in watching inmates who might commit suicide."[14] On January 31, 2005, the state of California signed an agreement to settle the lawsuit, putting as top priority the goal of treatment.[15] Also in 2005, the CYA was renamed the Division of Juvenile Justice (DJJ) within the newly reorganized and renamed Department of Corrections and Rehabilitation.[16]

If the proposals calling for the closing of the remainder of the CYA institutions are approved, the remaining wards will either be released outright or will be housed in county facilities—bringing the CYA to an end almost exactly 70 years after it was created.[17]

Notes

[1] Lerner, S. (1986). *Bodily Harm: The Pattern of Fear and Violence at the California Youth Authority.* Bolinas, CA: Common Knowledge Press; Lerner, S. (1982). *The CYA Report, Part I: Conditions of Life at the California Youth Authority.* Bolinas: CA: Commonweal; Lerner, S., P. Demuro, and, A. Demuro (1988). *The CYA Report, Part III: Reforming the California Youth Authority—How To End Crowding, Diversify Treatment and Protect the Public Without Spending More Money.* Bolinas: CA: Commonweal.

[2] Byrnes, M., D. Macallair, and A. D. Shorter (2002). "Aftercare as Afterthought: Reentry and the California Youth Authority." San Francisco: Center on Juvenile and Criminal Justice.

[3] Teji, S. (2011, July 10). "Goodbye Preston." Retrieved from http://cjcj.org/post/juvenile/justice/goodbye/preston

[4] Leovy, J. and J. Chong (2004, February 6). "Youth Authority to Review Use of Cages." *Los Angeles Times.* Retrieved from http://articles.latimes.com/2004/feb/06/local/me-cage6

[5] Cannon, A. (2004, August 3). "Special Report: Juvenile Injustice." *US News and World Report.* http://www.usnews.com/usnews/news/articles/040809/9juvenile.htm

[6] Warren, J. (2004, May 7). "Attack by Prison Dog Revealed." *Los Angeles Times.* Retrieved from http://articles.latimes.com/2004/may/07/local/me-youth7

[7] Bell, J. and J. Stauring (2004, May 2). "Serious Problems Festering in Juvenile Justice System Require Serious Reforms." *Los Angeles Times.* Retrieved from http://articles.latimes.com/2004/may/02/opinion/oe-bell2

[8] *Farrell v. Cate.* Retrieved from http://www.prisonlaw.com/cases.php#juvi

[9] Warren, J. (2004, November 17). "State Youth Prisons on Road to Rehab." *Los Angeles Times.* Retrieved from http://articles.latimes.com/2004/nov/17/local/me-cya17/3

[10] James, S. (2004, December 30). "CYA Goes to Reform School." Retrieved from http://www.newsreview.com/sacramento/cya-goes-to-reform-school/content?oid=33045

[11] Macallair, D., M. Males and C. McCracken (2009). *Closing California's Division of Juvenile Facilities: An Analysis of County Institutional Capacity.* San Francisco: Center on Juvenile and Criminal Justice. http://cjcj.org/files/closing_californias_DJF.pdf

[12] Furillo, A. (2005, January 4). "CA Inspector General's Report Finds Fault with Education and Mental Health Care." *Sacramento Bee.* Retrieved from http://realcostofprisons.org/blog/archives/2005/01/cainspector_gen.html

[13] Warren, "State Youth Prisons on Road to Rehab."

[14] *Farrell v. Cate.*

[15] Warren, J. (2005, February 1). "For Young Offenders, a Softer Approach." *Los Angeles Times.*

[16] Retrieved from http://www.cdcr.ca.gov/Juvenile_Justice/DJJ_History/index.html

[17] A complete discussion can be found on the website of the Center on Juvenile and Criminal Justice (www.cjcj.org). See especially the following report: http://cjcj.org/files/Renewing_Juvenile_Justice.pdf

could receive better support at the local level. "In county juvenile halls, you don't have the entrenched gang culture and violence you have at the state youth authority. The counties can offer a continuum of options—maximum security, minimum security, intensive services in the community—that the state could never come close to matching."

In March 2011, Brown presented a revised budget that would allow counties to continue sending violent youth offenders to state correctional institutions.[90] The new proposal would still share the annual DJJ budget with counties and would allow the option of sending none or all of their juvenile offenders to DJJ. If counties opt to send the youths, they would pay the state the current cost: $200,000 per ward annually. The cost of incarcerating a juvenile offender at the county level ranges from $25,000 to $90,000 a year, depending on the county and the needs of the offender. Macallair doubts that many counties will want to pay several times that rate to send youths to the state. Contra Costa County's chief probation officer, Philip Kader, said he wants to keep more local youth offenders close to home. "Community-based services are always better."[91]

The counties are marked by a hodgepodge of juvenile justice practices; some rely on DJJ, and some do not.[92] San Francisco placed a moratorium on sending youth to DJJ in 2004 after *Farrell v. Harper*. Although it had more youth felonies per capita than any other California county in 2009 (the most recent year for which data are available), San Francisco had only seven juvenile offenders serving time in state institutions. Enhanced rehabilitative programming and partnerships with community organizations have created alternatives to locking youths up in large state institutions rife with gang activity. There is no systematic oversight of county programs, and the quality varies from county to county—as does their reliance on the state. Krisberg notes that "There are no real standards, and as a result, practices can be good in some places and horrible in other places."[93] In 2010, the counties with the most juveniles in state facilities were: Los Angeles County (370), Kern County (100), and Fresno County (85). Several counties (Santa Clara, Santa Cruz and San Diego) have implemented variations of the Missouri model (see chapter 14) that emphasizes treatment in small groups and alternatives to incarcerations. Krisberg refers to "justice by geography" and says if juveniles are committed in San Diego, they will receive decent treatment, while if they're committed in Los Angeles, they will suffer some of the worst conditions in the country.

Critics are concerned that city and county detention programs are uneven and poorly monitored.[94] Sara Norman, managing attorney of the Prison Law Center that filed the *Farrell* lawsuit, says: "Ideally the counties would have the resources to address the needs of these youth so they could stay close to their families and communities. The reality is that many counties are in far worse shape than the state system now." She believes a compromise between a county or a state system would be viable; regional centers could treat the most violent offenders from several counties. Macallair is concerned that the March proposal will allow counties that have delayed reforming their juvenile justice programs to continue to drag their feet:

The concern I have is that it will allow counties that are currently underperforming and have become overly reliant on committing youth to state institutions to continue do so without forcing them to change. In the field of corrections, necessity is the mother of invention.[95]

New York

A federal investigation from 2007 to 2009 found that "excessive physical force was routinely used to discipline children at several juvenile prisons in New York, resulting in broken bones, shattered, teeth, concussions, and dozens of other serious injuries."[96] Although rules stated force was allowed only as a last resort, physical force was frequently the first response to any perceived insubordination by juveniles. "Staff at the facilities routinely used uncontrolled, unsafe applications of force, departing from generally accepted standards. Anything from sneaking an extra cookie to initiating a fistfight may result in a full prone restraint with handcuffs." After continuing to laugh after being ordered to stop, one juvenile was forcibly restrained and handcuffed. A boy who had glared at a staff member suffered a broken collarbone from the force with which he was forced into a sitting position with his arms secured behind his back.

Officials at the institutions routinely failed to follow state rules requiring reviews whenever force is used. Even if a review determined that excessive force had been used, staff members often escaped punishment or received minimal reprimands. After a youth counselor with a documented record of using excessive force threw a youth to the ground so hard that stitches were required, officials suggested firing. The union intervened, and the punishment was downgraded to a letter of reprimand, an $800 fine, and a two-week suspension—that was itself suspended.[97]

Facing the threat of a Justice Department takeover of New York State's juvenile prisons, the governor appointed the Task Force on Transforming Juvenile Justice. Both the federal and state investigations produced scathing reports documenting excessive use of force by staff and a chronic lack of adequate funding that resulted in an inability to meet the most basic needs of the juveniles in their care. One example—more than half of the 800 to 900 incarcerated youths have been diagnosed as suffering from at least one mental illness, yet there is no full-time psychiatrist on staff. The majority of the incarcerated youths are black or Latino.[98] Three-quarters of the children entering New York's juvenile justice system have drug or alcohol problems and a third have developmental disabilities.[99]

The institutions are not centers of rehabilitation; rather incarcerated residents face danger in the facilities and a likely descent into greater degradation after release. The Task Force stated: "It comes as no surprise then, that not only do youths leave facilities without having received the support they need to become law-abiding citizens, but many are also more angry, fearful or violent than they were when they entered."[100] Critics refer to the shameful treatment of juveniles housed in these facilities as systemic neglect of society's most vulnerable youths. By failing to rehabilitate the troubled juveniles, the institutions compound the social and economic problems of families and home communities. "New York's facilities are so disastrous and inhumane that state officials recently asked the courts to refrain from sending children to them, except in cases in which they presented a clear danger to the public."[101] The task force recommended replacing most residential youth prisons in smaller centers closer to the home communities of the young offenders.[102]

The Task Force described a failed system that damages young people and costs the state millions of dollars; 89% of boys released from the state's juvenile prisons are re-arrested by the time they're 28.[103] Half of the youths in New York's juvenile institutions were placed there for minor, nonviolent infractions. The Legal Aid Society of New York City filed a class-action suit in 2010 on behalf of youths in confinement, arguing that conditions in the system violate their constitutional rights.[104] As mentioned in chapter 10, The New York Civil Liberties Union filed a suit against New York City charging that police and school guards were violating the civil rights of students through wrongful arrests.[105]

A young boy died at Tryon Detention Center for juveniles in New York in 2007. The facility was eventually closed. There were no juveniles there in 2010, but there were 25 to 30 staffers collecting almost $90,000 a year with benefits because a New York law requires that union members at juvenile prisons receive a year's notice before being dismissed.[106] The empty detention center costs taxpayers $3 million a year. The state system incarcerates 661 juveniles yet has 2,134 employees. It costs $228,000 a year to keep a juvenile in a secure facility and $298,000 in a non-secure facility. Cities and counties pay half. New York City filed a lawsuit in 2010 claiming the state is overcharging the city and counties throughout the state for services that it is not providing.

Governor Cuomo wants to close the juvenile prisons that house 700 youths despite opposition over lost jobs. New York City, which accounts for more than half the youths in state custody at a cost of $270,000 per youth per year, wants to opt out of the state system entirely and to keep youths closer to their families.[107] Detroit began handling almost all of its juvenile cases in 2000; the number of youths sent to state facilities dropped from more than 730 in 1998 to 18 in 2009. Advocates fear county prosecutors will increasingly charge juveniles in adult court if the state option is no longer available. While state prisons are problematic, adult prisons are worse. The number of juveniles tried as adults has increased in California. In 2010, almost twice as many juvenile offenders (43) in New York were transferred to adult prisons than in any of the previous five years.[108]

In July 2010 the federal government placed four of New York's youth prisons under federal oversight—limiting the use of physical force to situations that threaten personal safety or attempted escapes and introducing the most significant expansion of mental health services in years for youths in custody.[109] The assistant attorney general for the Justice Department's civil rights division said: "It is New York's fundamental responsibility to protect juveniles in its custody from harm and to uphold their constitutional rights." Two monitors, jointly chosen by federal and state officials, will oversee the state's efforts to meet the terms of the agreement. Although the agreement covers only four institutions, state officials hoped to use it as a springboard to make changes throughout the entire juvenile system, which had 26 facilities around the state that housed 667 youths in 2010. Advocates for youths in state custody said they would continue to try to transform the juvenile justice system in New York, which they allege warehouses youths who primarily need psychiatric care and counseling rather than imprisonment. "The changes will only affect those kids who have mental health needs who are already incarcerated. It doesn't get to the fact that any of those young people could be safely treated in their communities without ever seeing the inside of a prison cell."[110]

In December 2010, New York City merged its Department of Juvenile Justice into the Administration for Children's Services. The city had reduced its placements in state juvenile institutions by 56% since 2002.[111] The goal of the merger was to reduce recidivism by programs to place youths on the path toward school, work, and successful adulthood.

Texas

In 2007, the Texas Youth Commission faced allegations of abuse and severe lack of treatment programming. The intense scrutiny generated by the revelation that two senior TYC administrators had been accused of sexually abusing several youths in 2005 but had not been prosecuted led to sweeping reforms. In March 2007, investigators were dispatched to every TYC facility and an abuse reporting hotline was established—which received thousands of calls. The TYC Board was disbanded, and the agency was placed under conservatorship.[112] The legislature outlined reforms, which included: creating the Office of the Inspector General and the Office of the Independent Ombudsman, forming a Release Review Panel to ensure juveniles were not held in TYC unnecessarily or longer than beneficial, reducing the maximum age of confinement from 21 to 19, eliminating misdemeanant commitments to TYC, reducing residential populations, adopting a Parents' Bill of Rights, and creating a new general treatment program. After implementing the reforms, the conservatorship was removed in October 2008.

In 2011, the website for the Texas Youth Commission concludes with a section titled "renewal."

> The present focus is on changing the culture of TYC system-wide, which takes time. TYC must concentrate on its basic mission with the dual responsibility of providing public safety by holding youth accountable and providing treatment to youth in hopes they will learn to become law-abiding adults. Primarily, the agency will see a continued departure from housing youth in large, centralized institutions and, instead, develop community-based, regionalized treatment programs. These treatment programs will be evidence-based and will incorporate national best practices. They will better serve youth, because youth services will be focused and individualized.[113]

The reorganization of the Texas juvenile justice system was endorsed by both the liberal Texas Appleseed and the conservative Texas Public Policy Foundation (TPPF) based on the shared belief that prisons cost too much and accomplish little. The most recent milestone in the five-year transformation of the Texas system was legislation that closed 3 of 10 youth prisons and shifted state money to local rehabilitation programs. The bill is projected to save the state $150 million. TYC has 1,400 juveniles in custody, down from 5,000 in 2006.[114] The juvenile crime rate also has fallen.

Handicapped by rural settings, TYC is challenged to hire well-trained personnel and provide the mental health treatment most youth offenders need. In many cases, therapy was provided via teleconference. Now, county probation departments will receive money from the state to provide mental health services if the offender is kept in the community. Locking kids up without dealing with root causes increases the probability of another offense. Deborah Fowler, deputy director of Texas Appleseed, noted: "One thing we know is that kids committed to TYC have a much greater likelihood of becoming involved in the adult criminal justice system. What these programs are doing is diverting kids from that path."[115]

Ohio

In May 2008, the state Department of Youth Services (ODYS) settled a federal class-action lawsuit that had found confinement conditions at ODYS unconstitutionally unsafe for youth. The settlement mandated specific steps toward a safer and more humane environment and moving toward regional, small facilities rather than large institutions. Children are isolated inappropriately for lengthy periods of time; facility violence remains high; and mental health services are severely lacking. In one facility, the juveniles designated as management problems wear physical restraints whenever outside of their rooms. "It is impossible to imagine this type of treatment having a positive impact on their development."[116] Ohio spends a little more than $300 per day (well over $100,000 per year) to incarcerate a single young person. An estimated 53–57% of juveniles released from ODYS facilities will reoffend.

Ohio's juvenile justice system has made significant progress in reducing the number of youth confined in state facilities and has closed three facilities. Like many states, Ohio faces the need to remedy the costly mistake of creating a juvenile justice system that mirrors the adult criminal justice system. The director of the Juvenile Justice Coalition in Columbus, Sharon Weitzenhof, remarked:

> The tough-on-crime approach has proved ineffectual and even harmful to communities and youth, meaning that Ohio and other states have been sinking money into futile systems. Society benefits when we get it right with these troubled youth. We avoid wasting tax dollars on ineffective services and we reduce the potential costs of future victimization and criminal behavior. When it comes to crime and kids, it's about time we went beyond "getting tough" and began to get smart.[117]

Life in youth prisons is violent and harsh. Thousands of youths have spent their adolescence in institutions where their physical and emotional safety is threatened daily. The developments described above have been dramatic. If California and New York close their remaining state institutions, it would represent one of the most—if not the most—significant change in juvenile justice ever. Unfortunately, those attempting to change the status quo often confront vested interests in keeping the system the way it is.

A Failed Program

On many occasions, a treatment program has been announced for a juvenile institution, usually with much fanfare and great promise. Most fail for one of two reasons: either the theory behind the program (i.e., a theory of why people commit crime) is not sound or the program is not implemented correctly. Sometimes both reasons are present. Such was the case with a program that promised to reduce youth crime in Arizona.

A "model" program was established at a juvenile prison near Tucson after a class action lawsuit charged that the conditions of confinement at the prison were cruel, unconscionable, and illegal.[118] The program was designed to replace inflexible rules with collective problem solving and self-empowerment in a respectful atmosphere. The demise of the program and the failure to live up to its promises was not a new story; it has recurred repeatedly throughout the history of juvenile prisons.

Three months into the program, it became apparent that the only people who hoped it would succeed were the youths themselves and a small number of dedicated staff. Officials were primarily interested in meeting the demands of the lawsuit quickly. There was constant resistance from staff, authoritarian administrators, and political opposition. Perhaps the largest impediment to success was that the working conditions for most staff members did not improve. They continued to receive "low salaries, demanding working conditions, menial tasks, and perceptions of lack of support and respect from superiors."[119]

Good intentions notwithstanding, even the best programs initiated in juvenile and adult prisons are doomed to failure if the various social and personal contexts that resulted in a person's problems with drugs, gangs, and violence are not addressed.

> For most youths, going home meant a return to poverty and unemployment, troubled homes, the allure of alcohol and drugs, the dominance of gangs, and daily hardships. . . . Unresolved problems awaited the youths when they were released from prison. Outside the prison, fundamental social conditions remained unchanged. When they were paroled, within a few days or a few hours youths confronted the same old pressures and many reverted to familiar responses and solutions.[120]

Juveniles face an almost impossible task when they are encouraged to change their behavior and to develop high aspirations, only to return to their virtually unchanged communities. For example, the Arizona program originally planned to establish three intensive programs. The first addressed sexually aggressive behaviors, although less than 10% were charged with such crimes. The second treated violent behavior; less than 40% of those confined had committed violent offenses. The third program, substance abuse, was never implemented, although 90% of the youths had used drugs. The program's "failure to confront the youths' extensive drug and alcohol problems mirrored society's failure."[121]

There are some hopeful signs regarding juvenile prisons; states are moving in the direction of sending youths to alternative residential programs. At a minimum, the numbers of juveniles confined in state institutions are declining rapidly. Perhaps changes will occur because of the budget crises—recall Macallair's "necessity is the mother of invention" remark. If good juvenile justice practices are also good fiscal policies, everyone benefits.

> Imprisoning youth can have severe detrimental effects on youth, their long-term economic productivity and economic health of communities. Youth who are imprisoned have higher recidivism rates than youth who remain in communities, both due to suspended opportunities for education and a disruption in the process that normally allows many youth to "age-out" of crime.[122]

High Recidivism Rates Plague Juvenile Prisons

Recidivism generally refers to the commission of another crime by someone who had been convicted of a previous crime. There are several variations, however. Recidivism can be operationally defined as only a rearrest, or it can be defined as being convicted, or it can be defined as being returned to prison or jail. In juvenile cases, it can be measured as either an arrest, a referral to juvenile court, a petitioned filed, or a recommitment to an institution.[123] Whatever method is used, it is one of the best methods of measuring the effectiveness of a policy.

As noted repeatedly above, juvenile prisons have not reduced recidivism.

> A growing body of research shows that young people incarcerated in large institutions get rearrested more frequently, and for more serious crimes than their counterparts with similar delinquency histories who are not incarcerated. For example, a study that compared matched samples of offenders in Arkansas found that the incarceration experience was the single greatest predictor of future criminal conduct, dwarfing the effects of gang membership or family dysfunction.[124]

A comprehensive study in Oregon found that among a cohort of more 3,000 juvenile offenders, about half of those released from Oregon youth prisons at age 17 or 18 ended up in the adult prison system; about 40% of those released at age 16 ended up in adult prison.[125] The total recidivism rate was 42%. The study also found that females had a significantly lower rate of recidivism (21%) than males (45%). Note here that the definition of "recidivism" was an arrest as an adult. Consistent with other longitudinal studies, the earlier the age of first contact with the juvenile court, the higher the proportion of those who ended up in the adult system (e.g., 57% of those age 12 ended up in the adult system versus 43% of those whose first referral was at age 17).[126] Another interesting finding (also consistent with prior research), was that the longer a youth spent time in a juvenile institution, the higher the recidivism rate.[127]

A recidivism study in California looked at 28,000 juveniles who were released between 1988 and 2000. The overall recidivism rate, based upon police arrest records, was 74%. Property offenders had a higher recidivism rate than violent offenders (80% versus 70%). The recidivism rate was lower for females (52%). It also was lower for the youngest and oldest youths released; those under 17 had a rate of 60%, which was the same rate as for those over 21. This age group was a minority; most releasees were between 17 and 21 years of age and their recidivism rate was 76%.[128]

Barriers to Reentry

Research emphatically demonstrates that recidivism rates are significantly lower among youths who are not sent to youth prisons. Holding constant other variables, those who are given probation and a variety of intensive services (e.g., drug treatment, tutoring, mental health counseling, family counseling, etc.) have much lower recidivism rates. The Center on Juvenile and Criminal Justice found the following barriers to successful re-entry:[129]

- Lack of educational options.
- Lack of housing options.
- Limited skills and education.
- Gang affiliations and related racial tensions.
- Institutional identity.[130]
- Drug problems.
- Mental health problems.
- Lack of community support and role models.
- Legislative barriers.

In California, most committed youths had math scores at about the seventh- or eighth-grade level and reading scores in the eighth- to ninth-grade level. Less than 5% passed the high school exit exam in math, while only 17% passed the English-language arts test. Releasees often run into resistance to enrollment in school from teachers, school administrators, parents, and other students.[131] There have been cutbacks in education grants (Pell) across the nation, despite the fact that education is a proven antidote to criminal activity. The majority of releasees have serious drug problems (74% of the males and 68% of the females), while 45% of the males and 65% of the females have mental health problems (national averages are between 50% and 75%).[132]

Cash assistance and food stamps are almost impossible for parolees to obtain, since the 1996 Welfare Reform Act prohibits offenders with a felony offense that involves drugs from receiving any cash assistance for the rest of their life. Some youths on parole rely on Supplemental Security Income (SSI), but may be denied this if they violate a condition of their parole.[133]

Finding work and a place to live become the most important needs for these youths—and the major obstacles. Consider Mercer Sullivan's description of one of the youths in his case study of young offenders reentering society. "Reggie," 20 years old, had just been rearrested for cashing a check that had been entrusted to him as part of his part-time job as a messenger. At the time, his social support network was falling apart.

He had been raised mostly by his grandfather, who died. He had then lived with his own father, who had spent many years in prison. Reggie attributed his own (relatively) law-abiding behavior to his father's warnings to him to stay away from heroin. Then his father died also, and Reggie was left living with his father's girlfriend. She had a drug habit and kept stealing his wages from the program [a program called Neighborhood Work Project in New York City]. As a result he needed his own place, but he could not afford it. The program itself was supposed to be time-limited, although there were always a few workers like Reggie who were allowed to stay beyond the limit because they were reliable. He sold a little marijuana on the side and got arrested for that but then managed to settle the case for a sentence of probation. Reggie was thus barely surviving in a highly unstable situation.[134]

Simplistic rhetoric like "take responsibility" and "obey the law" has little meaning in life circumstances like Reggie's. The key to "going straight" centers around finding work, a place to live, and developing an intimate relationship. Years of research have confirmed this principle.[135]

Aftercare/Parole for Ex–Juvenile Offenders

Every offender committed to a juvenile institution eventually gets released into *parole* or *aftercare*. The term "aftercare" is commonly used, even though technically a youth has been paroled and is being supervised by a parole officer. There are an estimated 200,000 young offenders released from juvenile institutions each year. Some come directly from juvenile institutions, while others are released from an adult prison. Some enter into the world of juvenile prisons as juveniles (under 18) but leave as adults (ranging in age from 18 to 24, depending upon the jurisdiction).[136]

A profile of those released reveals that they have several characteristics that need to be taken into account when discussing the barriers to reentry.[137] Most had been in custody for at least four to six months; 88% were male; 19% were 14 or younger and 36% age 17 or older; the majority were nonwhites (56%); and 38% had committed a violent crime. Most had grown up in a single-parent home and had relatives who were incarcerated.[138] Over half of those between 15 and 17 years of age had not completed the eighth grade, while almost one-fourth (23%) had never entered high school. Between 20% and 50% have attention deficit hyperactivity disorders, and about one out of eight is mentally retarded. Indeed, mental health problems were pronounced (68%). Most used alcohol and drugs on a regular basis and began using at around ages 12 and 13. A good portion of their formative years had been spent in various placement facilities ("state-raised youth").

One survey of aftercare systems found that there were eight different types of aftercare or parole supervision.[139] There were four variations of *determinate parole*, ranging from one that computes the time spent since the start of a youth's period of institutional confinement to a version known as *presumptive minimum*, where the time on parole ends at some specified time but the aftercare officer can extend supervision for a period of time not to exceed the maximum age for juvenile court jurisdiction (normally 21). There are four variations of what is known as *indeterminate parole*, ranging from one where the supervision period can be extended for an indefinite period of time to one that is purely discretionary, where the decision to discharge is left entirely in the hands of aftercare staff (this latter version is the most common, with 30% of the jurisdictions using it).

Intensive Aftercare Programs

Since traditional parole/aftercare has often not been successful, most states have devised *intensive aftercare programs* (IAPs). These programs emerged because of several interrelated factors: (1) inadequate communication between the institutional and aftercare personnel, (2) failure to identify the appropriate services for released youths, (3) excessively high case loads for parole officers (up to 100 or more), and (4) the selection of youths who were not appropriate for parole supervision.[140]

One of the problems with aftercare is that the majority of the youths released from juvenile institutions face a number of hurdles related to backgrounds of poverty, family conflicts, drug and alcohol use, lack of education and skills, and many more. The recent emphasis on accountability and responsibility ignores several important facts: (1) the released juveniles are still adolescents, with many experiencing "delayed emotional and cognitive development" largely because of emotional abuse and early drug use; (2) most of them "have never successfully used problem-solving or coping skills outside of the correctional setting"; (3) most "still have no adults in their lives to help them learn the skills they need to deal with" everyday life challenges.[141]

As noted in chapter 1, children previously became adults at a much earlier age. In modern societies, adolescence extends to the ages of 23 or 24. By late adolescence, most youths have developed a strong sense of independence and healthy relationships with their parents, peers, and adults in general based on trust, empathy, self-disclosure, and loyalty. The vast majority of young offenders serving time are far behind their nondelinquent peers in terms of psychological development.[142] At the time of reentry, most of the released juveniles could be described as in the stage of adolescence usually exhibited at the ages of 11–14. Correctional facilities are not conducive to normal development; most inmates live in fear and distrust, blocking the acquisition of effective life skills.[143]

The institutional structure, which dictates every move, does not prepare youths to cope with the outside world—a world that has already rejected them and presented them with numerous problems. They are released into *the same hostile environment that spawned their delinquent behavior in the first place.*

Summary

This chapter reviewed what are euphemistically called "correctional institutions"—in reality they are public or private *prisons*. Some confinement facilities are short-term (usually ranging from a few days to a couple of months); others are long-term (ranging from three or four months to one or two years). Detention centers, adult jails, and shelter care facilities are examples of short-term institutions. Over the years there have been many reports of substandard care. A high proportion of youths confined in these institutions suffer serious mental disorders, and the staff often are not professionally trained.

Long-term institutions are an extension of the nineteenth century houses of refuge. Treatment is nonexistent, and recidivism rates are high. Minority youths are the most likely to be housed in such prisons. Within many of these institutions, physical abuse is a daily occurrence. Budget constraints have pushed states to divert increasing numbers of troubled juveniles away from juvenile prisons. The fiscal restraints may result in better programs and better results.

"Aftercare" remains one of the most underfunded portions of the juvenile justice system—to such an extent that any assistance is more realistically termed "afterthought." Released juveniles are totally unprepared for independent living. If the diversion to local facilities continues and is accompanied by treatment and skills programs, the next step in successful rehabilitation is an aftercare system that identifies the areas of greatest need.

NOTES

[1] Bickel, C. (2010). "From Child to Captive: Constructing Captivity in a Juvenile Institution." *Western Criminology Review* 11(1): 37–49. Retrieved from http://wcr.sonoma.edu/v11n1/Bickel.pdf

[2] War rhetoric is similar—killing innocent civilians is called "collateral damage."

[3] I will refrain from using the term "corrections" wherever possible in this chapter.

[4] Mendel, Richard A. (2010) "The Missouri Model: Reinventing the Practice of Rehabilitating Youthful Offenders: Summary Report." The Annie E. Casey Foundation, p. 3. Retrieved from http://www.aecf.org/~/media/Pubs/Initiatives/Juvenile%20Detention%20Alternatives%20Initiative/MOModel/MO_Fullreport_webfinal.pdf

[5] Ibid.

[6] Griffin, P. and M. King (2006). "National Overviews." *State Juvenile Justice Profiles*. Pittsburgh, PA: National Center for Juvenile Justice. Retrieved from http://70.89.227.250:8080/stateprofiles/overviews/faq12t.asp#combo

[7] Ibid. Retrieved from http://70.89.227.250:8080/stateprofiles/overviews/faq12.asp; The National Center for Juvenile Justice maintains a website for state juvenile justice profiles that allows viewers to choose specific states to learn procedures or national overviews.

[8] Ibid.

[9] Clark, M. (2011, May 3). "Maryland Comes to Compliance with Juvenile Detention Rules." *The Daily Record*. Retrieved from http://thedailyrecord.com/2011/05/03/md-comes-to-compliance-with-juvenile-detention-rules/

[10] Ibid.

[11] Minton, T. D. (2011, April). "Jail Inmates at Midyear 2010—Statistical Tables." Retrieved from http://www.bjs.gov/content/pub/pdf/jim10st.pdf

[12] Arthur, P. J. and R. Waugh (2009). "Status Offenses and the Juvenile Justice and Delinquency Prevention Act: The Exception that Swallowed the Rule." *Seattle Journal of Social Justice* 7: 555–77.

[13] Ibid. Such exceptions are generally because the extent of noncompliance is insignificant in terms of the total juvenile population in the state or plans are underway to significantly reduce the population of status offenders.

[14] Macallair, D. and M. Males (2004). "A Failure of Good Intentions: An Analysis of Juvenile Justice Reform in San Francisco During the 1990s." *Review of Policy Research* 21: 63–78.

[15] Teplin, L. A., G. M. McClelland, K. M. Abram, and D. Mileusnic (2005). "Early Violent Death among Delinquent Youth: A Prospective Longitudinal Study." *Pediatrics* 115: 1586–93.

[16] Chen, S. (2009, February 23). "Pennsylvania Rocked by 'Jailing Kids for Cash' Scandal." CNN. Retrieved from http://www.cnn.com/2009/CRIME/02/23/pennsylvania.corrupt.judges/index.html; Editorial (2009, January 28). "Judges Sentenced Kids for Cash." *Philadelphia Inquirer*.

[17] Southern Poverty Law Center (2009). *E.W., et al, v. Lauderdale County, Miss.* Case filed October 19, 2009; settled April 30, 2010. Retrieved from http://www.splcenter.org/get-informed/case-docket/ew-et-al-v-lauderdale-county-miss.

[18] Shufelt, J. L. and J. J. Cocozza (2006, June). "Youth with Mental Health Disorders in the Juvenile Justice System: Results from a Multi-State Prevalence Study." National Center for Mental Health and Juvenile Justice. Retrieved from http://ncmhjj.com/pdfs/publications/PrevalenceRPB.pdf

[19] Abram, K. M., J. Y. Choe, J. J. Washburn, L. A. Teplin, D. C. King and M. K. Dulcan (2008). "Suicidal Ideation and Behaviors Among Youths in Juvenile Detention." *Journal of the American Academy of Child and Adolescent Psychiatry* 47: 291–300.

[20] Fazel, S., H. M. Doll and N. Langstrom (2008). "Mental Disorders among Adolescents in Juvenile Detention and Correctional Facilities: A Systematic Review and Metaregression Analysis of 25 Surveys." *Journal of the American Academy of Child & Adolescent Psychiatry* 47: 1010–19.

[21] Moore, S. (2009, August 10). "Mentally Ill Offenders Strain Juvenile System." *New York Times*. Retrieved from http://www.nytimes.com/2009/08/10/us/10juvenile.html

[22] Chief Probation Officers of California and the California Mental Health Directors Association (2008). *Costs of Incarcerating Youth with Mental Illness.* Cited in Justice Policy Institute (2009, May) "The Costs of Confinement: Why Good Juvenile Justice Policies Make Good Fiscal Sense." Retrieved from http://www.justicepolicy.org/images/upload/09_05_REP_CostsOfConfinement_JJ_PS.pdf

[23] Southern Poverty Law Center (2010, March 10). "SPLC Sues Mississippi Over Mental Health System for Children on Medicaid." Retrieved from http://www.splcenter.org/get-informed/news/splc-sues-mississippi-over-mental-health-system-for-children-on-medicaid

[24] *Missouri Revised Statutes.* Chapter 211, Juvenile Courts, Section 211.021.

[25] Kaufman, L. (2005, January 15). "Foster Care Contracts Canceled after City Finds Files Doctored." *New York Times*.

[26] *Los Angeles Times*, "Stories of 98 Child Deaths in 2009." Retrieved from http://www.latimes.com/news/local/traffic/la-me-migueltable,0,4580955.htmlstory

[27] *Los Angeles Times* (2010, March 28). "A Timeline of Death: 12 Troubled Years for L.A. County's Department of Children and Family Services." Retrieved from http://www.latimes.com/news/local/la-me-child-death-chronology2-2010mar28,0,5124634.story; see also Therolf, G. and K. Christensen (2010, March 28). "As More L.A. County Children Die, Reform Still Falters." *Los Angeles Times*. Retrieved from http://www.latimes.com/news/local/la-me-child-deaths28-2010mar28,0,3567747.story; Therolf, G. (2010, March 24). "L.A. County to Develop Foster Care Investigative Unit." *Los Angeles Times*. Retrieved from http://www.latimes.com/news/local/la-me-dcfs18-2010mar24,0,984019.story.

[28] Therolf, G. (2010, March 31). "L.A. County Drops Foster Care Agency." *Los Angeles Times*. Retrieved from http://www.latimes.com/news/local/la-me-child-death31-2010mar31,0,1785580.story

[29] Therolf, G. (2010, March 18). "Foster Mother Had 5 Abuse Complaints." *Los Angeles Times*. Retrieved from http://articles.latimes.com/2010/mar/18/local/la-me-child-death18-2010mar18

[30] Boys Town Nevada. Retrieved from http://www.boystown.org/nevada

[31] OJJDP Model Programs. Retrieved from http://www.ojjdp.gov/mpg/mpgProgramDetails.aspx?ID=99

32 Indiana Department of Corrections. Retrieved from http://www.in.gov/idoc/dys/2348.htm

33 Virginia Department of Juvenile Justice. Retrieved from http://engage.richmond.edu/opportunities/lists/VaDeptJuvJustice.html

34 Oklahoma Department of Corrections (n.d.). "The R.O.C." Retrieved from http://www.state.ok.us/~oja/roc.htm

35 California Department of Corrections and Rehabilitation (2011, June). "Youth Conservation Camps." Retrieved from http://www.cdcr.ca.gov/Juvenile_Justice/Facility_Locations/Youth_Conservation_Camps/index.html

36 Parent, D. G. (2004, June). *Correctional Boot Camps: Lessons From a Decade of Research.* Washington, DC: National Institute of Justice. Retrieved from http://www.ncjrs.gov/pdffiles1/nij/197018.pdf; MacKenzie, D. L., A. R. Gover, G. S. Armstrong, and O. Mitchell (2001). *A National Study Comparing the Environments of Boot Camps with Traditional Facilities for Juvenile Offenders.* Washington, DC: National Institute of Justice; Peters, M., D. Thomas, C. Zamberlan, and Caliber Associates (1997). *Boot Camps for Juvenile Offenders.* Washington, DC: Office of Juvenile Justice and Delinquency Prevention.

37 Macallair, D. (2002, August 5). "Boot Camp Blunder." *Chronicle.* Retrieved from http://articles.sfgate.com/2002-08-05/opinion/17557013_1_military-training-youth-programs-military-boot-camp

38 OJJDP (n.d.). "Juvenile Justice Reform Initiatives in the States 1994–1996." Juvenile Boot Camps. Retrieved from http://www.ojjdp.gov/pubs/reform/ch2_g.html

39 Parent, "Correctional Boot Camps," pp. 2, 7.

40 Walker, S. (2011). Sense *and Nonsense about Crime, Drugs and Communities: A Policy Guide* (7th ed). Belmont, CA: Cengage.

41 Libit, H. (2002, August 8). "State Approves $4.6 Million for Former Boot Camp Inmates: Settlement Likely to Play Role in Governor's Race." *Baltimore Sun.*

42 Government Accountability Office (October 10, 2007). "Residential Treatment Programs: Concerns Regarding Abuse and Death in Certain Programs for Troubled Youth." Statement of Gregory D. Kutz, Managing Director Forensic Audits and Special Investigations, and Andy O'Connell, Assistant Director Forensic Audits and Special Investigations. Retrieved from http://www.gao.gov/new.items/d08146t.pdf

43 Ibid., p. 1.

44 "Six Camp Counselors Charged in Death." (2005, July 20). *Chicago Tribune*, p. 17.

45 "Florida Boots Harsh Tactics." (2006, May 8). *U. S. News and World Report*, p. 6.

46 Garcia, J. (2006, May 6). "Teen's New Autopsy Shows He Suffocated." *Orlando Sentinel.* Retrieved from http://articles.latimes.com/2006/may/06/nation/na-bootcamp6; CBS News, (2006, August 13). "13-Year-Old Cadet Dies at Boot Camp." Retrieved from http://www.cbsnews.com/stories/2006/08/13/national/main1890432.shtml; CBS News (2006, November 28). "8 Charged In Teen's Boot Camp Death." Retrieved from http://www.cbsnews.com/stories/2006/11/28/national/main2211680.shtml; a video of this incident can be viewed at http://www.nospank.net/anderson.htm#fdle

47 Schnurer, E. B. and C. R. Lyons (2004). "Juvenile Boot Camps: Experiment in Trouble." Washington, DC: Center for National Policy.

48 A website entitled "Mississippi Gulag" reports the abuses that took place in Mississippi. Retrieved from http://www.nospank.net/msgulag.htm

49 "CRIPA Investigation of Oakley and Columbia Training Schools in Raymond and Columbia, Mississippi" (2003, June 19). Retrieved from http://www.splcenter.org/sites/default/files/legacy/images/dynamic/main/report/6/oak_colu_miss_findinglet.pdf

50 Southern Poverty Law Center (2006, April 6). "Violations Continue at Mississippi Training Schools." Retrieved from http://www.splcenter.org/get-informed/news/violations-continue-at-mississippi-training-schools

[51] Southern Poverty Law Center (2003, December 1). "SPLC Works to Improve Mississippi Juvenile Justice." Retrieved from http://www.splcenter.org/get-informed/news/splc-works-to-improve-mississippi-juvenile-justice

[52] "BOOT CAMP FOR KIDS: Torturing Teens for Fun and Profit." Retrieved from http://www.nospank.net/boot.htm#gina

[53] Montgomery, B. and W. A. Moore (2009, April 19). "For Their Own Good: A *St. Petersburg Times* Special Report on Child Abuse at the Florida School for Boys." *St. Petersburg Times*. Retrieved from http://www.tampabay.com/features/humaninterest/article992939.ece

[54] Sickmund, M., T. J. Sladky, and W. Kang (2011). "Census of Juveniles in Residential Placement Databook 2007." Retrieved from http://www.ojjdp.gov/ojstatbb/ezacjrp/asp/glossary.asp#Facility

[55] Livesay, S., M. Sickmund, and A. Sladky (2009, January). "Juvenile Residential Facility Census, 2004: Selected Findings," p. 2. Retrieved from http://www.ncjrs.gov/pdffiles1/ojjdp/222721.pdf

[56] Sedlak, A. J. and K. S. McPherson (2010, April). "Youth's Needs and Services: Findings from the Survey of Youth in Residential Placement." OJJDP. Retrieved from http://www.ncjrs.gov/pdffiles1/ojjdp/227728.pdf

[57] Sickmund et al., "Census of Juveniles in Residential Placement Databook." Retrieved from http://www.ojjdp.gov/ojstatbb/ezacjrp/asp/Offense_Race.asp?state=0&topic=Offense_Race&year=2007&percent=rate

[58] Bickel, "From Child to Captive," p. 38.

[59] Sickmund et al., "Census of Juveniles in Residential Placement Databook." Retrieved from http://www.ojjdp.gov/ojstatbb/ezacjrp/asp/State_Race.asp?state=&topic=State_Race&year=2007&percent=rate

[60] Ibid. Retrieved from http://www.ojjdp.gov/ojstatbb/ezacjrp/asp/State_Race.asp?state=&topic=State_Race&year=2007&percent=row

[61] Ibid.

[62] Shelden, R. G. (1999, August 13). "If It Looks Like a Prison . . ." *Las Vegas City Life*. For an update, visit the website: http://www.sheldensays.com/i_told_you_so.htm

[63] Equal Justice Initiative (2007, November). *Cruel and Unusual: Sentencing 13 and 14-Year-Old Children to Die in Prison*. Montgomery, AL: Equal Justice Initiative, p. 25. Retrieved from http://www.eji.org/eji/files/20071017cruelandunusual.pdf

[64] Rainville, G. A. and S. K. Smith (2003). *Juvenile Felony Defendants in Criminal Courts*. Washington, DC: Bureau of Justice Statistics. Retrieved from http://bjs.ojp.usdoj.gov/content/pub/pdf/jfdcc98.pdf

[65] Austin, J., K. D. Johnson, and M. Gregoriou (2000, October). "Juveniles in Adult Prisons and Jails." Washington, DC: U.S. Department of Justice, pp. x–xi. Retrieved from http://www.ncjrs.gov/pdffiles1/bja/182503.pdf

[66] Struckman-Johnson, C., D. Struckman-Johnson, L. Rucker, K. Bumby, and S. Donaldson (1996). "Sexual Coercion Reported by Men and Women in Prison." *The Journal of Sex Research* 33: 67–76.

[67] Goffman, I. (1961). *Asylums*. New York: Doubleday.

[68] Bickel, "From Child to Captive," p. 38.

[69] Kupers, T. A. (2008). "Prison and the Decimation of Pro-social Life Skills." In A. Ojeda (Ed.), *The Trauma of Psychological Torture*. New York: Praeger, p. 5.

[70] For a particularly gruesome account of actions within one of these "correctional" institutions see the movie *Sleepers* (starring Brad Pitt, Robert DeNiro, and Dustin Hoffman).

[71] Vinter, R. D. et al. (Eds.) (1976). *Time Out: A National Study of Juvenile Correctional Programs*. Ann Arbor: National Assessment of Juvenile Corrections, The University of Michigan.

[72] Irwin, J. (1970). *The Felon*. Englewood Cliffs, NJ: Prentice-Hall, p. 74. These types still can be found in many prisons today. See Austin, J. and J. Irwin (2001). *It's About Time: America's Incarceration Binger* (3rd ed.). Belmont, CA: Wadsworth.

[73] Bartollas, C., S. H. Miller, and S. Dinitz (1976). *Juvenile Victimization: The Institutional Paradox.* Beverly Hills, CA: Sage.

[74] Miller, S. H., C. Bartollas, and S. Dinitz (n.d.). *Juvenile Victimization Revisited: A Study of TICO Fifteen Years Later* (unpublished manuscript).

[75] Kaiser, D. and L. Stannow (2010, January 7). "The Crisis of Juvenile Prison Rape: A New Report." Retrieved from http://www.nybooks.com/blogs/nyrblog/2010/jan/07/the-crisis-of-juvenile-prison-rape-a-new-report/

[76] Beck, A. J., P. M. Harrison, and P. Guerino (2010, January). "Sexual Victimization in Juvenile Facilities Reported by Youth, 2008–09." Bureau of Justice Statistics, p. 1. Retrieved from http://bjs.ojp.usdoj.gov/content/pub/pdf/svjfry09.pdf

[77] Kaiser and Stannow, "The Crisis of Juvenile Prison Rape."

[78] Beck et al., "Sexual Victimization in Juvenile Facilities," p. 10.

[79] Ibid., p. 11.

[80] Kaiser and Stannow, "The Crisis of Juvenile Prison Rape."

[81] Moore, M. (2011, March 16). "States Making Juvenile Detention More Localized." *USA Today.* Retrieved from http://www.usatoday.com/news/nation/2011-03-16-juvenileWEB2_ST_N.htm

[82] Moore, S. (2009, March 26). "Missouri System Treats Juvenile Offenders with Lighter Hand." *New York Times.* Retrieved from http://www.nytimes.com/2009/03/27/us/27juvenile.html; Bundy, T. (2011, January 22). "Can Counties Handle Young Offenders on Their Own?" Retrieved from http://www.baycitizen.org/crime/story/can-counties-handle-young-offenders-own/

[83] Burrell, S. and J. Laba (2006, April 26). "Violence-Prone Youth Authority Still Fails Its Children, Its Taxpayers." Youth Law Center. Retrieved from http://www.ylc.org/articleDetail.php?id=13&type=article

[84] Warren, J. (2005, February 1). "For Young Offenders, a Softer Approach." *Los Angeles Time.*

[85] Krisberg, B. (2009, October 23). *Farrell v. Cate: Update on Safety and Welfare Remedial Plan Progress.* Retrieved from http://www.prisonlaw.com/pdfs/OSM13,AppA.pdf

[86] Ibid, p. 22.

[87] Little Hoover Commission (2008, July). "Juvenile Justice Reform: Realigning Responsibilities," pp. i–ii. Retrieved from http://www.lhc.ca.gov/studies/192/report192.pdf

[88] Bundy, "Can Counties Handle Young Offenders on Their Own?"

[89] de Sá, K. (2011, January 14). "Brown Calls for Elimination of Youth Prison System and Shifting of State Prisoners to County Jails." *San Jose Mercury News.*

[90] Bundy, T. (2011, March 1). "Gov. Brown Scratches Plan to Eliminate Youth Prisons." Retrieved from https://www.baycitizen.org/crime/story/gov-brown-scratches-plan-eliminate-youth/1/

[91] Ibid.

[92] Macallair, D., C. McCracken, and S. Teji (2011, February). "The Impact of Realignment on County Juvenile Justice Practice: Will Closing State Youth Correctional Facilities Increase Adult Criminal Court Filings?" Retrieved from http://www.cjcj.org/files/The_impact_of_realignment_on_county_juvenile_justice_practice.pdf

[93] Freedberg, L. (2011, March 14). California Watch. Retrieved from http://californiawatch.org/dailyreport/browns-plan-shut-down-youth-correctional-facilities-derailed-9158

[94] Moore, "Missouri System Treats Juvenile Offenders with Lighter Hand."

[95] Ibid.

[96] Confessore, N. (2009, August 24). "4 Youth Prisons in New York Used Excessive Force." *New York Times*, p. A1. Retrieved from http://www.nytimes.com/2009/08/25/nyregion/25juvenile.html?_r=1&hp

[97] Ibid.

[98] Editors (2010, February 19). "Juvenile Detention Facilities in New York State: The Ghetto Dynamic at Work." The Defenders Online. Retrieved from http://www.thedefendersonline.com/2010/02/19/juvenile-detention-facilities-in-new-york-state-the-ghetto-dynamic-at-work/

[99] Confessore, "4 Youth Prisons."

[100] Ibid.

[101] Editorial (2010, January 5). "Juvenile Injustice." *New York Times.* Retrieved from http://www.nytimes.com/2010/01/06/opinion/06wed2.html?_r=1

[102] Confessore, N. (2010, July 14). "Federal Oversight for Troubled N.Y. Youth Prisons." Retrieved from http://www.nytimes.com/2010/07/15/nyregion/15juvenile.html?_r=1

[103] Gonnerman, J. (2010, January 24). "The Lost Boys of Tryon." Retrieved from http://nymag.com/news/features/63239/

[104] Editorial, "Juvenile Injustice."

[105] New York Civil Liberties Union (2010, January). "NYCLU, ACLU File Class Action Lawsuit Against NYPD Over Excessive Force, Wrongful Arrests in New York City's Schools." Retrieved from http://www.nyclu.org/news/nyclu-aclu-file-class-action-lawsuit-against-nypd-over-excessive-force-wrongful-arrests-new-yor

[106] Taylor, B. N. (2010, November 22). Staff Watches Over Empty Juvenile Detention Facility. Retrieved from http://www.myfoxny.com/dpp/news/investigative/staff-watches-over-empty-juvenile-detention-facility-20101122#

[107] Ibid.

[108] Associated Press (2011, March 17). "More New York Juvenile Offenders Moved to Adult Prisons Last Year than in Previous Five Years." Retrieved from http://www.syracuse.com/news/index.ssf/2011/03/more_new_york_juvenile_offende.html

[109] Confessore, N. (2010, July 14). "Federal Oversight for Troubled N.Y. Youth Prisons." Retrieved from http://www.nytimes.com/2010/07/15/nyregion/15juvenile.html?_r=1

[110] Ibid.

[111] NYC Administration for Children's Services (n.d.). "Youth and Family Justice." Retrieved from http://www.nyc.gov/html/acs/html/yfj/youth_family_justice.shtml

[112] Texas Youth Commission (n.d.). "A Brief History of the Texas Youth Commission." http://www.tyc.state.tx.us/about/history.html

[113] Ibid.

[114] Hart, P. K. (2011, May 21). "Lawmakers in Lockstep on Juvenile-Justice Bills." Retrieved from http://www.chron.com/disp/story.mpl/metropolitan/7575646.html

[115] Ibid.

[116] Weitzenhof, S. (2010, December 20). "With Kids and Crime, Smart Works Much Better than Tough." *Akron Beacon Journal.* Retrieved from http://www.juvenilecoalition.org/news

[117] Ibid.

[118] Bortner, M. A. and L. Williams (1997). *Youth in Prison: We the People of Unit Four.* New York: Routledge, p. 2. This is one of the best books ever written on the subject. It discusses in great detail the emergence and ultimate failure of a program to reduce juvenile crime. The lawsuit was *Johnson v. Upchurch*, 1986.

[119] Ibid., p. 134.

[120] Ibid., p. 148.

[121] Ibid., p. 151.

[122] Justice Policy Institute (2009, May). The Cost of Confinement: Why Good Juvenile Justice Policies Make Good Fiscal Sense. Retrieved from http://www.justicepolicy.org/images/upload/09_05_REP_CostsofConfinement_JJ_PS.pdf

[123] See Shelden, R. G. (1999). "Detention Diversion Advocacy: An Evaluation." *OJJDP Juvenile Justice Bulletin* (September). In this analysis I used several different measurements of recidivism.

[124] Bell, J. and J. Stauring (2004, May 2). "Serious Problems Festering in Juvenile Justice System Require Serious Reforms." *Los Angeles Times*. Retrieved from http://articles.latimes.com/2004/may/02/opinion/oe-bell2

[125] State of Oregon, Oregon Youth Authority (2003, May 23). "Previously Incarcerated Juveniles in Oregon's Adult Corrections System." Salem: State of Oregon, Office of Economic Analysis. Retrieved from http://www.oregon.gov/DAS/OEA/docs/oya/oya-to-corrections.pdf?ga=t

[126] Concerning "age of onset" see Dryfoos, J. G. (1990). *Adolescents at Risk: Prevalence and Prevention.* New York: Oxford University Press for a good review.

[127] An earlier study documenting this was Vinter et al., *Time Out*; see also Beck, J. L. and P. B. Hoffman (1976). "Time Served and Release Performance: A Research Note." *Journal of Research in Crime and Delinquency* 13: 127–32; Orsagh, T. and J. R. Chen (1988). "The Effect of Time Served on Recidivism: An Interdisciplinary Theory." *Journal of Quantitative Criminology* 4: 155–71; an Australian study also found that the longer the period of confinement the higher the recidivism rate: Makkai, T., J. Ratcliffe, K. Veraar, and L. Collins (2004). "ACT Recidivist Offenders." Canberra: Australian Institute of Criminology.

[128] Bailey, B. and G. Palmer (2004, October 17). "High Rearrest Rate: Three-Fourths of Wards Released Over 13 Years Held on New Charges." *San Jose Mercury News.*

[129] Byrnes, M., D. Macallair, and A. D. Shorter (2002). "Aftercare as Afterthought: Reentry and the California Youth Authority." San Francisco: Center on Juvenile and Criminal Justice.

[130] An interesting concept is what some researchers call the *Post-Incarceration Syndrome,* defined as a "set of symptoms that are present in many currently incarcerated and recently released prisoners caused by prolonged incarceration in environments of punishment with few opportunities for education, job training, or rehabilitation. The severity of symptoms is related to the level of coping skills prior to incarceration, the length of incarceration, the restrictiveness of the incarceration environment, the number and severity of institutional episodes of abuse, the number and duration of episodes of solitary confinement, and the degree of involvement in educational, vocational, and rehabilitation programs." See Gorski, T. T. (2001, March 1). "Post Incarceration Syndrome." *Addiction Exchange,* Volume 3, No. 4. Retrieved from http://www.mid-attc.org/addex/addex3_4.htm; see also http://www.tgorski.com/criminal_justice/cjs_pics_&_relapse.htm

[131] Byrnes et al., "Aftercare as Afterthought," p. 11.

[132] Ibid., p. 13.

[133] For an excellent study on this problem see Schiraldi, V. and B. Holman (2000). "Poor Prescription: The Costs of Imprisoning Drug Offenders in the United States." San Francisco: Center on Juvenile and Criminal Justice. See also Allard, P. (2002). "Life Sentences: Denying Welfare Benefits to Women Convicted of Drug Offenses." Washington, DC: The Sentencing Project.

[134] Sullivan, M. (2004). "Youth Perspectives on the Reentry Experience." *Youth Violence and Juvenile Justice* 2: 59.

[135] This research includes the pioneering work of Joan McCord (McCord, J. [1983]. "A Forty Year Perspective on Effects of Child Abuse and Neglect." *Child Abuse and Neglect* 7) and the work of Sampson, R. J. and J. H. Laub (1993). *Crime in the Making: Pathways and Turning Points Through Life.* Cambridge, MA: Harvard University Press; also, Sampson, R. J. and J. H. Laub (1997). *A Life-Course Theory of Cumulative Disadvantage and the Stability of Delinquency.* New Brunswick, NJ: Transaction.

[136] Mears, D. P. and J. Travis (2004). "Youth Development and Reentry." *Youth Violence and Juvenile Justice* 2: 3–20.

[137] Snyder, H. (2004). "An Empirical Portrait of the Youth Reentry Population." *Youth Violence and Juvenile Justice* 2: 39–55.

[138] One of the best predictors of a lengthy juvenile criminal career is having at least one parent who had been in jail or prison. See Dryfoos, *Adolescents at Risk*; West, D. (1982). *Delinquency: Its Roots, Careers and Prospects*. Cambridge, MA: Harvard University Press; and West, D. and D. P. Farrington (1977). *The Delinquent Way of Life*. London: Heinemann.

[139] Ashford, J. B. and C. W. LeCroy (1993). "Juvenile Parole Policy in the United States: Determinate versus Indeterminate Models." *Justice Quarterly* 10: 187–91.

[140] Gordon, J. (2003). "Aftercare." In M. McShane and F. P. Williams (Eds.), *Encyclopedia of Juvenile Justice*. Thousand Oaks, CA: Sage, pp. 4–5.

[141] Todis, B. et al. (2001). "Overcoming the Odds: Qualitative Examination of Resilience among Formerly Incarcerated Adolescents." *Exceptional Children* 119–39, cited in Byrnes et al., "Aftercare as Afterthought," p. 3. This is also discussed in Steinberg, L., H. L. Chung, and M. Little (2004). "Reentry of Young Offenders from the Justice System: A Developmental Perspective." *Youth Violence and Juvenile Justice* 2: 21–38.

[142] Altschuler, D. and R. Brash (2004). "Adolescent and Teenage Offenders Confronting the Challenges and Opportunities of Reentry." *Youth Violence and Juvenile Justice* 2: 72–87.

[143] Ibid., pp. 76–77.

THE DOUBLE STANDARD
OF JUVENILE JUSTICE

Women serve on the Supreme Court, in Congress, and on boards of directors of corporations. At first glance, it might appear that the twenty-first century has conquered gender inequality. Looking deeper, reality is much less equitable. More women than men have a high school education, university degrees, and graduate degrees, but women earn about 75% of what men earn.[1] Only one-quarter of the CEO positions are held by women; 13% of architects and engineers are women; 31.5% of attorneys; 32.3% of physicians.[2]

In *Beyond the Double Bind*, Kathleen Hall Jamieson reveals the false choices women have been offered. The "double bind" of either/or choices traps women—equality or difference; femininity or competence; nurture or endanger the family.

> Binds draw their power from their capacity to simplify complexity. Faced with a complicated situation or behavior, the human tendency is to split apart and dichotomize its elements. So we contrast good and bad, strong and weak, for and against, true and false, and in so doing assume that a person can't be both at once—or somewhere in between. . . .
>
> In the history of humans, such choices have been constructed to deny women access to power and, where individuals manage to slip past their constraints, to undermine their exercise of whatever power they achieve. The strategy defines something "fundamental" to women as incompatible with something the woman seeks—be it education, the ballot, or access to the workplace.[3]

As Judith Lorber notes, gender is a social structure that originates in culture, not in biology. "Like any social institution, gender exhibits both universal features and chronological and cross-cultural variations that affect individual lives and social interaction in major ways."[4] Gender establishes expectations for behavior. These conceptions are woven through all social organizations of society, including the family, the economy, politics, and the criminal justice system.

Normative beliefs about femininity and masculinity begin in the family.[5] Despite many advances for women, there is little evidence that gender role socialization within families has changed much. Although many parents are concerned about sex-role equality, particularly for their daughters, stereotypic gender roles are still reinforced.[6]

Adolescent girls live in a world that has not changed much despite alterations to the adult female role. Modern girls, like girls in the past, are more closely watched than their brothers.[7] As girls approach puberty, parents begin to monitor them more closely—at the very stage of their lives when they desire more freedom and rely more on peer groups for approval. Clashes between daughters and parents may be more likely during late adolescence. Much of the family disharmony is an outgrowth of the long-standing sexual double standard (see discussion in chapter 5) that tacitly encourages male sexual exploration and punishes female sexuality. Despite recent cultural changes and the growth of the feminist movement, the double standard persists.[8] Research has amply documented the dichotomy between the "culture of romance" and the specter of the "slut."[9] The sexual double standard generally means that parents, concerned that too much freedom will result in poor behavior choices, try to exert more control to protect their daughters.

Some parents, who are not sure how to manage their children, turn to the juvenile court to enforce their authority.[10] Parents whose communication with their children has broken down "look to the court for outside help and relief, yet find their children locked away as a result—sometimes repeatedly—without any resolution of the underlying problems."[11] One major reason for the presence of girls in juvenile courts is the insistence of their parents that they be arrested. Historically, conflicts with parents were by far the most significant referral source. In Honolulu, 44% of the girls who appeared in court in 1929–1930 were referred by parents.[12] In less dramatic ways, this pattern continues, as girl status offenders are still more likely to be referred to court by their parents.[13]

The history of the juvenile justice system was reviewed in some detail in chapter 1. In this chapter we will focus on how the system has historically responded to the behavior of girls. Looking at the emergence of the juvenile court at the end of the nineteenth century, we find solid evidence of a double standard.

The Child-Saving Movement and the Juvenile Court

Attitudes toward youths in U.S. society shifted during the Progressive Era (1890–1920). The stubborn-child law (see chapter 1) established the legal relationship between children and parents. The Progressive Era extended that concept and ushered in unprecedented government involvement in family life, and more specifically in the lives of adolescents. The child-saving movement made much rhetorical use of the value of such traditional institutions as the family and education: "The child savers elevated the nuclear family, especially women as stalwarts of the family, and defended the family's right to supervise the socialization of youth."[14] But while the child savers were exalting the family, they were also crafting a governmental system that would have authority to intervene in familial areas and, more specifically, in the lives of young people. The child savers regarded their cause as a moral one and "viewed themselves as altruists and humanitarians dedicated to rescuing those who were less fortunately placed in the social order."[15]

As discussed in chapter 1, the culmination of the child savers' efforts was the juvenile court. The legislation that established the first juvenile court in Chicago in 1899 became a prototype for legislation in other states. Juvenile courts soon appeared in Colorado (1900), Wisconsin (1901), New York (1901), Ohio (1902), and Maryland (1902). By 1928 all but two states had a juvenile court system.

Based on an assumption of the natural dependence of youth, the juvenile court was charged with determining the guilt or innocence of accused under-age persons and with acting for or in place of defendants' parents. The concern of the child savers went far beyond removing the adolescent criminal from the adult justice system. Many of their reforms were actually aimed at "imposing sanctions on conduct unbecoming youth and disqualifying youth from the benefit of adult privileges."[16] One of the unique features of the new juvenile courts was that they monitored and responded to youthful behaviors believed to indicate future problems. For instance, part of the Tennessee juvenile code included the phrase "who are in danger of being brought up to lead an idle or immoral life."[17]

Some observers assert that the pervasive state intervention into the life of the family was grounded in colonial laws regarding "stubborn" children. Those laws incorporated the thinking prevalent at that time that "parents were godly and children wicked."[18] Many child savers actually held an opposite opinion—that children were innocent and either the parents or the environment was morally suspect. Although the two views are incompatible, they have nevertheless coexisted in the juvenile court system since its inception. At various times one view or the other has predominated. Both bode ill for young women.

The Reformers

Privileged women devoted their energies to the establishment of family courts. As the legitimate guardians of the moral sphere, middle-class women were seen as uniquely suited to patrol the normative boundaries of the social order. Women carved out a role for themselves in the policing of women and girls. Many early activities of the child savers revolved around monitoring the behavior of young girls, particularly immigrant girls, in order to prevent their "straying from the path."[19] Lisa Pasko describes the changing boundaries of the court regarding girls.

> Whereas the first juvenile court originally defined "delinquent" as those under sixteen who had violated a city ordinance or law, when the definition was applied to girls, the court included incorrigibility, associations with immoral persons, vagrancy, frequent attendance at pool halls or saloons, other debauched conduct, and use of profane language in its definition.[20]

Scientific and popular literature on female delinquency expanded enormously during this period, as did institutions specifically devoted to the reformation of girls.[21]

The child-saving movement was keenly concerned about prostitution and other social evils such as white slavery.[22] Just exactly how women, many of them highly educated, became involved in patrolling the boundaries of work-ing-class girls' sexuality is a depressing but important story. Middle-class women reformers initially focused on regulating and controlling male sexual-ity. They had a Victorian view of women's sexuality and saw girls as inherently chaste and sexually passive. These women waged an aggressive social move-ment to raise the age of consent (which in many parts of the country ranged from 10 to 12 years of age) to 16 or above.

The pursuit of claims of statutory rape against men was another compo-nent of their efforts. Charges were brought in a number of cases. If a girl lost "the most precious jewel in the crown of her womanhood," it was the fault of men who had forced them into sexual activity.[23] Later research found that in almost 75% of the cases reviewed in Los Angeles, the girls entered into sexual relationships with the young men willingly. Led largely by upper- and upper-middle-class women volunteers, many of whom were prominent in the tem-perance movement (like Frances Willard), this campaign—not unlike the Mothers Against Drunk Driving campaign of later decades—drew an impres-sive and enthusiastic following, particularly among white citizens.

African-American women participated in other aspects of progressive reform, but they were less aggressive in pursuing statutory rape complaints. Mary Odem speculates that they rightly suspected that any aggressive enforce-ment of these statutes was likely to fall most heavily on young African-Ameri-can men (while doing little to protect girls of color), which is precisely what occurred.[24] Although the number of cases was small, African-American men were sent to prison to reform their "supposedly lax and immoral habits," while white men were either not prosecuted or were given probation.

The statutory rape complaints met staunch judicial resistance, particularly when many (but not all) cases involved young, working-class women who had chosen to be sexually active. Reformers (many of them now professional social workers) began to shift the focus of their activities. The "delinquent girl" her-self became the focus of reform. Moral campaigns to control teenage female sexuality began to appear. Reformers during this later period (1910–1925) assumed that they had the authority to define what "appropriate" conduct was for young working-class women and girls—based, of course, on middle-class ideals of female sexual propriety. Girls who did not conform to these ideals were considered "wayward and in need of control by the state."[25]

Alice Stebbins Wells was a social worker who became the first police-woman in the United States. She illustrates the ironies of child saving perfectly. In 1910 she was hired by Los Angeles because she argued that she could not serve her clients (young women) without police powers. Her work, and the work of five other female police officers hired during the next five years, was to monitor "dance halls, cafes, picture shows and other public amusement places" and to escort girls who were "in danger of becoming delinquent to their homes and to make reports to their parents with a proper warning."[26]

Women reformers played a key role in the founding of the juvenile court in Los Angeles in 1903 and vigorously advocated the appointment of women court workers to deal with the "special problems" of girls. This court was the first in the country to appoint women "referees," who were invested with nearly all the powers of judges in girls' cases. Women were also hired to run the juvenile detention facility in 1911. As Cora Lewis, chairman of the Probation Committee that established Juvenile Hall, declared, "In view of the number of girls and the type of girls detained there . . . it is utterly unfeasible to have a man at the head of the institution." The civic leaders and newly hired female court workers "advocated special measures to contain sexual behavior among working-class girls, to bring them to safety by placing them in custody, and to attend to their distinctive needs as young, vulnerable females."[27]

The Girl-Saving Movement

Girl-saving efforts evolved through a coalition between feminists and other Progressive Era movements. Concerned about female victimization and distrustful of male (and to some degree female) sexuality, prominent women leaders, including Susan B. Anthony, found common cause with the more conservative social purity movement around such issues as the regulation of prostitution and raising the age of consent. Once the focus had shifted to the delinquent girl, the solution became harsh, "maternal justice" meted out by professional women.[28]

Girls were the losers in this reform effort. Studies of early family court activity reveal that almost all of the girls who appeared in these courts were charged with immorality or waywardness.[29] The sanctions for such misbehavior were extremely severe. For example, the Chicago family court sent half the girl delinquents (but only a fifth of the boy delinquents) to reformatories between 1899 and 1909. In Milwaukee and Memphis, twice as many girls as boys were committed to training schools.[30] A detailed study of the Cook County Juvenile Court between 1906 and 1927 found that the two most common charges against girls were immorality and incorrigibility. The third most common charge was larceny.[31] Identical findings have been reported in a study examining the juvenile court in St. Louis in the first years of the twentieth century.[32]

From 1929 to 1930, over half the girls referred to juvenile court in Hawaii were charged with "immorality," which meant there was evidence of sexual intercourse; 30% were charged with "waywardness." Evidence of immorality was vigorously pursued by both arresting officers and social workers, who questioned the girls and, if possible, the males with whom they were suspected of having sex. Other evidence of "exposure" was provided by routinely ordered gynecological examinations. Doctors, who understood the purpose of such examinations, noted the condition of the hymen. Girls were twice as likely as males to be detained for their offenses and spent five times as long in detention. They were also nearly three times more likely to be sentenced to the training school. Indeed, half of those committed to training schools in Honolulu well into the 1950s were girls.[33]

Large numbers of girls' reformatories and training schools were established during the Progressive Era, in addition to places of "rescue and reform." Twenty-three facilities for girls were opened during the decade from 1910 to 1920 (in the previous 60 years the average was 5 reformatories a decade), and they did much to set the tone of official response to female delinquency. These institutions were obsessed with precocious female sexuality and were determined to instruct girls to overcome their wayward behavior.[34]

There was a slight modification of the *parens patriae* doctrine during this period. The "training" of girls was shaped by the image of the ideal woman that had evolved during the early part of the nineteenth century. Women belonged in the private sphere, performing such tasks as rearing children, keeping house, caring for husbands, and serving as the moral guardians of the home. In this capacity, women needed qualities like obedience, modesty, and dependence. The domain of men was the public sphere: the workplace, politics, and the law. By virtue of this public power, men were the final arbiters of public morality and culture.[35] This white, middle-class "cult of domesticity" was, of course, very distant from the lives of many women in lower socioeconomic classes who were in the labor force by necessity. The Ladies Committee of the New York House of Refuge summed up their approval of the goals of institutions for girls.

> The Ladies wish to call attention to the great change which takes place in every girl who has spent one year in the Refuge; she enters a rude, careless, untrained child, caring nothing for cleanliness and order; when she leaves the House, she can sew, mend, darn, wash, iron, arrange a table neatly and cook a healthy meal.[36]

The institutions established for girls isolated them from all contact with males and trained them in feminine skills, while housing them in bucolic settings. The intention was to hold the girls until marriageable age and to teach them domesticity during their sometimes lengthy incarceration. The child savers had little hesitation about such extreme intervention in girls' lives. They believed delinquency to be the result of a variety of social, psychological, and biological factors, and they were optimistic about the juvenile court's ability to remove girls from influences that were producing delinquent behavior.

The juvenile court judge served as a benevolent yet stern father. The proceedings were informal, without the traditional judicial trappings. Initially no lawyers were required; constitutional safeguards were not in place; no provisions existed for jury trials; and so on. Consistent with the *parens patriae* doctrine, juvenile courts were not constrained by the legal requirements of criminal courts because of the rationale that they were acting in the best interests of the child. Nowhere has the confusion and irony of the juvenile court been more clearly demonstrated than in its treatment of girls labeled as delinquent. Many of these girls were incarcerated for noncriminal behavior during the early years of the court.

The Juvenile Court and the Double Standard of Juvenile Justice

The offenses that bring girls into the juvenile justice system reflect the system's dual concerns: adolescent criminality and moral conduct. Historically, they have also reflected a unique and intense preoccupation with girls' sexuality and their obedience to parental authority.[37]

Relatively early in the juvenile justice system's history, a few astute observers became concerned about the abandonment of minors' rights in the name of treatment, saving, and protection. One of the most insightful was Paul Tappan.[38] He evaluated several hundred cases in the Wayward Minor Court in New York City during the late 1930s and early 1940s and concluded that there were serious problems with a statute that brought young women into court simply for disobeying parental commands or because they were in danger of becoming depraved. Tappan was particularly disturbed that the court was essentially legislating what is and is not morally acceptable. Noting that many young women were being charged with sexual activity, he asked, "What is sexual misbehavior—in a legal sense—of the nonprostitute of 16, or 18, or of 20 when fornication is no offense under criminal law?"[39]

When one group imposes their own definition of morality onto another group (a common method of social control), those efforts can be termed "moral imperialism." The major problem of such an imposition from a legal standpoint, as noted in chapter 1, is that it punishes someone for something they *might* do in the future. Tappan believed that the structure of the Wayward Minor Court invested the judge with judicial totalitarianism, and he cautioned that "the fate of the defendant, the interest of society, the social objectives themselves, must hang by the tenuous thread of the wisdom and personality of the particular administrator."[40]

Mary Odem and Steven Schlossman reviewed the characteristics of the girls who entered the Los Angeles Juvenile Court in 1920 and in 1950. In 1920, 93% of the girls accused of delinquency were charged with status offenses; of those, 65% were charged with immoral sexual activity (even though the majority had engaged in sex with only one partner, usually a boyfriend). The parents of the girls referred 51% of the cases to the court. Odem and Schlossman attributed these actions to parental fears about their daughters' exposure to the "omnipresent temptations to which working-class daughters in particular were exposed to in the modern ecology of urban work and leisure."[41]

Women court officials attempted to instill a middle-class standard of respectability by "dispensing the maternal guidance and discipline supposedly lacking in the girls' own homes. Referees and probation officers scolded their charges for wearing too much makeup and dressing in a provocative manner."[42] Court officials were obsessed with the sexuality of these young women. Odem notes that after a girl was arrested, "probation officers questioned her relatives, neighbors, employers, and school officials to gather details about her sexual misconduct and, in the process, alerted them that she was a delinquent in trouble with the law."[43]

Between 1920 and 1950 the makeup of the court's female clientele changed very little: "the group was still predominantly white, working class, and from disrupted families. Girls were more likely to be in school and less likely to be working in 1950. Status offenses (78%) continued to be the most frequent charges, although somewhat different from those in 1920. Thirty-one percent of the girls were charged with running away from home, truancy, curfew, or "general unruliness at home." The percentage charged with sexual misconduct declined to less than 50% (once again usually with a single partner). Referrals from parents declined to 26% (referrals from police officers increased to 54% from 29% in 1920; referrals from schools decreased to 21%, versus 27% in 1920). Although the rationale for detention had changed, concerns about female sexual conduct "remained determinative in shaping social policy" in the 1950s.[44]

As mentioned repeatedly throughout this book, contemporary status offense categories are extremely vague. They can serve as "buffer charges" for suspected sexuality. Researchers in the 1960s observed that although girls were incarcerated in training schools for what they called the "big five" (running away from home, incorrigibility, sexual offenses, probation violation, and truancy) "the underlying vein in many of these cases is sexual misconduct by the girl delinquent."[45]

A review of cases of ungovernability in New York in 1972 revealed that judges based their decisions on personal feelings. Consider this comment by one of the judges: "She thinks she's a pretty hot number; I'd be worried about leaving my kid with her in a room alone. She needs to get her mind off boys."[46] Another admonished a girl:

> I want you to promise me to obey your mother, to have perfect school attendance and not miss a day of school, to give up these people who are trying to lead you to do wrong, not to hang out in candy stores or tobacco shops or street corners where these people are, and to be in when your mother says.[47]

Empirical studies of the processing of girls' and boys' cases between 1950 and the early 1970s documented the impact of these sorts of judicial attitudes. Girls charged with status offenses were often more harshly treated than their male or female counterparts charged with crimes. A study of court dispositions in Washington State between 1953 and 1955 found that girls were far less likely than boys to be charged with criminal offenses—but more than twice as likely to be committed to institutions.[48] Some years later a study of a juvenile court in Delaware discovered that first-time female status offenders were more harshly sanctioned (as measured by institutionalization) than males charged with felonies. For repeat status offenders, the pattern was even starker: female status offenders were six times more likely than male status offenders to be institutionalized.

Despite the eventual changes detailed below, judicial discretion continues to impact girls in the twenty-first century.

> Studies indicate that judges continue to have sexist, paternalistic attitudes toward young girls. Courts believe that girls must be protected from the evils of the outside world. . . . Because of this view, judges continue to perceive a need to intervene in girls' lives to save the young females through the authority of the juvenile justice system. Moreover, as status offenders are not afforded procedural due process rights, they have no protections against the paternalistic attitudes of juvenile court judges.[49]

The nature of status offenses facilitates discretionary enforcement based on culturally fostered attitudes. Criminal cases have relatively clear guidelines;

standards of evidence are delineated; elements of the crime are laid out in the statutes; and civil rights are, at least to some extent, protected by law. Judges have few legal guidelines in status offense cases. Many judges accepted one of the orientations built into the juvenile justice system: the puritan stance supportive of parental demands or the progressive stance, whereby the court assumes parental roles. It was inevitable that such attitudes and the resulting actions would result in significant legal challenges. In the 1970s, critics mounted a major drive to deinstitutionalize status offenders and to divert them from formal court jurisdiction.

Deinstitutionalization and Judicial Paternalism

By the mid-1970s, correctional reformers had become concerned about juvenile courts' abuse of the status offense category. However, very little of the concern was based on the history of gender bias that characterized some, but not all, of these categories. Instead, the argument was that noncriminal youth should be treated and helped—not detained and institutionalized.

As discussed in chapters 3 and 5, the Juvenile Justice and Delinquency Prevention Act (JJDPA) of 1974 required that states receiving federal delinquency prevention money begin to divert and deinstitutionalize status offenders. "Despite inconsistent enforcement of this provision and some resistance from states to decriminalize status offenders, girls were the clear beneficiaries of the reform, as they no longer could be directly incarcerated for filial disobedience, running away, truancy, or immorality."[50] Incarceration of young women in training schools and detention centers across the country fell dramatically. Studies of court decision making found less clear evidence of discrimination against girls in parts of the country where serious diversion efforts were occurring.[51]

The Conservative Backlash

There was resistance to deinstitutionalization. When the JJDPA was first being implemented, the director of the National Center of Juvenile Justice claimed that status offenses were offenses against the country's values. He said girls were "seemingly overrepresented as status offenders because we have had a strong heritage of being protective toward females in this country" and continued that it offended sensibilities when a fourteen-year-old girl engaged in sexually promiscuous activity.[52] He offered the opinion that the police, the church, or vigilante groups would probably act if their values were offended, and he preferred that action be taken in the court where the rights of the parties could be protected.

Resistance permeated official agencies, including the Law Enforcement Assistance Administration (LEAA)—the agency implementing the legislation. A 1978 General Accounting Office (GAO) report concluded that the LEAA had "downplayed its [the act's] importance and to some extent discouraged states from carrying out the Federal requirement."[53] The GAO declared that: monitoring of states' compliance with the law was lax or nonexistent (only nine states had what the GAO deemed complete data); definitions of what constituted detention and correctional facilities were confusing (children in jail, for example, were frequently not counted); LEAA was apparently reluctant to take action against states in noncompliance.

The extent of anti-deinstitutionalization sentiment among juvenile justice officials was obvious. Judge John R. Milligan, representing the National Council of Juvenile and Family Court Judges, testified:

> The effect of the Juvenile Justice Act as it now exists is to allow a child ultimately to decide for himself whether he will go to school, whether he will live at home, whether he will continue to run, run, run, away from home, or whether he will even obey orders of your court.[54]

Chapter 3 discussed the 1980 modification of JJDPA to allow judges discretion if a juvenile had violated a valid court order (VCO).[55] The change, never publicly debated in either house, effectively gutted the act by permitting judges to reclassify a status offender who violated a court order as a delinquent. This meant that a young woman who ran away from a court-ordered placement (a halfway house, foster home, or the like) could be relabeled a delinquent and locked up. In 1988, 37 states invoked VCO exclusions; twenty-four states reported using 4,990 of these exclusions.[56]

Before the enacted change, judges engaged in less public efforts to circumvent deinstitutionalization. These included "bootstrapping" status offenders into delinquents by issuing criminal contempt citations, referring or committing status offenders to secure mental health facilities, and referring them to "semi-secure" facilities.[57] A study of 162,012 cases referred to juvenile justice intake units in Florida from 1985–1987 revealed the damage of contempt proceedings to female status offenders. The researchers found only a weak pattern of discrimination against female status offenders compared with male status offenders. However, contempt citations had a far different pattern. Females referred for contempt were more likely than females referred for other criminal offenses to be petitioned to court. They were substantially more likely to be petitioned to court than males referred for contempt and far more likely than boys to be sentenced to detention. The typical female offender in the study had a probability of incarceration of 4.3%, which increased to 29.9% if she was held in contempt—a circumstance that was not observed among males. The researchers concluded that "the traditional double standard is still operative. Clearly neither the cultural changes associated with the feminist movement nor the legal changes illustrated in the JJDPA's mandate to deinstitutionalize status offenders have brought about equality under the law for young men and women."[58]

The 1992 Reauthorization of the Juvenile Justice and Delinquency Prevention Act

The subcommittee deliberating on the 1992 reauthorization of the Juvenile Justice and Delinquency Prevention Act addressed for the first time the "provision of services to girls within the juvenile justice system."[59] The chairman opened with the following remarks:

> In today's hearing we are going to address female delinquency and the pro-visions of services to girls under this Act. There are many of us that believe that we have not committed enough resources to that particular issue. There are many of us who realize that the problems for young ladies are increas-ing, ever increasing, in our society and they are becoming more prone to end up in gangs, in crime, and with other problems they have always suffered.[60]

He continued by commenting on the high number of girls arrested for status offenses, the high percentage of girls in detention as a result of violation of court orders, and the failure of the system to address girls' needs. He ended with the question, "Why are there no other alternatives than youth jail for her?"[61] Representatives from organizations serving girls, such as Children of the Night, Pace Center for Girls, and Girls, Incorporated, testified at the hear-ing, as did girls active in these programs.

The 1992 reauthorization included specific provisions requiring plans from each state receiving federal funds to include "an analysis of gender-specific ser-vices for the prevention and treatment of juvenile delinquency, including the types of such services available and the need for such services for females and a plan for providing needed gender-specific services for the prevention and treatment of juvenile delinquency."[62] Additional monies were set aside for states wishing to develop policies to prohibit gender bias in placement and treatment and to develop programs that assure girls equal access to services.[63] The act also called for the GAO to conduct a study of gender bias within state juvenile justice systems, with specific attention to "the frequency with which females have been detained for status offenses." While not specifically related to gender, the reauthorization of the act made "bootstrapping" of status offend-ers into delinquents more difficult. It specified that youth who were being detained due to a VCO violation had to have received "the full due process rights guaranteed to such juvenile by the Constitution of the United States." Before issuance of the order, "both the behavior of the juvenile being referred and the reasons why the juvenile might have committed the behavior must be assessed." The reauthorization also mandated that all dispositions (including treatment) be exhausted or deemed inappropriate before placement in a secure detention or correctional facility. Finally, the court has to receive a "written report" stating the results of the review.[64]

The next revision of JJDPA did not focus on girls. As discussed in chapter 12, the 2002 Act established four core protections: deinstitutionalization of sta-tus offenders (DS), with some VCO exclusions; separation of juveniles from adults in institutions; removal of juveniles from adult lockups and jails; and reduction of disproportionate minority contact.

The JJDPA has not been reauthorized since 2002. The Senate Judiciary Committee approved a revision in 2009, and the House introduced a reauthori-zation in 2010. Both proposals would strengthen the requirement to reduce dis-proportionate minority contact; strengthen support for community-based delinquency prevention programs as alternatives to detention; and increase funding levels.[65] Child advocates are pushing for a three-year phase-out of the VCO exception.[66]

Continuing Evidence of Gender Bias

Although gender bias is not as blatant as in earlier years, it is still visible.[67] The legacy continues today, as Pasko notes.

> With a focus on their physical appearance and sexuality, the characterizations of girls in their official court records and case files regularly deem them to be deceitful, manipulative, hysterical, wildly sexual, and verbally abusive. Under a paternalistic ideology, the current juvenile justice institutions—police, courts, and corrections—exercise the repeated need to protect their daughters, usually from sexual experimentation and other dangers on the streets. At the same time, the court frequently labels girls as sexually promiscuous, untrustworthy, and unruly, without connecting such behaviors to their life histories and social contexts.[68]

Getting into the System

Many youths come to the attention of the juvenile court because of a complaint or referral from sources other than law enforcement agencies—particularly for status offenses. For example, 83% of all delinquency referrals but 46% of all status offense referrals came from law enforcement personnel in 2007. There are important gender differences within the status offense category. Schools are the major source (75%) of referrals for truancy; relatives are the major source (41%) of referrals for ungovernability.[69]

> Parents often struggle to find an effective response when their children persistently skip school, run away from home, or exhibit troubling or rebellious behavior. Many turn to the courts for assistance, despite the fact that the court system lacks the resources to provide the necessary social services.[70]

Chapter 5 discussed arrests of girls in detail; a brief synopsis follows. Three of every 10 juveniles arrested in 2009 was a girl, but for serious crimes of violence the ratio drops to 18 of every 100 juvenile arrests.[71] Only 2.6 out of every 100 arrests of a girl was for violent crime. Not much has changed over almost two decades; the percentage in 1986 was 2.1%. Running away accounts for 9.2% of all arrests of girls (versus 3.3% for boys) even though self-report studies show both being equally as likely to run away from home. Girls account for 55% of all arrests for running away. As noted in table 5-2, "other assaults" (juvenile court data use the term "simple assault") and disorderly conduct are two of the five categories of the most frequent arrests for girls. The increase is attributable to formal responses to ordinary fights at school and in domestic situations (see chapter 3).

Girls on the Streets

As we know, girls are more likely than boys to be arrested for minor property offenses and status offenses. This circumstance is stable despite efforts to de-emphasize the official processing of youths arrested for noncriminal status offenses. Research that compares or links self-report data to arrest data suggests that girls may be overrepresented among those charged with minor or status offenses when arrests are compared to actual behavior. There is also some indication that girls may be committing some serious offenses for which they are not being arrested.

Researchers conducted a self-report survey among California high school students in the late 1960s and then checked official records for evidence of police contact (not necessarily official arrests). They found sizable gender differentials in the frequency of such contacts. The researchers had gathered data on auto theft that showed a male–female self-report ratio of 2:1 and a ratio of police contacts of 26:1.[72] Police contacts occurred in only 1% of the serious offenses admitted by females, in contrast to 4% of boys' serious offenses. "Although females perceive themselves as partners in the theft of automobiles, apparently police officers apprehended only their male companions." Unfortunately, these researchers were not able to compare self-reported and official arrests for sexual offenses; hence their data could not address the treatment of girls suspected of such offenses.

Early sociological studies of police behavior in the field rarely examined the effect of gender on the decision to make an arrest. One exception was an investigation of police dispositions of juvenile offenders in Philadelphia, which discovered that police were more likely to release a girl than a boy they suspected of committing a crime, equally likely to apprehend males and females they suspected of running away, and more likely to arrest girls they suspected of sex offenses.[73]

Christy Visher examined 785 police–suspect encounters during 1977 in 24 police departments in three geographically separate communities. She excluded morals offenses (prostitution and drug-related offenses), confining her study to routine criminal and public-order offenses. Scrutinizing many aspects of the arrest situation, Visher concluded that age was irrelevant in police interactions with males but relevant in interactions with females, with younger females receiving harsher treatment.[74] Visher noted that police officers act in a paternalistic manner toward young females and adopt a harsh attitude to deter any further violation of appropriate sex-role behavior. Demeanor was an extremely important factor in the arrest decision. If a female suspect violated typical middle-class standards of behavior (i.e., submissive) she was not treated chivalrously.[75] Women suspected of property offenses were actually more harshly treated than their male counterparts, many of whom were suspected of minor crimes of violence, such as fighting.

Police have increased arrests of girls for simple assault. One study compared the arrest rate ratio between simple and aggravated assault (arrest rate for simple assault divided by the arrest rate for aggravated assault) for boys and girls between 1980 and 2003. In 1980 the ratio for girls was 2.9—the police were almost three times more likely to arrest girls for simple assault than for aggravated assault; for boys the ratio was 1.9. In 2003, however, the girls ratio was 5.4 (meaning that the police were more than five times more likely to arrest them for simple assault), while the boys ratio was 3.5.[76]

There has been little research demonstrating overt police bias against girls in recent years. In fact, some studies suggest that police are far more likely to refer boys to court than girls, simply because their offenses are much more serious.[77] At the same time, the fact remains that despite the less serious nature of girls' offenses, court referrals for them have increased significantly in recent years. Perhaps rather than overt bias, the police are simply following local policy directives, especially when it comes to domestic violence and school-related offenses. Some research suggests a more subtle form of police bias.[78]

Gender and Delinquency Referrals

What kinds of behavior result in referral to juvenile court? Are there significant differences between girls and boys in referrals? Juvenile court referrals include youths charged with both criminal violations and status offenses, such as incorrigibility (in some jurisdictions called unmanageability or ungovernability, and in others the child is labeled "in need of supervision") and truancy. In some parts of the country, youths who are abused or neglected are also handled in juvenile courts.

> When a child is brought before the court for behavior felt to be beyond the control of the parent/guardian, ideally there would be many alternatives to filing a petition in court, such as mental health services, family intervention and support, mediation or alternative dispute resolution, and other community-based services and supports aimed at helping these children in the context of their family and community life.[79]

Between 1985 and 2007, the number of delinquency cases involving girls increased 101% (from 223,100 cases to 448,900 cases); the percentage increase for boys was 30% (from 933,600 to 1,217,100).[80] Males were involved in 73% of the delinquency cases handled by the juvenile court in 2007. As shown in Table 13-1, 36% of both males and females are referred to court for a property offense—declining from 61% for boys in 1985 and 58% for girls. In 1985 only 16% of girls were referred for "person" offenses, in 2007 the percentage was 27; for boys these percentages were 16 and 24 respectively. This of course does not mean girls are more violent, for the bulk of these cases (as noted in earlier chapters) are for simple assault, stemming mostly from domestic violence cases and fighting at school (the Juvenile Court Statistics source does not break down these offenses so that we can tell what proportion are referred for "simple assaults"). Property offenses have dropped dramatically for both boys and girls, while the proportion of boys brought in on drug offenses has almost doubled. Public order offenses also increased for both boys and girls.

The nature of status offenses petitioned to court has also changed. Table 13-2 shows 24% of girl status offenders were runaways in 1995 versus 16% in 2007;

Table 13-1   Juvenile Court Referrals, by Offense and Gender

Offense	Male		Female	
	1985	2007	1985	2007
Person	16%	24%	16%	27%
Property	61	36	58	36
Drugs	7	13	6	8
Public Order	16	28	19	30

Source: Puzzanchera, C., B. Adams, and M. Sickmund (2010, March). *Juvenile Court Statistics 2006–2007.* Pittsburgh: National Center for Juvenile Justice, p. 13. Retrieved from http://www.ojjdp.gov/ojstatbb/njcda/pdf/jcs2007.pdf

the percentage decreased for boys as well.[81] The proportion of girls and boys brought in for truancy increased, while the proportion for liquor law violations declined for boys and increased slightly for girls. The female caseload for petitioned status cases increased 33%; the male caseload increased 29%. Males accounted for 57% of all petitioned status cases. As a reminder, these figures are for the cases petitioned to court; many status cases are handled informally by local social service organizations, making gender comparisons difficult.

On the surface these data reveal a drop in status offense referrals, although not as dramatic a decline as some expected in the wake of legal efforts to divert and deinstitutionalize status offenders. It has become increasingly difficult to obtain national data on status offenses, with the exception of arrest data (and these data only show arrests for runaways and curfew violations). Most revealing, however, are the numbers of status offenders that end up in juvenile correctional facilities. As noted in chapter 5, 11% of girls, but only 3% of boys, confined in juvenile correctional facilities were status offenders.[82]

The author's longitudinal study found that males and females differed in significant ways in terms of length of careers and type of offenses committed. The majority of the girls (60.7%) had only one contact with the court, compared

Table 13-2   Petitioned Status Offense Cases and Gender

	Male		Female	
	1995	2007	1995	2007
Runaway	12%	9%	24%	16%
Truancy	27	36	33	40
Curfew	12	11	7	7
Ungovernability	14	13	15	13
Liquor	28	24	17	19
Miscellaneous	7	8	5	5

Source: Puzzanchera, C., B. Adams, and M. Sickmund (2010, March). *Juvenile Court Statistics 2006–2007.* Pittsburgh: National Center for Juvenile Justice, p. 77. Retrieved from http://www.ojjdp.gov/ojstatbb/njcda/pdf/jcs2007.pdf.

with 43.3% of the boys. Boys were about twice as likely as girls to be "chronic delinquents" (those with five or more referrals to court), and about 10 times as likely to be "chronic serious offenders" (the majority of their offenses being felonies). In terms of the overall distribution of offenses, girls were twice as likely as boys to be referred for status offenses and for petty larceny; boys were far more likely than girls to be referred for traditional "male" offenses, such as robbery, aggravated assault, burglary, and grand larceny.[83]

What is not often discussed is the nature of referrals to various service providers. Here we see some clear gender differences. One study found that girls were more likely to be referred by school officials and private practitioners for various "family issues," in addition to depression and mental health issues. In contrast, boys were more likely to be referred by juvenile courts and probation officers for delinquency.[84]

Comparing Girls and Boys in Court

Not all research has confirmed the existence of judicial sexism. One study examined court dispositions of youthful offenders in five states. By controlling for "offense type" and prior record, they found that "status offenders are consistently given harsher treatment than delinquent offenders" but "this is as true for boys as it is for girls." From this, they concluded that treatment within the court was "relatively even-handed."[85] Several other studies also found little evidence that female status offenders were more harshly sanctioned than their male counterparts once the effects of a variety of extralegal variables were controlled for.[86]

Some of the findings could reflect actual changes attributable to the deinstitutionalization movement. However, it is also possible that bias against girls may be less overt. For instance, one study observed that many of the girls taken into custody for crimes had actually exhibited behavior that earlier would have been classified as status offenses. For example, girls who broke into their parents' homes to take food and clothing to help themselves survive while maintaining their runaway status were charged with burglary.[87] Such reclassification of female status offenders into female criminals occurred during a period characterized by a "get-tough" attitude toward juvenile crime. Some observers suggest that the hardening of the public mind has particularly burdened female offenders because their behavior was being redefined as criminal at precisely the time that courts were increasingly likely to process their cases formally and punish them more harshly.[88]

Other observers, however, have failed to uncover evidence that girls and boys charged with status offenses are treated equally. In one study females referred to court for status offenses were more likely than males referred for the same offenses to receive formal processing (that is, a court hearing). Girls were also more likely to be detained for status offenses than boys (though the differences were not statistically significant).[89] Similar findings came from a study of runaway youths in the Midwest, which found that girls were more likely than boys to be detained and to receive harsher sentences.[90]

The most recent studies continue to find that girls are treated more harshly for status offenses—and that the variables of race and ethnicity impact decisions. For example, one study found that Native American boys are treated the most severely, followed by black girls and Hispanic girls.[91] Several other recent studies have documented the impact of race and ethnicity. A Florida study found that black girls received harsher dispositions than white girls. However, the dispositions for Hispanic girls were no harsher than for white girls.[92]

Differences in the labels given to the noncriminal behavior of males and females may play a major role in producing harsher treatment for girls. We have seen that girls are far more likely to appear before a court for running away from home or for being ungovernable. As might be expected, the predominantly female status offenses are those that bring on the greatest use of detention, despite the fact that research suggests that male status offenders are more likely to have committed criminal violations. One study looked at whether youths charged with status offenses tended to escalate into criminal offenses; they found significant sex differences. The majority of youths charged with status offenses failed to return to court for any offense. Among those who did return, females (particularly white females) were the least likely to appear again before the court for a delinquent offense; it was usually for another status offense.[93]

Several studies have examined the role of probation officers and their assessments of male and female offenders. One study found that probation officers described boys as "fun loving with a spirit of adventure," while their female counterparts were described as "willful and destructive."[94] Another study found that probation officers tended to describe girl offenders as having "interpersonal problems" and "psychiatric problems."[95] When girls commit new offenses after being released from a residential treatment center, they are much more likely than boys charged with similar new offenses to be returned to that treatment center.[96]

Girls under Lock and Key

Barry Feld researched the interaction of gender and geography.[97] He found evidence that girls referred to juvenile court in Minnesota were more likely than boys to be detained, particularly for minor and status offenses. In rural juvenile courts, larger proportions of females are removed from their homes for minor offenses. Female juveniles are processed differently and more severely than are either rural males or female offenders in other settings.[98] He also noted that these courts tended to deal with the smallest proportions of juveniles charged with serious criminal activity and the largest proportion charged with status offenses. Feld found that judicial paternalism was less marked in urban courts, which he characterized as more formal and procedural, than in suburban and rural courts. Although urban courts tended to be more severe in sanctioning, that fact alone does not mean girls are better off in more informal circumstances.

National figures on juveniles in correctional facilities show strong gender differences. First, consider the detention population, as shown in table 11-3 (on p. 376). Girls are less likely than boys to be detained for all offenses except technical violations, other person, public order, and status offenses. Almost one third of the girls compared to less than one fourth of the boys are detained for a technical violation. Although a small percentage of girls are detained for a status offense (6%), the proportion for boys is even less (2%).

The American Bar Association (ABA) found that girls are far more likely to be detained for relatively minor offenses like public disorder, probation violations, status offenses, and even traffic offenses (29% of the girls versus 19% of the boys). Such gender bias was found to be especially evident for violations of probation and parole where more than half of the girls (54%), but only 19% of the boys were detained.[99] The report also noted the growing tendency to relabel family conflicts in which girls are involved as "violent" offenses, which impacts minority girls in particular. The ABA study concluded that even though the recidivism rate of girls is much lower than boys: "The use of contempt proceedings and probation and parole violations make it more likely that, without committing a new crime, girls will return to detention."[100] More than half (53%) of the girls and 41% of the boys were returned for technical violations. Girls returned to detention three times within a year were far more likely than their male counterparts to be returned on these kinds of violations (72% of girls versus 49% of boys).

Among youths committed to a juvenile facility, girls are more than four times as likely to be committed for status offenses as boys (see table 13-3). For example, an investigation by the Southern Poverty Law Center found that 75% of the girls at the Columbia Training School for Girls in Mississippi had been committed for status offenses, probation violations, or contempt of court.[101]

Table 13-3   Offense Profile of Committed Residents by Sex, 2007 (Column Percent)

	Male	Female
Total	100%	100%
Delinquency	97	87
Person	**38**	**33**
Violent Index	28	15
Other Person	10	18
Property	**26**	**22**
Property Index	22	18
Other Property	5	4
Drug	**9**	**8**
Public Order	**13**	**9**
Technical Violation	**11**	**16**
Status Offense	**3**	**13**

Note: Committed juveniles include those placed in the facility as part of a court ordered disposition.

Source: Sickmund, M., T. J. Sladky, and W. Kang (2011). "Census of Juveniles in Residential Placement Databook." Retrieved from http://www.ojjdp.gov/ojstatbb/ezacjrp/asp/Offense_Committed.asp?state=0&topic=Offense_Committed&year=2007&percent=column

Girls, Race, and the New Double Standard of Juvenile Justice

This chapter has reviewed numerous examples of how deinstitutionaliza-tion of status offenders has not yet been implemented in all jurisdictions. There is another problem—a *two-track* juvenile justice system in which girls of color are treated differently from white girls. Jody Miller examined the impact of race and ethnicity on the processing of girls' cases from one area probation office in Los Angeles during 1992–1993. Comparing the characteristics of the youth in Miller's group with Schlossman's earlier profile of girls in Los Ange-les in the fifties, we find how radically (and racially) different the current girls in the Los Angeles juvenile justice system are from their earlier counterparts. Latinas comprised the largest proportion of the population (45%), followed by white girls (34%), and African-American girls (23%).[102]

Predictably, girls of color were more likely to be from low-income homes, but this was especially true of African-American girls (53% were from AFDC families, compared to 23% of the white girls and 21% of Latina girls). Most importantly, Miller found that white girls were significantly more likely than either African-American or Latina girls to be recommended for treatment—75% of the white girls were recommended for a treatment facility compared to 35% of the Latinas and only 20% of the African-American girls.[103]

Examining a portion of the probation officer's reports in detail, Miller found key differences in the ways that girls' behaviors were described—reflect-ing what she called "racialized gender expectations." In particular, African-American girls were often framed as making "inappropriate 'lifestyle' choices," while white girls' behavior was described as resulting from low self-esteem, being easily influenced, and the result of "abandonment." Latina girls, Miller found, received "dichotomized" treatment, with some receiving the more paternalistic care white girls received, while others received the more punitive treatment (particularly if they committed "masculine" offenses like auto theft.[104]

A study of girls in the social welfare and juvenile justice system in Massa-chusetts also documents the racialized pattern of juvenile justice. The social welfare sample was 74% white, and the juvenile justice sample was 53% Afri-can American or Hispanic.[105] The researchers' interviews document remark-able similarities of the girls' backgrounds and problems. As an example, 80% of those committed to the juvenile justice system reported being sexually abused compared to 73% of the girls in the social welfare group. The difference between these girls was in the offenses for which they were charged. All of the girls in the social welfare system were charged with traditional status offenses (mostly running away and truancy), while most of the girls committed to the justice system were charged with criminal offenses. The interviews offer clear evidence of "bootstrapping." One 16-year-old girl was committed to juvenile justice for "unauthorized use of a motor vehicle"—she had "stolen" her mother's car for three hours to go shopping with a friend.[106] She had previ-ously been in the social welfare system for "running away from home repeatedly." Her mother had been advised by the social worker to press charges so that the girl would be sent to secure detention if she ran away again.[107]

More recently, Joseph P. Ryan and his colleagues found both a racial and gender bias in cases originating in the welfare system. Specifically, youth that came from the state welfare system were far more likely to be committed than those originating in the courts.[108]

Mike Males has found that in San Francisco "black girls are 11.4 times more likely to be arrested for felonies, 10.6 times more likely to be arrested for assault, and 18.9 times more likely to be arrested for felony drug offenses than are San Francisco girls of other races." He further notes that black girls in San Francisco are about 29 times more likely to be arrested for drug felonies than black girls in California generally. Expressed somewhat differently, he observes that "San Francisco has 1.8% of the state's young black women but accounts for 35.2% of the arrests of young black women for drug felonies, and 7.5% for all felonies, in the state." Within San Francisco itself, around 12% of girls are black, but they represent about 61% of all girls arrested for felonies, two-thirds of those arrested for robbery, and almost three-fourths (72%) of those arrested for drug felonies.[109]

One study, however, arrived at a different conclusion when it was found that in the specific county studied white girls were more likely than black girls to receive out-of-home placement. The authors of the study attribute this to the belief among judges and probation officers that white girls were more likely to be in violation of "sex role expectations" and more likely to benefit from the treatment offered in out-of-home placements.[110]

A Human Rights Watch report on girls in youth prisons in New York State details the connection between race and gender. The girls in the institutions investigated were 54% African American, 19% Hispanic, and 23% white.

> Across the U.S., 70% of delinquency cases involving white girls are dismissed, while only 30% of cases involving African-American girls are dismissed. Nationally, 34% of 12 to 17 year olds in the U.S. are girls of color, yet they account for 52% of those detained for juvenile offenses. . . . The disproportionately high number of African-American girls incarcerated in the highest security juvenile prisons in New York State echoes the overall over-representation of black children in OCFS [Office of Children and Family Services]. Since 1995, African-American boys and girls have consistently accounted for close to 60 percent of children taken into OCFS custody.[111]

Taken together, these studies suggest that deinstitutionalization pressures may have differentially affected girls depending on their race. For girls of color, particularly African-American girls, bootstrapping may be the response to their acting out while white girls face transinstitutionalization into the world of private institutions and placements. In either case, the true intent of the deinstitutionalization initiative is being subverted.

Pasko describes how we have arrived at a situation not all that different from earlier incarnations of the double standard in juvenile justice.

Despite, and occasionally due to, transformations in juvenile justice processing and corrections (deinstitutionalization, demise of rehabilitation, increase in direct files and punitive sanctions, growth of private treatment centers, and re-characterization of juvenile sexual offense), the correctional focus—through one definition or another—continues to be on girls' sexual behavior as cause for legal response, detention, and commitment. . . . While girls are not directly arrested and adjudicated for sexual immorality, they are indirectly sanctioned: a higher risk assessment score and probation violations place them at a higher possibility of being incarcerated. Regardless of structural constraints and difficulties, the focus remains on girls' "bad" choices; they are still told to take responsibility for their decisions, as the context of such decisions remains recorded but rarely used as mitigation.[112]

Summary

This chapter focused on the encounters girls have with the police and the juvenile court. Boys are far more likely to experience contacts with the police. The police are more likely to release a girl than a boy suspected of committing a crime, but they are more likely to arrest girls suspected of sex offenses. Girls tend to be overrepresented in arrest statistics for status offenses, especially running away and incorrigibility. Much of this has to do with girls' alleged sexual behavior, which is so often associated (at least from the standpoint of adult authorities) with the two offenses. One critical variable in police decision making on the streets is a young person's demeanor or attitude. In general, a boy or girl who is hostile or in any way aggressive is the most likely to be arrested. Especially important for girls is whether or not they follow middle-class standards of "proper" behavior for girls.

Juvenile court statistics show that girls are more likely than boys to be referred to court for the status offenses of running away and incorrigibility. Males, in contrast, are more likely to be referred for violent crimes. Property offenses bring large numbers of both girls and boys to court, but for girls the bulk of such offenses fall within the larceny-theft category (most are for shoplifting).

Evidence of changes in official responses to girls who appear in the juvenile courts is somewhat mixed. Some studies have found more evenhanded treatment in recent years; others have not. The types of status offenses that girls and boys commit seem to account for some of the courts' differential responses. Girls typically appear for running away and other offenses that signal that they are beyond parental control, and boys appear for curfew and liquor-law violations. Recent research has specifically identified the need to address an undue focus on race as well as gender in the handling of youths.

Notes

[1] Reuters (2011, March 2). "Snapshot of U.S. Women Sees Educational Strides, Workforce Lag." *Chicago Tribune*, p. 12.

[2] Current Population Survey (2010). "Employed Persons by Detailed Occupation, Sex, Race, and Hispanic or Latino Ethnicity." Labor Force Statistics, table 11. Retrieved from http://ftp.bls.gov/pub/special.requests/lf/aat11.txt

[3] Jamieson, K. H. (1995). *Beyond the Double Bind.* New York: Oxford University Press, pp. 5, 14.

[4] Lorber, J. (1994.). *Paradoxes of Gender.* New Haven, CT: Yale University Press, p. 1.

[5] For an extended discussion of the topic of this chapter, see chapters 7, 8, and 9 in Chesney-Lind, M. and R. G. Shelden (2004). *Girls, Delinquency and Juvenile Justice* (3rd ed.). Belmont, CA: Wadsworth. The material has been revised and updated. Some portions were originally written by Meda Chesney-Lind, and some were written by me. Various editorial changes and the passage of time may have caused confusion as to who wrote what. I thank Meda for her collaboration on our successful book and for her gracious contributions to this chapter.

[6] Berns, R. M. (2010). *Child, Family, School, Community: Socialization and Support.* Belmont, CA: Cengage; Marks, J. L., C. Bun Lam, and S. M. McHale (2009). "Family Patterns of Gender Role Attitudes." *Sex Roles* 61: 221–34; Bohanek, J. G., K. A. Marin, and R. Fivush (2008). "Family Narratives, Self, and Gender in Early Adolescence." *The Journal of Early Adolescence* 28: 153–76; Kite, M. E., K. Deaux, and E. L. Haines (2008). "Gender Stereotypes." In F. L. Denmark and M. A. Paludi (Eds.), *Handbook on the Psychology of Women* (2nd ed.). Westport, CT: Greenwood Press, pp. 205–36; Raley, S. and S. Bianchi (2006). "Sons, Daughters, and Family Processes: Does Gender of Children Matter?" *Annual Review of Sociology* 32: 401–21.

[7] Morrongiello, B. A. (2010). "Child Injury: The Role of Supervision in Prevention." *American Journal of Lifestyle Medicine* 4: 65–74; Morrongiello, B. A., N. Klemencic, and M. I. Corbett (2008). "Interactions between Child Behavior Patterns and Parent Supervision: Implications for Children's Risk of Unintentional Injury." *Child Development.* Retrieved from http://www.srcd.org/journals/cdev/0-0/Morrongiello.pdf; Nebbitt, V. E., M. Lombe, and M. A. Lindsey (2007). "Perceived Parental Behavior and Peer Affiliations among Urban African American Adolescents." *Social Work Research* 31: 163–69.

[8] Valenti, J. (2008). *He's a Stud, She's a Slut, and 49 Other Double Standards Every Woman Should Know.* Berkeley, CA: Seal Press; Siegel, D. (2007). *Sisterhood, Interrupted: From Radical Women to Girls Gone Wild.* New York: Palgrave Macmillan; McCann, C. and S. Kim (Eds.) (2009). *Feminist Theory Reader: Local and Global Perspectives.* New York: Routledge.

[9] Muehlenhard, C. L. and M. L. McCoy (2006). "Double Standard/Double Bind: The Sexual Double Standard and Women's Communication about Sex." *Psychology of Women Quarterly* 15: 447–61; Lauzen, M. M. and D. M. Dozier (2005). "Maintaining the Double Standard: Portrayals of Age and Gender in Popular Films." *Sex Roles* 52: 437–46; Thorne, B. (1994). *Gender Play: Girls and Boys in School.* New Brunswick, NJ: Rutgers University Press; Adler, P., S. J. Kless, and P. Adler (1992, July). "Socialization to Gender Roles: Popularity among Elementary School Boys and Girls." *Sociology of Education* 65: 169–87.

[10] Coalition for Juvenile Justice (2011, May). "Deinstitutionalization of Status Offenders (DSO): Facts and Resources." Retrieved from http://juvjustice.org/media/factsheets/factsheet_14.pdf

[11] Hornberger, N. G. (2010, Summer). "Improving Outcomes for Status Offenders in the JJDPA Reauthorization." *Juvenile and Family Justice Today,* p. 19. Retrieved from http://www.juvjustice.org/media/announcements/announcement_link_156.pdf

[12] Chesney-Lind, M. (1973). "Judicial Enforcement of the Female Sex Role." *Issues in Criminology* 8: 51–70.

[13] Chesney-Lind and Shelden, *Girls, Delinquency and Juvenile Justice.*

[14] Ibid., p. 98.

[15] Platt, A. (1977). *The Child Savers* (revised edition). Chicago: University of Chicago Press, p. 3.

[16] Ibid., p. 199.

[17] Shelden, R. G. (1981). "Sex Discrimination in the Juvenile Justice System: Memphis, Tennessee, 1900–1917." In M. Q. Warren (Ed.), *Comparing Male and Female Offenders*. Newbury Park, CA: Sage, p. 432.

[18] Teitelbaum, L. E. and L. J. Harris (1977). "Some Historical Perspectives on Governmental Regulation of Children and Parents." In L. E. Teitelbaum and A. R. Gough (Eds.), *Beyond Control: Status Offenders in the Juvenile Court*. Cambridge, MA: Ballinger, p. 34.

[19] Chesney-Lind, "Judicial Enforcement"; Valenti, *He's a Stud*; Freedman, E. (1981). *Their Sisters' Keepers*. Ann Arbor: University of Michigan Press.

[20] Pasko, L. (2010). "Damaged Daughters: The History of Girls' Sexuality and the Juvenile Justice System," p. 1100. *The Journal of Criminal Law & Criminology* 100(3): 1099–1130. Retrieved from http://www.law.northwestern.edu/jclc/symposium/v100/n3/1003_1099.Pasko.pdf

[21] Odem, M. E. (1995). *Delinquent Daughters: Protecting and Policing Adolescent Female Sexuality in the United States, 1885–1920*. Chapel Hill: University of North Carolina Press; Messerschmidt, J. (1987). "Feminism, Criminology, and the Rise of the Female Sex 'Delinquent,' 1880–1930." *Contemporary Crises* 11: 243–62; Schlossman, S. and S. Wallach (1978). "The Crime of Precocious Sexuality: Female Delinquency in the Progressive Era." *Harvard Educational Review* 48: 65–94.

[22] Odem, *Delinquent Daughters*; Rafter, N. H. (Ed.) (1988). *White Trash: The Eugenic Family Studies, 1899–1919*. Boston: Northeastern University Press, p. 54; Schlossman and Wallach, "The Crime of Precocious Sexuality."

[23] Odem, *Delinquent Daughters*, p. 25.

[24] Ibid., p. 81.

[25] Ibid., p. 4.

[26] Odem, M. E. and S. Schlossman (1991). "Guardians of Virtue: The Juvenile Court and Female Delinquency in Early 20th Century Los Angeles," p. 190. *Crime and Delinquency* 37(2): 186–203.

[27] Ibid., pp. 190–92.

[28] Odem, *Delinquent Daughters*, p. 128.

[29] Chesney-Lind, M. (1971). "Female Juvenile Delinquency in Hawaii." Master's thesis, University of Hawaii; Schlossman and Wallach, "The Crime of Precocious Sexuality"; Shelden, "Sex Discrimination."

[30] Schlossman and Wallach, "The Crime of Precocious Sexuality," p. 72; Shelden, "Sex Discrimination," p. 70.

[31] Knupfer, A. M. (2001). *Reform and Resistance: Gender, Delinquency, and America's First Juvenile Court*. New York: Routledge, p. 199.

[32] Bright, C. L., S. H. Decker, and A. M. Burch (2007). "Gender and Justice in the Progressive Era: An Investigation of Saint Louis Juvenile Court Cases, 1909–1912." *Justice Quarterly* 24: 657–78.

[33] Chesney-Lind, "Female Juvenile Delinquency in Hawaii."

[34] Schlossman and Wallach, "The Crime of Precocious Sexuality," p. 70.

[35] Pisciotta, A. W. (1983). "Race, Sex, and Rehabilitation: A Study of Differential Treatment in the Juvenile Reformatory, 1825–1900." *Crime and Delinquency* 29: 254–68; see also Daly, K. and M. Chesney-Lind (1988). "Feminism and Criminology." *Justice Quarterly* 5: 497–538.

[36] Pisciotta, "Race, Sex, and Rehabilitation," p. 265.

[37] Pasko, "Damaged Daughters."

[38] Tappan, P. (1947). *Delinquent Girls in Court*. New York: Columbia University Press.

[39] Ibid., p. 33.

[40] Ibid.

[41] Odem and Schlossman, "Guardians of Virtue," p. 196.

[42] Odem, *Delinquent Daughters*, p. 142.

[43] Ibid.

[44] Odem and Schlossman, "Guardians of Virtue," p. 200.

[45] Vedder, C. B. and D. B. Somerville (1970). *The Delinquent Girl*. Springfield, IL: Charles C. Thomas, p. 147.

[46] Andrews, R. H. and A. H. Cohn (1974). "Ungovernability: The Unjustifiable Jurisdiction," p. 1388. *Yale Law Journal* 83(7): 1382–1408.

[47] Ibid., p. 1404.

[48] These and other studies are summarized in Chesney-Lind and Shelden, *Girls, Delinquency and Juvenile Justice*, ch. 7.

[49] Kim, J. J. (2010). "Left Behind: The Paternalistic Treatment of Status Offenders within the Juvenile Justice System," p. 862. *Washington University Law Review* 87(4): 843–67. Retrieved from http://lawreview.wustl.edu/inprint/87/4/kim.pdf

[50] Pasko, "Damaged Daughters," p. 1108.

[51] Teilmann, K. and P. Landry (1981). "Gender Bias in Juvenile Justice." *Journal of Research in Crime and Delinquency* 18: 47–80.

[52] Hurst, H. (1975, June 20). "Juvenile Status Offenders." Speech delivered to the New Mexico Council on Crime and Delinquency, Albuquerque, p. 7. The reader can easily guess whose values were being challenged here and whose rights would be upheld.

[53] General Accounting Office (1978). *Removing Status Offenders from Secure Facilities: Federal Leadership and Guidance Are Needed*. Washington, DC: General Accounting Office, p. 10.

[54] United States House of Representatives, Committee on Education and Labor (1980). *Juvenile Justice Amendments of 1980*. Washington, DC: U.S. Government Printing Office, p. 136.

[55] U.S. Statutes at Large. Ninety-Sixth Congress, 2d session (1980, December 8). Public Law 96–509. Washington, DC: U.S. Government Printing Office.

[56] Blume, J. M. (1990). "Status of Court-Ordered Detention of Juvenile Status Offenders." Paper presented at the annual meeting of the American Society of Criminology.

[57] Costello, J. C. and N. L. Worthington (1981–82). "Incarcerating Status Offenders: Attempts to Circumvent the Juvenile Justice and Delinquency Prevention Act." *Harvard Civil Rights-Civil Liberties Law Review* 16: 42.

[58] Frazier, C. E. and D. Bishop (1990). "Gender Bias in Juvenile Justice Processing: Implications of the JJDP Act." Paper presented at the annual meeting of the Academy of Criminal Justice Sciences, Denver, p. 22.

[59] U.S. House of Representatives (1992). *Hearings on the Reauthorization of the Juvenile Justice and Delinquency Prevention Act of 1974*. Hearings before the Subcommittee on Human Resources of the Committee on Education and Labor. One Hundred and Second Congress, Serial No. 102–125. Washington, DC: U.S. Government Printing Office.

[60] Ibid., p. 2.

[61] Ibid.

[62] Public Law 102-586–November 1992.

[63] Girls, Incorporated (1996). *Prevention and Parity: Girls in Juvenile Justice*. Indianapolis: Girls, Incorporated National Resource Center, p. 26.

[64] United States House of Representatives, *Hearings*, p. 4998.

[65] Moeller, M. (2011, February). "Reauthorizing the Juvenile Justice and Delinquency Prevention Act: The Impact on Latino Youth." Retrieved from http://www.njjn.org/media/resources/public/resource_1712.pdf; Education and the Workforce Committee (2010). "Reforming the Juvenile Justice System to Improve Children's Lives and Public Safety." Retrieved from http://edworkforce.house.gov/Calendar/EventSingle.aspx?EventID=193080

[66] Bilchik, S. and E. Pinheiro (2010). "What the JJDPA Means for Lawyers Representing Juvenile Status Offenders." In American Bar Association, *Representing Juvenile Status Offenders*, p. 6. Retrieved from http://www.americanbar.org/content/dam/aba/migrated/child/PublicDocuments/rjso_chapter1.authcheckdam.pdf

67 Shelden, R. G. (1998). "Confronting the Ghost of Mary Ann Crouse: Gender Bias within the Justice System." *Juvenile and Family Court Journal* 49: 11–25; Faludi, S. (1991). *Backlash: The Undeclared War against Women*. New York: Crown; Connell, R. W. (1987). *Gender and Power*. Palo Alto, CA: Stanford University Press; Lerner, G. (1986). *The Creation of Patriarchy*. New York: Oxford University Press; Fuentes, A. and B. Ehrenreich (1983). *Women in the Global Factory*. Boston: South End Press.

68 Pasko, "Damaged Daughters," p. 1112.

69 Puzzanchera, C., B. Adams, and M. Sickmund (2010). *Juvenile Court Statistics 2006–2007*. Pittsburgh: National Center for Juvenile Justice, p. 82. Retrieved from http://www.ojjdp.gov/ojstatbb/njcda/pdf/jcs2007.pdf

70 Kapur, T. D. (2010, Fall). "Status Offender Systems Reform in Louisiana and Washington State." Vera Institute of Justice. Retrieved from http://www.vera.org/blog/status-offender-systems-reform-louisiana-and-washington

71 Federal Bureau of Investigation (2010). *Crime in the United States, 2009*. Retrieved from http://www2.fbi.gov/ucr/cius2009/data/table_33.html

72 Elliott, D. and H. L. Voss (1974). *Delinquency and Dropout*. Lexington, MA: Lexington Books, pp. 84–87.

73 Monahan, T. P. (1970). "Police Dispositions of Juvenile Offenders." *Phylon* 31: 139.

74 Visher, C. A. (1983). "Gender, Police Arrest Decisions, and Notions of Chivalry." *Criminology* 21: 5–28.

75 Ibid., pp. 15, 22–23.

76 Girls Study Group (2008). *Violence by Teenage Girls: Trends and Context*. Washington, DC: OJJDP, p. 6. Retrieved from http://www.ncjrs.gov/pdffiles1/ojjdp/218905.pdf

77 Farrington, D. P., D. Jolliffe, J. D. Hawkins, R. F. Catalano, K. G. Hill, and R. Kosterman (2010). "Why Are Boys More Likely to Be Referred to Juvenile Court? Gender Differences in Official and Self-Reported Delinquency." *Victims and Offenders* 5: 25–44.

78 Sealock, M. D. and S. S. Simpson (1998). "Unraveling Bias in Arrest Decisions: The Role of Juvenile Offender Type-Scripts." *Justice Quarterly* 15: 417–57; see also Donley, R. M. (2007). "Girls in the Juvenile Justice System." Master's Thesis, Marshall University. http://www.marshall.edu/etd/masters/donley-ryan-2007-ma.pdf.

79 Hornberger, N. G. (2010, Summer). "Improving Outcomes for Status Offenders in the JJDPA Reauthorization." *Juvenile and Family Justice Today*, p. 18. Retrieved from http://www.juvjustice.org/media/announcements/announcement_link_156.pdf

80 Puzzanchera et al., *Juvenile Court Statistics 2006–2007*, p. 12.

81 Ibid., p. 77.

82 Sickmund, M., T. J. Sladky, and W. Kang (2011). "Census of Juveniles in Residential Placement Databook: Detailed Offense Profile by Sex (column percent)." Retrieved from http://www.ojjdp.gov/ojstatbb/ezacjrp/asp/Offense_Sex.asp?state=0&topic=Offense_Sex&year=2007&percent=column

83 Shelden, R. G. (1987). "The Chronic Delinquent: Gender and Racial Differences." Paper presented at the annual meeting of the American Society of Criminology, Montreal.

84 Maschi, T., C. S. Schwalbeb, K. Morgenc, S. Gibsond, and N. M. Violette (2009). "Exploring the Influence of Gender on Adolescents' Service Needs and Service Pathways." *Children and Youth Services Review* 31: 257–64.

85 Teilmann and Landry, "Gender Bias in Juvenile Justice," p. 47.

86 See Chesney-Lind and Shelden, *Girls, Delinquency and Juvenile Justice*, ch. 7, for a review of this research and relevant citations.

87 Mahoney, A. R. and C. Fenster (1982). "Female Delinquents in a Suburban Court." In N. Rafter and E. Stanko (Eds.), *Judge, Lawyer, Victim, Thief*. Boston: Northeastern University Press.

88 Curran, D. (1984). "The Myth of the New Female Delinquent." *Crime and Delinquency* 30: 386–99.

[89] Shelden, R. G. and J. Horvath (1986). "Processing Offenders in a Juvenile Court: A Comparison of Male and Female Offenders." Paper presented at the annual meeting of the Western Society of Criminology, Newport Beach, California.

[90] Mann, C. (1979). "The Differential Treatment between Runaway Boys and Girls in Juvenile Court." *Juvenile and Family Court Journal* 30: 37–48.

[91] Freiburger, T. L. and A. Burke (2011, March 15). "Status Offenders in the Juvenile Court: The Effects of Gender, Race, and Ethnicity on the Adjudication Decision." *Youth Violence and Juvenile Justice*. doi:1541204011399933.

[92] Moore, L. D. and I. Padavic (2010). "Racial and Ethnic Disparities in Girls' Sentencing in the Juvenile Justice System." *Feminist Criminology,* 5: 263–85. See also M. J. Leiber, S. J. Brubaker, and K. C. Fox (2009, October). "A Closer Look at the Individual and Joint Effects of Gender and Race on Juvenile Justice Decision Making." *Feminist Criminology* 4: 333–58.

[93] Datesman, S. and M. Aickin (1984). "Offense Specialization and Escalation among Status Offenders." *Journal of Criminal Law and Criminology* 75: 1246–75; Shelden, R. G., J. Horvath, and S. Tracy (1989). "Do Status Offenders Get Worse? Some Clarifications on the Question of Escalation." *Crime and Delinquency* 35: 202–16.

[94] Sagatun, I. J. (1989). "Gender Biases in Probation Officers: Attributions of Juvenile Delinquency." *International Journal of Offender Therapy and Comparative Criminology* 33: 131–40; see also Mallicoat, S. L. (2007). "Gendered Justice: Attributional Differences between Males and Females in the Juvenile Courts." *Feminist Criminology* 2: 4–30.

[95] Horn, R. and M. Evans (2000). "The Effect of Gender on Pre-Sentence Reports." *The Howard Journal* 39: 184–97.

[96] N. T. Carr, K. Hudson, R. S. Hanks, and A. N. Hunt (2008, January). "Gender Effects along the Juvenile Justice System: Evidence of a Gendered Organization." *Feminist Criminology* 3: 25–43.

[97] Feld, B. (1990). "Justice by Geography: Urban, Suburban, and Rural Variations in Juvenile Justice Administration." *The Journal of Criminal Law and Criminology* 82: 156–210.

[98] Ibid., p. 209.

[99] American Bar Association (2001). *Justice by Gender.* Chicago: American Bar Association.

[100] Ibid., p. 20.

[101] Southern Poverty Law Center (2003). Mississippi Youth Justice Project. http://www.splcenter.org/what-we-do/children-at-risk/mississippi-youth-justice-project. The specific lawsuit is *J.A. v. Barbour et al.* http://www.splcenter.org/get-informed/case-docket/ja-et-al-v-barbour-et-al; the reference to the Columbia Training school is found in a report to the governor of Mississippi found on this website: http://www.splcenter.org/sites/default/files/legacy/images/dynamic/main/report/6/oak_colu_miss_findinglet.pdf

[102] Miller, J. (1994). "Race, Gender and Juvenile Justice: An Examination of Disposition Decision-Making for Delinquent Girls." In M. D. Schwartz and D. Milovanovic (Eds.), *The Intersection of Race, Gender and Class in Criminology.* New York: Garland Press, p. 11.

[103] Ibid, p. 18.

[104] Ibid, p. 20.

[105] Robinson, R. (1990). "Violations of Girlhood: A Qualitative Study of Female Delinquents and Children in Need of Services in Massachusetts." Ph.D. dissertation, Brandeis University.

[106] This is why it is very important to consider the *context* of every offense. Technically speaking, this is an index crime called "motor vehicle theft" and will be included along with more serious actions such as stealing a car and stripping it down to sell the parts, which would be part of an ongoing car theft ring. The reader should always be cautious when interpreting the labels that are used, like "felon." In this case, the girl is technically a "felon."

[107] Robinson, "Violations of Girlhood," p. 202.

[108] Ryan, J. P., D. Herz, P. M. Hernandez, and J. M. Marshall (2007). "Maltreatment and Delinquency: Investigating Child Welfare Bias in Juvenile Justice Processing." *Children and Youth Services Review* 29: 1035–50.

[109] Males, M. (2004, July 8). Testimony to San Francisco Board of Supervisors on Disproportionate Arrest/Confinement of African-American Young Women for Drug Offenses.

[110] Guevara, L., D. Herz, and C. Spohn (2006). "Gender and Juvenile Justice Decision Making: What Role Does Race Play." *Feminist Criminology* 1: 258–82.

[111] Human Rights Watch/ACLU (2006, September 24). *Custody and Control: Conditions of Confinement in New York's Juvenile Prisons for Girls.* Retrieved from http://www.hrw.org/en/node/11152/section/7

[112] Pasko, "Damaged Daughters," p. 1129.

SOME SENSIBLE SOLUTIONS

> We can't solve problems by using the same kind of thinking we used when we created them.
>
> —Albert Einstein

It has become evident that many—if not most—traditional approaches to the prevention and treatment of delinquency have not fared too well. It is time to "think outside the box." After almost 40 years of studying and teaching the subject of crime and delinquency I am convinced that some very fundamental changes need to be made in the way we live and think before we see any significant decrease in problems. Adults have referred to the "problems" with youths for centuries with such value-laden questions as "what's wrong with kids these days?"[1]

We Need a New Paradigm

In 1962, Thomas Kuhn wrote *The Structure of Scientific Revolutions,* which presented his argument that scientific advancement consists of a "series of peaceful interludes punctuated by intellectually violent revolutions" that lead to replacing one conceptual view of the world with another. He described how scientists move from disdain through doubt to acceptance of a new theory and detailed the effect of social and psychological factors on science.

When the prevailing paradigm cannot provide an explanation for anomalies that occur, there can be a crisis in the paradigm itself. Sometimes dramatic shifts in the thinking about a phenomenon create scientific revolutions. Classic examples include the discoveries of Copernicus who challenged the conventional paradigm of viewing the sun revolving around the earth, Darwin's work on evolution, the work of Isaac Newton and Galileo, and in the field of linguistics the work of Noam Chomsky (often called the "Chomskian Revolution"). The development of Renaissance Humanism and the Reformation also come to mind. More recent examples include the Human Genome Project.

The prevailing paradigm runs into a brick wall when it cannot answer the questions being asked or provide solutions for pressing problems. Einstein's quotation above identifies that type of crisis. The answers to difficult questions must come from a totally different way of thinking—from people who think outside the box.

The myopic view that youths are the only ones who need to change is usually accompanied with various labels that clearly describe the source of the problem. The labels keep changing, along with changing times. As Jerome Miller has noted, we began with *possessed* youths in the seventeenth century, moved to the *dangerous classes* in the eighteenth and late nineteenth centuries, and to the *constitutional psychopathic inferiors* of the early twentieth century. We continued in the twentieth century with the *psychopath* of the 1940s, the *sociopath* of the 1950s, the *compulsive* delinquent, the *unsocialized aggressive*, and finally the *bored* delinquent. "With the growth of professionalism, the number of labels has multiplied exponentially."[2]

Miller asserts that the problem with these labels is that they maintain the existing order, buffering it from threats that might arise from its own internal contradictions. They reassure

> that the fault lies in the warped offender and takes everyone else off the hook. Moreover, it enables the professional diagnostician to enter the scene or withdraw at will, wearing success like a halo and placing failure around the neck of the client like a noose.[3]

More importantly, the labels reinforce the belief that harsh punishment works, especially the kind of punishment that includes some form of incarceration, so that the offender is placed out of sight and, not coincidentally, out of mind.

A recurring problem in juvenile justice reform—and with other reforms—is that after all the political maneuvering, the end result is that nothing changes or the changes are cosmetic. Daniel Macallair and Mike Males reviewed reforms in San Francisco.

> Despite the city's investment in juvenile justice reform from 1996–1999 there is no evidence of *system* change. Instead it appears that new services and programs were simply marginalized. Marginalization occurs when new programs are designed as simple *adjuncts to current operations*, rather than intended to replace core system elements.[4]

As noted in chapter 1, we continue to succumb to the "edifice complex." We love to build these "edifices," no matter what they are called. Perhaps it is because politicians like to point to a permanent structure as a legacy that they have done something about crime. Or perhaps these buildings—whether a new juvenile detention center, a new prison, a new correctional center, a new police station, a new courthouse, etc.—are a profitable part of the huge "crime control industry."

I believe otherwise. I believe that we need to quit looking solely at the "troubled youth" or "criminals" as the source of the problem. It is time that those of us among the more privileged sectors of society consider that we too contribute to the problem; perhaps we are the primary contributors. A change in paradigms was actually suggested almost 40 years ago by sociologist Edwin Schur. His views certainly have relevance today.

Radical Nonintervention

Chapter 7 discussed the labeling perspective. One of the best illustrations of the labeling perspective as it applies to delinquency was *Radical Nonintervention: Rethinking the Delinquency Problem*, written by Edwin Schur.[5] His approach seemed quite novel in 1973 when he challenged a number of previously unchallenged assumptions about the problem of delinquency. I believe that his approach has even more relevance in today's punitive climate.

Resurrecting an Old Perspective

Schur noted that the traditional response to delinquent behavior was that the system needed improvement. Thus, more facilities were built, accompanied by elaborate studies of cost-benefit and systems analyses.[6] Whether or not the system has improved, it is certainly much larger and making more arrests than ever before. Obviously something different is needed to stem this growth and to provide better solutions for at-risk youths.

Schur outlined five general proposals.[7]

1. *"There is a need for a thorough reassessment of the dominant ways of thinking about youth 'problems.'"* Schur maintained that many, if not most, behaviors youth engage in (including many labeled as "delinquent") are "part and parcel of our social and cultural system" and that "misconduct" among youth is inevitable within any form of social order. We pay a huge price, he charged, for criminalizing much of this behavior.

2. *"Some of the most valuable policies for dealing with delinquency are not necessarily those designated as delinquency policies."* Addressing education needs, mental-health issues, and poverty/inequality could have a larger impact on delinquency than many of the legal sanctions currently enacted.

3. *"We must take young people more seriously if we are to eradicate injustice to juveniles."* Schur notes that many young people lack a sound attachment to conventional society (one of Hirschi's "social bonds"; see chapter 7). In conjunction with addressing the inequalities noted above, we need to build more respect for young people into our culture. The lack of respect that Schur noted seems to be even greater today, marked by conflicting feelings of fear and admiration toward young people. Policies such as "leave no child behind" is evidence of the latter; increasing punishments for relatively minor offenses under "zero tolerance" policies is evidence of the former.

4. *"The juvenile justice system should concern itself less with the problems of so-called 'delinquents,' and more with dispensing justice."* Schur was talking specifically about narrowing the jurisdiction of the juvenile court, specifically over status offenses. Little did Schur realize the extent to which net widening would occur in the intervening years. While status offenders have been diverted from the juvenile justice system, many have also been returned through bootstrapping or VCO exceptions (see chapter 13).

5. *"As juvenile justice moves in new directions, a variety of approaches will con-tinue to be useful."* Schur specifically suggested approaches such as pre-vention programs that have a community focus plus programs that are voluntary and noninstitutional in nature. One such approach is the Detention Diversion Advocacy Project (DDAP) discussed below.

An Assessment of Schur's Ideas

As already indicated, much of what Schur articulated four decades ago remains relevant today, as does the labeling approach itself. The juvenile justice system extends far too broadly into the lives of children and adolescents. Mike Males has made this point perhaps more forcefully that most others when he accuses criminologists and public policy makers of blaming kids for most ills of society while ignoring the damage done by adults (see chapter 3).[8]

One of the questions posed by the labeling perspective is: why are certain acts labeled criminal or delinquent while others are not? Another pertinent question is: how do we account for differential rates of arrest, referral to court, detention, adjudication, and commitment based on race and class? Also, why do we overburden juvenile court workers with dealing with behavior that would not be criminal if committed by an adult? Why criminalize adolescent behavior like disturbing the peace and minor altercations? (One may reason-ably ask: Whose peace is being disturbed?) These are not merely academic questions; the lives of real people are impacted by policies that ignore such questions and focus only on punishment.

We continue to criminalize behavior that should be dealt with informally, outside of the formal juvenile justice system. Criminalizing truancy has always puzzled me. Why take formal police action because a child is not going to school? Certainly, children should stay in school, because an education is a pre-requisite for a decent life. Why use the immense power of the state to enforce compliance? Likewise, kids should obey the reasonable demands of their par-ents, but families should be left alone to figure things out for themselves. There is no need for state involvement in private family matters, unless some direct physical or other obvious harms are being committed. As noted several times throughout this book, zero-tolerance policies have labeled youths as delin-quent or worse for behavior that formerly would have been ignored or handled informally without the policies.

Intervention Typologies

Prevention and intervention strategies come in many different forms. In understanding where to go from here it may be helpful to distinguish among different types of interventions. One of the most comprehensive overviews of delinquency prevention programs is provided by Joy Dryfoos.[9] She addresses four interrelated problems: delinquency, teen pregnancy, drug abuse, and school failure. Her review of the research found that the majority of prevention programs fall into one of three broad categories: (1) early childhood and family interventions, (2) school-based interventions, and (3) community-based and/ or multicomponent interventions. Programs that fall within the early childhood and family intervention category include two major types: (1) preschool/ Head Start programs and (2) parent training/support programs. Programs found within the school-based intervention category include three main types: (1) curricula, (2) organization of school (teacher training, school team, and alternative schools), and (3) special services (counseling and mentoring programs, health services, and volunteer work). Community-based interventions include three main types: (1) school–community collaboration programs, (2) community education, and (3) multicomponent comprehensive programs.

Several recent studies have confirmed the success of early intervention programs like Head Start and similar preschool programs. A longitudinal study of a Head Start program in Ypsilanti, Michigan, followed participants to the age of 40 and found success, as measured by higher income and lower involvement in the criminal justice system.[10] A longitudinal study of a preschool intervention program in Chicago of more than 1,500 low-income youths (93% of whom were African American) found that there were significant reductions in not only the incidence of delinquency but its frequency and severity by age 18.[11] The most comprehensive research was a "meta-analysis" of 123 comparative studies of early childhood interventions. Positive effects were found for children who attend a preschool program prior to entering kindergarten. The most significant impact was on the children's cognitive behaviors, social skills, and school progress, all of which are correlated with reduced rates of delinquency.[12]

Components of Successful Programs

Programs should target medium- to high-risk youths with intensive, multifaceted approaches that focus on the development of social skills (for example, conflict resolution) and address the attitudes, values, and beliefs that reinforce antisocial behaviors. Ideally, the community should offer alternatives to activities and associations (such as gangs) that could lead to delinquent or criminal behavior. Recreational programs, after-school events, and jobs allow juveniles to spend their time on enjoyable and rewarding pursuits. Programs should model alternatives to criminal styles of thinking, feeling, and acting and provide explicit reinforcement for positive choices. Programs that focus on families and schools promote bonding with those institutions. Programs staffed with well-trained, skilled individuals who have developed empathy and an understanding of a youth subculture are more likely to be well received. Link programs with the world of work to assist youths in developing job skills. The goals of the program should be specific and culminate in some kind of award (for example, a diploma). It is important to recognize that relapse is normal (whether we are dealing with drug or alcohol abuse or any pattern of negative antisocial behavior) and that treatment is a continual process rather than a single episode.

In short, the programs that succeed in helping the children and families . . . are intensive, comprehensive, and flexible. . . . Their climate is created by skilled, committed professionals who establish respectful and trusting relationships and respond to the individual needs of those they serve.[13]

In a meta-analysis of research on interventions with juveniles, Mark
Lipsey found that the most successful programs had a therapeutic intervention
philosophy serving high-risk offenders with high quality implementation.[14]
Lipsey grouped evaluations into seven categories: counseling, deterrence, discipline, multiple coordinated services, restorative programs, skill building,
and surveillance. Comparing the effects, he found that interventions based on
punishment and deterrence appeared to increase criminal recidivism, whereas
therapeutic approaches based on counseling, skill building and multiple services had the greatest impact in reducing further criminal behavior. Cognitive
behavioral skill-building approaches were more effective in reducing further
criminal behavior than any other intervention. The Missouri Model, discussed
below, has been highly successful and employs the elements Lipsey identified
as most effective.

A Blueprint for Juvenile Justice Reform

Recently an organization called the Youth Transition Funders Group, consisting of academics, practitioners, city and county agencies, nonprofits and
foundations came together and wrote a series of recommendations that they
called a "blueprint" for the reform of the juvenile justice system. After a review
of the existing system and its problems they concluded that "No experience
may be more predictive of future adult difficulty than having been confined in
a secure juvenile facility." They also noted that "The time is ripe to fundamentally change the juvenile justice landscape." With this in mind they identified
nine tenets for improved outcomes.[15]

1. Reduce Institutionalization
2. Reduce Racial Disparity
3. Ensure Access to Quality Counsel
4. Create a Range of Community-Based Programs
5. Recognize and Serve Youth with Specialized Needs
6. Create Smaller Rehabilitative Institutions
7. Improve Aftercare and Reentry
8. Maximize Youth, Family and Community Participation
9. Keep Youth Out of Adult Prisons

Within this document several model programs were cited to serve as examples. One was Missouri, a state that has been in the forefront of modern juvenile justice reform movements and one whose practices are being copied all
over the country.

Missouri's Model System of Juvenile Justice

Like most other states, Missouri had a history of confining young offenders in large institutions. Starting in the 1980s they began experimenting with regionally based, smaller facilities. Over the years the Missouri system has been the recipient of constant praise from all over the United States. It has been written about in the *New York Times, USA Today, Los Angeles Times* and *Huffington Post*, among other media outlets.[16] An editorial in the *New York Times* stated:

> With the prisons filled to bursting, state governments are desperate for ways to keep more people from committing crimes and ending up behind bars. Part of the problem lies in the juvenile justice system, which is doing a frighteningly effective job of turning nonviolent childhood offenders into mature, hardened criminals. States that want to change that are increasingly looking to Missouri, which has turned its juvenile justice system into a nationally recognized model of how to deal effectively with troubled children.[17]

Many other states, including Florida, Illinois, Louisiana, and California, as well as the District of Columbia, have followed Missouri's lead. The Missouri Division of Youth Services (DYS) won the 2008 Annie E. Casey Innovations Award in Children and Family System Reform, awarded by the Ash Institute for Democratic Governance and Innovation at Harvard Kennedy School.[18]

Missouri has an agency-wide commitment to helping troubled youth change their antisocial, self-destructive behaviors and to prepare them to return to their communities and to continue their pathways to success. Youths are confined in small facilities located near their homes and families. In most states, youths are sent to institutions housing more than 150 juveniles. DYS has 32 residential programs; the largest has 50 beds. The seven secure facilities have 36 or fewer residents. DYS divided Missouri into five regions. Each has 4 levels of programs: community (nonresidential) care for the least serious offenders; group homes housing 10–12 less serious offenders; moderate security facilities with 20–50 youths; and secure facilities.

DYS uses the case-management approach to develop a unique treatment plan for each youth.[19] Everyone is assigned to a group of 10–12. The youths together, eat together, study together, exercise together, and attend daily treatment sessions together. The treatment process is enhanced by remaining with the same group and encouraging members to trust and feel responsible toward one another. The rooms at all levels are carpeted and resemble those in college dormitories—no concrete cells. "There is no barbed wire around facilities like Missouri Hills, on the outskirts of St. Louis. No more than 10 youths and 2 adults called facilitators live in cottage-style dormitories in a wooded setting, a far cry from the quasi penitentiaries in other states. When someone becomes unruly, the other youths are trained to talk him down."[20]

The Missouri program emphasizes keeping youths safe physically and emotionally. It eliminates ridicule and emotional abuse through constant staff supervision and positive peer relationships. Coercion and demeaning treatment are not part of the process. The youths spend 6 hours each day on education; each group has its own teacher. Staff members work to help youths develop self-awareness and communication skills—critical to future success. Missouri recruits family members as partners in the treatment process and for success after release—rather than treating them as the source of the delinquency. There is intensive support and supervision to help youths transition to life outside the facility. There is intensive aftercare planning before release and close monitoring and mentoring after release.

The core DYS philosophy is that every young person wants to—and can—succeed. The hunger for approval, acceptance, and achievement is universal. "No matter how serious their past crimes, and no matter how destructive their current attitudes and behaviors, DYS considers every young person a work in progress. Each is redeemable and deserves help."[21]

> The three most important DYS beliefs are: (1) that all people—including delinquent youth—desire to do well and succeed; (2) that with the right kinds of help, all youth can (and most will) make lasting behavioral changes and succeed; and (3) that the mission of youth corrections must be to provide the right kinds of help, consistent with public safety, so that young people make needed changes and move on to successful and law-abiding adult lives.[22]

Delinquent youth can't be reformed through a military-style treatment, and few will be deterred from crime by fear of punishment. "Rather, change can only result from internal choices made by the young people themselves—choices to adopt more positive behaviors, seek out more positive peers, and embrace more positive goals."[23]

Missouri built a unique youth corrections model focused on fostering the personal growth of adjudicated youth in small, supportive facilities rather than confining them in large, impersonal prisons. The DYS advisory board faced perhaps its most difficult challenge in the mid-1990s. As discussed throughout this text, that was the height of fear about a juvenile crime wave based on isolated, high-profile cases. States endorsed "adult time for adult crime." While juvenile crime actually declined during this period, the vast majority of states passed laws that mandated punishment for juveniles in adult prisons. Many state legislators in Missouri made similar demands, but DYS worked with groups in the legislature and the governor's office to preserve its treatment approach. "Rather than widespread transfers to criminal court, the legislature created the blended sentence alternative, which gives DYS the opportunity to retain custody and treat serious youth offenders—and to void adult prison sentences for those who respond well to DYS treatment."[24]

Cynthia Osborne studied the Missouri youth corrections model intensively. She cautions that specific ideas, strategies, and practices are not the key. Any system seeking to change and replicate the success in Missouri "must relinquish the traditional correctional values of punishment and slowly grow a new system rooted in the values of treatment, compassion, and accountability. Practices cannot produce good results when used apart from the values."[25] Missouri has refined and revised its approach over three decades; the process in other states may be slow and painstaking and requires concentrating on four areas: (1) everyone in the organization must embrace the core values and beliefs; (2) operationalizing those core values requires changes in facilities, staffing, treatment programs, and organizational structure; (3) to avoid drifting back to previously accepted standards, administrators must hire educated personnel who believe in the core values and train them to be effective in working with youths; there must also be accountability procedures and all procedures must be transparent; and (4) the program must be supported by key constituencies in state government, courts, and communities, and employees must work to cultivate and sustain that support.

The case management approach incorporated in the Missouri model is the foundation of the Detention Diversion Advocacy Project in San Francisco.

The Detention Diversion Advocacy Project

If diversion is to work effectively, it is of paramount importance that *youths truly be diverted from the system itself.* This becomes especially important when dealing with the continual problem of overcrowding within the detention system of the juvenile justice system. If a particular detention center (or any other correctional center) is plagued by chronic overcrowding, then the obvious solution is to either (1) increase the space available (e.g., add rooms to the current structure or build a new one) or (2) remove a certain percentage from the correctional system in question and deal with them in an alternative program.

The Center on Juvenile and Criminal Justice (CJCJ) in San Francisco, California, developed the original Detention Diversion Advocacy Project (DDAP) in 1993. The program's major goals are to reduce the number of youth in court-ordered detention and to provide them with culturally relevant community-based services and supervision. Youths selected for the program would likely have been detained pending their adjudication—youths destined for what Jerome Miller calls the deep end of the juvenile justice system.[26] This is a very important aspect of the program. By focusing on *detained* youth, the project ensures that it is a true diversion alternative; it is not an example of widening the net to ensnare lower-level offenders. Youths are screened by DDAP staff to determine if they are likely to be detained and whether they present an acceptable risk to the community. DDAP provides an intensive level of community-based monitoring and advocacy. The program has been replicated in two other parts of the country (Washington, D.C., and Montgomery County, Maryland).

Disposition case advocacy, the type of approach used in this program, has been defined as "the efforts of lay persons or nonlegal experts acting on behalf of youthful offenders at disposition hearings."[27] It is based in part on the more general concept of case management that has been defined as a "client-level strategy for promoting the coordination of human services, opportunities, or benefits." Case management seeks two major outcomes: (1) "the integration of services across a cluster of organizations" and (2) continuity of care.[28] The main focus of case management is to develop a network of human services that integrates the development of client skills and the involvement of different social networks and multiple service providers.

DDAP was designed to accomplish the following goals: (1) provide multi-level interventions to divert youth from secure detention facilities; (2) demonstrate that community-based interventions are an effective alternative to secure custody and that the needs of both the youths and the community can be met at a cost savings to the public; and (3) reduce disproportionate minority incarceration.[29] There are two primary components.

1. ***Detention Advocacy:*** This component involves identifying youth likely to be detained pending their adjudication. Once a potential client is identified, DDAP case managers present a release plan to the judge. The plan includes a list of appropriate community services that will be accessed on the youth's behalf. Additionally, the plan includes specified objectives as a means to evaluate the youth's progress while in the program. Emphasis is placed on maintaining the youth at home. If the home is not a viable option, the project staff will identify and secure a suitable alternative. If the plan is deemed acceptable by a judge, the youth is released to DDAP's supervision.

2. ***Case Management:*** The case management model provides frequent and consistent support and supervision to youth and their families. The purpose of case management is to link youths to community-based services and to closely monitor their progress. Case management services are "field oriented," requiring the case manager to have *daily contact* with the youth, his or her family, and significant others. Contact includes a minimum of three in-person meetings a week. Additional services are provided to the youth's family members, particularly parents and guardians, in areas such as securing employment, day care, drug treatment services, and income support.

Clients are primarily identified through referrals from the public defender's office, the probation department, community agencies, and parents. As noted above, admission to DDAP is restricted to youths currently held, or likely to be held, in secure detention. The youths selected are those deemed to be "high risk" in terms of their chance of engaging in subsequent criminal activity (based on a risk assessment instrument developed by the National Council on Crime and Delinquency). Qualification for participation in the project is based on whether youths can reside in the community under supervision without unreasonable risk and on their likelihood of attending court hearings. This is similar in principle to what occurs in the adult system when someone is released on bail pending his or her court hearings.

Client screening involves gathering background information from probation reports, psychological evaluations, police reports, school reports, and other pertinent documents. Interviews are conducted with youths, family members, and adult professionals to determine the types of services required. Once a potential client is evaluated, case managers design individualized community service plans that address a wide range of personal and social needs, including linguistic or medical needs. DDAP staff presents a comprehensive community service plan at the detention hearing and requests that the judge release the youth to DDAP custody.

DDAP staff monitor both the youth's participation and the quality of services provided. Using multiple service providers helps to insure that the project represents and addresses the needs of the various communities within San Francisco in the most culturally appropriate manner. Historically, youth services in San Francisco have been fragmented by ethnicity, race, and community. DDAP is trying a more unified approach. It has become a neutral site within the city, staffed by representatives from CJCJ and several other community-based service agencies.

More specific goals include: (1) ensuring that a high proportion of the program clients are not rearrested while participating in the program; (2) achieving a high court reappearance rate; (3) reducing the population of the Youth Guidance Center; (4) reducing the proportion of minority youths in detention. Currently, the Youth Guidance Center is the only place of detention in the city. It has a capacity of 137, but the daily population typically ranges from 140–150. The average length of stay is around 11–12 days.

The author conducted an evaluation of DDAP which consisted of comparing a group of youths referred to DDAP with a similarly matched control group that remained within the juvenile justice system.[30] The results showed that after a three-year follow-up, the recidivism rate for the DDAP group was 34%, compared to a 60% rate for the control group. Detailed comparisons holding several variables constant (e.g., prior record, race, age, gender, etc.) and examining several different measures of recidivism (e.g., subsequent commitments, referrals for violent offenses) showed that the DDAP youths still had a significantly lower recidivism rate.

There are several reasons for the success of this program. First, the caseloads of the DDAP caseworkers are extremely low in comparison to the caseloads of probation officers. The DDAP workers average about 10 cases each. Regular probation officers in major urban areas have caseloads ranging from 50 to 150. Smaller caseloads mean more quality time with clients *in the field* (e.g., in their homes, on the street corners, at school), rather than visits to an office with interruptions of phone calls and other bureaucratic chores.

Second, DDAP is a program that is "out of the mainstream" of the juvenile justice system. As a true alternative program, rather than one of many bureaucratic extensions of the system, normal bureaucratic restrictions do not generally apply. For instance, the qualifications for being a caseworker with DDAP are not as strict as you might find within the juvenile justice system (e.g., age restrictions, educational requirements, arrest records, "street" experience, etc.). In casual observations of some of these caseworkers, I was impressed with their dedication and their passion for helping youths. Moreover, the backgrounds of these workers were similar to the backgrounds of some of their clients (e.g., similar race, neighborhood of origins, language, etc.).

Third, the physical location of DDAP is "user friendly," lacking the forbidding appearance of the formal system. There are no bars, no concrete buildings, no devices for screening for weapons as you enter the building, no "cells" for "lockdown," etc. Further, the DDAP workers are not "officers of the court" with powers of arrest, and they do not don the usual accoutrements of such occupations (e.g., badges, guns).

There could also be a possible fourth explanation—speculative at this time because the data are insufficient. It could be that given the low caseloads, DDAP caseworkers are more likely than regular probation officers to be "on top of the case," that is, to be in constant contact with the youth and thus able to sidetrack potential problems. If a police officer learns that a youth in a possible arrest situation is a DDAP case, he or she may contact the caseworker, who might be able to persuade the officer that the situation could be handled without a formal arrest. We do not know whether this occurs with any degree of regularity. If it did, it would be a positive sign, since youths from more privileged backgrounds often reap such benefits. Many a youth has been saved the stigma of formal juvenile processing by an intervention of significant adults in their lives.

Since this evaluation was completed, DDAP has expanded into several new locations, notably in Baltimore, Washington, DC, and Philadelphia. An evaluation was conducted on the program in Philadelphia, also showing positive results.[31]

I followed my initial evaluation with a closer look at how girls fared in this program. About one-fifth of the sampled cases were girls, so there were sufficient numbers to draw some conclusions. In general, the recidivism rates for the girls in DDAP pretty much paralleled those for the boys. Specifically, 30% of the DDAP girls were recidivists, compared to 48% of the girls in the control group. Although this difference was not statistically significant, further analysis found that the control group was far more likely to have two or more subsequent referrals (43.5% versus 11.6%). In other words, while the overall recidivism rates were not statistically significant (including no differences as far as serious and minor recidivists are concerned), it appears that the DDAP girls had only one subsequent appearance in court, if they returned at all.[32]

Models for Change

The John D. and Catherine T. MacArthur Foundation supports Models for Change—programs for juvenile justice reform that "accelerate progress toward a more effective, fair, and developmentally sound system that holds young people accountable for their actions, provides for their rehabilitation, protects them from harm, increases their life chances, and manages the risk they pose to themselves and to the public."[33] Programs have been initiated in Illinois, Pennsylvania, Louisiana, and Washington.

Redeploy Illinois

Redeploy Illinois began in 2005. The program provides financial assistance to counties that reduce by 25% the number of juveniles they commit to state facilities. State funds are used to provide counseling, substance abuse and mental health treatment, life skills education, cognitive therapies, and other direct services to young offenders in their communities. Illinois saved more than $9 million in 2010 by diverting 184 juveniles away from expensive incarceration inside state youth prisons. In the six years of its existence, Redeploy Illinois has diverted almost 800 youth from commitment to the Illinois Department of Juvenile Justice. The chair of the Illinois Juvenile Justice Commission, a retired judge, said:

> The $2.5 million the state devotes annually to Redeploy Illinois will more than pay for itself by more than threefold, and we can't even measure the positive impact on the lives of these young people and the improved public safety for their communities.... Without Redeploy Illinois, those youth could easily have gone to prison and returned home as nothing more than better criminals. Redeploy Illinois gave them a chance to escape the likelihood of an adult life revolving in and out of the adult prison system.[34]

There are eight Redeploy sites in Illinois. The average reduction in youths diverted from commitment was 53%.[35]

Pennsylvania Academic and Career/Technical Training (PACTT)

Annually, Philadelphia communities experienced the return of 1,300 youths who had been committed to residential placements for delinquency. Usually one-third of them were returned to facilities within six months. Philadelphia was by no means unique.

> Each year, as many as 100,000 young people return to their home communities following periods of residential placement in delinquency institutions. In general, their prospects are grim. Besides all the other strikes against them (they suffer disproportionately from mental illness, they are often alcohol and drug-dependent, their families tend to be fragile and their neighborhoods distressed, etc.), returning youth have too often burned their bridges to school, and lack the skills, credentials, and connections needed to access the legal job market. And their median age is 17.[36]

The cycle of reentry failure prompted the Reintegration Initiative, an ambitious multi-agency collaboration that worked to change almost everything about how youths released from placement were reconnected to their communities.

Organizers of the Reintegration Initiative realized that successful reintegration was linked inextricably with core problems: academic failure, disconnection from school, and lack of job preparation and marketable skills. Efforts to improve education and job training eventually prompted the partnership known as PACTT. Pennsylvania has a highly decentralized juvenile justice system that relies heavily on private placement service providers. Agencies affiliated with PACTT treat about one-third of the juveniles in placement facilities in Pennsylvania.

PACTT concentrates on improving education programs for committed youths. Their assessments found that education programs were uneven, fragmented, and unrelated to the educational requirements in the school districts to which delinquent youth would return. Candace Putter, the director of PACTT, noted: "No one was really paying attention to education in placement. Not the state, not probation, and not the local schools. Young people were showing up in facilities years behind academically, and just getting their educational records was extremely difficult."

PACTT has worked to help facilities align their curricula with state standards and to solicit cooperation from local schools. Teaching staff in the institutions are trained in literacy strategies and techniques for remedial education. The goal is to standardize instruction in the skills every young person needs to succeed in the job market—skills needed to find a job, to understand and meet employer expectations, and to handle typical workplace issues and conflicts. PACTT facilities have excelled in the area of career/technical education, offering programs in high-demand areas—culinary arts, indoor/outdoor maintenance, auto body, welding, and office support. Putter commented:

> The re-entry process for our young people is not easy, and employers aren't standing in line waiting to hire them. But by preparing them well, giving them a strong foundation to continue their education, and helping them earn certifications that employers value, we give them a leg up—something to counter the negative mark that their delinquent history puts on them.[37]

About 200 youths have jobs in the facilities where they are committed—in the kitchens, maintenance plants, and offices. Many are earning wages for the first time in their lives, establishing work histories, and developing confidence. A new program, "Learn to Earn" will provide jobs for some youths for 6 weeks while in placement and then 6 weeks in the community after their release.

> The next task for PACTT is to make those crucial connections to employers—to convince them that by giving our kids a chance, they're actually helping themselves by acquiring trained and enthusiastic employees. And of course we need to build connections to ongoing training, so these kids can continue their education and keep building their technical skills.[38]

Jefferson Parish, Louisiana

One-third of the arrests of juveniles in Jefferson Parish, Louisiana, occurred in schools. The overwhelming majority of the school arrests were for nonviolent misdemeanor offenses—primarily "interference with an education facility" or "disturbing the peace." While disruptive, the offenses did not threaten public safety. The problem was the culture. Roy Juncker, Director of the Jefferson Parish Department of Juvenile Services, commented: "It's built into the way the school system operates. Kids get arrested, suspended, expelled, and that's how you get rid of the problem. As opposed to focusing on the problems causing the misbehavior and dealing with that."[39]

In 2008, the Jefferson Parish Public School System held a special training session to help school staff intervene more effectively. Carol Mancuso, the Director of School Safety, said: "It's learning what not to call the police for. You don't pick up the phone because a kid is running down the hall. You can't pick up the phone just because you don't know what else to do."[40] That said, she also sympathized with teachers and administrators having to deal with emotional and learning problems, saying it is tempting to call the police to get some relief.

Shauna Epps, with the Center for Children's Law and Policy, describes a common problem. When kids act out in school, sheriffs remove them from the classroom, yell at them, and the kids yell back. The incident escalates and frequently results in a charge of "'disturbing the peace."[41] Avoiding calls to the police and rewriting common scenarios requires practical intervention techniques. The parish offers training in crisis intervention to help law enforcement officers respond to situations without making them worse by overreacting or misinterpreting signals. The Department of Juvenile Services is working to minimize unnecessary formal processing and confinement—which disproportionately affect minorities—when youths are arrested. It instituted a "Graduated Sanctions Ladder" policy in 2010 to respond to probation violations without resorting to secure detention. Detention alternatives have expanded, and overall detention usage is 40% below 2004 levels.

United for Youth in Washington

In other chapters, child maltreatment was identified as a risk factor for delinquency. Abused or neglected children are at greater risk of offending when they are older.[42] They are also more likely to suffer mental illness, to have learning disabilities, and to have substance-abuse problems. They are sometimes called multisystem or crossover youth because they come to the attention of multiple agencies. The unfortunate fact is that efforts are rarely coordinated.

Employees of the King County Juvenile Court and the Children's Administration of the Washington Department of Social and Health Services embarked on a collaboration with other local agencies serving multisystem youth and their families in 2004. The planning partnership is called Uniting for Youth.

The impetus for the sharing of data and collaboration among multiple agencies was a study that found that two-thirds of the 4,475 youth referred to the juvenile court for offenses in 2006 had a history of contact with the state's child welfare agency. More than a third (37%) had family issues serious enough to merit agency action. Youth with agency histories offended at earlier ages, spent longer periods in detention, penetrated deeper into the juvenile justice system, and recidivated at higher rates than those with no child welfare history. The jurisdiction began an extensive program of multisystem cross training. Each agency details and shares its goals and responsibilities, resources and programs, methods, and services. Participants form teams to develop case plans for crossover cases. People learn "how the systems can and should work together. They talk through the issues and understand what resources are available from each of them, how they all fit into that puzzle."[43] They become accountable as a group for the outcomes.

Other Model Programs

Youth Courts

There were more than a thousand youth court programs (also called teen, peer, and student courts) in every state except Connecticut in 2010.[44] The number of youth courts increased exponentially from 1994, when there were less than 80. Youth Court offers an alternative solution for first-time, relatively minor offenses. Perhaps most importantly, youth courts increase awareness in the community about issues that affect juveniles. It engages other youths and community members in finding workable resolutions to problem behavior. Youthful offenders learn to confront the consequences of their actions. Offenders and volunteers learn citizenship and the law as well as developing skills in public speaking, mediation, and pro-social leadership. Communities recover losses from crime and regain confidence and pride in local youths.[45]

About half of the programs are justice-system based—operated by law enforcement agencies, juvenile probation, or prosecutor's offices. Slightly more than a quarter are community based and are operated by private, nonprofit organizations; about 8% are school based. Almost all youth courts (90%) require participants to admit guilt; the courts then decide the appropriate sentence. Offenses most frequently include theft, vandalism, alcohol use, disorderly conduct, assault, marijuana possession, tobacco offenses, curfew violations, traffic violations, truancy, and trespassing. Sentences can include community service (usually 30 to 60 hours), apologies, essays, educational workshops, jury duty on a youth court, restitution, curfew, tutoring, counseling, curfew, drug testing, victim-awareness classes, victim/offender mediation, peer mediation, or driver's license suspension. Just over 60% of youth courts dismiss the charges when defendants complete the program; 19% immediately expunge the record.

Youth courts are endorsed by police departments and local governments looking for cost-effective solutions. A youth-court trial takes less than an hour, and the average cost per case is less than $500. In contrast, probation costs more than $1,600; a criminal court trial ranges from $21,000 to $84,000. In addition to cost savings, youth court lets juveniles know that their behavior has consequences but also that the community cares about their place in society. As Jeffrey Butts, who directed an Urban Institute study on youth courts, states: "youth courts provide a more thorough and personal response."[46]

Volunteer defenders and prosecutors serve for at least a year. The eight weeks of training enhances their understanding of the judicial process, useful beyond their term of service. Jurors are untrained volunteers ranging in age from 12 through 18.[47] There are four types of youth courts: adult judge, peer jury, youth judge, and youth tribunal. In the latter two forms, youths perform all courtroom roles, including that of judge. Youth tribunals involve a panel of (usually three) judges that hears cases presented by youth attorneys. The youth judge model replicates traditional hearings with opposing counsel and a jury.

In adult judge programs (about half of all teen courts), youths perform all court functions except the role of judge. The peer jury model resembles a grand jury. An adult or youth volunteer presents each case to a jury of teens, who then question the defendant directly. Jury members choose the sentence, sometimes guided by the adult judge.[48]

While programs differ considerably, all youth courts are premised on the belief that if peer pressure can influence delinquent behavior, it can also influence pro-social behavior. Other theoretical perspectives that have been associated with youth courts are procedural justice (offenders who are treated fairly by the legal process are more likely to comply with sanctions and less likely to re-offend), labeling (stigmatizing youths as "delinquents" or "criminals" increases the probability that they will accept the label and continue to engage in illegal behavior), and restorative justice (a legal process that engages the community rather than the court system provides a means to repair the damage caused and to encourage pro-social behavior).[49]

Drug Courts

When some members of the criminal justice system and the public health system in Dade County, Florida, began to recognize in 1989 that drug abuse and the crimes associated with it would not go away simply by arresting people, they established the first drug courts. The main goals of drug courts are:

> to reduce drug use and associated criminal behavior by engaging and retaining drug-involved offenders in programmatic and treatment services; to concentrate expertise about drug cases into a single courtroom; to address other defendant needs through clinical assessment and effective case management; and to free judicial, prosecutorial and public defense resources for adjudicating non-drug cases.[50]

Drug courts typically include identifying defendants in need of drug treatment and referring them to treatment as soon as possible after their court appearance. They also include regularly scheduled court hearings to monitor the treatment program progress, plus mandatory drug testing. While the judge is a key player in the program, most drug courts try to function as a

> team in which prosecutors, defense attorneys and counselors work together to help offenders overcome their drug problems and resolve other issues relating to work, finances and family. Defendants who complete the drug court program either have their charges dismissed (in a diversion or pre-sentence model) or their probation sentences reduced (in a post-sentence model).[51]

Juvenile drug courts began in the mid-1990s. As of December 31, 2007, there were 455 juvenile drug courts in 47 states and the District of Columbia.[52] Although a few have been evaluated, there remains at least one unresolved issue, namely "whether the juvenile justice system really needs juvenile drug courts." The approach used in adult drug courts (based on what has been called "therapeutic jurisprudence"[53]) is not a new concept in the juvenile justice system, since it was founded (at least in theory) on a treatment orientation. Few juveniles have drug problems anywhere near as severe as the typical adult drug court participant. The typical youth is referred to a juvenile drug court at age 15 or 16 for drinking alcohol or smoking marijuana. Drug-involved youths usually need family counseling and improved relationships to support them in making positive choices.

> Why then does the juvenile justice system need a "new" court model to handle drug-involved youthful offenders? Perhaps because juvenile courts have strayed too far from their historic problem-solving mission to mimic the "just deserts" orientation of criminal courts. The drug court process may be an important change in style and procedure for today's juvenile courts, albeit one that returns them to their traditional mission. Maybe the introduction of juvenile drug courts allows local juvenile justice systems to acquire treatment resources they otherwise would not be able to access. Juvenile drug courts may be valued not because they offer a new or innovative court process for juvenile offenders but because they enable local officials to leverage new resources for responding to teen drug use.[54]

Evaluations of juvenile drug courts have been positive. For example, after five years of operation, almost 70% of the participants in a Kalamazoo, Michigan, court had no new adjudications while enrolled in the program.[55] An evaluation of drug courts for both juveniles and adults in Ohio and Arizona showed positive results.[56]

Model Community Mental Health Programming

The National Center for Mental Health and Juvenile Justice recommends that each youth involved in the juvenile justice system be screened for mental illness.[57] At least two-thirds of the youth in the juvenile justice system have diagnosable mental health disorders, and there are critical intervention points within the juvenile justice process where interventions should occur. These include: initial contact with law enforcement, intake, detention, judicial processing, secure placement, probation supervisor, and re-entry. The Center on Juvenile and Criminal Justice summarizes the issue as follows:

> Diverting youth with mental disorders from confinement to community-based programs is a vital piece on the continuum of care that should be available to youth involved with the juvenile justice. State correctional facilities and local detention facilities have not demonstrated the capacity to properly serve this population when it comes to providing appropriate mental health services, thus placing even more weight on the need to improve community mental health agencies' ability to serve this population. As long as the juvenile justice and mental health systems remain in opposition of each other, the youth will continue to suffer from lack of needed services. Reducing the tension between the juvenile justice systems and combining forces with the community agencies enhances the county's ability to provide appropriate services to these youth. By creating a better network system among community agencies and government agencies, a more efficient system can be cultivated to locate the necessary services for this specific high-needs population.[58]

Programs exist in several parts of the country that utilize a team of professionals trained to identify and treat various mental health issues, including a program at the Bernalillo County Juvenile Detention Center in Albuquerque, New Mexico, a special clinic within the Boston Juvenile Court, the Cayuga Home for Children's Multi-Dimensional Treatment program in Auburn, New York, the Colorado Crisis Intervention Team, the Cook County Juvenile Court Clinic, a Court for the Individualized Treatment of Adolescents in Santa Clara, CA, a program called Crossroads in Summit County, Ohio, and the Family Integrated Transitions Project in Seattle, Washington.[59]

One of the nine tenets for improving juvenile justice discussed earlier is the creation of a range of community-based programs. The Youth Transition Funders Group highlights three therapies that have proven effective.

> Three evidence-based programs are scientifically proven to prevent crime, even among youth with the highest risk of re-offending. Functional Family Therapy, Multidimensional Treatment Foster Care, and Multi-Systemic Therapy (MST) all focus on the family. None involve incarceration. All deliver results. Evaluations of MST for serious juvenile offenders demonstrate reductions of 25 to 70 percent in long-term rates of re-arrest, reductions of 47 to 64 percent in out-of-home placements, improvements in family functioning and decreased mental health problems, all at a lower cost than other juvenile justice services.[60]

Their ninth tenet of juvenile justice reform is the participation of youth, parents, and the community "both in an adolescent's treatment and rehabilitation, as well as in systemic reform efforts. True reform tackles not just the system; it engages the people who youth encounter in their day-to-day lives."[61] When people care, when they believe that young people can change, then positive things happen. This is a vast improvement from the lock-'em-up philosophy of the past.

Another New Paradigm: Restorative Justice

Restorative justice is an emerging idea that has great potential. Space does not permit a thorough analysis of this interesting concept. However, the reader should at least be aware of some of the basic tenets. Seeking to find alternatives to a punitive response to crime, restorative justice emphasizes the needs of the victims, the offender, and the community. The movement began in Canada with the case of two teenagers who vandalized 22 properties in 1974. The outcome was determined by a direct meeting between the victims and the two teenagers. Since that time efforts to seek peaceful and nonpunitive solutions have evolved all over the world.[62]

The central thrust of restorative justice is to end the pain and suffering of the victims of crime—all types of crimes, including all forms of human rights abuses. The usual response to crime—especially violent crime—is the desire for retribution, seeking "just deserts" against offenders. But this response has always proven to be counterproductive. In fact, it goes against virtually every religious tenant.[63] As taught and practiced by Gandhi and Martin Luther King, nonviolence is the only way to stop the endless cycle of violence followed by retaliation in kind. Martin Luther King, in his acceptance speech for the Nobel Peace Prize in 1964, said: "The choice today is not between violence and nonviolence. It is either nonviolence or nonexistence."[64]

The idea of forgiveness as a path to ending hurt and anger has existed for centuries. The English poet Alexander Pope (1688–1744) famously said "To err is human, to forgive divine."[65] Unfortunately, forgiveness seems out of step in our current political/economic system. Such forgiveness would be more in line with an economic/political system "that sees acknowledgment of a harm-done, and apology for it, and forgiveness offered in return, as processes that are personally healing for all involved and simultaneously restorative of community."[66]

The underlying aim of the restorative justice process is to cease further objectification of those who have been involved in the violent act—the victim, the offender, the families connected to these two individuals, and the community at large. Everyone engages in a healing process. Traditional mediation and conflict resolution techniques "help those affected by the harm dissolve their fears, and hates, and resentments and thereby recover a sense of their former selves."[67]

Proponents of restorative justice recognize the difficulty of convincing a capitalistic culture to reject power and control over others. As Dennis Sullivan and Larry Tifft observe, the change necessary for restorative justice "transforms all of our conceptions of political economy, that is, how we view power and money, and how we assess human worth."[68]

Many programs are based on restorative justice principles. The Mural Arts Program in Philadelphia, Pennsylvania, is one. It offers a constructive, creative outlet for chronically truant/delinquent youth.[69] It began in 1984 as a program to remove graffiti for youths who had been adjudicated for engaging in graffiti. The mural-painting component was designed to help adolescents learn more positive ways to express their creativity and to provide positive role models, structured activities, and opportunities to develop job skills. Over 3,000 murals have been created and are a tourist attraction in Philadelphia.[70] The program works with adjudicated youth at the city's detention center, a correctional center for young adults, a residential program for boys, and with adjudicated youths in supervised independent-living homes around the city.

Another program with a history of success is Peacemaking Circles in Peoria, Illinois. The city was concerned about disproportionality in its detention center. Analyses of juvenile arrest and detention data pointed to aggravated battery referrals from Manual High School as the largest contributor to the disproportionate detention of minorities. Surveys and focus group interviews with Manual students and teachers revealed substantial anxiety about gangs and violence and a reliance on force to resolve problems. The fears and reactions created a culture of insecurity, broken relationships, and lack of trust. The effort to shift responsibility for responding to juvenile offending away from police, courts, and correctional systems began with an experiment in school-based restorative conflict resolution techniques—Peacemaking Circles.

The Circles were introduced on a voluntary basis in Manual classrooms in 2006. They allowed participants to raise issues, explain their feelings, work out misunderstandings, resolve differences, and support one another in a protected setting. Students participating in the programs reported better attendance, improved relationships with classmates and teachers, successful avoidance of trouble, and better schoolwork. Lori Brown, the coordinator for Peoria Models for Change, praised the program for its extraordinary ability to open lines of communication and understanding. Like other restorative justice practices, Circles emphasize "changing relationships by engaging people: doing things with them, rather than to them or for them. It's the relationships, not specific strategies, that bring about meaningful change."[71]

The program was so successful that Manual introduced MANYO (Motivating and Nurturing Youth Opportunity), a peer jury program that provides an alternative approach to school discipline. It emphasizes consensus-based conflict resolution by youths, with active efforts to repair harm and make peace. Holly Snyder, the local Restorative Justice Coordinator, describes the program as: "Holding youth responsible for their decisions and giving them a chance to repair the harm they've caused. It's easy to suspend them—no one talks to them, no one holds them accountable. And then they come back to school, and again no one deals with them."[72] Two other schools in Peoria introduced peer juries. In two years, school administrators have referred 119 cases involving fighting, intimidation, classroom insubordination, or other disruptive misconduct to the peer juries. Only 6 of the cases (5%) had to be referred back to school administration for further disciplinary action.

Restorative alternatives are expanding out of the schools and into the Peoria community. In the summer of 2010, the Covenant with Black America and the Peoria Police Department, with help from Models for Change coordinators, launched Community Peace Conferencing—a diversion program for nonviolent, first- and second-time juvenile offenders. Police refer the young offenders to community volunteers trained in restorative justice techniques. As Brown comments, "If we want peace in our community, the community itself must take an active role in obtaining it. This program is about ordinary citizens partnering with the police to fight crime and improve the lives of youth."[73]

Recent research has generally concluded that programs based on the restorative justice model are effective. A meta-analysis covering evaluations through the early twenty-first century found a high degree of effectiveness compared to other types of interventions.[74] An evaluation of a program focusing specifically on juvenile offenders based in a large urban area found that youth who participated in a restorative justice diversion program had a lower recidivism rate than a control group.[75] A study that did a long-term follow-up (up to four years) of a sample of juvenile offenders that participated in a restorative justice program found significantly lower recidivism rates than a control group left within the juvenile court system.[76] Finally, a study of a program for girl offenders found a restorative justice approach to be especially effective in reducing recidivism.[77]

Broad-Based National Strategies

Addressing the delinquency problem will require a national strategy; the problem is not just local in nature. More than 20 years ago, criminologist Elliot Currie suggested five general categories for a national strategy to address the general problem of crime. These are just as relevant today; the nine tenets detailed above urge similar reform.[78]

1. *Early educational interventions.* These would include programs such as Head Start, based on the assumption that delinquency is related to poor school performance and dropping out, which in turn are related to lack of preparedness for school, especially among lower-class minorities.[79]

2. *Expanded health and mental health services.* Such services would focus on high-risk youths and include pre- and postnatal care. This is based on evidence that the most violent youths suffer from childhood traumas of the central nervous system, exhibit multiple psychotic symptoms, and have also experienced severe physical and/or sexual abuse.[80]

3. *Family support programs.* Programs should be designed to address child abuse and other forms of domestic violence. Abused children are far more likely than nonabused children to become abusers themselves. Some recent research indicates that the majority of prison inmates, especially violent ones, experienced severe physical, emotional, or sexual abuse or some combination of all three.

4. *Reentry programs.* There should be careful planning for helping offenders after they have broken the law, rather than merely warehousing them in a correctional setting. The key ingredient in virtually all successful rehabilitation programs is improving skills—work skills, reading and verbal skills, problem-solving skills, and so on.

5. *Drug and alcohol abuse treatment programs.* The war on drugs targets the manufacturing and distribution (the supply side) of drugs, rather than the use (the demand side). The nation needs to emphasize treatment of addictions.

Social Capital

About the same time Currie wrote his proposals, sociologist Mark Colvin also wrote about the need for national strategies.[81] He focuses on the concept of social reproduction—the process through which institutions (primarily families and schools) prepare children for productive roles in society. His main thesis is that these institutions have largely failed to establish the necessary social bonds to link young people to legitimate avenues to adulthood. The result is that many are becoming marginal to the country's economic institutions. This has been caused by a failure to invest in human development and human capital. This failure has resulted in a growing crime rate and increasing expenditures for welfare and prisons. There is a need for a "national comprehensive program aimed at spurring economic growth, human development, and grassroots, democratic participation in the major institutions affecting our lives and those of our children."[82]

Crime may be less likely to occur in communities with stronger social capital. Higher levels of community participation create social networks, consensus, and an environment of mutual support and trust.

> Improving social capital through volunteerism and political activism could alter the social norms surrounding crime and a community's reaction to crime. Civic engagement seems to mitigate those cultural norms that allow violence and crime to take root. Increasing youth participation in community activities could be an important tool in stemming the adverse effects of crime, as well as keeping individual youth more bonded to conventional social norms.[83]

A comprehensive approach must aim at broader economic and human-development programs that affect large segments of the population (for example, the social security system versus welfare for the poor). The country must do what other industrialized nations do and consider seriously the need to develop human capital for the continued overall well-being of society. In the United States, the system is so privatized that public or social needs are often undermined by private investment decisions that result in moving capital all over the world but eliminate jobs at home. Education is the key here. However, as Colvin notes, education must be more than what the term has traditionally meant—namely, formalized public schooling leading to a diploma. Education should be a comprehensive policy that includes families, schools, workplaces, and communities working to reduce the marginalization of young people. "For youth, who often feel the effects of social exclusion, social capital can be as simple as a positive relationship or affiliation with neighborhood and community associations. Thus, collective as well as personal efficacy can be achieved through volunteerism and political participation."[84]

Positive Youth Development

Another national strategy that has attracted attention is positive youth development (PYD). For most of the twentieth century, adolescence was viewed as a period of turmoil. The deficit-based approach to adolescence focused on what could go wrong in a young person's development. The individual treatment philosophy of the original juvenile court movement was based on this approach. Studies, however, noted that most youth succeed even in the presence of multiple risk factors and applied the label "resilience" to describe qualities that promote healthy development in the face of adversity. Youth advocates began to see adolescence as a process of positive opportunities for youth to learn, serve, and benefit from interactions with pro-social adults and communities.

The strength-based, resilience-oriented perspective on adolescence of PYD is "a comprehensive way of thinking about the development of adolescents and the factors that facilitate their successful transition from adolescence to adulthood."[85]

The basic premise of PYD is that even the most disadvantaged young person can develop positively when connected to the right mix of opportunities, supports, positive roles, and relationships. Having a wide range of prosocial experiences during adolescence allows a young person to practice and demonstrate competency and to embrace his or her responsibilities and value to the larger community. The central purpose of PYD is action. Communities are encouraged to break down barriers to opportunity, and provide positive roles and relationships for all youth, including the most disadvantaged and disconnected.[86]

PYD involves building connections, valuing community, and emphasizing learning/doing and attaching/belonging. A key concept involves changing the frame—looking at youth as resources rather than as victims of villains. People are beginning to question the rationale for interventions based solely on the punishment or individual treatment model.

- If delinquent behavior stems from a lack of integration and habilitation, why do correctional strategies focus on isolation of offenders?

- If the goal is to make offenders more responsible and accountable, why do we place them in positions (e.g., in most treatment programs) where others assume responsibility for their activities and behaviors?

- If many sources of delinquency are to be found in communities, families, and schools, why do probation strategies often target only the individual offender?

- If youth justice professionals are experts in delinquent behavior, why are youth justice agencies so often viewed by policy makers as an all-purpose "dumping ground" for troubled youth rather than a resource for resolving problems in schools and communities?[87]

Addressing the Problem of Social Inequality

As noted in chapter 8, delinquency is strongly related to social inequality. Social inequality in the United States has reached its highest point since the start of the Great Depression. Most commentary focuses on the impact of the economic crisis on the "middle class"—ignoring the poor and especially the growing marginality of the urban underclass. One important function of the punishment business is processing this underclass into the prison system. As noted in chapter 10, there is a school-to-prison pipeline for the inner-city black underclass.[88]

To break this "pipeline" we might very well need something like what Paul Krugman has called a "new New Deal."[89] He suggests starting with universal health care and continuing on to job creation and other reform measures, just like FDR did with the original "New Deal." Perhaps a kind of "Public Works Program" like the WPA in the 1930s would be required. Some have suggested instituting a kind of "Marshall Plan" for the inner cities.[90]

Figure 14.1   Changing the Frame

Changing the Frame

ASSUMPTIONS	PRIMARY LENS		
	Youth as Victim	Youth as Villain	Youth as Resource
Origins of Most Delinquent Behavior	Symptom of underlying disturbance	Anti-social impulses, lack of restraint due to permissiveness and the absence of punishment	Normative response to adolescent needs for status, belonging, power & excitement, lack of empathy
How Delinquent Youth Compare with Other Adolescents	Fundamentally different in psychological and emotional makeup	Fundamentally different motivations and impulses toward different behavior	Largely similar to other adolescents but with fewer social assets
Delinquent Youth Capacity for Behavior Change	Incapable of conventional behavior without therapeutic interventions	Incapable of conventional behavior without strict discipline and the threat of punishment	Inherently capable of conventional behavior with sufficient access to supports and pro-social opportunities
Primary Intervention Strategy	Individual or family-based therapeutic treatment	Deterrence and retributive punishment	Skill development, attachment and engagement
Role of Treatment	Primary	Secondary	Secondary
Risks of Treatment	Could fail to address underlying cause(s)	Could delay or impede deterrence	Could introduce stigma or harm—i.e., iatrogenic effects

What about Girls?

Because the majority of delinquency prevention programs are co-ed, the specific needs of girls are either shortchanged or simply ignored because the population of boys greatly outnumbers the population of girls.

There are several sources that provide reviews of programs for girls, especially Prevention and Parity: Girls in Juvenile Justice by Girls Incorporated and the Girls Study Group.[91] Few of these programs have been subjected to rigorous evaluation, so judge elements of the programs against what we currently know about effective and ineffective strategies for working with troubled girls.

Children of the Night

The current director of Children of the Night, Lois Lee, started the program in 1979 in southern California, while she was a graduate student in sociology at

UCLA. Lee asked herself, "Why would a girl stand on a street corner and do something deplorable, then give all the money she earned to a pimp?" Soon she began to offer her apartment as a temporary shelter to the young males and females who wanted to escape.[92] The majority of girls in the program were runaways from abusive homes.

The program (see also chapter 5) consists of: (1) a 24-hour hot line; (2) a walk-in center that provides medical aid, clothing, crisis intervention, and referrals for housing, drug counseling, schools, jobs, and foster home placement; (3) professional counseling by volunteer psychologists and psychiatrists; (4) an outreach component whose trained volunteers walk the streets distributing informational materials to potential clients and engaging in on-the-spot counseling; and (5) a "turn-in-a-pimp" component that entails cooperation among the youths, the agency, the police, and the court system (the aim here is to obtain court testimony against pimps to assist in the prosecution of individuals who otherwise might go free because of lack of evidence).

National Programs of Girls Inc.

Girls Inc. (formerly the Girls Clubs of America) sponsors a number of programs (some of which are listed below) to help girls.[93] These programs are offered by trained professional staff at 1,000 sites nationwide.

Friendly PEERsuasion. This program helps young women avoid substance abuse. It approaches prevention as a peer issue.[94] Participants learn decision-making, assertiveness, and communication skills at the ages of 11 through 14 to resist peer pressure to use drugs and to develop healthy ways to manage stress. They also learn the short- and long-term effects of substance abuse. They practice how to leave situations where they feel pressured to use alcohol or drugs. After successfully learning these skills, the girls conduct substance-abuse prevention activities for children aged 6 through 10. Their status as leaders reinforces their commitment to resist using drugs and alcohol.

Preventing Adolescent Pregnancy. This program, which teaches skills, insights, and peer support, consists of four age-appropriate components.[95] The first stage, "Growing Together," consists of five sessions designed to start conversations between young girls (ages 9–11) and a trusted adult about sexuality. "Will Power/Won't Power" is the next stage. Throughout the 10 sessions, girls (ages 12–14) learn to resist pressure and to avoid risky situations. The positive aspects of abstinence and the value of a positive sister-support system are stressed. The third stage is "Taking Care of Business" (for girls 15–18). Ten sessions stress smart choices, provide facts on contraception, and teach communication and success skills for career goals. "Health Bridge" links girls to community health-care services; it is a resource for girls who choose to be sexually active, providing them with reproductive health information, testing, and contraception services. Teenagers in the United States have the highest pregnancy rate in the industrialized world. An evaluation found that those who participated in one or more components of the program were less likely to experience pregnancy than those who did not. Those who participated in two or more components were less likely to engage in sexual intercourse without birth control than those who participated in a single program component.[96]

Local Programs Sponsored by Girls Inc.

A program in Baltimore known as the *Female Intervention Team* (FIT) supervises and provides various treatment services for adjudicated delinquent girls or those in need of services. The founder of this program, Marian Daniel, wanted to design a program to "make it look as if girls might want to come." They have an "infant and toddler" program to help young women learn good parenting skills. They also provide family counseling and tutoring, recreation activities, and close monitoring by FIT "case managers" who, by using the "case management approach," are able to provide more intensive services than do regular probation officers.

The *Harriet Tubman Residential Center* in Auburn, New York is a research-based program for girls who have been adjudicated in juvenile court. It focuses on women's issues and development and tries to offer services that relate to these issues. The program description includes four specific "outcome objectives": (1) self-management (such as personal hygiene and developing responsibility for one's own physical well-being); (2) relationship building (interacting with peers and parents and developing an understanding of nonviolent methods of solving problems); (3) empowerment and self-direction (focusing on such issues as academics, vocational development, and independent living); and (4) future orientation (includes setting personal goals and a sense of future direction). The program takes into account the differences between the way boys and girls develop and how they view their surrounding world (e.g., boys tend to be "task oriented" whereas girls focus on "building relationships").

Professionals working in the juvenile court system in Jacksonville, Florida, in the early 1980s recognized that girls involved in delinquent activities were either not being held accountable or were placed further into the system for their protection or they were placed in programs designed for boys. Founder Vicki Burke created a research-based alternative to institutionalization in 1985—The *PACE* (Practical, Academic, Cultural, and Educational) *Center for Girls Inc.* The basement of a downtown Jacksonville church was the first location, which served 10 girls. PACE now has 17 centers throughout Florida and has served over 21,000 Florida girls.

> Its purpose is to intervene and prevent school withdrawal, juvenile delinquency, teen pregnancy, substance abuse and welfare dependency in a safe and nurturing environment. PACE programs provide the following services: academic education, individualized attention, a gender-specific life management curriculum (SPIRITED GIRLS®), therapeutic support services, parental involvement, student volunteer service projects and transition follow-up services.[97]

PACE takes a holistic approach and focuses on providing services such as life management skills, community service, counseling, and self-esteem building. It offers both day programs and aftercare services. The Department of Justice and OJJDP praises the program and gives it very high ratings. The University of Florida does yearly evaluations, and thus far the outcomes have been very positive.

OJJDP Model Programs for Girls

OJJDP provides a model programs guide (MPG) listing more than 200 evidence-based programs covering a continuum of youth services from prevention through sanctions to reentry.[98] Some of the programs are listed below.

Girls' Circle.   This support group addresses the specialized needs of girls between the ages of 9 and 18 to counteract social and interpersonal forces that impede girls' growth and development. The program consists of a 10-week curriculum. Each week, a group of girls of similar age and development meets with a facilitator for either 90- or 120-minute sessions. During this time, the girls take turns talking and listening to one another respectfully about their concerns and interests. They further express themselves through creative or directed activities such as role-playing, drama, journaling, poetry, dance, drawing, collage, and clay. Gender-specific themes and topics are introduced that relate to the girls' lives, such as body image, goals, sexuality, drugs, alcohol, tobacco, competition, decision-making, friendships, and trusting oneself. A key component in the model is the council-type format of one group member speaking at a time, with the expectation of attentive listening from other participants to increase empathy skills and mutual understanding among the whole group. An evaluation found significant increases in body image scores, perceived social support, and level of self-efficacy. However, self-esteem and locus of control did not improve.[99]

Movimiento Ascendencia (Upward Movement).   Located in Pueblo, Colorado, this program provides girls with positive alternatives to substance use and gang involvement. Activities are designed around three main components: cultural awareness, mediation or conflict resolution, and self-esteem or social support. The program includes mentoring, recreational activities, tutoring, cultural enhancement, and close involvement with parents. The location also provides a safe haven for girls. An evaluation found that girls in the treatment group showed a greater reduction in delinquency, along with higher grades than those in the control group.[100]

Nurse–Family Partnership (NFP).   This program provides low-income mothers with home visitation services from public health nurses. NFP nurses work intensively with these mothers to improve maternal, prenatal, early childhood health, and well-being with the expectation that this intervention will help achieve long-term improvements in the lives of at-risk families. The program is designed to improve five broad domains of family functioning: parental roles; family and friend support; health (physical and mental); home and neighborhood environment; major life events (e.g., pregnancy planning, education, employment). The program addresses such issues as substance abuse, poor maternal and infant outcomes, suboptimal childcare, and a lack of opportunities for the children. Every member of the family gets involved in the program. An evaluation was done through three large studies (Elmira, NY; Memphis, TN; Denver, CO). The study found that not only did the mother's prenatal health (especially in relation to their use of cigarettes) improve (compared to a control group), but the number of preterm deliveries decreased, there were fewer injuries to children, and the mothers made better use of the social welfare system. A 15-year follow-up of the Elmira program found that there was a significant reduction in child abuse and neglect, reduced problems associated with drug use, reduced arrests among the mothers and a significant reduction (54%) in arrests among the 15-year-olds.[101]

Urban Women against Substance Abuse (UWASA).   This is a 28-week, school-based program targeting Puerto Rican, Latina, African-American, and Caribbean-American girls (ages 9–11) and their female caregivers. They use a self-development curriculum that teaches girls to build their cultural and gender identity, while discouraging alcohol and drug use, promoting HIV awareness, and exploring possible career options. They also have a curriculum to apply to mothers that includes "mother-daughter sharing sessions." An evaluation of this program found that the girls in the program were more likely than a comparison group not in the program to exhibit much greater awareness of issues related to HIV, a better record of substance use, and exhibited an improvement in their attitudes about sexual activity. Especially noteworthy was the fact that the mother-daughter relationships improved significantly for the treatment group.[102]

Some Closing Words

Saul Alinsky, the social reformer and agitator of the early twentieth century, offered a parable that is highly informative for readers who need a perspective to guide their own individual efforts to seek change. Imagine a large river with a high waterfall. At the bottom of this waterfall, hundreds of people are working frantically to rescue those who have fallen into the river. One individual looks up and sees a seemingly never-ending stream of people cascading down the waterfall, and he begins to run upstream. One of his fellow rescuers hollers, "Where are you going? There are so many people that need help here." The man replied, "I'm going upstream to find out why so many people are falling into the river."

Now imagine that the scene at the bottom of the waterfall represents the criminal justice system responding to crimes that have been committed and dealing with both victims and offenders. If you look more closely, you will begin to notice that there are more people at the bottom of the stream, that they work in relatively new buildings with all sorts of modern technology and that those working here get paid rather well, with excellent benefits. And the money keeps flowing into this area, with all sorts of businesses lined up to provide various services and technical assistance. If you look upstream, you will find something far different. There are not too many people; the buildings are not as modern; the technology is old or nonexistent. The people working upstream are not paid very much, have few benefits, and the turnover is quite high. Businesses do not offer assistance. Budgets are insufficient, and workers constantly need to beg for money. More women work upstream, and the culture does not value their work as highly as the work of men (men are in charge downstream). Prevention does not seem to be very macho in this culture, and it is not linked to profits.

Some people choose to respond to problems related to crime and delinquency by working downstream. This is certainly a noble goal and good people are always needed. As for me, I picture myself as being one who is constantly running upstream, asking "why?" Which way you want to go is up to you. You just have to be able to look yourself in the mirror each day and be able to say, "I tried." A lot of work lies ahead. The answer begins and ends with people—with "highly motivated, highly trained staff constantly interacting with youth to create an environment of trust and respect."[103]

In this chapter, we reviewed Missouri's model of juvenile justice reform that focuses on fostering the personal growth of adjudicated youth in small, supportive facilities rather than punishment in large, harsh, prisons. The lives of adolescents have been enhanced, tax dollars saved, and crimes averted.

> For states struggling to combat deep problems in their youth corrections systems, Missouri's message is twofold: (1) no matter how troubled your system may be today, success is possible, and (2) the answer lies not in any single reform, but rather a long-term commitment to continuous improvement.[104]

The Annie E. Casey Foundation believes that the winds of change are "beginning to blow in juvenile corrections. A new wave of reform is gathering force, dual-powered by a growing recognition that the conventional practices aren't getting the job done, and by the accumulating evidence that better results are available through a fundamentally different approach."[105] The formal juvenile justice system is no substitute for strong families, schools, and communities. The best responses are informal and close to home, "guided by the community's traditions and restrained by its common sense. It's not just cheaper than arrests, petitions, court hearings, detention stays, and everything else that comes with formal processing. It's more effective in the long run."[106]

To narrow the pipeline of adolescents entering the system, we must eliminate the reliance on secure detention—the gateway to the deep end of the system. Diverse and effective interventions in the community are far more effective for most youths than confinement in an institution. If we want a smaller, more effective juvenile justice system, we need improved diversion programs, probation, and alternatives to incarceration.

Summary

This chapter reviewed some promising approaches in dealing with juvenile delinquency, but it merely scratched the surface of the vast literature that is available. Interested readers should consult the sources cited in this chapter for additional information.

There are two critical points emphasized in this chapter. First, it is mandatory that we begin to think "outside the box." Before we attempt to change youthful behaviors we don't like or fear, we need to change ourselves first, especially the way we perceive youths and their potential. The second point is that we need to change the surrounding culture and social structure. In the richest society in world history, we fail miserably in providing good opportunities to all our citizens.

I suppose it is part of our nature to blame individuals for their shortcomings while failing to see what is so obvious. Human behavior, both delinquent and nondelinquent, is shaped by outside forces. Our culture and our social institutions teach certain values, but the avenues for reaching those goals are often closed to some members of society. We need to work hard at providing the services that youth in trouble desperately need. Even if we succeed in teaching the necessary skills, the effort will be wasted if they return to the same environment that had so much to do with their original delinquent activities. I urge each reader to remember the upstream/downstream parable and to use his or her unique talents to blaze new trails in how we deal with delinquency.

NOTES

[1] For an excellent discussion of this subject see Sternheimer, K. (2006). *Kids These Days: Facts and Fictions about Today's Youth.* Lanham, MD: Rowman & Littlefield.

[2] Miller, J. (1998). *Last One Over the Wall* (2nd ed.). Columbus: Ohio State University Press, p. 234.

[3] Ibid.

[4] Macallair, D. and M. Males (2004). "A Failure of Good Intentions: An Analysis of Juvenile Justice Reform in San Francisco during the 1990s." *Review of Policy Research* 21: 63–78. Emphasis added.

[5] Schur, E. (1973). *Radical Nonintervention: Rethinking the Delinquency Problem.* Englewood Cliffs, NJ: Prentice-Hall.

[6] Ibid., p. 117.

[7] Schur, *Radical Nonintervention*, pp. 166–70.

[8] Males, M. (1999). *Framing Youth: Ten Myths about the Coming Generation.* Monroe, ME: Common Courage Press; and Males, M. (1996). *The Scapegoat Generation: America's War on Adolescents.* Monroe, ME: Common Courage Press.

[9] Dryfoos, J. (1990). *Adolescents at Risk.* New York: Oxford University Press.

[10] Belfield, C. R., N. Milagros, S. Barnett, and L. Schweinhart (2006). "The High/Scope Perry Preschool Program: Cost-Benefit Analysis Using Data from the Age-40 Follow-Up." *Journal of Human Resources* 41(1): 162–90.

[11] Mann, E. A. and A. J. Reynolds (2006). "Early Intervention and Juvenile Delinquency Prevention: Evidence from the Chicago Longitudinal Study." *Social Work Research* 30(3): 153–67.

[12] Camilli, G., S. Vargas, S. Ryan, and W. S. Barnett (2010). "Meta-Analysis of the Effects of Early Education Interventions on Cognitive and Social Development." *Teachers College Record* 112: 579–620.

[13] Schorr, L. (1989). *Within Our Reach: Breaking the Cycle of Disadvantage.* New York: Anchor, p. 259.

[14] Lipsey, M. W. (2009). "The Primary Factors that Characterize Effective Interventions with Juvenile Offenders: A Meta-Analytic Overview." *Victims and Offenders* 4: 124–47.

[15] Youth Transition Funders Group (2006, Spring). *A Blueprint for Juvenile Justice Reform* (2nd ed.). Retrieved from http://www.ytfg.org/documents/Platform_Juvenile_Justice.pdf

[16] See the following: Moore, S. (2009, March 27). "Missouri System Treats Juvenile Offenders with Lighter Hand." *New York Times.* http://www.nytimes.com/2009/03/27/us/27juvenile.html; Moore, M. T. (2010, May 28). "For DC, Hope in Treating Young Offenders." *USA Today.* http://

www.usatoday.com/news/nation/2010-05-18-offenders_N.htm?csp=obinsite; Wright, M. E. (2010, March 15). "Juvenile Justice Reform: Making the 'Missouri Model' an American Model." *Huffington Post.* http://www.huffingtonpost.com/marian-wright-edelman/juvenile-justice-reform-m_b_498976.html; Warren, J. (2004, July 1). "Spare the Rod, Save the Child." *Los Angeles Times.* http://articles.latimes.com/2004/jul/01/local/me-juvie1

17 Editorial (2007, October 28). "The Right Model for Juvenile Justice." *New York Times.* Retrieved from http://www.nytimes.com/2007/10/28/opinion/28sun2.html

18 Annie E. Casey Foundation (2008, December). "Missouri Juvenile Justice System Honored by Harvard University & Casey Foundation." http://www.aecf.org/MajorInitiatives/JuvenileDetentionAlternativesInitiative/Resources/Dec08newsletter/JJNews5.aspx

19 This information is provided on their website: http://www.dss.mo.gov/dys/articles/progservice.pdf

20 Moore, "Missouri System Treats Juvenile Offenders with Lighter Hand."

21 Mendel, R. A. (2010). "The Missouri Model: Reinventing the Practice of Rehabilitating Youthful Offenders." The Annie E. Casey Foundation, p. 37. Retrieved from http://www.aecf.org/~/media/Pubs/Initiatives/Juvenile%20Detention%20Alternatives%20Initiative/MOModel/MO_Fullreport_webfinal.pdf

22 Ibid., p. 36.

23 Ibid., p. 37.

24 Ibid., p. 49.

25 Ibid., pp. 50–51.

26 Miller, *Last One Over the Wall.*

27 Macallair, D. (1994). "Disposition Case Advocacy in San Francisco's Juvenile Justice System: A New Approach to Deinstitutionalization." *Crime and Delinquency* 40: 84. Dan Macallair, the director of the Center on Juvenile and Criminal Justice in San Francisco, was instrumental in developing DDAP. He can be reached at: dmacallair@cjcj.org.

28 Moxley, R. (1989). *Case Management.* Beverly Hills, CA: Sage, p. 11.

29 The ability of case advocacy and case management to promote detention alternatives was demonstrated by the National Center on Institutions and Alternatives (NCIA). Under contract with New York City's Spofford Detention Center, NCIA significantly augmented the efforts of that city's Department of Juvenile Justice to reduce the number of youth in detention and to expand the range of alternative options. A similar case management system has been in use in Florida through the Associated Marine Institutes. The Key Program, Inc., also uses the case management approach. In this instance, the youth are *closely supervised*, meaning that they are monitored on a 24-hour basis and must conform to some very strict rules concerning work, school, counseling, victim restitution, etc. (Krisberg, B. and J. Austin. [1993]. *Reinventing Juvenile Justice.* Newbury Park, CA: Sage, pp. 178–81). Additional evidence in support of the use of case advocacy comes from a study by the Rand Corporation. This study compared two groups of randomly selected youths, a control group that was recommended by their probation officers for incarceration, and an experimental group that received disposition reports by case advocates. Of those who received case advocacy disposition reports, 72% were diverted from institutional care, compared to 49% of the control group. The Rand study also found tremendous resistance from juvenile justice officials (especially probation officers) to alternative dispositions, particularly those coming from case advocates. It appeared that the probation staff resented the intrusion into what had heretofore been considered their "turf" (Greenwood, P. W. and S. Turner [1991.] *Implementing and Managing Innovative Correctional Programs: Lessons from OJJDP's Private Sector Initiative.* Santa Monica, CA: Rand Corporation, p. 92).

30 Shelden, R. G. (1999). "Detention Diversion Advocacy: An Evaluation." Washington, DC: OJJDP. Retrieved from http://www.ncjrs.gov/pdffiles1/ojjdp/171155.pdf

31 Feldman, L. B. and C. E. Jubrin (2002). *Evaluation Findings: The Detention Diversion Advocacy Program Philadelphia, Pennsylvania.* Washington, DC: Center for Excellence in Municipal Management, George Washington University.

32 Shelden, R. G. (1998). "The Detention Diversion Advocacy."

33 Griffin, P. (2010, November 30). "Models for Change: Innovations in Practice." National Center for Juvenile Justice, p. 2. Retrieved from http://www.modelsforchange.net/publications/287

[34] Illinois Models for Change (2011, June 3). "Redeploy Illinois Saving Millions and Changing Lives." Retrieved from http://www.modelsforchange.net/reform-progress/123?src=hometxt

[35] Illinois Department of Human Services (2011, May 19). "Redeploy Illinois Initiative Saves State Millions." Retrieved from http://www.dhs.state.il.us/page.aspx?item=55824&newssidebar=27893

[36] Griffin, "Models for Change," p. 2.

[37] Ibid., p. 4.

[38] Ibid.

[39] Ibid., pp. 7–8.

[40] Ibid., p. 8.

[41] Ibid.

[42] Ibid., p. 9.

[43] Ibid., p. 11.

[44] National Association of Youth Courts. "Facts and Stats." Retrieved from http://www.youthcourt.net/?page_id=24

[45] Schneider, J. M. (2008). "Youth Courts: An Empirical Update and Analysis of Future Organizational and Research Needs." Hamilton Fish Institute. The George Washington University, p. 11. Retrieved from http://www.youthcourt.net/wp-content/uploads/2010/09/222592.pdf

[46] Caplan, J. (2005, July 18). "A Jury of Their Peers." *Time*, p. 63.

[47] Ibid.

[48] Butts, J. and J. Buck (2002, Winter). "The Sudden Popularity of Teen Courts." *The Judges' Journal*, 41(1): 29–33.

[49] Butts, J., J. Buck, and M. Coggeshall (2002). *The Impact of Teen Court on Young Offenders*. Washington, DC: Urban Institute.

[50] Belenko, S. (1998, June). "Research on Drug Courts: A Critical Review." *National Drug Court Institute Review, I* (1): 4. Retrieved from http://www.pretrial.org/Docs/Documents/casa.pdf

[51] Ibid., p. 5.

[52] Huddleston, C. W., D. B. Marlowe, and R. Casebolt (2008, May). "Painting the Current Picture: A National Report Card on Drug Courts and Other Problem-Solving Court Programs in the United States." National Drug Court Institute, II (1). Retrieved from http://www.ndci.org/sites/default/files/ndci/PCPII1_web%5B1%5D.pdf

[53] Rottman, D. and P. Casey (1999, July). "Therapeutic Jurisprudence and the Emergence of Problem-Solving Courts." *National Institute of Justice Journal*.

[54] Butts, J. and J. Roman (2004). *Juvenile Drug Courts and Teen Substance Abuse*. Washington, DC: The Urban Institute. http://www.urbaninstitute.org/pubs/JuvenileDrugCourts/preface.html

[55] Hartmann, D. J. and G. M. Rhineberger (2003). "Evaluation of the Kalamazoo County Juvenile Drug Treatment Court Program." Kalamazoo: Kercher Center for Social Research, Western Michigan University.

[56] Shaffer, D. K., S. J. Listwan, E. J. Latessa, and C. T. Lowenkamp (2008). "Examining the Differential Impact of Drug Court Services by Court Type: Findings from Ohio." *Drug Court Review* 6: 33–66; Ruiz, B. S., S. J. Stevens, J. Fuhriman, J. G. Bogart, and J. D. Korchmaros (2009). "A Juvenile Drug Court Model in Southern Arizona: Substance Abuse, Delinquency, and Sexual Risk Outcomes by Gender and Race/Ethnicity." *Journal of Offender Rehabilitation* 48: 416–38.

[57] Skowyra, K. R. and J. J. Cocozza (2007). *Blueprint for Change: A Comprehensive Model for the Identification and Treatment of Youth with Mental Health Needs in Contact with the Juvenile Justice System*. Delmar, NY: The National Center for Mental Health. http://www.ncmhjj.com/Blueprint/pdfs/Blueprint.pdf

[58] Ishii, R. (2010). "Model Community Mental Health Programming." San Francisco: Center on Juvenile and Criminal Justice. Retrieved from http://cjcj.org/post/juvenile/justice/model/community/mental/health/programming

[59] Skowyra and Cocozza, *Blueprint for Change*, Section Five.

[60] Youth Transition Funders Group, *A Blueprint for Juvenile Justice Reform*, p. 8.

[61] Ibid., p. 10.

[62] Bonita, J., S. Wallace-Capretta, J. Rooney, and K. Mcanoy (2002). "An Outcome Evaluation of a Restorative Justice Alternative to Incarceration." *Contemporary Justice Review* 5: 319–38; see also Bazemore, G. (2005). "Whom and How Do We Reintegrate? Finding Community in Restorative

Justice." *Criminology and Public Policy* 4: 131–48; Braithwaite, J. (2002). *Restorative Justice and Responsive Regulation.* Oxford: Oxford University Press. See also: "Two Stories on Restorative Justice" posted on my website: http://www.sheldensays.com/two_stories_on_restorative_justi.htm

[63] Ironically, it is not practiced much by most religions, despite the fact that they preach this and similar principles. In the name of Christianity a multitude of horrors have been committed worldwide (see Ellerbe, H. [1995]. *The Dark Side of Christian History.* San Rafael, CA: Morningstar Books). Thus, "restorative justice" may be a hard sell to so-called "Christians."

[64] Quoted in Seldes, G. (Ed.) (1996). *The Great Thoughts.* New York: Ballantine Books, p. 253.

[65] Ibid., p. 376.

[66] Sullivan, D. and L. Tifft (2003). *Restorative Justice as a Transformative Process.* Voorheesville, NY: Mutual Aid Press, p. 6.

[67] Ibid., p. 9.

[68] Ibid., p. 34.

[69] Butts, J. A., G. Bazemore, and A. S. Meroe (2010, May). "Positive Youth Justice—Framing Justice Interventions Using the Concepts of Positive Youth Development." Washington, DC: Coalition for Juvenile Justice, p. 14. Retrieved from http://juvjustice.org/media/resources/public/resource_390.pdf

[70] Visit the website at muralarts.org

[71] Griffin, "Models for Change," p. 5.

[72] Ibid., p. 6.

[73] Ibid.

[74] Latimer, J., C. Dowden, and D. Muise (2005). "The Effectiveness of Restorative Justice Practices: A Meta-Analysis." *The Prison Journal* 85: 127–44.

[75] Rodriguez, N. (2007). "Restorative Justice at Work: Examining the Impact of Restorative Justice Resolutions on Juvenile Recidivism." *Crime & Delinquency* 53: 355–79.

[76] Bergseth, K. J. and J. A. Bouffard (2007). "The Long-Term Impact of Restorative Justice Programming for Juvenile Offenders." *Journal of Criminal Justice* 35: 433–51. Retrieved from http://www.co.clay.mn.us/depts/attorney/PDFs/BerBou07.pdf

[77] Davis, K. L. (2009). "Restorative Justice Experiences of Juvenile Female Offenders: School, Community, and Home." PhD dissertation, Drake University. http://escholarshare.drake.edu/bitstream/handle/2092/1109/Davis_Kim.pdf?sequence=1

[78] Youth Transition Funders Group, *A Blueprint for Juvenile Justice Reform.*

[79] Currie, E. (1989). "Confronting Crime: Looking toward the Twenty-First Century." *Justice Quarterly* 6: 5–25.

[80] See also Dryfoos, *Adolescents at Risk.*

[81] Colvin, M. (1991). "Crime and Social Reproduction: A Response to the Call for 'Outrageous' Proposals." *Crime and Delinquency* 37: 436–48.

[82] Ibid., p. 437.

[83] Butts et al., "Positive Youth Justice," p. 27.

[84] Ibid., p. 26.

[85] Ibid., p. 9.

[86] Ibid.

[87] Ibid., p. 15.

[88] Western, B. (2006). *Punishment and Inequality in America.* New York: Russell Sage Foundation.

[89] Krugman, P. (2008, November 8). "New Deal Economics." Retrieved from http://www.krugman.blogs.nytimes.com/2008/11/08/new-deal-economics/. Others have suggested this. See Dodd, R. (2008, April 16). "Politically Incorrect Solutions: What about a New Deal-Style Jobs Program?" *Dollars and Sense.* Retrieved from http://www.alternet.org/story/81921/

[90] Pogrebin, R. (2007, November 6.). "Rebuilding New Orleans, Post-Katrina Style." *New York Times.* Retrieved from http://www.nytimes.com/2007/11/06/arts/design/06ecle.html Named after the Secretary of State George Marshall, this was officially called the "European Recovery Program" that aimed at rebuilding much of Europe through economic aid from the United States.

[91] Girls Inc. (1996). *Prevention and Parity: Girls in Juvenile Justice Report.* New York: Girls Incorporated National Resource Center; Girls Study Group (2008). *Violence by Teenage Girls: Trends and Context.* Washington, DC: OJJDP, p. 6. Retrieved from http://www.ncjrs.gov/pdffiles1/ojjdp/218905.pdf

[92] For additional information on Children of the Night, see http://www.childrenofthenight.org/

[93] Girls Inc. http://www.girlsinc.org/index.html

[94] Ibid., http://www.girlsinc.org/about/programs/friendly-peersuasion.html

[95] Ibid., http://www.girlsinc.org/about/programs/adolescent-pregnancy.html

[96] Postrado, L. T. and H. J. Nicholson (1992). "Effectiveness in Delaying the Initiation of Sexual Intercourse of Girls Aged 12–14: Two Components of the Girls Incorporated Preventing Adolescent Pregnancy Program." *Youth and Society* 23(3): 356–79.

[97] PACE. *Believing in Girls*. (n.d.) "History." Retrieved from http://www.pacecenter.org/pace-history.html

[98] Model Programs Guide. Retrieved from http://www.ojjdp.gov/mpg/; prevention programs are listed at http://www.ojjdp.gov/mpg/prevention.aspx?continuum=prevention

[99] Irvine, A. (2005). *Girls' Circle: Summary of Outcomes for Girls in the Juvenile Justice System*. Santa Cruz, CA: Ceres Policy Research. More information can be found on the following website: http://www.girlscircle.com/

[100] Williams, K., G. D. Curry, and M. I. Cohen (1999). *Evaluation of Youth Gang Drug Intervention/Prevention Programs for Female Adolescents Volume 1: Final Report*. Washington, DC: U.S. Department of Justice, National Institute of Justice.

[101] Olds, D. L., et al. (1998). "The Promise of Home Visitation: Results of Two Randomized Trials." *Journal of Community Psychology* 26(1): 5–21; Olds, D. L., et al. (2002). "Home Visiting by Paraprofessionals and by Nurses: A Randomized, Controlled Trial." *Pediatrics* 110(3): 486–96; Olds, D. L., et al. (2004). "Effects of Home Visits by Paraprofessional and by Nurses: Age 4 Follow-Up Results of a Randomized Trial." *Pediatrics* 114(6): 1560–68.

[102] Berg, M. J. (2000). *Urban Women against Substance Abuse, Final Report*. Hartford CT: Institute for Community Research.

[103] Mendel, "The Missouri Model," p. 28.

[104] Ibid., p. 17.

[105] Ibid., p. 5.

[106] Griffin, "Models for Change," p. 4.

GLOSSARY OF JUVENILE JUSTICE TERMS

Abuse   See **Child Abuse**

Adjudication   The process of rendering a judicial decision as to whether the allegations in a petition or other pleading are true. An adjudicatory (also called a jurisdictional or evidentiary) hearing in a delinquency case is a fact-finding hearing to determine whether the accused committed the alleged acts; in civil cases, it is a fact-finding hearing to determine the rights and duties of the parties.

Adoption   A legal proceeding in which an adult takes a minor who is not the adoptive parent's natural offspring as his or her lawful child. The adopted minor loses all legal connection to the previous parent(s), and the adoptive parent undertakes permanently the responsibility of providing for the child. See also **guardianship**.

Aftercare   Supervision of a juvenile who has been returned to the community from training school.

Allegation   A charge or claim set forth in a petition, which must be proven true or false at a hearing.

Bootstrapping   The tendency within the juvenile justice system to relabel a status offense or a violation of a court order (i.e. a violation of probation rules) as a more serious delinquent offense. The JJDPA prohibits juvenile courts from locking up status offenders, but if the charge is for a delinquent offense, the prohibition does not apply.

CASA   A Court Appointed Special Advocate who is a trained volunteer appointed by a family/juvenile court judge to represent the best interests of abused, neglected, or dependent children who are the subject of court proceedings.

Child Abuse   Traditionally, any physical mistreatment of a child, as opposed to child neglect or negligent care. However, the term is increasingly used to cover any physical or mental injury, sexual abuse, negligent treatment, or maltreatment of a child by a person responsible for the child's welfare.

Child Neglect   Failure by a parent or custodian to render appropriate care to a child; an act of omission by the person legally responsible for a child's care which threatens the child's well-being. Failure to provide a child with suitable food, shelter, clothing, hygiene, medical care, or parental supervision.

Child Protection Action   The filing of legal papers by a child welfare agency when its investigation has turned up evidence of child abuse. A civil rather than criminal charge designed to take preventive action (such as appointment of a guardian) for at-risk children before abuse occurs.

Civil Protection Order   A form of protective custody in which a child welfare or police agency orders an adult suspected of abuse to leave the home.

Commitment   An order by which the court directs an officer of the court to take a person to a penal institution or mental health facility.

Complainant   The person who applies to the court for legal redress by filing a complaint.

Complaint   (1) An oral statement, usually made to police, charging criminal, abusive or neglectful conduct; (2) District Attorney's document that starts a criminal prosecution (also known in many states as an "information"); and (3) Initiating pleading in a criminal or civil case, filed by the moving party and setting out the cause of action. In family court, the complaint is usually called a "petition."

Consent   An agreement of the parties resolving pending matters before the court.

Contempt   The action of a person who willfully disobeys a court order or fails to comply with a court decision.

Continuance   The adjournment or postponement of a session, hearing, trial or other proceeding to a subsequent day or time.

Counsel   The advice or assistance given by one person to another in regard to a legal matter; often provided by an attorney.

Custody   The responsibility for a child's care and control, carrying with it the duty of providing food, shelter, medical care, education, and discipline. Custody can be joint or sole.

Deep End   Jerome Miller first used the term while he was the commissioner of youth corrections for the state of Massachusetts in the 1970s. It refers to those youth who are deemed the worst offenders housed in juvenile detention centers and other correctional facilities. They occupy the deepest end of the juvenile justice system. The theory behind Miller's approach was that if you could demonstrate that these offenders could be treated through alternative methods, then the rationale for locking up less serious offenders would be weakened. Miller and others who followed proved that most deep-end youths could be successfully treated in alternative locations.

Deinstitutionalization of Status Offenders (DSO)   The practice of diverting juveniles who have committed a status offense from being committed/detained in an institution.

Delinquency   The commission of an illegal act by a juvenile.

Delinquency Proceeding   A court action to officially declare someone a juvenile delinquent. A "delinquent" is a person under the age of majority who has been convicted in juvenile court of committing an act that would be classified as a crime in adult court.

Delinquent Child   A child who commits an act, which if committed by an adult, would constitute a crime.

Dependent Child   A child under the age of maturity who relies on an adult for care and protection.

Detention   The confinement of a juvenile by a legally authorized person.

Detention Hearing   A court hearing held to determine whether a minor who is alleged to be delinquent should be kept away from his parents until a full trial can be held. Detention hearings must usually be held within 24 hours of the filing of a detention request.

Detention Diversion Advocacy Project (DDAP)   A program developed in San Francisco in 1993 to reduce the number of youth in court-ordered detention and to provide them with culturally relevant community-based services and supervision.

Dismiss   To dispose of an action or suit without any further consideration or hearing.

Disposition   A phase of a delinquency proceeding similar to the "sentencing" phase of an adult trial. The judge must consider alternative and individualized sentences rather than imposing standard sentences. The judge (1) considers evidence about the juvenile's needs, available resources, and other relevant factors and (2) designs a plan to meet the juvenile's needs and the interests of the state. Case dispositions include: waived to criminal court; placement; probation; dismissed; and other (fines, restitution, community service, referrals outside the court for services with minimal or no further court involvement anticipated).

Disproportionate Minority Contact (DMC)   At every stage of contact with the juvenile justice system, minorities are overrepresented compared to their representation in the general population; with each decision—to arrest, to refer, to commit—the differences are amplified.

Diversion   An alternative to trial wherein the child is referred to counseling or other social services at intake.

Due Process   The constitutionally guaranteed right of persons to be treated by the law with fundamental fairness. In criminal proceedings, due process means the right to adequate notice in advance of hearings, the right to counsel, the right to confront and cross-examine witnesses, the right to refuse to give self-incriminating testimony, the right to notification of allegations of misconduct in advance of the hearing, and the right to have allegations proven beyond a reasonable doubt.

Evidence   Any sort of proof submitted to a court for the purpose of influencing the court's decision.

Ex Parte   A judicial proceeding or order which is held or granted at the instance and for the benefit of one party without notice to the other party.

Felony   An offense that differs legally from a misdemeanor because of the punishment imposed if found guilty—imprisonment for longer than a year and/or a fine greater than $1,000. Felonies include murder, rape, kidnapping, assault, robbery, burglary, and arson.

Fifth Amendment   The Fifth Amendment to the United States Constitution guarantees the right of a defendant not to self-incriminate. A defendant can refuse to answer a question (by "taking the Fifth") on the basis that the answer might incriminate him or her.

Foster Care   A form of substitute care, usually in a home licensed by a public agency, for children without parents or guardians or whose welfare requires that they be removed from their own homes.

Fourteenth Amendment   The Fourteenth Amendment to the U.S. Constitution secures to every person due process rights to life, liberty, and property.

Fourth Amendment   The Fourth Amendment to the U.S. Constitution protects every person against unlawful search and seizure.

Guardian   An adult appointed by a probate or family court to serve as custodian of a minor until the minor's parent proves renewed ability to provide proper care to the child. A guardian has almost all the rights and powers of a natural parent, but the relationship is subject to termination or change.

Guardian Ad Litem   An adult who is appointed by a court to act in the minor's behalf *ad litem* (in a lawsuit), because minors lack the legal capacity to sue or defend against a legal suit. The guardian is considered an officer of the court.

Guardianship   The power and duty of taking care of and/or managing property and rights of a child or an individual who is considered incapable of taking care of him/herself.

Habeas Corpus   A writ ordering a public officer holding a person in confinement to bring the person before the court for release. It is used to secure the release from custody of minors or adults being illegally held.

In Loco Parentis   The role of a custodian, guardian, or other person acting in the parent's place and stead.

Incarceration   The confinement of a juvenile or adult in a secured correctional institution.

Intake   A procedure prior to preliminary hearing in which a group of people (intake officer, police, probation, social worker, parent, and child) meet to decide to approve a complaint for filing as a petition or divert the matter from court.

Juvenile Justice and Delinquency Prevention Act (JJDPA)   Enacted in 1974, the Act prohibits the placement of status offenders in locked detention in states receiving federal funds. The Act was modified in 1980 to allow judges discretion if status offenders violated a valid court order (VCO). The 1992 reauthorization focused on protections for girls; the 2002 reauthorization extended requirements for the deinstitutionalization of status offenders (DSO).

Judge   A lawyer (in some states an elected official and in others one who is appointed by the governor and confirmed by the senate) who presides over court hearings and has the power to enter orders affecting the parties.

Judgment   A final decision of the court resolving the dispute and determining the rights of the parties involved in the case.

Jurisdiction   The power of a particular court to hear and dispose of cases involving certain categories of persons or allegations. Family/juvenile court has jurisdiction over most juvenile delinquency cases, adult misdemeanor domestic violent crimes, and family civil actions, such as divorce and custody.

Juvenile   A person under age 18 (in some states the age is 17).

Juvenile Court   A court that has jurisdiction (legal power) over minors only, usually handling cases of suspected delinquency as well as cases of suspected abuse or neglect. In many states, terminations of parental rights occur in juvenile court proceedings, but that is generally the limit of the juvenile court's power over adults.

Juvenile Delinquency   A person under age 18 is found guilty of committing an act which would be a crime if the person were an adult.

Master   A person appointed by the juvenile or family court judge to hear cases as assigned. Masters' orders may be reviewed before a judge of family court.

Mediation   The process by which court mediators assist parties to reach voluntary agreement in domestic relation matters (e.g., support, custody, visitation) without a formal court hearing before a judge. This is an informal dispute resolution process in which a neutral third party (mediation officer) helps litigants reach an agreement. The mediator has no power to impose a decision on the parties.

Miranda Rule   In *Miranda v. Arizona*, the U.S. Supreme Court ruled in 1966 that confessions are inadmissible at trial if the police do not advise the subject of certain rights before questioning him or her: (1) the right to remain silent and to refuse to answer any questions; (2) the right to know that anything he or she says can and will be used against him or her in a court of law; (3) the right to consult with an attorney and to have an attorney present during questioning; (4) the right to have counsel appointed at public expense prior to any questioning if the subject cannot afford counsel. The Miranda ruling applied only to people in the custody of police; it was rarely used for juveniles under the theory that they were not under police custody and were free to leave any interview. Some states did require that a minor be advised of the right to have a parent, relative, or other advisor present during questioning. In *J. D. B. v. North Carolina*, the Supreme Court ruled in 2011 that police officers who remove students from a class to question them about a crime must inform them of their right to remain silent. The justices ruled that age is a critical factor in determining whether someone would understand the freedom to walk away from an interview.

Misdemeanor   A category of crime for which the punishment can be no more than one year of imprisonment (usually in a county jail rather than state prison) and/or a fine of $1,000. Distinguished from a felony, which is more serious, and from an infraction, which is less serious (e.g., loitering).

Nonsecure Custody   The physical placement of a juvenile in a licensed foster home or other home or facility before disposition and pursuant to a written court order.

Order   The decision of a court or judge directing the disposition of a case.

Parens Patriae   From English law, the legal doctrine under which the Crown assumed the protection of certain minors, orphans, and other persons in need of protection. It is a concept used by courts when acting on behalf of the states to protect and control the property and custody of minors and incompetent persons. Translated literally, it means "the father of his country."

Petition   A formal written application to a court describing the grounds by which the court should take jurisdiction of the case and the relief requested.

Petitioner   The person initiating a legal action, usually in a civil case; the person who presents a petition to a court.

Placement   The residential and/or custodial arrangements determined for a child by the court. The removal of a child from his or her natural home and placement in a different custodial setting for more than a short period of time. Placement may be in a foster home, group home, relative's home, or an institution. Juvenile or family courts sometimes place minors but usually commit delinquents or dependent children to other agencies for placement services.

Pre-Disposition Report (PDR)   A report to the court on the youth's offense, family history, community involvement, and recommendations for disposition.

Probable Cause   A reasonable ground for belief in the existence of facts warranting some action on the court's part.

Probation   Allowing a convicted criminal defendant or a juvenile found to be delinquent to remain at liberty, under a suspended sentence of imprisonment, generally under the supervision of a probation officer and usually under certain conditions.

Probation Officer   One who supervises a person placed on probation by a court in a criminal proceeding.

Prosecution   In a criminal action, a proceeding instituted for the purpose of determining guilt or innocence of a person charged with a crime.

Protective Custody   In child abuse and neglect cases, the emergency removal of a child from his home when the child would be in imminent danger if allowed to remain with the parent(s) or custodian(s).

Public Defender   An attorney appointed by a court to defend indigent defendants in criminal cases.

Referral   When a youth is directed to the court based on an allegation of a criminal law violation.

Recidivism Rate   The rate at which juveniles reoffend, are rearrested, or are readmitted to correctional facilities.

Restitution   A process by which a juvenile or adult reimburses the victim for any loss or damage to person or property.

Revocation   Rescinding a conditional release—returning a juvenile conditionally released from an institution after a violation of the terms of the release.

Risk Assessment   A method of estimating the chances that a juvenile will commit a future offense. Factors considered include: the juvenile's age, the most serious prior conviction, any prior assaults, runaway history, substance use, school behavior, positive or negative peer relationships, and parental supervision. The assessment, along with the current offense and delinquency history, are considered by the court counselor in making a recommendation during the intake process, and by judges in determining a sentence.

Sealing   The closing of records to inspection by all but the parties involved.

Secure Custody   The physical placement of a juvenile in an approved detention facility pursuant to a court order.

Sentence (Disposition)   The hearing officer's written order as to how a case was decided. In a criminal case, it is the punishment determined from the defendant.

Social Report   The document prepared by a probation officer or social worker for the family court hearing officer's consideration at the time of disposition of a case. This report addresses the minor's history and environment.

Standard of Proof   The level of proof required in a particular legal proceeding. In criminal and delinquency cases, the offense must be proven beyond a reasonable doubt. In neglect and dependency proceedings, and in civil cases generally, the standard of proof is by a preponderance of the evidence, a significantly lower standard which requires that the judge believe that it is more likely than not, on the evidence presented, that neglect occurred. In some cases, the standard of proof is by clear and convincing evidence, a standard more stringent than preponderance of the evidence and less demanding than beyond a reasonable doubt.

Stare Decisis   Legal doctrine that requires adherence to legal precedents (decisions of appellate courts) until they are overruled by the same or higher courts.

Status Offense   An activity illegal when engaged in by a minor, but not when done by an adult. Examples include truancy, curfew, running away, or habitually disobeying parents.

Taken into Custody   The physical control of a youth who is detained by a law enforcement officer due to a violation of law or a court order.

Termination of Parental Rights (TPRS)   A legal proceeding to free a child from his or her parents so that the child can be adopted by others without the parents' written consent.

Temporary Custody   The physical taking and holding of a juvenile under personal supervision before a petition is filed and without a court order.

Training Schools   Residential facilities for delinquent juveniles who are a danger to persons or property in the community and for whom no less restrictive placement is available or appropriate.

Transfer   Changing the jurisdiction of a case from one court to another.

Valid Court Order (VCO)   Rulings by the court, which can include orders requiring a juvenile to stop engaging in certain noncriminal behaviors such as running away or skipping school. If the juvenile continues the status offenses, he or she may be incarcerated for violating the court's order.

Waive   To transfer a case to criminal court by a waiver hearing in juvenile court.

Waiver   The understanding and voluntary relinquishment of a known right, such as the right to counsel or the right to remain silent during police questioning.

Ward   As used in some states (e.g., California), a minor who is under the jurisdiction of the juvenile court for a delinquent act or an allegation or finding of abuse, neglect, or dependency. Also used for juveniles with a legally appointed guardian.

Writ   An order issued by a court commanding that a certain act or acts be done or not done.

Writ of Habeas Corpus   A legal paper issued by the court ordering a person to produce the body of another person. It is sometimes used in disputed custody cases where one parent refuses to turn over the child to the other parent (the legal guardian) at the end of a visitation period.

INDEX

513